Modern Europe and the Wider World

DERMOT LUCEY

My-etest
Packed full of extra questions, **my-etest** lets you revise
– at your own pace – when you want – where you want.

Test yourself on our FREE website www.my-etest.com and check out how well you score!

Teachers!
Print an etest and give it for homework or a class test.

Gill & Macmillan

Gill & Macmillan Ltd
Hume Avenue
Park West
Dublin 12
with associated companies throughout the world
www.gillmacmillan.ie

© Dermot Lucey 2004
Illustration p.146 © Kate Shannon
ISBN-13: 978 07171 3517 2

Design, maps and print origination in Ireland by Designit
Colour reproduction by Typeform Repro

Acknowledgments

'Imagine' by John Lennon Copyright © 1971 renewed 1999 by Lenono Music. All rights reserved. Used by permission.
'Eve of Destruction' Words & Music by P.F. Sloan © Copyright 1965 American Broadcasting Music Incorporated, USA. Universal/MCA Music Limited. Used by permission of Music Sales Limited. All Rights Reserved. International Copyright Secured.
'57 Channels' Words & Music by Bruce Springsteen © Copyright 1992 Zomba Music publishers Limited. Used by permission of Music Sales Limited. All Rights Reserved. International Copyright Secured.

Picture Credits

For permission to reproduce photographs and other material, the author and publisher gratefully acknowledge the following:
240T/254 both/256/262B/267T/305B/384/398/399T/444/460 © The Advertising Archive Ltd; 327B/326R © Alamy Images; 327C/343/358BL/358TR/378 406L/408/417L/426/427/437T/440B/477TR © AP/World Wide Photos; 48/78T/121B/131T/136/137B/147 © The Art Archive; Corbis: 11/12L/13/17/25 26/31/52/62B/93/94T/96/97TL/104B/107/108B/115T/116/121T/123/156R/173/178R/182B/183/186TL/194T/195/199R/209/212/214/215/220R/227 both/228 both/229/230/231/232/239/244/257/261/270BR/273B/282T/286/295/296/301T/305T/314/316/324/326L/331B/331C /333/345/347/358TL 359T/361/365B/366/369/370/375/377/381/382/387/388/392/399B/400/401/404/414/415/416 both/423T/425/431T/439B/440T 445B/449/454B/457 465/477BR/478 © Bettmann, 12R/14/18T/60BL/62T/78B/94B/95T/97B/104T/105/108T/113T/117/135T/146/154/164/165/176B/186TR/187T/213B 217/255T/269T/302/307T © Hulton-Deutsch, 19/53T/101/128/151/194B/210/334/335/336/340T/350/356/360/365T/423B/445T © Corbis, 10/43B/331T © Underwood & Underwood, 92 © Minnesota Historical Society, 95B/103 © Swim Ink, 98 © John Springer Collection, 145T © Leonard de Selva, 181 © National Archives, 204/237 © Alain Nogues, 224 © Julia Waterlow/Eye Ubiquitous, 238/338 © Owen Franken, 245T © Yevgeny Khaldei, 245B © Shepard Sherbell, 246/468 © Rykoff Collection, 249 both/250 © Peter Turnley, 251B © Les Stone, 251TR © Marc Garanger, 251TL © David Forman/Eye Ubiquitous, 262T © Paul Thompson/Eye Ubiquitous, 263B/397B © H. Armstrong Roberts, 270T/447 © Henry Diltz, 270BL © Richard Olivier, 273T © Mike King, 274/299/475 © Roger Ressmeyer, 278 © David Turnley, 283 © Tim Graham, 287/297 © David Lees, 306 © Charles O'Rear, 307B © Gabe Palmer, 308 © Jose Fuste Raga, 317T © Sprio Gino, 317B © Bryn Colton/Assignments Photographers, 374 © Francoise de Mulder, 380 © Dean Conger, 407 © Charles E. Rotkin, 459B © William Gottlieb, 466/476/477BL © Corbis Sygma, 469/477TL © NASA, 470 © Jerry Cooke; 396 © Mike Luckovich, Creators Syndicate; Getty Images: 255B/260/264/313/319/348/359C/376/389/433/454T © Hulton Archive, 402/439T/450 © Time Life; 27 © David King Collection; 397T © Hagley Museum and Library; Kobal Collection: 312L © MGM, 459T © Lucasfilm/20th Century Fox, 418 © Warner Bros; 417R/429/431B © Magnum Photos; Mary Evans Picture Library: 8B/32R/41 both/43C/43T/45 (2ndL)/45L/45R/55/56/59T/60B (2ndR)/65/72/80/84/97TR/113B/125/126B/133 both/137T/141B/150 271T/223T/268T © MEPL, 54/60B2L/60BR/63/64/68/69/73B/145B/162 © Weimar, 141T © Explorer, 143BL/143BR/143T © Meledin, 446 © Jeffrey Morgan; 81 both/82/126T/156L/166 Brow/269BL/301B/303B © Mirrorpix; 20/21/22 all/248 © Novosti (London); 18B/44/45(2ndR)/46/ 47/51/53B/59B/60T/73T 77/85/89/90/115B/122B/124/131B/135B/138/148/153/161/163/166 T&C rows/175/178L/185R/187B/344 © popperfoto.com; 122T/176T/213T/479 © Punch Ltd; 327T © Larry Downing, Reuters; 182T/185L/186B/193/196 both/198/199L/200/201/203/220L/221/223B/263T/268B/269BR/271B/272/275 280/282B/288/298/303T/312R/318/358BR/419/448/456/472 © Rex Features; 294 both Science Photo Library: 437B © Photo SCALA, Florence/Smithsonian American Art Museum, 2004; 8T © Topham Picturepoint.
Note: T=Top, B=Bottom, C=Centre, L=Left, R=Right.

The author and publisher have made every effort to trace all copyright holders, but if any has been inadvertently overlooked we would be pleased to make the necessary arrangements at the first opportunity.

The paper used in this book is made from the wood pulp of managed forests. For every tree felled, at least one tree is planted, thereby renewing natural resources.

Contents

Note:
The sections of this book, parts 1 to 3, cover Topics 3, 4 and 6 of the syllabus. They will be labelled Topic 3, Topic 4 and Topic 6 on your exam paper.

Topic 3: Dictatorship and Democracy in Europe, 1920–45

PERSPECTIVE	ELEMENTS	CASE STUDIES
Politics and administration	Origins and growth of the Fascist regimes in Europe; the Nazi state in peace and war. Communism in Russia: the regimes of Lenin and Stalin; the Stalinist state in peace and war. France: the Third Republic, 1920–40, and the Vichy state. Wartime alliances, 1939–45.	Stalin's Show Trials
Society and economy	Economic and social problems of the inter-war years, with particular reference to Britain and Germany. The Soviet alternative. Society during World War II: The Home Front; Rationing/evacuees; refugees; collaboration/resistance. Anti-semitism and the Holocaust.	The Jarrow March, October 1936
Culture, religion and science	Nazi propaganda – state control and use of mass media. Church-state relations under Mussolini and Hitler. Anglo-American popular culture in peace and war: radio and cinema. The technology of warfare.	The Nuremberg Rallies

In their study of the topic, students should become aware of the role of certain key personalities.

Another 'key' to developing understanding will be learning to identify the main issues through a familiarity with certain key concepts.

KEY PERSONALITIES

Students should be aware of the contribution of the following to the development listed under the elements above:

J M Keynes, Adolf Hitler, Benito Mussolini, Vladimir Ilyich Lenin, Josef Stalin, Winston Churchill, Joseph Goebbels, Leni Riefenstahl, Bing Crosby, Charlie Chaplin.

KEY CONCEPTS

Inflation, the Depression, protectionism, collectivisation, Communism, Fascism, dictatorship, personality cult, totalitarianism, democracy, propaganda, anti-semitism, herrenvolk Reichskirche, the Holocaust, collaboration, resistance, lebensraum, blitzkrieg.

DIFFERENTIATION – HIGHER AND ORDINARY

While students at both levels will study the same topics, for Ordinary level students a particular emphasis will be placed on Key Personalities and Case Studies associated with their topics. Higher level students will be expected to study all aspects of topics to a greater depth and to develop a greater level of conceptual understanding.

Topic 4: Division and Realignment in Europe, 1945–92

PERSPECTIVE	ELEMENTS	CASE STUDIES
Politics and administration	Origins of Cold War: division of Germany; 'Sovietisation' of Eastern Europe; military alliances; main crises of Cold War; emergence of reform movements in Eastern Europe; collapse of Soviet Union; fragmentation and realignment in Europe. Moves towards European unity, 1945–57; establishment and evolution of EEC.	The Hungarian Uprising, 1956
Society and economy	The Western economies 1945–73: the era of economic growth; Marshall Aid: moves towards free trade; immigration; the Welfare State. The Western economies 1973–90: Impact of the Oil Crisis; recession and the rise in unemployment. The Communist economies: problems and outcomes. Marriage, the family and the changing role of women. Affluence, leisure time and the consumer society.	The Oil Crisis, 1973
Culture, religion and science	Literature and social criticism, East and West. Changing patterns in religious observance. Youth and popular culture (including sport) and the mass media. The impact of (a) advances in the biological sciences, (b) nuclear power, and (c) the computer	The Second Vatican Council

In their study of the topic, students should become aware of the role of certain key personalities.

Another 'key' to developing understanding will be learning to identify the main issues through a familiarity with certain key concepts.

KEY PERSONALITIES

Students should be aware of the contribution of the following to the development listed under the elements above:

Imre Nagy, Nikita Khrushchev, Pope John Paul II, Mikhail Gorbachev, Jean Monnet, Jacques Delors, Margaret Thatcher, Alexander Solzhenitsyn, Simone de Beauvoir, John Lennon.

KEY CONCEPTS

Capitalism, Communism, Sovietisation, Cold War, Iron Curtain, nuclear deterrence, détente, satellite state, glasnost, common market, federal Europe, welfare state, feminism, dissident writer, ecumenical movement, mass media, information technology, pop star, teenager.

DIFFERENTIATION – HIGHER AND ORDINARY

While students at both levels will study the same topics, for Ordinary level students a particular emphasis will be placed on Key Personalities and Case Studies associated with their topics. Higher level students will be expected to study all aspects of topics to a greater depth and to develop a greater level of conceptual understanding.

Course Outline

Topic 6: The United States and the World, 1945–89

PERSPECTIVE	ELEMENTS	CASE STUDIES
Politics and administration	US politics: structures and tensions – federal government and the states; the separation of powers.	Lyndon Johnson and Vietnam, 1963–8
	The Presidency from Roosevelt to Reagan.	
	Domestic factors in US foreign policy: McCarthyism, the anti-war movement, race relations.	
	US foreign policy, 1945–72: Berlin, Korea, Cuba, Vietnam.	
	Decline of Cold War certainties, 1973–89: withdrawal from Vietnam, détente, SALT and Star Wars.	
Society and economy	Sources of the US economic boom; the war, public investment and international financing, 1945–68.	The Montgomery Bus Boycott, 1956
	The development of the US industrial structure: the multinational corporation, 1945–68.	
	The Vietnam War; the federal deficit; domestic recession; international competition from Japan and Europe, 1968–89.	
	Demographic growth; affluence – consumerism, leisure, the role of work, the changing role of women and the family.	
	Troubled affluence: racial conflict, urban poverty, drugs and crime.	
Culture, religion and science	Consensus? 1945–68: Hollywood – the American Dream; the 'red scare'.	The Moon landing, 1969
	Collapse of consensus, 1968–89: youth culture, 'counter-culture' and multiculturalism.	
	Religion in modern American culture; the mass media in modern American culture; mass higher education.	
	Advances in military, space and information technology.	

In their study of the topic, students should become aware of the role of certain key personalities.

Another 'key' to developing understanding will be learning to identify the main issues through a familiarity with certain key concepts.

KEY PERSONALITIES

Students should be aware of the contribution of the following to the development listed under the elements above:

Harry Truman, Joe McCarthy, Martin Luther King, Lyndon Johnson, the 'Organisation Man', Betty Friedan, Norman Mailer, Muhammad Ali, Billy Graham, Marilyn Monroe.

KEY CONCEPTS

Corporate capitalism, globalisation, internationalism, imperialism, consumerism, technological development, the military-industrial complex, discrimination, liberalism, presidential bureaucracy, mass media, public opinion, fundamentalism, moral majority, feminism.

DIFFERENTIATION – HIGHER AND ORDINARY

While students at both levels will study the same topics, for Ordinary level students a particular emphasis will be placed on Key Personalities and Case Studies associated with their topics. Higher level students will be expected to study all aspects of topics to a greater depth and to develop a greater level of conceptual understanding.

NOTE: It is proposed to prescribe the topic 'The United States and the World, 1945–89' for the compulsory documents-study section of the Leaving Certificate examination in 2008 and 2009. Questions will be based on the Case Studies in this topic and on a wider knowledge of the topic overall.

PART 1:
DICTATORSHIP AND DEMOCRACY IN EUROPE, 1920-45

The Rule of Lenin

[handwritten notes: Karl Marx (communist ... manifesto) "let the ruling class tremble" at a communist revolution. The proletarians have nothing to lose but their chains ... they have a world to win. The workers of the world unite]

Introduction – The Communists Take Over

Lenin Arrives in Petrograd, 1917, at the start of the Communist Revolution in Russia.

In 1917, Russia was a huge empire ruled over by **Tsar** (emperor) **Nicholas II**, a member of the Romanov family which had ruled Russia for 300 years. He had great power; *'The Emperor of all the Russias is an autocratic and unlimited monarch. God himself commands that his supreme power be obeyed.'* There was also a parliament or Duma which had little power but wanted the Tsar to share more power. At this time, the Russian Empire was fighting in the First World War (1914–18) and the chaos and destruction caused by the war led to two revolutions.

Key Personality: Lenin

Lenin was born in Russia in 1870. He joined the Social Democratic Party which was the Russian Marxist or Communist party. He wanted to form a small group of elite revolutionaries to plan revolution. This group became known as the **Bolsheviks**. Lenin spent most of his time in exile in England or Switzerland. He returned to Petrograd, the capital of Russia, after the first revolution in February 1917. He began to plan the second revolution.

In the **October Revolution** 1917, Lenin and the Bolsheviks took over Russia but they had little support. They signed a peace agreement with Germany, and then in order to retain power they had to fight the opposition forces – the Whites – in the **Russian Civil War**. The Bolsheviks (now called Communists) were led by Lenin and Trotsky (who organised the Red Army). Lenin was in charge of **War Communism**. He took over the main industries and sent out Communist groups to the countryside to confiscate food from the peasants (farmers). He also set up the Cheka, a secret police, to eliminate opposition. By the end of the Civil War, Lenin had to change his policy. A revolt by the sailors in the **Kronstadt** naval base near Petrograd made him realise the severity of his policies. He now brought in the **New Economic Policy** (NEP) which allowed farmers to sell more of their produce for profit.

But Lenin's health was declining. In 1921, he had been shot by Dora Kaplan in an assassination attempt. He also suffered from a series of **strokes** which gradually took away his movement and speech. He was worried about who would succeed him. In his Last Testament, he preferred a collective leadership (a group sharing power) and he warned about the dangers of **Stalin**. He died in 1924. He had founded the Union of the Soviet Socialist Republics which was the **first Communist state**. His views about revolution were imitated by others during the twentieth century.

Somehow the means of production, distribution and exchange should be owned and controlled by the state (achieving more equality in society)

In the first revolution, in February 1917, Tsar Nicholas II was overthrown by the Provisional Government drawn from members of the Duma. Eight months later, in October, Lenin and the Bolsheviks overthrew the new Provisional Government.

Lenin wanted to introduce **Communism** to Russia, which would mean:

- the abolition of private property,
- government control of agriculture and industry,
- a one-party dictatorship.

> **KEY CONCEPT: COMMUNISM** was based on the writings of Karl Marx, a German writer of the nineteenth century. He outlined his ideas in *The Communist Manifesto* and *Das Kapital*. Communists believed that the working class would revolt against the middle class who controlled industry. This would result in a Communist society where private property was abolished. The government would run the land and the factories for the benefit of the people and everybody would be equal.

LENIN HOLDS ONTO POWER

Having taken over the country, Lenin's biggest challenge was to hold onto power. Lenin first obtained a majority in the All-Russian Congress of Soviets when the opposition walked out. Over the next year Lenin took steps to maintain his power.

1. By the **Decree on Land** *(absolute power)*, he allowed the peasants to take over private land.
2. Lenin had to allow elections for the **Constituent Assembly** (parliament) to take place. The elections resulted in a majority of seats for the other political groups, especially the Social Revolutionaries. But having allowed it to meet for one day in January 1918, the next day Lenin used **Bolshevik Red Guards** to dissolve the Assembly.
3. The Bolshevik Party was renamed the Communist Party.
4. Freedom of the press was abolished.
5. Lenin set up the **Cheka** (or secret police) to protect the Bolshevik revolution. There were widespread arrests and executions of those the Cheka considered were opposed to Lenin and the Bolsheviks.
6. Lenin wanted to take Russia out of the First World War. The victorious Germans imposed harsh terms on Russia in the **Treaty of Brest-Litovsk** (1918) but Lenin persuaded his colleagues to accept them. *'We gained a little time, and sacrificed a great deal of space for it,'* he said. *'The Russian Revolution must sign the peace to obtain a breathing space to recover.'* He promised to renege on the terms once the world war was over.

> In the Treaty of Brest-Litovsk, Russia lost
> 25% of its land
> 26% of its population
> 33% of its farming land
> 80% of its coalmines
> 33% of its manufacturing industry

After Brest-Litovsk, Lenin faced his greatest threat in the Civil War.

THE RUSSIAN CIVIL WAR, 1918–21

In the Civil War, the Whites opposed Lenin and his party, now called the Communist Party. Lenin and Trotsky led the Communists or **Reds**. Lenin concentrated on economic and political problems, while Trotsky organised the military. The Whites were composed of many different groups, such as:

- Social Revolutionaries, → *(those who where disclosed from government) also the kulaks.*
- former Tsarists who wanted to restore the Tsar,
- supporters of the Provisional Government,
- landlords,
- industrialists, and
- national minorities such as the Cossacks who wanted independence from Russia.

They were helped by the Allied powers (Britain, France, US and Japan) who wanted Russia to continue fighting in the First World War.

(i) The Military Conflict

The Red Army was led by **Trotsky**, Commissar of War, as Chairman of the Supreme War Council. It controlled only the centre of Russia at the beginning of the Civil War. However, this territory included the main cities of Russia (Moscow and Petrograd), the main industrial areas and the best farming land. The Red Army was attacked from all sides by the White armies but it defeated each in turn.

There were three major White armies:
The Siberian army under General Kolchak.
The southern Volunteer army under General Denikin.
The north-western army under General Yudenich.

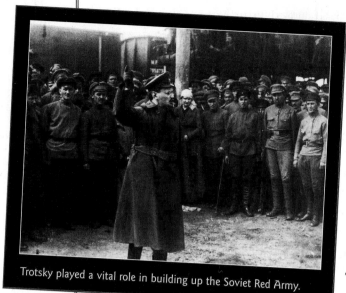
Trotsky played a vital role in building up the Soviet Red Army.

The East: In Siberia, the Communists were threatened by a Czech Legion and by the Siberian army of General Kolchak. They took over territory along the Trans-Siberian railway and advanced through the Ural Mountains towards Moscow. Lenin feared their advance would lead to the rescue of Tsar Nicholas II and his family, who were held in Ekaterinberg. So he ordered their execution. However, Kolchak was defeated and later executed by the Reds (February 1920). The Red Army then made an agreement with the Czech Legion which allowed the Legion to leave Russia through the eastern port of Vladivostok.

The South: General Denikin attacked from the south (the Crimea and the Ukraine) and came within 200 miles of Moscow, which was now the capital of the Soviet Union. But he too was defeated.

The North-West: General Yudenich advanced from the Baltic states (Lithuania, Latvia, Estonia) towards Petrograd. In 1919 he reached the suburbs of Petrograd but stubborn resistance by the Reds, encouraged by the presence of Trotsky, led to his defeat.

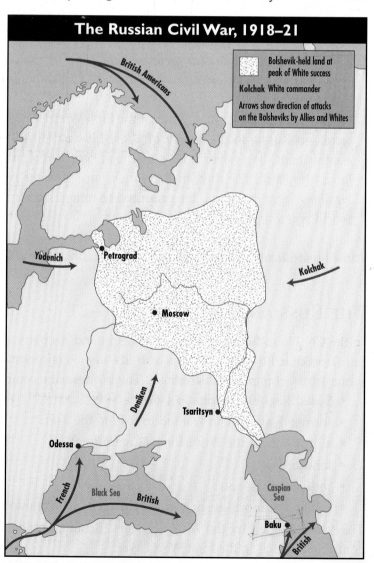

The Russian Civil War, 1918–21

British Americans

Bolshevik-held land at peak of White success

Kolchak White commander

Arrows show direction of attacks on the Bolsheviks by Allies and Whites

Yudenich
Petrograd
Kolchak
Moscow
Denikin
Tsaritsyn
Odessa
French
Black Sea
British
Caspian Sea
Baku
British

The Rule of Lenin

Allied Intervention: When the Bolsheviks (Communists) pulled Russia out of the First World War, Allied troops were landed in Murmansk and Archangel in the north, in the Crimea in the south, and in Vladivostok in the east, (see map of allied intervention in the Russian civil war). The Allies intervened in Russia for a variety of reasons: they wanted to <u>bring Russia back into the war; they feared the spread of Communism to the West;</u> they were horrified at the execution of the Tsar and they were opposed to the nationalisation (taken into government ownership) of foreign-owned business by the Communists. Apart from sending in troops, the Allies gave large quantities of arms and ammunition to the Whites which helped prolong the Civil War. However, when the First World War ended in November 1918, the Allies were not interested in Soviet Russia and gradually withdrew their help. As Lloyd George, the British Prime Minister, said, *'If we were going to do any good we should need a million men at least.'*

> **The Czech Legion**: The Czech Legion had fought on the side of the Russians against Austria-Hungary in the First World War. But when the Communists pulled Russia out of the war, the Legion wanted to get to Western Europe to continue fighting in the war.

So, by the beginning of 1920 Trotsky's Red Army had strengthened their position, but it had yet to face one of its greatest threats.

The Russo-Polish War, 1920–21: The Russian Civil War was complicated by the intervention of Poland. The Peace Treaties at the end of the First World War created Poland. The eastern border with Russia was marked as the **<u>Curzon Line</u>**. Pilsudski, the Polish leader, took advantage of the chaos in Russia to take over territory for Poland and to create an <u>independent</u> <u>Ukraine</u> under <u>Polish influence</u>. He advanced rapidly into Russia and took Kiev in May 1920. However, the Red Army regrouped and soon defeated the Poles.

Bolshevik (Communist) officers take over cars for use in the Russian Civil War.

The Red Army then advanced towards Warsaw, the Polish capital, to set up a Communist government there. However, the Poles, advised by the French general, Weygand, defeated the Reds just east of the city in the **Battle of Warsaw**. After this the Poles advanced into Russia, but peace negotiations were soon begun and concluded with the **Treaty of Riga** in March 1921. In this Treaty, Poland gained substantial territory from Russia.

The Last of the White Armies: By this time the Reds were distracted by another attack, the last White attack. After Denikin's failure in the south, General Wrangel replaced him. Wrangel took advantage of the Reds' campaign in Poland to advance into the Ukraine. However, after early successes, he was defeated by larger Red forces who also stopped his efforts to link up with the Polish army. Wrangel retreated to the Crimea, evacuating his troops and about 150,000 civilians to Turkey. In November 1920, the Red or Soviet commander in the south sent Lenin news of the final victory: *'Today our cavalry took Kerch. The southern front is destroyed.'* The Communist Red Army was victorious.

(ii) War Communism

While Trotsky was mainly in charge of the Red Army and the military conflict, Lenin took control of economic and political problems. Lenin followed a policy of **War Communism**. With this

Russian revolutionary poster: encouraging people to sign up immediately to join the co-operative.

policy, he ensured that all industry and agriculture within the Communist-controlled territory was geared solely towards the war effort. But he was also putting Communist ideas into practice.

Industry: Private trading was banned and factories with more than ten workers were taken over by the government. Production was planned and organised by the government. There was forced mobilisation of workers for industry. Strikes were also banned and strikers were shot. Rapid inflation (price rises) made money worthless, so bartering (swapping) of goods became widespread.

Lenin with military commanders in Red Square.

Agriculture and food supplies:

Surplus crops were taken (requisitioned) by the government to feed the workers and the soldiers. Food detachments were sent to the countryside to get the food. They were made up of *'not less than 75 men and two or three machine guns.'* Food was rationed and given to people depending on their contribution to the economy. Industrial workers, for example, received three times more rations than professionals, such as lawyers.

War Communism achieved its aim of winning the war but it caused great suffering. Industrial production declined, though this was partly caused by shortages of raw materials such as cotton, coal and iron. There were severe shortages of fuel, and transport ground to halt except for the war effort. The peasants cut back in grain production so that, along with bad weather in 1920 and 1921, Russia experienced famine in 1921. It is estimated that between five and seven million people died of hunger.

(iii) The Red Terror

The **Cheka**, led by Felix Dzerhinsky, began the **Red Terror**. Any opposition to Lenin and the Communists was dealt with by violence. Peasants, striking workers, former government officials, landlords or anybody accused of co-operating with the White armies could be punished or executed. The Red Terror became more severe after the attempt on the life of Lenin by Dora Kaplan (August 1918). It was a systematic (organised) terror designed to ensure the continuation of Bolshevik or Communist rule. Some party officials were opposed to it but Lenin encouraged and organised the Red Terror, although he tried to distance himself from it as much as possible. By the end of the Civil War, it was estimated that between 12,000 and 50,000 people were killed by the Cheka and 85,000 prisoners were put into concentration camps.

WHY DID LENIN AND TROTSKY WIN THE RUSSIAN CIVIL WAR?

(i) Trotsky and the Red Army

Trotsky said he had to construct *'an army all over again'*. *'What was needed for this?'* he asked. *'It needed good commanders – a few dozen experienced fighters, a dozen or so Communists ready to make any sacrifice; boots for the bare-footed, a bath house, propaganda, food, underwear, tobacco, matches.'* He introduced conscription for all men between 18 and 40. By 1920 the Red Army was five million strong. To train these inexperienced soldiers, Trotsky forced former **Tsarist officers** to join the army. In some cases he took families hostage to ensure the loyalty of officers. But he also appointed **political commissars** to watch them. The commissars were loyal Communist Party workers who were responsible for the morale of the troops.

Trotsky imposed a harsh discipline on the army but he also won the respect of the soldiers by moving from front to front giving orders and raising the spirit of the troops. He used a special armoured train equipped with a printing press, a radio station and a telegraph office. Trotsky took advantage of internal supply lines by using the rail system which centred on Moscow and Petrograd. He could move troops around quickly to face each new threat from the Whites.

> **KEY CONCEPT: PROPAGANDA** is spreading information to convince people of your point of view. Governments and politicians use propaganda to achieve or retain power. Newspapers, posters, leaflets, speeches, word of mouth and (in more recent times) radio and television, can be used to spread the information. The information may be true, partly true or lies.

(ii) The Weaknesses of the White Armies

The White armies were disunited and poorly led with each group following different aims, so they failed to co-ordinate their attacks. They were also responsible for atrocities in the lands they conquered. Their soldiers were badly disciplined and were prone to drunkenness and looting. In southern Russia 100,000 Jews were killed in anti-semitic attacks. Overall they caused far more suffering to the peasants than the Red Terror of the Communists. One British officer who was helping Kolchak in Siberia said, *'I think most of us were secretly in sympathy with the Bolsheviks after our experiences with the corruption and cowardice of the other side.'*

(iii) Lenin and War Communism

Lenin was responsible for supplying the army with weapons and food. He also had control of much of the war material produced for use in the First World War. He and Trotsky provided a united leadership.

(iv) Use of Propaganda

The Communists used propaganda more effectively. They used posters and leaflets to frighten the peasants and workers that the Tsar and the landlords would return under the Whites. They also appealed to Russian nationalism against the intervention of Allied armies; they were fighting for Russia against foreign invaders.

ТОВ. ЛЕНИН ОЧИЩАЕТ ЗЕМЛЮ ОТ НЕЧИСТИ.

Lenin sweeps away the opposition: effective Communist propaganda.

(v) The Attitude of the Peasants

The peasants did not like the Communists but they feared the Whites even more because they would bring back the landlords, as they did in some areas.

Famine: seven million Russians died in 1921, largely due to the First World War and Civil War.

(vi) The Red Terror

The Communists used the Red Terror to force people to concentrate on the war effort and to eliminate any opposition.

(vii) The Allied Withdrawal

The Allies lost interest in Russia when the First World War was over. The Whites lost the sympathy of the Allied governments because of their atrocities, their anti-semitism and their plans to restore the Tsar. Allied armies were withdrawn and supplies of weapons dried up. Eventually Britain signed a new trade agreement with Soviet Russia.

(viii) Conclusion

The Red Army won the Civil War but at great cost. During the Civil War 10 million people were killed for various reasons. Besides the fighting and the terror, disease also killed many; 2 million were killed by typhus alone. In the famine of 1921, 5 to 7 million died. Compared with 1913, factory production was only one-fifth and food production was halved.

Many of the defeated Whites emigrated from Russia. Some settled in Eastern Europe but others moved to Paris, Berlin and other western cities. Soviet Russia lost many of its educated class – writers, scientists and engineers – and later suffered from a shortage of managerial talent.

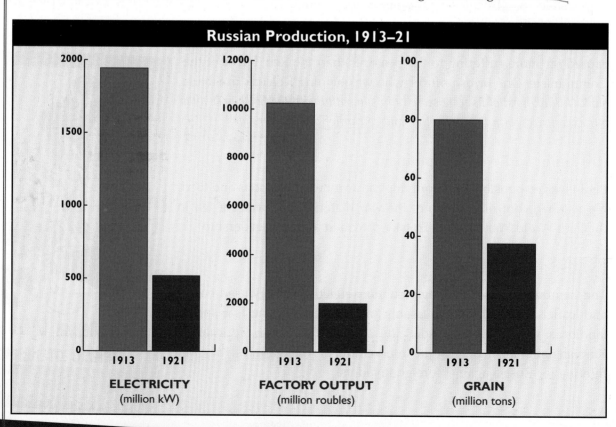

Russian Production, 1913–21

ELECTRICITY (million kW)

FACTORY OUTPUT (million roubles)

GRAIN (million tons)

The Rule of Lenin

While the Civil War was in progress, between 1918 and 1921, Lenin established a **Communist dictatorship:**

- The newly named Communist Party grew in membership from about 250,000 in 1917 to 700,000 in 1921.
- All government power was concentrated in the hands of party members.
- All opposition were banned, with dissenters imprisoned, exiled or shot.

In March 1921, Lenin banned all factions or groups within the Party.

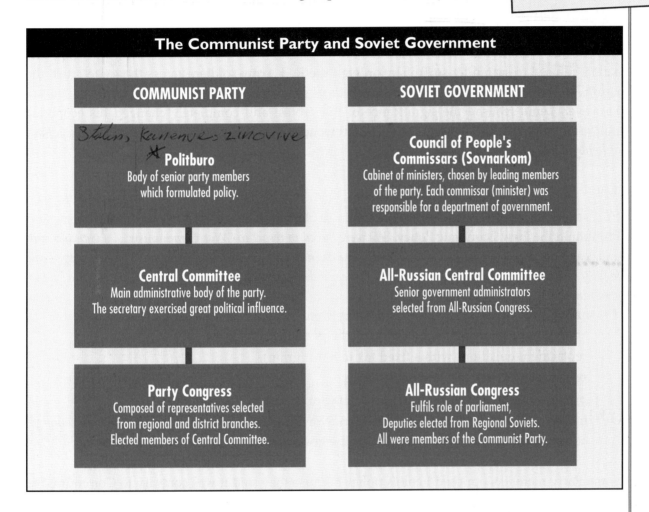

The Communist Party and Soviet Government

COMMUNIST PARTY

Stalin, Kamenev, Zinoviev

✗ Politburo
Body of senior party members which formulated policy.

Central Committee
Main administrative body of the party. The secretary exercised great political influence.

Party Congress
Composed of representatives selected from regional and district branches. Elected members of Central Committee.

SOVIET GOVERNMENT

Council of People's Commissars (Sovnarkom)
Cabinet of ministers, chosen by leading members of the party. Each commissar (minister) was responsible for a department of government.

All-Russian Central Committee
Senior government administrators selected from All-Russian Congress.

All-Russian Congress
Fulfils role of parliament, Deputies elected from Regional Soviets. All were members of the Communist Party.

LENIN AND THE NEW ECONOMIC POLICY

Ending War Communism

In March 1921, Lenin announced the end of War Communism and the beginning of the **New Economic Policy** (NEP). Social and economic life in Russia was badly disrupted by the First World War, the Civil War, the policy of War Communism and the Allied blockade of Russia. This resulted in serious discontent which undermined support for Communism:

- There were peasant risings against food requisitioning and the abolition of private trading.
- Workers' discontent increased as factories closed due to shortages of fuel and raw materials.
- Strikes in Petrograd in early 1921 led to the imposition of martial (military) law.

But the Kronstadt rising presented the most serious difficulties for Lenin and the Communist Party.

The Kronstadt Rising, 1921

Kronstadt was a naval base on an island near Petrograd. In March 1921 the Kronstadt sailors rose in revolt against the Communist Party and War Communism. These sailors had played a major role in the victory of the Bolsheviks in the October Revolution, 1917. Now they were very critical of the new regime brought in by Lenin. They said the Communist government *had taken away the fruits [of the Revolution] from the workers and peasants in whose name it had been made.'*

They demanded new elections to the soviets, freedom of speech for other political parties, freedom for trade unions, the end of food requisitions and the right of peasants to hold land.

Lenin and **Trotsky** took immediate action against the revolt because they saw the danger it posed to their survival. Trotsky stated his intention to have the rebels *'shot down like partridges'*. The sailors refused to surrender so Trotsky ordered the Red Army soldiers across the ice to crush the rising. The Kronstadt fortress fell and hundreds of prisoners were killed.

However, Lenin realised the significance of the protest and completely changed his economic policy to revive the Russian economy. The Kronstadt rising, he said, *'illuminated reality like a flash of lightning'*.

The New Economic Policy (NEP)

In a speech to the Party in April 1921 Lenin explained why he ended War Communism and brought in the New Economic Policy. *'We were forced to resort to "War Communism" by war and ruin ... it was a temporary measure ... Our poverty and ruin are so great we cannot hope to restore large-scale factory socialist production at one stroke.... Hence, it is necessary, to a certain extent, to help to restore small industry....'*

The **main points of the New Economic Policy** were:

- ending requisitions (taking food) from the peasants,
- replacing requisitions with a fixed tax in kind (grain),
- peasants could sell the surplus produce,
- private enterprise was allowed in small factories and in trade,
- heavy industry (coal, iron, electricity, railways) – *'the commanding heights of the economy'*, as Lenin said – were still controlled by the government.

Some Party members opposed Lenin's policy because they said it was contrary to Communist or Marxist ideas. Lenin justified his policy as a temporary retreat from Communism to give the Russian economy the time to recover and to ensure the survival of the Communist Party.

The Results of the NEP

The NEP was successful:

- By increasing agricultural and industrial production, it helped Lenin and the Communists survive.
- In farming, production reached pre-war levels by 1925. Peasant unrest declined and the richer peasants (kulaks) benefited.
- A new class of merchant or trader developed – **nepmen** – who controlled trade between country and towns.
- Heavy industry increased production but in some areas it did not yet reach pre-war levels.

Lenin saw that the country was not ready for communist. He said "The boat must take one step back, far then steps forward (socialist) Trotsky, a poor marxist was not interested with city acceptance of limited capitalism.

By the end of the 1920.s it seemed that the country had removed from the miseries of war.

Lenin's New Economic Policy increased farming production. Richer farmers (kulaks) could afford new machinery.

Industrial and Agricultural Production in Russia before and after NEP, 1913–25

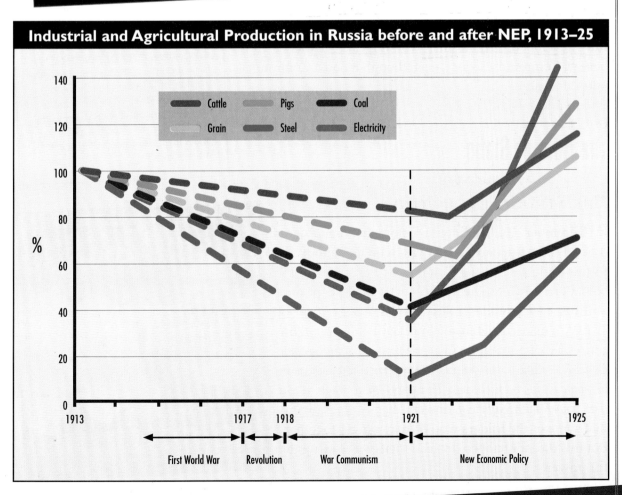

THE DEATH OF LENIN

Lenin did not live to see the full effects of the New Economic Policy. He suffered a series of strokes in 1922 and 1923 and died in January 1924, at the age of fifty-three. His body lay in state for a week as thousands of Russian people marched past in the freezing cold. Afterwards, his body was embalmed and placed in a special mausoleum in Moscow. Petrograd was renamed Leningrad in his honour.

Thousands of people attended Lenin's funeral.

ASSESSMENT OF LENIN

[handwritten margin note: Trotsky called Lenin "engine driver of revolution"]

A cult of Lenin was developed after his death but it is unlikely he would have wanted this. His widow, Krupskaya, wrote, *'Do not build monuments to him, name palaces after him, do not hold magnificent celebrations in his memory. All of this meant so little to him.'*
He created the Communist Party of the Soviet Union and led it to the first Communist revolution and Communist state. He showed how a small group of dedicated revolutionaries could win a revolution. He ensured the survival of Communism in Russia after the revolution and he created a one-party Communist dictatorship which others later imitated.

But, he left many problems for his successor(s). Russia was still a peasant society with eighty per cent of its people earning their living from the land. It was still relatively poor compared to France, Britain and Germany. Since manufacturing industry was not fully developed it had a small working class. It was far from being a Communist society, even though it had a Communist party in charge.

> **KEY CONCEPT: CULT OF PERSONALITY.**
> In politics, the cult of personality is the worship of a leader. This involves the use of propaganda to create an image of the leader who is all-wise and powerful. The leader speaks for the people and guides them. They put their trust entirely in the leader.

The Rule of Stalin

[handwritten note: mausoleum]

THE STRUGGLE FOR POWER

In December 1923, a month before he died, Lenin drafted his Testament. He was worried about the future leadership of the Communist Party and of the Soviet Union. In it, he wrote about the **exceptional abilities** of Comrade Trotsky. But he was critical of Trotsky's **over-confidence**. However, Lenin was more concerned about Stalin. *'Comrade Stalin, having become General Secretary, has concentrated an enormous power in his hands, and I am not sure he always knows how to use that power with sufficient caution.'* Lenin was hoping that some of the leaders would share power together. But this did not happen. Instead there was a **struggle for power**.

Lenin was concerned that Stalin (right) would misuse power after his own death.

Trotsky Versus Stalin

The contest for Lenin's successor rested between Trotsky and Stalin. Many thought Trotsky would become the new leader because he had clear advantages over Stalin. He had commanded the Red Guards in the October Revolution, 1917. He had also created and led the Red Army in the Civil War. He was a great organiser and a very able speaker. But he also suffered certain disadvantages. He was personally arrogant and some feared he might use the army to take over Russia. Stalin, on the other hand, was like a **grey blur** – nobody was sure what he stood for. He initially joined two other Communist leaders, **Zinoviev** and **Kamenev**, in opposition to Trotsky. All were members of the Politburo, the main ruling body of the party, and they

From left: Stalin, Rykov, Kamenev and Zinoviev defeat Trotsky after Lenin's death.

had a strong influence over the party organisation in other ways. Zinoviev was dominant in Petrograd (Leningrad) and Kamenev was strong in Moscow. Stalin was not only **Commissar of Nationalities**, he was also **General Secretary** of the party. This gave him great influence over party membership and allowed him to appoint supporters in key positions in the party.

Stalin deliberately spread the cult of Lenin, beginning with the stage-management of Lenin's funeral. He was able to promote his own image as **the best, the staunchest, the truest comrade-in-arms of Lenin**.

Stalin was also helped by the mistakes of others. Trotsky failed to attend Lenin's funeral and also attacked Lenin's New Economic Policy. Zinoviev and Kamenev helped Stalin by refusing to publish Lenin's Testament, with its damaging verdict on Stalin.

Permanent Revolution and Socialism in One Country

But the major battle between Trotsky and Stalin was fought over the future of Communism and the development of Soviet Russia. Trotsky supported the idea of **permanent revolution** in which workers in other countries would be encouraged to revolt and set up Communist states. He took the view that Communism was weak in Russia and could not be developed unless Communism was spread to other countries, particularly in western Europe.

Stalin, on the other hand, believed in '*socialism in one country*'. He said Communism should be developed in Russia first, so that the country would be a modern, powerful state, rather than encouraging world revolution. Stalin was supported in this policy by Zinoviev and Kamenev. This was also the policy supported by party members who felt that Russia had suffered enough through war and revolution from 1914 to 1921.

Victory for Stalin

Stalin soon turned against Zinoviev and Kamenev and when they joined Trotsky, it was too late. The three were voted out of the **Politburo** in 1926, and Trotsky and Zinoviev were expelled from the party in 1927 along with seventy-five supporters. Trotsky was then exiled to Siberia before he was eventually banished from the Soviet Union (1931) and later assassinated in Mexico (1940). By the end of 1929, Stalin had filled all positions in the Politburo with his own supporters. He was now fully in control of the Soviet Union.

KEY PERSONALITY: STALIN

Stalin was born in Georgia, in the southern part of the Russian Empire, in 1879. He joined the **Bolsheviks** and was a follower of Lenin. He did not come to prominence until after the October revolution in 1917. He took part in the **Russian Civil War**, being involved in the defence of **Tsaritsyn**, which was later called Stalingrad.

After the Bolshevik (Communist) Revolution, he began a slow rise to power. He became **General Secretary** of the Communist Party. He used this position to put loyal followers in power. When Lenin died, there was a **struggle for power** between **Trotsky**, **Kamenev**, **Zinoviev** and **Stalin**. Stalin was the least favoured but he first of all combined with Kamenev and Zinoviev to defeat Trotsky. Then he defeated Kamenev and Zinoviev so that by 1928 he was the most powerful person in the Soviet Union. He now set about the huge transformation of Soviet society – building **Socialism in One Country**. He brought in **Five Year Plans** to industrialise Russia. He concentrated on heavy industry – iron, steel and electricity. He also **collectivised** the farms. By 1938, Stalin had made Russia into the world's second industrial power. But in the process he had created great suffering for the workers and the peasants (farmers). Stalin also crushed any opposition to himself. He made Russia into a **totalitarian state** by controlling press and radio, creating a **cult of personality** and suppressing any criticism. He organised the **Great Purges** which resulted in the deaths of millions. As part of the Great Purges, he set up the **Moscow Show Trials** of high ranking Communist party members such as Kamenev and Zinoviev, and others.

By 1939, Stalin was aware of the dangers posed by Hitler. He signed the **Nazi-Soviet Pact** to give himself time to prepare for war. In 1941 Hitler invaded Russia. Stalin organised the defence of the country in the **Great Patriotic War**. The **Battle of Stalingrad** was one of the turning points of the war. After that, the Russian army pushed back the German army to Berlin. Stalin took part in the **wartime conferences** with Churchill and Roosevelt. He was able to take credit for playing a big part in defeating Hitler. He continued in power until his death in 1953.

The Stalinist State in Peace

> **KEY CONCEPT: TOTALITARIANISM** is a term which was first used in the 1920s to describe the type of government in Italy, Germany and Russia. Totalitarian governments control all aspects of life, from the actions of people to their thoughts. These governments make great use of propaganda, secret police, terror and a strong political party.

In Stalin's Russia, all adults had the right to vote. They elected the local soviets (councils) who in turn selected representatives for the higher soviets at district and provincial level. At the top there was the Congress of Soviets. The Soviet Constitution of 1936 guaranteed freedom of speech, freedom of the press and the right to work and education. However, even though this had the appearance of a democratic structure, real power lay with the Communist Party, the secret police and the army. Stalin created a **totalitarian state** where the party controlled all the people and the state.

The Party: The Communist Party grew in size from 1·3 million members in 1928 to 3·3 million in 1933. It became less a party of workers and more a party of **intelligentsia** (the educated class). Party members were in control of press, radio and industry.

The secret police: The Party used the OGPU, later called the NKVD, to enforce Party policy and to ensure conformity to the Party's wishes. It supervised some of the major projects of the Five Year Plans, purged the Party in the 1930s and controlled the labour force of the prison camps.

The Soviet army: The army also came under the direct control of the party. Most of the army commanders were party members. At any rate, military commanders worked alongside political commissars who ensured party policy was followed.

Stalin used posters to develop a cult of personality.

THE CULT OF STALIN

An important feature of Stalin's totalitarian state was the **cult of personality**. *'Stalin is our hope, Stalin is the beacon which guides all progressive mankind. Stalin is our banner. Stalin is our will. Stalin is our victory.'* These are the words of Khrushchev, one of the new Communist leaders promoted during the 1930s. Stalin and the Communist Party deliberately promoted this worship of Stalin. History was rewritten to make Stalin a hero of the October Revolution and the Civil War. Posters, photographs and statues of Stalin were everywhere. Cities and streets were named after him. Music, art and poetry were used to praise him. Propaganda made him the equal of Lenin; *'Stalin is the new Lenin of today.'* Soon he was exceeding Lenin in importance – he was the *'most learned of men'*, *'the fount of all wisdom'*. He was treated like a god.

O great Stalin, O leader of the peoples,

Thou who brought man to birth,

Thou who fructifies the earth,

Thou who restores to centuries,

Thou who makes bloom the spring,

Thou who makes vibrate the musical chords,

Thou, splendour of my spring, O thou,

Sun reflected by millions of hearts.

A O Avidenko, published in *Pravda*, 1938

The Soviet Alternative

THE FIVE YEAR PLANS

Why Did Stalin Introduce the Five Year Plans?

In 1928, Stalin introduced the first **Five Year Plan**. This meant that the New Economic Policy was abandoned and a **centrally planned economy** was put in its place. This would ensure forced economic growth. This huge change in Soviet economic policy was due to a number of factors:

- Stalin wanted to get greater control of the economy so that he would have greater control of the Soviet Union.
- He wanted to overcome the failure of agriculture to produce enough grain for the towns.
- Stalin wanted to modernise Russia so that it would match the economies of the western world as quickly as possible. *'We are 50 to 100 years behind the advanced countries. Either we make good the difference in 10 years or they will crush us.'*

The Operation of the Five Year Plans

Industry: The First Five Year Plan, 1928–32

The economic planning was directed by the **Central Planning Commission (Gosplan)**. In industry, Gosplan decided on production targets in manufacturing, transport and raw materials. These targets were set for the regions and the factories.

The first Five Year Plan concentrated on heavy industry – coal, iron, gas, and electricity. Their expansion formed the basis for future industrial growth.

autarky = self-sufficient

Overall, the targets were too high but yet by the end of 1932 significant progress was made:

- **machinery** production increased by four times,
- **oil** production doubled,
- **electricity** almost trebled,
- **new towns** such as Magnitogorsk were constructed,
- but there was also **poor quality or faulty production** because of the concentration on quantity.

Left: in 1928 the gloating rich man calls the Five Year Plan a 'fantastic dream'; in 1933 he is angry because he is proved wrong. Middle: fulfil the Five Year Plan in four years. Right: you are now a free woman – help build socialism.

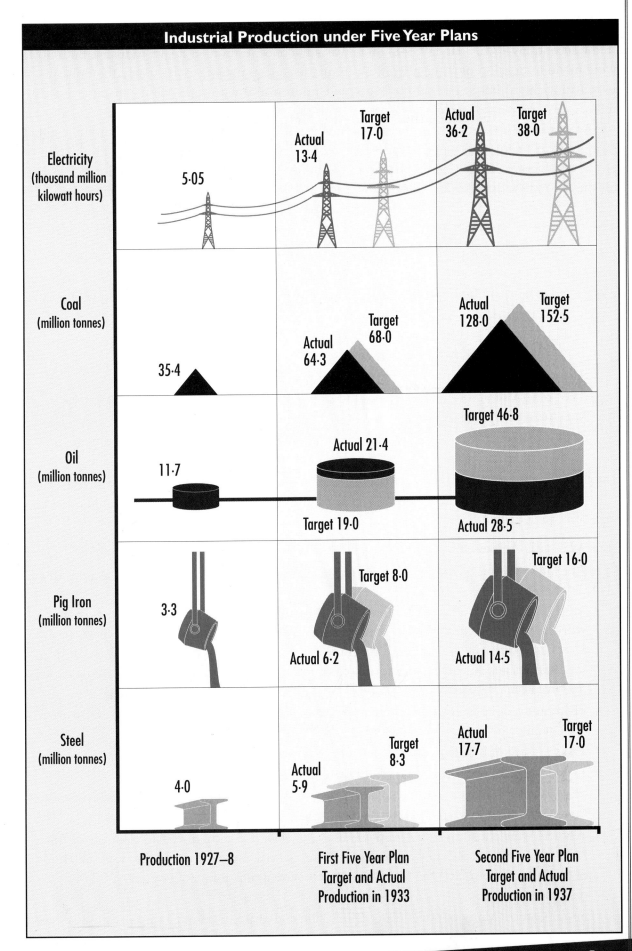

Electricity (thousand million kilowatt hours)

5·05

Actual 13·4 Target 17·0

Actual 36·2 Target 38·0

Coal (million tonnes)

35·4

Actual 64·3 Target 68·0

Actual 128·0 Target 152·5

Oil (million tonnes)

11·7

Actual 21·4 Target 19·0

Target 46·8 Actual 28·5

Pig Iron (million tonnes)

3·3

Target 8·0 Actual 6·2

Target 16·0 Actual 14·5

Steel (million tonnes)

4·0

Actual 5·9 Target 8·3

Actual 17·7 Target 17·0

Production 1927–8

First Five Year Plan Target and Actual Production in 1933

Second Five Year Plan Target and Actual Production in 1937

The Soviet Alternative

The Second and Third Five Year Plans

In the second Five Year Plan (1933–8) there was still concentration on heavy industry. But efforts were made to develop new metalworking industries and transport, particularly the railways. It was during the second plan that the **Moscow Underground** was built. More consumer goods – radios, washing machines etc. – were also promised.

However, during the progress of the second Five Year Plan, the troubled state of Europe resulted in more investment in armaments, and this led to a cutback in consumer goods. Production of armaments became even more important in the third Five Year Plan (1938–41) as Europe headed for the Second World War. The German invasion in 1941 shortened the life of the plan.

The Results of the Five Year Plans

By 1941, the Soviet economy was transformed. A backward, mainly agricultural country was changed into a leading industrial power. The Russian economy grew far more rapidly than the western economies of the US, Britain and France. Russia was now the second largest economy in the world, after the US:

- Production of industrial goods almost trebled.
- Iron, oil and electricity production grew even faster.
- The urban working class grew from 11 million in 1928 to 33 million in 1938.
- The Soviet Union did not experience the Depression suffered by the West; instead there was full employment.
- Russia had a better educated workforce as illiteracy was wiped out and the numbers in secondary schools grew six times between 1928 and 1938.

The changes in the economy meant that Russia was now better prepared to face the German invasion when it came in 1941. Indeed, it can be argued that Stalin's industrialisation and modernisation saved the Soviet Union.

How Was This Achieved?

(i) All the authority and power of the state was used to force through industrialisation rapidly.

(ii) The Workers:

- Much of Stalin's success was due to the hard work and reduced living standards of the workers. Working conditions were severe and there was the risk of punishment as a **wrecker**, if targets were not met. **Absenteeism** from work was punished by loss of job, food rations and housing. An **internal passport system** was introduced to prevent workers moving from job to job.
- There was a large increase in **women workers**. By 1940, forty per cent of industrial workers were women as the government set up crèches and day care centres.
- The standard of living of workers fell and they were worse off in 1938 compared to 1928.
- They lived in overcrowded and badly maintained buildings.
- There were also incentives for workers. There were **bonus payments** for those who exceeded targets and **holidays** were paid for by the state.
- Workers were encouraged by **propaganda**. The work of **Stakhanov** is an example of this. He along with his colleagues produced 102 tons of coal in one shift. He became the **Hero of Socialist Labour**, and the **Stakhanovite movement** encouraged workers to follow his success.

(iii) Labour Camps: Many opponents of Stalin's rule ended up in **labour camps** or **gulags**. Here, as many as ten million were used as **slave labour** in building roads, bridges and canals. The greatest project was the building of the 500 km canal from the White Sea to the Baltic Sea.

COLLECTIVISATION – THE REVOLUTION IN AGRICULTURE

What Was Collectivisation?

The changes in industry were accompanied by equally huge changes in agriculture. Indeed the changes in agriculture contributed to the success of industry. A new policy – collectivisation – was introduced. In **collectivisation**, individual farms were taken over by the government and combined into collective farms in which the land was jointly owned and worked by the peasants. The **collectives** hired machinery from the **Machine Tractor Stations** run by the government and they had to sell quotas to the state at low prices. Some farms were combined into **state farms** where the peasants were paid as labourers. Initially Stalin encouraged voluntary collectivisation, but in 1929 he insisted on forced collectivisation.

> **KEY CONCEPT: COLLECTIVISATION.** This was the policy of Stalin's government to force the peasants (farmers) to give up their farms and form large collective farms. The work, machinery and the profits were shared.

Why Did Stalin Introduce Collectivisation?

Stalin introduced collectivisation for economic and political reasons.

(i) Economic Reasons: Stalin wanted to increase the output of grain to feed the workers in the industrial cities. He believed that more grain would be produced in larger farms run by the state. With larger farms, tractors and other machinery could be shared to improve efficiency. Stalin also wanted to export food to buy industrial machinery and raw materials needed for industrialisation.

Collectivisation: Soviet women cleaning grain.

(ii) Political Reasons: Many Communists disagreed with the New Economic Policy because it created a rich farming class (kulaks) who owned their own land. These Communists wanted to put their ideas into practice and this meant state control of agriculture. They supported Stalin's proposal for collectivisation.

Collectivisation in Progress

There was huge resistance to Stalin's collectivisation among the **kulaks** (or rich peasants). They slaughtered their animals and burnt or hid their grain rather than hand it over to the collectives. Food production fell and there was a **famine** in Russia in 1932–3, which killed over five million people. Stalin responded with harsh measures – he said the kulaks must be eliminated. He sent out groups from the towns to the countryside to seize grain. He had kulaks rounded up and killed or sent to labour camps (gulags).

'Trainloads of deported peasants left for the icy north, the forests, the steppes, the deserts. These were the whole populations ... the old folk starved to death in mid-journey, new born babies were buried on the side of the road, and each wilderness had its crop of little crosses of white wood.'

By the middle of the 1930s the whole kulak class (about five million people) had been wiped out. But the strong resistance against collectivisation forced Stalin to make concessions. He allowed the peasants to hold onto **small private plots** around their houses. The produce was sold to the state or at private markets.

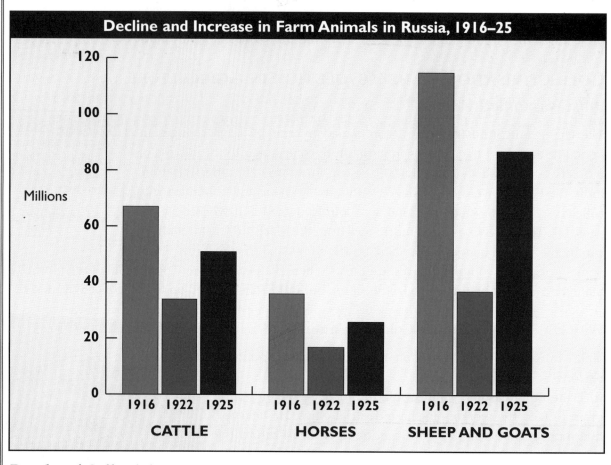

Decline and Increase in Farm Animals in Russia, 1916–25

Millions

	1916	1922	1925	1916	1922	1925	1916	1922	1925
	CATTLE			HORSES			SHEEP AND GOATS		

Results of Collectivisation

- Stalin's harsh methods meant that by 1940, 97% of the farms were collectivised.
- But the **cost in lives** was very great. About 10 million people died as a result of collectivisation, either because of famine or the labour camps.
- In spite of the changes, the collectives were still **inefficient**. Indeed, by the end of the 1930s, most of the country's milk and meat and half of its wool was produced on the private plots.
- Collectivisation helped the **growth of industry** – many peasants left farming to work in industry and industrial workers were sold cheap grain by the government.

THE PURGES AND SHOW TRIALS

Why Did Stalin Begin the Purges?

Stalin's policies of forced industrialisation and collectivisation led to increased opposition to him in the Communist Party. He was worried that his enemies were plotting against him. Criticisms by **Trotsky**, who was now in exile outside

Show Trials in the House of Trade Unions. Posters of Marx, Engels, Lenin and Stalin.

Russia, angered Stalin. Stalin claimed that Trotsky was plotting with others in the country to overthrow him. In the middle of the 1930s Stalin began a series of **purges** (cleaning out) of all opposition to him.

The Assassination of Kirov

Stalin was suspicious of **Kirov**, the leader of the Communist Party in Leningrad. But, historians are divided on whether he ordered the assassination of Kirov in December 1934. However, he took advantage of Kirov's death and used it as an excuse to begin purging his enemies. The assassin and thirteen of his colleagues were shot, and over 100 others unconnected to Kirov's death were also executed. Over the next year, there was a witch hunt throughout the Party and hundreds were arrested. But this was nothing like the Great Purge which began one year later in 1936 and lasted for two years.

The Great Purge

The Great Purge began with the arrest of **Zinoviev** and **Kamenev** in August 1936. They were tried in Moscow in the first of the public trials (called **Show Trials**) and were executed. After this Stalin purged his enemies in the main institutions of the country, beginning with the Communist Party.
The Party: Members at all levels in the Party were accused of plotting against Stalin and spreading **Trotskyite** propaganda. One historian writes:

> 'The records of all members were scrutinised for dangerous tendencies. One comrade might have given a testimonial ten years previously to a member since convicted of Trotskyism ... Another's wife's aunt might have emigrated from Russia in 1918 ... Their fate was the same; they were **unmasked** by one or other of their colleagues, invited to confess before a mass meeting, were rarely found not guilty, lost their jobs, were usually deported to work camps ... and their families and associates were next to be **unmasked**.'

The Army: Stalin next purged the Soviet Red Army. The Commander-in-chief, Tukhachevsky, and 35,000 officers – half the officer corps – were either shot or jailed. These included most of the army commanders and generals.

The Secret Service: Not even the secret police, the NKVD, were safe. **Yagoda**, the head of the secret police, and responsible for the interrogation and execution of all the accused, was tried and executed. He was replaced by Yezhov, who was later accused of **excessive zeal** in carrying out the purges and executed.

An American newspaper published photos of Soviet leaders killed in Stalin's purges.

More Trials and Purges

During this time also, there were **two further Show Trials**. In January 1937, a further 17 Communist leaders were tried and executed. This was followed in March 1938 by the last of the trials when **Bukharin**, **Rykov** and **Yagoda** along with 18 others were either shot or jailed. (See Case Study: Stalin's Show Trials, 1936–8 on p. 31.)

'Visit the pyramids of the USSR': anti-Soviet cartoon published by exiled Russians living in France. What is its message?

But the Purges went far beyond the leaders and the main organisations. They reached into all areas of Soviet life. Nobody was safe. Between 1936 and 1938 millions of ordinary Russians were arrested by Stalin's secret police. Some were tried, some were executed, many ended in the **labour camps (gulags)** in Siberia. Very often family members never heard from them again. One woman later described what happened to her father when she was young. *'They came in the middle of the night and took my father away. I never saw him again.'*

Why Were the Purges So Cruel?

At the end of 1938, the Purges ended almost as suddenly as they began when Beria replaced Yezhov. There had been other purges in Russia during Lenin's life and earlier in Stalin's rule. But historians disagree on how to explain the **savagery and cruelty** of the Great Purge:

- Some historians say that Stalin was suffering from paranoia (suspicious of everybody).
- Others suggest that he was corrupted by great power.
- Some say he was sadistic (cruel) by nature.
- Others blame the structures laid down by Lenin with a one-party state and a secret police under its control.
- Defenders of Lenin say he would not have allowed the purges to happen if he was still ruling.

The Results of the Purges

1. There was now **no challenge** to the leadership of Stalin.
2. Stalin had destroyed the remaining leaders of the October Revolution and replaced them with a **new generation of leaders**.
3. The **Red Army** took time to recover from its purging. Not surprisingly, the army performed badly in the early stages of the Second World War.
4. Many skilled workers, scientists and engineers were killed. This slowed down the expansion of the economy and the progress of the Five Year Plans.

The Soviet Alternative

ORDINARY LEVEL

1. Study the map, The Russian Civil War, 1918–21 (p. 10) and answer the following questions:

(i) Name three White commanders.

(ii) What foreign countries sent help to the Whites?

(iii) Which cities were controlled by the Bolsheviks/Communists?

2. Study Lenin's Hanging Order (p. 12) and answer the following questions:

(i) Who were the kulaks?

(ii) What did Lenin say must happen to the kulaks?

(iii) Why must the Penza Communists do this?

3. Study the graph of Industrial and Agricultural Production in Russia before and after NEP, 1913–25 (p. 17) and answer the following questions:

(i) When was the lowest and highest production for each of the products listed?

(ii) Why did production decline from 1913 onwards?

(iii) Why did production increase after 1921?

(iv) Which product had the fastest growth after 1921?

4. Study the graphs on Industrial Production under Five Year Plans (p. 23) and answer the following questions:

(i) Which of the products achieved their target in 1933?

(ii) Which of the products reached their target in 1937?

(iii) Why do you think Stalin selected these products for increased production?

(iv) If production did not reach its target, do you think that was a failure?

5. Study the graph of Decline and Increase in Farm Animals in Russia 1916–25 (p. 26) and answer the following questions:

(i) Describe the changes in the numbers of cattle, horses, sheep and goats from 1916 to 1925.

(ii) How do you explain the changes in the number of animals over these years?

(iii) What do you think were the effects of the decline in the number of animals between 1916 and 1922?

6. Study the documents on Stalin's industrialisation and answer the following questions.

> The enormous influx of peasant workers in the first plan raised many problems. Despite emergency measures, it was impossible to train them properly so that much inefficiency, as well as accidents to people and machinery, resulted. The peasant was not used to factory discipline. By tradition he tended to slacken his effort as soon as his earnings covered his necessities . . . He was used to working hard and long at certain seasons and taking things easy at other times . . . The new worker did not always realise that work could go on when it rained, or that punctuality was essential.
>
> J. N. Westwood, *Endurance and Endeavour: Russian History, 1812-1971*

> The city of Magnitogorsk [in the Urals] grew and developed from the dirty, chaotic construction camp of the early thirties into a reasonably healthy and habitable city. A street car line was constructed . . . New stores were built and supplies of all kinds made their appearance in quantity and at reasonable prices. Fuel, clothing and other elementary necessities became available. It was no longer necessary to steal in order to live. The city had 50 schools, 3 colleges, 2 large theatres,

half a dozen small ones, 17 libraries, 22 clubs, 18 clinics, and a large park.

> John Scott, a British engineer who worked in Magnitogorsk

(i) What caused inefficiency and accidents?

(ii) Explain the term 'factory discipline'.

(iii) Why did the peasant slacken his effort?

(iv) How was the pattern of work by the peasant different to factory work?

(v) What was Magnitogorsk like in the early 1930s?

(vi) What improvement did Magnitogorsk experience?

(vii) Why do you think Magnitogorsk grew so rapidly?

(viii) In what ways do these accounts help us understand the problems and possibilities of Stalin's Five Year Plans?

7. Write **paragraph answers** on each of the following questions:

(i) The Allied and White attacks in the Russian Civil War.

(ii) War Communism.

(iii) The Red Terror.

(iv) Lenin's New Economic Policy.

(v) The struggle for power after Lenin's death.

(vi) Stalin's dictatorship of the Communist Party.

(vii) Collectivisation under Stalin.

8. Write **long answers** on each of the following questions:

(i) Why did Lenin, Trotsky and the Communists win the Russian Civil War?

(ii) Lenin's role in Russian History, 1920–24.

(iii) Stalin's Five Year Plans.

(iv) Stalin's rule in the Soviet Union, 1928–39.

(v) How did the Show Trials consolidate Stalin's power? (Department of Education, Sample Paper)

HIGHER LEVEL

1. Evaluate the part played by Lenin in the history of the Soviet Union from 1920 until his death in 1924.

2. How and why did the Communists win the Russian Civil War?

3. Discuss the economic changes experienced by the Soviet Union between 1921 and 1939, OR between 1928 and 1939.

4. How did Stalin win the struggle for power to succeed Lenin, and how did he consolidate that power in the 1930s?

5. How and why did Stalin organise political purges in the 1930s and what was their impact on the Soviet Union?

6. How successful were Stalin's economic policies from 1928 to 1939?

7. 'Under Stalin's rule, up to 1945, there occurred the decisive shift that was to propel the Soviet Union from a backward country to a superpower.' Discuss how this transformation took place. (Department of Education, Sample Paper)

TEST YOURSELF AT
my-etest.com

CASE STUDY: Stalin's Show Trials, 1936-8

INTRODUCTION

During the Great Purge, three show trials were held in Moscow, where senior Communist Party leaders were tried in public. This was part of Stalin's efforts to ensure **greater power** for himself and to **condemn critics** of his collectivisation and industrialisation.

THE FIRST SHOW TRIAL, 1936

The first show trial was held in August, 1936. **Zinoviev**, **Kamenev** and fourteen other leaders were tried. Later trials followed a similar pattern to the first trial:

- accusations of treachery and plotting,
- written confessions,
- a bullying prosecutor,
- no rules of evidence, and
- a final judgment, usually of execution.

In the first trial, Zinoviev, Kamenev and the others were accused of the **murder of Kirov**, the leader of the Communist Party in Leningrad, and **planning to kill Stalin**. Even though **Trotsky** was in exile, he was as much on trial as they were.

Workers voting to demand severe punishment for 'enemies of the people'.

SOURCE 1 – Indictment (charges) of the accused

'On the strength of newly revealed circumstances ascertained by the investigating authorities in 1936 in connection with the discovery of a number of terrorist groups of Trotskyites and Zinovievites, the investigation has established that ... the Zinovievites pursued their criminal terroristic practices in a direct bloc [group] with the Trotskyites and with **L Trotsky**, who is abroad. [They] prepared a number of practical measures for the assassination of Comrades Stalin, ... and others.

One of these terrorist groups ... carried out the foul murder of Comrade **S M Kirov** on 1 December 1934, on the direct instructions from **Zinoviev** and **L Trotsky**.'

Transcript of the trial

SOURCE 2 – Breaking the defendants

'From the start, the rigging of the [Zinoviev] trial was closely planned by Stalin in person ... Stalin would shout that Zinoviev and Kamenev were to be **given the works** until they came crawling on their bellies with confessions in their teeth. Zinoviev was influenced by threats to his family, being also subjected to the physical ordeal of a cell deliberately overheated in the height of the summer, which was additionally troublesome in view of his poor health.'

R Hingley,

Joseph Stalin: Man and Legend

Show Trial: These are public trials held by governments for political purposes. They are used for propaganda purposes. When the government establishes the guilt of the accused, it is sending out a message to its own people and foreign observers that it is following the law.

Terrorist: a person who uses systematic (organised) terror (killings, bombings) as a means of achieving his/her aims.

Fascist: followers of Hitler or Mussolini.

Bourgeois: middle class.

The secret police, the NKVD, interrogated (closely quest- ioned) the accused and forced confessions from them. The NKVD had a great variety of ways to ensure **Zinoviev** and **Kamenev** confessed. They used forced confessions from minor Party officials against the two; they were held in isolation; they were regularly interrogated and deprived of sleep; they were subjected to beatings and threats were made against family members.

SOURCE 3 – Stalin's promise

'Stalin gave his personal word that neither Zinoviev or Kamenev would be executed if they would stand trial on his terms.'

R Hingley, *Joseph Stalin: Man and Legend*

SOURCE 5 – Vyshinsky's cross-examination of Kamenev

Vyshinsky: 'What appraisal should be given of the articles and statements you wrote in 1933, in which you expressed loyalty to the Party? Deception?'

Kamenev: 'No, worse than deception.'

Vyshinsky: 'Perfidy' [Treachery]

Kamenev: 'Worse.'

Vyshinsky: 'Worse than deception, worse than perfidy – find the word. Treason?'

Kamenev: 'You have found it.'

Vyshinsky's summing-up speech:

'The entire people rose to their feet at the first announcement of this villainy. The entire people is trembling with rage. And I, too, as a representative of the State Prosecutor's office, add my indignant and outraged voice of a State Prosecutor to the roar of the millions! I demand that the mad dogs be shot – every single one of them!'

Transcript of the Trial

SOURCE 4 – Zinoviev's admission of guilt

'I want to say once again, that I admit that I am fully and completely guilty. I am guilty of having been an organiser of the Trotskyite-Zinovievite **bloc** second only to Trotsky, the **bloc** which set itself the aim of assassinating Stalin, ... and a number of other leaders of the Party and the government. I plead guilty to having been the principal organiser of the assassination of Kirov.'

Transcript of the Trial

An imaginative drawing of the execution of Karakhan.

SOURCE 6

An American newspaper cartoon from the 1930s.

Zinoviev broke first and then he was used to get a confession from Kamenev. Once the confessions were signed, the defendants had to **memorise** their lines for the trial.

At the trial, three judges sat facing the selected audience of about 200. These included ordinary workers and international observers including journalists and diplomats. The accused sat on four rows of chairs, behind a low wooden barrier. Armed soldiers escorted the accused to their seats.

Across the room from them was the prosecutor's table. **Vyshinsky** was the prosecutor for all three trials. There were no lawyers for the defence and there was no jury. Very often the daily court sessions lasted eight hours.

The only evidence produced at the trial were the **confessions** of Zinoviev, Kamenev and their co-accused. Each of the defendants was cross-examined and they made public statements admitting their guilt.

The prosecutor, Vyshinsky, took the defendants through their pre-arranged testimony and bullied them. All the accused were found guilty and they were shot early the next morning.

THE SECOND SHOW TRIAL, 1937

At the second Show Trial, which lasted eight days, the defendants included **Radek, Pyatakov** and fifteen others. These were all former supporters of Trotsky but they did not hold positions of great power. They were described as members of the **Anti-Soviet Trotskyite Centre**.

They faced similar accusations as Zinoviev and Kamenev faced in the first trial.
The trial followed a similar pattern with Vyshinsky demanding the death penalty and the defendants confessing their guilt. But Radek provided an unusual view of torture. At this trial, 13 were executed and 4 were sent to labour camps, including Radek.

SOURCE 8 – Radek's confession at the trial

'The question has been raised whether we were tortured while being investigated. I have to say that it was not I who was tortured, but it was I who tortured the investigators and made them do a lot of useless work...'

Transcript of the Trial

SOURCE 9 – Soviet newspaper headlines

'We demand the spies' execution!'
'No mercy for the Trotskyite degenerates, the murderous accomplices of Fascism!'

(Note: degenerate = immoral person)

SOURCE 10 – VYSHINSKY'S CROSS-EXAMINATION

Vyshinsky: 'Can the conclusion be drawn from this that Karakhan, with your knowledge, engaged in negotiations with Fascist circles regarding support for your treasonable activity on definite conditions? Was that the case?'
Rykov: 'Yes.'
Vyshinsky: 'And what were the conditions?'
Rykov: 'First, a number of economic concessions, and secondly the so-called dismemberment [break-up] of the USSR.'
Vyshinsky: 'Allow me to ask Bukharin. Did you know?'
Bukharin: 'I did.'

Transcript of the Trial

SOURCE 11 – Krestinsky's admission

The President (of the court): 'Accused Krestinsky, do you plead guilty to the charges brought against you?'
Krestinsky: 'I plead not guilty. I am not a Trotskyite.'
On the following day, Krestinsky changed his mind.
Krestinsky: 'In the face of world public opinion, I had not the strength to admit the truth that I had been conducting a Trotskyite struggle all along. I request the Court to register my statement that I fully and completely admit that I am guilty of all the gravest charges brought against me personally, and that I admit my complete responsibility for the treason and treachery I have committed.'

Transcript of the Trial

The last of the three show trials was held in March 1938. **Bukharin**, **Rykov**, **Yagoda** and eighteen others were tried. This trial is sometimes called the **Great Show Trial** because Bukharin and Rykov had been members of Lenin's Politburo. In Yagoda's case, this was a man who knew more about the Purges than most other people except Stalin. They were accused of:

- being members of the 'Anti-Soviet bloc of Rightists and Trotskyites',
- wrecking and sabotage to weaken the economy,
- attempting to assassinate Stalin,
- some doctors in the group were accused of assisting in the murders of Party members.

Before the trial, the newspapers demanded a clear verdict.

Vyshinsky questioned the defendants about their plotting. They admitted a plot involving **Fascist circles** (Germany). Some defendants moved away from the lines they had learnt, but they were quickly brought back.

One of the defendants, Krestinsky, another Politburo member under Lenin, refused to admit his guilt. But the next day he returned and changed his mind.

Bukharin denied he was guilty of individual charges. However, as part of an agreement to save the lives of his wife and child, he still pleaded guilty to the charges in general terms. All the defendants, except three minor officials, were executed.

Reaction to the Trials

Stalin had to ensure that the trials were accepted by people, both inside and outside Russia, as legal and properly conducted. Prior to the trial, the Soviet newspapers carried full reports of the indictment (charges) of the accused. During the trials, the newspapers carried daily reports and their headlines demanded severe punishment for the accused.

SOURCE 12 – Bukharin's admission of guilt

'I plead guilty to being one of the outstanding leaders of this **Bloc of Rights and Trotskyites**. Consequently, I plead guilty to what directly follows from this, the sum total of crimes committed by this counter-revolutionary organisation, irrespective of whether or not I knew of, whether or not I took direct part, in any particular act.'

Transcript of the Trial

SOURCE 13 – The International Association of Lawyers' statement on the Zinoviev-Kamenev trial

'We consider the claim that the proceedings were unlawful to be totally unfounded.... We hereby categorically declare that the accused were sentenced quite lawfully.'

Report of the US Ambassador, Joseph E Davies, to the State Department

'I have talked to many if not all of the members of the diplomatic corps here, and with possibly one exception, they were all of the opinion that the proceedings established clearly the existence of a political plot and conspiracy to overthrow the government.'

International observers were invited to the trials. These included the US Ambassador, British diplomats and reporters from the *New York Times*. They believed that the Show Trials were legal and fair. By the time the trials ended there was a sense of panic in Russia. The trials indicated that there was a widespread conspiracy with links to foreign countries, including Germany and Japan.

Stalin's role

The Purges and the Show Trials were **directed** by Stalin. He took a close and detailed interest in the interrogation of the accused and in the trials themselves. There is even the suggestion that he observed the Great Show Trial from behind the dark glass of a small window at the rear of the courtroom. But that role was disguised from the people and even from those who were arrested. Instead the Purges were known in Russian as the **Yezhovshchina**, after Yezhov, the head of the NKVD.

ASSESSMENT

The Show Trials have a special place in the general history of the Purges. Stalin used them to **discipline the Soviet population**, as well as close associates in the Party who feared they could be next. The Trials left him in **complete charge** of the Party. He also used the Trials as **propaganda** because, for example, various problems in Russian society could be blamed on **wreckers** or outside agents. These internal and external enemies were used to create unity in the Soviet Union and support for Stalin as leader.

People living in fear and dread

During Stalin's lifetime, one view was expressed in Russia about the Show Trials. While speaking during the Bukharin Trial, Vyshinsky passed his judgment on 'the odious traitors' and on the future of the Soviet Union. Soviet history books provided similar views about what happened.

In 1953, Stalin died and **Khrushchev** took over as leader of the Soviet Union. He set up a Commission to investigate the Purges. At the twentieth Party Congress he condemned Stalin in a wide-ranging speech, which included the findings of the Commission on the Purges and Show Trials.

PRESENT-DAY CONTROVERSY

The Stalin Purges and Show Trials still cause controversy. Historians differ on their interpretations concerning what happened in the 1930s. Present-day admirers of Stalin and Trotsky also differ on what happened then. One of those who experienced the gulags (labour camps), Alexander Solzhenitsyn, who was neither a supporter of Stalin or Trotsky, took a very different view of the Show Trials.

SOURCE 17 – Khrushchev's speech to the twentieth Party Congress, 1956

'The Commission has become acquainted with a large quantity of materials in the NKVD archives and with other documents, and has established many facts relating to false accusations and glaring abuses of Soviet law which resulted in the death of innocent people. Many Party, Soviet and economic activists who were branded in 1937–8 as **enemies** were actually never enemies, spies, wreckers etc., but were always honest Communists. Often, no longer able to bear barbaric tortures, they charged themselves with all kinds of grave and unlikely crimes.'

Quoted in N Khrushchev,
Khrushchev Remembers

SOURCE 18 – UK: Stalin Society Meeting – Moscow Trials, 20 May 2001, London

The Moscow Trials

Misinformation concerning the Moscow Trials abounds in the bourgeois [middle-class] media and in the papers of various Trotskyite outfits who sought then, as now, to undermine the achievements of the USSR and instil scepticism in the minds of workers regarding the practice of socialism. In the 1930s, the Soviet Union stood as a glorious example of how the peoples of the world could rid themselves of unemployment, poverty, hunger – and the bourgeoisie did all it could to prevent this example being followed.

This presentation will give ample evidence of the truth concerning the Trials, namely, that it was a revolutionary purge ... against those who committed treasonable acts against the Soviet state, terror against leaders of the Soviet Union, wrecking and sabotage of Soviet industry, and collaborated with imperialist powers in order to bring about the restoration of capitalism in the USSR.

Sunday, 20 May 2001, 2 p.m.

**Conway Hall,
Red Lion Square, London, WC1**

SOURCE 19 – The Show Trials as plays

'Dumbfounded, the world watched three plays in a row, three wide-ranging and expensive dramatic productions in which the powerful leaders of the fearless Communist Party, who had turned the entire world upside down and terrified it, now marched forth like doleful, obedient goats and bleated out everything they had been ordered to, vomited all over themselves ... and confessed to crimes they could not in any way have committed.'

**Alexander Solzhenitsyn,
*The Gulag Archipelago***

COMPREHENSION

1. Study Source 1. What are the <u>names</u> of the <u>terrorist groups</u>? Who were they planning to assassinate? Who gave direct orders for the murder of Kirov?

2. Who were the **Trotskyites** in Source 1?

3. According to Source 2, who <u>planned</u> the rigging of the <u>Zinoviev trial</u>? Name <u>one factor</u> which <u>influenced</u> Zinoviev <u>to confess.</u>

4. In Source 2, what do you think Stalin meant by saying that Zinoviev and Kamenev were to be 'given the works'?

5. In Source 4, what promise did Stalin make to Zinoviev and Kamenev?

6. To what did Zinoviev plead guilty?

7. Who was the leader of the Trotsky-Zinoviev bloc according to Zinoviev?

8. In Source 5, who were the 'mad dogs' referred to by Vyshinsky?

9. What did Vyshinsky want to happen to the **mad dogs**?

10. In Source 7, what accusations were made against Radek and the others in the second trial?

11. What was Pyatakov accused of?

12. What is **wrecking**?

13. Explain Woodward's view that Pyatakov 'was a convenient scapegoat for the shortcomings of the industrialisation programme'. (Source 7)

14. Did Radek admit to being tortured in Source 8?

15. In the Great Show Trial, what did the newspapers want to happen to Bukharin and the others? (Source 9)

16. According to Source 10, who was Karakhan in negotiations with?

17. According to Source 11, why did Krestinsky say he pleaded not guilty on the first day?

18. In Source 13, what did the International Association of Lawyers say about the Zinoviev-Kamenev trial? Does their view agree with that of the US Ambassador?

19. According to Source 14, what did the Old Bolsheviks believe about Stalin's involvement in the Show Trials and the Purges?

20. In Source 15, what is Vyshinsky's view of Stalin?

21. Does Source 16 support what Vyshinsky said in Source 15?

22. What was the conclusion of the Commission which Khrushchev set up to investigate the Purges and Show Trials (Source 17)?

23. According to Source 18 what were the Trotskyite papers trying to do?

24. What were the 'three plays' Solzhenitsyn referred to in Source 19?

COMPARISON

1. Study Sources 2 and 3. <u>Which</u> of the sources is more <u>helpful</u> in providing an understanding of <u>Stalin's cruelty</u>? Explain your answer.

2. Using <u>evidence taken</u> only from the transcripts of the trial above, what was Stalin able to **prove**?

3. <u>How</u> do the <u>views</u> in Sources <u>13</u> and <u>18 compare</u>?

4. Examine the cartoon in Source <u>6</u>. What are its views about <u>justice</u> in the <u>Soviet Union</u>? What <u>impression</u> does the <u>cartoon give</u> of <u>Stalin</u>? In what <u>ways</u> can it be regarded as <u>propaganda</u>?

5. What do Sources <u>5</u>, <u>10</u> and <u>15</u> tell us about Vyshinsky's <u>style</u> of <u>prosecution</u>?

6. In Source 11, examine <u>Krestinsky's explanation</u> for his <u>change of mind</u>. Do you <u>agree</u> with his explanation <u>or would you support any other</u>?

7. How do the <u>views</u> of the <u>prisoners</u> in Source <u>14</u> compare with Vyshinsky's in Source <u>15</u>?

8. Examine Sources 15, 16 and 17. How do these sources <u>differ</u> on their <u>views</u> of what happened

during the Purges and Show Trials? Which of these is the most reliable? Give reasons for your answer.

9. What are the similarities in the views of Vyshinsky (Source 15) and the advertisement for the Stalin Society meeting (Source 18)? Can you explain the similarities?

10. Do you think Solzhenitsyn (Source 19) agrees with the version of history written in Source 16?

CRITICISM

1. What type of sources are 1, 2 and 3? Is there any evidence of <u>bias</u> or <u>propaganda</u> in any of the sources? <u>Explain your answer.</u>

2. Is the admission of guilt in Source 4 a primary or secondary source? How reliable is it as an admission of guilt?

3. What would you want to know about Source 5 to judge its reliability?

4. How useful are political cartoons as sources for historians? What are their strengths and weaknesses? (Source 6)

5. How useful and reliable are imaginative drawings, such as the drawing of the execution of Karakhan (p. 32), as sources for historians?

6. Why would you expect the views of (i) the International Association of Lawyers, and (ii) the US Ambassador in Source 13, to be reliable?

7. Is the report of the U.S. ambassabor both an **eyewitness** account and a **public record**? Explain your answer. What are the strengths and weaknesses of (i) eyewitness accounts, and (ii) public records, as sources for historians?

8. If historians are now sure that Stalin's Show Trials were set up by him, how do you explain the views in Source 13? What does this tell us about the reliability of sources in general?

9. Which of the Sources 13, 17 and 19 is likely to be more reliable? Give reasons for your answer.

10. How useful is Source 18 as evidence for Stalin's Show Trials?

CONTEXTUALISATION

1. Write an account of the Purges and Show Trials.

2. What were the effects of (i) the Purges, and (ii) the Show Trials, on the Soviet Union?

3. Why was Trotsky the chief defendant in the Show Trials?

4. 'The Purges and Show Trials were part of Stalin's scheme to establish a totalitarian state.' Explain fully how Stalin established a totalitarian state.

OR

How did Stalin hold onto power in the USSR in the 1930s?

5. How did the Show Trials consolidate Stalin's power? (Department of Education, Sample Paper)

The Growth of Dictatorships

Many dictatorships were established in European countries between the First and Second World Wars, from 1918 to 1939. Most of southern and eastern Europe was ruled by **dictatorships**. Only in countries in western Europe, and in two in central Europe, did **democracies** survive. (See map of Dictatorships and Democracies in Europe, 1918–39.)

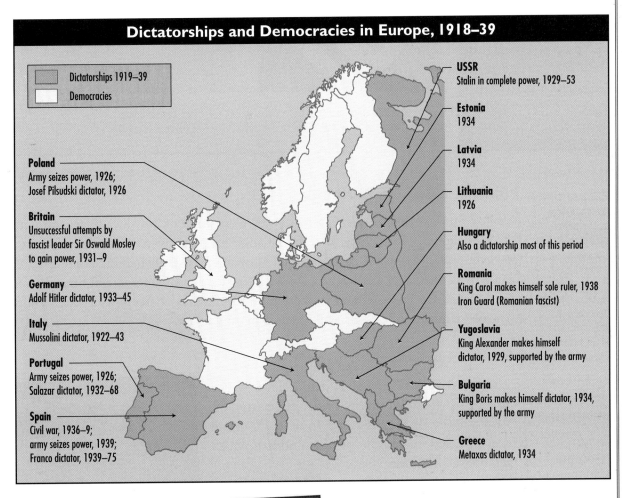

Dictatorships and Democracies in Europe, 1918–39

- Dictatorships 1919–39
- Democracies

Poland
Army seizes power, 1926;
Josef Pilsudski dictator, 1926

Britain
Unsuccessful attempts by fascist leader Sir Oswald Mosley to gain power, 1931–9

Germany
Adolf Hitler dictator, 1933–45

Italy
Mussolini dictator, 1922–43

Portugal
Army seizes power, 1926;
Salazar dictator, 1932–68

Spain
Civil war, 1936–9;
army seizes power, 1939;
Franco dictator, 1939–75

USSR
Stalin in complete power, 1929–53

Estonia
1934

Latvia
1934

Lithuania
1926

Hungary
Also a dictatorship most of this period

Romania
King Carol makes himself sole ruler, 1938
Iron Guard (Romanian fascist)

Yugoslavia
King Alexander makes himself dictator, 1929, supported by the army

Bulgaria
King Boris makes himself dictator, 1934, supported by the army

Greece
Metaxas dictator, 1934

CHARACTERISTICS OF A DICTATORSHIP
Rule by one man (dictator) or party.
No other political parties allowed.
Control of the media (press).
Police and army used to maintain control.

CHARACTERISTICS OF A DEMOCRACY
Rule by the people, usually through elected representatives.
Political parties allowed.
Freedom of speech and a free press (media).
Judges free to apply the rule of law.

The style of government in a dictatorship differed greatly from a democracy. (See box.)

Most of the European dictatorships followed these features. Sometimes the word **authoritarian** is used to describe their rule, such as Franco's dictatorship in Spain and Salazar's in Portugal.

	Germany	**Italy**
Leader	Adolf Hitler	Benito Mussolini
Title	Der Führer (The Leader)	Il Duce (The Leader)
In Power	1933–45	1922–43
Party	Nazi Party	Fascist Party
Symbol of the Party	The Swastika	The Fasces
Armed Force of the Party	Storm Troopers (known as 'Brownshirts')	Combat Groups (Known as 'Blackshirts')

FASCIST DICTATORSHIPS

In many European countries, Fascist parties were popular. Mosley's Blackshirts in Britain, Belgium's Rex Party and the Falange in Spain were examples of these. However, very few Fascist parties came to power and established dictatorships. Of the few who took over government, only two lasted for any significant time. These were **Mussolini's Fascist Party** in Italy and **Hitler's Nazi Party** in Germany. They advocated a new political idea called **Fascism** or **Nazism**.

What Was Fascism?

The word **Fascist** was Italian in origin. It was used by Mussolini to describe his party, the Fascist Party. It was derived from the Ancient Roman **fasces** or bundle of rods and axe which symbolised authority there.

TOTALITARIAN DICTATORSHIPS

The dictatorships of Mussolini and Hitler were also **totalitarian**. In this way they were similar to Stalin's dictatorship in Soviet Russia. They believed that they should control all aspects of a person's life – social, economic, political, cultural and religious. They wanted to create a new person. They differed from **authoritarian regimes** who maintained the power of the ruling classes – church, land and army – and who were happy to keep the people down.

CHARACTERISTICS OF FASCISM

Fascists were:
against democracy and political parties, against the Treaty of Versailles, anti-semitic, anti-Communist.

Fascists favoured:
Extreme nationalism – the individual was subject to the nation; the nation must expand and conquer.
Cult of the leader – everything depended on a **wise** leader, he must be obeyed.
Use of violence – to achieve power, the strong rule over the weak.
Racialism – the people of the nation must be kept **pure**.

WHAT CAUSED THE RISE OF FASCIST REGIMES?

The stories of the rise to power of Mussolini and Hitler differ in some respects but there were many common factors in explaining their rise to power. These were:

- The effects of the First World War.
- Economic depression.
- Unstable government and weak democracy.
- Fear of Communism.
- Strong leadership.
- Use of violence and propaganda.

> **CHARACTERISTICS OF TOTALITARIANISM**
> A single ideology (set of political beliefs) that everyone must follow.
> A single party led by a dictator.
> Control of propaganda (all means of communication).
> Control of police and army and the use of terror.
> Central control of the economy.

Mussolini and Fascist Italy

WHAT CAUSED MUSSOLINI'S RISE TO POWER?

1. Post-war Italy

At the end of the First World War (1914–18), there was great dissatisfaction in Italy with the war. Italians had joined the war in the hope of gaining more land from the defeated Austro-Hungarian Empire. At the Paris Peace Conference, Italy gained most of the land but failed to get **Dalmatia** and the city of **Fiume**. Italian nationalists were bitterly disappointed because they had lost over 600,000 men in the war. They now claimed that Italy had won the war but lost the **mutilated peace**, as they called it. **D'Annunzio**, a nationalist poet and war hero, took action by capturing Fiume with a small revolutionary group. He established a Fascist-style government with ceremonies, flags, symbols, parades and speeches. Nationalists throughout Italy supported him. But he soon turned many people, including his own supporters against him. After fifteen months in Fiume, he was expelled by the Italian army. His failure led to increased nationalist bitterness.

The war also affected the **Italian economy**. By 1919 the economy was in a **depressed** state. Soldiers were demobilised and there were two million unemployed. **Inflation** had risen by over 500 per cent between 1914 and 1920, and this wiped out wages and savings. Italians, from all different classes, felt betrayed that their sufferings during the war did not lead to improvements after the war.

> **KEY CONCEPT: COMMUNISM** was based on the writings of Karl Marx, a German writer of the nineteenth century. He outlined his ideas in **The Communist Manifesto** and **Das Kapital**. Communists believed that the working class would revolt against the middle class who controlled industry. This would result in a Communist society where private property was abolished, the government would run the land and the factories for the benefit of the people and everybody would be equal.

> **KEY CONCEPT: FASCISM.** This was the word used to describe the beliefs of Mussolini and his followers in Italy, and the ideas of Hitler and the Nazis in Germany. Fascism believed in nationalism, dictatorship, racism and the use of violence. It was against democracy and Communism.

Hero: the Italian nationalist poet D'Annunzio took over the city of Fiume after the First World War.

Street fighting in Italy after the First World War. The chaos helped Mussolini to power.

2. Social and Political Discontent

There was widespread discontent in Italy because of the economic depression. In the **towns and cities**, there were large-scale strikes and workers occupied factories. In 1920, there were over 1,800 strikes affecting a million workers. They wanted higher wages and factory councils. They were inspired by socialist and Communist leadership, who wanted *'the violent conquest of political and economic power ... to be entrusted to workers' and peasants' councils'*. There was also widespread conflict in the **countryside** where peasants (farmers) and labourers took over land, often supported by priests.

Industrialists and landlords reacted angrily against these actions. They believed this discontent was due to the spread of Communism. They feared that Italy would soon follow the example of Soviet Russia. They were disappointed at the failure of the Italian governments to stop the lawlessness, so they organised groups of their own to attack workers and peasants.

3. Weak Government

The two largest parties in Italy, the Socialist Party and the Catholic Popular Party, failed to agree so Italy was ruled by **five** different coalition governments between 1919 and 1922. The Italian governments were shown to be weak on many occasions. They failed to control the lawlessness and to solve the political, economic and social problems. Democracy seemed to be failing in Italy so many people looked for a strong leader.

4. Mussolini's Fascist Movement

In March 1919, Mussolini founded his first **combat group** (or **fascio di combattimento**) in Milan. They were also known as **Blackshirts**. Soon other groups were set up in cities in northern and central Italy. At first they had a socialist programme but Mussolini changed that quickly after gaining only two per cent of the vote in elections in Milan in November 1919. After the election, Milan socialists mocked him by carrying a coffin with his name on it past his apartment. Indeed, Mussolini was so disappointed that he thought about emigrating or becoming a pilot.

When Mussolini changed his policies to supporting the monarchy and dropping anti-clericalism (against the power of the Church in politics), he gained support. The Fiume affair also helped. D'Annunzio's adventure was very popular throughout Italy and Mussolini gained from his support for it.

With a more conservative and nationalist policy, Mussolini's Fascist movement grew more rapidly. His Fascist groups took advantage of the disorder and the weakness of the government to gain support. Industrialists and landlords got the help of Fascist squads to put down the workers and the peasants. Over 400 Fascists were killed in clashes with socialists and Communists between 1919 and 1922, but there were twice as many socialists killed.

'We passed through the province destroying and burning all the offices of the socialist and Communist organisations.... Our passage was marked by high columns of fire and smoke.'

By 1922 the Fascists had 3,000 groups and over 250,000 members. The membership was made up of war veterans and ex-officers, professional and landowning sons, and middle class and better-off peasant families.

Mussolini and Fascist Italy

March on Rome

In May 1921, Mussolini's Fascists gained thirty-five seats in parliament and later that year he formed the **Fascist Party** out of his combat groups. The Party claimed to follow *'a policy based on three principles: order, discipline, hierarchy'*. Mussolini's next success was the crushing of socialist-led strikes in August 1922. It appeared as if Mussolini and the **Fascist squads** saved the country from the **red** threat while the government was helpless. This success encouraged him and his fellow leaders to organise a **March on Rome** in October 1922.

After Mussolini was made Prime Minister, he led the Fascist March on Rome.

Fascist groups approached Rome from three directions. As 25,000 **Blackshirts** gathered on the edge of Rome, the Italian government was divided on what to do. Some ministers wanted to resist the march and declare a state of emergency; others believed that the Fascists should be given a share of government. The army could have easily scattered the Fascists. But by now **King Victor Emmanuel III** was tired of all the changes in government and he also feared a civil war. He refused to bring in the army and the Prime Minister resigned. Mussolini did not want to be part of any government unless he was made Prime Minister. The King was left with no alternative but to appoint Mussolini as Prime Minister. At 39, he was the youngest Prime Minister in Italian history.

Two days after Mussolini's appointment as Prime Minister the March on Rome went ahead. It was more of a **victory parade** than a march. But Mussolini gave the impression that he had come to power in a **coup d'etat (takeover of the state)**. The Fascists were now creating another one of their myths – that the March on Rome toppled the government. While the Fascist march was well prepared, it could easily have been stopped. It owed its success to the support of many conservative groups who believed that Mussolini should be given a chance to rule.

Mussolini on the throne. What is the message of the cartoon?

5. Mussolini's Role

Mussolini had played an important role in his own rise to power. Mussolini changed his policies to gain popularity. He believed that Fascism was not a system of unchanging beliefs but **a path to political power**. He made use of the discontent of the soldiers after the war. He was also a clever propagandist and a very able speaker. When he was offered a place in the Italian government he refused it because he knew there was no alternative to making him Prime Minister.

Mussolini was an outstanding speaker and he attracted huge crowds.

KEY PERSONALITY: MUSSOLINI

Mussolini was born in northern Italy. His mother was a schoolteacher and his father was a blacksmith. Mussolini worked at different jobs – he was a teacher, a soldier and a journalist. He was a member of the **Socialist Party** and became **editor** of their newspaper, *Avanti*. He was expelled from the Socialist Party when he wanted Italy to join the First World War. He now became more nationalistic. After the war, he founded the **fascio di combattimento** (combat groups) in 1919. He opposed the growth of socialism and Communism in Italy. His followers used violence to attack socialists. He formed a political party, the **Fascist Party**, out of the combat groups. Mussolini became Prime Minister when the government failed to persuade **King Victor Emmanuel** to use the army against the **March on Rome**.

After becoming Prime Minister, he established a **totalitarian dictatorship**. He controlled all the means of propaganda, set up the **Corporate State**, built roads and drained marshes, made an agreement – the **Lateran Agreement** – with the Pope. In the 1930s he expanded Italy's power by attacking **Abyssinia** and helping Franco in the **Spanish Civil War**. He made agreements with Hitler – the **Rome-Berlin Axis** and the **Pact of Steel**. He stayed out of the Second World War at the beginning. When he joined, the Italian army performed badly. After the Allies invaded Italy he was deposed. Hitler rescued him, but when he was next caught, he was shot.

> **KEY CONCEPT: PROPAGANDA** is spreading information to convince people of your point of view. Governments and politicians use propaganda to achieve or retain power. Newspapers, posters, leaflets, speeches, word of mouth and, in more recent times, radio and television, can be used to spread the information. The information may be true, partly true or lies.

HOW DID MUSSOLINI ESTABLISH DICTATORSHIP?

Mussolini's new government had only four Fascist ministers so Italian nationalists hoped to tame him. But over the next few years, Mussolini used democratic and legal means – parliament and the king – to become a totalitarian dictator.

Parliament

Mussolini first set about destroying the power of parliament. He began by passing the **Acerbo Law** in 1923. This law proposed that the party which got the greatest number of votes in the next election should have two-thirds of the seats. Mussolini argued that this would provide political stability and parliament agreed. In the general election the following year, Mussolini used his Fascist groups to ensure the Fascist Party got the greatest number of votes. He enrolled his Blackshirts into a **Volunteer Militia** and this made their violence legal. He also had success in foreign policy when he got Fiume from Yugoslavia. Not surprisingly, the Fascists won sixty-five per cent of the vote. *Mussolini blackshirt became champions of law and order.*

Matteoti's Murder and the Aventine Secession

One of Mussolini's fiercest critics was **Giacomo Matteoti**, a socialist member of parliament. He was kidnapped by a group of Fascists and brutally killed. There was widespread anger at the murder and Mussolini's position as Prime Minister seemed in great danger. However, two factors saved him. First, the socialists pulled out of parliament in protest, in what became known as the **Aventine Secession**. This only strengthened Mussolini's position and gave greater control to the Fascists. Second, King Victor Emmanuel continued to support Mussolini.

Four years later a new electoral law stated that the Fascist Grand Council, headed by Mussolini, would nominate members of parliament. The Council drew up a list of 400 people which the electorate would vote on as a group. In this way, Mussolini had eliminated the power of the democratic parliament.

Dictatorship

Mussolini was encouraged by his own survival after Matteoti's murder. He even claimed that he had done nothing wrong. *'I declare that I, and I alone, assume the political, moral, and historical responsibility for all that has happened.... Italy wants peace and quiet, and to get on with its work. I shall give it all these, if possible in love, but if necessary by force.'*

Over the next few years he took further steps to impose dictatorship. There were constant house-to-house searches, the free press was stopped, there was harassment of political opponents, political parties were banned and the secret police, OVRA, was set up. Mussolini also banned trade unions and strikes. But his most important step to dictatorship was the power to **rule by decree** which he got in 1926. Over the next 17 years Mussolini signed more than 100,000 decrees.

Totalitarianism

But Mussolini intended to establish not just a dictatorship, but also a **totalitarian dictatorship**. He wanted to control all aspects of the lives of the people, their thoughts as well as their actions. Fascist propaganda played a key role in this.

The cult of the leader: A cult of personality was developed around Mussolini. He was called **Il Duce (the Leader)**. Mussolini used photographs, newspapers, radio and newsreel film to create the image of the all-wise, all-talented leader. *'Mussolini is always right'*, was the motto. There was Mussolini the animal lover – he liked to be photographed with his pet lioness, **Italia**; Mussolini the sportsman – the skier, the horseman, the pilot; Mussolini the worker – the light was left on in his office all night; and Mussolini the ordinary man – he helped out cutting corn.

Mussolini's image as a **superman** was helped when he survived a number of assassination attempts. After one of these, a Fascist leader announced to huge crowds; *'God has put his finger on the Duce! He is Italy's greatest son, the rightful heir of Caesar!'*

Mussolini's image in Italy was also helped by the praise he got from foreign leaders. Churchill, later Prime Minister of Britain, said he would have worn the Blackshirt had he been an Italian.

> **KEY CONCEPT: CULT OF PERSONALITY.**
> In politics, the cult of personality is the worship of a leader. This involves the use of propaganda to create an image of the leader who is all-wise and powerful. The leader speaks for the people and guides them. They put their trust entirely in the leader.

> **KEY CONCEPT: TOTALITARIANISM**
> is a term which was first used in the 1920s to describe the type of government in Italy, Germany and Russia. Totalitarian governments control all aspects of life, from the actions of people to their thoughts. These governments make great use of propaganda, secret police, terror and a strong political party.

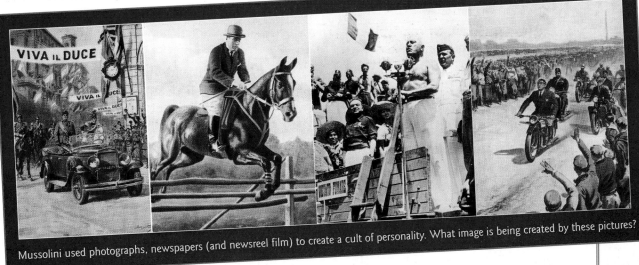

Mussolini used photographs, newspapers (and newsreel film) to create a cult of personality. What image is being created by these pictures?

Young Italian boys were encouraged to join the Balilla.

Education: For the Fascists, the main purpose of education was to teach children the **Fascist values** of **obedience** and **patriotism**. Children were taught that Il Duce would make Italy great again. Textbooks were changed and teachers critical of Fascism were sacked. History was rewritten to highlight the glories of the Roman Empire and only committed Fascists could teach the subject. Mussolini wanted boys to be ready for fighting and girls to be good mothers, in line with the Fascist slogan, *'War is to the male what childbearing is to the female.'*

Youth organisations: Young boys and girls had to join youth organisations outside school. From the age of 4 up to the age of 18, they progressed through a series of these organisations, such as the **Balilla**. After 18, the most dedicated members joined the Young Fascists.

FASCIST YOUTH ORGANISATIONS		
AGE	**BOYS**	**GIRLS**
4 to 8	Sons of the She Wolf	
8 to 14	Balilla	Piccole Italiana
14 to 18	Avanguardisti	Giovanni Italiana

Press and radio: No opposition press was allowed and the existing press and radio was made serve the Fascist regime. The number of radios increased from 27,000 in 1926 to over 1 million by 1939. The Fascists encouraged the production of low-cost radios because they believed the radio was an important means of maintaining contact with the people.

Sport: Sport was important to Fascists because it created fit young men and achievements in sport could be used for nationalist propaganda. Italy organised the **1934 World Cup** and won it, and retained it in 1938. In boxing, **Primo Carnera** became a national hero by winning the world Heavyweight championship.

The police state: The secret police, the OVRA, was set up, along with a special court to try anybody critical of the Fascist state. Individual freedom was abolished. Over 4,000 were imprisoned and others were sent to remote islands, but only about 10 people were sentenced to death. While Mussolini's Italy was brutal and oppressive, it was not as murderous as Hitler's Germany or Stalin's Russia. The power of the OVRA was not as great as the SS in Germany. As well as this, Mussolini's Italy did not have the labour camps of Soviet Russia or the harsh concentration camps of Nazi Germany.

The Limits of Totalitarianism

There were limits to Mussolini's power. Even though Mussolini attempted to gain total control, many groups in Italy were able to hold onto much of their power. Very often he was satisfied by appearances. As one biographer of Mussolini said, *'Mussolini's own mental processes never ceased to be governed by slogans and eight-column headlines.'* The Fascist Party was not as powerful as Stalin's Communist Party or Hitler's Nazi Party. *'In reality, however, the Fascist regime fell well short of the totalitarianism claimed by its spokesmen.... monarchy, industry, landowners, armed forces, and the church formed an integral part of Mussolini's regime, making it less profoundly Fascist ... and less totalitarian in scope than it pretended to be.'* (M Blinkhorn, *Mussolini and Fascist Italy*)

CHURCH-STATE RELATIONS UNDER MUSSOLINI

The Catholic religion was the religion of most Italians and the head of the Catholic Church, the Pope, was based in Rome. However, relations between the Pope and the Italian state had been poor since Italy was united in 1870 and the Pope lost land to the new state.

However, relations between Mussolini's government and the Catholic Church improved during the 1920s. Mussolini was anti-clerical (against the power of the Church in politics) but he knew he could not control the Church. On the other hand, the Catholic Church saw Fascism as the best hope of resisting the spread of Communism.

Mussolini took a series of steps which **improved relations**:

- He brought back compulsory religious education in primary schools.
- Crosses were allowed in the classrooms.
- He had his own civil marriage blessed by a Catholic ceremony.
- Fascist support for the family in the Battle of Births (to increase the Italian population) pleased the Catholic Church.

In return, the Pope withdrew his support for the Catholic Popular Party and this helped Mussolini.

Lateran Agreements, 1929

Following on the improved relations came two years of negotiations which led to the **Lateran Agreements (Treaty and Concordat) of 1929**. Three documents laid out the terms of the agreement:

Mussolini being saluted as the Fascist Prime Minister of Italy by naval and military cadets.

- The Pope recognised the Italian state.
- Italy recognised the Pope's control of the Vatican City.
- Italy paid £30 million compensation for taking Rome in 1870.
- In the Concordat, the Catholic religion was recognised as *'the sole religion of the state'*.
- The Pope appointed all the bishops of Italy, subject to Mussolini's agreement.
- The government agreed to pay the salaries of bishops and priests.
- Religious instruction was to be given in public (state) schools.

This agreement was a major achievement for Mussolini following a dispute which lasted for sixty years. The agreement increased his prestige in Italy and abroad. He became more acceptable to Catholics in Italy and in the rest of Europe. Some historians regard the Lateran Agreements as Mussolini's **greatest political success**.

Further Conflicts

conflict between church and state over education.

However, the agreement did not end the conflicts between church and state. The Fascists claimed that *'the education and instruction of youth can be entrusted only to the state.'* So, in 1931, Mussolini disbanded the Catholic youth and student groups. But a strong reaction from the Pope led Mussolini to place lesser restrictions on these organisations. This incident illustrated the limitations of Fascist power. While the Catholic Church did not openly oppose Fascism, it remained a separate organisation. Fascism was not strong enough to bring the Church under the control of the state.

THE CORPORATE STATE *(organises society in economic unit)*

The idea of the Corporate State was influenced partly by Catholic teaching. Fascists believed that the class conflict between workers and employers should be replaced by **class co-operation**. Fascists also hoped the Corporate State would increase their control of the country.

A **Ministry of Corporations** was set up in 1926 but it took over 10 years to establish the Corporate State. The economy was divided into **22 Corporations**. Each Corporation represented a major area of economic activity such as agriculture, industry and the professions. Employers, workers and the government were represented on each Corporation. They decided wages and working conditions. Finally, Parliament was abolished in 1939 and replaced by a Chamber of Fasces and Corporations.

Did the Corporate State represent a Fascist revolution? It did not. Instead of providing greater class co-operation, *'it represented,'* as one historian said, *'a means of disciplining labour (the workers) in the interest of the employers and the state.'* It also added another layer of bureaucracy (officials and rules) and led to greater corruption and inefficiency.

Mussolini taking in the wheat in the Battle of Wheat, another of Mussolini's 'battles', this time to increase wheat production.

THE ECONOMY

Mussolini knew little about economics and Fascism was not an economic system like Communism. Between 1922 and 1925, Mussolini left the running of the economy in the hands of the Minister of Finance, **Alberto de Stefani**. He cut government spending, promoted free trade and benefited from the improved European economy of the time. Even though he successfully reduced unemployment to 120,000, de Stefani was fired by Mussolini and replaced with a financier and industrialist.

New Policies

This signalled a change in economic policy. **Protectionism** (duties or taxes on imports) was introduced to protect heavy industry and some agricultural products such as grain. Next, Mussolini revalued the currency to 90 lira to the £sterling (Quota 90). This was done for reasons of national pride but it made Italian exports dearer and damaged the economy.

By the early 1930s Mussolini was advocating a policy of **autarky** (economic self-sufficiency). This took the form of a series of **battles**. Already in 1925, Mussolini began the **Battle of Grain** – to increase grain production and make the country self-sufficient. Grain production increased steadily during the 1920s and 1930s, but often at the expense of other crops which would have been better suited to some of the land. As well as this, the duties which protected Italian grain increased the price of bread.

The Battle for Land Reclamation – a scheme for reclaiming land for grain production, accompanied the Battle of Grain. Its greatest success was the draining of the **Pontine Marshes** near Rome which added thousands of extra acres of land and reduced malaria.

There were other advances made by the Italian economy. Electricity production was increased significantly, so also was motor car production. New motorways (autostrada) connected Italy's major cities and towns, much of the railway system was electrified and the mainline trains ran on time. The Fascists made good use of propaganda to boast about these achievements.

State Control of the Economy

As the 1930s progressed, Mussolini was more conscious of the need for **economic self-sufficiency** in preparation for war. By 1939, the beginning of the Second World War, most of Italy's ship-building, shipping, iron and steel industries were controlled by the state. The state owned a greater proportion of industry in Italy than in any other country outside the Soviet Union.

Who Benefited?

Some groups benefited more than others from Fascist economic policies. In particular the industrialists and larger landowners and farmers benefited – their produce was protected by tariffs and wages were kept low. The greatest losers were the working class in the cities and the labourers in the country, in spite of the **Labour Charter** of 1927. This was a list of workers' rights – the right to good working conditions and fair wages. But the workers had no trade unions, the right to strike was abolished and they were not properly represented on the Corporations. Unemployment rose from 110,000 in 1926 to 1 million in 1933 due to the Great Depression. Their living standards declined as the value of their wages fell by ten per cent between 1925 and 1938. However, workers did benefit from the **Dopolavoro (After Work)** which was set up in 1925 to control leisure time. It controlled athletic and sports clubs, choirs, bands, night schools and libraries. It sponsored day outings and tours, and it promoted cinema and theatre.

Cultural

MUSSOLINI'S FOREIGN POLICY

Mussolini took a strong interest in foreign policy. Mussolini looked on relations with other powers as a means of gaining prestige for Italy, and himself. As well as being Prime Minister, he was also Foreign Minister for much of the time between 1922 and 1939. Even when he handed over the Foreign Ministry to his son-in-law, Count Ciano, in 1936, Mussolini still took a controlling interest. His declared **aims** in foreign policy were: *'I want to make Italy great, respected and feared'*. He wanted to expand the power of Italy around the Mediterranean Sea in imitation of the Roman Empire. The Mediterranean was to become **Mare Nostrum** (Our Sea).

Foreign Policy in the 1920s

Mussolini began his rule with a number of foreign policy successes. His first success was the **Corfu incident** (1923). When four Italians were killed redrawing the Greek-Albanian border for the League of Nations, Mussolini took over Corfu, a Greek island, after the Greek government refused to pay 50 million lira compensation to Italy. Mussolini continued to hold Corfu until the League ordered Greece to pay the 50 million lira which was demanded. This encouraged Mussolini to establish a protectorate over Albania and he took it over completely in 1939. Thereby, the Corfu incident had launched Mussolini's <u>**expansionist**</u> programme. In his second success, he acquired **Fiume** in January 1924 after negotiations with Yugoslavia.

However, after these initial successes, Mussolini spent the rest of the 1920s <u>building up an image of an international</u> **statesman and man of peace**. Mussolini attended the **Locarno Conference** (1925) at which Italy and other European powers, including Germany, agreed to the **Locarno Pact** which guaranteed Germany's existing borders with France and Italy. Three years later, Mussolini signed the **Kellogg-Briand Pact** <u>outlawing war</u> as an instrument of national policy. Mussolini also supported disarmament and the League of Nations. In all he signed over 130 international agreements in two years but he had no intention of being bound by **paper** agreements.

Fascism for Export – the 1930s

By the 1930s, Mussolini had established full control of Italy – now he could expand. He wanted to **found an empire** and **to win glory and power**. *'The growth of empire, that is to say, the expansion of the nation, is an essential sign of vitality'*, he said. His main areas of interest were the <u>Balkans</u>, southern <u>Europe and Africa.</u>

MUSSOLINI AND HITLER DISAGREE

However, the first problem he faced in the 1930s was the rise to power of Hitler in Germany. While Mussolini was delighted that Fascism, **his doctrine**, was in power in another state, he was fearful of the creation of a <u>**Greater Germany**</u> through the union of Germany and Austria **(Anschluss)**.

Mussolini wanted to ensure the independence of Austria so he helped the Austrian Prime Minister, **Dollfuss**, break up the Nazi movement in Austria. When <u>Dolfuss was assassinated</u>, Mussolini sent troops to the Austro-Italian border to stop Hitler's plan to unite Germany and Austria.

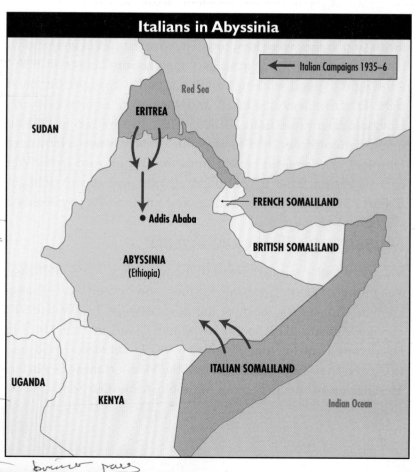

Italians in Abyssinia

← Italian Campaigns 1935–6

Red Sea
SUDAN
ERITREA
• Addis Ababa
FRENCH SOMALILAND
BRITISH SOMALILAND
ABYSSINIA (Ethiopia)
UGANDA
KENYA
ITALIAN SOMALILAND
Indian Ocean

Mussolini and Fascist Italy

Mussolini then formed the **Stresa Front** with Britain and France to oppose the break-up of treaties *'which may endanger the peace of Europe'*. Mussolini hoped the Stresa Front would limit Hitler's ambitions and that he would be able to expand his own empire in Africa. However, Mussolini's invasion of Abyssinia destroyed the Stresa Front and drove him into the arms of Hitler.

THE INVASION OF ABYSSINIA

Italy already controlled Libya after a long war in the 1920s. She also controlled two countries – Italian Somaliland and Eritrea – bordering on Abyssinia, (see map of Italians in Ethiopia). There were a number of reasons for Mussolini's invasion of Abyssinia:

The badly-armed Abyssinian tribesmen had little chance against the well-armed Italian army with tanks and planes.

- Mussolini wanted to enlarge the Italian empire.
- Italians wanted revenge for a humiliating defeat by the Abyssinians in Adowa in 1896.
- Some historians suggest Mussolini wanted to distract the Italian people from economic problems at home in the middle of the 1930s.

Mussolini used a border incident with Abyssinia to build up his army and attack in October 1935. He claimed his invasion aimed to restore order in a huge country left in the most atrocious slavery and the most primitive conditions. Over 400,000 Italian soldiers using tanks, planes and poison gas overran the lightly armed tribesmen of Abyssinia. Their Emperor, **Haile Selassie**, appealed to the **League of Nations**. The League condemned Italy and imposed economic sanctions. The sanctions, which excluded oil from the list, had little effect on the war and Italy took the capital, Addis Ababa, by May 1936.

Results of the Invasion

- The invasion of Abyssinia ended the Stresa Front. Britain and France, as key members of the League, were involved in imposing sanctions on Italy.
- The failure of the sanctions showed up the weakness of the League of Nations.
- At the same time, Hitler supported Mussolini, whose attitude to Hitler now changed. When he first met Hitler in Rome in 1934, he was unimpressed. *'In politics,'* he said, *'it is undeniable that I am more intelligent than Hitler.'* But he was very impressed by German military strength after a visit there in 1937.

Other factors also drew the two countries closer together. One was the similarity between Fascism and Nazism, in particular, their anti-Communism. They were also drawn together by helping Franco in the **Spanish Civil War** (1936–9). In Mussolini's case he sent 75,000 men, 100 aircraft, weapons and ammunition to help Franco to victory.

AGREEMENTS BETWEEN MUSSOLINI AND HITLER

A series of agreements cemented their relationship:

- They first of all formed the **Rome-Berlin Axis** (October 1936), a loose agreement between the two countries.

- This was followed by the **Anti-Comintern Pact** (November 1937) with Germany and Japan to present a united front against Communism.

When Hitler invaded Austria in March 1938 to form Anschluss, Mussolini did not intervene.

- In May 1939, Italy and Germany signed the **Pact of Steel**. Both sides agreed to back each other in any future war.

Mussolini was very impressed with German military might when he visited there in 1937.

ANTI-SEMITIC LAWS

Mussolini was now increasingly under Hitler's influence. This can be seen in the anti-semitic laws – the **Charter of Race** – which were brought into Italy for the first time in October 1938. There was no experience of racial persecution in Italy before this and even Mussolini said he was opposed to the ideas of racial superiority. Now Jews were deprived of Italian nationality; they were not allowed to have state jobs and they were not allowed to marry non-Jewish Italians. But many Italians objected and the Pope wrote to Mussolini in protest. The anti-semitic laws were one factor in Mussolini's declining popularity.

THE ROAD TO WAR

Italy was the junior partner in the alliance with Germany. In March 1938, Mussolini acted as a peacemaker in **Munich** to get agreement between Germany, France and Britain over Czechoslovakia (see Chapter 6). Even though Mussolini liked to think he had **saved Europe** from war, his role in Munich was very limited. When Germany took over the rest of Czechoslovakia in 1939, Mussolini took over Albania. ← reactionary

As Europe headed for war in 1939, Mussolini realised that the Italian army was not ready. Wars in Libya (1920s), Abyssinia and Spain ensured that Italy was economically and militarily weakened. Mussolini himself said Italy would not be ready until 1943. When Hitler declared war in September 1939, Mussolini asked for huge quantities of arms and ammunition which he knew Hitler could not give him. In this way, Mussolini was able to declare Italy's **non-belligerence**.

FASCISM AT WAR

By the beginning of the Second World War, **Mussolini's popularity** was already in decline:

- Italians were worse off in the 1930s, self-sufficiency made products dearer and the standard of living fell.

- Mussolini came more under Hitler's influence and Italians did not like that.

- Many Italians did not like anti-semitism which Mussolini introduced.

Mussolini was drawn into the war as he envied Hitler's success in Poland and France. But this was a fatal mistake on his part. His army invaded southern France when Hitler had conquered Belgium and northern France. But the war exposed the weaknesses of Mussolini's planning and exposed his bluff:

- He made himself commander-in-chief and therefore was held responsible for Italy's defeats.
- The Italian army was badly equipped and poorly led.
- He hoped for a quick victory so he made no provision for rationing.
- He also failed to fully mobilise Italy for war, he even allowed luxury restaurants in Rome to remain open.

After Mussolini was removed from power and imprisoned in a mountain-top hotel, he was rescued by Nazi paratroopers.

Italian Defeats and the Death of Mussolini

Not surprisingly, Italy was beaten in Libya, Egypt and Greece (see Chapter 7). Mussolini failed to prepare for the Allied invasion of Sicily and Italy, and this led to his downfall. He was removed by King Victor Emmanuel and the Fascist Grand Council and imprisoned in a mountain-top hotel. Hitler sent German commandos to rescue him. He set up a rebel Fascist government in northern Italy called the **Salo Republic**. But he was captured by Italian resistance fighters and shot. His body and that of his mistress, who was shot with him, were hung upside down from a lamppost in Milan. His participation in the Second World War led to his own downfall, and contributed to the defeat of his ally, Hitler.

ASSESSMENT OF MUSSOLINI

Mussolini was the **first** of the Fascist dictators. His tactics were later copied by Hitler to achieve power. However, Mussolini's rule was never as totalitarian as Hitler's – the king was still head of state in Italy and he eventually dismissed Mussolini. Neither could Mussolini control the Catholic Church. Mussolini's Fascist Party did not control the Italian state in the same way that Hitler's Nazi Party did in Germany.

Much of what Mussolini did was **superficial**. Some historians claim that Italian Fascism was built on a series of myths – the **mutilated peace**, the March on Rome, Mussolini the Superman and the myth of the military might of the Italian army. These myths were shattered by the Second World War.

Italian Fascism died with Mussolini. His only long-lasting legacy was the Lateran Agreements; his Corporate State was a failure and his foreign policy led Italy into the Second World War and to his downfall. His genius lay in his ability to manipulate the Italian people through mass meetings, press and radio.

Mussolini was recaptured, shot dead and hung upside down in Milan, along with his mistress.

The Nazi State in Peace – Origins and Growth

[handwritten top margin: the survival of the new german republic would ultimately rest on two factors]

INTRODUCTION – THE BACKGROUND

In 1918, the **Weimar Republic** was established in Germany. It faced many problems. Germany was defeated in the First World War (1914–18) and the Weimar government had to sign the harsh **Treaty of Versailles** imposed by the victorious Allies (Britain, France and the US):

- Germany lost territory,
- her armed forces were reduced,
- she had to agree to a war guilt clause,
- she had to pay reparations of £6·6 billion.

[handwritten notes: the ability and willingness of the german people to counter the authoritarian and anti-disruptive & imperial germans to the liberties and the democracy of the weimar republic]

In 1929, the Wall Street Crash led to the Great Depression. German dole queues grew as unemployment rose from 8% in 1928 to 30% in 1932.

The failure of the Weimar Republic to pay reparations led to the French occupation of the **Ruhr** (1923) and to very rapid **inflation**. However, after this the Weimar Republic experienced economic and political stability under the leadership of **Gustav Stresemann**. A new currency was introduced, reparations were reduced and American loans were provided under the **Dawes Plan**. By 1929 Germany was the leading industrial country on the continent.

But this stability obscured (covered over) many of the weaknesses of the Republic. These were exposed by the economic crisis caused by the **Wall Street Crash** (1929) and the **Great Depression**. These led to the rise of Hitler and the downfall of the Weimar Republic.

[handwritten note: the chancellor's ability to command reichstag and so command a clear majority in the coalitions.]

The Great Inflation of 1923

After the First World War, Germany continued to experience inflation. The Weimar Government printed money to pay for war debts and reparations. Inflation increased from 1919 to 1922, but the biggest problems came when the government failed to pay reparations in 1922. As a result, the French and Belgian armies invaded the Ruhr industrial region, and this led to the collapse in the value of the Mark and to very rapid inflation (hyperinflation). In 1922 one dollar could buy 500 Marks; by November 1923, one dollar could buy four trillion Marks. The Mark had become worthless.

The German middle class was ruined; the value of their savings and pensions collapsed and workers were made poorer. They had to bring suitcases or carts to work to take home the paper money. Some lost work, but industrialists and landowners gained, some making huge fortunes.

The German economy was rescued by a new currency and the Dawes Plan (1924) which lessened reparation payments and brought American loans to Germany. The economy revived from the middle of the 1920s. Industrial production grew, wages increased and unemployment fell to eight per cent by 1928. *[handwritten: ✻ Gustav Stresemann]*

WHAT CAUSED THE RISE TO POWER OF HITLER AND THE NAZIS?

1. The Wall Street Crash and German Economic and Social Problems

German economic growth in the second half of the 1920s was due largely to American loans. But, in 1929 the value of shares in the New York Stock Exchange on Wall Street collapsed. This led to an **economic depression** in America. When American banks and companies called in loans from Germany, Germany too faced economic depression. As Gustav Stresemann warned in 1928, '*Germany is dancing on a volcano. If the short-term credits (loans) are called in, a large section of our economy would collapse.*'

Businesses went bankrupt, factories and mines closed and workers were laid off. In 1929, there were already 1·5 million unemployed in Germany. This rose rapidly over the next few years. By January 1932 there were six million unemployed, but many more were on short-time working.

The economic crisis led to poverty and hunger. Many middle-class families suffered. Some had to sell their houses, others could not afford to rent. They moved to makeshift shanty towns on the edge of cities. Many had to rely on soup kitchens for food. Some provoked arrest to get food and shelter in jail. Others joined the Red Front (Communists) or Hitler's **Storm Troopers (SA)**. One worker explained how he became a Nazi. In the Depression, '*Hunger was the daily companion of the German working man ... Many an honest worker had to steal to get food ... All people looked for better times. As for me, like many another, I lost all I possessed so, in early 1930, I joined the Nazi Party.*'

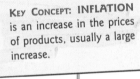

> **KEY CONCEPT: DEPRESSION**
> is a term used to describe when an economy is doing badly; industrial production declines, factories and businesses close and there is widespread unemployment. The unemployment leads to poverty which affects all classes. The Great Depression which began with the Wall Street Crash in 1929 was the most severe depression in the early twentieth century.

2. The Failure of the Weimar Republic

Already the **reputation of the Weimar Republic** was damaged among some Germans because of the Treaty of Versailles and the notion that the Weimar Republic had **stabbed the army in the back**. For this they were called the **November criminals**. The ruling classes of the old Imperial Germany who were still in power also weakened the Republic. The judges, generals, civil servants and teachers all favoured a more **authoritarian** government and they used their positions of influence to undermine the Weimar Republic.

> **KEY CONCEPT: INFLATION**
> is an increase in the prices of products, usually a large increase.

The actions of the Weimar government worsened the economic crisis. The **Chancellor (Prime Minister), Brüning**, cut back on government spending. He reduced wages, pensions and unemployment benefit. This earned him the nickname **Hunger Chancellor** and increased dissatisfaction and disorder in the streets.

Brüning made two further mistakes. He used **President Hindenburg's** power to **rule by decree** to bring in some of his unpopular measures. This showed the failure of democracy. Brüning also called a general election for June 1930. Instead of gaining a majority, the results of the election showed a swing to **extremism** – to an increase in the popularity of Hitler and the Nazi Party, and of the Communists.

Hitler expounding his ideas at an early Nazi meeting in the Nazi headquarters in Munich.

3. Hitler's Leadership of the Nazis

Hitler and the Nazis owed much of their rise to power to the economic and social problems caused by the Wall Street Crash and the Great Depression. But it was also due to Hitler's ability as a political leader.

Nazi Tactics and Policies: In 1923 Hitler organised the **Munich Putsch** (rising) which was a failure. After this he decided to change tactics. He now believed that the use of force was not the best way to

Hitler taking the salute at the first Nuremberg Rally in 1927.

achieve power. He intended to use democracy to destroy democracy. *'If outvoting them takes longer than outshooting them, then at least the result will be guaranteed by their own constitution.'* He began the **reorganisation** of his party. He established branches throughout Germany and appointed regional leaders (or gauleiters) – but all authority came from him. The **SA (Brownshirts)** or **stormtroopers** were a paramilitary wing of the Nazi Party. The **SS (Blackshirts)** were Hitler's bodyguards. Other branch organisations were also formed such as the **Hitler Youth** and the **Women's League**.

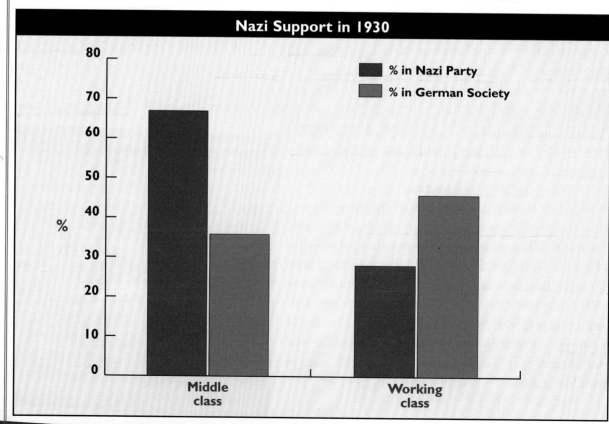

The Nazi State in Peace – Origins and Growth

He shaped his **policies** to make them attractive to many different groups:

- He appealed to **nationalists** through his attack on the Treaty of Versailles – *'the disgrace of Versailles'* – and the *'November criminals'*. He also promised to unite German-speaking people in a Greater Germany.
- Hitler was very strongly **anti-Communist** and this pleased the middle class, the industrialists and the farmers. They feared a Communist state and workers' soviets, as in Russia, when the Communists increased their seats in each of the elections in Germany. Hitler was able to use the violence of the SA and SS against the socialists and Communists.
- The support of **industrialists and business leaders** was important because they helped finance his elections.
- The support for the Nazi Party came mostly from the lower middle class – small merchants, farmers, craftsmen, white-collar workers and civil servants.

But other parties had policies similar to the Nazis. The Nazis succeeded because of their **propaganda techniques**.

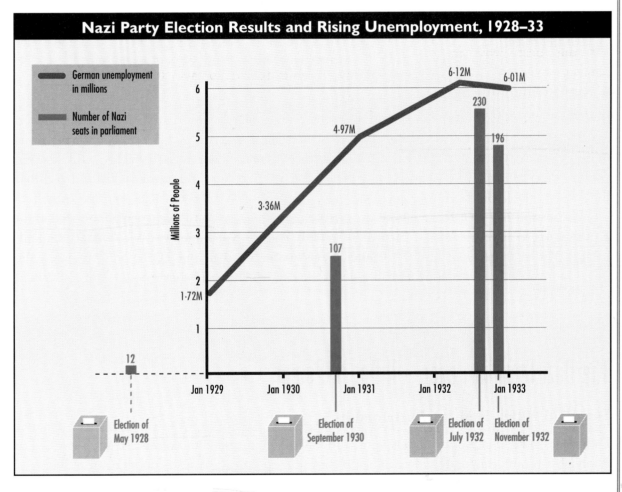

Nazi Party Election Results and Rising Unemployment, 1928–33

Nazi Propaganda Techniques: Hitler used very effective propaganda techniques to get across his message. Hitler was an **outstanding speaker**, a Hitler speech was superb theatre. Hitler himself said, *'To be a leader means to be able to move the masses.'* One of his followers said, *'He enters a hall. He sniffs the air. For a moment he feels his way, senses the atmosphere. Suddenly he bursts forth. His words go like an arrow to their target; he touches every private wound on the raw, liberating the mass unconscious,* *expressing its innermost aspirations, telling it what it most wants to hear.'* He reduced his policies to simple **slogans**, *'It's [Nazi propaganda] intellectual level must be adjusted to the most limited intelligence'*, he said. *'When you lie, tell big lies.'*

The use of **uniforms, salutes and mass rallies** gave an impression of strength. They made good use of films and gramophone records (of Nazi speeches), the talker spouting forth from loudspeakers on trucks. One German explained how the Nazis fought the elections in his state. *'Hitler himself spoke at sixteen major rallies. Columns of SS troops shouted slogans and marched the villages and towns from morning to night. In every market square an SA band or Nazi minstrels played marches for hours on end.'*

Albert Speer, later Hitler's chief architect, explained how the Nazis appealed to him after listening to Hitler in 1931:

> *'Here, it seemed to me, was hope. Here were new ideals, a new understanding, ... The perils of Communism could be checked, Hitler persuaded us, and instead of hopeless unemployment, Germany could move towards economic recovery. It must have been during these months that my mother saw an SA parade in the streets of Heidelberg. The sight of discipline in a time of chaos, the impression of energy in an atmosphere of universal hopelessness, seems to have won her over too.'*

4. Right-wing Plotting

By 1932 the Nazi Party was the **largest** in the Reichstag. Many conservative politicians believed that Hitler must be part of any government. The Nazis lost seats and votes between the elections in July and November 1932 (from 230 seats to 196 seats). Former Chancellor and leading conservative politician, **Von Papen**, now believed that Hitler was in a weaker position and that the conservatives could control him. *'I have roped him in. In two months we'll have pushed Hitler into a corner so hard that he'll be squeaking.'* In these circumstances, Von Papen persuaded **President Hindenburg** to appoint Hitler as Chancellor in January 1933. Von Papen was Vice-Chancellor and, besides Hitler, there were only two other Nazis in the cabinet. But Hitler only accepted the position provided he was allowed call a general election. Little did they know it but Hitler had outwitted them.

The Nazi State in Peace – Hitler in Power

How Did Hitler Establish Dictatorship?

Hitler had come to power by largely constitutional (legal) means. But he was already planning to establish a **totalitarian state** where all aspects of life – political, social, economic and religious – would be controlled by the state.

Hitler's first step was to call a **general election** for March 1933. This became a huge propaganda campaign for the Nazis. Goebbels wrote in his diary: *'Now it will be very easy to carry on the fight as we can call on all the resources of the state. Radio and press are at our disposal. We shall stage a masterpiece of propaganda.'* This was accompanied by street violence as the SA clashed with the Communists. Over 400,000 SA were enlisted in the police so they now could use legal terror.

Two weeks before the election, a Dutch Communist, **van der Lubbe**, set fire to the Reichstag.

Hitler exploited this by talking about the *'Communist threat'*. In the election, the Nazis increased their seats to 288 and, with the help of the Nationalist Party, Hitler had a parliamentary majority. He passed the **Enabling Law** which allowed him to **rule by decree**. Weimar democracy was at an end.

KEY PERSONALITY: ADOLF HITLER

Hitler was born in **Austria** in 1889, the son of a customs official. As he grew up he wanted to become an **artist**, but suffered the humiliation of being turned down by the Vienna Academy of Fine Arts. He spent the next five years of *'misery and woe in Vienna'* doing odd jobs, living on charity or selling some of his sketches.

It was in Vienna that he developed his **hatred** of the Jews, Communists and democracy. It was here also that he dreamt of a Greater Germany. He went to Munich and joined the German army in the First World War. He took part in 47 battles, mostly as a messenger.

He was wounded twice and was also awarded the Iron Cross on two separate occasions. He was in hospital suffering from a gas attack when the war ended.

After the war, he joined the German Workers' Party, soon becoming its leader and changing its name to the **National Socialist German Workers' Party**. The Party's Twenty-five Point programme emphasised anti-semitism, extreme nationalism, racial superiority and leadership. Hitler felt the Weimar Republic was about to collapse, so he organised the **Munich Putsch**, which failed miserably.

He spent some time in jail where he dictated *Mein Kampf* (My Struggle). When he came out of jail, he reorganised the Party but Hitler had to wait for the Great Depression before he gained significant popularity. After his Party became the largest in the Reichstag, he was invited by **President Hindenburg** to become Chancellor in January 1933.

Over the next few years he established a **totalitarian state** under his control and that of the Nazi Party. His campaign against the **Jews** became a significant feature of his state. He also promoted an aggressive **foreign policy** in breaking the Treaty of Versailles and expanding Germany's borders. However, this caused the Second World War.

Even though his armies were initially successful, conquering most of mainland Europe, he experienced defeat in the Battle of Britain, North Africa and, most important of all, in Russia. As the Russians advanced from the east and the Americans and British from the west, Hitler committed **suicide** in his bunker in Berlin rather than be captured by the Russians and be shown off naked in a cage, as he feared.

Hitler aimed what he called "gleichschaltung" "coordination" where by political, social and religious would be brought all aspects of germans life under state control

Nazi 'Co-ordination'

Hitler extended his power further by a policy of co-ordination – by limiting or destroying the power of groups and institutions which were opposed to the Nazis:

- He **outlawed** the Communists and the SDP (Social Democrats) and seized their property.
- The Nazis were the **only political party** allowed in Germany.
- He **abolished** the elected State assemblies (parliaments) and appointed Nazi governors instead.
- Trade unions were abolished and replaced by the **German Labour Front**.
- The **press** was put under Nazi control.

This led to nazification of Germany there to be dominated by the party. every aspect of German life was

Hitler's SS rounding up left-wing 'undesirables' to be questioned and searched.

The SA and the Night of the Long Knives

Next, Hitler eliminated opposition within his own party organisation in the **Night of the Long Knives**. By 1934 the **SA**, under the leadership of **Ernest Röhm**, had grown to over two million members. Röhm planned a **people's army** where the German army would merge with the SA with Röhm at its head. The army generals were opposed to this and Hitler needed the regular army for his plans. Hitler decided to use the SS to kill the leadership of the SA (including Röhm). Up to 400 people were killed, mostly from the SA but also some old scores were settled. *'I alone during those twenty-four hours was the supreme court of justice of the German people. I ordered the leaders of the guilty shot,'* said Hitler. The **SS under Himmler** became the most important of all Nazi organisations.

Himmler (right) used the SS, under Hitler's orders, to kill Röhm (left) and the SA leadership in 1934.

Der Führer

Hitler's next step, on the death of President Hindenburg in 1934, was to combine the offices of the Chancellor and the President. He was now called **Führer (Leader)**. *'The Führer unites in himself all the sovereign authority of the Reich.'* He was now head of the armed forces and all the members had to swear a new **oath** to him, *'the Führer of the German Reich and People.'* In little over 18 months Hitler had established a **Nazi dictatorship**.

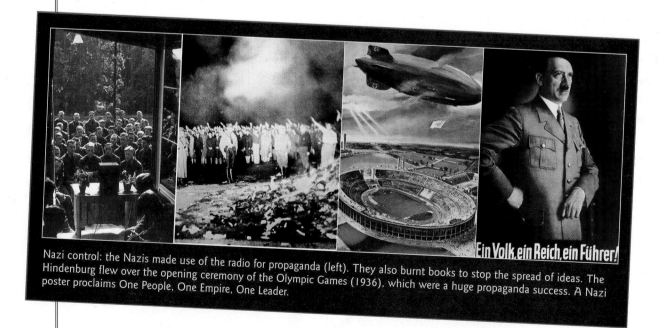

Nazi control: the Nazis made use of the radio for propaganda (left). They also burnt books to stop the spread of ideas. The Hindenburg flew over the opening ceremony of the Olympic Games (1936), which were a huge propaganda success. A Nazi poster proclaims One People, One Empire, One Leader.

The Totalitarian State – Propaganda and Terror

The Nazis now proceeded to introduce what Goebbels called *'the national revolution'*. This resulted in Germany becoming a **totalitarian state**. Two methods were used – **propaganda and terror**.

Nazi Propaganda: Propaganda played a key role in Nazi control of Germany.

> *'Hitler's dictatorship differed in one fundamental point from all its predecessors in history. His was the first dictatorship in the present period of modern technical development.... Through technical devices like radio and the loudspeaker, eighty million people were deprived of independent thought. It was thereby possible to subject them to the will of one man.'*

> Albert Speer

Hitler appointed **Goebbels** as **Minister of Enlightenment and Propaganda**. Goebbels was totally loyal to Hitler and he used every means at his disposal to ensure the loyalty of the German people to Hitler. The **Ministry of Propaganda** was divided into sections called chambers such as the Chamber of Archives, the Press Chamber, the Radio Chamber. In this way all media were used to influence public opinion. Goebbels believed that, *'If you tell a big lie often enough, people will believe it.'* The Nazis also controlled the publication of **newspapers and books**. In 1933, Goebbels organised a **book burning** to destroy any books with anti-Nazi – unGerman – ideas. In the case of newspapers, Goebbels created only one official German News Bureau. He held a daily press conference for editors and they were instructed on what view they should take on various issues. Jewish editors were fired and any anti-Nazi newspapers were closed down.

Goebbels also used the newer mass media of **radio and cinema**. *'I consider,'* he said, *'radio to be the most modern and most crucial instrument that exists for influencing the masses.'* People were encouraged to buy a **People's Radio** – a small black wireless or radio which could only receive Nazi radio stations. By 1939 there were four times more radios in Germany than in 1933. Loudspeakers were placed in streets and bars for those who were not within reach of a radio. He also used short-wave radio stations to broadcast to areas outside Germany.

Goebbels also knew how effective **cinema and film** were. Newsreels were used to boast about Germany's greatness and the achievements of Hitler. Germany's most famous film maker – **Leni Riefenstahl** – produced many very influential propaganda films. *The Triumph of the Will* (1934) was based on the **Nuremberg Rally** and *Olympia* told the story of the 1936 Berlin Olympics. Film was also used as a powerful weapon in anti-semitism. *The Eternal Jew* and *Jud Suss* were two films used to target Jews and to get across Nazi racialist ideas.

Goebbels also used huge **gatherings** to influence public opinion – marches, parades, torchlight processions and rallies. They created a feeling of order, strength and togetherness. The **Berlin Olympics in 1936** became one huge propaganda exercise for Nazi Germany. A new 100,000 seater stadium was built and the latest technology was used in running the Games. But the **Nuremberg Rally** held in August or September was the highlight of each year. Hitler knew the importance of the rally as it sent thousands of Nazis home to all corners of Germany fired with new enthusiasm (see Case Study: The Nuremberg Rallies).

Cult of Personality

Central to all Goebbels' propaganda was the **Cult of the Leader**. He was following Hitler's belief, *'The most important part of Fascism is absolute trust in a wise and able leader.'* Slogans such as *'Ein Reich, Ein Volk, Ein Führer'* (One Country, One People, One Leader) were used to get across the worship of Hitler. Goebbels created the image of Hitler through carefully staged photographs, portraits, posters and meetings. He was idolised by the youth and by women.

KEY PERSONALITY: JOSEPH GOEBBELS

Goebbels was born in the **Rhineland** in Germany in 1897, the son of a manual worker in a strict Catholic family. He was rejected by the German army in the First World War because of a **club foot and a limp**, a rejection which affected him for the rest of his life. Instead he studied philosophy, history and literature in a number of German universities. He joined the **Nazi Party** in 1922 and became editor of one of the Nazi newspapers. He developed an intense **loyalty** to Hitler: '*Adolf Hitler, I love you*', he wrote in his diary. Hitler rewarded him by making him, first, a regional leader (gauleiter) and later Propaganda leader of the Nazi Party in 1929. He showed outstanding ability by organising Hitler's two campaigns for the Presidency and the general elections of 1930–32, which brought the Nazis to power.

He was a **master of propaganda** so when he was appointed **Minister of Public Enlightenment and Propaganda**, he used the full resources of the state to bring all the means of communication (media) under Nazi control. His role was crucial in developing and maintaining Nazi power in the totalitarian state. During the Second World War, he had the difficult task of maintaining morale, particularly when the war went against the Germans.

As the Russians closed in on Hitler at the end of the war, Goebbels remained loyal to the end. After Hitler's suicide; Goebbels, his wife and six children also committed **suicide**. In his final testament, he wrote, '*I express an unalterable resolution not to leave the Reich capital, even if it falls, but rather, at the side of the Führer, to end a life which will have no further value to me if I cannot spend it in the service of the Führer, and by his side.*'

KEY PERSONALITY: LENI RIEFENSTAHL

A German film actress and director, Leni Riefenstahl was born in Berlin in 1902. She began her career as a **ballet dancer** but after an injury to her knee, she became a **film actress** in the mid-1920s. In 1931, she founded her own **film company** and won awards for *The Blue Light*, a film which she wrote, directed and acted in the leading role.

Hitler asked her to produce a film documentary of the 1934 Nuremberg Rally, called the *Triumph of the Will*. (See Case Study at the end of this chapter.) She also filmed the 1936 Berlin Olympics in *Olympia*, which she divided into two parts. She was the first to use many of today's film-making techniques. In 1939, the International Olympic Committee honoured her for directing and producing that film.

After the Second World War, she was **cleared** of being a Nazi. She always claimed that she only directed films and was not a follower of Hitler's ideas. She said that in 1934, '*Nobody knew what was going to happen.*' '*All they have written about me is nothing. I had no position and no love story with Hitler.*' However, *Triumph of the Will* destroyed her career as a film director after the Second World War because of its association with the Nazis.

In her later life, she became well-known as a **still photographer**, particularly photographing the Nuba tribe in Sudan. She also got recognition as an **underwater photographer**. However, her life is still **controversial**; a proposal to make a film of her *Memoirs* was condemned by Jews in America. She died in 2003 at the age of 101.

EDUCATION AS PROPAGANDA: THE YOUTH

Hitler paid particular attention to young people. The **Law Concerning the Hitler Youth** said; *'It is on the youth that the future of the German nation depends.... It is not only at home and school, but in the Hitler Youth as well that all of Germany's youth is to be educated physically, mentally and morally, in the spirit of National Socialism, to serve the nation and the racial community.'*

The Nazis believed that **the whole purpose of education is to create Nazis**. All school subjects were used to get across Nazi ideas. A Nazi maths book had the following problem, *'The Jews are aliens in Germany. In 1933 there were 66,060,000 people living in the German Reich. 499,862 of these were Jews. What is the percentage of aliens in Germany?'*

Boys and girls were educated differently. **Boys** were geared towards military service and **girls** towards housekeeping. Children were taught to love their Führer and Hitler was often photographed with children. On Hitler's birthday, they put flowers beside his photograph at home and in school. In these ways, children were **indoctrinated** (brainwashed/moulded) into Nazi ideas.

Outside school, children were encouraged to join **Nazi youth organisations**. This became compulsory after 1936. Boys joined the **Hitler Youth** and girls joined the **League of German Maidens**. At younger ages, boys learned camping and hiking, but in older organisations they were taught Nazi ideas and military discipline. Girls, on the other hand, were encouraged to care for their health and prepare for motherhood.

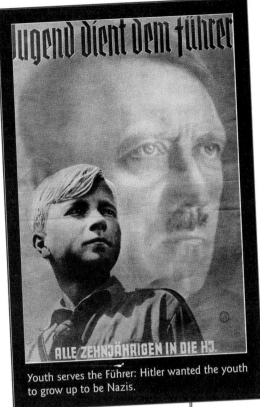

Youth serves the Führer: Hitler wanted the youth to grow up to be Nazis.

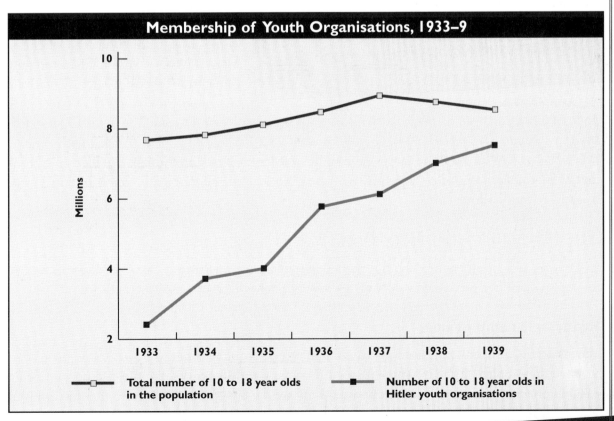

Membership of Youth Organisations, 1933–9

Millions

Total number of 10 to 18 year olds in the population

Number of 10 to 18 year olds in Hitler youth organisations

The 'Swingers' – Youth Opposition

However, not all young people followed Nazi ideas. Some were **swingers** who listened to American and English music. Others formed their own groups such as the **Navajos** and the **Edelweiss Pirates**. They disrupted Hitler Youth patrols and were severely punished if caught. Their anti-Nazi activity in the Second World War resulted in public hangings of some of them.

The Police State and the Use of Terror: As well as propaganda, Hitler used a variety of organisations to create a **police state**. The most important of these was the **SS** led by **Himmler**. The main job of the SS was to destroy opposition to Hitler and to carry out Nazi racial policies. The SS had three main sections: one dealing with security, the second called the Waffen SS were special army units and the third – the Death's Head Units – were responsible for the concentration camps.

Jewish women in a Nazi concentration camp. It was not until the Second World War that concentration camps were used for extermination.

Of all Hitler's organisations, the **Gestapo** (Secret State Police) were the most feared by ordinary Germans. They were led by **Reinhard Heydrich** who was ruthless with all opposition. They had wide powers of arrest and they used torture to gain confessions and information.

The **police and courts** also maintained Hitler's totalitarian state. Nobody could get a **fair trial** since justice had to serve the Nazi state. Between 1934 and 1939 over 500 were tried and executed for political opposition. By 1939, over 16,000 were in jail for political offences. Many of these were held in the new **concentration camps** such as **Dachau**, near Munich. Prisoners were forced to do hard labour and punishments such as beatings were severe. In Dachau, the regulations stated, *'Anyone who discusses politics, carries on controversial talks and meetings, forms cliques, loiters around with others, will be hanged.'* The camps held **undesirables** such as Communists, intellectuals, trade unionists, tramps and Jews. During the Second World War, many of the concentration camps became **extermination camps**.

THE NAZIS AND THE ECONOMY

Hitler was faced with two economic challenges when he came to power – one was to reduce unemployment, the second was to develop self-sufficiency in raw materials (**autarky**).

Reducing Unemployment

The rising unemployment caused the discontent which brought Hitler to power. Now he needed to solve the problem. The government spent money on **public works**, the most important being 7,000 kilometres of motorways (**autobahn**). Many workers were recruited from the unemployed so the unemployment figures fell from 6 million in 1932 to 2·5 million in 1936. Further declines in employment occurred with the introduction of **conscription** (compulsory military training) and the **growth of heavy industry** as Germany rearmed.

The rearmament was based on the **Four Year Plan**, introduced by Hitler in 1936. It led to huge increases in coal, iron and steel production. By 1939, unemployment was down to 200,000. Germany was much more successful than the US which reduced unemployment from 13 million (1933) to 8 million (1939) and Britain which still had ten per cent unemployment in 1939.

Hitler admires one of the products of German industry, a Mercedes sports car.

German Military Spending 1933–9

Year	Million Marks
1933	1,900
1934	1,900
1935	4,000
1936	5,800
1937	8,200
1938	18,400
1939	32,300

Self-sufficiency

The Plan also sought to develop **self-sufficiency (autarky)** in food and raw materials to prepare Germany for war. The food policy was not fully successful. There was a decline in grain and potatoes, and some foodstuffs had to be imported. In the case of raw materials there was a recycling of products and the development of synthetic products such as wool. But Germany still needed imports of oil, copper and rubber. Hitler's policy of self-sufficiency was only partly successful. Eventually Hitler would have to conquer lands in Eastern Europe to provide living space (**Lebensraum**) and supplies.

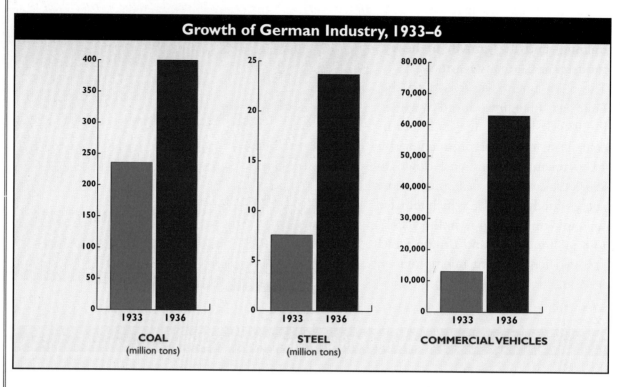

Who Benefited from Nazi Economic Policies?

The Workers

Workers benefited from the increased jobs. Wages also increased but so did working hours, and profits increased much faster. The Nazis tried to help workers by setting up two other organisations. **Beauty through Joy** aimed to improve working conditions, while the **Strength through Joy** movement was used to improve leisure time. Cheaper holidays, coach tours, concerts and cheaper sports facilities were provided. In 1938, 180,000 went on a holiday cruise, while 10 million took other holidays. The Strength through Joy movement also encouraged the development of the **People's Car – the Volkswagen** – which ordinary Germans could own.

> **KEY CONCEPT: LEBENSRAUM.** Hitler borrowed the idea of lebensraum from previous German thinkers. He believed that having additional living space would strengthen Germany by making it **self-sufficient** in food and raw materials. He wanted the living space in Eastern Europe, particularly Russia. This idea of lebensraum became the basis of German foreign policy during Hitler's Third Reich.

The Nazis and 'Big Business'

Big business gained most from German economic growth. Production came into the hands of fewer capitalists. By 1937, seventy per cent of German production was in the hands of **cartels** (monopolies). Even though the industries were owned by private individuals and companies, the overall aims of economic policy were decided by the Nazis: rearmament and self-sufficiency.

CHURCH-STATE RELATIONS IN NAZI GERMANY

Hitler hated **the Jewish-Christ creed**. He **condemned Christianity** for defending the weak and the lowly. But he could not openly attack it since most Germans were either Protestant or Catholic.

He did not want to make martyrs of the priests. Instead he intended to use indirect methods to undermine the churches.

When he came to power, relations between the Nazis and the Catholic and Protestant churches seemed good. In his first speech as Chancellor, Hitler said he would respect the churches. *'Christianity'*, he said, *'is the unshakeable foundation of the moral and ethical life of our people.'* In return, the churches thought Hitler would be better than the Weimar Republic in maintaining family values.

The Nazis and the Catholic Church: Not surprisingly, therefore, Hitler made a **Concordat** with the Catholic Church (July 1933). He promised to respect the rights of the Catholic Church if the priests stayed out of politics. But less than two months later the Vatican protested in vain that the Concordat was being broken by the Nazis. The Nazis fired Catholic civil servants, Catholic youth organisations were undermined and priests were put on trial for sexual immorality and currency smuggling. The Nazis defended their actions by saying that these were not attacks on the Church, but against Churchmen involved in politics.

The Pope responded in 1937 with an encyclical, **With Burning Anxiety**. This was smuggled into Germany and read at masses. The Pope criticised the Nazis treatment of the Catholic Church and urged Catholics to resist. The Nazis responded with further attacks on Catholics. A further clash between the Nazis and the Catholic Church occurred during the Second World War. The Nazis began a programme of **euthanasia** (mercy killing). When word of this leaked out, one of the leading Catholic churchmen, Cardinal Galen, wrote a letter which was read at masses condemning the execution of mentally ill people. Whether for this reason or others, the euthanasia programme stopped soon after.

The Nazis and the Protestant Churches: The Protestant churches were in a more difficult situation. There were many different Protestant churches and Nazism had greater influence on them. Some members of these churches founded a **German Christian** movement and got their candidate elected as Bishop of The Reich. This was an attempt to set up a **Reichskirche** (national church) to replace the Protestant churches. *'Adolf Hitler is the new messiah'*, was one of the beliefs of the new church. Hitler also ordered that a copy of *Mein Kampf* and a sword be placed on the altar of each church. Hitler also gave permission for a pagan church – the **German Faith Movement**.

But opposition also built up within the Protestant churches led by **Pastor Martin Niemoller**. This opposition founded their own church – the **Confessional Church**. But Niemoller's resistance led to his arrest in 1937 and his later internment in a concentration camp until 1945. Other individuals also resisted. In all, 800 Protestant clergymen were arrested for opposition to Hitler.

Hitler had succeeded in weakening and controlling the churches but he had failed to crush them. But, the Churches as organisations did not provide effective opposition to Hitler, only individuals provided effective opposition.

THE NAZIS AND THE JEWS: ANTI-SEMITISM AND THE HOLOCAUST

Nazi Racialism

Hatred of the Jews (**anti-semitism**) was a very important part of Hitler's ideas. This hatred formed part of his thinking on race. He said the Germans were the **master race** or **Herrenvolk**, of Aryan descent. They were depicted as blond, blue-eyed, tall and strong. As a master race, the Germans were superior to other races. They produced the great civilisations in history – the great artists,

An anti-semitic cartoon used in a schoolbook. What is its message?

writers, thinkers and sportspeople. Hitler wanted to protect the **purity** of the German race from the untermenschen (subhumans), the Jews and Slavs.

Hitler and the Nazis reserved their greatest hatred for, and fear of, the Jews. In *Mein Kampf*, Hitler said, *'The Jew is and remains a parasite, a sponger, who, like a germ, spreads over wider and wider areas.'* The Jews were regarded as the source of all evil. They were blamed for Germany's loss in the First World War and the Great Depression. They were associated with **Communism** because Karl Marx, the father of Communism, was Jewish. Nazi propaganda portrayed the Jews as rich, even though a quarter of Berlin's Jews were in poverty. But they were easy targets as a greater proportion of German bankers, lawyers, doctors and dentists were Jewish.

Nazi newspapers spread wild **stories** about the Jews. They were accused of slaughtering children and *'the blood of the slaughtered child is used by young married Jewish couples, by pregnant Jewesses, for circumcision and so forth.'*

Holocaust: This is the word used to describe the Nazis' attempt to exterminate the Jews during the Second World War. It resulted in the death of about six million Jews.

Persecution Begins

KEY CONCEPT: HERRENVOLK. This was the Nazi idea of the Germans as a **master race**, superior to all other races.

When Hitler and the Nazis came to power in 1933, they did not have a clear plan on how they would deal with the Jews. They began by excluding them from positions of social and political influence. They were barred from the civil service, universities and newspapers. Hitler ordered a boycott of Jewish shops, lawyers and doctors. *'If you buy from a Jew, you are a traitor to your German country.'* There were also random attacks by the SA on Jews in the streets or on their businesses.

KEY CONCEPT: ANTI-SEMITISM. The hatred for, and persecution of, the Jews. This hatred was based on religious and economic factors. Modern anti-semitism can be traced mainly to Tsarist Russia and eastern Europe in the nineteenth century, where there were large numbers of Jews. It spread into central and western Europe, e.g. Austria and France, where it became associated with the rise of nationalism. Many nationalists believed that the Jews were not part of their nation. Anti-semitism became an important part of Nazi racial views which saw the Jews as an inferior race. It led to the Nuremberg Laws against the Jews, and later, the Holocaust during the Second World War.

Systematic Persecution

However, for the first couple of years in power, Hitler moved slowly against the Jews because of the fear of upsetting world opinion and because of his need for foreign loans. But by 1935 his position at home was secure. Persecution of the Jews became more systematic. Jews were banned from other areas of German life. They were excluded from parks, swimming pools, restaurants and public buildings. In September 1935, Hitler announced the **Nuremberg Laws**. Jews were forbidden to marry Aryans, and sexual relations between Jews and **citizens of German or kindred blood were forbidden**. Jews were also deprived of German citizenship.

Night of the Crystal Glass

During the Berlin Olympics in 1936, the Nazis reduced the persecution of the Jews and got rid of some of the anti-Jewish signs. But this was short-term. Soon Jews were deprived of other rights such as choosing names for their children except from an approved list; also the qualifications of Jewish doctors were cancelled.

However, the worst oppression came on the **Night of the Crystal Glass (Kristallnacht)** in November 1938. The killing of a minor official in the German embassy in Paris by a Polish Jew was used as an excuse for widespread attacks on Jews by the SA. Jewish shops and synagogues

The overcrowded conditions and the thin bodies in a Nazi concentration camp.

were destroyed, over 100 Jews were killed and others were sent to concentration camps. Hitler imposed a fine on the Jewish community to pay for the damage.

The Holocaust

By 1939, nearly half of Germany's Jews had emigrated including the great scientist, **Einstein**. They were lucky to escape from the systematic repression and killing of the Second World War. During the war, 300,000 German Jews were joined by about six million more from the countries of Nazi-occupied Europe. Jews from these countries were sent to concentration camps in Germany and Poland. *The adr erete set up agreency first connunloather coump in Dakere*

From 1942, the Nazis went ahead with the **Final Solution** or extermination of the Jews. The most systematic killing was carried on in **Auschwitz** but there were other large camps at **Treblinka** and **Chelmo**. In all, six camps in Poland were involved in the scheme of **genocide** (extermination of a race or people).

Jews arrived by train and were separated into those fit for work and those unfit. The unfit were **gassed** in chambers designed like large shower rooms. The commandant of Auschwitz, Hoess, said, *'We tried to fool the victims into thinking they were going through a delousing process. Sometimes they realised our intentions and we had riots.'* The others were used as **slave labour** until they died. Jews were also used for live experiments such as operations without anaesthetic. In all about six million Jews were killed during the war, over four million of those during the Final Solution. After the war many of those responsible for the Holocaust were put on trial in Nuremberg. They claimed they were *'only obeying orders'*. (See Chapter 7, The Second World War, 1939–45.)

Hitler: "Denmark in the breeding ground in which the bairler of the marxist would pest can go and prosper."

ORDINARY LEVEL AND HIGHER LEVEL HOMEWORK EXERCISES

ORDINARY LEVEL

1. Study the map of Dictatorships and Democracies in Europe, 1918–39 (p. 39) and answer the following questions:

(i) How many countries experienced dictatorships in Europe between 1919 and 1939?

(ii) How many were established as dictators in (a) 1920s, and (b) 1930s?

(iii) Who was the longest serving dictator?

(iv) How many countries were democracies?

2. Study the illustrations about Mussolini on p. 45 and answer the following questions:

(i) Who is referred to as Il Duce in the first illustration?

(ii) In what activities is Mussolini participating in each of the other illustrations?

(iii) What image is Mussolini creating of himself in those illustrations? How does it compare with the image of Mussolini in other photographs in this chapter?

3. Study the photograph of the Balilla (p. 46) and answer the following questions:

(i) Describe the activity of the boys.

(ii) What impression is being created by the Balilla in this photograph?

(iii) Why, do you think, are there large crowds along the road?

4. Study the map of Italians in Abyssinia (p. 50) and answer the following questions:

(i) Name two Italian colonies.

(ii) What advantage did these give Italy in carrying out its attack on Abyssinia?

(iii) Why did Italy attack Abyssinia?

(iv) Why was Italy able to defeat Abyssinia so easily?

5. Study the graph of Nazi Support in 1930 (p. 56) and answer the following questions:

(i) Which class had the higher percentage in German society?

(ii) Which class had the higher percentage in the Nazi Party?

(iii) Suggest reasons to explain the information provided in this graph.

6. Study the graph of Nazi Party Election Results and Rising Unemployment, 1928–33 (p. 57) and answer the following questions:

(i) In which of these elections did Hitler win his greatest number of seats in parliament?

(ii) How many were unemployed in Germany in (a) 1929, and (b) 1932?

(iii) Do you think there is a connection between the Nazi election results and the rising unemployment? If so, how do you explain the connection?

(iv) Hitler and the Nazis lost seats in the November 1932 election. How did this help Hitler become Chancellor?

7. Study the illustrations of Hitler and Nazi Germany on p. 60 and answer the following questions:

(i) How does the first illustration show the power of radio?

(ii) Why did the Nazis burn books?

(iii) What is the message of the poster of the 1936 Olympics?

(iv) What impression does the poster on the right give of Hitler?

8. Study the cartoon on p. 68 and answer the following questions:

(i) What is the story of the cartoon?

(ii) How is the Jewish man portrayed compared to the children?

(iii) What do you think is the purpose of such a cartoon?

(iv) Why would this cartoon be considered propaganda?

9. Write **paragraph answers** on each of the following:

(i) Mussolini and the March on Rome.

(ii) Mussolini's relations with the Catholic Church. (Department of Education, Sample Paper)

(iii) Mussolini and the use of propaganda.

(iv) The Corporate State.

(v) Mussolini and the Italian economy.

(vi) Relations between Mussolini and Hitler.

(vii) Italy at War.

(viii) Economic and social problems in Weimar Germany, 1920–33.

(ix) The Great Depression in Germany.

(x) Anti-semitism in Germany, 1933–45. (Department of Education, Sample Paper)

(xi) The SA and the SS.

(xii) The Nazis and Youth.

(xiii) Nazi economic policies in the 1930s.

(xiv) Hitler's relations with the Christian Churches in Germany, 1933–45.

(xv) Leni Riefenstahl and Nazi propaganda.

10. Write **long answers** on each of the following:

(i) Mussolini's rise to power in Italy.

(ii) Mussolini's foreign policy.

(iii) Hitler's rise to power up to 1933.

(iv) Hitler's dictatorship of Germany, 1933–9.

(v) How did Joseph Goebbels use propaganda to support the Nazi state? (Department of Education, Sample Paper)

HIGHER LEVEL

1. Why did stable democratic institutions survive in so few European countries during the inter-war years? (Department of Education, Sample Paper)

2. How and why was Mussolini able to achieve power in Italy?

3. Assess the aims and progress of Mussolini's foreign policy between 1922 and 1940.

4. What was Hitler's contribution to the rise of the Nazis to power in Germany?

5. What was the role of propaganda in totalitarian dictatorships in the 1920s and 1930s?

6. How did Hitler and the Nazis consolidate power and create a totalitarian dictatorship after 1933?

7. Discuss the Nazi policy of anti-semitism and its effect on German history.

8. How did Mussolini in Italy, and Hitler in Germany, try to limit the power and influence of the Christian Churches?

CASE STUDY: The Nuremberg Rallies

Mass (large scale) rallies were an integral part of Nazi organisation and propaganda. The most important of these rallies was the annual party rally held in Nuremberg in southern Germany each August or September. The medieval city of Nuremberg was chosen by Hitler because of its links with German history. It also had a central location with seven railway lines converging there.

Sense of History

THE FIRST RALLIES

Prior to Hitler's coming to power, the rallies were used to show the strength of the Nazi Party and to impress German public opinion. The first of the Party rallies was held there in August 1927. It featured a torchlight procession, the consecration of the flags, and Hitler's speech. The next Rally, held in 1929, was on a much greater scale.

THE NAZIS IN POWER – EXPANSION OF THE RALLIES

But it was not until 1933, after Hitler came to power, that the Nuremberg Rallies took on the shape so well known to the world. Hitler declared Nuremberg to be the *'city of the Nazi Party rallies'* and the venue for the main gatherings moved outside the city. At the 1933 rally, **Albert Speer**, a young architect, became involved in the organisation of the rally. He constructed a huge wooden framed eagle behind the podium. The next year he was asked by Hitler to draw up an overall plan for the Nazi Party grounds, which were eleven square kilometres in extent.

SOURCE 1 – Plan of Nuremberg Rally Grounds

GESAMTPLAN
1. Luitpoldhalle
2. Luitpoldarena
3. Turm d. Ehrentribüne in der Luitpoldarena
4. Gefallenendenkmal
5. Kongreßbau
6. Bau für die Kulturtagungen
7. Ausstellungsbau
8. Zeppelinfeld
9. Tribünenbau des Zeppelinfeld
10. Altes Stadion
11. Das Deutsche Stadion
12. Märzfeld

LAGER

DUTZEND   TEICH

Reichsparteitag-Gelände in Nürnberg Entw.: Arch. Prof. Speer

The grounds were designed by Albert Speer. The Nazis began building them during the 1930s after Hitler came to power but they were not completed by 1939.

LOCATION OF THE RALLIES

The area had a series of large open spaces such as the **Zeppelin Field**, the **Luitpold Arena** and the **March Field**. The plans also included a number of large buildings such as the **Congress Hall**. These were linked by the **Great Road**, 2 kilometres long and 60 metres wide. Much progress was made in constructing the site but the construction was not completed when war broke out in 1939.

- The **Zeppelin Field** was built on an old airfield. It could accommodate over 100,000 spectators. Speer's design for a stone structure *'was a mighty flight of stairs topped and enclosed by a long colonnade, flanked on both ends by stone abutment…. The structure had a length of thirteen hundred feet and a height of eighty feet.'*

- The **Luitpold Arena** could hold 150,000 people. It was used for the mass gatherings of the SS and the SA.

- The **Congress Hall** – a huge hall based on Roman architecture.

THE ORGANISATION OF THE RALLIES

Each Rally had to be carefully planned. In 1933, 500,000 Nazis had to be accommodated in factories, public buildings and in a camp with kitchens, washing facilities and outdoor toilets.

SOURCE 2 – The Army Parade in the Zeppelin Field

The structure on the right is the Zeppelin Tribune, which is only partly built.

SOURCE 3 – The Flag Ritual at the Luitpold Arena

Hitler honours the flag of the Munich Putsch in this ceremony, with the partly built grandstand in the background. This picture was painted by an official Nazi artist.

SOURCE 4 – Planning

'The participants were already flooding into Nuremberg. Carefully selected months in advance, each had a number, a designated truck, a designated seat in the truck, and a designated cot in the vast tent city near Nuremberg. By the time the ceremonies began on 4 September the thousands of party members had been rehearsed to perfection.'

J Toland, *Adolf Hitler*

SOURCE 5 – Masterpieces of theatrical art

'The Nuremberg Rallies held every year ... were masterpieces of theatrical art, with most carefully devised effects. I had spent six years in St Petersburg before the war in the best days of the old Russian ballet,' wrote Sir Neville Henderson [a British diplomat], 'but for grandiose beauty I have never seen ballet to compare with it.'

A Bullock, *Hitler: a Study in Tyranny*

SOURCE 6 – The Hitler Youth

'On Sunday all Nuremberg was filled with the presence of young Germany. From the earliest hours of the morning, endless columns of Hitler Youth marched to the stadium. As always, it is a marvellous sight: In rows of 48, the youth stand with others from their area. It is a picture of discipline and strength. Other Hitler lads and girls sit in the seats around the field. Across from the Führer's platform are the choirs and music groups, and high above the watchtowers from which fanfares and drumbeats will sound. Rows of Naval Hitler Youth stand to the right and left of the Führer's platform.... A few minutes before ten a command thunders over the field. The units and detachments stiffen, then break out in thousand-fold jubilation: The Führer has arrived.'

From *The Ceremony of the Hitler Youth*, 1936

Each rally was also based around a **theme**. The 1933 Rally was called the Congress of Victory; in 1935 the Nuremberg Laws against the Jews were announced; in 1936 the key theme was Honour and Freedom focussing on the evils of Bolshevism (Communism), Germany's self-sufficiency in raw materials and Germany's demand for colonies lost after the First World War.

SOURCE 7 – Launching campaigns

'Lloyd George [former British Prime Minister] was predictably impressed by the 1936 Party Day at Nuremberg. More spectacular than ever, it was marked by the launching of two new campaigns: the Four-Year Plan for economic self-sufficiency and an anti-Bolshevik crusade against "the powers of disorder". On a bright Sunday morning, Hitler spoke of the Bolshevik menace to 160,000 massed Brownshirts and SS men in the huge Nuremberg stadium, then drove back to the city in an open Mercedes acknowledging the plaudits of the multitude who jammed the narrow streets and hung from the dormer windows.'

J Toland, *Adolf Hitler*

Each Rally was preceded the night before by the performance of the opera, *Die Meistersinger von Nürnberg*, by Wagner, Hitler's favourite composer. The Rally was opened with the **Party Roll of Honour** of those who died for the Party. Each part of the Nazi organisation *creating a sense of history* presented themselves before Hitler over the six or seven days of the rally – the Hitler Youth, the German Women's League, the Reich Labour Service, the SA and the SS, as also did the Wehrmacht (the German armed forces). **Hitler's speech** was the highlight of the occasion.

SOURCE 8 – Rally of Greater Germany

'The Party Congress at Nuremberg that year served as a dramatic prelude to the developing political crisis by its impressive display of Nazi power and discipline. The title of the 1938 festivities was appropriate: "First Party Rally of Greater Germany", as was the trappings. Hitler had brought from Vienna ... the insignia of the First Reich – the Imperial crown, the Orb of Empire, the Sceptre and the Imperial Sword. At the presentation of these symbols of imperialism he solemnly vowed that they would remain in Nuremberg.'

J Toland, *Adolf Hitler*

SOURCE 9 – Spectacular

'200,000 party faithful with more than 20,000 unfurled flags crowded into Zeppelin Field and lined up with military precision. The effect of Speer's 130 giant searchlights was more breathtaking than imagined.... In the awesome silence, Hitler's voice came across the field from loud-speakers with eerie effect. "We are strong and will get stronger!" he said, and made it as much a threat as a promise.'

J Toland, *Adolf Hitler*

NUREMBERG – A SYMBOL OF NAZISM

The 1939 Rally, with a theme of the **Party Rally of Peace**, was cancelled due to the outbreak of the Second World War on 1 September 1939. By then Nuremberg had become a key **symbol** of Nazism. Consequently, during the war the city suffered from Allied bombing. After the war, the US army held a victory parade there and blew up the swastika which was behind the reviewing stand. The **trials** of the Nazi war criminals were deliberately held in that city. Nuremberg has now become the centre of a museum but long after its rallies have ended, their spectacle still causes controversy.

SOURCE 10 – Hitler speaks

'The sense of power, of force and unity was irresistible, and all converged with a mounting crescendo of excitement on the supreme moment when the Führer himself made his entry. Paradoxically, the man who was most affected by such spectacles was their originator, Hitler himself, and ... they played an indispensable part in the process of self-intoxication.'

A Bullock, *Hitler: a Study in Tyranny*

SOURCE 11 – Berlin questioning 2000 light show

'Berlin – Two Berlin officials are calling for the cancellation of the centerpiece of the city's millennium celebration: a huge, animated "light sculpture" around a towering column that they charge is reminiscent of the spectacles put on at Nazi rallies in the 1930s.... The millennium "Cathedral of Light" even shares the same name as the spectacle designed by Hitler's state architect Albert Speer at the Nuremberg Nazi rallies, the two said... The millennium show is centred around the Victory Column in Tiergarten Park.... Adding to the controversy is the fact that it was Speer who moved the monument to its current location as part of his master architectural plan for Berlin.'

Maurice Frank, Associated Press, 9 December 1999

TRIUMPH OF THE WILL

In 1934, Hitler commissioned **Leni Riefenstahl** to film the Nuremberg rally. Preparations for the Rally were linked with preparations for the filming. Nuremberg became a giant stage with flags, banners, marches and torches. Riefenstahl used 30 cameramen and over 100 technicians. She also used planes, cranes, roller skates and tracking rails to shoot the documentary. In all, 61 hours of footage was reduced to two hours of documentary, called the *Triumph of the Will*. 'At the premiere [of the film] she was greeted coolly by party officials but even Goebbels, her greatest critic, realised it was an outstanding achievement and, in its way, far more effective propaganda for the Führer and National Socialism than any other film yet made.' (Toland) Often regarded as one of the master-pieces of film propaganda, it was banned from public viewing for over fifty years. Now it can be bought on video or DVD.

CASE STUDY QUESTIONS

COMPREHENSION

1. In Source 1, how many different buildings and open spaces were planned for in the Nuremberg Rally grounds? Identify the Luitpold Arena, the Zeppelin Field, the March Field, the Great Road and the Congress Hall.

2. Who designed the Zeppelin Tribune in Source 2?

3. What is the emblem on the large banners behind the grandstand in the Luitpold Arena?

4. In Source 4, what evidence is there that everything was carefully planned?

5. In Source 5, why does the writer say the Nuremberg Rallies were 'masterpieces of theatrical art'?

6. Why does the Hitler Youth break out in 'thousand-fold jubilation'?

7. In Source 7, what two new campaigns were launched at the 1936 Party rally?

8. In Source 8, what was the theme of the 1938 Party rally?

9. Who, according to Source 10, was the originator of the 'spectacle' at Nuremberg? What is meant by the process of 'self-intoxication'?

COMPARISON

1. What aspects of Sources 2 and 3 show that the Nuremberg Rallies were carefully planned?

2. What different features of the Nuremberg Rallies do Source 4 and Source 5 highlight?

3. Does Source 6 tell us more about the features of Source 4 or Source 5?

4. What do Sources 7 and 8 tell us about Nazi policy?

5. What aspects of the Rally in Source 9 illustrate the 'sense of power, of force and unity' mentioned in Source 10?

6. What is common to both Source 9 and Source 11?

CRITICISM

1. How useful are photographs (Source 2) and artists' drawings (Source 3) compared to written accounts (Sources 4, 5 and 6) as evidence of what happened at the Nuremberg Rallies?

2. How would photographs and written accounts compare with film, such as *Triumph of the Will*, of the Nuremberg Rally as evidence of the events of the Rally?

CONTEXTUALISATION

1. Write an account of the Nuremberg Rallies.

2. What role did the Nuremberg Rallies play in Nazi propaganda?

3. How did the Nuremberg Rallies enhance the leadership of Hitler?

4. How were the Nuremberg Rallies used to get across Nazi policy to party members?

5. Why would Nuremberg be seen as a symbol of Nazism?

6. Were the two Berlin officials (Source 11) justified in their reaction to the 2000 Light Show?

3. Economic and Social Problems in Britain during the Inter-war Years, 1920–39

Introduction

In 1918, when the First World War ended, Britain counted the cost. Although the country suffered little physical damage, 750,000 soldiers were killed and many more were wounded. **Inflation** doubled and government spending on the war increased the National Debt by ten times. This was paid for out of increased taxation and borrowing from home and abroad, especially America. However, there was hope at the end of the war. The Prime Minister, David Lloyd George, promised a *'Land fit for Heroes'* – a better society for all to live in. But this did not happen. After a brief post-war boom, the British economy went into **depression** from which it never fully recovered until the Second World War. In 1921, unemployment rose to 2·2 million and it never fell below one million in the inter-war years. (See graph of Unemployment in Britain, 1920–39.)

> **KEY CONCEPT: DEPRESSION** is a term used to describe when an economy is doing badly; industrial production declines, factories and businesses close and there is widespread unemployment. The unemployment leads to poverty which affects all classes. **The Great Depression** which began with the Wall Street Crash in 1929 was the most severe depression in the early twentieth century.

> **KEY CONCEPT: INFLATION** is an increase in the prices of products, usually a large increase.

Causes of the British Economic Depression in the 1920s

The **depressed state** of the British economy in the 1920s was due to a number of factors:

- the decline of Britain's **staple industries** (coal, iron and steel, shipbuilding, cotton),
- the development of industry in other parts of the world,
- the decline of British trade,
- American competition,
- British wage costs.

Britain experienced high levels of unemployment during the inter-war years, as witnessed by this unemployment queue in Glasgow.

In the nineteenth and early twentieth century British prosperity depended a great deal on its export trade. Iron and steel, shipbuilding, cotton textiles and coal were the staple industries. But after the First World War these **older** industries went into decline – in one year alone they lost one million of their 4·5 million workers – and the British economy suffered for the next 20 years.

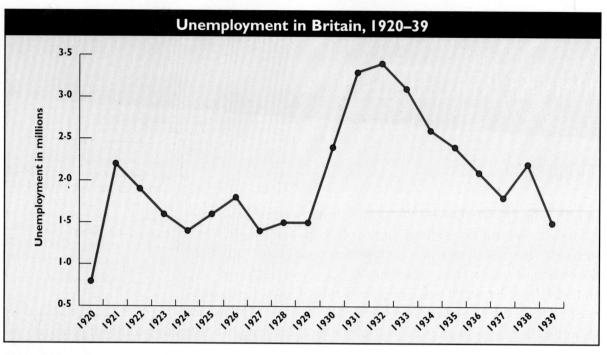

Unemployment in Britain, 1920–39

(Graph: Unemployment in millions, y-axis from 0.5 to 3.5; x-axis years 1920 to 1939)

Even though many suffered unemployment in Britain, the Rich were still rich.

Inefficient British coalmining could not compete with the more mechanised American, German or Polish mines.

Shipbuilding: After the First World War, there was a general decline in world trade so there was a **surplus of ships**. During the war, other countries such as the US and Japan began to produce their own ships. British shipyards fell behind in design and construction techniques. This decline in shipbuilding, and the end to armaments production, meant a drop in iron and steel production.

Cotton: Britain was the leading cotton producer before the First World War. But during the war, Britain lost some of its **traditional markets** such as China and India. They were replaced by the growth of home industries in those countries and by products from the US and Japan. In its Survey of Industries, the Balfour Committee reported that, '*China is approaching self-sufficiency as a result of the enormous development of modern spinning plant which has taken place in recent years.... Japanese competition has become formidable in China, India and other great markets of the Far East.*'

Coal Mining: Coal was another of Britain's staple industries. But after the war, British coal lost markets to American, German and Polish coal. A British magazine reported in 1921; '*American coal can be mined cheaply because it is near the surface and in thick seams.... British coal is hard to obtain because it is very deep, often in thin seams and therefore expensive to mine.*'

British coal was mined largely by **shovels and picks**, but mechanical mining was more developed in Germany and the US. Many British mines were too small and could not

[handwritten annotation at top:] Britain fundamental problem was lack of Diversification and over concentration on a few basic industries, cotton shipping, coal. cotton and shipping

invest in machinery. The only alternative was to cut wages or close the mines.

Coal also faced **competition** as a source of energy from petrol, oil and electricity.

The economic difficulties facing coal mining brought the mine owners and the miners into conflict in strikes and lockouts.

[handwritten annotation:] market were filled by new competitors (US etc)

The Location of Industry – Depressed Areas

Not all of Britain was affected by the decline of these industries. They were mainly concentrated in:

- **Clydeside** (Shipbuilding and engineering).
- **Tyneside** (North-east England) (Shipbuilding and coal mining).
- **Lancashire** (Cotton and engineering).
- **South Wales** (Coal mining).

The result of this industrial concentration was **depressed areas**, marked by high unemployment, low labour participation by women and other social problems such as a high infant mortality.

In contrast, the **Greater London area** and the **Midlands** were more prosperous. The contrast was great enough that people differentiated between **inner Britain** and the depressed state of **outer Britain**. In inner Britain the newer industries such as motor cars, electrical and consumer goods were being manufactured. These industries were more productive and were dependent on the home market.

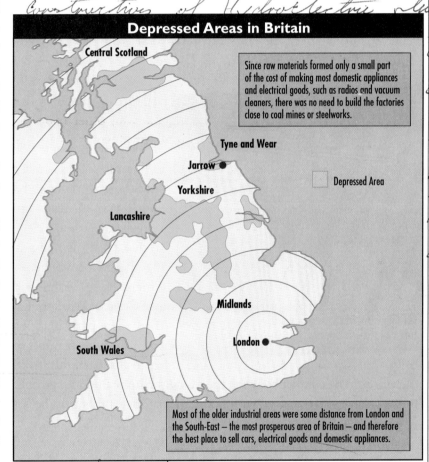

Depressed Areas in Britain

Central Scotland

Since raw materials formed only a small part of the cost of making most domestic appliances and electrical goods, such as radios and vacuum cleaners, there was no need to build the factories close to coal mines or steelworks.

Tyne and Wear

Jarrow

Yorkshire

Depressed Area

Lancashire

Midlands

London

South Wales

Most of the older industrial areas were some distance from London and the South-East – the most prosperous area of Britain – and therefore the best place to sell cars, electrical goods and domestic appliances.

[handwritten annotation in right margin:] Construction of Hydroelectric plant, in ... and middle ... sorts ... and oil refineries brought in a decline of demand for coal, as the world ... of electricity and oil.

Government Policy

[handwritten annotation:] * the sharp decline in exports meant that the British economy will not absorb all of the 6 million de-mobbed troops. There disablement at there jobs fers

The government followed the traditional economic policy of the nineteenth and early twentieth century of intervening very little in the economy. The government wanted to **balance the budget** so it was not prepared to borrow money to help industry. Instead it was more concerned about the large National Debt which had developed during the war.

[handwritten annotation at bottom:] because many believed Lloyd George when he spoke about ... November 1918 ...

[handwritten annotation right margin:] home coming was all the more acute

In 1925, the government decided to fix the value of the £sterling to the **Gold Standard**. It was fixed at $4·86 to the £ and many economists, including J M Keynes, said this was too high. The government hoped to control inflation by fixing the exchange rate (between different countries), but it also made British **exports dearer**, and thereby damaged British trade.

The Dole

By December 1920 over 800,000 had lost their jobs in Britain. This increased to over two million by June 1921. By this time the **National Insurance Act** had extended unemployment benefit to most workers. However, there were problems with the scheme. It only provided 15 shillings a week for men and 12 shillings a week for women. This was not enough to support families for food, rent, electricity and heating. The benefit was also limited to 15 weeks a year because it was aimed at short-term unemployment. The scheme could not cope with the new long-term unemployment. To solve this problem the government allowed workers get the additional benefits – called the **dole** – from the Poor Law Guardians. They had to queue each week to obtain this.

The General Strike in 1926 led to clashes between the workers and the police.

Wage Cuts

Those who had jobs also suffered from the economic depression. Cotton, engineering, shipbuilding and mine workers all had wages cut. But after the First World War, the trade unions were in a stronger position to resist those wage cuts. There were about eight million trade union members in 1921 and some unions joined together to form bigger and stronger unions, such as the Amalgamated Engineering Union and the Transport and General Workers Union.

There were particular problems in the **coal industry**, and clashes between mine owners and workers eventually led to the General Strike in 1926. It was inevitable that there would be conflict between the owners who wanted wage cuts and longer working hours and the workers who wanted **nationalisation** (government ownership), higher wages and shorter working hours.

The General Strike, 1926

The conflict came to a head in 1925 when mine owners looked for further wage cuts. The selling price of coal in export markets had increased by ten per cent when Britain went back on the Gold Standard. The workers' leader, A J Cook, responded with, *'Not a penny off the pay! Not a minute off the day!'* This time the miners were backed by the **Trades Union Congress** (TUC). The government agreed to pay a subsidy to maintain the miners' wages until a government commission, the **Samuel Commission**, enquired into the coal industry.

Coping with the General Strike: some travelled by lorry (left); a food convoy guarded by soldiers (right).

The Samuel Commission recommended that the mines be modernised, but also supported wage cuts and longer hours. The workers refused to accept this. When the government subsidy ended on 31 April 1926, the mine owners locked out the workers. The TUC supported the miners and when negotiations with the government broke down, a General Strike began on 3 May 1926.

THE GENERAL STRIKE IN PROGRESS

Transport, railway, building, printing, gas and electricity workers were called out on strike in support of the miners. This involved about two million workers, including one million miners. The remaining workers were held **in reserve**.

But, the Strike only lasted nine days as the government plans to counter it worked. The government set up the **OMS** (Organisation for the Maintenance of Supplies) which distributed food from Hyde Park, food convoys were protected by soldiers and thousands of volunteers – mostly middle class – drove cars, lorries, buses and even trains. While many people were sympathetic to the miners, they felt that the country was being held to ransom for their cause.

The TUC leaders called off the Strike when the government said there would be no victimisation if the strike ended. The miners were left to carry on their own strike. But they had to accept defeat six months later with longer hours and less pay.

EFFECTS OF THE GENERAL STRIKE

- The TUC was hurt by the failure of the strike – over the next few years **union membership fell** by almost two million.
- Individual workers also suffered – some were sacked, others lost pay.
- The government passed the **Trades Dispute Act (1927)** which outlawed general strikes. It also said trade unions could no longer use members' dues (subscriptions) to support the Labour Party unless they agreed.
- The spirit of **trade union militancy** was broken. The unions adapted a new strategy – more negotiation and co-operation instead of conflict. Industrial relations generally were improved, as there were fewer strikes after 1926. Neither were there any wage cuts for the next three years.

The Great Depression in Britain

The Wall Street Crash affected Britain in the same way as other countries. When the New York Stock Exchange crashed in October 1929, its effects spread worldwide. International trade fell, factories closed and unemployment rose.

The collapse of trade affected Britain's export industries so they had to cut production. Britain's unemployment, at 1·5 million in 1929, was high even before the Depression began. By 1932, unemployment rose to 3·4 million or one-fifth of the labour force.

Unemployment caused poverty so unemployed men had to find pickings in a rubbish heap.

Most of the **rise in unemployment** was in the older industries already in difficulties in the 1920s – coal, iron and steel, shipbuilding and cotton. In 1932, one-third of miners were unemployed, over 40% of cotton workers, almost 50% of iron and steel workers and over 60% of shipyard workers. The greatest losses were also in the areas where these industries were located – Lancashire, South Wales, North-east England and Central Scotland.

In Britain, there was a government **financial crisis** in 1931. There was a large **budget deficit** – the government spent £120 million more than it got in taxes, mostly in unemployment benefit and on the National Debt. The problem of how to tackle the budget deficit – cut the unemployment benefit or leave the Gold Standard – led to the downfall of the Labour Government. However, the new government – the **National Government** – was led by the same Prime Minister, **Ramsay McDonald**; and Chancellor of the Exchequer, Philip Snowdon, mainly supported by the Conservative and Liberal Parties, and only twelve Labour MPs.

The government took difficult decisions:

- It took Britain off the Gold Standard; very quickly the £sterling fell 30% in value.
- The government also cut unemployment benefit by 10% and introduced a **Means Test** (people lost benefit if they had other income, savings or if any of the family had a job).
- **Wages** of civil servants, soldiers and teachers were **cut**.

These actions balanced the budget.

- An **Import Duties Act** was introduced which put a tariff (tax) on imports (protectionism). This was the end of Britain's Free Trade policy, but since the tariffs increased the price of goods in Britain they may not have helped the country.
- **Special Areas Act, 1934**. The Government proposed to give help to Special Areas (depressed areas) to encourage the building of factories. But this was not a success. Less than 15,000 jobs were created.
- The bank **interest rate** was lowered so people could borrow to buy cars and houses.

BRITAIN AND GERMANY

But the British depression was mild compared to that of Germany:

- British unemployment was **half** the German level.

- British banks survived the Depression.

- Britain also imported a great deal of its food and since food prices fell, those who had jobs were better off.

- Unemployment was less in the **newer industries** – cars, electrical goods – so the areas where these were produced had lower unemployment; London, for example, had only ten per cent unemployment.

- The high and long-term unemployment of the north of England, south Wales and central Scotland was in **contrast** to the prosperity of the south-east of England and the Midlands. Unemployment there fell as soon as the economy picked up. Those who had jobs in the 1930s got better off as interest rates and food prices fell (rising standard of living). They increased the demand for electrical and consumer goods.

- The **British recovery** began sooner in 1934 than the German recovery.

- It also began **without rearmament** which was not begun until 1935 and was not significant until 1938.

- Also, the British recovery did not depend on government investment in the economy as the German recovery under Hitler did. Britain continued to balance the budget from 1932 to 1937 and it did not begin the large-scale public works which were used in Germany.

However, even though Britain recovered quickly from the Depression, unemployment remained high – it was still 2.2 million in 1938. This was largely due to the older industries in the depressed areas. These older industries lost 1.3 million workers between 1920 and 1938.

> **KEY CONCEPT: PROTECTIONISM** is the use of tariffs (taxes) to protect home industry and employment from foreign competition. This is the opposite of Free Trade.

Unemployment in Britain and Germany, 1929–38

The Condition of the People – Social Problems

Unemployment benefit was now based on a **means test** – once the insurance benefits were ended, any additional payments (the dole) depended on any earnings by other members of the family. This was assessed by officials visiting the homes of workers to check on the income and savings of the family. In *The Road to Wigan Pier*, George Orwell described the effect this had; '*the most cruel effect of the Means Test is the way in which it breaks up families. An old age pensioner, for instance, if a widower would live with one of his children.... Under the Means Test, however, he counts as a lodger and if he stays at home his children's dole will be docked. So, perhaps at seventy or seventy-five years of age, he has to (move) into lodgings.*'

Unemployment benefit was looked on as a **charity, not a right**. This affected the esteem and self-respect of the workers. J B Priestley wrote in an *English Journey* of '*men who, though they knew they were idle through no fault of their own, felt defeated and somewhat tainted.*' Orwell said, '*The middle classes were still talking about "lazy idle loafers on the dole".*' Unemployment lasted a long time for some workers. In 1936, a quarter of the unemployed were out of work for over a year. Some young men had never worked.

> '*In the distressed areas, there was a gloomy atmosphere of sadness, of bored resignation and despair. Forced inaction led to demoralisation. In the streets of towns, large and small, the unemployed walked aimlessly up and down.... Beggars in rags sold matches, boot polish, boot-laces; pilferers took bits of coal from railway sidings.... Everywhere one found shops closed and houses shut with their windows boarded up.*'
>
> F Bedarida, *A Social History of England, 1851–1990*

Unemployment was the **main cause of poverty**. A survey carried out in York in 1935–6 by Seebohm Rowntree found that thirty-one per cent of the people were living below the poverty line, and this was mostly caused by unemployment. Even many of the employed were on such low wages that they did not have enough for food after spending money on rent, clothing, fuel and light.

Hunger Marches were organised to protest about unemployment. They sometimes led to clashes with the police.

Poverty contributed to death and disease among the poorer classes. Orwell wrote, '*in any large industrial town the **death rate and infant mortality rate** of the poorest districts are always about double those of the well-to-do residential quarters.*' His views were supported by studies at the time. This was partly due to the poor diet of the unemployed.

HUNGER MARCHES

To highlight the long-term unemployment in the depressed areas, a series of marches, called **hunger marches**, were organised. These were organised by the **National Unemployed Workers' Movement (NUWM)**. This organisation was active since the early 1920s but the Labour Party and the TUC shunned it because the Communist Party dominated its leadership. The NUWM organised a march to London of 2,000 people in 1932, and further marches in 1934 and 1936. There were also local demonstrations and marches in Belfast, Glasgow and elsewhere. These sometimes resulted in clashes with the police. The **Jarrow March** or **Crusade** in 1936 had the same aims as the **hunger marches**, but it was organised separately. (See Case Study at the end of this chapter.)

In spite of increased unemployment during the Great Depression, Britain did not experience the growth of extremist parties in the same way as Germany. The **Communist Party** remained small and **Oswald Mosley's British Union of Fascists** made little impact. Most people still supported the traditional parties – Conservative and Labour.

Conclusion

The 1920s and 1930s saw the decline of the **traditional** British economy – the coal, steel, ship-building and cotton industries which had dominated since the nineteenth century. Their decline created many **depressed areas**, particularly in the northern half of England and in Wales and Scotland. However, southern England prospered with the progress of newer industries. The policy of Free Trade also came to an end and **protectionism** was brought in during the 1930s.

The government policy of **not intervening** in the economy was also questioned, especially as there seemed to be no end to unemployment. People did not want to experience again the bleakness of unemployment and they demanded that the government take a more active role in ending it. After the Second World War, the policies of **J M Keynes** who advocated government intervention to create full employment were put into practice. People also demanded that government take greater care of its citizens and this led to the creation of the **Welfare State**.

KEY PERSONALITY: JOHN MAYNARD KEYNES

J M Keynes was born in Cambridge, England, and educated at Eton and Cambridge. During his life he worked as a civil servant, taught economics at Cambridge and wrote many books and articles.

At the end of the First World War, he was economic adviser to **David Lloyd George, the British Prime Minister**, at the Paris Peace Conference. He disagreed with the Allied treatment of Germany, and published his criticism in ***The Economic Consequences of the Peace***. His belief that reparations were too great a burden on Germany was proven correct. Keynes was brought up in the economic thinking of the time. This stated that the government should not intervene in the economy. Instead it should balance the budget and not spend money on public works. In a depression, the economy would get itself right – unemployment would lead to a fall in wages and cheaper prices; this would lead to greater demand and a return to employment.

In the 1920s, Keynes **opposed** Britain's return to the Gold Standard at $4.86. He also believed that the government should help the depressed areas where shipbuilding, cotton and coalmining were declining. But it was the Great Depression which undermined the accepted economic thinking. Economists and politicians were baffled by the Great Depression and could not explain it with their economic theories.

Keynes provided the explanation in his great book, ***The General Theory of Employment, Interest and Money*** (1936). He said the current economic policies would not cure unemployment. This would only be done by the government borrowing money to create public works. The government should also lower interest rates (a **cheap money** policy). This began the **Keynesian Revolution** but it was a slow process because many resisted his ideas. However, after the Second World War, governments came to intervene in the economy, and gave commitments to full employment. Keynes's ideas and the **Beveridge Report** (1942) were the foundation of the **Welfare State** in Britain after the war. This established that the state through its social, economic and educational policies should protect its citizens **from the cradle to the grave**.

ORDINARY LEVEL

1. Study the graph of Unemployment in Britain, 1920–39 (p. 78) and answer the following questions:

(i) In which years was unemployment in Britain (a) lowest, and (b) highest?

(ii) How many years was unemployment over two million?

(iii) Which year(s) showed the most rapid rise in unemployment?

(iv) What reasons can you give to explain this?

2. Study the map of Depressed Areas in Britain (p. 79) and answer the following questions:

(i) List three of the depressed areas.

(ii) Apart from being depressed areas, what else had these areas in common?

(iii) Why was there no need to build factories for newer industries near coalmines or steelworks?

(iv) Why is the focus of this map on London and the South-East of England?

3. Study the graph of Unemployment in Britain and Germany, 1929–38 (p. 83) and answer the following questions:

(i) How many years was German unemployment (a) greater than, and (b) less than British unemployment?

(ii) Which country showed the more rapid rise in unemployment?

(iii) Which country showed the more rapid decline in unemployment?

(iv) What can the graphs tell us about how the Great Depression affected each country?

4. Write **paragraph answers** on each of the following:

(i) Unemployment in Britain in the 1920s.

(ii) The decline of British industry in the 1920s.

(iii) The General Strike in Britain, 1926.

(iv) The Hunger Marches.

(v) J M Keynes.

(vi) Poverty in Britain in the 1920s and 1930s.

5. Write **long answers** on each of the following:

(i) The Great Depression in Britain, 1929–39.

(ii) The Great Depression in Britain and Germany, 1929–39.

(iii) The role of the British government in the economy, 1920–39.

(iv) Economic and social problems in Germany under the Nazis, 1933–39. (See Chapter 2.)

HIGHER LEVEL

1. Why was the British economy in depression for most of the inter-war years, 1920–39?

2. Discuss the causes and effects of unemployment in Britain in the inter-war years.

3. How did the Great Depression affect Britain and Germany?

OR

Discuss the social and economic problems of Britain and Germany between 1929 and 1939.

4. With reference to Britain and Germany, discuss the role of governments in the economy between 1929 and 1939.

TEST YOURSELF AT
my-etest.com

INTRODUCTION

Jarrow, a town in the north-east of England, on the south bank of the river Tyne, was a depressed town in the 1920s and 1930s. In the nineteenth and early twentieth century its main industries were iron and steel manufacture and shipbuilding. In 1931, the steelworks closed down. Jarrow then depended on one shipyard, **Palmer's**, which suffered like other shipyards in the inter-war years, 1919–39.

In 1934, Palmer's yard closed down. **Unemployment** in Jarrow reached 72%, compared to 15% in the country. Of 8,000 skilled workers in steel manufacture and shipbuilding, only 100 were employed. The increased unemployment added to the existing problems of a depressed area – poverty, overcrowding, poor housing and high mortality.

1931 led to the fall of the Labour Ramsey McDonald

ORGANISATION OF THE CRUSADE

On 20 July 1936, **Jarrow Borough Council** decided to present a **petition to Parliament** in London. There was considerable planning for the march. Two hundred men were selected, after medical examination. The Council raised £1,500 to fund the march, including pocket money for the men. The route and stops along the way of the 300-mile journey were also planned. The Council also ensured cross-party support for the march, including support from the local Conservative Party. The Council did not want the march to be linked to the **hunger marches** organised by the **National Unemployed Workers Movement** (NUWM), who had connections with the Communist Party. They also called it a **crusade rather than a march** – partly to reflect the religious background of the area, but also to distance it from the **hunger marches**.

SOURCE 1 – No work in Jarrow

'There was no work. No one had a job except a few railwaymen, officials, the workers in the co-operative stores and a few workmen who went out of the town.... the plain fact (is) that if people have to live and bear and bring up their children in bad houses on too little food, their resistance to disease is lowered and they die before they should.'

MP for Jarrow.

Ellen Wilkinson, *The Town That Was Murdered*

SOURCE 2 – Poverty

'My mother used to keep us in bed in the morning because she couldn't afford to feed us. There was real starvation on Tyneside. It was hard for my parents ... I was one of ten children but all of us survived.... I went to school in my bare feet ... In hot or cold, in winter with six inches of snow, I would get home and my mother would have to rub a towel on my feet to stop me getting frostbite.'

Bill Batty, a Jarrow resident recalling his youth in Jarrow

SOURCE 3 – Closure of Palmer's

'Now when Palmer's went, not only did the actual funds of the company go, but the pension funds, the benevolent funds in which workers had invested their savings also went.'

Guy Waller, a journalist who reported on the March

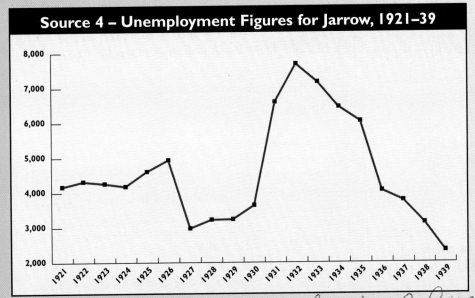

Source 4 – Unemployment Figures for Jarrow, 1921–39

Brit. PM, 1936 = Stanley Baldwin

SOURCE 5 – Jarrow petition

'To: The Honourable the Commons of the United Kingdom of Great Britain and Northern Ireland in Parliament Assembled.

The humble petition of the inhabitants of the Borough of Jarrow sheweth as follows:

During the last fifteen years Jarrow has passed through a period of industrial depression without parallel in the town's history. The persistence of unemployment has reduced us to a deplorable condition – homes are impoverished and acute distress is prevalent ... your petitioners humbly and anxiously pray that H.M. Government realise the urgent need that work be provided for the town without further devastating delay, actively assist resuscitation [revival] of industry and render such other actions as may be meet.

Signed by the under-mentioned, being inhabitants of the town of Jarrow of the age of 18 years and over.'

D Dougan, Jarrow March 1936

THE PROGRESS OF THE CRUSADE

There were 11,000 Jarrow people who signed the petition, which the marchers were carrying to London in an oak box with gold lettering. Over 68,000 Tyneside people signed a further petition. The marchers set off from the Town Hall, watched by most of the townspeople. They were led at the start by the Mayor, local councillors and **Ellen Wilkinson**, Labour Member of Parliament for Jarrow, who had encouraged the organisation of the march. They carried large banners saying **Jarrow Crusade**.

Each day followed a similar pattern. They began around 8.45 a.m. and marched an average of 13 miles a day. Some marched army-style – 50 minutes marching and 10 minutes resting. They marched in all conditions, though they were fortunate that there were only a few days of rain along the route.

SOURCE 6 –

Jarrow Appeal – Money collected for the march

Donations from general public:

Jarrow	£183.15.2	
Tyneside towns	£55.1.9	
Rest of UK	£442.0.0	£680.16.11
Donations from Conservative, Labour and Liberal Party organisations		£61.1.10
Donations from Trade Unions		£134.6.5
Donations from Co-operatives		£323.2.7
Collections en route		£317.12.8
Special Supper Donation		£50.0.0
Total		£1,567.0.5

D Dougan, Jarrow March 1936

SOURCE 7 – Organisation of march

'The organisation seems well nigh perfect. It includes a transport wagon – a bus bought for £20 and converted – which goes ahead with the sleeping kit, waterproofs for every man worn bandoleer fashion, 1s 6d pocket-money and two 1d stamps a week, medical attention, haircutting (and shaving for the inexpert), cobbling, accommodation at night in drill halls, schools, church institutes, and even town halls, and advance agents in the persons of the Labour agent at Jarrow, Mr. Harry Stoddart, and the Conservative agent, Mr. R Suddick, who work together in arranging accommodation and getting halls for meetings.'

With the Jarrow Marchers in the Manchester Guardian, 13 October 1936

SOURCE 8 – Support of march

'There is no political aspect to this march. It is simply the town of Jarrow saying "Send us work". In the ranks of the marchers are Labour men, Liberals, Tories (Conservatives), and one or two Communists, but you cannot tell who's who.'

With the Jarrow Marchers in the Manchester Guardian, 13 October 1936

SOURCE 9 – A town march

'... there was something which set the Jarrow march apart from all the others. It was partly the discipline and sense of order, but, more important than that, it was its origin as a town march. It did not represent a faction or a dissatisfied segment of society.... It was not a demonstration for food and charity. It was a means of presenting a petition to Parliament and its object was to ask for work.'

D Dougan, Jarrow March 1936

Sometimes they broke the monotony by singing, led by their mouth organ band. During the day, they were fed from their transport wagon. At the end of a day's marching, they were usually warmly welcomed – and fed – in the towns where they stopped. The leaders presented the case of Jarrow at public meetings in the towns.

LONDON AND HOME

After 23 days marching and two weekend rests, they reached London on Saturday, 31 October. They were led into the city by Ellen Wilkinson, Jarrow's Mayor, 11 councillors and a Labrador mascot dog. But their crusade made little impact on those in power. The marchers held a demonstration in Hyde Park on 1 November. A couple of days later the petition was presented to Parliament by their MP, Ellen Wilkinson, along with the petition from the wider Tyneside area.
The marchers returned to Jarrow by train. They were welcomed by cheering and shouting crowds; *'Never before in the history of the town has there been such an exhibition of mass enthusiasm,'* reported the *North Mail.*

SOURCE 10 – Start of march

'They were all issued with kit bags to carry their bedding and changes of clothing. Then they marched to Christ Church in Grange Road for a special service. The church was full to capacity with family and well-wishers. Bishop Gordon of Jarrow gave them a blessing.'

D Dougan, Jarrow March 1936

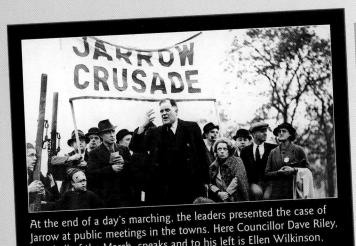

At the end of a day's marching, the leaders presented the case of Jarrow at public meetings in the towns. Here Councillor Dave Riley, Marshall of the March, speaks and to his left is Ellen Wilkinson, MP for Jarrow.

SOURCE 11 – Not a hunger march

'With eggs and salmon and such sandwiches as I saw today being consumed on the menu it is emphatically not a hunger-march. The men are doing well on it, and only two of them have fallen out for reasons of health in nearly 90 miles of marching.'

With the Jarrow marchers in the *Manchester Guardian*, 13 October 1936

SOURCE 12 – Welcome at Harrogate

'Harrogate welcomed the Jarrow marchers today as cheerfully as if they were a relief column raising a siege. The music of the mouth-organ band might have been that of the bagpipes so surely did it bring the people flocking, and when the two hundred reached the Concert Rooms there were hundreds of folk drawn up on the slopes around to cheer them. The police were in attendance and there was a big banner raised saying, "Harrogate workers welcome the Jarrow marchers". At the Drill Hall, the headquarters for the night, the crowd was denser.... A meeting is to be held at the Winter Gardens with Miss Ellen Wilkinson as one of the speakers. At every stopping-place there is such a meeting so that the world should know of Jarrow.'

With the Jarrow marchers in the *Manchester Guardian*, 13 October 1936

SOURCE 13 – Speeches on the march

'There were four main speakers. Alderman Thompson (Mayor) spoke about Jarrow's plight in general. "First we lost the Steelworks and 3,000 men lost their jobs. Then we lost our shipyard and another 5,000 were out of work." Councillor David Riley developed the economic theme. Poor towns like Jarrow had to subsidise their own poverty because a higher rate (local tax) had to be levied to cover substantial unemployment benefits that were being paid out. The third speaker, Councillor Paddy Scullion, dealt with the impact of unemployment on the health of the community. Finally, Ellen Wilkinson, the town's Member of Parliament, spoke. She concentrated her attack on the complacency – or cruelty – of the Government and the inertia of its leaders.'

D Dougan, Jarrow March 1936

The next day they got a shock when the Unemployment Assistance Board reduced their unemployment benefit by between four and eleven shillings a week – because they had not been available for work.

SOURCE 15

The band leads the Jarrow marchers.

Source 14 – Route of Jarrow March

- Jarrow
- Chester le Street
- Ferryhill
- Darlington
- Northallerton
- Ripon
- Harrogate
- Leeds
- Wakefield
- Barnsley
- Sheffield
- Chesterfield
- Mansfield
- Nottingham
- Loughborough
- Leicester
- Market Harborough
- Northampton
- Bedford
- Luton
- St Albans
- Edgware
- London

SOURCE 16 - Opposition to the march

'... the Labour Party Conference in Edinburgh rebuked Ellen Wilkinson for organising the march, on the grounds that hunger marches were associated with Communist organisations, such as the NUWM, and their use might lead to disorder....'

Stevenson and Cook,
The Slump. Society and Politics during Depression

SOURCE 17 – Opposition to the march

'The presentation of petitions was followed by a question from Ellen Wilkinson to the Prime Minister, Mr. Stanley Baldwin, asking how many resolutions he had received since 1 July regarding the position of Jarrow. He replied that he had received 66 resolutions, eight letters, one telegram and five postcards. And that was that.... It seemed such a let-down.... They [the men] had expected something more dramatic, a debate, a discussion, a statement, but they were left with – nothing.'

D DOUGAN, JARROW MARCH 1936

CONCLUSION

Jarrow's economy improved in the next few years but this had little to do with the Crusade. In 1938, a ship-breaking yard and engineering works were set up, and a year later a steelworks. Finally, the approach of the Second World War gave a boost to rearmament and to shipbuilding.

However, the Jarrow Crusade had an impact beyond the confines of the town. Along with the other hunger marches, it sparked the conscience of the middle classes. The march, more than any of the other marches, symbolised the **despair** of unemployed men and depressed areas. The effect of mass unemployment in the 1920s and 1930s contributed to the setting up of the **Welfare State** in Britain after the Second World War. '*The legacy of bitterness and suffering caused by mass unemployment helped spur the creation of the Welfare State.*' (Stevenson and Cook, *The Slump. Society and Politics during the Depression*)

COMPREHENSION

1. Study Sources 1, 2 and 3. Who had work in Jarrow? Why did people 'die before they should'? Why did Bill Batty's mother keep him in bed? Apart from losing their jobs, how else were workers affected by the closure of Palmer's?

2. Study Source 4. Which year had the highest unemployment? Which year had the lowest unemployment? Do the figures for unemployment in this source match those in other accounts? If not, can you explain the difference?

3. According to the Jarrow Petition (Source 5), how long had the industrial depression lasted? Is their view supported by the figures in Source 4? What did the petition ask the government to do?

4. How do the figures in Source 6 show the widespread appeal of the Jarrow Crusade?

5. According to Source 7, what use was made of the transport wagon? Where did the marchers get accommodation?

6. What was the purpose of the march according to Sources 8 and 9? Why do you think it was called the Jarrow Crusade?

7. How did the Jarrow March differ from the other marches according to Source 9?

8. How do we know from Source 12 that the marchers got a good welcome in Harrogate?

9. What messages did the speakers give in Source 13 'that the world should know about Jarrow' (Source 12)?

10 In Source 13, how was it shown that Jarrow suffered a double blow?

11. According to Source 14, how many stops were made along the way by the marchers – 18, 21, 23 or 24?

12. In Source 16, why did the Labour Party Conference rebuke Ellen Wilkinson for supporting the march?

13. Why did the men feel let-down after the petition was presented to Parliament (Source 17)?

COMPARISON

1. What is the evidence from Sources 7, 8 and 9 that the marchers had widespread support?

2. Using a variety of sources, what evidence is there that Jarrow was in a 'deplorable condition'?

3. Do you agree that the marchers showed 'discipline and a sense of order'?

4. Do you agree that the march was well-planned?

5. Was the criticism of the march by the Labour Party Conference justified?

CRITICISM

1. Sources 1 and 2 are primary sources. Would you consider them reliable and unbiased?

2. Examine the newspaper accounts from the *Manchester Guardian*. Assess their reliability and the journalist's view of the marchers? In general, what are the strengths and weaknesses of newspapers as sources for History? What evidence of these strengths and weaknesses can you see in these reports?

3. Does the evidence from the photo (Source 15) match the accounts given of the marchers in other sources? How do written and pictorial sources compare as historical sources?

4. List some of the secondary sources used above. How do they compare for reliability and bias with the primary sources used?

5. What other types of sources do you think would be useful for a study of the Jarrow March?

CONTEXTUALISATION

1. Write an account of the economic background to the Jarrow March.

2. What was the impact of unemployment on Britain in the inter-war years?

3. What were the policies of various British governments for solving unemployment in the 1920s and 1930s? How successful were they?

4. What was Keynes's view of government economic policies in the 1920s and 1930s?

In the 1920s the American economy boomed. Skyscrapers were built, cities expanded, consumer goods were bought, motor car sales trebled and road mileage doubled. It was a time of mass-production and new advertising. This prosperity formed the basis of the **Roaring Twenties** – a time of fun, music and good times. Very quickly, some of these **American influences** spread to Britain and to continental countries, such as France and Germany.

The motor car had a great influence on society in the 1920s and 1930s. Even before Henry Ford introduced mass-production techniques in his factory, the car was popular – it represented freedom and adventure. It became America's largest industry. It influenced people's way of life and the shape of towns.

Popular Culture: This term refers to activities, styles and aspects of the way of life which are enjoyed by ordinary people or the majority of people. This can include music, dance, clothes, advertising, sport and entertainment generally.

Popular Culture

Popular culture of the 1920s and 1930s was associated with radio, cinema, jazz and sport. In these decades, the entertainment industry expanded rapidly:

- the working week shortened,
- there were more women working,
- average wages rose so spending power increased,
- holidays with pay became more common by the late 1930s.

Much of the extra time and money was spent on entertainment and leisure. This was helped by the influence of the **motor car** which gave greater mobility. **Mass-production** reduced the cost of consumer goods and loans made them easier to buy. The **Great Depression** only slowed down the spread of these trends but it did not stop them.

The popular culture of the 1920s and 1930s was a **young culture**. It reflected a **difference** in generations between young and old, sons and daughters and their parents. It was also very much a **city culture**, as rural areas in both the US and Britain remained conservative.

Popular Culture

Radio

RADIO IN THE US

Popular culture was spread rapidly by the two new forms of **mass-entertainment**: radio and cinema. Cinema had begun before the First World War (1914–18) but radio was almost entirely new. In 1921, there was only one licenced radio station in the US. By the end of 1922 there were over 500 stations. By the late 1920s, NBC and CBS had networked stations across America. American radio was based on **advertising** and **competition**. A survey in 1932 said that the usual programmes of a station were music (63%), educational (21%), literature (12%), religion (2·5%) and **novelties**.

The impact of radio was instant. A young schoolboy described how he first heard radio in a friend's house and stayed up most of the night to listen. He was amazed. *'A man in ... Pittsburgh said it was snowing there ... someone sang in New York ... A banjo plucked in Chicago ... It was sleeting in New Orleans.'*

As well as being a source of entertainment and news for all the family in the 1920s and 1930s, the radio became part of the furniture.

RADIO IN BRITAIN

In Britain radio was first broadcast in 1922, and four years later the **British Broadcasting Corporation** (BBC) got a **monopoly** (control) of radio broadcasting. By the 1930s the quality of radio reception had improved and the radio unit was often like a piece of **furniture** in the living room. By 1939, seventy-five per cent of British families had a **wireless**, for which they paid a licence fee.

The BBC wanted to maintain **high standards** and set a good moral tone in its broadcasting. Its programmes were mainly news, information and entertainment. It believed in broadening the interests of the public, and very quickly it developed educational programmes.

THE INFLUENCE OF RADIO

- Radio was a new form of **entertainment**. It boosted popular music and the music industry soon realised that radio helped sales of records.
- It also kept people **better informed** – and more quickly informed – with its news programmes.
- **Newspapers** were affected by the arrival of this competitor for news. Now the newspapers had to become more **sensational** and **scandalous** to compete with radio news.
- Governments realised very quickly the **propaganda value** of radio.
- The influence of radio could be seen when Orson Welles broadcast a programme on CBS in America based on H G Wells's *War of the Worlds* in October 1938. This caused **huge panic** among hundreds of thousands of listeners who believed that aliens had invaded Earth.

Cinema

Even though cinema had been popular before the 1920s, it expanded enormously in that decade and in the 1930s. The huge expansion centred on **Hollywood**, a suburb of Los Angeles, with its all-year-round sunshine. Thousands of silent, black and white movies were produced to satisfy the huge demand for them. The advent of sound films in 1927, when **Al Jolson** featured in *The Jazz Singer*, gave an added boost to cinema. Then Disney produced the first animated film, *Steamboat Willie*, in 1929, introducing **Mickey Mouse**. In the 1930s, colour films also became available. British audiences depended on mostly American films because the First World War led to a fall-off in the production of British films. It was not until the 1930s that British films made an impact again.

Sound movies arrived in 1927 when Al Jolson starred in *The Jazz Singer*.

Rudolf Valentino, Italian-born star of American movies, who was idolised by women. He was widely mourned after his early death in 1926.

THE POPULARITY OF CINEMA

Cinema was hugely popular in America. In cities such as **Chicago** there were hundreds of cinemas showing four performances a day. In 1920, 40 million cinema seats were sold each week; this had increased to 100 million a week by 1929.

In **Britain**, the small cinemas – or **flea-pits**, as they were called – of the pre-First World War era expanded rapidly in the 1920s and 1930s. A huge number of **super-cinemas** which could hold up to 3,000 people were built in the main cities, particularly London. They had plush seats with space for an orchestra, or an organist, up front to accompany the film. But the introduction of sound soon made these redundant.

Going to the **pictures,** or the **flicks** as they were called in Britain, was the most popular form of entertainment in the 1930s. By 1939, fifty per cent of the people went to the cinema once a week, and twenty-five per cent went twice a week. It was entertainment for **all classes**, even the unemployed. As George Orwell wrote in *The Road to Wigan Pier*: '*Even people on the verge of starvation will readily pay two pence to get out of the ghastly cold of a winter afternoon.*' For others it was a form of escapism – '*a private day-dream of yourself as Clark Gable or Greta Garbo.*'

THE INFLUENCE OF CINEMA

- Cinema was the **most popular** form of entertainment in the 1920s and 1930s. It added a new world of **romance** and **adventure**.
- The **stars** of the new cinema influenced the **lifestyle** of the young in particular. The films influenced fashions, mannerisms, the perfume women wore, the hairstyle of men and, even sometimes, slang. One Welshman complained that the nice local accents were broken by '*such words and phrases as "Attaboy!", "Oh, Yeah" and "Sez you"* '.
- In this way, cinema spread **American culture** to Britain and the continent of Europe.
- Cinema used **sex** to sell itself. It contributed to the **gap** between the younger and older generations. In the years before the First World War, sex was not mentioned. But in the 1920s,

whether through scandalous stories in newspapers or the appeal of the cinema, sex was more **openly discussed**. Hollywood produced *Forbidden Path, Where a Woman Sins* and *Up in Mabel's Room* and many more films with a sexual tone. **Mary Pickford** (the world's sweetheart), and **Clara Bow** (the **It** girl of the 20s), were the female sex symbols of the decade while **Rudolf Valentino** was the male sex symbol.

- **Sound** revolutionised cinema in the 1930s. Some of the old stars failed to transfer from silent to sound. But the female stars of the 1930s such as **Greta Garbo** and **Claudette Colbert** were still alluring while often playing career women. In this way, they provided a **role model** for some young women. On the other hand, **Clark Gable** represented the glamorous lover and the man of action, features he combined in the great 1930s movie, *Gone with the Wind*.

- **Musicals** were now added to the list of adventure, comedy, romance, western and gangster movies already being produced in the 1920s. The new musical stars such as **Bing Crosby** had to be able to sing and dance but also look just **ordinary**.

Mary Pickford, known as 'America's Sweetheart', was very popular in the 1920s.

KEY PERSONALITY: CHARLIE CHAPLIN

Charlie Chaplin was the greatest actor of the silent movies, but his talent went well beyond that.

He was born in **London** of mixed French-Irish parents. He had a difficult early life, experiencing poverty and the workhouse. After playing music halls and theatres in England, he was signed up for a **film career** in America. He began working in films in 1914 and was already a well-established star by the beginning of the 1920s. When he visited Europe at that time, he was hailed as a hero and swamped by huge crowds. By now he had developed the style which made him famous – **the tramp**. This was the *'little fellow'*, as he said himself, with the tight jacket, the baggy trousers, the over-sized shoes, the bowler hat and the cane. He combined **humour** with **sadness**; he was the underdog who appealed to everybody.

He had great success with *The Kid, The Gold Rush* and *The Circus* in the 1920s. He wrote, directed, produced and acted in these films, as he did with later ones. In *The Kid* it was said, *'There are almost as many tears as laughs in this movie.'* But *The Gold Rush* is regarded as his greatest film.

When the silent era ended, Chaplin refused to go along with **sound**; instead, he maintained the tramp as his main character in *City Lights* (1931) and *Modern Times* (1936). *The Great Dictator* (1940) was his **first talking** film. In it he warned against the rise of Hitler's power in Europe. His political comments here, which seemed to be urging America to join the war, led to criticism.

More serious was his support for **Russian War Relief**. Given the suspicion of Communism in America, it was indeed likely that he would be accused of being a **Communist**. His lifestyle of three marriages and three divorce cases was also criticised. In 1947, he was called before Senator Joe McCarthy's **Senate Committee on Un-American Activities**. He was able to show he wasn't a Communist. But a number of years later, while on a trip to Europe with his family, he was informed that his re-entry permit had been cancelled.

Fortunately for Charlie Chaplin some years before he had met and married **Oona O'Neill**, the daughter of Eugene O'Neill, one of America's greatest playwrights. He was 54 and she was 18. Chaplin spent the remainder of his life in Switzerland. In 1972, he returned to America once more when he was awarded a special honorary Oscar *'for the incalculable effect he has had in making motion pictures **the art form of this century**.'*

Cinema

KEY PERSONALITY: BING CROSBY

Bing Crosby was born in Washington State, America, of Irish descent. He went to university but wanted to be a **singer**, so he headed for California in the mid-1920s. He quickly began a remarkable career, which gave him outstanding success as a singer, a recording artist, a radio and film star; and later, a TV star, to a lesser extent. Bing Crosby began his **recording career** in 1926 and became the most successful recording artist of the twentieth century. His relaxed singing style – his **crooning** – along with his wide range of songs from romantic ballads to Jazz classics appealed to the people. His hits in the 1930s included *Brother Can You Spare a Dime*, *Red Sails in the Sunset* and *Alexander's Ragtime Band*. But his biggest hit came in 1942 with *White Christmas*, the most successful single of all time.

He first appeared on **radio** in 1928 and very quickly realised how radio could promote his records. From 1931 he had his own show, singing live on CBS and NBC with sponsored radio programmes.

His **film career** was even more successful. For 15 years in the 1930s and 1940s he was a **top, box office attraction**. He usually played light-hearted comedy or musical roles. But he won an **Oscar for Best Actor** in 1944 for his portrayal of Father O'Malley in *Going My Way*. It was during the 1940s that he began the **Road** movies with Bob Hope – the first was *Road to Singapore* – and the movie format lasted into the 1960s.

During the **Second World War** he contributed to the **war effort** by entertaining at military camps and promoting government war bonds. He also took his radio show to Europe and broadcast from England, France and Germany. At the end of the war a magazine poll voted him the individual who had done most for soldiers morale.

When Bing Crosby died in 1977, President Carter of America paid a **fitting tribute** to him. He described him as '*a gentleman, proof that a great talent can be a good man despite the pressures of show business.*' He was '*successful, yet modest; casual but elegant.*'

The 'Flappers' and the 'Bright Young Things'

Some of the biggest changes in the 1920s occurred in the lives of **young women**. Women had experienced independence during the First World War when they had worked at men's jobs. In the 1920s this trend continued as there were increased numbers of working women (ten million more in the US).

These younger women – known as the **flappers** in America or the **bright young things** in Britain – cut their hair short, abandoned corsets and wore knee-length skirts, make-up and lipstick. They drove cars, danced, smoked and went to the movies. In Britain, there were parties and clubs in **Soho** in London with the new American cocktail drinks. At the seaside some wore bathing suits that left their legs uncovered.

They were the **modern** young ladies of the 1920s and in part they were rebelling against the older generation. They symbolised the **Roaring Twenties** but they were still a **small proportion** of the population, though their lives often hit the headlines. They were mainly **middle and upper middle-class** young women. Most other women were still concerned with managing the home.

All That Jazz

Jazz music characterized the spirit of the 1920s, to such an extent that the decade is sometimes called the **Jazz Age**. Jazz spread out from **New Orleans** where it originated to other cities and parts of America, and beyond. It was spread by the migration of black people to the northern cities. But **radio and cinema** also helped spread it everywhere. It spread to Europe – to Britain and the continent, especially Paris and Berlin. Jazz brought new dances, especially the **Charleston**, and it was particularly popular among the young.

A **dance craze** swept the countries. In America it became the time of the **dance marathons**; in Britain it was Saturday nights in lavishly decorated halls when the **foxtrot** and the **Charleston** combined with the older waltzes. The new style upset the older generation.

'If these up-to-date dances are within a hundred miles of all I hear about them then I should say that the morals of a pig-sty would be respectable in comparison.'

Flappers dancing the Charleston, one of the popular dances of the 1920s.

Flappers chatting at the bar: modern young ladies of the 1920s.

Sport

Radio and cinema contributed to the spread of another aspect of popular culture – sport. These decades were the great decades of **mass spectator sport**. It was also a time of more **professionalism** (people earning a living from sport). Sport also had its **heroes or stars**, just like cinema. Indeed, these helped spread the popularity of their sport.

In America, **baseball** was the most popular summer sport. It had its hero in **Babe Ruth** whose exploits could be heard on **radio commentaries**. But baseball was largely confined to America and it did not spread like other aspects of American culture. In Britain, in contrast, **soccer** became the national sport. In 1923, 200,000 attended the Cup Final in **Wembley**, among them King George V. By 1939, thirteen million were attending First Division matches in England.

Boxing and **athletics** were also popular. **Tennis** spread to all classes though the spectators at **Wimbledon**, the highlight of the tennis season, were mainly middle class. **Golf** still remained middle class, even retaining elements of **privilege** and **exclusion**. Generally, Americans competed aggressively and with a determination to win in the sports in which they were interested. This partly explains why the **star performers** in many of these sports were American.

Jesse Owens, the great American athlete, winning the long jump in the 1936 Olympic Games in Berlin.

Radio and Cinema in the Second World War

The role of radio and cinema became even more important when the Second World War began. As the war became **a total war** where all the resources of each country were needed to fight the enemy, radio and cinema played a very important role in **propaganda**. Since they could reach **mass audiences** easily, they were used to create **national unity** and to **keep up morale** in difficult times. Leaders such as **President Roosevelt** of America and **Winston Churchill**, the Prime Minister of Britain, used radio to reach into people's homes. The importance which governments placed in radio can be seen in Germany where the government made listening to **foreign radio broadcasts** a capital offence (subject to the death penalty).

Radio also continued with its role as a provider of news. Most people first heard about the **major war events** – the invasion of Poland and France, the attack on Russia, the bombing of Pearl Harbour and the D-Day landings in Normandy – from radio broadcasts.

Before America entered the war in December 1941. Charlie Chaplin directed and acted in *The Great Dictator*. It was seen by some in America as encouraging the country to join the war.

CINEMA IN WAR

Cinema too played its part. In both America and Britain there were many films produced with a war message. Films such as *Action in the North Atlantic, Desert Victory* (a documentary) and *Escape* were important morale boosters. The Allies were always portrayed as good and brave; the Nazis (or Japanese) were the villains, both cruel and evil.

But the stars too contributed in another way – they visited and entertained the troops in their camps and promoted government bonds. Two of the most popular performers among the soldiers were **Bing Crosby** and **Bob Hope**.

Conclusion

By 1945, all the trends in radio, cinema, music and sport which were established in the 1920s and 1930s continued. **Television** had not yet made the impact which it did from the 1950s onwards. Greater amounts of leisure time and a higher standard of living ensured that **popular culture** depended on radio and cinema to reach the mass audiences.

ORDINARY LEVEL

1. Study the following extract on early radio broadcasting and answer the following questions:

   'There was ... great argument about what the impact of [radio broadcasting] might be. Some people thought reading would come to an end; others that no one, in future, would go to concerts. Some people thought that everyone would become passive [inactive], head-phones firmly clamped to the head.'

   A Briggs, 'The Birth of Broadcasting',
   History of the 20th Century

   (i) Why was there a great argument about the impact of radio broadcasting?

   (ii) Why do you think that some people thought (a) reading would come to an end, and (b) that no one would go to concerts?

   (iii) What influences had radio which are not listed above?

2. Study the extract on Charlie Chaplin and cinema and answer the following questions:

   'Charlie Chaplin became the world's most prominent film-maker during the period of the silent film, which ended with the introduction of sound-on-film in 1928. His reputation grew first as a comedian of unique character and talent in American slapstick comedy, at the time when the impact of popular, international stardom was being experienced for the first time. The film was an entirely new kind of entertainment industry, and the first to be industrialised. It was Chaplin's good luck to arrive at the right time....
   Hollywood, the principal centre for American film-making, became legendary for what were termed its "dream factories", the great studios of the leading motion picture companies.... The pivot on which the industry turned was the world-wide appeal of its stars.... These stars rose to the top because their personalities, talents or "images" were attuned [in step with] to some world-wide heart's desire in the public who used their local cinemas as a weekly channel for excitement and daydream.'

   R Manvell, 'Charles Chaplin and Charlie',
   History of the 20th Century

   (i) When did the silent era in film-making end and why?

   (ii) What type of actor was Charlie Chaplin?

   (iii) Why was it Charlie Chaplin's 'good luck to arrive at the right time'?

   (iv) Why was Hollywood famous?

   (v) Why did the stars rise to the top?

   (vi) Why did the people [public] go to the cinema?

3. Study the extract on Charlie Chaplin's View of Talking Pictures and answer the following questions:

   Paris, 1 November 1930
   'Charlie Chaplin is the last great star to hold out against the arrival of sound, and it is perhaps a measure of his greatness that he can still defy the march of progress. Chaplin continues to believe that the talkies are only a passing fad.... In an interview for the American magazine, *Silver Screen*, he predicts the imminent disappearance of pictures which are '100 per cent talking'.... In his latest film, *City Lights*, ... he has made only limited use of the technical resources of sound. *City Lights* is a silent film ... synchronised music and simplistic sound effects accompany the action.'

   Cinema Year by Year, 1894–2002

   (i) Why does Charlie Chaplin 'hold out against the arrival of sound'?

   (ii) What is a measure of Chaplin's greatness?

   (iii) What does Chaplin say will happen to pictures which are '100 per cent talking'?

   (iv) Did Chaplin get it wrong? Explain your answer.

4. Study the photograph of Charlie Chaplin in *The Great Dictator* (p. 98) and answer the following questions:

(i) Who, according to Charlie Chaplin, is the Great Dictator?

(ii) What do the emblems on the armbands and on the hat of the Great Dictator signify?

(iii) Is this film propaganda? Explain your answer.

5. Write **paragraph answers** on each of the following questions:

(i) The spread of radio in the US and Britain in the 1920s and 1930s.

(ii) The growth of cinema in the US and Britain in the 1920s and 1930s.

(iii) The influence of radio and cinema.

(iv) Charlie Chaplin and the early cinema.

(v) Bing Crosby.

(vi) The Flappers and the Bright Young Things.

(vii)The role of radio and cinema during the Second World War in the USA and Britain.

(viii)The role of radio and cinema in spreading popular culture.

6. Write **long answers** on each of the following questions:

(i) The origins, growth and influence of radio in the USA and Britain between 1920 and 1945.

(ii) The origins, growth and influence of cinema in the USA and Britain between 1920 and 1945.

(iii) Charlie Chaplin and the growth of cinema.

OR

How did Charlie Chaplin contribute to the popularity of cinema? (Department of Education, Sample Paper)

(iv) Bing Crosby, a star of radio and cinema.

HIGHER LEVEL

1. What was the role and influence of cinema in the US, OR Britain, from 1920 to 1945?

2. What was the role and influence of radio in the US, OR Britain, from 1920 to 1945?

3. What part did Charlie Chaplin play in the success of silent cinema and how did he adjust to sound-on-film?

5. Politics and Administration in France: The Third Republic, 1920–40 and the Vichy State, 1940–44

The Impact of the First World War

France suffered greatly in the First World War (1914–18). Even though the country was on the winning side, the impact of the war was felt all during the inter-war years (1919–39) and beyond. Of the 8 million Frenchmen who fought in the war: 1·3 million died; 3 million were wounded; and about 1 million of the wounded were badly injured. Large areas of northern France were destroyed – factories, mines, towns and prosperous farming land. The cost of reconstruction was estimated at over 100 million francs. During the war, inflation rose by over 400 per cent and France owed a great deal of money which the country had borrowed to pay for the war.

Government and the Political System in France

France was a democratic republic with a parliament composed of a Chamber of Deputies and a Senate. But while all men had the vote, women were barred from voting. The country had a large number of political parties which were divided into **Left** (reforming or revolutionary), **Right** (conservative) and **Centre** (moderate). All governments in the inter-war period were **coalitions** (groups of parties).

There was a great deal of **political instability** as governments changed on average every six months when they lost the support of some sections of the coalition through disagreements over domestic or foreign policy. The **electoral system** caused some of the political instability in France. A small change in votes resulted in huge changes in the number of seats won in general elections. Victory for the right wing in one election was followed by victory for the left wing in the next election. In such a situation, governments sometimes had to resort to **rule by decree** to bring in laws.

Nevertheless, in spite of the rapid changes of government, France experienced **greater stability** than this would suggest. While new Prime Ministers formed new governments, often the ministers remained the same. Secondly, most governments in the inter-war years included the **Radical Party**. Coalitions were usually from either Left- or Right-wing groups, but these groups had to join up with the main moderate or centre party, the Radical Party, to form the government.

French wounded of the First World War being treated in a ruined church in Northern France.

A New Government – the Bloc National

In November 1919, the **Bloc National** – a coalition of right-wing parties – won the general election. They succeeded because they favoured punishing Germany after the war and because of the fear of Communism after the Russian Revolution of 1917. The government was immediately faced with the problem of industrial unrest. In 1919, the previous government passed the **eight-hour working day** but demands for further improvements in working conditions and pay led to a **general strike** in May 1920. The increased militancy of the trade unions was due to a number of factors:

- Union membership of the **CGT**, the largest federation of trade unions, increased threefold during the war.
- Instead of wage increases driven by wartime inflation, there were **wage cuts** after the war.
- The increased militancy of the unions was partly inspired by the success of the **Communist Revolution** in Russia in 1917.

But the Bloc National government reacted strongly to the general strike of May 1920. The government put it down ruthlessly; the leaders were arrested and when workers gave in at the end of May, 18,000 railwaymen were sacked. The CGT was split after the strike and union membership fell by almost two million.

Changes of Government in France, 1919–44

1919–24	1924–6	1926–32	1932–4	1934–6	1936–8	1938–40	1940–44
	Cartel des Gauches – left-wing parties		Cartel des Gauches – left-wing parties		Popular Front – left-wing parties		Vichy France
Bloc National – right-wing parties		Government of National Union – right-wing parties		Right-wing governments		Government of National Defence – right-wing parties	

SOCIALIST DIVISIONS

The political party representing the workers – the Socialists – also divided. Some favoured closer ties with Russian Communism by joining the (Communist) **Third International** (or Comintern). The majority formed the **French Communist Party** (PCF) and followed instructions from Moscow, while the remainder led by **Leon Blum** favoured moderate socialism and they retained the name **Socialist Party**. During the 1920s divisions continued between the two parties and this prevented the formation of some coalition governments.

RECONSTRUCTION

The Bloc National government began a programme of **reconstruction** in the war-torn areas of northern France which was completed by 1926. Roads and railways were repaired, factories were rebuilt with modern machinery, new houses were constructed and agricultural land was made productive again. One historian has written, *'The reconstruction of the devastated areas was the greatest economic achievement of postwar Europe.'* But, due to the effects of the First World War, the French economy suffered from a **shortage of manpower**. Two million immigrant workers who came from Italy, Spain, Belgium and Poland between 1920 and 1930 replaced this shortage.

The greatest difficulty facing the government was the **cost** of reconstruction. The French people, in particular the ruling class of industrialists and bankers, wanted the costs to be paid for out of German **reparations** (compensation). The **Treaty of Versailles** imposed a **war guilt** clause on Germany and made the country responsible for reparations after the war. This was calculated at £6·6 billion, over fifty per cent of which was to be paid to France. French people wanted to ensure that this was paid so that Germany was kept weak and to gain revenge for German destruction during the war. But they also wanted to ensure that the costs of the war and of reconstruction would not lead to increased taxation in France. This showed how domestic and foreign policy influenced each other.

> **KEY CONCEPT: COMMUNISM** was based on the writings of Karl Marx, a German writer of the nineteenth century. He outlined his ideas in *The Communist Manifesto* and *Das Kapital*. Communists believed that the working class would revolt against the middle class who controlled industry. This would result in a Communist society where private property was abolished, the government would run the land and the factories for the benefit of the people and everybody would be equal.

FOREIGN POLICY

French Security and the Peace Treaties

At the Paris Peace Conference (1919) after the First World War, **Clemenceau**, the French Prime Minister, tried to ensure the **security** and **safety** of France by demanding harsh measures on Germany. (See the Treaty of Versailles in Chapter 2.) He succeeded in many points in the Treaty of Versailles – apart from reparations, Germany was largely disarmed and it lost its empire. But Clemenceau failed in his demand that Germany should give up all land west of the Rhine River.

Many French people were therefore concerned that the Treaty did not provide enough security for France – after all France had been invaded twice in 50 years by Germany. They had little confidence in the League of Nations. As well as this, American and British guarantees to help France in future wars against German aggression collapsed when the American Senate rejected the Treaty of Versailles. France felt betrayed.

Helping with reconstruction in post-war France: subscribe to the National Loan.

Protecting France

French foreign policy was guided by French fear of a revived Germany. The French army was the largest in Europe and there was no threat from the much-reduced German army but this still did not provide security. The government tried to provide greater security by two principal methods: (i) isolating Germany, and (ii) enforcing the terms of the Treaty of Versailles.

Isolating Germany

To provide better security, France made a series of **military treaties** which attempted to encircle Germany. By isolating Germany, France hoped to keep it weak. Treaties with Belgium (1920) and Poland (1921) began the encirclement. These were followed in 1924 with an alliance with Czechoslovakia, which linked France to the **Little Entente** of Czechoslovakia, Yugoslavia and Romania.

French Occupation of the Ruhr

French occupation of the Ruhr in Germany: French gunboats arriving (top) and French troops on German trains (below).

But also the French people wanted to enforce all the terms of the Treaty of Versailles on Germany. The question of reparations was the one which caused the most trouble during the 1920s.

By 1921, it seemed that Britain was prepared to reduce the total reparations figure to allow the revival of the German economy. When the French Prime Minister, **Aristide Briand**, appeared to favour this, he was replaced by Poincaré, a more hard-line Prime Minister. **Poincaré** was a lawyer who saw the issue in legal terms. He believed firmly in the rightness of the French case. When Germany failed to pay some of the instalments due under reparations, Poincaré ordered a French army takeover of the Ruhr, the industrial heart of Germany (1923). The Ruhr occupation dragged on due to passive German resistance and French relations with Britain and America were embittered. In 1924, the Germans agreed to revised payments under the **Dawes Plan** and the French troops were withdrawn. *believed in (american bankers) a realisable scheme.*

For many French people this was **not a satisfactory outcome**. In the first place, the occupation showed that France was not strong enough on its own to enforce the Treaty of Versailles. Secondly, the cost of sending in French troops resulted in increased taxation and the decline in the value of the franc. This contributed to the defeat of Poincaré and the Bloc National in the general election of 1924.

Based on germanys ablity to pay back loans. us gave 800 mill to germany.

The Cartel des Gauches

The Bloc National was replaced in the 1924 general election by the **Cartel des Gauches** (Coalition of the Left). This was an alliance or coalition of the Radicals and the Socialists, led by a Radical Prime Minister, **Edouard Herriot**. The Cartel des Gauches benefited in the election from:

- the failure of the Ruhr occupation,
- the effect of the Ruhr occupation on the French economy,
- better party organisation.

Very soon the Cartel des Gauches faced a **financial crisis**, brought on partly by the Ruhr occupation. But the government also continued to borrow to pay for reconstruction and as the debt got larger, the value of the franc fell. French investors invested their money abroad to force the government not to tax the rich. When the government tried to take action, it collapsed in April 1925. Over the next year, six more Cartel des Gauches governments were formed but they all failed to solve the economic problems; the government had no money, the franc continued to decline in value and prices continued to rise.

Government of National Union

In 1926, the Cartel des Gauches government was replaced by a more conservative **Government of National Union** headed by **Raymond Poincaré** as Prime Minister and Minister of Finance. He now took the decisions which the Cartel failed to take in 1924. He increased taxation for everybody, though more on the poor than on the rich, and he balanced the budget. He was helped by German reparations payments under the Dawes Plan. The franc was stabilised, investors grew confident and Poincaré was regarded as **the saviour of the franc**. Not surprisingly, the parties which supported him, including the Radicals, were returned to government after the 1928 general election. However, Poincaré had to retire the next year due to ill-health.

Briand and French Foreign Policy

In spite of many changes of government between 1925 and 1932, French foreign policy during this time was largely in the hands of one man, **Aristide Briand**. He realised that it was not possible for France to get support for forcing Germany to adhere to the terms of the Treaty of Versailles. He also realised that he had to come to some agreement with Germany. He believed that by bringing Germany fully into the political and economic life of Europe, Germany would be so dependent on other European countries that she would not go to war with France again.

Briand was fortunate that the German Foreign Minister, **Gustav Stesemann**, also wanted European acceptance of Germany. In the **Locarno Pact** (1925), France and Germany, with British and Italian support, pledged to accept the borders established between them by the Treaty of Versailles. Germany was also invited to join the League of Nations. French people were delighted with the pact and Briand was given a hero's welcome when he returned to Paris.

The Locarno Pact was followed by the **Kellogg-Briand Pact** (1928). Briand and Kellogg, the US Secretary of State, agreed, along with 63 other countries, including Germany, to renounce the use of war as an instrument of national policy.

After these successes, Briand continued to work for better relations with Germany. The **Young Plan** (1929) further eased German reparation payments. In 1930, five years ahead of schedule, French troops left the Rhineland.

Maginot Line

However, in spite of these improvements in Franco-German relations, the French still felt insecure. In 1929, they began the building of the **Maginot Line** – a huge line of fortifications along the German border. When it was completed in 1934, it gave the French a greater sense of security. But by that time also the Great Depression was affecting France, German reparations were cancelled in 1932, and Hitler became German Chancellor in January 1933.

Rows of posts in front of the Maginot Line, the French defensive line facing Germany.

[Handwritten margin notes:] Young Plan. Owen Young american Berceos man reduced the amount owed by Germany to be reduced to 2 billion 200 mil

The Great Depression and its Effects

ECONOMIC PROGRESS IN THE 1920S

KEY CONCEPT: DEPRESSION. This term is used to describe when an economy is doing badly; industrial production declines, factories and businesses close and there is widespread unemployment. The unemployment leads to poverty which affects all classes. The **Great Depression** which began with the Wall Street Crash in 1929 was the most severe depression in the early twentieth century.

In spite of political difficulties and many changes of government, the French economy prospered in the 1920s. Electricity, metal industries and chemicals made rapid progress, while older industries such as textiles, leather and food products also grew, though not as fast. Some industries were modernised. Car production, for example, imitated American-style mass production and the number of cars grew from 135,000 in 1920 to 1·8 million in 1939.

KEY CONCEPT: PROTECTIONISM is the use of tariffs (taxes) to protect home industry and employment from foreign competition. This was the opposite of Free Trade.

The Great Depression in France

Unlike other European countries, the **Wall Street Crash** of 1929 did not affect France immediately. The economy was protected by high tariffs (taxes on imports), the Bank of France had huge reserves of money, French companies had borrowed very little and France did not depend on American loans. But the effect was only delayed until 1931. Once it hit, however, the **Great Depression** lasted longer in France than most other countries.

The Great Depression affected France in two main ways. **French exports** declined and the country had a huge **balance of payments deficit** (more imports than exports). French goods, especially luxury goods, were too expensive so production dropped and profits declined. The French tourist industry also suffered from falling numbers of visitors.

All sections of society were hit by the Depression; the farmers suffered from falling prices; wages fell and unemployment hit the workers, though this mainly affected migrant workers; the middle and upper classes feared for the future.

GOVERNMENT POLICIES

Governments of the Third Republic found it difficult to solve the economic problems. They followed traditional policies of cutting public (government) spending, usually by cutting the salaries of civil servants and the pensions of ex-soldiers. The governments introduced more **protectionism** as well. They also took over ownership or part ownership of some companies such as Air France and the railways. But the dissatisfaction of the social classes (the middle class, workers and peasants) and the pressure they put on the political parties made it difficult for governments to find solutions. This resulted in many changes of government and in criticism of the Third Republic.

CARTEL DES GAUCHES AGAIN IN POWER

Politics in the Third Republic was not immediately affected by the Depression. When Poincaré retired in 1929 due to ill-health, his government of National Union continued. He was succeeded briefly as Prime Minister by **Aristide Briand**, and then by **André Tardieu**. But as the Great Depression affected France by 1931 and 1932, the government failed to agree on economic policies. They lost popularity because they did not provide solutions for the economic problems. Instead, a new left-wing **Cartel des Gauches** won the 1932 general election with 344 seats to the

The Great Depression in France

259 seats of the right-wing parties. Once again the **Radicals**, led by **Herriot**, formed the government. But support from the Socialists collapsed when the government brought in a policy of cutting public spending to solve the economic problems. The very problems which brought them to power were now causing their undoing. But the government was faced not only with an economic and financial crisis: these were compounded by the rise of the right-wing leagues and, in foreign policy, with the threat to French security from the rise of Hitler.

THE RIGHT-WING LEAGUES

A series of right-wing groups or leagues were formed largely in the 1920s and 1930s. These groups were **anti-parliament, anti-Communist, anti-semitic and very nationalistic**. They had many Fascist traits or characteristics but they could hardly be regarded as Fascist. They had similarities to Mussolini's Blackshirts and Hitler's Brownshirts. They wore coloured shirts, jackboots, beat up people and called for the downfall of the Republic. They had the support of business and banking groups and they called for authoritarian government:

- The oldest group dated back to the late nineteenth century. This was the royalist **Action Française**. It drew its support from minor nobles, the professional classes, small businessmen and shopkeepers. Its younger members were mainly university students who joined **Camelots du Roi** for street brawls and protests.
- **Jeunesses Patriotes** (set up in 1924) favoured a stronger Presidency. It had a membership of about 90,000 and most of the support came from university students.
- **Solidarité Française** (1933) had similar beliefs. It was founded and financed by a rich perfume manufacturer and it proclaimed 'France for the French'.
- **Croix de Feu** (1927), formed for war veterans, was the strongest. It had a paramilitary style and it wanted to wipe out Communism and reform the Republic. One-third of its 60,000 members were in Paris.

> **KEY CONCEPT: FASCIST.** Followers of Hitler or Mussolini. See Chapter 2, 'What Was Fascism?'

The Leagues provided all the elements of propaganda, private army and terror which in Italy and Germany produced **Fascist revolutions**. Between 1934 and 1936 conditions appeared favourable in France for such a revolution – economic depression, failure of governments to cope, rapidly changing governments and the example of Hitler. The opportunity to exploit these conditions was provided by the **Stavisky Affair**.

> **KEY CONCEPT: ANTI-SEMITISM** is the hatred for, and persecution of, the Jews. This hatred was based on religious and economic factors. Modern anti-semitism can be traced mainly to Tsarist Russia and Eastern Europe in the nineteenth century, where there were large numbers of Jews. It spread into central and Western Europe, e.g. Austria and France where it became associated with the rise of nationalism. Many nationalists believed that the Jews were not part of their nation. Anti-semitism became an important part of Nazi racial views which saw the Jews as an inferior race. It led to the Nuremberg Laws against the Jews, and later the Holocaust, during the Second World War.

A Croix de Feu meeting: the Croix de Feu was one of the right-wing leagues in France in the 1920s and 1930s.

THE STAVISKY AFFAIR

The Great Depression worsened in France, unemployment rose and a series of short-lived Cartel des Gauches governments – six during 1932–4 – failed to improve the economy. But economic problems were soon overshadowed by the **Stavisky Affair** (or Scandal) which did great damage to members of the Radical Party and also to the Third Republic.

Theft and Fraud

Serge Stavisky, a Russian-born Jew, had been charged in 1927 with the theft of millions of francs. However, his trial was postponed 19 times over the next 6 years. But his involvement in the Bayonne Affair – where he floated a loan of 200 million francs based on the false evaluation of the municipal pawnshop in Bayonne – led to his end. After the scheme collapsed in December 1933, he was wanted by the police. He went missing, but in January 1934 he shot himself.

Corruption

It was soon clear that Stavisky had many friends in high places. The right wing went on the attack. They said that Stavisky had been murdered to hide the names of his friends in the police, politics and business. They produced letters to show the involvement of a government minister. The right-wing groups – particularly those known as the **Leagues** – used the Affair to blame parliamentary democracy. They were supported by the right-wing press who worked to undermine morale and confidence in the Third Republic. During January 1934, there was nightly rioting in Paris against the government, often ringing with the shouts of *'Down with the Robbers'* or *'Hang the Deputies'*.

The Prime Minister, **Chautemps**, attempted a cover-up. He refused to hold an inquiry, but he had to resign when it became known that the public prosecutor was his brother-in-law – the man responsible for the nineteen postponements of Stavisky's earlier trial. It now seemed that the governments of the Third Republic were not just incompetent because they could not solve the economic crisis, but they were also corrupt.

Stavisky (left) at his trial for corruption (top) and anti-Stavisky demonstrators in riots in Paris (below).

RIOTS

When the new Prime Minister, **Edouard Daladier**, sacked the Prefect of Police, Chiappe, who favoured right-wing groups, this resulted in a major street demonstration the day the new government met parliament. On that day, 6 February 1934, a huge rally close to the Chamber of Deputies turned into rioting and a battle with the police. The rally and riots were largely organised and led by the Leagues, in particular

Action Française and **Solidarité Française**. The strongest of the Leagues, **Croix de Feu**, was involved in the protest but did not participate as actively in the rioting. Fourteen rioters were killed and 236 wounded, and one policeman was killed and about 100 injured in 6 hours of rioting. The rioting led to the immediate **resignation of Daladier**. But it also resulted in a counter-strike a few days later organised by the left wing and trade unions to show that workers were prepared to defend the Republic.

ATTEMPTED COUP?

The **riots of 6 February** shocked republican politicians who saw this as an attempt to overthrow the Republic. A later Investigating Committee concluded, *'the Sixth of February was a revolt against Parliament, an attempt against the regime. The intention was, by means of a popular uprising, to disperse the deputies, to take possession of the Chamber and to proclaim an authoritarian government.'* However, the left wing greatly exaggerated the possibility of a Fascist takeover of France, similar to Italy and Germany:

- The groups were **not co-ordinated** and they **lacked a leader** like Hitler or Mussolini.
- Many of the groups had **small membership**.
- Unemployment was not as severe in France.
- Parliamentary democracy had a stronger tradition.

But the riots reflected serious dissatisfaction with the Third Republic and its failure to solve the economic, social and political problems.

The Popular Front Government

One effect of the riots of February 1934 and the rise of the Leagues was the coming together of left-wing parties; **the Socialists**, **Communists** and the **Radical Party**, to form the **Popular Front**. The main motivation came from the Communists who were ordered by Moscow to change policy – the rise of Nazism in Germany, and the failure of socialists and Communists to combine to stop Hitler, forced a change in Communist thinking. Now they wanted to **co-operate with other parties** to resist the rise of Fascism.

On Bastille Day, 14 July 1935, almost 400,000 people marched together in Paris and were addressed by the leaders of the three parties. In early 1936 they published a programme for government:

- They wanted **economic and social reform** and the **abolition** of the Leagues.
- In foreign policy they favoured **collective security** and **the League of Nations**.
- Their **slogan** was *'Bread, Peace and Liberty'* and they attacked *'the two hundred families'* who represented organised wealth in France.

The Popular Front won the 1936 general election with a clear majority of seats over the right-wing parties. The Socialists became the largest party and the Socialist leader, **Léon Blum**, became Prime Minister.

SIT-IN STRIKES AND THE MATIGNON AGREEMENT

The victory of the Popular Front raised the hopes of workers who expected the factories would be handed over to them. A spontaneous wave of **sit-in strikes** swept the country. As industry ground to a standstill, the new government was faced with its first serious problem. Blum called a conference of employer's representatives and the CGT (the trade union federation) in the **Hotel**

Matignon, the official residence of the Prime Minster. Fear of widespread revolution forced the employers to make significant concessions in the **Matignon Agreement**:

- An **increase in wages** of about twelve per cent.
- The establishment of a **forty-hour working week** and **holidays with pay**.
- **Collective bargaining** between trade unions and employers.
- The **nationalisation** (government ownership) of the armaments industry and government control of the Bank of France.

For the moment both the workers and employers were pleased: the workers because they had made great gains – *'the greatest victory which the working class has won in its whole history'*, as one union leader exaggerated – and the employers because they had avoided a revolutionary situation.

PAUSE IN REFORMS

But economic problems continued. The government borrowed to pay for the cost of some of its proposals and the franc lost value in relation to other currencies. This forced the government to **devalue the franc**. Even though this reduced export prices, inflation and unemployment remained high in France and industrial production stayed well below the 1929 level. In March 1937, Blum called a **pause** in the programme of reforms of the Popular Front government.

DIVISIONS IN FRENCH SOCIETY AND POLITICS

The divisions in French society and politics became greater. Right-wing politicians and press criticised the government viciously for bringing in the reforms. The government's attempts to dissolve the Leagues were only partially successful as they formed again under different names; the Croix de Feu, for example, became a political party. French industrialists and financial classes continued sending their money abroad and this worsened the economy. Blum was harassed by right-wing groups who spread the slogan, *'Better Hitler than Blum'*. His Jewishness was also attacked in a wave of **anti-semitism**.

But Communists and some socialists also attacked the government now for the pause in reforms. Workers discontent was expressed through further strikes, and when they crowded the traditional middle-class seaside resorts on paid holidays, this only led to middle-class resentment of their gains.

COLLAPSE OF THE POPULAR FRONT

Blum now proposed to use **decree laws** to bring in economic policies. But his proposals were turned down by the Senate and he resigned in June 1937. *'I have had enough,'* he said. *'Everything I attempted to do has been blocked.'* Further Popular Front governments, including another period with Blum as Prime Minister, failed to resolve France's difficulties. In April 1938, the Popular Front government finally collapsed and a conservative Government of National Defence headed by Edouard Daladier of the Radical Party replaced it.

Government of National Defence

The new government suspended the reforms of the Popular Front and brought in economic policies favoured by the business classes. The government allowed some industries to break the forty-hour week and they cut government spending. This led to conflict with the trade unions.

However, the government had a clear victory over the **CGT** who organised a **one-day strike** for November 1938. The government, encouraged by the right-wing press, organised troops and police, and intimidated public sector workers who were forced not to join the strike. After the strike, workers were fired and disciplined and the CGT lost members once again. The left wing was weakened even more.

PROBLEMS CONTINUE

By 1939, all the main problems that French society had suffered from in the inter-war years still remained.

Population: The loss of 1·3 million men in the First World War and the falling birth rate, meant there was a shortage of labour and, by the end of the 1930s, soldiers. The French population was also older than that of other countries. The total population was much the same as twenty-six years earlier in 1913, and this was only due to migrant labour of three million. However, the use of migrant labour increased **social and political tensions**.

Agriculture: Agriculture stayed inefficient. It was protected by a system of tariffs so that farm prices were higher than elsewhere. Changes in government policy to modernise farming were prevented by the large rural vote.

Industry: Industry also suffered from small-scale production. These small producers kept prices up and their large number prevented the implementation of social and economic reforms by the government. They were supported by richer financiers and industrialists.

Summary: Overall, France was economically backward with a great deal of class conflict. The biggest section of society was comprised of small producers, traders and farmers. The governments of the Third French Republic followed policies which suited their interests. They wanted low taxes and little social reform. This caused political instability which led to the many changes of government between 1920 and 1939. It also prevented the many improvements and reforms in French society which would have better prepared the country for the Second World War.

Foreign Policy in the 1930s

French foreign policy in the 1930s was still haunted by a feeling of insecurity. Their fear of Germany dictated their agreements and alliances. Initially, however, the arrival of Hitler to power in 1933 did not create any greater insecurity in France. Few French people realised how much Hitler hated France or the nature of Hitler's expansionist policies. Instead they believed his assurances of peace and his support for the Locarno Pact. Indeed, in 1934 France entered a **Four Power Pact** along with Britain, Italy and Germany to guarantee peace.

Soon after the Four Power Pact a new foreign minister, **Louis Barthou**, changed the emphasis of French foreign policy. He maintained a firm line towards Germany and he believed that only an efficient **system of alliances** could protect France. He reinforced French ties with Poland and the Little Entente (Czechoslovakia, Hungary and Romania). He also began talks with Italy and the Soviet Union. Even though he was assassinated in 1934, his successor, **Pierre Laval**, concluded an agreement with the Soviet Union. However, this agreement fell short of a military alliance.

FRANCE AND ITALY

Instead, Laval was more interested in an agreement with **Mussolini** in Italy. In 1935 he signed the **Rome Agreements** which ended differences between the two countries. Laval next agreed to the

Stresa Front (1935) which brought Britain, Italy and France together. Their fear of Germany led them to reaffirm the Locarno Pact to contain Germany and guarantee the borders. France had maintained the isolation of Germany – but very soon French foreign policy was in ruins.

TURNING POINTS IN FRENCH FOREIGN POLICY

The Invasion of Ethiopia: Mussolini's invasion of **Ethiopia** (Abyssinia) in late 1935 had a major impact on French foreign policy. At the League of Nations, Laval had to agree with sanctions on Italy but he opposed British plans to include oil in the sanctions. He then privately persuaded the British Foreign Secretary, **Sir Samuel Hoare**, to agree that Ethiopia should be given to Italy. When news of the **Hoare-Laval Plan** leaked out it led to Hoare's resignation and, soon after, to Laval's also. Laval also upset Mussolini by not supporting Italy's attack on Ethiopia. The Stresa Front collapsed and the League of Nations was defeated. As one historian concluded, *'France was left alone to defend herself as best she could against a restless, aggressive Germany which very soon ... would be stronger on land and in the air than she.'*

Hitler breaks Versailles: Hitler's breaches of the Treaty of Versailles clearly showed the **weakness** of French foreign policy. The French failed to act as Hitler introduced conscription, created the Luftwaffe and expanded the navy in agreement with the British. But the **greatest defeat** for French foreign policy occurred when Hitler took advantage of another rift between France and Britain, and a weak government in France, to **remilitarise the Rhineland** in 1936.

The French refused to act against Hitler on their own, partly because of a **defeatist attitude** in the army and in the right-wing press. The Minister of War expressed this view at a cabinet meeting, *'The Foreign Minister talks of entering the Rhineland.... There are risks in this. The present state of the French army does not allow us to run risks.'* Instead they looked to Britain for support. But the British were following a **policy of appeasement** and allowed Hitler break the Treaty of Versailles in order to avoid a major war. Hitler scored a major victory in the Rhineland, and France was badly weakened. She was now dependent on weak Eastern European countries and on ties with Britain.

France and Britain: France had to follow Britain's policy of appeasement even though it allowed Germany to get stronger:

- France needed Britain's resources for rearmament.
- France also needed the British army to fit into their war plan against Germany. The French army with the help of the British intended to block the Germans west of the Maginot Line.

Therefore, for the remainder of the 1930s, the French government made efforts to maintain good relations with Britain.

The Spanish Civil War: French foreign policy was next tested by the **Spanish Civil War** where a Popular Front republican government was attacked by a nationalist army backed by Germany and Italy. Blum, the leader of the French Popular Front government, opted for **non-intervention** in the war because of social and political divisions in France – the Right and Left were bitterly divided – and the need to maintain relations with Britain who also favoured non-intervention. Once again French foreign policy had failed.

MORE FAILURES

By now French foreign policy was effectively tied to the British. Neither country made any serious protest when Hitler took over Austria in **Anschluss** (March 1938). But the biggest French sell-out came when Hitler demanded the **Sudetenland** from Czechoslovakia. The French Prime Minister, **Daladier**, attended the **Munich Conference** (September 1938) along with Hitler,

Mussolini and Neville Chamberlain, the British Prime Minister. Daladier signed the **Munich Agreement** which forced Czechoslovakia to hand over the Sudetenland to Germany in spite of French agreements with Czechoslovakia. **Daladier** was supported in this policy of appeasement by a majority of French people so as to avoid a European war. The right wing in particular looked on Hitler as less of a danger than Russian Communism.

THE APPROACH OF WAR – PEACE AT ALL COSTS

During 1939 the French government tried to avoid war at all costs. They first tried to break the **Franco-Polish Alliance** (1921) to avoid going to war on behalf of Poland. They were prepared to give Hitler a free hand in Eastern Europe. But France was now tied to Britain and British opinion was changing. After Hitler took over the **rest of Czechoslovakia** (March 1939), Britain gave a formal guarantee of help to Poland. France also agreed to follow Britain. The French and British tried to form a pact with Soviet Russia against Germany. But this was destroyed by the **Nazi-Soviet Pact** (August 1939). Even when Germany invaded Poland on 1 September 1939, the French still tried to break their commitments. However, they had no choice but to go along with Britain and both declared war on Germany on 3 September 1939.

The Defeat of the Third French Republic, May–June 1940

Instead of uniting France against the German danger, the beginning of the Second World War divided the country further. Because of the Nazi-Soviet Pact, **French Communists** opposed the French war against Germany. They were directed by Moscow to denounce the war as an imperialist war. They also attempted to undermine French morale. On the other hand, the right wing developed a **peace party** one of whose members was **Pierre Laval** who favoured a separate peace with Germany.

GERMAN INVASION

It was a divided France which faced the German blitzkrieg of May 1940. The Daladier government fell in March 1940 so a new government led by **Paul Reynaud** faced the German invasion. But the defeat of France was mainly due to **faulty military strategy** which could not cope with the German blitzkrieg tactics of speed and mobility. The French High Command still thought in terms of the First World War. On hearing of the German attack, they sent their best troops, along with the **British Expeditionary Force** (BEF), into Belgium. They were easily cut off by the German tanks who raced across from the Ardennes and reached the English Channel in ten days. (See Chapter 7, The Second World War.)

German troops occupying Paris in May 1940 (top) and Hitler posing with the Eiffel Tower in the background.

FRENCH SURRENDER

The government left Paris and eventually went to Bordeaux. The French army was ordered to retreat and millions of Parisians left the city by every means possible. Reynaud wanted to continue the fight in North Africa but the Army Commander and the cabinet were opposed to this so he was forced to resign. He was replaced by **Marshal Pétain**, hero of the First World War, who sued for peace. On 22 June, France signed an **armistice** with Germany in the same railway carriage in Compiègne in which Germany had surrendered in 1918:

- France was now divided into an **Occupied Zone** (northern and western France) and an **Unoccupied Zone** (southern or Vichy France).
- The French army was reduced to 100,000 men.
- France had to pay the cost of German occupation.

This was a humiliating end for the Third French Republic.

Vichy France, 1940-44

The new French government was based in the town of **Vichy**. **Pétain** was head of government but Laval played a dominant role in the government. He got the Parliament to agree to abolish itself and the Third Republic. The Vichy government replaced the Third Republic with a **corporate state** similar to Mussolini's where the interests of the employers, workers and the State were represented. Pétain replaced Parliament with a **Veterans' League** of ex-soldiers. He also restored the influence of the Catholic Church to education and he protected the better-off classes. The Vichy government introduced **anti-semitic laws** and rounded up Jews for deportation to Germany. Over 75,000 of these died in the Holocaust.

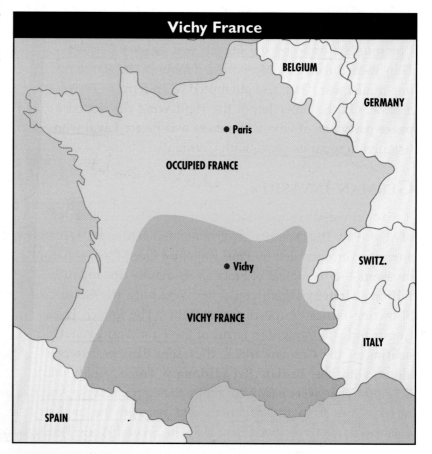

Vichy France

BELGIUM

GERMANY

• Paris

OCCUPIED FRANCE

• Vichy

SWITZ.

VICHY FRANCE

ITALY

SPAIN

> **KEY CONCEPT: COLLABORATION** is co-operating with the enemy especially when they have taken over your own country. During the Second World War, this happened in Norway with Quisling, and in France under the Vichy government. But collaboration was not confined to **puppet** governments (governments under the control of the Nazis). Individuals and groups also collaborated with the Germans.

> **KEY CONCEPT: RESISTANCE.** This was the act of resisting when enemy troops have taken over the country. The Resistance was usually a secret, or underground, organisation involved in sabotage against the occupying forces and collaborators. The Resistance members were also called **partisans** in some countries, or **Maquis** in France.

COLLABORATION

Laval believed that Germany was going to win the war and he wanted France to adjust to the new order in Europe. In October 1940, Pétain and Laval met Hitler. Afterwards, Laval said, '*I enter into the way of collaboration*.' But Laval's arrogance and desire for power led to his replacement for a short time. However, by April 1942 he was restored by Pétain, this time as Prime Minister, partly under pressure from the Germans. Laval continued to look for a role for France in the new Europe which he believed the Germans were creating. He wanted France to be the **favourite province of Germany**. Both he and Pétain thought that the only alternative to collaboration was direct Nazi rule.

French troops released by the Germans praised Pétain and Laval: Vichy France exchanged three French workers for each freed French soldier.

GERMAN POLICY TOWARDS VICHY

But Vichy collaboration did not win greater respect from the Germans. Instead, Hitler looked on Vichy France as a cheap way of policing the area and as a source of raw materials and foodstuffs for the war. The Vichy government paid very large occupation costs. They also agreed to the conscription of French workers for the German war industry in return for the release of some French prisoners of war. Further, they put down the French Resistance which attacked supply routes to Germany.

In November 1942, Vichy France lost most of the little power it had. On 11 November, Hitler ordered his army to take over Vichy France when Americans and British troops invaded North Africa and took over Vichy-controlled Morocco and Algeria. A Vichy government continued to exist in France until 1944, but only in name.

FRENCH RESISTANCE

While those in charge of Vichy collaborated with Germany, a French Resistance movement opposed German occupation in many different ways: collection of military intelligence; helping British airmen to escape; distribution of anti-German leaflets; boycotting Germans in public or in bars; sabotage of railways or guerrilla attacks on German soldiers. German treatment of those who were caught was ruthless; they were arrested, tortured and often executed. Sometimes there were even mass executions as in the town of **Oradour-sur-Glane** where 642 men, women and children were massacred.

The French Resistance planning another ambush.

Resistance Grows

In the early months of the German occupation, Resistance was sporadic, usually carried out by small groups. But gradually groups such as **Combat, Franc-Tireur, Liberation Nord** and **Front National** developed. The Resistance got a huge boost in June 1941 when Hitler invaded Soviet Russia. Then the **French Communists**, who up to this had been neutral towards Germany, became the most active leaders of the Resistance. A further boost to the Resistance came when French workers were being conscripted to work in German war industries. This enlarged the Resistance as many of the young men took to the hills and forests.

General de Gaulle, leader of the Free French, led a triumphant march down the Champs Elysees after Paris was recaptured by the Allied forces.

Co-ordination of Resistance

As the war progressed there was greater co-ordination between the Resistance groups. Eventually, the leadership of the French Resistance was taken over by **General Charles de Gaulle**. In 1940, on the fall of France, de Gaulle escaped to London where he set up the **Free French**. He wanted all patriotic Frenchmen to join him. However, he struggled to receive recognition from **Churchill** and the British who found him difficult to deal with. The **Americans** were even more hostile and accepted Vichy France as the legitimate French government. They installed **General Giraud** in North Africa but he maintained a Vichy-style regime with repressive laws, including laws against the Jews. Instead, de Gaulle was able to create unity among the many resistance groups through his representative, **Jean Moulin**, who was parachuted into France. He first created links between the northern and southern resistance groups. Then he persuaded the Communists to accept de Gaulle as a replacement for Pétain when liberation came. Moulin organised the CNR, the **National Resistance Council**, which represented all resistance groups. Moulin, however, was soon betrayed and executed by the Nazis.

De Gaulle Takes Over

The Americans saw little role for the Resistance as they planned the Normandy landings (1944). However, the Resistance increased their attacks but very often at the expense of huge reprisals by the Germans. When Paris was liberated in August 1944, American troops were accompanied by French troops as they took over the city. De Gaulle ensured that he was recognised by all as leader of France when he led a triumphal march from the Arc de Triomphe to Notre Dame.

Revenge on Collaborators

After the Liberation, the Resistance took revenge on the collaborators. About 9,000 were executed without trial and there was a danger these executions would get out of control. But de Gaulle's government began the **systematic punishment** of the collaborators. They arrested and tried 125,000 people over the next two years; about 90,000 were punished, about half of these were imprisoned, and 767 were executed after trial. Some of these included the leaders of Vichy France including **Laval**, but **Pétain's** death sentence was commuted to life imprisonment. By taking control of the punishment of the collaborators, de Gaulle's government contained the violence and established the authority of the State.

Assessment of Resistance

Overall, the numbers involved in the Resistance were relatively small – about two per cent of the adult French population. However, the Resistance played a major role in boosting French morale. It helped wipe out the memory of Vichy collaboration. Even though the military impact of Resistance was small, it kept alive the hope that Germany would be defeated. It also gave French people a role in their own liberation, even if it was small compared to the armies of America and Britain.

Women collaborators' heads were shaved.

ORDINARY LEVEL AND HIGHER LEVEL HOMEWORK EXERCISES

ORDINARY LEVEL

1. Study the extracts on French security and answer the following questions:

   'What France wanted from Germany, after two damaging invasions in fifty years was above all, security. As M. Clemenceau [the French Prime Minister] told the [Paris] Peace Conference in January 1919: "If a new war should take place, Germany would not throw her forces upon Cuba or upon Honduras, but upon France; it would always be upon France."'

   J Terraine, *The Mighty Continent: View of Europe in the Twentieth Century*

   'France is, and will remain, the ... enemy of Germany.'

   A Hitler, *Mein Kampf*

(i) How many times did Germany invade France in fifty years?

(ii) What did France want from Germany?

(iii) According to M. Clemenceau, who would Germany attack in a new war?

(iv) Does Hitler's attitude support Clemenceau's view?

2. Study the extract on Vichy France and answer the following questions:

   'The German pressure upon unoccupied France is growing stronger as indicated by messages from France and by the tone of German propaganda towards the Vichy Government. The Germans, it seems, are now bluntly demanding that Vichy should clear up her attitude and are making it quite clear that they expect her to comply completely with their requests.

The official Vichy protest against the German terror does not necessarily imply any genuine resistance. It is pointed out in Free French quarters that the protest may well have been made with ulterior [hidden, underhand] motives:

To allay the widespread unrest and uneasiness in the country and to conceal, if possible, the extent of Vichy's subservience to Germany.

There are grounds for the belief – though this belief can be proved true only by events – that the worst fears may be confirmed and the Vichy Government has already entered into far-reaching commitments to the Axis.'

The *Manchester Guardian*, 16 December 1941

(i) What was Vichy France?

(ii) What was another name for 'unoccupied France'?

(iii) How did the Vichy Government react to the German demands?

(iv) Who were the Free French? What reasons do the Free French give for the Vichy reaction?

(v) What 'belief can be proved true only by events'?

(vi) The *Manchester Guardian* is an English newspaper. How would this affect the reliability of the report?

3. Write **paragraph answers** on each of the following questions:

(i) Reconstruction in France in the 1920s.

(ii) French foreign policy in the 1920s.

(iii) The French occupation of the Ruhr.

(iv) French foreign policy in the 1930s.

(v) Aristide Briand and French foreign policy.

(vi) The Right-wing Leagues.

(vii) The Stavisky Affair.

(viii) The Popular Front Government.

(ix) The German invasion and the downfall of the French Third Republic, May 1940.

4. Write **long answers** on each of the following questions:

(i) French policy towards Germany, 1920–39.

(ii) Pierre Laval and Vichy France.

(iii) Collaboration and Resistance in France during the Second World War.

HIGHER LEVEL

1. How successful were French governments in solving the internal and external problems which the country faced in the 1920s?

2. Discuss Franco-German relations in the inter-war years, 1920–39.

3. How and why was France affected by political instability in the 1930s?

4. Account for the fall of France in 1940 and describe the consequences of the fall for France.

5. Assess the part played by Pierre Laval in French politics during the 1930s and the Second World War.

TEST YOURSELF AT
my-etest.com

6. Hitler's Foreign Policy, 1933-9 and the Causes of the Second World War

Hitler's Aims

'the generation to which I belong fail in its task' - Leon Blum (P.M. - 1936. Popular Front)

In 1939, the Second World War began when Germany invaded Poland. Hitler's aims in foreign policy and the aggressive way in which he carried them out were the main causes of the war.

Hitler stated his aims in foreign policy in *Mein Kampf* (1924) and in a series of speeches by himself and his fellow Nazi leaders. He had **three main aims** in foreign policy:

1. He wanted to **destroy the Treaty of Versailles** – to rearm the German army, navy and air force; to remilitarise the Rhineland; to form Anschluss (union) with Austria; to change the borders on the east with Poland.
2. He wanted to create a **Greater Germany** (Grossdeutschland) by uniting all German-speaking people.
3. He wanted to create **Lebensraum** – living space in Eastern Europe to make Germany self-sufficient in food and raw materials for his master race. *'The new Reich must ... obtain by the German sword, sod for the German plough and daily bread for the nation.'* (*Mein Kampf*)

> **KEY CONCEPT: LEBENSRAUM.** Hitler borrowed the idea of lebensraum from previous German thinkers. He believed that having additional living space would strengthen Germany by making it **self-sufficient** in food and raw materials. He wanted the living space in Eastern Europe, particularly Russia. This idea of lebensraum became the basis of German foreign policy during Hitler's Third Reich.

A German postcard produced in 1935 highlighted German disarmament compared to that of her neighbours. The aim of the postcard was to show British people that Germany had been treated unfairly by the Treaty of Versailles. How does it get this message across?

Hitler's Successes

After coming to power in 1933, Hitler proceeded cautiously in foreign policy for the first year. He wanted to be seen as a man of peace while he consolidated his power at home. He withdrew from the **Disarmament Conference** and the **League of Nations** but he was able to blame it on France's refusal to disarm like Germany. He was part of the **Four Power Pact** of Britain, France, Italy and Germany itself to preserve the peace of Europe. He formed a ten-year **Non-Aggression Pact** with Poland. This broke the isolation of Germany which France had achieved. A further success was the **Saar Plebiscite** (vote of the people). In the Treaty of Versailles (1919), the Saar had been given to France for fifteen years to extract coal. Now the people of the Saar voted to become part of Germany.

Setback

But Hitler also suffered a setback. The **union** of Austria with Germany (Anschluss) was one of his main aims. Austrian Nazis were encouraged and helped by Hitler. In 1934, they murdered the Austrian Chancellor, **Dollfuss**, in an attempted Nazi coup (or takeover). Hitler was ready to invade the country, but Italy feared a German takeover. The Italian leader, **Mussolini**, rushed troops to the Austrian border and Hitler backed down.

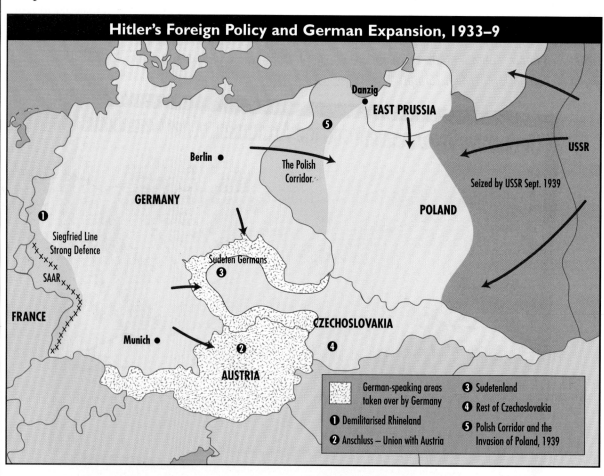

Destroying Versailles

By 1935, Hitler had consolidated his power at home. He began a more aggressive foreign policy by breaking the terms of the Treaty of Versailles. Initially, the terms he broke applied directly to Germany. In early 1935, Hitler began German **rearmament**. He introduced conscription (compulsory military service) and announced the existence of the **Luftwaffe** (air force), which had been set up secretly. Hitler's actions led to the formation of the **Stresa Front** (1935) by **Britain, France and Italy** because of fear of German expansion.

Luftwaffe pilots receiving orders: in the background is a Stuka dive bomber which became an important part of German military success in the early years of the Second World War.

However, within a few months, Britain undermined the Stresa Front and helped Hitler dismantle the Treaty of Versailles further by agreeing to the **Anglo-German Naval Agreement** (1935). This allowed Hitler to increase his navy up to thirty-five per cent of the British navy, but have the same amount of submarines (U-boats) as the British. France was very upset by the agreement because they had not been consulted. But Hitler was delighted. He felt that Britain was prepared to allow German breaches of the Treaty of Versailles and this encouraged him to try again.

Some British politicians were fooled by Hitler. One said, *'I am convinced that Hitler does not want war ... what the Germans are after is a strong army which will enable them to deal with Russia.'* But one observer noted the danger for Britain; *'Germany gets a U-boat tonnage equal to Britain's. Why the British have agreed to this is beyond me. German submarines almost beat them in the last war, and may in the next.'*

Signing the Pact of Steel between Italy and Germany: they were committed to help each other in war.

Timeline: The Build-up to the Second World War

1933	1934	1935	1936	1938	1939
	Hitler withdrew from the League of Nations and the Disarmament Conference		Hitler remilitarised the Rhineland / The Spanish Civil War began		Hitler took over the rest of Czechoslovakia / The Nazi-Soviet Pact / Hitler invaded Poland
Hitler came to power in Germany		Hitler began rearmament / The Anglo-German Naval Agreement / Mussolini invaded Abyssinia		Anschluss with Austria / The Munich Conference / Hitler took over the Sudetenland	

Italian Invasion of Abyssinia

In October 1935 Mussolini invaded Abyssinia. Abyssinia turned to the League of Nations for help. The League imposed economic sanctions on Italy but these sanctions excluded oil. However, the League failed to take any other effective action. At the same time, Britain and France secretly agreed the **Hoare-Laval Plan** (called after the British and French foreign ministers) to give most of Abyssinia to Italy. When news of this plan leaked out, it was dropped and it led to the resignation of both foreign secretaries. Abyssinia was quickly and easily defeated by the modern technology of Italy.

The invasion of Abyssinia had a number of important **results**:

- Britain and France fell out over the **Hoare-Laval Plan**.
- British and French support for sanctions upset Mussolini and the **Stresa Front** broke up.
- On the other hand, Hitler supported Mussolini and this brought them closer together.
- The **weaknesses of the League of Nations** were shown up. It appeared to be very ineffective because it could not prevent one of its own members attacking and conquering another member. This showed that **collective security** – countries working together to protect other countries – did not seem to work:
  - Economic sanctions did not work because they did not apply to non-members such as the US and Germany.
  - The League had no army to enforce its decisions.
  - The absence of the US was a major weakness since it was the most powerful country in the world.

THE GOOSE-STEP
"GOOSEY GOOSEY GANDER,
WHITHER DOST THOU WANDER?"
"ONLY THROUGH THE RHINELAND—
PRAY EXCUSE MY BLUNDER!"

Hitler had an important success when he remilitarised the Rhineland in 1936. A British cartoon commented on the remilitarisation (top) – what is the message of the cartoon? German troops crossing the Rhine (below).

Remilitarisation of the Rhineland, 1936

Hitler took his next gamble. He was encouraged by his early success to remilitarise the Rhineland. The remilitarisation of the Rhineland was banned by the Treaty of Versailles and agreed to by Germany in the **Locarno Pact** (1925).

Hitler **timed** his action well. He took advantage of the crisis in 1936 over Abyssinia between Italy, Britain and France. He also said that Germany was under threat because of a recent agreement between France and Russia. In March 1936 he moved about 10,000 troops, backed up by police, into the Rhineland.

The **League of Nations** condemned his action but did nothing else because of the Abyssinian crisis. France was the country most threatened by the remilitarisation but it failed to act. *'Oh, the stupidity (or is it the paralysis?) of the French,'* wrote one journalist. The country was about to hold a general election; the Left and Right were bitterly divided; the French army overestimated the

The Siegfried Line: the German defensive line which ran along the Franco-German border.

numbers of German soldiers and France did not get British support. Instead, Britain looked on the remilitarisation as the Germans going into their **own back garden**.

Hitler had gambled and won. He later said that *'...at that time we had no army worth mentioning... If the French had taken any action we would have been easily defeated.'* The remilitarisation of the Rhineland allowed him to build the **Siegfried Line** – a line of fortifications along the Franco-German border – and this prevented France invading Germany. It also protected his back as he turned his attention to Eastern Europe. But the result for France was disastrous. A demilitarised Rhineland was vital for French security so that it could attack the industrial heart of Germany. Now that was gone.

The Influence of the Spanish Civil War

The **Spanish Civil War** (1936–9) broke out between the Republican government and the Nationalist army led by Franco. Hitler and Mussolini gave help to Franco by providing ships, planes, equipment and soldiers. This help ensured victory for Franco.
The Republican government was helped by the Soviet Union but Britain and France did not help either side. Instead they formed a **Non–Intervention Committee** which did more harm to the Republican side. The war showed the weakness of Britain and France, and it also brought Hitler and Mussolini closer together.

Mussolini's dispute with Britain and France over Abyssinia and the events of the Spanish Civil War led Hitler and Mussolini to form the **Rome-Berlin Axis** (November 1936). They made an agreement over Austria (Hitler gave up his claim to the German-speaking people of the South Tyrol); in return Mussolini agreed to Hitler's takeover of Austria. One month later, Germany and Italy joined with Japan in the **Anti-Comintern Pact** to stop the spread of Communism.

The Hossbach Memorandum and Plans for War

In November 1937 Hitler met his senior military commanders. The **Hossbach Memorandum**, notes taken at the meeting by Colonel Hossbach, recorded Hitler's plans for the future. That future depended on getting **lebensraum** (living space) for food and raw materials. *'Germany's problem could only be solved by means of force,'* he said. He believed that his first objective must be to overthrow Austria and Czechoslovakia. He used the same tactics in both cases of **outside pressure** combined with **internal disruption**.

German military parade showing the strength of rearmament.

Hitler could feel confident of success because, by this time, Germany was rearming quickly. The army was expanded from 100,000 in 1933 to 750,000 by 1939, with one million reserves; large numbers of tanks were produced; the navy was equipped with new battleships and submarines; and the Luftwaffe had about 4,500 aircraft. The other European powers had been overtaken because their rearmament began later. Hitler believed that the latest Germany could go to war was 1943–5 because after that other countries would have caught up with it.

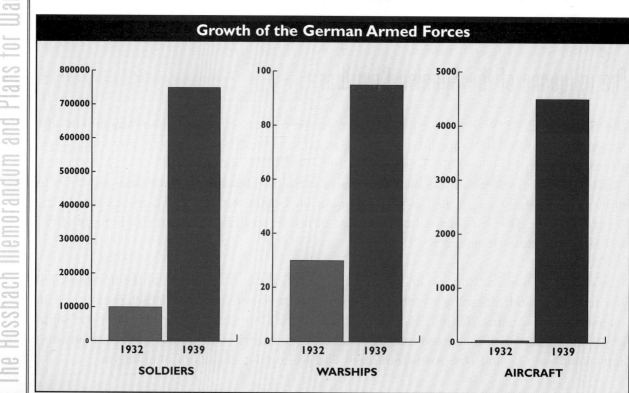

Growth of the German Armed Forces

SOLDIERS — WARSHIPS — AIRCRAFT (1932 and 1939)

Anschluss with Austria, 1938

Hitler took a special interest in Austria where he was born. He encouraged the Austrian Nazi Party to demand union with Germany (Anschluss). He used bullying tactics with Austria to get his demands. He demanded of the Austrian Chancellor, **Dr Schuschnigg**, that the Nazi Party be legalised and that the Nazi, **Dr Seyss-Inquart**, be appointed Minister of the Interior. Schuschnigg had to agree. However, Schuschnigg decided to hold a **plebiscite** (referendum or vote of the people) on union with Germany, knowing that the Austrian people would reject it. But Hitler acted before the plebiscite. He forced the resignation of Schuschnigg. Seyss-Inquart then invited the German army into Austria to *'help preserve the peace'*. Austria was taken over and Hitler returned triumphantly to Vienna on 15 March 1938. One month later a Nazi-supervised referendum produced a 99·75% vote in favour of Anschluss.

Hitler had gambled and won again. Once more the Treaty of Versailles was broken. Anschluss consolidated Germany's relations with Italy. Hitler was grateful to Mussolini for allowing the German takeover; *'Tell Mussolini I will never forget him for this,'* he said. The British did not try to stop the union because they felt that the Austrians and Germans had a right to be united. Now the Austrian army was added to the German army and Czechoslovakia was surrounded on three sides by German territory.

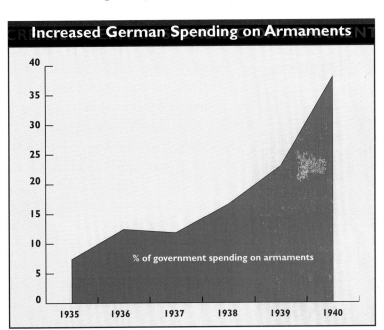

Increased German Spending on Armaments

% of government spending on armaments

1935 1936 1937 1938 1939 1940

The Sudetenland, 1938

Across the border from Germany was the **Sudetenland**, a German-speaking part of Czechoslovakia which included three million Germans. The Sudeten Germans complained they were discriminated against. Their leader, **Konrad Henlein**, demanded to be united with Germany. He was encouraged and supported by Hitler who sent troops to the border.

But the Czechs had a modern army and strong defences. They also had a military alliance with France, while Britain and Russia promised support. They were prepared to resist the German threats, so Europe seemed on the verge of war during the summer of 1938.

Hitler received a great reception after he entered the Sudetenland, the German-speaking part of Czechoslovakia, which he took over in 1938.

France favoured action but Britain was cautious. **Neville Chamberlain**, the British Prime Minister, expressed his views; *'How horrible, fantastic, incredible it is that we should be digging trenches and trying on gas masks here because of a quarrel in a faraway country between people of whom we know nothing. I am myself a man of peace to the depths of my soul.'* When he visited Hitler in Germany he was delighted that Hitler only demanded parts of Sudetenland. However, when Hitler changed his demands a few days later, war seemed likely again and the British navy was mobilised.

The Munich Agreement

The **Munich Conference** was organised to prevent war. **Chamberlain, Daladier (France), Mussolini and Hitler** met in Munich (September 1938) to decide the future of the Sudetenland. The Soviet Union was not invited, and neither was Czechoslovakia. The four leaders agreed that the Sudetenland should be given to Germany and Czechoslovakia had to give in. In a joint declaration, Chamberlain and Hitler said, *'We regard the [Munich] Agreement signed last night … as symbolic of the desire of our two peoples never to go to war with one another again.'* Chamberlain returned home with **peace for our time** and a hero's welcome. In France the view was, *'We can go back to work and sleep soundly again.'*

Once again Hitler had gambled and won. His tactics of taking Europe to the brink of war had succeeded. This crisis encouraged Hitler to believe that neither Britain nor France would back up their words with action. Now Germany was in a much stronger position – in taking over the Sudetenland, Germany had taken most of Czechoslovakia's heavy industries and defences.

Chamberlain, the British Prime Minister, believed that the policy of appeasement was working. What do the photos tell us about the response of the British people?

European leaders – Chamberlain (Britain), Mussolini (Italy), Daladier (France) and Hitler (Germany) – agreed at the Munich Conference to hand over the Sudetenland to Germany.

Britain, France and the Policy of Appeasement

Britain's policy towards Hitler was characterised by **appeasement**. Britain believed that if they gave in to Hitler's demands, this would prevent a European war. Instead they believed in the League of Nations and disarmament as the best way of achieving peace. This policy was mainly associated with Neville Chamberlain, but it was supported by all sections of the British people:

- Many British leaders had fought in the First World War and they did not want to see the horrors of war repeated. This anti-war attitude was reinforced by books and poems published in the 1920s and 1930s.
- Many British people felt that Germany had been too harshly treated by the Treaty of Versailles; they believed that Hitler's demands were reasonable.
- Hitler and Nazi Germany was seen as a barrier to the spread of Communism from the Soviet Union.
- Britain was not ready for war – the politicians did not want to cut spending on social welfare programmes to pay for rearmament.

The **French government and people** also longed for peace and supported appeasement for many of the same reasons. But France was also affected by the **Maginot mind** – the belief that France could defend itself behind the **Maginot Line**, the huge system of fortifications built along the eastern border with Germany. France was also a very **divided society** between the **Left** (Communist/Socialist) and the **Right** (Conservative/Fascist). The fear of these divisions often resulted in France doing nothing. (See Chapter 5, Politics and Administration in France: the Third Republic, 1920–40 and the Vichy State, 1940–44.)

The Destruction of Czechoslovakia, March 1939

In March 1939 Hitler took over the rest of Czechoslovakia. Britain and France only protested. This clearly showed **the weaknesses** of the policy of appeasement. However, this was also the first non-German area taken over by Hitler. British policy began to change. Prior to this, the British believed that Hitler's aims were limited; now they knew he sought European domination. It was clear that Poland would be Hitler's next target.

Poland and the Polish Corridor

The Treaty of Versailles had separated East Prussia from the rest of Germany by the **Polish Corridor** – a narrow strip of land which gave Poland access to the sea through the port of **Danzig**. (See map of Hitler's Foreign Policy and German Expansion, 1933–9, p. 120) In 1939, Hitler demanded the return of Danzig and a road and rail link to East Prussia through the Polish Corridor. Poland rejected Hitler's demands.

In March 1939, Britain and France agreed to support Poland against *'any action which clearly threatened Polish independence'*. But after years of appeasement, Hitler did not believe that Britain and France would act. Hitler also made his own agreement – the **Pact of Steel** with Italy. This was a military alliance in which each country would help the other in war. Europe was divided into two armed camps and once again it faced the prospect of war.

The Nazi-Soviet Pact, 1939

However, the key to the safety of Poland was the Soviet Union. Britain and France made a half-hearted effort to negotiate an alliance with **Stalin**, the Soviet leader, during 1939. But the British and French mistrusted Stalin and the Poles hated the Russians as much as they hated the Germans.

Stalin was worried about the safety of Russia since Hitler came to power. He joined the League of Nations but saw it was too weak. He wanted an alliance with Britain and France during the Sudetenland crisis, but now he did not trust them after the Soviet Union was not included in the Munich Conference. Instead, **Ribbentrop, the German Foreign Minister**, and **Molotov, the Soviet Foreign Minister**,

WONDER HOW LONG THE HONEYMOON WILL LAST?

A British cartoon on the Nazi-Soviet Pact. What is its message?

stunned the world when they agreed a **ten-year non-aggression pact**. The arch-enemies of Fascism and Communism also secretly agreed to divide Poland between themselves.

The **Nazi-Soviet Pact** was very important to Hitler. He feared that if he invaded Poland, he would be involved in a two-front war against Russia in the east and France and Britain in the west. Now the Pact allowed him to attack Poland without Russia intervening. It also gave Stalin time to prepare his army. Later Stalin said, *'It will be asked why the Soviet government signed a non-aggression pact with a deceitful nation led by criminals like Hitler and Ribbentrop ... We secured peace for our country for eighteen months which allowed us to make military preparations.'*

The War Begins

Hitler believed everything was now in his favour. He had the non-aggression pact with Russia; the Siegfried Line protected him from attack in the west; he believed Britain and France would not fight, and if they did they were too far away to help Poland; and he had Poland surrounded on three sides. He also had the strongest army in Europe.

But Poland still refused to give in to his demands, so on 1 September 1939 Hitler invaded the country. To his surprise, Britain and France backed Poland and declared war on Germany on 3 September.

British and French opinion had changed quickly after the Munich Conference. They felt Hitler could not be trusted and they backed rearmament. There was a determination to face war if it was necessary.

The Causes of the Second World War

Hitler's Aims and Methods

- Hitler wanted to create a Greater Germany with living space (lebensraum) in the east.
- He broke the terms of the Treaty of Versailles.
- He used outside pressure and internal disruption to take over Austria and Sudetenland.
- When he took over the rest of Czechoslovakia, Britain and France supported his next target, Poland.

Weakness of the League of Nations

The League could not stop Mussolini and Hitler (and Japan in Asia) from taking over other countries:

- Economic sanctions were not effective.
- There had to be unanimous agreement among the members for action.
- The US was not a member and other powers were members for short periods.
- The League did not have an army to enforce decisions.

Isolation of the US

America was the strongest country but it followed a policy of isolation:

- It was only interested in affairs on its own continent.
- It did not want to send troops to fight in faraway wars.
- America rejected the Treaty of Versailles and did not become a member of the League of Nations.
- In the 1930s America passed the Neutrality Acts which stopped aid or trade with warring countries.

Policy of Appeasement

Britain and France followed this policy:

- They believed that if they gave in to Hitler's small demands they would stop a European war.
- The policy was influenced by:
  - Their experiences of the First World War.
  - In Britain they believed that Germany had been harshly treated by the Treaty of Versailles.
  - They wanted a strong Germany to stop the spread of Communisim.

In a radio broadcast, Chamberlain expressed his own views and those of many other people.

'[Hitler] gave his word that he would respect the Locarno Treaty; he broke it. He gave his word that he neither wished nor intended to annex Austria; he broke it. He declared that he would not incorporate the Czechs in the Reich; he did so. He gave his word after Munich that he had no further territorial demands in Europe; he broke it. He gave his word that he wanted no Polish provinces; he broke it. He has sworn to you for years that he was the mortal enemy of bolshevism [Communism]; he is now its ally. Can you wonder his word is, for us, not worth the paper it is written on!'

ORDINARY LEVEL AND HIGHER LEVEL HOMEWORK EXERCISES

ORDINARY LEVEL

1. Study Hitler's speech on disarmament which he made to the Reichstag soon after he became Chancellor, and answer the following questions:

   'Germany is at any time willing to undertake further [disarmament] ... if all other nations are ready ... to do the same.... Germany would also be perfectly ready to disband her entire military [force] and destroy the small amount of arms remaining to her if the remaining countries will do the same thing with equal thoroughness.'

   A Hitler speaking to the Reichstag, 17 May 1933

(i) What is disarmament?

(ii) Under what condition would Germany disarm, according to Hitler?

(iii) Do you think this condition would be fulfilled? Explain your answer.

(iv) How do you think political leaders in France and Britain would react to Hitler's speech?

(v) Why do you think Hitler made this speech?

2. Study the map of Hitler's Foreign Policy and German Expansion, 1933–9 (p. 120) and answer the following questions:

(i) What was the name of the German defence line in the west along the border with France?

(ii) Explain the term **Demilitarised Rhineland**.

(iii) Name two German-speaking areas taken over by Hitler.

(iv) Why did Hitler lay claim to the Polish Corridor?

(v) Under what agreement did the USSR invade and take over Eastern Poland in September 1939?

3. Study the cartoon and photograph on the remilitarisation of the Rhineland (p.122) and answer the following questions:

(i) What do each of the following mean in the cartoon (a) the weapons, (b) the flags, and (c) the olive branch with the Pax Germanica label on it?

(ii) Who was the goose-step associated with? How does this help us understand the cartoon?

(iii) The goose tears up Locarno. What was Locarno?

(iv) What is the message of the cartoon?

(v) Is the cartoon propaganda? Explain your answer.

(vi) From the photograph of the crossing of the Rhine bridge, would you say that the people were surprised to see the German army coming?

4. Study the radio broadcast by Neville Chamberlain (pp. 128–9) and answer the following questions:

(i) What did the Locarno Treaty say?

(ii) What was the German annexation of Austria called?

(iii) What was the German-speaking part of Czechoslovakia called?

(iv) Explain the meaning of **Reich**.

(v) What happened at Munich?

(vi) How did Hitler become the ally of Bolshevism (Communism)?

(vii) What is the main point that Chamberlain is making?

5. Write **paragraph answers** on each of the following questions:

(i) The aims of Hitler's foreign policy.

(ii) German Remilitarisation and Hitler's Plans for war.

(iii) Hitler, Mussolini and the Spanish Civil War.

OR

The Influence of the Spanish Civil War.

(iv) The Nazi takeover of the Sudetenland.

(v) The Policy of Appeasement.

(vi) The Nazi-Soviet Pact and the invasion of Poland.

6. Write **long answers** on each of the following questions:

(i) German expansion in the 1930s.

(ii) The causes of the Second World War.

(iii) How did Hitler contribute to the causes of the Second World War?

OR

Hitler's foreign policy from 1933 up to the outbreak of the Second World War, 3 September 1939.

HIGHER LEVEL

1. Discuss critically, the view that 'Hitler's aggressive foreign policy was the main cause of the Second World War.'

2. Discuss the extent to which Hitler had destroyed the Treaty of Versailles by 1939.

3. To what extent were the foreign policies pursued by Hitler and Mussolini responsible for the outbreak of the Second World War?

4. Discuss the reaction of European states to Hitler's foreign policy up to the outbreak of the Second World War.

5. Why did war break out in Europe in 1939?

TEST YOURSELF AT
my-etest.com

The Nazi State at War

THE INVASION OF POLAND, 1939

At dawn on 1 September 1939, the German invasion of Poland began. The German army employed the bold new tactics of **Blitzkrieg or lightning war**, based on surprise and speed. The **Luftwaffe**, led by Stuka dive-bombers, attacked the Polish Air Force, knocking most of the planes out of action on the ground. Within two days the air force had ceased to exist and the Luftwaffe had **control of the air**.

At the same time, the **Panzer (tank) units** advanced rapidly into Poland. They bypassed the main Polish army units. They worked with the air force and used a **pincer movement** to cut off the supply and communication lines of the Polish army. As one tank commander said, *'There was virtually no resistance ... There was a certain amount of sporadic fighting when we got to the river barriers, but the Luftwaffe had already cleared the way for us.'* Following behind the Panzers, **the infantry units** broke down any remaining resistance.

Hitler reviewing troops going into Poland on 1 September 1939.

Within a week, German units were on the outskirts of Warsaw, others then progressed halfway into Poland. As part of the secret clauses of the **Nazi-Soviet Pact**, the Soviet army attacked from the east, almost three weeks into the war. Warsaw held out until 27 September but the Polish government had fled to Romania long ago. Poland had been humiliated in a month.

The results of the invasion: Britain, France and even Hitler were surprised by the speed of the victory. A country of 33 million with an army of 1·7 million was crushed before it could fight back. The Poles had fought by the rules of the First World War; the Germans had invented new ones.

The cost to Germany was 10,000 killed and 20,000 wounded. In accordance with their pre-war Pact, Poland was divided between Germany and the Soviet Union. Within a few months the victorious countries had executed 18,000 Poles for **offences**, and the Germans began the process of herding Jews into **ghettoes**.

Victims of German success in Poland: Polish Jews being rounded up for the Warsaw ghetto.

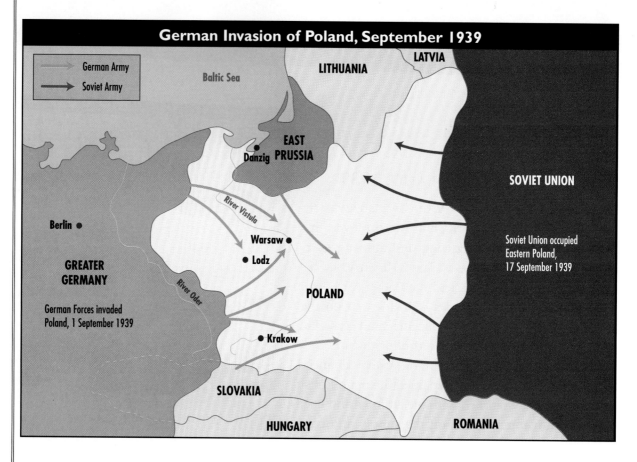

German Invasion of Poland, September 1939

German Army
Soviet Army

Baltic Sea
LITHUANIA
LATVIA

EAST PRUSSIA
Danzig

River Vistula

Berlin

GREATER GERMANY

German Forces invaded Poland, 1 September 1939

River Oder

Warsaw
Lodz

POLAND

Krakow

SLOVAKIA

HUNGARY

SOVIET UNION

Soviet Union occupied Eastern Poland, 17 September 1939

ROMANIA

THE WEST

Meanwhile in the West virtually nothing happened. Hitler left just enough forces to defend the **Siegfried Line** knowing that the French and British would be slow to **mobilise** (get their armies ready). There were no British forces on the continent and the French made a half-hearted advance towards the **Siegfried Line** before retreating. Once again the French showed their weakness.

Hitler, on the other hand, was triumphant. He had Central and Eastern Europe at his mercy. He offered peace to the British and French, which they rejected. At the same time, he gave orders for an attack on France. But eleven times the weather forced cancellation of the order. The West settled into a winter of phoney war.

> **KEY CONCEPT: BLITZKRIEG (LIGHTNING WAR)** was developed by German generals at the beginning of the Second World War in campaigns against Poland, France, North Africa, the Balkans and Russia. It involved close **co-operation** between tanks (Panzer) units, air force and motorised infantry. They were linked by a good **communications system**. Later in the war, Allied generals, e.g. General Patton, used Blitzkrieg tactics in North Africa and France. Blitzkrieg was later used by the Israeli army in Arab-Israeli wars, and by the Americans in Desert Storm and in Iraq:
> • The air force attacks the enemy air force, as well as roads and railways.
> • Concentrated tank divisions break through the enemy lines and advance well into enemy territory, cutting off supplies and reinforcements coming to the main army.
> • The main infantry defeats the weakened enemy infantry units.

THE WINTER WAR – THE RUSSO-FINNISH WAR

After taking over the eastern half of Poland, the Soviet Union then took control of the Baltic States, **Latvia, Estonia and Lithuania**. However, **Stalin**, the Russian leader, was concerned about the future defences of **Leningrad**. He wanted Finland to hand over some territory to Russia to strengthen Leningrad. When the Finns refused, Russia invaded Finland on 30 November 1939. This appeared an unequal contest – a country of 180 million with an army of one million and

The Nazi State at War

much greater numbers of tanks and planes, against a country of 3 million with just over 30,000 soldiers. However, much to the surprise of the Russians, the Finns held out for over three months, finally surrendering in March 1940. The Russian army could not progress in the snow, while the Finns used ski patrols to ambush and harass them. The Finns had built a strong defence line – the **Mannerheim Line** – and this held up the Russians. But the main reason for the slow progress of the Russians was **Stalin's purges** in the 1930s which weakened the Soviet officer corps. By the end of the Winter War, the victorious Russians had suffered losses ten times greater than the Finns.

THE PHONEY WAR

While the Russo-Finnish War was in progress, the western front experienced the **phoney war** – a period of seven months after the defeat of Poland when there was no fighting along the western front between France, Britain and Germany. The French took up a **defensive position** along the **Maginot Line**. This huge system of fortifications, which cost £160 million to construct, had underground barracks, power stations, and a miniature railway.

But the Maginot Line only protected the border with Germany. The French army protected the rest of the French border from Luxembourg to the sea, now at last with the support of the British Expeditionary Force. Both the Allies and the Germans waited and built up supplies and armaments for the next round of fighting.

THE INVASION OF DENMARK AND NORWAY, APRIL 1940

The invasion of **Denmark and Norway** brought the phoney war to an end. Hitler needed Norway to protect valuable **Swedish iron ore** supplies which came through the Norwegian port of **Narvik** in winter. The loss of Swedish ore would cripple his war effort; a British report said, it would *'bring German industry to a standstill'*. Hitler also saw the value of the long **Norwegian coast** which could be used for sheltering ships and submarines. Britain was also planning to take Norway but when Hitler became aware of these plans he got there before them.

First, however, Hitler captured **Denmark** in less than a day. At the same time his warships transported troops to attack and capture six Norwegian cities, including Trondheim and Bergen. He also used **paratroopers** to take bridges and

A Soviet air attack during the Russo-Finnish War of 1939–40.

The German army invaded Norway in April 1940 to protect iron ore supplies coming from Sweden.

airfields. But British and French forces also landed, particularly around Narvik. The **Luftwaffe** gave the Germans an advantage and eventually the British and French troops had to be evacuated. Hitler imposed **Vidkun Quisling**, a Norwegian Nazi, in government but a Nazi official soon replaced him due to his incompetence.

Results: Hitler's success in Norway undermined the position of **Neville Chamberlain**, the British Prime Minister. **Winston Churchill** replaced him as Prime Minister the day Hitler began his new campaign, the attack on France. Churchill told the House of Commons, *'I have nothing to offer but blood, toil, tears and sweat.'* A Member of Parliament wrote the same day, *'Winston – our hope – he may yet save civilisation.'*

THE INVASION OF FRANCE, MAY 1940

Now that Hitler had safeguarded his northern side, he again turned to plans for **invading France**. He was not happy with the original war plans which seemed to him too much like the failed German war plan of the First World War. Hitler was presented with an alternative plan by **General Manstein** which he ordered to be carried out in spite of the objections of the Army High Command. Manstein's plan took full advantage of the **speed** and **mobility** of blitzkrieg.

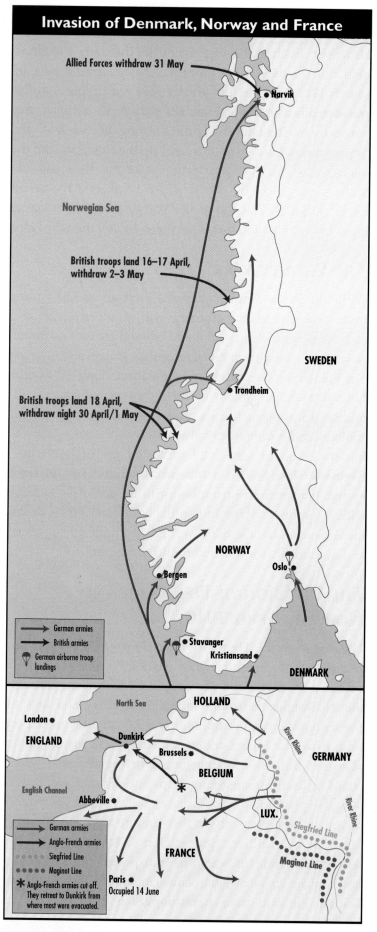

Invasion of Denmark, Norway and France

Allied Forces withdraw 31 May

Narvik

Norwegian Sea

British troops land 16–17 April, withdraw 2–3 May

SWEDEN

British troops land 18 April, withdraw night 30 April/1 May

Trondheim

NORWAY

Bergen

Oslo

→ German armies
→ British armies
⍭ German airborne troop landings

Stavanger
Kristiansand

DENMARK

HOLLAND
North Sea
London
ENGLAND
Dunkirk
Brussels
River Rhine
GERMANY
BELGIUM
English Channel
Abbeville
✳
LUX.
Siegfried Line
River Rhine
FRANCE
Maginot Line
Paris
Occupied 14 June

→ German armies
→ Anglo-French armies
○○○○ Siegfried Line
●●●● Maginot Line
✳ Anglo-French armies cut off. They retreat to Dunkirk from where most were evacuated.

THE MAIN ALLIES AND AXIS POWERS

ALLIES	AXIS POWERS
Britain	Germany
France	Italy (after June 1940)
Soviet Union (after June 1941)	Japan (after December 1941)
US (after December 1941)	

The Invasion Begins

The invasion began on 10 May 1940. Early that morning 2,500 Luftwaffe aircraft attacked airfields in Holland, Belgium, France and Luxembourg, destroying many enemy planes.

The right wing of the German army swung into Belgium, easily capturing the huge Belgian fort at Eben Emael. But the Belgian attack, and the takeover of Holland, were mainly **decoys**. At the first signs of the attack the British and French armies advanced into Belgium. This ideally suited the main German attack which came through the **Ardennes** mountains and forests. Here **General Guderian's** Panzer units advanced rapidly towards **Sedan**, breaking through the French lines. After this they moved westwards towards the English Channel, cutting off the British and French armies in Belgium.

A torched village as the German army invaded France.

Dunkirk

The British Expeditionary Force (BEF) and the French army fell back to Dunkirk when they realised what was happening. Fortunately for the 300,000 soldiers in Dunkirk, Hitler ordered a halt to the advancing tanks. This breathing space allowed the British to put **Operation Dynamo** into action. With the **Royal Air Force** (RAF) defending the air, 860 boats and ships crossed and recrossed the English Channel over a period of about 10 days to rescue 300,000 soldiers, two-thirds English and one-third French. The British army had been saved even though they lost many tanks, trucks, heavy guns and rifles. British propaganda turned the defeat into victory and a morale booster at home.

The Fall of France, June 1940

The remainder of the French army, aided by 100,000 British troops, continued the fight for the next few weeks. But they had no hope against the overwhelming superiority of the Germans. They controlled the air and bombed French cities behind the front. They advanced southwards and took the Maginot Line from the rear.

Eventually the outstanding German successes enticed **Mussolini** into the war. He failed to honour the Pact of Steel when the war broke out in September 1939. Now he wanted to share in Hitler's glory. On 10 June, he invaded southern France. He said, *'I need a thousand dead in order to take my seat at the table with the victors.'*

British and French troops being rescued at Dunkirk in Operation Dynamo.

Why Was Germany So Successful in 1939-40?

1. The Military Balance

Germany had a **stronger army** than either Poland, Norway, France or Britain:

- In 1939, it had 125 divisions compared to 80 for the French and 4 for the British.
- It had over 4,000 aircraft compared to 1,200 French and 1,700 British. Its planes were faster and better armed than the French.

2. Military Tactics

Germany had better military tactics. Its **use of blitzkrieg** explains why the enemy countries collapsed so quickly. Tanks and aeroplanes worked together for a rapid advance, cutting off the enemy supplies. Paratroopers were also used behind enemy lines. In contrast, the Poles and French used tanks in the same way as in the First World War in support of the infantry, and therefore slowly.

3. Failure to Help Poland

France failed to act when Hitler invaded Poland. At the time France had a far greater army along its border with Germany. But the French military leaders still believed in a defensive stance, as had been used in the First World War.

4. Failure to Act Decisively against Norway

The British and French realised the importance of Norway for German iron ore supplies coming from Sweden. They planned to cut them off, but they delayed their attack and gave Hitler the chance to get there before them.

5. The Weakness of France

France had failed to prepare fully for the war. It was late rearming, it neglected its air force and the new methods of fighting. Its war plan, which involved invading Belgium, was a failure. Its people were divided between Left and Right.

Armistice

The French government survived for another couple of weeks. They moved from Paris to Bordeaux. A new Prime Minister, **Marshal Pétain**, a hero of the First World War, sought an armistice with Germany. Hitler ensured that the armistice was signed on 21 June in the same railway carriage, and in the same place in Compiègne, where Germany had signed its surrender in 1918 at the end of the First World War. Now Germany dictated the terms to France:

- The Germans controlled the north and west of France while the rest, Vichy France, was under French government control.
- France kept control of its navy and empire.
- The French army was disarmed and demobilised.
- France had to pay the cost of occupation.

Results: The defeat was a disaster and shame for France. The country and its army had been destroyed in 40 days. Over 80,000 French soldiers had been killed, 120,000 injured and 1·5 million captured. The British navy destroyed the French fleet at **Mers-el-Kebir** in Algeria to ensure it did not get into German hands. The future of France rested with either the Vichy government or with **General de Gaulle's Free French** movement which he set up in London. Hitler and his allies now ruled most of Europe from the Atlantic seaboard to the border with the Soviet Union.

Hitler the man-eater, a propaganda cartoon in 1942: what is its message?

THE BATTLE OF BRITAIN, AUGUST–SEPTEMBER 1940

Hitler now planned the invasion of Britain – **Operation Sealion**. He had between 20 and 45 divisions ready to be transported across the English Channel. But he needed **control of the air** to protect the ships and barges. He knew the Luftwaffe had to defeat the RAF. This was the Battle of Britain.

Winston Churchill urged on the British people,

> 'We shall defend our island whatever the cost may be.... We shall fight on the beaches, we shall fight on the landing grounds, we shall fight in the fields and the streets, we shall fight in the hills, we shall never surrender.... Let us therefore brace ourselves to our duty and so bear ourselves that if the British Commonwealth and Empire last for a thousand years men will still say, "This was their finest hour." '

The RAF Spitfires matched the speed and manoeuvrability of German fighter planes in the Battle of Britain.

The Battle

The Battle of Britain was fought in a number of **stages**. First, Hitler began by attacking ships in the English Channel to draw the RAF into battle. Then he followed this with attacks on the **airfields** and **radar stations**. The RAF was stretched as pilots not only from Britain but also from Commonwealth countries (Australia, Canada, New Zealand), as well as Poland and Czechoslovakia, battled against wave after wave of German planes. On **Eagle Day** (13 August) the Luftwaffe sent in five waves of bombers and fighters. This pattern was followed on many other days. However, even though the RAF pilots were exhausted, they were inflicting heavy losses on the Luftwaffe.

In spite of some success against the RAF, Hitler changed his target to the **bombing of London** in September in response to a British attack on Berlin. He hoped to break the **morale** of the civilian population. London was attacked twenty-four times that month and people took to living in cellars and in the Underground. From November onwards, the Luftwaffe raided only at night because of the heavy daytime losses. But this was not successful either. London was protected by 1,500 barrage

A German air raid on London on 11 September 1940, during the Blitz.

balloons, 2,000 anti-aircraft guns and, most importantly, 750 Spitfire and Hurricane fighter planes. Instead, the bombing of London relieved pressure on the RAF and the airfields. In the middle of September Hitler **postponed** the invasion of Britain and by October he **called it off**. He had lost the Battle of Britain.

The Blitz

The aerial bombing of British cities, known as the **Blitz**, continued after the Battle of Britain. The Blitz lasted from September 1940 to May 1941. From November onwards, the Luftwaffe raided only at **night** because of the heavy daytime losses. In that period, Luftwaffe bombers not only attacked London, which was bombed many more times, but also industrial cities such as Coventry, Manchester, Birmingham and Liverpool. The Luftwaffe dropped 35,000 tons of bombs and lost 650 aircraft. By May 1941, 43,000 people in Britain had been killed and 1·4 million had been made homeless. By that time Hitler needed the Luftwaffe to lead the attack on Russia.

Why Did Britain Win the Battle of Britain?

- Germany had a clear advantage in planes – over 2,000 bombers and fighters to Britain's 900 fighters. But the British **Spitfire** and **Hurricane** fighter planes were a match for the German **Messerschmitts** and easily defeated the slow **Stuka**. The Luftwaffe lost nearly twice as many planes as the RAF.
- Churchill rightly praised the **pilots** of the RAF; *'Never in the field of human conflict was so much owed by so many to so few.'*
- **Radar** helped in this battle by giving advance warning of attack. British fighters were able to conserve fuel while German fighters had limited time over Britain.

The Battle of Britain was Hitler's first defeat. Britain now became the centre of resistance to Hitler.

AIRCRAFT LOSSES IN THE BATTLE OF BRITAIN		
	RAF	**LUFTWAFFE**
10 July–23 August 1940	264	576
24 August–6 September 1940	286	380
7–30 September 1940	242	433
Total	792	1,389

KEY PERSONALITY: WINSTON CHURCHILL

Winston Churchill had a **long career** in politics behind him when the Second World War broke out in 1939. In the 1930s he warned against the danger of the Nazis and was opposed to the policy of appeasement. In 1939, Neville Chamberlain appointed Churchill to the War Cabinet in charge of the Royal Navy.

Churchill succeeded Chamberlain as Prime Minister in May 1940. He took over at a time when Britain needed **strong leadership** during the Battle of Britain and the Blitz. Churchill was the **ideal war leader**. He spoke with enthusiasm, inspiring British people to resist. He also had great energy. In 1943 he travelled 40,000 miles, at the age of 70, to encourage and co-ordinate efforts to defeat Hitler.

He **worked well** with the American President, Roosevelt. He was delighted with the **Lend-Lease Act** which gave military goods to England without payment. He strengthened the relationship with the US when he met Roosevelt in Newfoundland in 1941 and they agreed the **Atlantic Charter**. He attended the **Allied Conferences** in Casablanca, Teheran, Yalta and Potsdam and so was involved in the **major decisions** in running the war, and the peace after the war.

After the war, Churchill, as a leader of the Conservative Party, was defeated in the general election in Britain. He continued to advocate the US-British link, now in opposition to Communism and **the Iron Curtain**. He also called for European unity.

THE WAR AT SEA

The War at Sea played a vital role in deciding who won the war. Britain was dependent on supplies reaching the country from its empire and above all, from the US. **President Roosevelt** of America responded to urgings from **Churchill** and provided the vital supplies:

- In September 1940, he gave **50 warships** to Britain.
- In January 1941, under the **Lend-Lease Act** Roosevelt could supply military equipment to Britain without payment.

When the war began, Britain faced danger from **commerce-raiders** such as the **Admiral Graf Spee**, and the **Scharnhorst**. These operated in the North and South Atlantic attacking convoys coming from the US or West Africa. The most powerful of these ships was the **Bismarck** but it too was sunk like most of the others. The threat from these had been alarming and spectacular, but not serious.

A much more serious threat came from the **U-boats**. From the middle of 1940, German U-boats were able to use bases in Norway and France to advance into the North Atlantic. **Wolf packs** (groups of U-boats) moved out from strongly protected submarine lairs. They had considerable success in attacking convoys of ships protected by destroyers. In April–June 1941, for example, the U-boats sank one million tons of Allied shipping.

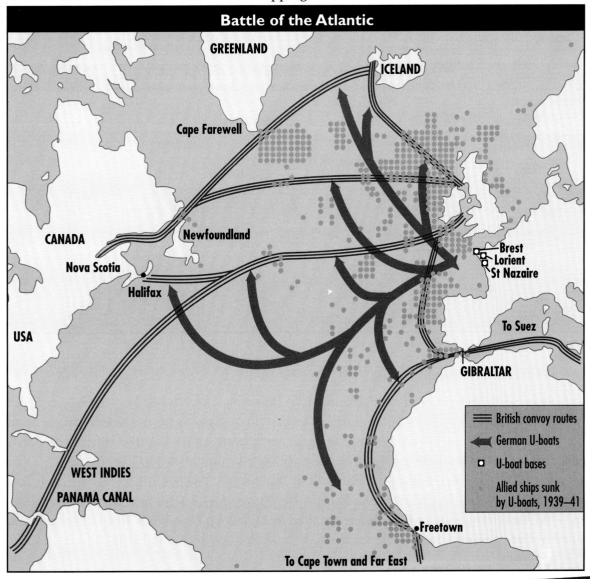

Battle of the Atlantic

GREENLAND
ICELAND
Cape Farewell
CANADA
Newfoundland
Nova Scotia
Halifax
USA
WEST INDIES
PANAMA CANAL
Brest
Lorient
St Nazaire
To Suez
GIBRALTAR
Freetown
To Cape Town and Far East

British convoy routes
German U-boats
U-boat bases
Allied ships sunk by U-boats, 1939–41

Allied Counter-measures

Allied losses were at their highest in 1942, but by 1943 counter-measures by the Allies began to work – greater protection for the convoys with more warships, the use of **Ultra** to crack the German navy codes and follow the path of the submarines, the use of long-range aircraft, depth charges, sonar, a huge programme of shipbuilding to replace sunken ships and the entry of the US into the war in December 1941. By 1943 the Allies had won the war at sea, but in the process over 2,700 Allied merchant ships and 100 warships had been sunk by the U-boats.

GERMAN INVOLVEMENT IN THE MEDITERRANEAN AND THE BALKANS

THE WAR IN THE DESERT – ITALIAN AND GERMAN FAILURE IN NORTH AFRICA

Italy Loses its African Empire

At the start of the war, Italy had an African Empire which included Libya, Ethiopia and Somaliland. In September 1940, the Italians attacked **Egypt**, hoping to capture the Suez Canal which was vital for control of the Mediterranean, the Middle East and the route to Asia. The Italian advance failed and a counter-offensive by **Wavell**, the British commander in the Middle East, led to Italy losing its entire African Empire by the spring of 1941.

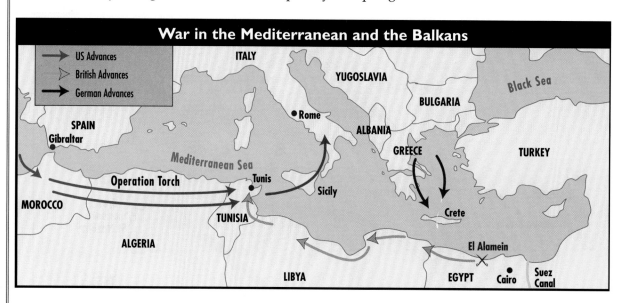

The Battle of El Alamein

British successes forced Hitler to send **Rommel** (the Desert Fox) and the **Afrika Korps** to Libya in April 1941. Rommel recaptured all the territory lost by the Italians along the North African coast into Egypt. Churchill now installed **Montgomery** as commander of the Eighth Army. He prepared for the **Battle of El Alamein** by using information obtained from breaking German codes. Montgomery defeated Rommel at the Battle of El Alamein in October 1942. Over the next few months, Rommel was forced to retreat to Tunisia. He was in great danger here when a new Allied army – the **Americans** – under **Eisenhower**, landed in Algiers (in **Operation Torch**). Rommel was recalled to Germany, and the Desert War ended in an Allied victory (May 1943).

Results of the Desert War: Victory for the **Axis Powers** (Germany and Italy) would have given them control over Egypt and the Suez Canal and access to oil in Saudi Arabia. Instead, this was the first victorious Allied campaign; it was a **turning point** in war. The Axis powers lost control of North Africa. In contrast, the Allies maintained their grip on the Mediterranean Sea, and they prepared for the invasion of Italy.

The War in Eastern Europe

Germans and Italians in the Balkans

In October 1940, **Mussolini** attacked Greece from Albania. He wanted to impress Hitler but

Rommel, the Desert Fox, reviewing battle plans. Rommel and his Afrika Korps were sent to North Africa by Hitler to help the Italians.

the attack failed. Germany had to come to Mussolini's rescue. In the process, Bulgaria, Yugoslavia and Greece were occupied by the Germans (1941). The **British** who had helped the Greeks were expelled from the mainland, and their naval base in **Crete** was captured. Germany ensured **control of the Balkans** so that Hitler was protected from attack when he invaded Russia.

The Stalinist State at War

OPERATION BARBAROSSA – THE GERMAN INVASION OF SOVIET RUSSIA, 1941

Hitler's Reasons

Both Hitler and Stalin knew that the Nazi-Soviet Pact (1939) only postponed the day when they would go to war with each other. Hitler wanted the **open spaces** of Eastern Europe and Russia to provide the oil, grain and the living space (lebensraum) for his master race. *'The Russian space is our*

German tanks and troops advanced rapidly using blitzkrieg tactics in the invasion of the Soviet Union (Operation Barbarossa).

India,' Hitler said. *'Like the English, we will rule this empire with a small number of men. We will supply grain to all in Europe who need it. The Crimea will give us its citrus fruits, cotton and rubber.'* In the process he wanted to **destroy Communism** in Russia. *'The fight which is about to begin is a war of extermination,'* he said.

German contacts with the Soviet army in Poland, and the poor performance of the Russians against Finland in the Winter War (1939–40) convinced Hitler that, *'We have only to kick in the door and the whole rotten structure will come crashing down.'* Hitler was sure he *'would not make the same mistake as Napoleon.'*

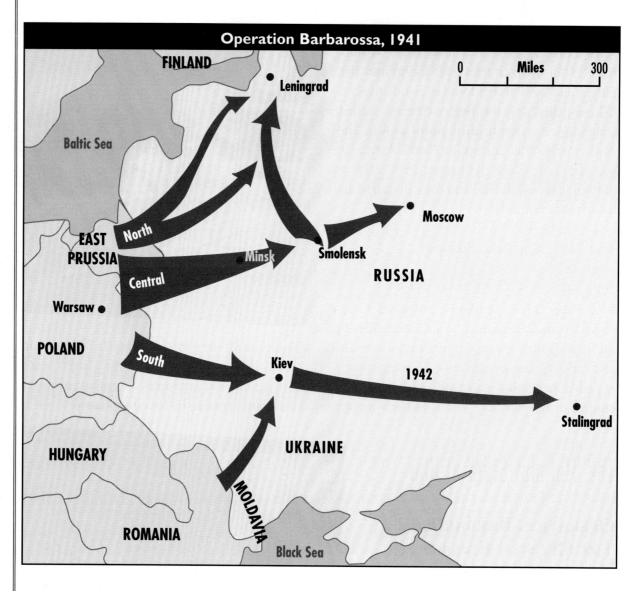

Operation Barbarossa, 1941

The Invasion Begins

The invasion code-named **Operation Barbarossa** had to be postponed from mid-May to 22 June because Hitler had to help Italy in the Balkans. This delay proved to be crucial to the outcome of the plan.

Three million men, 4,000 aircraft and 3,000 tanks began the invasion in a **three-pronged attack** towards:

- **Leningrad** in the north,
- **Moscow** in the centre, and
- **Kiev** in the south.

German Success

The Germans were very successful. The Russian landscape with its rolling countryside was ideal for blitzkrieg (lightning war). In 18 days the Germans advanced 400 miles and the Russians lost 2,000 aircraft, 1,500 tanks and 300,000 prisoners. In the north **Leningrad** was put under siege, in the centre the Germans got to within 15 miles of **Moscow**, and in the south they captured and advanced beyond **Kiev**.

The German advance was so rapid that **Stalin** was surprised by its speed. He did not believe the warnings of invasion he got beforehand. His initial reaction was confusion and fear as he shut himself up in the Kremlin for three days. But once he overcame his depression, he provided the **strong leadership** which Russia needed to overcome the invasion.

Russian Retreat

The Soviet (Red) army lost heavily in men and machines even though it tried to avoid direct clashes with the Germans. However, the Red army was kept **intact** and retreated in an **orderly fashion**. The Russians also used a **scorched earth policy** – destroying crops, buildings and bridges. They kept pressure on the German army as **Communist guerrilla fighters** harassed the enemy lines. But the Germans' advance ran into trouble – they had bad maps, the autumn rains brought mud and soon these were changed to snow. Radiators burst, petrol solidified and soldiers froze. Night temperatures fell to minus 40 degrees. They had to light fires under the tanks to try to get them started. The Germans were halted short of **Moscow** by the severe winter and a Russian counter-offensive led by **Marshal Zhukov**.

A victorious German soldier with a burning Russian village in the background.

Tough street-by-street fighting in the Battle of Stalingrad (left): the German commander Von Paulus eventually had to surrender (right).

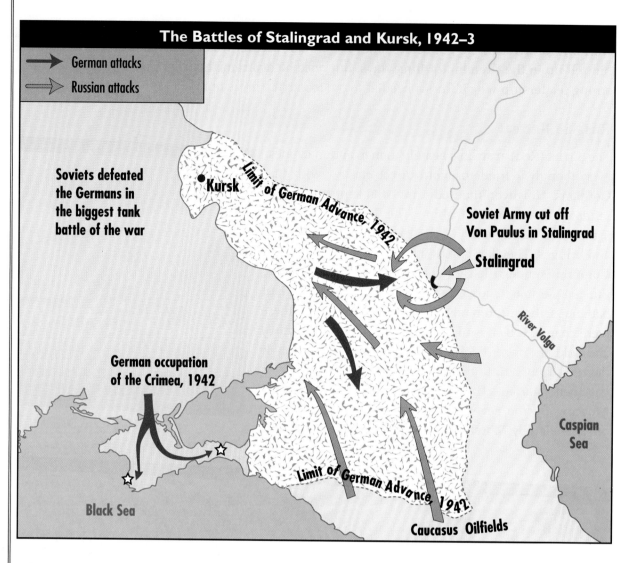

The Battles of Stalingrad and Kursk, 1942–3

→ German attacks

⇒ Russian attacks

Soviets defeated the Germans in the biggest tank battle of the war

Kursk

Limit of German Advance, 1942

Soviet Army cut off Von Paulus in Stalingrad

Stalingrad

River Volga

German occupation of the Crimea, 1942

Caspian Sea

Black Sea

Limit of German Advance, 1942

Caucasus Oilfields

The Battle of Stalingrad, 1942–3

In 1942, the Germans began the offensive again. This time they concentrated their attack in the south towards **Stalingrad** and **the oilfields of the Caucasus**. The Germans were running short of oil but instead of concentrating solely on the Caucasus, Hitler sent part of his army to attack Stalingrad. By dividing his forces, Hitler failed to achieve either target.

The German attack on **Stalingrad** was slowed down by vicious street fighting. The Germans captured most of the city but the Russians held on to a small area of land along the River Volga. Each night more men and supplies were ferried across the river. Then in November 1942, the Russian general, **Marshal Zhukov**, broke through the German lines to the north and south of Stalingrad. His attack trapped the German Sixth Army under **von Paulus** in Stalingrad. Hitler refused permission for von Paulus to attempt a breakout. Instead, efforts to break through to von Paulus failed so the Battle of Stalingrad continued over the winter. But he was forced to surrender, against Hitler's wishes, in February 1943. (See map of The Battles of Stalingrad and Kursk, 1942–3.)

This was a **major turning point** in the war in the east. At the same time the **siege of Leningrad** was lifted after 900 days. From now on the Russians went on the offensive. In July 1943 they won the **Battle of Kursk** where more tanks were involved than in any other battle in history. A year later in the **Battle of Minsk** a much larger Red army again defeated the Germans.

The Stalinist State at War

Why Were the Germans Defeated in Russia?

1. **The delay in starting the campaign** in 1941 meant that Hitler did not have enough time to capture Moscow before the autumn rains and winter snow slowed progress. Many of the soldiers were exhausted from the huge distances travelled.

2. Instead of a short campaign, Hitler was now fighting a **total war** against a country with much **greater resources** of population, soldiers and industry.

3. **Relocation of factories:** Stalin gave orders between 1939 and 1941 to dismantle many factories and move them over the Ural Mountains out of the range of German planes. Tank, plane and munitions production kept going during the invasion.

4. **German use of terror** – the SS executed thousands of Jews, thousands of Soviet prisoners-of-war were killed or allowed to die, and the civilian population were terrorised behind the German lines – rather than crushing the people, these actions ensured greater resistance from the Russians.

5. Stalin used the **call of nationalism** to motivate the Russian people to resist. In a message to the Russian people, he said, '*Comrades, Red Army and Red Navy units, officers and political workers, men and women partisans!... The war you are waging is a war of liberation, a just war. May you be inspired in this war by the heroic figures of our great ancestors....*' Stalin set an example in the **Great Patriotic War** by staying in the **Kremlin** in Moscow during the war.

A Soviet war poster encourages the production of armaments.

THE WAR TURNS

By 1942, the war had turned against Hitler. From now on the defeat of Germany was only a matter of time:

- In December 1941, Hitler had made the mistake of **declaring war** on the US. After the Japanese attack on Pearl Harbour which brought America into war in the Pacific Ocean and Asia, America and Germany were still at peace. But Hitler **underestimated** the power of the US – he saw it as corrupt because of its mixture of races and the influence of the Jews. By declaring war on the US, Hitler gave Roosevelt the opportunity to make Hitler's defeat in Europe the **main objective** of US policy.

- All of Hitler's plans up to 1942 were based on his belief that he would achieve his goals with **short wars**. But Germany's failure to defeat Britain and Russia meant the country had to mobilise for a **long war** and her resources would not match those of Russia and America.

Hitler looks at himself in the mirror during the Battle of Stalingrad in this Soviet cartoon. What is the message of the cartoon?

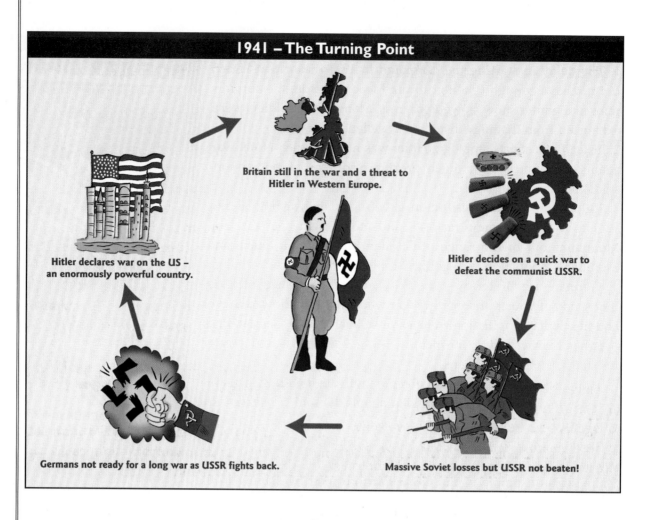

Britain still in the war and a threat to Hitler in Western Europe.

Hitler declares war on the US – an enormously powerful country.

Hitler decides on a quick war to defeat the communist USSR.

Germans not ready for a long war as USSR fights back.

Massive Soviet losses but USSR not beaten!

Wartime Alliances, 1939–45

ALLIED CONFERENCES

The leaders of Britain, Russia and America worked together to defeat Hitler. Up to 1941 Britain was largely alone, but when Hitler invaded Russia, Churchill formed the Anglo-Russian Alliance with Stalin. This provided supplies for Russia through Lend-Lease.

Churchill and Roosevelt formed a strong bond, even before America entered the war. Afterwards these leaders, along with Stalin, met at a series of key conferences which decided the shape of the war and made arrangements for the peace settlement after the war.

Allied leaders at the Yalta Conference (February 1945): Churchill (Britain), Roosevelt (USA) and Stalin (USSR).

Germany, Italy and Japan formed a war coalition. But they never developed a common strategy or co-operated to the same extent as the Allies.

The Atlantic Charter, 1941

Even before America entered the war, Roosevelt and Churchill met in Newfoundland and issued the Atlantic Charter. In this they made *'known certain common principles ... on which they base their hopes for a better future for the world.'*:

- All people have the right to decide their own form of government.
- All people should live their life in freedom from fear and want.
- There should be improved economic conditions and social welfare.
- All nations should abandon the use of force.

Casablanca Conference, January 1942

Roosevelt and Churchill met in Casablanca in North Africa. Stalin, who was not present due to the serious war situation in Russia, urged them to open a second front in the west. This would relieve pressure on the Soviet Army. They compromised on an invasion of Italy. They decided:

- to organise a major anti-submarine campaign,
- to organise the bombing of Germany,
- to invade Italy,
- to seek unconditional surrender from Germany.

Teheran Conference, November–December 1943

Roosevelt, Churchill and Stalin (the Big Three) met together for the first time. The issue of the **second front** was central to the conference. Stalin was annoyed at what he saw as the long delay in opening the **second front** in the west. Churchill favoured an invasion in the Balkans. Roosevelt and the Americans favoured the invasion of France. Other decisions also favoured Stalin. They decided:

- to plan the D-Day landings for May 1944,
- to form a new organisation for peace after the war to replace the League of Nations,
- Russia would get part of Poland after the war as a buffer zone,
- in compensation, Poland would get part of Germany – the decisions concerning Poland were kept secret.

Yalta Conference, February 1945

Roosevelt, Churchill and Stalin met at Yalta in the Crimea. This was the most controversial conference. Stalin was in a strong position in the war (he occupied most of Eastern Europe) and Roosevelt was sick. Many of the decisions favoured the Soviet Union. They decided:

- the Polish-Russian border would follow the partition line agreed between Stalin and Hitler in 1939;
- the Polish-German border would follow the line of the Oder-Neisse rivers;

A Soviet cartoon (1942): The Big Three will tie the enemy in knots. What is the message of the cartoon?

- countries liberated by the Allies would have free elections;
- the United Nations would be formed;
- Germany would be divided into four Occupation Zones after the war (US, British, French and Russian);
- Germany would pay reparations, mainly to the Soviet Union;
- the Soviet Union would declare war on Japan three months after defeating Hitler.

Potsdam Conference, July–August 1945

Truman, Churchill/Attlee and Stalin met in Potsdam, outside Berlin. The war in Europe was over, but the Japanese were still fighting in Asia. In America, Roosevelt died in April 1945 and he was replaced by President Truman; in Britain Churchill lost the general election so during the Conference Clement Attlee replaced him as Prime Minister.

The tension, which eventually developed into the Cold War, was evident. This was not helped by the revelation that America had the atomic bomb. They failed to agree on major issues. They decided:

- Nazi war criminals would be prosecuted,
- Nazis were to be dismissed from government posts,
- the Council of Foreign Ministers would draw up peace treaties with the Axis Powers,
- German reparations would include machinery and equipment from factories.

The Technology of Warfare

THE AIR WAR

In 1941, the Blitz on British cities ended as Hitler concentrated on the invasion of Russia. But it was not until after America joined the war in December 1941 that the Allies began the **systematic bombing** of Germany. Roosevelt and Churchill decided at the Casablanca Conference (1943) that the main aim of the strategic bombing was: *'The progressive destruction and dislocation of the German military, industrial and economic system, and the undermining of the morale of the German people to a point where their capacity for armed resistance is fatally weakened.'*

A British Stirling bomber being loaded with bombs for a night raid on Germany.

The Technology of Warfare

Technology played a vital role in the Second World War. As the war developed into a total war, all aspects of life – political, economic and propaganda as well as technological – were needed to ensure victory. Technological developments were needed to stay **one step ahead of the enemy** or **sometimes to catch up**.

The First World War (1914–18) was dominated by artillery, machine guns and trenches. But two new weapons – **tanks and aeroplanes** – which played a small part in the First World War, dominated the Second World War.

In between the wars, **military thinkers** came up with new strategies to make use of the new technology. German commanders, for example, favoured the use of tanks and planes together for greater speed and mobility. This was their **blitzkrieg** (lightning war) tactics.

There was also the **opposite development** between the wars, when France and Germany used the latest technology to construct huge fortifications, the Maginot Line and the Siegfried Line. But the Second World War showed that the new defensive fortifications were no match for the new faster tanks and planes:

- Tanks and planes **speeded up warfare** and made it **more destructive**.
- Tanks were used together to drive in behind the enemy troops and cut them off (blitzkrieg). The Germans used these tactics to great effect in the invasions of Poland and France.
- During the war tanks developed quickly. The **German Panzers** were successful at the beginning of the war. But they came up against stronger **Russian tanks** (T-34) so the Germans had to build a tank with stronger armour and more powerful guns (Tiger).
- **Aeroplanes** were used to get **control of the air**. Aeroplanes could be used to bomb enemy troops and ships. They could also be used to bomb cities and industries. Planes were also used to **transport** troops and supplies quickly. But motor transport (trucks) and railways were much more important for transport.
- During the war there were **rapid technological developments** in air warfare:
  - Much **larger bombers** were made which could carry more bombs, and fly faster and further.
  - Long-range **fighter planes** (Mustang) were developed to protect the bombers.
- **Air navigation** was very dependent on technological developments. The Germans used the **Knickbein** system when bombing Britain. On the other hand, the Allies developed the **Oboe** to allow them to bomb through cloud and smoke.

New Weapons: The most significant developments in air warfare came **too late** to affect the outcome of the war. Both sides developed **jet aircraft** which were far faster than existing aircraft.. The Germans also developed the **V1 flying bomb** and the **V2 rocket**. The V1 was no faster than an aeroplane so the British were able to defend against it. But the V2 was unstoppable.

Weapons of defence were just as important as weapons of attack. **Radar** (RAdio Direction And Range) was first developed by the British and it played a vital role in the **Battle of Britain**. Just as important, but much more secret, was the use of **Ultra** to crack the secrets of the German **Enigma** coding machine. This influenced land battles as well as the **war at sea**. Here Germany built larger and more powerful **submarines** which could stay at sea longer. These were countered by **Sonar** which tracked the movements of U-boats under the water.

By the end of the war, technology had developed the ultimate weapon which made all others obsolete – the **Atomic bomb**. Developed secretly in the US as the **Manhattan Project**, it was used against Hiroshima and Nagasaki to end the war against Japan.

The ABC of Technology and War

Some technological inventions which influenced the Second World War.

Air

Knickbein – Germans used radio beams to guide their bombers onto targets.

Oboe – a radar-based system to allow bombers to bomb accurately whatever the weather conditions.

Land

Bazooka – an important anti-tank weapon for the US infantry: it fired a rocket about 400 yards.

Katyusha – powerful Russian rocket launcher which could fire 36 rockets at once.

PLUTO (Pipeline Under The Ocean) – pipeline under the English Channel used for carrying oil to France after D-Day.

Sea

Hedgehog and Squid – launchers used for firing depth charges from a ship at a submarine.

General

Computers – the building of the first non-mechanical computer, **Colossus**, that was installed at Bletchley Park in December 1943 to read code produced on the Enigma machines.

Day and Night Bombing

The British and the Americans took **two different approaches**. British Bomber Command under Air Marshal Harris used **area bombing** of German cities at **night**. The British used Lancaster and Stirling bombers. On the other hand, the **Americans** used **precision bombing** by **daytime** because they had better bombers, the **Flying Fortresses**. However, they suffered huge losses at the hands of German fighters and anti-aircraft guns. By the **middle of 1944** the Allies had complete control of the air. They were helped by technological developments with better navigational and bomb sighting equipment, and the protection of the long-range fighter, the Mustang.

Most major German cities were attacked, in particular those in the **Ruhr** industrial area: so also was **Hamburg** for ten days in July-August 1943. The Americans bombed by day and the British by night. The use of incendiary bombs set fire to timber buildings which eventually created a **firestorm**. Sixty per cent of the homes were damaged or destroyed, 40,000 people were killed and a million people fled the city. Even more serious was the damage to **Dresden** (February 1945) when a quarter of a million people were killed in a city with no military importance.

Effects of the Air War

- The Allies disrupted factory production but the Germans quickly started up again.
- The most effective targets were the oil refineries. German oil production declined in 1944 and this hit the tanks and aircraft.
- The Luftwaffe had to be taken off campaigns, e.g. against Russia, where they were badly needed and transferred to defending German air space.
- The Allies lost a great deal of aircraft and men. About 30,000 aircraft were lost and 180,000 British and US airmen were either injured or killed.
- Hundreds of thousands of German civilians were killed and German morale was weakened.

The German city of Dresden was heavily bombed by the Allies in February 1945.

The Invasion of Italy, 1943

After defeating the Germans and Italians in North Africa, the Allies turned to Italy. They wanted to knock a weakened Italy out of the war. They also wanted to capture **Sicily** which would give them control of the Mediterranean Sea route to Asia.

In July 1943, in **Operation Husky**, an American army under **Patton** and a British army under **Montgomery** landed and captured Sicily in thirty-nine days. The fall of Sicily led to the dismissal of **Mussolini** as Prime Minister by **King Victor Emmanuel**. The new government, led by **Marshal Badoglio,** imprisoned Mussolini and began secret negotiations with the Allies.

Catching Italian warships: what is the message of this cartoon?

GERMAN DEFENCES

However, when the Italian government signed an armistice with the Allies, the Germans took over Rome and continued the fighting. American and British armies then invaded mainland Italy. They advanced northwards until they were held up by the strong German defensive line, the **Gustav Line**, centered on **Monte Cassino**. They tried outflanking the Germans by using an **amphibious landing at Anzio** but this was only partly successful. It took a number of attacks and the heavy bombing of the monastery on Cassino before the Allies broke through. In June 1944, Rome fell.

But there were many more months of bitter fighting before the Allies advanced into northern Italy. In the process, they had to capture a second German defence line, the **Gothic Line**. In the meantime, Hitler's commandos had rescued Mussolini and he set up the so-called **Salo Republic** in the north. But his capture by Italian resistance fighters led to his execution in April 1945. Shortly afterwards the German soldiers in northern Italy surrendered.

D-Day – The Normandy Landings, June 1944

The Americans and British knew that if they were to defeat Hitler they had to invade France. Stalin, the Russian leader, was pressing them to open a **second front**. The decision to invade was made at the **Teheran conference** between Roosevelt, Churchill and Stalin. Later, **General Eisenhower** was appointed Supreme Commander of the Allied Expeditionary Force to carry out the invasion plan, code-named **Operation Overlord**.

The Allies fooled the Germans into thinking that the invasion would occur around Calais. Instead they chose the beaches of Normandy because they were not as well defended and they gave direct access to Paris.

THE INVASION

On 6 June 1944, around 5,000 ships landed over 150,000 soldiers, 6,000 tanks and armoured vehicles on five beaches in Normandy. They were protected by Allied control of the air, and they were helped by paratroopers dropped behind the German lines. Over the next few days the Allies extended their control out from the beaches. (See D-Day Landings map.)

Allied reinforcements and supplies were brought in through **mulberry piers** – artificial harbours

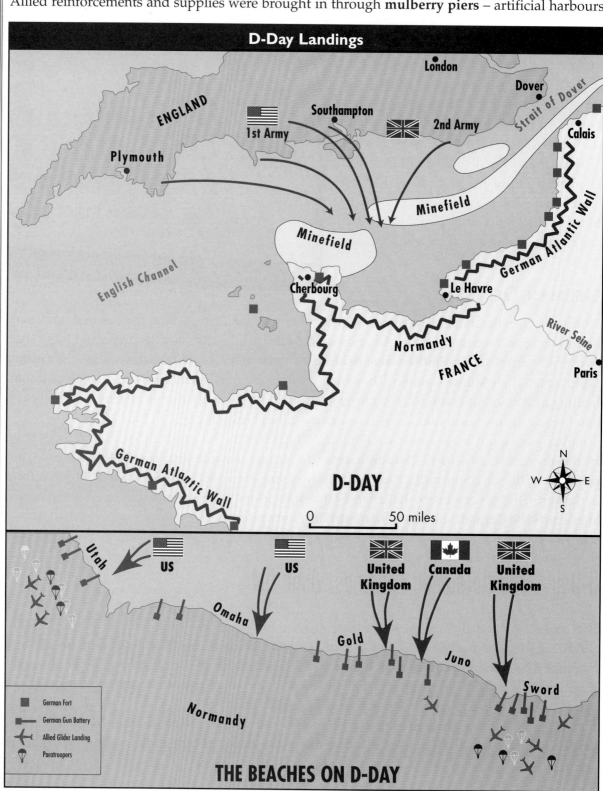

D-Day Landings

London
Dover
Strait of Dover
ENGLAND
1st Army
Southampton
2nd Army
Calais
Plymouth
Minefield
German Atlantic Wall
Minefield
English Channel
Cherbourg
Le Havre
River Seine
Normandy
FRANCE
Paris
German Atlantic Wall
D-DAY

N
W E
S

0   50 miles

THE BEACHES ON D-DAY

Utah
US
US
United Kingdom
Canada
United Kingdom
Omaha
Gold
Juno
Sword
Normandy

▪ German Fort
▪ German Gun Battery
✈ Allied Glider Landing
⛵ Paratroopers

towed across the English Channel. Oil supplies were brought by **PLUTO** – an undersea pipeline that crossed from England to France. The surprise landing, control of the air and the huge resources of the Allies ensured victory on D-Day and afterwards.

By August 1944, the Allies broke out of Normandy and headed for Paris. The city was liberated on 24 August. Two days later **General de Gaulle**, leader of the Free French, marched in triumph down the Champs Elysees. He claimed France for the French and for himself.

The Allies bring in supplies on Omaha Beach after the success of the D-Day landings in Normandy (June 1944).

Advance on Germany

By 1944, the Allies were advancing on Germany from **three sides**.(See map of Allied Advance on Germany from Three Sides.) The advance progressed as follows:

1. In the **east**, the Russians moved into Poland in March 1944. However, they refused to help the **Warsaw Uprising** organised by Polish resistance fighters. Over 200,000 Poles were killed as the Germans crushed the Uprising. A few months later, in early 1945, the Russians took Warsaw and set up a Communist-controlled government. This was the first of the **Communist satellite states** in Eastern Europe which were to last for forty-five years.

2. In the **west**, the British and Canadians pushed into Belgium and captured the sites of the **V1 flying bombs** and the **V2 rockets**. However, progress here was slowed when **Operation Market Garden** – an attempt to break through at **Arnhem** in Holland – failed. American progress was halted temporarily when the Germans attacked at the **Battle of the Bulge** in December 1944.

Allied Advance on Germany from Three Sides

Western Allies (British and American)
USSR
Third Reich

SOVIET UNION
Kursk
Berlin
POLAND
GERMANY
Stalingrad
Normandy
SLOVAKIA
AUSTRIA HUNGARY
FRANCE
ROMANIA
YUGOSLAVIA
BULGARIA
ITALY
GREECE
Sicily
El Alamein
North Africa

But the attempt failed, with a huge loss of German lives. A few months later the British and Americans crossed the Rhine.

3. In the **south**, there was slower progress in Italy because of the mountains and the German defence lines. But by April 1945 the Germans there surrendered.

HITLER'S SUICIDE

As the Americans and British advanced across Germany and the Russians attacked Berlin, Hitler committed suicide in his own bunker, along with his former mistress and then wife, **Eva Braun**, and close associate, **Goebbels**. On 7 May 1945, the German government, now led by **Admiral Doenitz**, surrendered unconditionally. The Allies had won **Victory in Europe**.

The Soviet army then joined in the **war against Japan**. But, by

A Russian soldier raised the Soviet flag over the Reichstag in Berlin.

then, the Japanese army had been weakened and the first atomic bomb had been dropped on Hiroshima. The Russians overran **Manchuria** and captured 500,000 Japanese troops before Japan surrendered.

Why Did the Allies Win the War?

Short war to Total war: Hitler planned for a series of short wars, using Blitzkrieg, to achieve his targets. In between the wars, he would build up his resources. But the war turned into a long war where all the resources of a country were needed (total war).

Failure to defeat Britain: Hitler's failure to defeat the British at Dunkirk, and in the Battle of Britain, meant that Britain continued to be a centre of resistance in the west when he turned to attack Russia.

Greater resources: Hitler attacked the Soviet Union and declared war on America, two countries with far greater resources than Germany:

- **Population:** The combined population of Britain, Russia and America was 344 million; Germany and her allies 181 million.

- **Army, navy, air force:** the Allies had 27·5 million; Germany and her allies had 17·5 million.

- **Oil production:** the Allies produced 2,200 million barrels a year; Germany and her allies 60 million barrels a year.

- **Military equipment:** Russia alone produced 24,700 tanks, 25,400 aircraft; Germany produced 9,300 tanks and 14,700 aircraft.

- **America** became the **arsenal of democracy** – under **Lend-Lease**, US war supplies were given free to her allies; America gave Britain $31 billion dollars and Russia $10 billion of supplies; America produced 300,000 aircraft and 86,000 tanks.

Italy's role: Because of the weakness of the Italian army, Hitler had to send Rommel and the Afrika Korps to Africa to help the country, and delayed the beginning of Operation Barbarossa to help the Italians in the Balkans. Hitler assumed that he would defeat Russia before winter set in, so he did not make adequate preparations for it.

Hitler's role: Hitler's over-confidence in his ability as a military leader. He supported the use of Blitzkrieg at the beginning of the war and this provided Germany with success. But as the war went on he made a number of mistakes, such as his refusal to allow von Paulus to break out of Stalingrad before he was fully encircled.

Brutal treatment: The Germans treated the people of the occupied countries badly and this increased their opposition to the Nazis.

The war at sea: The Allies won the war at sea and kept the sea route to America open.

Bombing raids: The Allied heavy bombing of Germany disrupted the economy and reduced civilian morale.

The success of D-Day: This opened the second front and the Allies advanced on Germany from east and west.

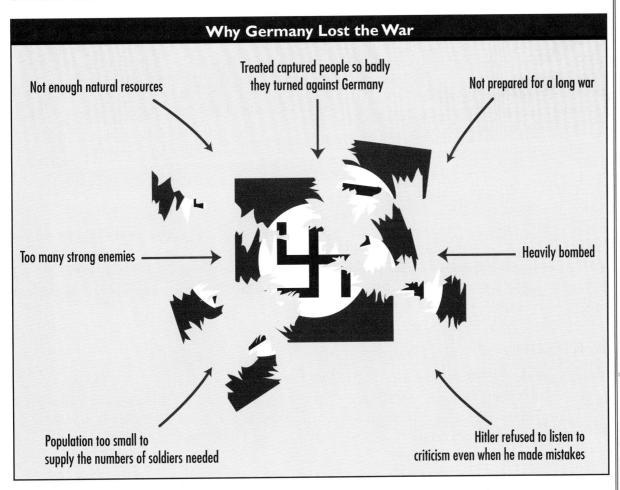

Why Germany Lost the War

Not enough natural resources

Treated captured people so badly they turned against Germany

Not prepared for a long war

Too many strong enemies

Heavily bombed

Population too small to supply the numbers of soldiers needed

Hitler refused to listen to criticism even when he made mistakes

The Results of the Second World War

The war is over: German troops captured during the D-Day landings (left), people waiting for bread in Berlin (right).

1. DEATH AND DESTRUCTION

The war resulted in huge loss of life and destruction of cities and countryside. The Soviet Union had about 20 million soldiers and civilians killed, as much as the total loss for all countries in the First World War. In total, between 40 and 50 million soldiers and civilians were killed in the war. Cities, towns and villages were devastated by aerial bombing and by street fighting. Russia and Poland were the worst affected. In Russia alone 1,700 towns, 70,000 villages and 40,000 miles of railway track were either totally or partially destroyed.

2. REFUGEES

There were about 20 million refugees at the end of the war:
- Most left home because of the dangers of war to seek refuge in a safer place. The largest group of these was about **10 million Germans** who left their homes in Eastern Europe, fleeing from the advancing Soviet army. They moved to the British, French and American Occupation Zones in Germany.
- **Other refugees** included those taken to Germany as **forced labour**. Some were trying to return to their home country.
- **Jewish refugees** left Europe after the war and headed for Palestine. They later founded the state of Israel.

Camps were constructed after the war to house them and they were helped by the United Nations or by Allied troops. Many died from cold, hunger or disease.

3. POLITICAL EFFECTS

- **Fascism** and **Nazism**, which had dominated the history of the 1930s, were largely wiped out.
- **Germany** was divided in two, east and west. It remained divided for the next forty-five years.
- **The Growth of Superpowers:** The **Soviet Union** replaced Germany as the strongest European power and it developed as a **superpower**. It spread its influence over satellite states in Eastern Europe, where it established Communist governments. The **US** became the other superpower after the war.
- The **conflicting ideologies** (political ideas and systems) of the two superpowers led to **the Cold War** which dominated post-war foreign policy until the fall of Communism in Russia in 1991.
- The other European powers, particularly Britain and France, lost the power they had before the war. They also lost their colonies in a process of **decolonisation** during the 1950s and 1960s.
- The horror of the war encouraged political leaders to create **organisations** that would prevent another war. The failure of the League of Nations led to the setting up of the **United Nations** to sort out disputes between countries peacefully. In Europe, leaders pushed for **European unity** and this led to the founding of the **European Economic Community** (1958).

4. SCIENTIFIC AND TECHNOLOGICAL EFFECTS

During the war huge efforts were made by all sides to use new technology to win the war. The new technology was often used for peaceful purposes after the war:

- In **medicine**, there were improvements in surgery and in the discovery of medicines to help against malaria, infection, and asthma.
- Improvements in **aircraft** led to a huge expansion in air travel after the war.
- The invention of the V2 rocket, and the engineers who worked on it, became the inspiration for the US and Russian **space programmes**.
- The invention of the atomic bomb led to a **nuclear arms race** and this became a key factor in relations between the superpowers during the Cold War.

ORDINARY LEVEL

1. Study the maps of the Invasion of Denmark, Norway and France (p. 134) and answer the following questions:

(i) Name three Norwegian cities which the Germans attacked.

(ii) Why was the city of Narvik important to the Germans?

(iii) What happened to the British and Allied troops in Norway?

(iv) Outline one problem that Germany faced in trying to capture Norway.

(v) What was the (a) Maginot Line, and (b) Siegfried Line?

(vi) What difficulties did the German army face crossing through Luxemburg (LUX. on the map)?

(vii)How were the British and French troops evacuated from Dunkirk?

2. Study the map of the Battle of the Atlantic (p. 139) and answer the following questions:

(i) What was a convoy?

(ii) Name the origin and destination of three convoy routes.

(iii) Where was the greatest number of Allied ships sunk between 1939 and 1941? Explain your answer.

(iv) Why did Germany build U-boat bases in France at Brest, Lorient and St Nazaire?

3. Study the extract on Operation Barbarossa from the Goebbels Diaries and answer the following questions:

'Sunday, 22 June 1941 The attack will begin at 3.30 a.m. 160 full divisions along a 3,000 kilometre-long battle front. Everything is well prepared. The biggest concentration of forces in the history of the world. The Führer seems to lose his fear as the decision comes nearer. It is always the same with him. He relaxes visibly. All the exhaustion seems to drop away. We pace up and down in his salon for three hours. I go over to the Ministry of Propaganda. It is still pitch dark. I put my colleagues in the picture. Total amazement in all quarters. Most had guessed half, or even the whole truth. Everyone sets to work immediately. Radio, press and newsreel are set in motion. Everything runs like clockwork.'

The Goebbels Diaries

(i) Why do you think the attack was planned to begin at 3.30 a.m.?

(ii) Why is this the biggest concentration of forces in the history of the world?

(iii) How does Hitler react to the invasion?

(iv) Why does Goebbels go to the Ministry of Propaganda?

(v) Goebbels was Nazi Minister of Propaganda. How does this affect the usefulness and reliability of this source?

4. Study the cartoon, The Big Three will tie the enemy in knots (p. 147), and answer the following questions:

(i) The caption refers to **The Big Three**. Who were **The Big Three** countries?

(ii) Which country produced the poster? Give a reason for your answer.

(iii) What message is the cartoon trying to get across?

(iv) Give ONE example of how the countries co-operated together in the war against Hitler.

(Department of Education, Sample Paper)

5. Study the map of D-Day Landings, (p. 152) and answer the following questions:

(i) What defences did the Germans build against an invasion?

(ii) Apart from the German defences, what other problem(s) can be seen on the maps that faced the Allies when invading Normandy?

(iii) How many beaches were used by the Allies for the invasion?

(iv) Using the map (p. 152), and the photograph (p. 153), list some of the methods the Allies used to invade Normandy.

6. Write **paragraph answers** on each of the following questions:

(i) Blitzkrieg tactics in the Second World War.

(ii) The Invasion of Poland, 1939.

(iii) The Invasion of Denmark and Norway.

(iv) The Invasion of France,

OR

The Downfall of France, May 1940.

(v) The Battle of Britain.

(vi) The Blitz.

(vii) The War at Sea,

OR

The Battle of the Atlantic.

(viii) The Air War.

(ix) The Battle of Stalingrad.

(x) D-Day, the Invasion of Normandy.

(xi) Advances in technology in the war at sea, OR in the air, 1939–45.

(Department of Education, Sample Paper)

7. Write **long answers** on each of the following questions:

(i) German success in the Second World War, 1939–41.

(ii) Operation Barbarossa and Soviet victory.

(iii) Wartime Alliances.

(iv) How effective a wartime leader was Winston Churchill between 1940 and 1945? (Department of Education, Sample Paper)

(v) The technology of war during the Second World War.

(vi) Why did the Allies win the Second World War?

OR

Why did Germany lose the Second World War?

(vii) The impact (results) of the Second World War.

Higher Level

1. Why was the German army so successful in 1939–41?

2. How and why did the German attack on Soviet Russia fail?

3. What role did the Soviet Union play in the Second World War?

4. Why did Germany lose the Second World War?

5. Account for the initial success and final defeat of Germany in the Second World War.

6. What was the impact of the Second World War on Europe?

7. Discuss the influence of technology on the progress of the Second World War.

8. What part did Winston Churchill play in bringing about the Allied victory in the Second World War?

TEST YOURSELF AT
my-etest.com

Hitler's Europe – Nazi-occupied Europe

By the end of 1941, Germany and her allies extended their control over most of the continent of Europe – from the Atlantic seaboard to central Russia. (See map showing Nazi-occupied Europe.) The war had also changed from the short campaigns of 1939 and 1940 with the German blitzkrieg winning large amounts of territory for small losses. Now the Russian campaign changed everything. Germany had to organise and mobilise all the resources at her disposal. This meant that all the conquered lands were forced to support the German war machine. The war had become a **total war**.

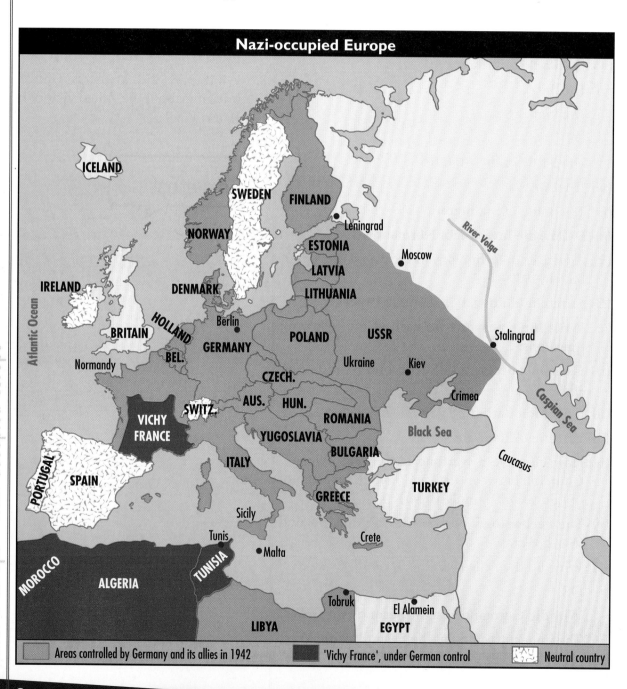

Nazi-occupied Europe

| Areas controlled by Germany and its allies in 1942 | 'Vichy France', under German control | Neutral country |

THE HOME FRONT IN GERMANY

Germany had to gear herself entirely for the war. **Civilians** were as much a part of the war as soldiers. Many had to work in war industries producing weapons and ammunition for the front. As the war went on these included many **women**, even though the Nazis did not approve of women workers. They also included foreign workers who were mostly **forced labour** from the occupied countries. By 1944, these amounted to 7,500,000. Added to these were 2 million **prisoners of war** who were forced to work in factories, mines or farms.

Germany suffered from **food shortages** so food had to be rationed, but some could get supplies on the black market. Civilians experienced the direct effects of war,

Forced labour in a German concentration camp.

especially from 1942 onwards. The Allies began to bomb German cities by day and by night. Thousands of civilians were killed as cities and towns were wrecked. These bombings and the food shortages made life in Germany very difficult by the end of the war.

ECONOMIC CONTROL

The Germans exploited the lands they took over by a variety of means:

- The cost of supporting the occupying troops was borne by the conquered people.
- Everything was priced in German Marks which were overvalued.
- Almost all exports from the occupied lands were sent to Germany. This included most of the food. In Denmark and Holland, for example, all the dairy and poultry produce went to Germany.
- Consequently, food was rationed and this resulted in inflation (price rises).
- Germany promised to pay her debt after the war.
- **Compulsory Labour Service** (forced labour) was used in local projects or sent to Germany – 600,000 were sent from France alone.

> **KEY CONCEPT: LEBENSRAUM.** Hitler borrowed the idea of lebensraum from previous German thinkers. He believed that having additional living space would strengthen Germany by making it **self-sufficient** in food and raw materials. He wanted the living space in Eastern Europe, particularly Russia. This idea of lebensraum became the basis of German foreign policy during Hitler's Third Reich.

GERMAN DAILY RATION OF FOOD	
Bread	12·5 oz
Jam	0·25 oz
Butter, fat	1·25 oz
Sugar	1·25 oz
Meat	2·5 oz (if it could be obtained)
Coffee	0·25 oz

REPRESSION

Germany imposed a harsh rule on its own people as well of those of the occupied lands. German rule in the east, in Poland and Russia, was brutal from the start. In the west, in France and Holland, for example, it became as brutal when the war turned against Germany and when the resistance became more active. Most of the repression was carried out by **Himmler's Gestapo** and the **SS**. Hostages were taken, and there were shootings or mass deportations to **concentration camps**. By 1944, there were **20 main camps** and **165 subsidiary camps** holding anybody the Nazis believed were opposed to their regime.

Transporting Jews to concentration camps.

> **KEY CONCEPT: ANTI-SEMITISM** is the hatred for, and persecution of, the Jews. This hatred was based on religious and economic factors. Modern anti-semitism can be traced mainly to Tsarist Russia and Eastern Europe in the nineteenth century, where there were large numbers of Jews. It spread into Central and Western Europe, e.g. Austria and France, where it became associated with the rise of nationalism. Many nationalists believed that the Jews were not part of their nation. Anti-semitism became an important part of Nazi racial views which saw the Jews as an inferior race. It led to the Nuremberg Laws against the Jews, and later the Holocaust during the Second World War.

Sometimes there were **extreme reprisals**. In Czechoslovakia, the men of the village of **Lidice** were shot and the women sent to concentration camps when Czech guerrilla fighters (partisans) ambushed and killed **Reinhard Heydrich**, the Nazi Protector of Czechoslovakia, in May 1942. Similar action was taken against the village of **Oradour-sur-Glane** in France in 1944, when the SS killed 648 people.

> **KEY CONCEPT: HOLOCAUST.** This is the word used to describe the Nazi's attempt to exterminate the Jews during the Second World War. It resulted in the death of about six million Jews.

THE JEWS IN THE HOLOCAUST

Some groups of people were subjected to even more repression, in particular the Jews. This was driven by **anti-semitism**. Hitler and the Nazis believed in the superiority of the **Aryan** race, and the need to protect it from **inferior races**, especially the Jews. The Nazis believed this could only be done by **extermination**. The organisation given the task of eliminating the Jews was the **SS**. Its leader, Himmler, was a firm believer in Nazi **racial ideas**.

> **KEY CONCEPT: HERRENVOLK.** This was the Nazi idea of the Germans as a **master race**, superior to all other races.

As Germany conquered more countries, the Germans took over more Jewish communities. To the three million Jews in Poland were added about four million more in other parts of Eastern Europe, particularly the Soviet Union. The Nazis first proposed to expel the Jews from Europe after the war to the island of **Madagascar** off the coast of Africa. But planning for this was dropped after a while. At the same time, the Nazis were herding Jews into **ghettoes**, the most notorious of which was the **Warsaw ghetto**. They were walled into the ghettoes in crowded conditions which got worse as the war progressed. In Russia, **Special Action Units** following the German army carried out **mass executions** of the Jews, such as the 33,000 killed in the Ukraine.

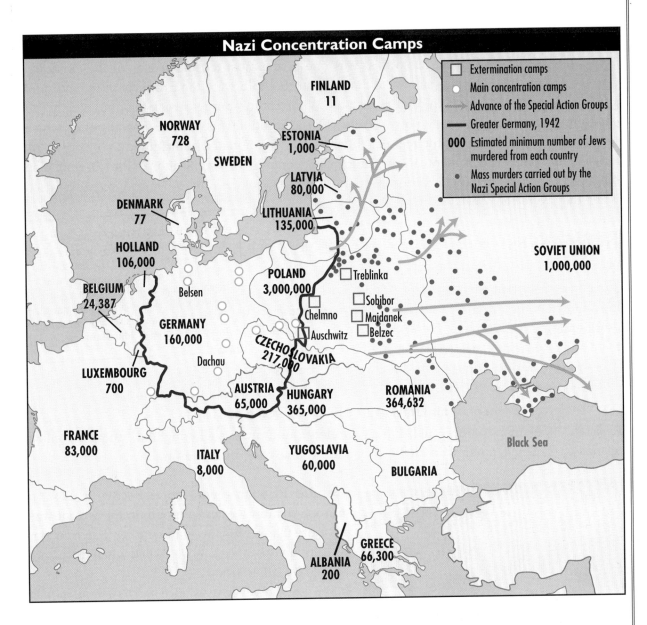

Nazi Concentration Camps

Legend:
- □ Extermination camps
- ○ Main concentration camps
- → Advance of the Special Action Groups
- ▬ Greater Germany, 1942
- **000** Estimated minimum number of Jews murdered from each country
- • Mass murders carried out by the Nazi Special Action Groups

FINLAND 11
NORWAY 728
SWEDEN
ESTONIA 1,000
LATVIA 80,000
DENMARK 77
LITHUANIA 135,000
HOLLAND 106,000
Belsen
POLAND 3,000,000
Treblinka
SOVIET UNION 1,000,000
BELGIUM 24,387
Chelmno
Sobibor
Majdanek
Belzec
GERMANY 160,000
Auschwitz
Dachau
CZECHOSLOVAKIA 217,000
LUXEMBOURG 700
AUSTRIA 65,000
HUNGARY 365,000
ROMANIA 364,632
FRANCE 83,000
ITALY 8,000
YUGOSLAVIA 60,000
BULGARIA
Black Sea
GREECE 66,300
ALBANIA 200

The Final Solution

In early 1942, Hitler and the Nazis decided to exterminate the Jews. The organisation of the **Final Solution** was planned at the **Wannsee Conference**, chaired by **Reinhard Heydrich**.

The extermination was conducted in concentration camps in Poland, especially in **Auschwitz-Birkenau**. After various experiments to get the most efficient method of killing, the SS decided on **gas chambers**, camouflaged as shower rooms, using **Zyklon-B**, a poisonous gas.

Jews were rounded up from all over Europe, including France and Holland, and sent to the camps in Poland. Some feared, or even knew, what was going to happen to them, but most went to their deaths still not realising what was happening. Once they got to the camps, the weak were separated from the able-bodied. The latter were worked until they too were weak. The weak were gassed, and their bodies were buried in mass graves or incinerated in ovens.

Victims of the Final Solution.

The Holocaust and Stalin's Purges Compared

The killing of the Jews in the Holocaust was one of the most terrible crimes of the twentieth century. In some ways it was similar to Stalin's purges. Both were the products of the **evil and suspicious mind** of a twentieth-century dictator. While Stalin's purges struck **fear** into people and ensured he retained his grip on power, Hitler's Final Solution was part of a **racial policy** which was one of the main aims of the regime. Hitler's Final Solution also contributed to his downfall, although in a small way, rather than ensuring greater control. The organisation of the extermination damaged the German war effort because trains, lorries, SS soldiers and other resources were used when they were badly needed by the Army.

RESISTANCE

In the first years of the war, resistance was scattered. Very often it was just passive resistance such as deliberately misunderstanding orders. The German army had come so quickly and with such force that it took time for resistance to be organised. After that, resistance grew because of:

> **KEY CONCEPT: RESISTANCE.** This was the act of resisting when enemy troops have taken over the country. The Resistance was usually a secret or underground organisation involved in sabotage against the occupying forces and collaborators. The Resistance was also called **partisans** in some countries or **Maquis** in France.

- **National pride** – doing something for their country.
- The **brutality of the German invader**, particularly the use of forced labour.
- The involvement of **Communists** after Hitler's invasion of Russia.

Resistance took many forms; publishing an underground press, sheltering and smuggling allied airmen, ambushing, passing on intelligence and in some cases open warfare.

Villagers bring in fresh food to Russian guerrillas.

Results: Resistance was more effective in Eastern Europe than in Western Europe. In the west it was no more than a **nuisance value** rather than a barrier to German operations. It was weak when it was not backed by Allied troops.

In the east, however, resistance had a definite impact on German operations. In **Yugoslavia**, for instance, **Tito's** partisans created considerable difficulties for German forces. In **Russia**, it is estimated that 150,000 partisans (or guerrilla fighters) were active behind German lines by 1942, cutting communications and holding down German troops. But even here resistance forces had their greatest effect when they were working with Allied forces, especially when Germany was weakening.

German Resistance

There was also resistance in **Germany**, particularly after 1941. Those such as **student groups** like the **White Rose** in Munich favoured **passive resistance**. But the most dangerous resistance came from within the German army. Here senior officers planned to overthrow Hitler's regime. A number of efforts were made to assassinate Hitler but the most serious was the **July Plot** in 1944. **Count von Stauffenberg** placed a bomb in Hitler's headquarters but Hitler escaped with minor injuries. The leaders of the plot were hanged with piano wire.

COLLABORATION

Collaboration (or active help) was needed by the Nazis to ensure control of the occupied countries or satellite states. There was active collaboration in many countries under Nazi control, though very little in Poland or Russia. Sometimes collaborators were members of **minority German communities** in countries such as Slovakia or Romania. In other countries they were members of **pre-war Fascist parties** who now believed that victory would gain them a share of the spoils. In Norway, Quisling held power briefly. In France these groups were active in the German-controlled area as well as in Vichy France. There was also **official collaboration**, as in Vichy France, and in Denmark where local or native governments collaborated with the Germans.

> **KEY CONCEPT: COLLABORATION.** This is co-operating with the enemy especially when they have taken over your own country. During the Second World War, this happened in Norway with Quisling, and in France under the Vichy government. But collaboration was not confined to **puppet** governments (governments under the control of the Nazis). Individuals and groups also collaborated with the Germans.

Why Did People Collaborate?

Collaborators had many **reasons** for working with the Nazis. Some admired the German **New Order**; others liked the Nazi control of trade unions and the protection of private property. Some traded with the Germans to make a living. Young women became friendly with German soldiers. These might supply cigarettes or stockings, or the women were attracted to them. Others had more specific reasons. In France, criminal gangs helped the Germans in the hope that their own crimes would be ignored. Still others in France used hatred of the English as an excuse.

Hitler was quite sure that he wanted collaborators and their countries for the benefit of Germany. He used collaborators to do **police work** or to send **recruits** to fight Bolshevik (Communist) Russia. In the latter case a number of countries contributed, including French and Dutch volunteers.

After the war was over, the collaborators were **punished** severely: by death, shaving of the hair in the case of women, or imprisonment. Collaboration became a shame on the country so the punishment of the collaborator was a way of regaining self-respect for the country.

A French collaborator is punished.

The Home Front in Britain

Conscription (compulsory military service) was introduced in Britain before the war so that by the end of 1940 there were two million men in the armed forces. Only men in **reserved occupations** – those which were vital to the war effort – were excused. These included working on farms or in the mines. After December 1941, single women could be conscripted into the WRNS (navy) and the WAAF (air force), the police or factory work.

Britain at war: (top, left to right) Soldiers on sentry duty; gas mask training; joining the Territorial Army; air raid shelters being built; railings removed for scrap iron; evacuating children; rationing; the WAAF (Women's Auxiliary Air Force) help out – driving a tractor, pulling bombs and helping with the harvest.

SHORTAGES AND RATIONING

Shortages of food and raw materials led to rationing. People became familiar with **ration books** and coupons as the necessities such as butter, sugar, meat and bacon were rationed. The black market was available for those who could afford it.

People were encouraged to contribute raw materials. Very often this was a **propaganda exercise**. People were asked to give up aluminium pans to make aircraft, even though many were thrown away because this was an expensive method of manufacture. Wartime shortages also affected clothes – men's trousers had no turn-ups and women's skirts and dresses were made shorter.

HOME DEFENCE

Britain's preparations for war included air raid shelters in back gardens, blacking out windows and the issuing of gas masks. The fear of the Luftwaffe also led to the **evacuation** of children, disabled people and pregnant women to the countryside where they were kept in local houses. Many were often unhappy there and returned to their homes in spite of the danger.

Apart from the regular army, navy and air force, Britain had the **Local Defence Volunteers** or **Home Guard** (Dad's Army). These were volunteers ranging from the age of 17 to 65, some of whom had served in the First World War. They often trained with very few weapons.

To further protect against invasion, road signs were removed, beaches were covered in barbed wire and church bells were prevented from ringing, only to signal an invasion.

WAR INDUSTRIES

Industry geared itself to the war. People worked longer hours and even during holidays. Factories making aeroplanes, tanks and ammunition boomed and unemployment disappeared. Seven million women came into the workforce to replace men who were fighting. Some women joined the Land Army to work on farms to increase food production.

INCREASED BRITISH FOOD PRODUCTION (million tons)		
	1939	1945
Wheat, Barley, Oats	3·3	7·3
Potatoes	4·4	8·9

INCREASED BRITISH AIRCRAFT PRODUCTION						
1938	1939	1940	1941	1942	1943	1944
2,800	8,000	15,000	20,000	24,000	26,000	26,500

CIVILIAN DEATHS

In spite of the fear of German bombers, the first civilian deaths did not occur until the war was seven months old. However, during the Blitz from September 1940, German bombers raided London and other cities (e.g. Coventry, Manchester, Liverpool) and civilian casualties grew rapidly. **Anti-aircraft guns** defended the cities but by the end of 1940, 22,000 civilians were killed. Even though one million people left London, two-thirds of the population stayed in the city, sheltering in cellars and underground stations at night. A few years later in 1944, London faced a second Blitz when Germany attacked the city with the **VI flying bombs** and the **V2 rockets**.

KEY CONCEPT: PROPAGANDA is spreading information to convince people of your point of view. Governments and politicians use propaganda to achieve or retain power. Newspapers, posters, leaflets, speeches, word of mouth and, in more recent times, radio and television can be used to spread the information. The information may be true, partly true or lies.

PROPAGANDA

Government propaganda was vital for the war effort to encourage people to contribute to the war and to keep up morale (spirits). During the Battle of Britain, for example, Luftwaffe plane losses were exaggerated. While the press still ran, the radio was an even more important means of propaganda. Churchill's speeches in his fine booming voice were very effective.

The government also used **censorship** to control the **bad** news. One example of this was the banning of all photographs which showed the effects of air raids.

ENTERTAINMENT

Entertainment also played an important role in the war. Again, the **radio** had a key role in providing entertainment especially through music. **Cinemas** and some **theatres** remained open, though they had been closed for a short time at the beginning of the war. This entertainment and occasional short holidays, for those who could take them, were needed to relieve the stress of war.

ORDINARY LEVEL AND HIGHER LEVEL HOMEWORK EXERCISES

ORDINARY LEVEL

1. Study the extracts about the Blitz in London and answer the following questions:

   'The legend of British self-control and coolness under fire is being destroyed. All reports from London agree in stating that the people are seized by fear ... The 7 million Londoners have completely lost their self-control. They run aimlessly about in the streets and are the victims of bombs and bursting shells.'

   German radio report, September 1940

   'There never was a trace of public panic. But the Blitz was not a picnic, and no fine slogan about "taking it" should hide the realities of human fear and heartache. So far was all this from panic that it took three months for the population of Central London to drop by about 25% from a little over 3 million in August [1940] to 2·3 million at the end of November.'

   British Government report, 1942

   (i) What was the **legend** of the British, according to the German radio report?

   (ii) How were the people affected by the Blitz, according to the radio report?

   (iii) According to the British Government report, how were the people affected by the Blitz?

   (iv) Explain the differences in the population figures given in each report.

   (v) Are both reports propaganda? Explain your answer.

   (vi) How reliable and useful are each of the reports?

2. Study the map of Nazi Concentration Camps (p. 163) and answer the following questions:

   (i) In which country were most of the extermination camps based?

   (ii) Name three of the extermination camps.

   (iii) Name two other concentration camps.

   (iv) Which country had (a) the largest, and (b) the second largest number of Jews murdered?

   (v) What were the Nazi Special Action Groups and in which countries did they mainly operate?

3. When Allied troops, advancing across Germany, came across the concentration

camps with gas chambers, they took local Germans through the camps to show them what was there. Study the extract from an American soldier and answer the following questions:

> 'When the [German] public saw what the camp was like and were led through the torture chambers and past the ovens, men and women screamed out and fainted. Others were led away crying hysterically. All swore that during the past years they had no idea of what was going on in the camp just outside their town. And yet, one heard other stories. One heard that it would be impossible not to know what was happening, that the greasy smoke and the unmistakable odour of burning bodies could be detected for miles around such concentration camps, that villagers got up petitions to have the camps moved elsewhere. I never knew what to believe.'

(i) What was the reaction of the Germans who were taken through the camps?

(ii) What stories did the soldier hear?

(iii) Why does he say, 'I never knew what to believe'?

(iv) How would you decide which was the truth? Could both be true?

4. Write **paragraph answers** on each of the following questions:

(i) Living conditions in Germany during the Second World War.

(ii) German control of the occupied lands in Europe during the Second World War.

(iii) Anti-semitism in Germany, 1933–45. (Department of Education, Sample Paper)

(iv) The French Resistance during the Second World War. (Department of Education, Sample Paper)

OR

Resistance in Nazi-occupied Europe.

(v) Collaboration in France during the Second World War.

OR

Collaboration in Nazi-occupied Europe.

(vi) Living conditions in Britain during the Second World War.

(vii) The role of propaganda in Germany and Britain during the Second World War.

5. Write **long answers** on each of the following questions:

(i) Nazi treatment of the Jews in Occupied Europe, 1939–45.

(ii) Civilian life in Germany.

OR

Britain during the Second World War.

(iii) Resistance and collaboration under the Nazis during the Second World War.

HIGHER LEVEL

1. Compare and contrast the experiences of the civilian populations in at least two of the countries involved in the Second World War. (Department of Education, Sample Paper)

OR

What was the impact of the Second World War on civilian life in at least two of the countries involved in the Second World War?

2. Discuss Nazi rule of the occupied territories in Europe, 1939–44.

3. What roles did collaboration and resistance play in Nazi-occupied Europe during the Second World War?

4. Why, and how, did the Nazis plan to exterminate the Jews?

TEST YOURSELF AT
my-etest.com

PART 2:
DIVISION AND REALIGNMENT IN EUROPE, 1945-92

This German cartoon of the late 1940s shows the US and the USSR dividing the world between them. In spite of the false smile of friendship, they are getting their weapons ready. Does the cartoon favour either side?

Introduction

During the Second World War, America, Britain and Russia had been allies. But even before the war was over, differences began to emerge. These differences grew after the war to eventually cause the **Cold War.**

The Cold War lasted from the end of the Second World War in 1945 to the downfall of Communism in Russia in 1991. It shaped relations between the East and West for those years. This was a time of great tension between the western countries – the US, Britain and their allies – and the Soviet Union and its allies. The tension was marked by a series of **crises** both in Europe and elsewhere which brought the world to the brink of a third world war.

> **KEY CONCEPT: COLD WAR.** This was a time of hostility, tension and propaganda rivalry between the USSR (Soviet Union) and the countries of Western Europe allied with the US. It developed after the Second World War (1945) and lasted until the collapse of Communism in the Soviet Union in 1991. It resulted in a series of crises which brought the world to the brink of nuclear war.

Origins of the Cold War

THE SUPERPOWERS

One of the results of the Second World War was the growth of two **superpowers**, the US and the USSR. These were much stronger economically and militarily than other powers, such as Britain and France. By 1945, the USSR had the largest army in the world, while the US was the world's most powerful economy.

Around the US and the USSR, two **blocs** (or groups of countries) were formed – the **western bloc** of the US, Britain, France and their allies and the **eastern bloc** of the Soviet Union and its allies.

Origins of the Cold War

MISTRUST OF COMMUNISM

The East and West represented two different sets of **beliefs** (ideologies) about how their countries should be run. There was the **Communist system** in the Soviet Union while the West had **capitalism and democracy**. Mistrust between the western countries and the Soviet Union began when the Communists took over control of Russia in 1917. Many people in the West feared the spread of Communism to their countries because they thought they would lose their property and freedom.

STALIN'S FEARS

Stalin, the ruler of Soviet Russia, feared the West. Stalin believed that war between

Soviet rocket launchers in the May Day parade in Red Square in Moscow in an annual display of Soviet military strength. These displays were meant to frighten the West. Who are the men in the two large posters in the background?

Communism and capitalism was inevitable. *'The development of world capitalism proceeds not in the path of smooth and even progress but through crisis and the catastrophe of war.'* Stalin's fears were reinforced by the events of the Second World War. He was angered by the **slowness** of the West in opening a **second front** against Germany. As well as that, the US had an **atomic bomb** and refused to share its secrets with the USSR. Stalin knew that the western leaders, **Truman** of the US and **Churchill** of Britain, were strongly anti-Communist. He felt that any western ideas would undermine the Soviet Union. He was so suspicious that he sent returning Russian soldiers and prisoners-of-war to labour camps (gulags) after the war.

SECURITY FOR THE SOVIET UNION

Russia had suffered a great deal during the German invasion in the Second World War. Stalin did not want another invasion from the West so he built up a **buffer zone** in Eastern Europe by establishing Communist governments in these countries.

'The Germans were able to make their invasion through these countries because, at the time, governments hostile to the Soviet Union existed in these countries. What can there be surprising about the fact that the Soviet Union, anxious for its future safety, is trying to see to it that governments loyal in their attitude to the Soviet Union should exist in these counties?' While Stalin believed he was only **defending** his country, the West looked on this as **Soviet** or **Communist expansion**.

> **KEY CONCEPT: CAPITALISM** is an economic system where the factories, banks, businesses and farms are privately owned and are operated for the profit of the owners (companies and individuals). This is the system of Western Europe and the US.

> **KEY CONCEPT: COMMUNISM** was based on the writings of Karl Marx, a German writer of the nineteenth century. He outlined his ideas in *The Communist Manifesto* and *Das Kapital*. Communists believed that the working class would revolt against the middle class who controlled industry. This would result in a Communist society where private property was abolished, the government would run the land and the factories for the benefit of the people and everybody would be equal.

> **KEY CONCEPT: SOVIETISATION.** The changing of governments to a Soviet-style Communist government which would be under the influence of the Soviet Union. This process began in Eastern Europe after the Second World War when countries such as East Germany, Hungary, Poland, Romania, Bulgaria and Czechoslovakia had Communist governments imposed on them. They became known as **People's Democracies**.

THE SOVIETISATION OF EASTERN EUROPE

The process of creating governments in Eastern Europe **friendly** to the Soviet Union – Sovietisation – was not an easy one for Stalin. In most of the countries Communists had only small support. Stalin had also to move cautiously because he did not want to upset the western countries too much. However, the establishment of Communist governments followed a similar pattern in most of the countries.

Stalin first insisted that **pro-Soviet governments** be formed in countries which he had liberated. He ensured that Communist exiles who had spent the war in Moscow were part of these coalition governments. Very often they got key ministries, such as the Ministry of the Interior which controlled the police. The Communists then used these positions to undermine non-Communists and establish **Soviet-style governments.** They called them **people's democracies.**

Poland: After the war, **16** of the 25 members of the Polish government were Communists. This resulted in an intense power struggle between the Communists (Polish Workers Party led by **Gomulka**) and the more popular Peasants Party and the Socialist Party. The Communists used **terror tactics** against the Peasants Party so that when a new election was held in January 1947 many of their leaders were killed or in prison. The Communists eliminated the Socialist Party when Stalin forced them to join with the Communists. Not surprisingly the Communists won eighty per cent of the vote in the 1947 election.

Hungary: Communists formed a small part of a national government after the war with other parties. However, their control of the **Ministry of the Interior** allowed them to terrorise members of the most popular party, the Smallholders Party. The leader of the Smallholders Party was arrested for *'offences against the state'*. In the next election the Communists won forty-five per cent of the vote and shortly after, the socialists merged with them. By 1949 they had established a **Soviet-style** government.

Romania: This followed a **similar pattern** to other countries. Communists joined a national government with other non-Communist parties. But, encouraged by Stalin, they attacked members of other parties. Then the Soviet army intervened and disarmed the Romanian army, and forced the abdication of the popular **King Michael**. The socialists merged with the Communists and won eighty per cent of the vote in the election of November 1946. Another Soviet-style government was set up.

Czechoslovakia: Czechoslovakia differed from the other countries. It had a tradition of **democracy** and **industrial development** and Communists were stronger there than in other Eastern European countries. After the war, Communists took part in a coalition government controlling the police and armed forces. That government was forced by Stalin to reject Marshall aid. When the non-Communist ministers resigned in February 1948, in the hope of defeating the Communists, it had the opposite effect and the Communists took over.

Yugoslavia and Albania: Communists in these two countries were strong enough to set up their own governments. In Yugoslavia, **Tito** and the Communists had led the resistance movement in the Second World War against the Nazis. Now they took over. In **Albania**, the Communists killed the king and also took power.

In a few years after the Second World War, Stalin had created a ring of **satellite states** which were Communist and pro-Soviet. As this was in progress, the fears of America and Britain were increased. They did not intervene because they saw Eastern Europe as part of the Soviet **sphere of influence** and they did not want to start another war.

THE WEST FEARED THE SPREAD OF COMMUNISM

In March 1946 **Churchill**, then leader of the Conservative Party in Britain, highlighted the division of Europe in his **iron curtain** speech in America. *'From Stettin in the Baltic to Trieste in the Adriatic, an iron curtain has descended across the continent of Europe.'* Many Americans agreed with this view but Stalin accused Churchill of *'warmongering'* and issuing a call to arms against the Soviet Union. The one-time allies of the Second World War were growing further apart.

> **KEY CONCEPT: SATELLITE STATES.** These are countries which are under the influence of more powerful neighbouring countries.

> **KEY CONCEPT: IRON CURTAIN.** This term was first used by Churchill to describe the line or border between the countries of Communist Eastern Europe and capitalist, democratic Western Europe.

THE PROBLEM OF GERMANY

Disagreements over what to do with defeated Germany after the war added to divisions between East and West. At the **Potsdam Conference** at the end of the Second World War, America, Britain and the Soviet Union had agreed to:

- divide Germany into four zones of occupation,
- divide the city of Berlin into four sectors,
- allow Russia to take reparations (compensation) from Germany for damage done during the war.

Stalin was happy with this arrangement because he wanted to keep Germany weak. But the Americans and British soon changed their views. They believed that the European

President Truman (US) (left) supported Winston Churchill's (right) **'Iron-Curtain'** speech in America. This speech heightened Cold War tensions.

economy would not recover until the German economy was strong again. America now wanted to build up Germany as a **buffer** against the expansion of Communism in the East.

THE TRUMAN DOCTRINE

By now American opinion was hardening against their former ally, Russia. The government took the next step which involved a major change in US policy to one of **confrontation** with Communism. This was the **Truman Doctrine.**

The American President, **Truman**, was forming a tougher attitude towards the Soviet Union. In January 1946 he wrote, *'Unless Russia is faced with an iron fist and strong language another war is in the making. Only one language do they understand – "How many [army] divisions have you got?" ... I'm tired of babying the Soviets.'*

At the end of the war, Britain supported **Greece** and **Turkey** in resisting the spread of Communism in their countries. But the British economy was very weak after the war, and Britain could no longer support either country. Britain wrote to America, *'devoutly hoping that [America] would assume the burden.'*

President Truman responded rapidly. In announcing in March 1947 what became known as the **Truman Doctrine**, he said, *'the seeds of **totalitarian regimes** [dictatorships] are nurtured in misery and want. They spread and grow in the evil soil of poverty and strife.'* He committed the US to providing $400 million dollars to help Greece and Turkey. *'I believe it must be the policy of the United States to support free peoples who are resisting attempted subjugation [control] by armed minorities and outside pressures.'*

America now followed a **policy of containment** – to limit the spread of Communism. This formed the basis of American policy for most of the Cold War. The American government believed that if Greece and Turkey fell to Communism then other countries in Western Europe and around the Mediterranean would be next. The Americans intended to confront **Communism** around the world.

THE MARSHALL PLAN

The Marshall Plan followed soon after the Truman Doctrine. **General George Marshall**, US Secretary of State, believed that Communism would take over in weakened European countries after the war. He wanted *'to restore the confidence of the European people in the economic future of their own countries and of Europe as a whole.... Our policy is directed not against any country or doctrine but against hunger, poverty, desperation and chaos.'* America also needed markets for its surplus goods and by reviving Europe they hoped to achieve this. This was the basis of the **European Recovery Programme** (ERP) or **Marshall Plan**, as it was known. (See also Chapters 10 and 11.)

Britain and France called a conference in **Paris** in July 1947 which was attended by fourteen other countries who wished to participate in the programme. They approved a programme which included:

- Plans to restore agricultural and industrial production.
- An organisation to promote economic cooperation. This became the **Organisation for European Economic Cooperation** (OEEC) through which requests for aid and the distribution of aid were channelled.

Over the next four years, from 1948 to 1952, the US provided **$13 billion aid** to Europe. Most of the aid was in **grant** form, only twenty per cent was in **loans**. The grants were usually in products, for example, grain or machinery.

A British cartoon which takes an optimistic view of the effects of Marshall Aid (European Recovery Programme) on Europe. What is its message? How useful are cartoons as sources for historians?

The first consignment of sugar under the Marshall Plan arriving in London in 1949. The onlookers include a politician and administrators of Marshall Aid. Marshall Aid was given in products such as tractors or grain or sugar, as in the photograph.

Effects of the Marshall Plan

- **Historians differ** on the impact of Marshall aid on the European economies. Some believe it was the crucial factor in giving a boost to the economies. Others believe that they were recovering and would have recovered even without Marshall aid. The European economies recovered rapidly, growing by twenty-five per cent in the first two years of the Plan. This growth continued into the 1950s and 1960s.
- Some countries such as **France** and **Italy** needed Marshall aid more than others. **Germany**, on the other hand, had other factors in its favour such as good industrial relations and skilled labour which meant it would have recovered anyway.
- But aid also benefited **the US** because Europe bought American goods and American industry prospered.
- However, one of the major effects of Marshall aid was **political**. It divided Europe in two, the western countries who participated and the Eastern European countries who did not.
- It was also an influence on the road to **European unity.**

The Soviet Reaction

Stalin believed that the US intended to use the Truman Doctrine and Marshall aid to undermine Soviet influence and to destroy the Communist system. As a result, Stalin rejected participation by the USSR and the people's democracies in Eastern Europe in the ERP. Instead he established **Cominform** to strengthen his control over Eastern Europe. Later he set up **Comecon**, as an alternative to the Marshall Plan, to co-ordinate the **economic development** of the USSR and its allies.

Main Crises of the Cold War

THE BERLIN BLOCKADE AND CRISIS, 1948–9

Background

The US and Britain believed that **reparations** (compensation) at the end of the First World War caused the rise of Hitler and the Nazis. Now after the Second World War, they planned to **revive** the German economy in order to help the European economy.

Russia was well aware of the plans of the western allies through spies. Russia did not want to see a revived Germany so gradually they put up **obstacles** to crossing from the western zones into Berlin. But the US and Britain, joined by France, went ahead with their plans. They agreed to allow a constituent assembly draw up a **constitution** for a West German state. They also launched a new currency – the **Deutschmark** – to revive the economy.

Blockade

In June 1948, Stalin and the Russians reacted immediately by sealing off the **borders** between the eastern and the western zones and cutting off all road, rail and canal routes between West Germany and West Berlin. Electricity supply from East Berlin was also cut off.

Berliners depended on air transport for their supplies during the Berlin Blockade. This large American 'Globemaster' plane brought 23 tons of flour from Frankfurt to Gatow airport in Berlin.

Before the Berlin Blockade was lifted, the Soviet government dismantled all rail lines leading into Berlin (April 1949).

All the factors seemed to favour Stalin because of the huge difficulty of supplying a city of 2·5 million people. But the Allies were determined to hold onto Berlin. *'We are going to stay, period.'* Truman said. West Berlin became a **symbol** for western democracy. The Allies took action which included:

- a **counter-blockade** of all railways into East Germany from the British and US zones,
- the organisation of a **massive airlift** to supply the people of West Berlin.

Airlift – Operation Vittles

The western allies used three **20-mile wide air corridors** to airlift tons of supplies each day into **three airports** in Berlin. In Operation Vittles, large transport planes or converted bombers brought in coal, petrol, medical supplies and food. At the height of the airlift, planes were flying in every 90 seconds and landing about 8,000 tons of supplies. They were helped by a milder winter than normal.

However, **conditions in Berlin** deteriorated. A total of 125,000 people lost their jobs, there was little heating, electricity was rationed to four hours a day and there was also rationing of food. Nevertheless, Berlin's political leaders kept morale high with massive demonstrations.

The airlift lasted until May 1949. By this time the Soviets realised that America and Britain could keep the city going. Stalin lifted the Blockade on 12 May.

Results

- The Berlin Blockade was a **huge propaganda victory** for the West. They were seen as the saviours of two million people, whereas the Soviet Union was portrayed as trying to starve them.
- The Blockade was also a victory for **western technology** which flew in the supplies.
- This was also a victory for the **policy of containment.**
- Two **separate countries** were created – West Germany and East Germany.
- Berlin became the **focal point** of the clash in Europe between the two sides in the Cold War.

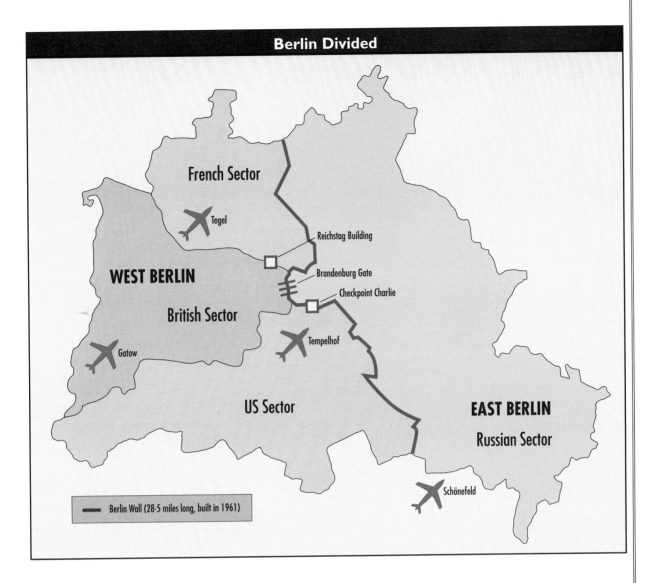

French Sector

Tegel

Reichstag Building

WEST BERLIN

Brandenburg Gate

Checkpoint Charlie

British Sector

Tempelhof

Gatow

US Sector

EAST BERLIN

Russian Sector

Schönefeld

—— Berlin Wall (28·5 miles long, built in 1961)

Military Alliances

NATO: Another of the results of the Berlin Blockade was the formation of **NATO** (North Atlantic Treaty Organisation) in April 1949. This was a **military alliance** of twelve countries – the **US, Canada and ten Western European countries**. The countries agreed *'that an armed attack against one or more of them ... shall be considered an attack against all.'* They pledged to help each other, if necessary by *'the use of armed force'*. One of the most significant aspects of NATO was that it committed **America** to the defence of Europe. A **unified military command** was set up, with a Council of foreign ministers representing each of the members. NATO expanded when Greece, Turkey (1952) and West Germany (1955) joined. But NATO also experienced differences when the **French** decided to develop their own nuclear weapons and withdrew their forces from NATO.

Warsaw Pact: The Soviet Union and it allies looked on the formation of NATO as a **hostile** act. However, it was not until 1955 that they formed an alternative military alliance, the **Warsaw Pact**. The Pact, agreed by the Soviet Union and seven other Eastern European countries, provided the same protection as NATO did for its members. The establishment of the Warsaw Pact was in direct response to West Germany joining NATO because Russia was opposed to **German rearmament**.

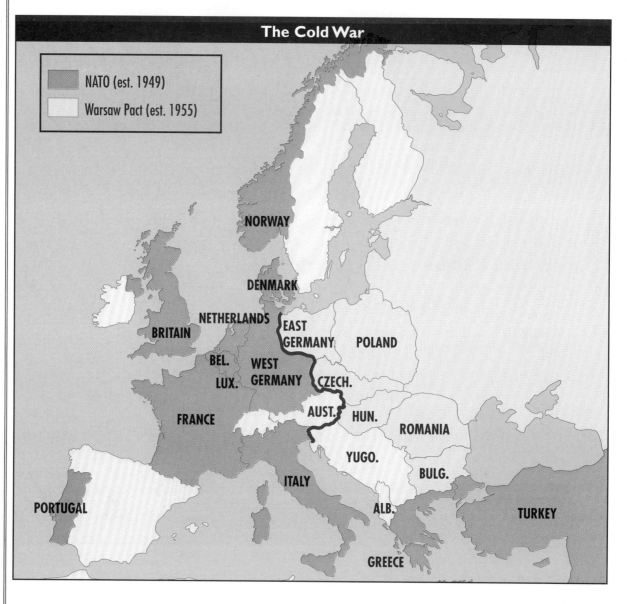

NATO (est. 1949)

Warsaw Pact (est. 1955)

NORWAY

DENMARK

NETHERLANDS

BRITAIN

EAST GERMANY

POLAND

BEL.

WEST GERMANY

LUX.

CZECH.

FRANCE

AUST.

HUN.

ROMANIA

YUGO.

BULG.

ITALY

ALB.

TURKEY

PORTUGAL

GREECE

Now Europe was divided into **two hostile military alliances**. However, the only occasion Warsaw Pact countries acted together was in the invasion of Czechoslovakia in 1968, while NATO's only joint military campaign was in Bosnia in 1995.

Thaw in the Cold War: Peaceful Co-existence

The death of Stalin in 1953 had a major influence on the Cold War. After he died, a collective leadership (group of leaders) took over in Russia. Within a few years, however, it was clear that **Nikita Khrushchev** was the most powerful man in Russia.

Very quickly the new Soviet leadership changed their foreign policy. This was highlighted by **Khrushchev's speech** at the twentieth Party Congress in 1956. He said war between capitalism and Communism was no longer inevitable. Communism would still spread, but now through the ballot box. It was Khrushchev's view that *'we stand as we have always stood, for the **peaceful co-existence** of the two systems.'*

ИЗВЕСТИЯ СОВЕТОВ ДЕПУТАТОВ ТРУДЯЩИХСЯ СССР

Год издания 36-й № 58 (11129) ПОНЕДЕЛЬНИК 9 МАРТА 1953 г. Цена 20 коп.

С глубокой болью прощается советский народ со своим вождем и учителем, отцом и другом—Иосифом Виссарионовичем Сталиным. Коммунистическая партия, все трудящиеся еще теснее сплачивают свои ряды вокруг Сталинского Центрального Комитета и Советского Правительства, клянутся отдать все свои силы великому делу построения коммунизма.

В Колонном зале Дома Союзов 8 марта 1953 года. На снимке слева направо: В. М. Молотов, К. Е. Ворошилов, Л. П. Берия, Г. М. Маленков, Н. А. Булганин, Н. С. Хрущев, Л. М. Каганович, А. И. Микоян у гроба товарища И. В. Сталина.

ДЕЛО СТАЛИНА БЕССМЕРТНО!

Прощание народов с великим вождем

В Колонном зале Дома Союзов

ГЛУБОКАЯ СКОРБЬ

The body of Stalin lying in state, from the front page of *Izvestia*, a Soviet newspaper (March 1953). All the main Communist leaders are lined up on either side of the coffin. Khrushchev, who succeeded Stalin, is third from the right.

However, a new American President, **Eisenhower**, adopted a more hardline attitude. He feared the advance of Communism in Asia. In the **Eisenhower Doctrine** (1957), he echoed Truman by promising American assistance *'against armed aggression from any country controlled by international Communism.'* But now the Americans were not just going to contain Communism, they wanted to **roll back** Communism and were prepared for massive **nuclear retaliation** to achieve this.

Nevertheless, the new Soviet policy of peaceful co-existence began to take hold. It led to a summit conference of the leaders in **Geneva** in 1955. Here the US, Britain, France and the Soviet Union created a **spirit of Geneva** which eased Cold War tensions. *'Socialists and capitalists have to live side by side on the one planet.'* However, relations between the two sides were soon influenced by events behind the Iron Curtain in the satellite states.

Thaw in the Cold War: Peaceful co-existence

KEY PERSONALITY: NIKITA KHRUSHCHEV

When Stalin died in 1953, a **collective leadership** took over the Soviet Union. But within a few years Nikita Khrushchev had established himself as more powerful than all the others.

In 1956 he made his famous **secret speech** to the twentieth Party Congress. In it he denounced Stalin for his cruelties and purges in the 1930s. Khrushchev began a process of **deStalinisation** – undoing the work of Stalin by giving greater freedoms, limiting the power of the secret service and removing Stalin's name and portraits.

In the Cold War he began a policy of **peaceful co-existence**. This led to a **thaw** in relations with the West. He met **President Eisenhower** of the US.

His friendly personality created a **human face for socialism** and his visits abroad made him popular and raised the prestige of the USSR. This was also increased by progress in the **Space Race** when Russian technology led the US. But peaceful co-existence faded when an American **U-2 spyplane** was shot down over Russia and the East Germans (with Khrushchev's support) were forced to build the **Berlin Wall** to stop the flow of emigrants to the West. However, the biggest crisis Khrushchev faced was over Soviet missile bases being built in **Cuba**. When these were photographed by an American spyplane, the world faced the prospect of a nuclear war. Khrushchev was forced to back down and remove the missiles. This failure weakened his control in Russia. His control was further weakened when he clashed with the other major Communist power, **China**. After his economic reforms failed, he was deposed as leader and replaced by **Brezhnev**.

KEY PERSONALITY: IMRE NAGY

Imre Nagy was born in Hungary in 1895. He served in the Austro-Hungarian Army in the First World War but was captured by the Russians. He escaped and helped the **Bolsheviks** (Communists) in the Russian Revolution in 1917. He spent most of the years 1929–45 in **Russia** and only came back to Hungary when the Soviet Army freed his country. He served as **Minister of Agriculture** in the coalition government after the war. As Minister, he introduced land reforms.

In 1947, he became **Speaker** of the Hungarian parliament and became associated with more **liberal Communism**. But Hungary was in the grip of **Matyas Rakosi** who established a strict **Stalinist-style** government and excluded Nagy from it. Rakosi crushed any criticisms of his system.

But Rakosi's economic plans were a failure and this led to discontent. When Stalin died in 1953, **Nagy** replaced Rakosi as **Prime Minister**. But Rakosi was still general secretary of the Communist Party and he opposed Nagy over the next two years until Nagy was forced to resign.

However, discontent built up in Hungary during 1956. Many people looked for the return of Nagy to government. So also did some of the Communist leaders who hoped that by bringing him back they would survive. Nagy became Prime Minister the day the Soviet army came into Budapest. He was caught between the hardline Communist leaders and the discontented people in the streets. He favoured the people and brought in more **reforms**. He also got the Soviet army to leave Budapest. But he continued to make changes. Eventually he said that he would withdraw Hungary from the **Warsaw Pact**.

This led to the **second invasion** by the Russian army. **Nagy** took shelter in the Yugoslav Embassy. But he came out when he was promised safe passage, arrested and sent to Romania. He was later brought back to Hungary, tried and executed.

Gomulka, leader of the Polish Communist Party, addressing half a million Poles in Warsaw in October 1956. Khrushchev, the Soviet leader, tried to enforce Soviet power in Poland but he had to allow Gomulka to continue to rule after Polish demonstrations and riots over low wages and bad working conditions.

Poland and Hungary

Soon after Stalin's death in 1953, workers in East Germany rebelled against the harsh rule of the East German Communist Party. This rebellion was crushed easily with the help of Soviet tanks.

Poland: However, a more serious situation arose in Poland in 1956. In **Poznan**, Polish workers rebelled against low wages and harsh working conditions. They also demanded greater political freedom. These demands led to the appointment of **Gomulka** as Secretary of the Polish Communist Party and the downfall of hardline Stalinist-style leaders. **Khrushchev** rushed to Poland to enforce Soviet power. But in spite of Soviet troops and tanks, Khrushchev had to back down and allow Gomulka to rule. He promised to maintain the Party and to keep Poland in the Warsaw Pact.

Hungary: As the Polish situation was being settled, Hungary rose in October 1956. Hungarian students and workers demanded **economic and political freedoms**. The Hungarian government invited in the **Soviet army** but this only led to further disturbances and deaths. As in Poland, a more popular leader, Imre Nagy, replaced the old hardline Communist leaders. After a few days, Russian troops were withdrawn from the capital, **Budapest**. However, Nagy upset the Russians when he declared he would make Hungary neutral and take it out of Warsaw Pact. In response to this **Khrushchev** ordered Soviet troops back into Budapest and the Hungarian Uprising was crushed. **Janos Kadar** replaced Nagy as leader.

INTRODUCTION

In the late 1940s and early 1950s, Hungary was ruled by a harsh Stalinist-style Communist government, headed by general secretary, Matyas Rakosi. He used **salami tactics** – he sliced up the opposition piece by piece – to gain power after the Second World War. He ran a ruthless dictatorship, crushing the Catholic Church and arresting its leader, **Cardinal Mindszenty**, and using the **AVH** (security police) to torture, imprison and execute thousands of Hungarians.

The Communist Party was backed by Stalin's Red Army. But conditions changed after Stalin's death in 1953, when a process of **deStalinisation** was begun in Russia. Pictures of Stalin were taken down and cities called after him, like Stalingrad, had their names changed. In 1956, Khrushchev denounced Stalin at the twentieth Party Congress in Moscow and this led to a further process of deStalinisation.

In the Soviet **satellite states** in Eastern Europe, Khrushchev's speech led to demands for greater freedom. In Hungary, the hardline (very conservative, dictatorial) leader, **Rakosi**, was dismissed by Moscow and replaced by Erno **Gero**. Gero made some changes to Communist rule. But these only raised expectations of more changes among the people.

> **DeStalinisation:** The process of removing the pictures and statues of Stalin and undoing the harsher aspects of his rule.

In **Poland**, in October 1956, demonstrations and riots forced Khrushchev to appoint a popular Communist leader, **Gomulka**. This encouraged Hungarians who wanted to see more changes in their country.

UPRISING

Discontent came to a head on 23 October 1956 when students and workers demonstrated in the capital, Budapest. The students marched into the city centre, and were joined by workers. They had sixteen demands: these included free elections, greater freedom from Moscow, and the return of popular Communist leader, **Imre Nagy**. At one point a large statue of Stalin was toppled. When an attempt was made to break into Radio Budapest, the crowd was fired on by the security police, the AVH. What had begun as a peaceful demonstration now turned into an intense street battle, and the beginning of an uprising.

SOURCE I – The beginning of the Uprising

'I have been the witness today of one of the great events of history. I have seen the people of Budapest catch the fire lit in Poznan and Warsaw (Poland) and come out into the streets in open rebellion against their Soviet overlords. I have marched with them and almost wept for joy with them as the Soviet emblems in the Hungarian flags were torn out by the angry and exalted crowds. And the great point about the rebellion is that it looks like being successful.

'As I telephone this dispatch I can hear the roar of delirious crowds made up of student girls and boys, of Hungarian soldiers still wearing their Russian-type uniforms, and overalled factory workers marching through Budapest and shouting defiance against Russia. "Send the Red Army home," they roar. "We want free and secret elections." And then comes the ominous cry which one always seems to hear on these occasions: "Death to Rakosi", death to the former Soviet puppet dictator – now taking a **cure** on the Russian Black Sea Riviera – whom the crowds blame for all the ills that have befallen their country in eleven years of Soviet puppet rule.'

S Delmar, *Daily Express*, 24 October 1956

The rebels or insurgents were soon joined by army and ordinary police who were called out to put down the Uprising. This led to further fighting with the AVH; but they had most of Budapest taken in a few hours.

CHANGE OF GOVERNMENT AND SOVIET TROOPS

The Central Committee of the Communist Party appointed **Nagy** as Prime Minister. The Party Secretary, **Erno Gero**, asked the Kremlin for help and the next day 30,000 Soviet troops marched into Budapest. Fierce fighting broke out and martial law was imposed. Janos Kadar replaced Gero as Party Secretary on the instructions of Moscow.

In an effort to end the fighting, Nagy proposed:

- an amnesty for everybody involved,
- political and economic reforms,
- negotiations with the Soviet government for the withdrawal of Soviet troops from Budapest.

> ### SOURCE 2 – Hungarian government appeal for Soviet troops
>
> 'Government organisations have called for help from Soviet troops stationed in Hungary under the terms of the Warsaw Pact. Responding to the Government's appeal, Soviet troops will help in the restoration of order.'
>
> Government statement quoted in T Meray, *Thirteen Days That Shook the Kremlin*

SOURCE 3

The Hungarian State Radio Headquarters after it was attacked by protestors in Budapest in October 1956.

SOURCE 4

The head of Stalin toppled by Hungarian protestors from a large statue in Budapest, the capital of Hungary.

A Hungarian protestor addressing a crowd during the Hungarian Uprising. The fellow protestor is holding the Hungarian flag.

The body of a Hungarian protestor covered by a Hungarian flag: behind him is the body of a secret policeman.

Anti-Soviet demonstration in Budapest in October 1956.

Russian (Soviet) soldiers in Budapest during the suppression of the Hungarian Uprising in 1956.

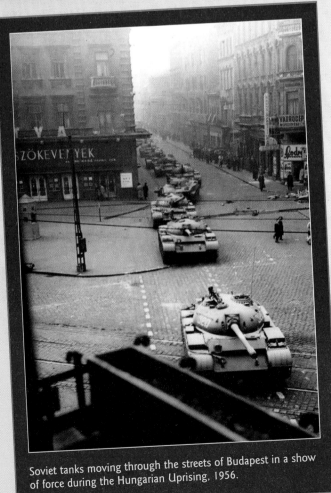

Soviet tanks moving through the streets of Budapest in a show of force during the Hungarian Uprising, 1956.

QUESTIONS

1. How useful are photographs as sources for the study of History?
2. What do you need to know about a photograph to judge its reliability?
3. What do these photos (and those in Sources 3 and 4) tell us about the Hungarian Uprising?
4. Is there any information in the photographs which would support the views that (i) the Hungarian Uprising was popular, and (ii) the Hungarian Uprising had little chance of success?

Hungarian resistance

But the fighting continued as the Hungarians fought back. For the next seven days they opposed the Soviet troops in street battles in Budapest. Small groups operated by attacking Soviet tanks, throwing **Molotov cocktails** (petrol bombs) and placing upturned soup plates on the road to resemble mines. They also overturned trams and tore up paving stones. Their advantage was that the Uprising had no leaders that could be easily arrested; it was not organised, instead it was spontaneous.

The government appealed to workers to resume working. But when peace was descending on the city, a peaceful demonstration was fired on and about twenty people were killed.

SOURCE 5 – Western broadcasts

'The various statements that the Western radios broadcasted ceaselessly to the Hungarian people exercised considerable influence in Hungary.... For the people of little Hungary, the news that the United Nations might take up their case was a powerful stimulant. The tide of revolutionary sentiment rose again. Most Hungarians were, in any case, suffering from nostalgia for the West ... They also had vague aspirations for liberty, for a better life.'

T Meray, Thirteen Days That Shook the Kremlin

SOURCE 6 – Radio reports

'From abroad, by radio, came word that the United States, Great Britain, and France had formally requested a meeting of the United Nations Security Council to take action on "foreign military intervention" in Hungary. But from Radio Moscow came the charge that the rebellion was incited and financed by the United States and other Western powers.'

T Meray, Thirteen Days That Shook the Kremlin

Timeline of Hungarian Uprising 1956

Demonstrations in Budapest. AVH (security police) fired on crowd.

Soviet troops withdrew from Budapest. Nagy formed a coalition government.

New Soviet troops invaded Hungary; Uprising crushed. New Communist government formed by Janos Kadar. Nagy arrested some days later; tried and executed in 1958.

23 Oct   24 Oct   30 Oct   1 Nov   4 Nov

Soviet tanks entered Budapest. Nagy appointed Prime Minister of Hungary. Fighting continued for the next seven days.

Nagy sought withdrawal of Soviet troops from Hungary. He repudiated the Warsaw Pact Treaty.

The Uprising spreads

The Hungarians grew in confidence and the Uprising spread to other parts of Hungary. Workers took over buildings and set up revolutionary councils. Free elections were held in villages and towns. Hungarian soldiers defected to the workers. The worst incident was at Magyarovar where the **AVH** (the security police) fired on a crowd, killing eighty-seven people. News of the massacre led to renewed attacks on the AVH.

Soviet withdrawal

But by Sunday, 28 October, Soviet troops had taken over the city and quelled most of the insurrections. Nagy ordered a cease-fire, said a new national police would be formed and the emblem of **Kossuth** would replace the Soviet Star in the national flag. But disturbances and strikes continued in the provinces and demands were made for the removal of Soviet troops from Hungary. The Catholic primate, **Cardinal Mindszenty**, was released from prison.

On 30 October, Khrushchev and the Soviet government agreed to **withdraw** their troops from Budapest and to engage in negotiations concerning the presence of Soviet troops in Hungary. They insisted, however, that Hungary must not endanger the socialist gains.

Reforms

On the same day that the Soviet Union agreed to withdraw troops from Budapest, Nagy announced a **series of reforms**:
- He abolished the one-party system.
- He formed a coalition government.

Former **political parties** were re-established – the Social Democrats, the Smallholders Party and the National Peasants Party – and became part of the new government, along with the Communists.

Nagy next sought the **total withdrawal of Soviet troops** from Hungary. He planned to leave the Warsaw Pact and to remain **neutral** between East and West.

Source 7 – The Moscow Declaration, 30 October 1956

'... Being of the opinion that the continued presence of Soviet units in Hungary could be used as a pretext for further aggravating the situation, the Soviet Government had now given instructions to its military commanders to withdraw their troops from the city of Budapest as soon as the Hungarian government feels they can be dispensed with.

At the same time, the Soviet government is prepared to engage in negotiations with the Hungarian People's government and the other signatories of the Warsaw Pact regarding the question of the presence of Soviet troops elsewhere in the territory of Hungary....'

T Meray, *Thirteen Days That Shook the Kremlin*

Source 8 – The attitude of the other people's democracies

'These testimonials of friendship (from Gomulka, Poland and Tito, Yugoslavia) were even more satisfying to Nagy because of the attitude [of] the other people's democracies – by Romania, Czechoslovakia, Bulgaria and East Germany – where the events in Hungary were met with open hostility. That this hostility should exist was, of course, easily understandable. The Czech, Romanian, Bulgarian and East German counterparts of Rakosi and of Gero were far from sure of their own popularity.'

T Meray, *Thirteen Days That Shook the Kremlin*

Source 9 – The Suez affair

'The Soviet leaders ... [took] advantage of the confusion created by the Suez affair, which had distracted attention from Hungary in the General Assembly [of the United Nations] ... Then, too, the Suez affair had divided the West: the French and British favoured pressing their intervention; the United States was for a peaceful settlement.'

T Meray, *Thirteen Days That Shook the Kremlin*

SOVIET INVASION

This was a step too far for **Khrushchev** and the Russian leadership. They were afraid that if Hungary left the Warsaw Pact, it would join the Western Alliance. On 4 November, he ordered Soviet troops to invade Hungary and to take over Budapest. The Soviet troops believed they were fighting **Fascists**, **landlords** and **capitalists**. Over the next six or seven days, the Soviet army crushed any resistance, even though Hungarian rebels resisted street-by-street. Many were imprisoned, some were killed.

When the Soviet army invaded, **Nagy** sought asylum in the Yugoslav Embassy and **Kadar** was imposed as leader of a new Communist government. Nagy left the Yugoslav Embassy twenty days later with guarantees of his freedom from the Kadar government. But this was a trick. No sooner had he left the protection of the Embassy than he, his family and friends were arrested. He was taken to Romania. Later he was brought back, tried for treason and executed in June 1958.

CONCLUSION

- Hungary suffered during the Uprising. Apart from the destruction, estimates vary on the numbers killed and injured. It is likely that 2,000 Hungarians were executed, more than 2,000 others killed and about 13,000 injured. Over 15,000 were jailed, thousands more were sent to Soviet forced labour camps and about 200,000 escaped to the West. Many of these were from the educated classes.

- The Soviet government had established control over one of its satellite states. In the process it showed that in spite of deStalinisation, there was a limit to the freedom which the Soviet Union would allow its satellite states.

- A new Communist government led by Janos Kadar was established which followed the Soviet position in foreign affairs. In internal politics, it allowed some measure of freedom and the standard of living improved.

- The western countries protested to the Soviet Union over its actions, but did little else. They believed that Hungary was in the Soviet sphere of influence (countries under direct or indirect Soviet control). They requested a meeting of the Security Council of the United Nations, but any action was blocked by the veto of the Soviet Union. At the same time, British, French and Israeli troops invaded the Suez Canal. This infuriated the Americans and it allowed the Soviet Union to invade Hungary while the western countries were distracted and disagreeing.

> **SOURCE 14 – A historian's view**
>
> 'The lesson for everyone was clear, the new Soviet leaders ... had acted as Stalin would have acted: loss of Party and international face took second place to Soviet security needs.'
>
> **M McCauley, *The Soviet Union Since 1917***

> **SOURCE 15 – A historian's view**
>
> 'The spectacle of the Red Army oppressing a genuine people's revolt against oppression caused yet another shock to the Communist world. There were more defections from Communist parties.'
>
> **J N Westwood, *Endurance and Endeavour: Russian History 1812–1971***

CASE STUDY QUESTIONS

COMPREHENSION

1. According to Source 1, what did the crowds do to the Hungarian flags and who did they blame for all the ills of Hungary?

2. In Source 2, who asked for help from Soviet troops?

3. Whose statue was knocked down in Budapest?

4. What gave the Hungarian people encouragement in Source 5?

5. Who requested a meeting of the UN Security Council?

6. What caused the Uprising according to Radio Moscow?

7. In Source 7, what action did the Soviet Government take?

8. What was it also prepared to do?

9. In Source 8, what countries in Eastern Europe were opposed to the Hungarian Uprising?

10. What leaders gave testimonials of friendship to Nagy?

11. In Source 9, what event distracted attention from Hungary at the United Nations?

12. What does the *Daily Mail* call the Soviet invasion of Hungary (Source 10)?

13. In Source 11, what actions did the Soviet troops take when they invaded?

14. What ludicrous lie did the puppet government put out about the Uprising?

15. What weapons did the Hungarians use against the tanks?

16. What are the Hungarian people doing, according to Nagy in Source 13?

17. In Source 15, who was shocked by the spectacle of the Red Army 'oppressing a genuine people's revolt'?

COMPARISON

1. What are the differences between Source 1 and Source 2 in their attitude to the Uprising?

2. Do you think that the evidence in Sources 1 and 3 supports the view that the Soviet troops were needed to restore order?

3. In Sources 5 and 6, how do the views of the Western broadcasts and the Western governments differ from those of Radio Moscow?

4. How does the attitude of the Soviet government in Source 7 differ from the attitudes of most of the leaders of the people's democracies in Eastern Europe (Source 8)?

5. Compare Sources 11 and 12. Are the attitudes of the Hungarian rebels the same in both sources?

6. Does Nagy's view in Source 13 agree with the historian's view in Source 14?

CRITICISM

1. Are both Source 1 and Source 2 biased?

2. What aspects of the Hungarian Uprising do Sources 3 and 4 help us understand?

3. Why does the author use the words **little Hungary** in Source 5?

4. How do Sources 5 and 6 help us understand the role of radio in propaganda?

5. Is the author trying to give a balanced report of the attitude of the people's democracies in Source 8?

6. Apart from the main headline, how does the *Daily Mail* show it is biased against the Soviet invasion of Hungary (Source 10)? What does this tell us about the reliability of newspapers as historical sources?

7. Give examples from Source 11 to show that the journalist favoured the Hungarian rebels.

8. Does the evidence in the Sources or in the report of the Hungarian Uprising support McCauley's view in Source 14 that 'loss of Party and international face took second place to Soviet security needs'?

9. Does the evidence in the Sources support Westwood's view in Source 15 that this was 'a genuine people's revolt against oppression'?

CONTEXTUALISATION

1. Why and how did Stalin impose Communist governments on the countries of Eastern Europe after the Second World War?

2. Write an account of Communism in Hungary in the decade after the Second World War.

3. Write an account of the career of Imre Nagy.

4. Using the account above and the sources, write a report on the Hungarian Uprising – causes, progress and results.

Continuation of Peaceful Co-existence

The West did not intervene in either Poland or Hungary. They believed those countries were in Russia's sphere of influence. This helped maintain the thaw in the Cold War. Over the next few years, Khrushchev made visits to many countries, including America, where his friendly personality made him popular. Nevertheless, there was **competition** between both sides over the numbers of heavy bombers, missiles and the Space Race. Then, tensions heightened again when an American **U-2 spyplane** was shot down over Russia in 1960. This led to the failure of a summit conference of the leaders in **Paris**. But a more serious cause of conflict arose over **Berlin** once again.

Berlin – Centre of Conflict

West Berlin and West Germany prospered during the 1950s. This prosperity attracted a constant stream of **immigration** from East Berlin into the West where there was a strong demand for labour. Between 1949 and 1961, 2·8 million people crossed to the West. This had a serious effect on the East German economy since many of these people were skilled workers and their families.

Soviet leader Nikita Khrushchev offering the hand to President John F Kennedy when they met in Vienna, Austria in 1961

Khrushchev decided to act when a new young President, **John F Kennedy**, was elected in America. They met in Vienna and Khrushchev demanded that the US withdraw from Berlin. He shouted at Kennedy, '*I want peace, but if you want war that is your problem.*' He gave America an **ultimatum** of six months for the withdrawal. Kennedy responded by increasing military spending and calling up reserves. He said, '*We seek peace, but we shall not surrender.*'

BUILDING THE BERLIN WALL

Khrushchev backed down. Instead the Soviet Union and East Germany went ahead with plans to cut off East Berlin from West Berlin in August 1961. They first built a **barbed wire fence** and then a **wall**. Watchtowers, machine gun posts and checkpoints marked the border between East and West. Since the Soviet Union did not interfere with West Berlin and the routes to West Germany, the western countries only protested but took no other action. West Berliners now had to have special permits to visit relations, and anyone caught escaping from the East to the West was shot.

A young woman, accompanied by her boyfriend, stands dangerously near the top of the Berlin Wall to talk to her mother on the East Berlin side.

Even though the wall **eased tension** by stopping the flow of migrants, serious incidents were likely to happen. Soon after the barbed wire was erected a dispute arose over passports. American and Soviet tanks faced each other across the dividing line. NATO was put on alert. After sixteen hours both sides backed down rather than **spark** a nuclear war.

Berlin became a **symbol** of Cold War divisions. When he visited there in June 1963, President Kennedy made the western viewpoint clear.

'There are many people in the world who really don't understand, or say they don't, what is the great issue between the free world and the Communist world. Let them come to Berlin. There are some who say that Communism is the way of the future. Let them come to Berlin. And there are some who say in Europe and elsewhere we can work with the Communists. Let them come to Berlin.'

SAM SITE
BAHIA HONDA, CUBA
23 OCTOBER 1962

NET COVERED LAUNCHERS

CANVAS COVERED MISSILE TRAIL IN HOLD REVETMENT

BULLDOZER BURYING TANK IN REVETMENT WALL

CANVAS COVERED FRUIT SET SURROUNDED BY VERTICAL NETTING

VEHICLE REPAIR RAMP

CANVAS COVERED MISSILE TRAILERS

An aerial reconnaissance photograph in October 1962 showing a surface-to-air missile site in Cuba during the Cuban Missile Crisis. The captions were added by US intelligence.

End of Peaceful Co-existence

Tensions between East and West were heightened by the incidents over the U-2 plane and the Berlin Wall and they brought peaceful co-existence to an end. This was emphasised by the **Cuban Missile Crisis** which brought the world to the brink of nuclear war again. But this time the crisis was so real that both sides realised something had to be done to control the nuclear arms race:

- A **hotline** was installed between Washington and Moscow to allow direct contact between the US and Soviet leaders.
- A Nuclear Test Ban Treaty was signed which confined testing of nuclear weapons to **underground**.

Background to Détente

During the 1960s, there was still a continual build-up of nuclear weapons. Heavy bombers, missiles or submarines could deliver nuclear bombs. Americans and Russians believed in a **policy of deterrence** – that a huge nuclear arsenal was necessary to deter (stop) the other side from attacking. But both sides also realised that the nuclear weapons which they held to deter each other would destroy the world if they went to war. This would result in **Mutually Assured Destruction (MAD)**.

The horror of a nuclear war with no winner also led to the growth of strong opposition in western countries. In Britain the **Campaign for Nuclear Disarmament** (CND) organised protests outside air bases and nuclear research centres. Protests were also organised by similar groups in continental countries.

> **KEY CONCEPT: NUCLEAR DETERRENCE.**
> This was the view that countries needed powerful nuclear weapons to deter (stop/frighten) other countries from attacking them. It resulted in an arms race to always keep ahead of the enemy.

De Gaulle's Independent Policy

Other events in the 1960s also had an impact on the Cold War. France, led by **President de Gaulle**, wanted to follow an independent foreign policy and to back this up with nuclear power. This led to a dispute with America and a (temporary) withdrawal of France from NATO.

Ostpolitik

Of greater importance was the development of **Ostpolitik** (Eastern Policy) by **Willy Brandt**, foreign minister and later Chancellor of West Germany. He wanted to improve relations with Eastern Europe because he realised that Germany would become the battleground of any future war. As part of this policy, Germany recognised Romania, renounced nuclear weapons, recognised the **borders with Poland** and signed a **non-aggression pact** with the Soviet Union. Eventually in 1972 Brandt signed a treaty of mutual recognition with East Germany.

West German Chancellor Willy Brandt welcoming Soviet leader Leonid Brezhnev to Bonn in May 1973. Brezhnev came on a five-day peace and trade mission which indicated the success of Brandt's Ostpolitik (Eastern Policy) of trying to improve relations with Eastern Europe.

Brandt's Ostpolitik led to a **relaxation of border controls** in Berlin and the city virtually disappeared from the list of Cold War trouble spots. In recognition of the way in which Ostpolitik had improved relations, in May 1973 the Soviet leader, **Leonid Brezhnev**, became the first such leader to visit Bonn, the capital of West Germany.

Reform Movements in Eastern Europe

Reform and Invasion in Czechoslovakia

But US-Soviet relations were stalled again by the Soviet invasion of Czechoslovakia in 1968. The year before, **Alexander Dubcek** replaced the hardline Communist leader of Czechoslovakia. Dubcek wanted *'socialism with a human face'* – more freedom, less censorship and less security police. He was a committed Communist and he assured Brezhnev he did not intend to pull out of the Warsaw Pact.

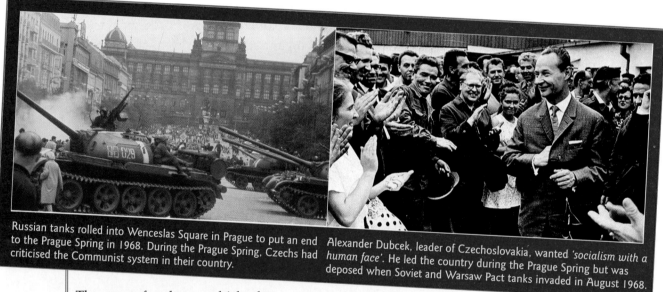

Russian tanks rolled into Wenceslas Square in Prague to put an end to the Prague Spring in 1968. During the Prague Spring, Czechs had criticised the Communist system in their country.

Alexander Dubcek, leader of Czechoslovakia, wanted *'socialism with a human face'*. He led the country during the Prague Spring but was deposed when Soviet and Warsaw Pact tanks invaded in August 1968.

The new freedoms which the Czechs enjoyed in the so-called **Prague Spring** of 1968 led to strong criticism of the Communist leadership for the way they had developed the country. The Soviet Union feared that these criticisms would lead to Communism collapsing in the country. They were concerned about the status of Czechoslovakia because of its central location in Europe and its strong industry. They tried to force Dubcek to call a halt to the freedoms. In this they were backed by the other Warsaw Pact countries who feared that these freedoms would spread to their countries.

To everybody's surprise, **Soviet and Warsaw Pact tanks** moved into Czechoslovakia in August 1968 and deposed Dubcek. Crowds protested in Prague; some threw petrol bombs and others argued with the Russian tank drivers. But overall, the Czechs put up little resistance. The experiment of socialism with a human face was stopped. Once again a country which seemed to be drifting away from a Soviet-style one-party system was crushed. This ended the possibility of liberal reform of the Communist system. The Soviet Union used the so-called **Brezhnev Doctrine** to justify their invasion - that the Soviet Union had the right to intervene in any eastern European country where Communism was under threat.

Détente

In spite of the invasion of Czechoslovakia, many factors now favoured a **policy of détente** – a relaxation of tension between the two sides. This was a policy mostly associated with **Brezhnev**, who succeeded Khrushchev as leader of the Soviet Union. One of the main factors was the danger posed by the **arms race**. Fortunately, as Brezhnev was changing Soviet policy, the election of **Richard Nixon** as President of America in 1969 heralded a new American policy.

> **KEY CONCEPT: DÉTENTE.** This was the easing, or relaxation, of tension between countries. It also involved greater co-operation in trade and cultural matters to improve relations and understanding.

This policy meant the **abandonment** of the Truman Doctrine of committing the US to defend freedom anywhere in the world. The costs of America's involvement in the **Vietnam War** were too great in men and money. Instead Nixon took up **peaceful co-existence**. Nixon said that *'after a period of confrontation, we are entering an era of negotiation.'* He said the greatest honour history could bestow on him was *'the title peacemaker'*.

Détente led to an immediate improvement in **US-Soviet relations**. Nixon visited Moscow on two occasions, while Brezhnev came to Washington once. Gradually Nixon pulled America out of Vietnam, made peace with Communist China, concluded the **Strategic Arms Limitation Treaty** (SALT) in 1972 which limited nuclear missiles and he made a trade agreement with the USSR.

THE HELSINKI ACCORDS

The Helsinki Accords of 1975 were the high point of détente. America, Russia and thirty-three other countries agreed at the **Conference on Security and Co-operation in Europe**:

- to recognise existing borders in Europe,
- to promote trade and cultural links between states, and
- to guarantee the free movement of people (human rights).

It seemed as if agreement had been reached on some of the key issues which divided East and West.

DÉTENTE BREAKS DOWN – FREEZE

However, détente broke down in the late 1970s. The US, led by **President Jimmy Carter,** supported human rights groups in the Soviet Union and Eastern Europe demanding greater freedoms. In Czechoslovakia a human rights group issued **Charter 77**; in the Soviet Union **Sakharov** (a nuclear scientist) and **Solzhenitsyn** (a poet and writer) protested about human rights abuses in their country, but human rights activists there were sent to **labour camps**. America also supported the **refusniks**, Jews in Russia, who wanted to be able to move to Israel. US support for the various **dissident groups** angered the Russians who saw it as interfering in their country.

In turn, the Soviet Union introduced new missiles in Eastern Europe which were aimed at Western European cities. This led to the introduction of more modern US missiles in these countries. The Soviet Union looked on the American missiles as an escalation of the arms race.

INVASION OF AFGHANISTAN

However, the biggest blow to détente and US-Soviet relations was the **Soviet invasion of Afghanistan** in 1979. The Soviet Union invaded the country to depose the existing Communist ruler and install one more favourable to Moscow.

The burnt-out remains of a Soviet convoy of fuel tankers after an ambush by Afghan rebels when the Soviet Union invaded Afghanistan in 1979 to install a Communist ruler more favourable to Moscow.

The Americans protested; they feared that the USSR wanted to move further south to control the oil states in the Persian Gulf. **President Carter** called the invasion *'the most serious threat to peace since the Second World War.'* America dropped its support for more talks on arms limitation and increased military spending. Détente had ended.

But even though this led to a severe crisis in relations between the US and the USSR, European countries, such as Britain, France and West Germany continued to maintain good relations with the USSR. They even participated in the **Olympic Games** in Moscow in 1980, in spite of an American-organised boycott.

When **Ronald Reagan** became President of the US in 1980 the freeze in relations continued. Reagan believed the Soviet Union was the *'evil empire'*. He expanded US nuclear forces and, in 1983, he announced the **Strategic Defence Initiative** (SDI) – popularly called Star Wars – a plan to use satellites to shoot down Soviet missiles.

Reform Movements in Eastern Europe

REFORM IN POLAND: SOLIDARITY

Relations deteriorated further due to events in Poland. During the years of Communist rule, workers had regularly protested over wages and food prices. The Communist government usually gave in to the workers' demands. But the Polish economy ran into serious trouble by the late 1970s. There were **shortages** of food and consumer goods. At the same time a Polish cardinal was elected **Pope John Paul II** and he made a return visit to Poland in June 1975. His visit, during which a quarter of the Polish people saw him, raised **expectations** and **self-confidence** in Poland.

Solidarity Formed

When the Communist government raised meat prices by 100 per cent in 1980, this led to strikes and factory stoppages. The great Lenin shipyard in Gdansk was the centre of the dispute. Here **Lech Walesa**, an electrician, led a strike which encouraged more strikes all over the country. Out of this dispute was formed **Solidarity**, which soon had ten million members. The government gave in to the demands of the Gdansk workers, including the right to form trade unions and the right to strike.

A Solidarity protest banner during a strike in Gdansk in Poland in August 1988, led by the Polish trade union leader Lech Walesa (right).

Pope John Paul II talking to old and handicapped Polish people during his visit to Poland. As a Polish pope, his visit raised the confidence of the Polish people and contributed to the downfall of Communism there.

Solidarity Banned

In 1981, economic conditions worsened in Poland. Solidarity asked for a vote on the Communist Party and on relations with the Soviet Union. **Brezhnev**, the Russian leader, put pressure on the Polish government to act by holding Soviet army manoeuvres on the Polish border. In December 1981, the Polish government, led by **General Jaruzelski**, proclaimed martial law and rounded up 10,000 Solidarity members, including Lech Walesa. The rights which Solidarity won in 1981 were rolled back – the free press was closed down, a curfew was imposed and Solidarity was banned.

But Jaruzelski failed to improve economic conditions. Instead he attacked the Catholic Church. The Polish situation worsened when the US and Western European countries imposed trade sanctions on Poland. The old mistrust and suspicion had returned.

Victory for Solidarity

Solidarity regrouped and operated openly. **Lech Walesa** was consulted by foreign governments on whether they should lift the trade sanctions. Further opposition rallied around the Catholic Church. When Solidarity threatened to call a nationwide strike against price rises in 1986, the government backed down. Two years later, the government agreed to lift the ban on Solidarity and to allow other political parties and free elections. In 1989, Solidarity had a major electoral victory which resulted in the **first non-Communist Prime Minister** in Eastern Europe. In 1990,

Solidarity had even greater success when **Walesa** became President of Poland. But by this time events in Poland were overtaken by reform in the Soviet Union itself.

KEY PERSONALITY: MIKHAIL GORBACHEV

Mikhail Gorbachev was born into a farming family in 1931. After studying law in Moscow, he worked his way up the Communist Party. He was known as an enemy of corruption and inefficiency.

As soon as he achieved power in 1985, he began reforming the Soviet Union with **glasnost** (openness) and **perestroika** (reconstruction). To ensure his reforms were a success, he needed to reduce military spending. This could only be done if the **arms race** with the West was ended. He had his greatest success in foreign policy where he convinced the Americans that he genuinely wanted to disarm the missiles and reduce the armies. He also wanted to allow greater freedom to the countries of the Warsaw Pact. This led to the downfall of Communism in these countries in 1989.

But Gorbachev was less successful in Russia. His economic reforms did not lead to improved conditions. He was criticised by conservative Communists and also by those who wanted him to speed up his reforms. But he had begun a process which he could not stop. He said, *'I'm doomed to go forward, and only forward. And if I retreat, I myself will perish and the cause will perish too!'*

The conservatives attempted a **coup** in August 1991 which failed. But it undermined his power. He was eventually forced to resign as President of the Soviet Union when it broke up into independent republics.

KEY CONCEPT: GLASNOST. This was the Russian word used by Gorbachev to describe more discussion, more openness in dealing with the problems facing the Soviet Union. Gorbachev linked glasnost with perestroika (restructuring or reform of the Soviet economy and the Communist Party) so that the Soviet Union would be improved. Glasnost ended the Cold War, but it also brought down the Soviet Union. Perestroika failed to reform the Soviet economy.

Reform in the Soviet Union

Mikhail Gorbachev became leader of the Soviet Union in 1985. He began a process of reform which brought an end to the Cold War and to the Soviet Union. He was known as a *'man with a nice smile but iron teeth'*.

REASONS FOR REFORM

By the mid-1980s, the Soviet economy was in difficulty. The arms race was too expensive, the country was fighting a costly war in Afghanistan, there was widespread corruption and the Communist system of production was inefficient. Russia also experienced high levels of alcoholism. Gorbachev knew that the Soviet system needed major reform if it was to survive. Gorbachev based his reform on **glasnost** (openness) and **perestroika** (reconstruction). He hoped that with greater discussion and economic reforms the Russian economy would improve. The key to reform was cutting military spending.

IMPROVED US-SOVIET RELATIONS

In order to reduce military spending Gorbachev needed to improve relations with the US and thereby ease Cold War tensions. *'The time is ripe,'* he said, *'for abandoning views on foreign policy which are influenced by an imperial standpoint. Neither the Soviet Union nor the US is able to force its will on others.'* He believed that *'adversaries must become partners'*.

Gorbachev met **President Reagan** in **Geneva** in November 1985. They got on well together and agreed that they would work towards cutting nuclear arsenals by half. They agreed that *'a nuclear war cannot be won and must not be fought.'* But the West was wary of Soviet propaganda while the Soviet Union feared SDI (Star Wars). Nevertheless, the two leaders made great progress when they met again in **Reykjavik** in October 1986. However, they failed to come to a final agreement because the Soviet Union insisted on America dropping SDI, which America felt was essential for its own security.

However, some progress was made a year later when they agreed to get rid of their **missiles in Europe** (Zero Option). Further progress was made when **President Reagan** visited Moscow in May 1988 and spoke with students at Moscow University. Then Gorbachev spoke at the **United Nations** in New York. He renounced war, rescinded the Brezhnev Doctrine, cut the Soviet army and said Communism was no longer relevant to the modern world.

The momentum towards peace continued in December 1989 when Gorbachev met the next American President, **George Bush**. They met on board ships off the coast of **Malta**. In spite of stormy weather, the two leaders had a wide-ranging discussion on economic and political problems that divided them. They developed a new spirit of co-operation and understanding. At the end, one Russian spokesman said, *'We buried the Cold War at the bottom of the Mediterranean Sea.'*

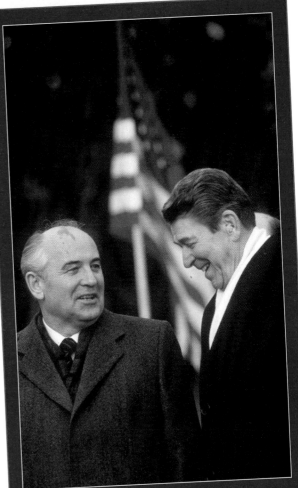

Gorbachev, leader of the Soviet Union, with the US President Reagan. They met a number of times and came to agreement on arms reduction in Europe.

Shortly after, Gorbachev lifted his objection to SDI. Also, by this time, the Americans could not afford the cost of SDI. So in 1991 **President Bush** and **President Gorbachev** signed the **START** Treaty. They agreed to cut missiles, and the US later stood down the 24-hour strategic alert status of the US Air Force. The Soviet Union was no longer considered a military threat. The Cold War was coming to an end.

Reform and the Collapse of Communism in Eastern Europe

In Eastern Europe, glasnost offered *'the right of every nation to choose its own path.'* In 1989 the Soviet Union said it *'could imagine no occasion in which Soviet troops might intervene in a Warsaw Pact country.'* Since the Warsaw Pact countries were held together by Soviet force, once that force was gone, Communism in Eastern Europe collapsed over the following six months.

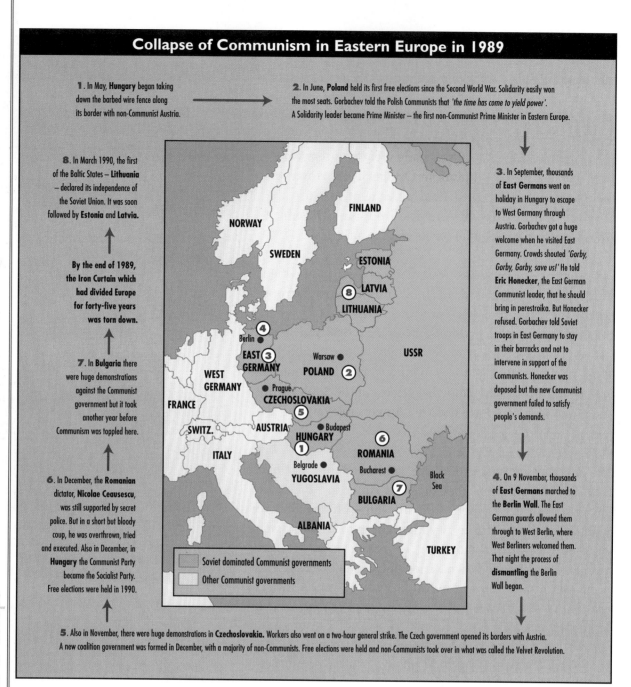

Collapse of Communism in Eastern Europe in 1989

1. In May, **Hungary** began taking down the barbed wire fence along its border with non-Communist Austria.

2. In June, **Poland** held its first free elections since the Second World War. Solidarity easily won the most seats. Gorbachev told the Polish Communists that *'the time has come to yield power'*. A Solidarity leader became Prime Minister – the first non-Communist Prime Minister in Eastern Europe.

8. In March 1990, the first of the Baltic States – **Lithuania** – declared its independence of the Soviet Union. It was soon followed by **Estonia** and **Latvia**.

By the end of 1989, the Iron Curtain which had divided Europe for forty-five years was torn down.

7. In **Bulgaria** there were huge demonstrations against the Communist government but it took another year before Communism was toppled here.

6. In December, the **Romanian** dictator, **Nicolae Ceausescu**, was still supported by secret police. But in a short but bloody coup, he was overthrown, tried and executed. Also in December, in **Hungary** the Communist Party became the Socialist Party. Free elections were held in 1990.

3. In September, thousands of **East Germans** went on holiday in Hungary to escape to West Germany through Austria. Gorbachev got a huge welcome when he visited East Germany. Crowds shouted *'Gorby, Gorby, Gorby, save us!'* He told **Eric Honecker**, the East German Communist leader, that he should bring in perestroika. But Honecker refused. Gorbachev told Soviet troops in East Germany to stay in their barracks and not to intervene in support of the Communists. Honecker was deposed but the new Communist government failed to satisfy people's demands.

4. On 9 November, thousands of **East Germans** marched to the **Berlin Wall**. The East German guards allowed them through to West Berlin, where West Berliners welcomed them. That night the process of **dismantling** the Berlin Wall began.

Map labels: NORWAY, SWEDEN, FINLAND, ESTONIA, LATVIA, LITHUANIA, Berlin, EAST GERMANY, Warsaw, POLAND, USSR, WEST GERMANY, FRANCE, Prague, CZECHOSLOVAKIA, SWITZ., AUSTRIA, HUNGARY, Budapest, ITALY, Belgrade, YUGOSLAVIA, ROMANIA, Bucharest, Black Sea, BULGARIA, ALBANIA, TURKEY

Legend:
- Soviet dominated Communist governments
- Other Communist governments

5. Also in November, there were huge demonstrations in **Czechoslovakia**. Workers also went on a two-hour general strike. The Czech government opened its borders with Austria. A new coalition government was formed in December, with a majority of non-Communists. Free elections were held and non-Communists took over in what was called the Velvet Revolution.

Fragmentation and Realignment in Europe

THE REUNIFICATION OF GERMANY

The opening of the Hungarian border and the fall of the Berlin Wall resulted in thousands of East Germans fleeing to the West. At the same time, huge crowds gathered in Berlin to demonstrate for German unity. The East German Communist Party tried to keep in control of the situation. They got rid of their leader, **Honecker**, and agreed to some reforms.

Outside Germany there was some concern about German unification. Other European leaders such as **Margaret Thatcher**, Prime Minister of Britain, feared the strength of a unified Germany.

Gorbachev also feared that a unified Germany would demand the revision of the borders which were established at the end of the Second World War when Germany lost land and Russia gained land.

However, **Helmut Kohl**, Chancellor of West Germany, gave guarantees about the borders with Poland, promised to limit the size of the German army, and to pay for the movement of Soviet troops back to Russia. There was also agreement between NATO and the Warsaw Pact about the size of their armed forces in Europe. In September, the four allied powers of the Second World War – the US, Britain, France and the USSR – agreed to end the occupation of Germany. Less than a week later, in October, 1990, **Germany was reunited**.

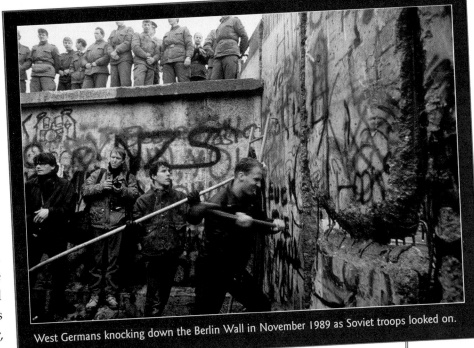
West Germans knocking down the Berlin Wall in November 1989 as Soviet troops looked on.

For many people this was the **end** of the Cold War. On 21 November 1990 the Conference for European Security and Co-operation declared the Cold War over. The once powerful Soviet empire in Eastern Europe was broken into separate countries which replaced their Communist systems with more capitalist and democratic systems.

THE COLLAPSE OF THE SOVIET UNION

The Downfall of Communism in the USSR

In the meantime, reforms made progress in the Soviet Union. In 1989, Gorbachev became President of the USSR and other political parties were allowed.

By now Gorbachev was attacked from both the **left** (reformers) and the **right** (conservatives). The right said that Gorbachev had gone too far with his reforms. The left (led By **Boris Yeltsin**) said he should speed up reforms and move more quickly towards democracy and a free market (capitalist) economy.

Slowly Gorbachev **lost control** of the situation. In February 1991 Yeltsin criticised Gorbachev at a huge demonstration in Moscow. Gorbachev brought out the troops but he was forced to back down. Further trouble occurred when **miners** in the Ukraine went on strike. When Yeltsin talked them back to work, conservatives in the Communist Party said Gorbachev should resign.

Gorbachev called a **conference of the Soviet republics**. Conservatives insisted on maintaining the Union of the Soviet Socialist Republics as they were. But Yeltsin, as leader of the Russian Republic, already supported the demand for independence from the Baltic States – Latvia, Estonia and Lithuania. Gorbachev got agreement on the **Union Treaty** which gave greater independence to the republics while still retaining a union of republics.

Attempted Coup

But when Gorbachev went on holiday to the **Crimea**, the conservatives organised a revolt. They placed Gorbachev under **house arrest** and announced that he was sick. They declared a state of emergency and tanks moved into Moscow. But Yeltsin took over control of the Russian Parliament Building and called on people to support him. He got huge support in Moscow – people did not want to return to the past.

The coup was badly organised. Gorbachev was soon back in power, but the power was largely in the hands of Yeltsin. The attempted coup actually led to the **collapse of the Soviet Union**. The Union Treaty was never voted on. Instead Russia and ten other republics formed the **CIS** (Commonwealth of Independent States) in December 1991 to replace the Soviet Union. Shortly afterwards, all the republics went their separate ways as **independent countries**. The Soviet Union was now fragmented; fifteen countries replaced one country.

Gorbachev's position as President of the Soviet Union did not exist anymore. Yeltsin as President of the Russian Republic held all the power. Communism was gone and so was the Soviet Union.

A pro-Yeltsin demonstration in Moscow in 1991 in opposition to Gorbachev. Yeltsin called for Gorbachev's resignation.

New Borders of European Countries

1. Czech Republic
2. Slovakia
3. Georgia
4. Armenia
5. Azerbaijan

The Effects of the Cold War

- The Cold War had **dominated** European and world affairs for forty-five years, since the end of the Second World War.
- It had resulted in **huge spending** – approximately $8 trillion – on nuclear missiles, tanks and planes. These were now dismantled or scrapped.
- Most of the military spending could have been used instead to improve **social conditions** in the West and in the USSR.
- The Cold War resulted in a number of **local wars** – Korea, Vietnam and Afghanistan – outside Europe; and **uprisings** in Poland, Hungary and Czechoslovakia. These resulted in millions dying in the wars, and thousands in the uprisings.
- The US claimed **victory** in the Cold War. It had contributed to the downfall of Communism in the Soviet Union and it left the US as the sole remaining superpower.

ORDINARY LEVEL

1. Study the cartoon below and answer the questions that follow.

(i) **'No admittance by order of Joe'**. Who is the **Joe** referred to here?

(ii) What do you understand by the term **Iron Curtain**?

(iii) What impression is given of life on the Russian side of the wall?

(iv) Who is trying to *'peep under the curtain'* and why?

(Department of Education, Sample Paper)

2. Study the extracts/quotations from Stalin and Churchill (below) and answer the following questions.

   Stalin:

   'The Germans were able to make their invasion through these countries because, at the time, governments hostile to the Soviet Union existed in these countries. What can there be surprising about the fact that the Soviet Union, anxious for its future safety, is trying to see to it that governments loyal in their attitude to the Soviet Union should exist in these counties?'

   Churchill:

   'A shadow has fallen upon the scenes so recently lighted by the Allied victory.... From Stettin in the Baltic to Trieste in the Adriatic, an iron curtain has descended across the continent of Europe. Behind that line lie all the capitals of the ancient states of Central and Eastern Europe, in what I must call the Soviet sphere. The Communist Parties [there].... have been raised to power far beyond their numbers. Police governments are prevailing in nearly every case. This is certainly not the liberated Europe we fought to build up.'

(i) How does Stalin justify/explain why Communist governments were established in Eastern Europe?

(ii) How does Churchill explain Stalin's actions in Eastern Europe?

(iii) Why do Stalin and Churchill give different explanations for what happened?

(iv) How do these extracts help us explain the cartoon above, **A Peep under the Iron Curtain**?

3. Study the cartoons on p. 207 and answer the following questions. Source A is a Soviet cartoon and Source B is British. In A, the documents on the ground state *'Occupation Laws'* and *'Bonn Constitution'*. In B, the caption reads, *'If we don't let him work, who's going to keep him?'*

(i) In Source A, which three countries are represented by the **mother hens**?

(ii) What country and political movement are represented by the **chick**?

(iii) What is the message of Source A?

Source A

Source B

(iv) In Source B, what countries are represented by the three men talking, and by the man tied on the ground?

(v) What is the message of Source B?

(vi) Is each cartoon giving the same message? Are they biased? Explain your answers.

4. Study the quotations from President Truman of the US on pp. 175 and 176 and answer the following questions:

(i) What does Truman mean when he refers to 'an iron fist and strong language'?

(ii) What is the only language Russia will understand, according to Truman?

(iii) What does Truman say is the cause of the rise of dictatorships?

(iv) Who are the 'armed minorities and outside powers' he is referring to?

(v) What help does the US give to resist these forces?

5. Study the map on the Collapse of Communism in Eastern Europe in 1989 (p. 202) and answer the following questions:

(i) Where did the first step in the break-up of Communism in Eastern Europe take place? When?

(ii) Where was the first non-Communist Prime Minister in Eastern Europe elected?

(iii) What did the East German crowds mean when they shouted 'Gorby, Gorby, Gorby save us'?

(iv) What orders did Gorbachev give to Soviet troops stationed in East Germany?

(v) Where was the Velvet Revolution? Why do you think it got that name?

(vi) In what two countries in Eastern Europe did Communism hold out the longest?

(vii) What were the Baltic states? How did they differ from the other countries of Eastern Europe?

6. Write **paragraph answers** on each of the following questions:

(i) The origins of the Cold War.

(ii) How the Truman Doctrine and the Marshall Plan contributed to the Cold War.

(iii) The Berlin Crisis, 1948–9. (Department of Education, Sample Paper)

(iv) The Sovietisation of Eastern Europe.

(v) Military Alliances in Europe after the Second World War.

(vi) Assess the contribution of Imre Nagy to the Hungarian Uprising in 1956.

(vii) Khrushchev and Peaceful Coexistence.

(viii) Reform in, and the invasion of, Czechoslovakia in 1968.

(ix) The Policy of Détente; its successes and failures.

(x) Solidarity and reform in Poland.

(xi) The overall effects of the Cold War in Europe.

7. Write **long answers** on each of the following questions:

(i) How, and why, did the Cold War develop in Europe after the Second World War?

(ii) How did Khrushchev respond to the Hungarian Uprising of 1956? (Department of Education, Sample Paper)

(iii) Write on the contribution of Nikita Khrushchev to developments in the Cold War in Europe.

(iv) How successful were reform movements in the countries of Eastern Europe from the 1960s to the 1980s?

(v) How, and why, did Communism collapse in Eastern Europe in the late 1980s?

(vi) Write on the contribution of Mikhail Gorbachev to developments in the Cold War in Europe.

OR

How did Gorbachev's reforms in the Soviet Union contribute to the downfall of Communism? (Department of Education, Sample Paper) (See also Chapter 12, The Communist Economies – Problems and Outcomes.)

HIGHER LEVEL

1. How, and why, did the Cold War develop in Europe after the Second World War?

OR

Why did a Cold War develop in Europe after 1945?

2. How, and why, did the Soviet Union establish control over Eastern Europe between 1945 and 1949?

3. How, and why, was Germany (East and West) a major centre of conflict during the Cold War?

4. How serious were the crises which faced the USSR in Eastern Europe after 1950?

OR

With reference to at least two countries, show how the Soviet Union dealt with opposition in Eastern Europe in the 1950s and 1960s.

5. Assess the impact of the Cold War on relations between Soviet Russia and the rest of Europe during the period 1945 to 1964 OR 1964 to 1992.

6. *'Between 1945 and 1992, relations between Western and Eastern Europe were dominated by a series of real crises and recurrent tensions.'* Discuss.

7. Assess the contribution of Nikita Khrushchev to developments in the Cold War in Europe.

8. How did the countries of Eastern Europe change during the rule of Gorbachev?

9. Discuss Gorbachev's role in improving relations with the West and in reforming Communism in the USSR.

OR

Assess the contribution of Mikhail Gorbachev to developments in the Cold War in Europe.

10. Why did the Cold War in Europe come to an end?

TEST YOURSELF AT
my-etest.com

10. European Unity

Moves toward European Unity, 1945–57

INTRODUCTION

The Cold War divided Europe in two – East and West. In Eastern Europe, unity was imposed by Soviet domination. In Western Europe, the divided countries began a process of co-operation which eventually led to greater unity. Many factors contributed to the growth of this unity.

Factors Encouraging European Unity

IMPACT OF THE SECOND WORLD WAR

The Second World War devastated Europe. Millions were killed, and cities, transport links and farmlands were destroyed. *'Over wide areas a vast quivering mass of tormented, hungry, care-worn and bewildered human beings gape at the ruins of their cities and homes.'* (Churchill) Many Europeans had already experienced the suffering of the First World War. Both of the wars were caused in Europe so many people began to think that the only way of guaranteeing European peace was through European unity. *'To build Europe is to build peace,'* said Jean Monnet.

The city of Dresden, Germany in 1945 after Allied bombing raids. The destruction of the Second World War led many Europeans to promote European unity to prevent future wars from happening in Europe.

In July 1944 a secret meeting of **Resistance leaders** issued a declaration which summarised the arguments in favour of European unity.

'Federal union alone:
- *can ensure the preservation of liberty and civilisation on the continent of Europe,*
- *bring about economic recovery, and*
- *enable the German people to play a peaceful role in European affairs.'*

CONTROLLING NATIONALISM

In the view of many of the Resistance leaders one of the principal causes of the two world wars was **nationalism** – the desire of nation-states to grow and expand. Some looked on the nation state as having *'the power to decide matters of war and peace, the power to control national armies … the power to create dictatorship'*, to become *'the tools of destruction and suppression.'* It was the belief of many leaders after the war that nationalism needed to be contained and directed towards peace. Instead of conflict, there should be **international co-operation**.

THE PROBLEM OF GERMANY

Even though Germany was defeated and destroyed during the Second World War, it was still a large country with seventy million people and centrally located in Europe. The **Russians** wanted to keep Germany weak so that it would not pose a danger to it in the future.

But the western countries, especially the **US and Britain**, learned from the mistakes of the First World War. They believed that if Germany was punished then Germans would feel a **sense of grievance** which would cause trouble in the future. They also felt that it was necessary to revive the German economy in order to revive Europe. Keeping the German economy weak would, according to British politicians, *'retard [hold back] Europe's economic recovery by reducing the export of essential supplies from Germany.'* Many European leaders now believed that Germany would be more easily controlled as part of a wider European organisation. They believed that bringing **Germany** into a united Europe would prevent a future war.

Support for European unity came from many different countries. But some countries wanted greater unity than others. This poster encouraged Europeans to work together.

THE GROWTH OF SUPERPOWERS

One of the results of the Second World War was the growth of **two superpowers**, the US and the USSR. These were much stronger militarily and economically than European countries. European countries had dominated the world for the previous 500 years. Now their economies were destroyed and they were too weak individually to compete against the superpowers. The only way they could do so was by combining and co-operating. Some believed that Europe could become a **Third Force**, competing with the two superpowers.

THE GROWTH OF COMMUNISM

The USSR posed another problem. It was controlled by **Communism** which now also controlled Eastern Europe. Western Europeans feared that Communism would spread to their countries and deprive them of their property and their freedom. They held the view that Western European countries needed to work together to ensure this would not happen.

ECONOMIC FACTORS

Many Western European countries such as Belgium, Holland and Luxembourg (Benelux) were small, and overall Western Europe was much smaller than the US and the USSR. European industries needed **larger markets** to become more efficient. *'The creation of a large internal market is indispensable to making it possible for Europeans to take their place in the world again.'* (Jean Monnet)

THE AMERICANS AND BRITISH FAVOURED EUROPEAN INTEGRATION

The **American government** wanted to rebuild Europe after the war. This was partly because of their fear of Communism. *'In these conditions freedom and democracy and the independence of nations could not long survive.'* A strong Europe would be a better ally in the fight against Communism. But America also needed a strong **trading partner** and a **customer** of US businesses. The American economy had expanded greatly during the war and the government now feared that the economy would decline if Europe remained poor.

The **British** attitude was different. The British were more interested in seeing the continental countries unite while they themselves maintained their **links** with their Empire (Commonwealth) and the US. Churchill, who had been Prime Minister of Britain during the war, expressed the view. *'We see nothing but good and hope in a richer, freer, more contented European commonality. But we have our own dream and our own task. We are with Europe, but not of it. We are linked ... but not absorbed.'*

ATTITUDES OF INDIVIDUAL COUNTRIES

In many countries after the war, there were groups promoting European unity. In France there was the **French Council for Europe**, in Germany there was the **Europa-Bund** while the **European Union of Federalists** drew members from many countries. The idea of European unity crossed many political boundaries – from Conservatives to Socialists to Christian Democrats, showing how widespread the support was.

Each country had its own reasons for wanting European co-operation and union. In **Germany** there was support for European unity because they felt it was the main way Germany would win back recognition from other countries. In **Italy**, they hoped European unity would help their economy. In **France**, they hoped that Germany would be controlled within a wider organisation. The **Benelux** countries also looked to the economic advantages but, in addition, they believed they needed greater protection because of their small size.

> **KEY CONCEPT: FEDERAL EUROPE.** The idea of a **federal Europe** influenced many of the leaders promoting European unity, such as Jean Monnet. They believed that two world wars had discredited the nation-state. Instead, a federal Europe where power was shared between a central authority and the countries of Europe would work better and provide peace. In the case of the EEC/EU many issues relating to economic and social issues are decided by European institutions. But other areas are controlled by the individual countries. Some leaders, such as Charles de Gaulle of France and Margaret Thatcher of Britain, were opposed to a federal Europe because they saw it as reducing the power of their countries (nation-states).

The Progress of Unity

At the end of the Second World War, those who advocated European unity thought in terms of all the countries of the continent. But within a short time it was clear that Europe was being divided between East and West in the Cold War. This made complete European unity impossible. (See Chapter 9, The Cold War in Europe.)

BENELUX

One of the first steps towards European unity was taken at a local level when Belgium, the Netherlands (Holland) and Luxembourg signed the **Benelux Treaty** in 1947. The three countries abolished **customs duties** (taxes) on trade between themselves and this led to increased prosperity. Ten years later Benelux trade had tripled. Benelux clearly showed the advantages of co-operation and **economic integration** (unity). But it was much easier to combine three countries compared to ambitious plans for a wider European union.

THE ROLE OF AMERICA

But the role of America was crucial in promoting European unity. Soon after the war, **America** was heavily committed to Europe through the **Truman Doctrine** and the **Marshall Plan** (see pp. 175–7). In the case of the Marshall Plan, European countries had to come together to plan the best use of the aid from America. This was done through the **Organisation for European Economic Co-operation** (OEEC) which was set up in April 1948 with sixteen countries. These excluded the countries from behind the Iron Curtain in Eastern Europe who were barred from taking aid by the Soviet Union.

The OEEC was an **international organisation** which had to:
- distribute Marshall aid money,
- help investment between countries,
- encourage the growth of European trade.

Through the workings of the OEEC, European countries could see the practical value of co-operation. It also helped break down opposition to the idea of **integration** (unity).

Konrad Adenauer (left), Chancellor of West Germany, shaking hands with Robert Schuman (right), French Foreign Minister, in 1952. Both politicians played important roles in establishing the European Coal and Steel Community (ECSC), which eventually led to the foundation of the EEC.

CONGRESS OF EUROPE

A further boost to European unity was given by **Winston Churchill's** speech in Zurich in September 1946. He said, *'We must build a kind of United States of Europe.'* This speech led to the **Congress of Europe** at the Hague in May 1948 with over 600 delegates from 16 European democracies. These included leaders who played a prominent part in the formation and development of later European organisations – **Konrad Adenauer** from Germany, **Robert Schuman** from France and **Alcide de Gasperi** from Italy.

The **Hague Congress** recommended that European countries should work for closer economic and political unity, that a European Assembly should be set up to discuss common issues and also a European Court of Human Rights.

COUNCIL OF EUROPE

Arising out of the Hague Congress, the **Council of Europe** was set up in 1949, with a headquarters in Strasbourg. Ten countries in Western Europe formed Western Europe's **first post-war political** organisation. Its aim *'is to achieve a greater unity between its members for the purpose of safeguarding and realising the ideals and principles which are their common heritage and facilitating their economic and social progress.'*

While many advocates of European union wanted to use the Council to further European union, it has **no power to make laws** or **to enforce its decisions**. Even though it was sometimes criticised as a *'talking shop'*, it was the main place to discuss views on further European unity. However, it was soon overtaken by other developments.

EUROPEAN COAL AND STEEL COMMUNITY (ECSC) – UNITY BY SECTORS

The formation of the **European Coal and Steel Community** (ECSC) was the most important step on the road to European unity. Once again the problem was what to do with **Germany**. By 1950, West Germany was well on the way to economic recovery. Even though the Allied governments were still in occupation, a West German government had taken over under Konrad **Adenauer**. In France there was still a fear that once Germany recovered it would attack France.

The Schuman Plan: The idea for a new European organisation was developed by **Jean Monnet** and announced by **Robert Schuman**, the French Foreign Minister. It was accepted by **Adenauer**, Chancellor of West Germany. In what became known as the **Schuman Plan**, Schuman proposed that France and Germany and any other countries in Western Europe should pool their **coal and steel** industries *'under a common High Authority'*. He said that this *'should immediately provide for the setting up of common foundations for economic development as a first step in the federation of Europe'*. He believed that *'Europe will not be made all at once, or according to a single plan. It will be built through concrete achievements which first create a de facto solidarity [unity]. The coming together of the nations of Europe requires the elimination of the age-old opposition of France and Germany.'*

ECSC: These countries were joined by **Italy** and the **Benelux** countries to sign the **Treaty of Paris** (1951) which set up the **European Coal and Steel Community** (ECSC) in 1952. The ECSC was a major step towards European unity because:

This British cartoon believes that the Schuman Plan and the ECSC will have an important influence on Europe. What is the message of the cartoon? Do you think the cartoon favours the Schuman Plan?

- For the first time these countries handed over some of their power to an outside body – the ECSC was a **supranational** organisation.
- Also, the **structures** of the ECSC with a High Authority, a Council of Ministers and a Parliament became the **model** for future European organisations.
- The ECSC was also a **success** in other ways. Steel production increased, and overall industrial production grew twice as fast as Britain.

But **Britain** refused to join because the country did not want to hand over control of an important part of her economy to a European authority.

The European Coal and Steel Community (ECSC) was set up under the Treaty of Paris (1951). The ECSC controlled the operation of steel and coal production in six Western European countries. Here a steel worker is tipping a huge vat of hot slag in a French steel mill (1952).

KEY PERSONALITY: JEAN MONNET

Jean Monnet is sometimes called the **Father of Europe** because of the part he played in working for European unity. He was born in France in 1888 and worked in business, finance and in the French civil service. He believed that *'The countries of Europe are not strong enough individually to be able to guarantee prosperity and social development for their peoples. The States of Europe must therefore form a federation or a European entity that would make them into a common economic unit.'* 'To build Europe', he said, 'is to create peace.'

In 1950 he drew up the **Schuman Plan** for pooling the coal and steel industries of France and Germany. He believed that by linking the industries of the two countries there was less likelihood of war. He presented his plans to **Robert Schuman**, the French Foreign Minister, who welcomed the ideas. Those ideas became the basis of the **European Coal and Steel Community** (ECSC) which was agreed by six countries in the **Treaty of Paris** (1951). A High Authority ran the ECSC, and Jean Monnet was its **first President**.

Monnet was **disappointed** with the failure of the **European Defence Community** (EDC) – a European army – which was rejected by France and Britain. He resigned from the High Authority to promote the idea of European unity. For this purpose, he founded the **Action Committee for the United States of Europe** with representatives of 20 political parties and 10 trade unions. He supported the idea of a **federal Europe** where power is shared between European organisations and individual countries.

Monnet believed that the best way to unite Europe was through a **step-by-step approach**. He also wanted to create **European institutions** rather than depend on governments to do the work. He was often in **conflict** with those whom he believed held up European unity, including the President of France, **Charles de Gaulle**.

The Action Committee for the United States of Europe continued until 1975 when it was disbanded. He was honoured a year later by the European Council when they proclaimed him **Honorary Citizen of Europe**. Three years later, in 1979, Monnet died and, in 1988, his body was later transferred to the Pantheon in Paris.

MILITARY UNITY

North Atlantic Treaty Organisation (NATO)

It was not surprising that some of the first efforts towards unity were **military** because of:

- The fear of Communism spreading from the East, particularly with the Soviet army in East Germany.
- Action by the French and Italian Communist Parties who worked towards establishing Communism in their own countries.
- The Communist takeover in Czechoslovakia in 1948.

Because of these circumstances, France, Britain, Belgium, the Netherlands and Luxembourg signed the **Treaty of Brussels** in March 1948. While the Treaty referred to economic and social matters, its main purpose was **military**. The countries would help each other if any one of them was attacked.

But the threat from the Soviet Union during the **Berlin Blockade** (1948–9) made these countries realise that they would not be able to stand up to the USSR on their own. In 1949 the Americans announced their intention of providing military help to Western Europe. This led to the formation of the **North Atlantic Treaty Organisation** (NATO) in 1949. The US, Canada and ten Western European countries pledged to help each other if attacked.

NATO provided a unified military command for the armies of the organisation. While NATO was not strictly European, it was a **further step** on the road to European unity.

European Defence Community (EDC)

During the Korean War (1950–53), America and Britain wanted to rearm West Germany to face the Soviet threat in Europe. But the French were fearful of **German rearmament**. They proposed the **Pleven Plan** – the formation of a **European Defence Community** within which a rearmed West Germany could be controlled. The European army would be under a single commander with individual army units from different countries, including West Germany. There was also included a plan for a Council of Ministers and European Parliament. This would have been a huge step towards European unity.

The **EDC Treaty** was signed by the six ECSC countries in 1952, but it was rejected by the **British** who did not want to hand over control to an outside body and by the **French parliament** (1954) who were still fearful of German rearmament.

This effort at European unity failed. It was the first serious defeat for those who favoured European unity. It showed that **military and political union** was still not possible. Instead **economic integration** was the best and most practical way towards a political union which was still a long way away.

THE TREATY OF ROME

In 1955, the foreign ministers of the ECSC decided to set up a committee, headed by the Belgian, **Paul-Henri Spaak**, to see what could be done to bring the countries of Europe closer together. The Spaak Report was debated by the six countries who agreed that Europe needed further unity because:

- of the Communist challenge;
- of the economic boom which Europe was experiencing;
- it was encouraged by America.

The **Spaak Report** was a turning point in the history of European unity. It formed the basis for the two treaties signed in Rome on 25 March 1957 by the representatives of the six ECSC countries.

They established the **European Economic Community** (EEC) and the **European Atomic Energy Commission** (Euratom) to pool information on atomic research. *'The Treaty of Rome,'* said Spaak, *'symbolises the triumph of co-operation over national selfishness.'*

Representatives of six Western European countries signing the Treaty of Rome in 1957 which brought into operation the European Economic Community (EEC) and Euratom. The signatories included Belgian Foreign Minister Paul Henri Spaak (extreme left) and West German Chancellor and Foreign Minister Konrad Adenauer (centre, signing).

Establishment and Evolution of the EEC, 1958-92

The Treaty of Rome laid out the aims, structure and policy of the **EEC**, or **Common Market** as it was popularly called. It came into effect on 1 July 1958. The Treaty of Rome represented a victory for the gradualist (step-by-step) approach to building the European Union, as advocated by Jean Monnet.

Aims: The aims of the EEC were:

- to promote economic activity;
- to raise the standard of living of the people;
- to bring the member states closer together – *'determined to lay the foundations of an ever closer union among the peoples of Europe'*.

Common market: The EEC established a **common market** to achieve the following aims:

- All **tariffs or customs duties** and **quotas** between members would be **abolished**. A **common tariff** (duty) would be levied on **imports** from outside the EEC.
- There would be **free movement** of goods, persons, services and capital. (The Four Freedoms)
- There would be **common policies** in agriculture and transport.
- A **Social Fund** would be set up to improve employment opportunities for workers.

Institutions: The institutions of the EEC reflected different interests. The **Council of Ministers**, with representatives from each of the countries, represented **national interests**; the **European Commission** – *'the engine of the Community'* – represented the Community interest; for the moment the third institution – the **European Parliament** – only indirectly represented the people's interest because it was made up of members from each of the national parliaments. Very often, progress, or the lack of it, in European unity depended on the **balance of power** between the Council of Ministers and the Commission.

> **KEY CONCEPT: COMMON MARKET.** A common market is a **group of countries** which removes customs duties (tariffs) between members, abolishes all barriers to the free movement of goods, people, services and capital; and puts the same tariff on imports from outside countries. The EEC was a common market between six countries. For that reason it was also called the Common Market.

PROGRESS IN THE 1960s

Prosperity and Policies

After the EEC began in 1958, the tariffs and quotas were abolished very quickly, establishing a market of 170 million people. As a result, the EEC countries enjoyed an **economic boom** in the 1960s; EEC economies grew faster than the US and Britain; trade between the member states doubled in a short time, the economies of the **Six** grew by fifty per cent and their unemployment fell by fifty per cent.

However, progress was made in only one of the 'Four Freedoms' – the free movement of **goods**. Free movement of **people, capital** and **services** was still limited. It took another thirty years before a full common market was established.

Common Policies

The EEC worked during the 1960s and 1970s to develop **common policies** in many areas. There were intense negotiations between countries to agree on these policies. But once agreed, decisions on the operation of these policies were taken by the EEC and not by national governments.

The most important of these policies was the **Common Agricultural Policy** (CAP). This gave **guaranteed prices** to farmers, but consumers paid higher prices for food. The **French** insisted on developing the CAP. De Gaulle wanted to use the CAP to modernise French agriculture. This would allow France to reduce the number of farmers and to make farming more efficient. **West Germany** was prepared to accept CAP because its industry benefited from the reduction in tariffs. But apart from CAP it took longer to develop common policies in Regional Policy, Fisheries Policy and Social Policy.

However, growing prosperity, the abolition of tariffs and the setting up of CAP illustrated the progress made by the EEC in the 1960s. But in other areas development slowed or even stopped. Central to this problem was the role of **de Gaulle and France**.

NATIONAL VERSUS COMMUNITY INTERESTS

One of the problems facing the EEC was balancing **national** and **community interests**. This problem could be clearly seen in de Gaulle's relationship with the EEC. He favoured French interests above community interests. He did not want a federal Europe, with strong Community institutions, such as the Commission and the Parliament.

In 1965, de Gaulle caused the **Empty Chair Crisis** when France refused to take its seat at the Council of Ministers because of a dispute concerning the funding of the CAP and majority voting. This crisis, which paralysed the Community for seven months, was the most serious **breakdown** in the operation of the EEC. It was finally resolved by the **Luxembourg Compromise** – France resumed its place in the Council in return for keeping **unanimous voting** (veto) when national interests were at stake.

The Empty Chair Crisis and the Luxembourg Compromise slowed developments in the EEC for the rest of the 1960s and during the 1970s. It weakened the Commission and it strengthened national interests. It also slowed down decision-making in the EEC when countries frequently used the argument of national interests.

General de Gaulle, President of France, who favoured French interests as opposed to Community interests. He was opposed to British entry to the EEC because he thought Britain was too much under American influence.

Britain's Attitude – The 'British Problem' and the Enlargement of the EEC in 1973

Why Britain Did Not Join the EEC

Britain refused to join the EEC in 1957 because:

- Britain wanted to maintain its close commercial and political links with Commonwealth countries.
- Britain also wanted to maintain a special relationship with the US.
- Britain did not want to give up political power to an outside body – a supranational or federal-type organisation.

Many in Britain still saw the country as a great power. But the British position had changed greatly over the previous fifty years. She had lost her lead in industry and her empire was now breaking up. It took a great deal of time for British people to realise that their position had changed.

For the moment however, instead of joining the EEC, Britain formed the **European Free Trade Association** (EFTA) with six other countries (Switzerland, Sweden, Norway, Austria, Denmark and Portugal). This made trade in **industrial goods** easier between themselves.

But very soon Britain changed its mind; the other six EFTA countries had a **small market** compared to the EEC, Britain's

A British cartoon commenting on Britain's application to join the EEC in 1961. Represented here are Macmillan (British Prime Minister), Adenauer (West Germany) and de Gaulle (France). What do Adenauer and de Gaulle mean when they say 'you want to join our club ... after all'?

trade with the EEC grew faster than with EFTA, and the EEC itself prospered. In 1961 the British Prime Minister, **Harold Macmillan**, proposed that Britain join the EEC, urged on by America. **Ireland, Denmark and Norway** also applied.

De Gaulle's Veto

There were difficulties in the negotiations concerning the Common Agricultural Policy (CAP), and also Britain's relationship with the **Commonwealth** and the **EFTA** countries. But the main difficulty was the **veto** of **President de Gaulle** of France, who said Britain was not European enough. As one historian commented, it was the view of some that *'From Hula-hoops to ... Rock 'n' Roll ... American habits crossed the Atlantic with a speed and certainty that suggested that Britain was now merely one more offshore island.'* De Gaulle felt that if Britain joined, the EEC would become *'a colossal Atlantic community under American domination'*. He wanted the EEC to become a **third superpower** – the Third Force – between the US and USSR, and so he was suspicious of Britain's close relationship with America. He also wanted to maintain **France's role** as the leading country of the EEC at that time.

President de Gaulle also vetoed **Britain's second application** in 1967. He said Britain was still not ready for the EEC. He claimed Britain's economy was too weak and **incompatible** with the EEC's. But de Gaulle's resignation in France in 1969, due to internal French difficulties, changed everything. The new President, **Pompidou**, lifted objections to British entry so **Britain applied once more**. While the talks were difficult and while there was strong opposition in Britain to joining, agreement was made. **Britain, Ireland and Denmark** joined together in 1973, while **Norway** rejected membership in a referendum.

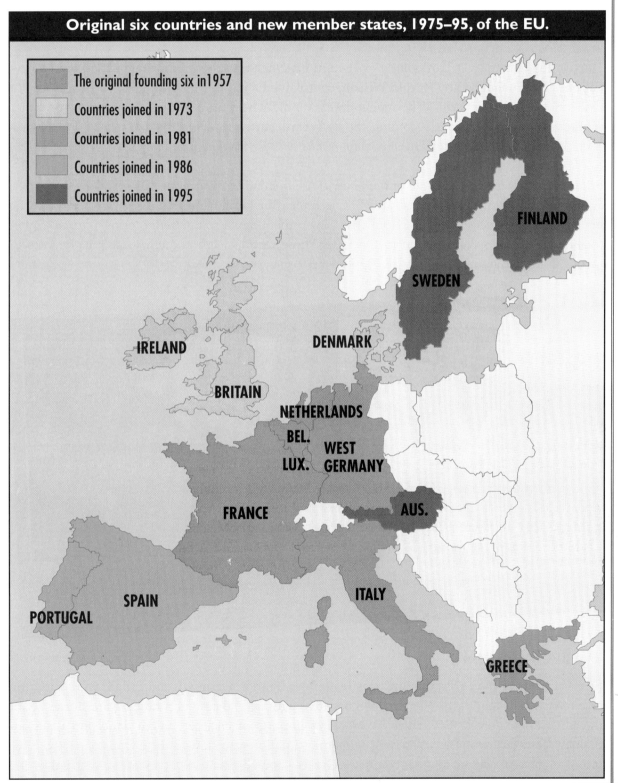

Original six countries and new member states, 1975–95, of the EU.

	The original founding six in 1957
	Countries joined in 1973
	Countries joined in 1981
	Countries joined in 1986
	Countries joined in 1995

FINLAND

SWEDEN

IRELAND

DENMARK

BRITAIN

NETHERLANDS

BEL.

LUX.

WEST GERMANY

FRANCE

AUS.

SPAIN

ITALY

PORTUGAL

GREECE

THE CHANGING EEC

Causes of Friction: Britain – the 'Awkward Partner'

This expansion or **enlargement** of the EEC occurred at a difficult time. Soon after, the **oil crisis in 1973** caused an economic recession. General economic problems of inflation and unemployment affected all countries. (See Case Study: The Oil Crisis, 1973, pp. 237–41.) This was aggravated by wide **currency fluctuations** (changes in value of European currencies) and the huge cost of CAP, which was creating **beef and butter mountains** and **wine lakes**. As a result there was some disillusionment with the EEC.

The disillusionment was particularly evident in Britain. No sooner had Britain joined than a new **Labour** government, led by **Harold Wilson**, complained about the conditions of entry and sought renegotiation of their terms. The renegotiations took eleven months and greatly angered other countries. Britain was now becoming the **awkward partner**. As one British pro-EEC politician said, the negotiation *'produced the minimum results with the maximum ill will'*.

Britain held a **referendum** (vote of the people) on the new terms in June 1975. This led to heated arguments between pro-EEC and anti-EEC groups. But Parliament, the press, the BBC and the main business interests were in favour. The government had also got better terms, particularly in relation to Britain's contribution to the EEC. These factors were enough to swing the vote in favour of remaining in the EEC.

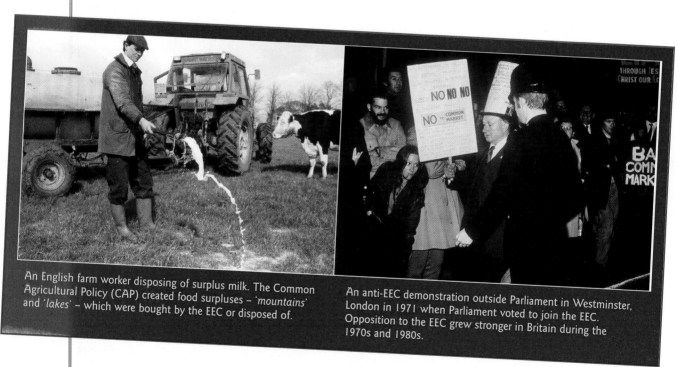

An English farm worker disposing of surplus milk. The Common Agricultural Policy (CAP) created food surpluses – 'mountains' and 'lakes' – which were bought by the EEC or disposed of.

An anti-EEC demonstration outside Parliament in Westminster, London in 1971 when Parliament voted to join the EEC. Opposition to the EEC grew stronger in Britain during the 1970s and 1980s.

The EEC Leaderless

By the middle of the 1970s, the EEC was **leaderless**. France, Germany and Britain were suffering economically, Britain's attitude remained negative with tabloid papers running scare stories about the EEC, France broke EEC rules by blocking imports of cheaper Italian wine and decision-making slowed down. The worsening economic situation also slowed the expansion of the EEC. It took eight years before another country – **Greece** – joined. Some experts were so worried by the lack of progress in the EEC that they concluded that *'If nothing is done, we are faced with the disintegration of the most important European achievement since the Second World War.'*

It was not surprising that a variety of reports commissioned by the EEC leaders proposing progress towards European unity were shelved (put to one side). One of those was the **Tindemans Report.** This report proposed moves towards a common foreign policy, progress on economic and monetary union, common policies for industry and energy, as well as strengthening the European Parliament. But it had no effect.

PROGRESS IN EUROPEAN INTEGRATION AND THE ENLARGEMENT TO 'EUROPE OF THE TWELVE', 1973–86

However, there was progress in other areas, which eventually in the 1980s led to significant progress in European unity:

- From 1975, the **European Council** was established as a regular meeting of **Heads of State or Government.** Major decisions were made by the Council.
- In 1979, the **European Monetary System** (EMS) was set up. This used the European Currency Unit (ECU), forerunner of the **euro**. It was the first significant step toward monetary union.
- The **first elections** to the European Parliament by **direct universal suffrage** were held in 1979.
- **Further enlargement:** The establishment of **democracy** in Greece and Portugal and the death of Franco in Spain resulted in the accession of these countries. Greece in 1981, and Spain and Portugal in 1986, became new members of the EEC.

KEY PERSONALITY: JACQUES DELORS

Jacques Delors was born in Paris in 1925. He was elected a Socialist member of the **European Parliament** in 1979 and was made chairman of the Monetary Affairs Committee. But he only served two years as he was appointed Minister of Finance in France in 1981. However, four years later he was back at the centre of European politics when he was appointed **President of the European Commission** in 1985, a position he held until 1995. In those ten years huge changes occurred in the EEC and Jacques Delors was very much involved in these. Some claimed his role in this period was as important as Monnet's in the 1950s.

Under Delors' **Presidency**, there were a number of major developments:

- The **Single European Act** was passed in 1986. This improved decision-making in the EEC and established the common market.
- The EEC was enlarged from **nine to twelve** countries.
- Germany was united and East Germany became part of the EEC.

The **Delors Report** in 1989 made proposals for **economic and monetary union**. But his efforts to further European unity were opposed by **Margaret Thatcher**, the British Prime Minister. They had two different views on Europe's future – one **federalist**, the other **nationalist**. But other European countries, especially Germany and France, favoured progress. This led to the **Maastricht Treaty** in 1991. This made huge changes to the EEC including establishing the **euro** and the **European Central Bank**.

Some historians say that Delors was the single **most influential President** of the European Commission. Delors' hard work and enthusiasm revived the European Community.

The British Budgetary Question

However, before further progress could be made there was more disagreement with Britain. **Margaret Thatcher**, who was elected the British Prime Minister in 1979, said that Britain paid too much into the EEC and did not get enough back in return. Britain had a strong case but Thatcher pursued her aim of getting a better deal for Britain with such **aggression** that she angered all the other leaders. The problem was not sorted out until 1984, that is five years and fifteen summits after it began.

The Single European Act, 1986

Once the British budgetary question was out of the way, the EEC could concentrate on reforming its institutions and on closer integration (unity). In the second half of the 1980s, this process got an important political boost, the work of **Jacques Delors** was crucial in this achievement. Delors, a French socialist, was elected **President of the European Commission** in 1985. He felt it was necessary to make changes as the EEC grew from **nine to twelve members** with the accession of Greece, Portugal and Spain.

The first step was the enacting of the **Single European Act** in 1986. It was realised that the EEC needed to **improve decision-making** and reform some of its institutions to cope with further enlargement. The Single European Act was the first change to the founding treaties of the European Communities, the Treaty of Paris in 1951 and the Treaty of Rome in 1957:

- The Act ratified the **European Council** (meeting of Heads of Government or State) as the body for major political negotiations among the member states.
- There was greater use of **majority voting**.
- The **powers** of the European Parliament were increased.
- Measures were adopted to establish a full **common** or **single market** by the end of 1992. There would be **no obstacles** to the free movement of goods, people, services and capitals. This target was **largely reached** and the common market became a reality.
- There was co-ordination of the **monetary policy** of the member States, paving the way for economic and monetary union.
- There were measures to promote integration in **social rights** (health and the workers' security), **research and technology**, and the **environment**.

TOWARD THE TREATY OF THE EUROPEAN UNION, 1986-92

The Single European Act entailed an important step forward in the **integration process**. It tried to balance the progress in free trade, which benefited industry, with the passing of a **Social Charter** that guaranteed minimum social standards to every European worker.

The British Prime Minister, Margaret Thatcher, opposed the policy of Delors. The Conservative leader favoured the **reduction** of State intervention in the economy and in social welfare. While Thatcher favoured the **single market**, she was **against any advancement** in European integration.

KEY PERSONALITY: MARGARET THATCHER

Margaret Thatcher was **leader** of the **Conservative Party** in Britain. She was elected Britain's **first woman Prime Minister** in 1979. The same year her Party won 60 out of the 78 British seats in the first direct elections to the European Parliament.

Margaret Thatcher campaigned for Britain to remain in the EEC in the 1975 referendum in Britain. But no sooner had she become Prime Minister in 1979 than she began to quarrel with the EEC over **Britain's contribution** to the EEC Budget. It took five years before this problem was solved. She also wanted to reform the **Common Agricultural Policy** (CAP) but found the opposition too strong.

However, she very much favoured the campaign for a **Single Market** – getting rid of all obstacles to the free movement of goods, services, capital and labour. She also favoured the **Single European Act** because it would speed up decision-making.

But overall Mrs Thatcher was **opposed to efforts** to strengthen Community institutions such as the Commission and the Parliament at the expense of the nation-states. She made this clear in a speech in Bruges in 1988 where she showed her **opposition** to the federal ideas of Jacques Delors, who was President of the European Commission; *'To try to suppress nationhood and concentrate power at the centre of a European conglomerate would be highly damaging.'* She was very reluctant to join the **Economic and Monetary Union** (EMU) and only did so when two of her chief ministers threatened to resign.

Margaret Thatcher had an **aggressive** style in politics – she was called the *Iron Lady* – which did not suit the methods of discussion and agreement in the EEC. Her opposition to the EEC was one of the reasons for the failure of the Conservative Party in the European elections in 1989 and for her own downfall in 1990.

Factors Influencing Integration

Conditions in Europe at the time forced on the **pace of integration and unification**. European economic problems experienced towards the end of the 1980s, especially **currency fluctuations** (changes in value), speeded up the process of integration. There was a need to control wide fluctuations in the value of currencies which were damaging trade. This could only be done through **monetary union**.

Much more influential though were **events in Eastern Europe**. The collapse of Communism in Eastern Europe in 1989 resulted in the **reunification of Germany** in October 1990. Germany became a country of eighty million people with one-third of the GNP of the EEC; it was a much larger economy than either France or Britain.

Once again, French and British fear of a revived Germany led to very significant progress in unification. The French President, **François Mitterrand**, believed that Germany might once again try to dominate Europe. He felt that the best way to control the country was to link it more firmly to Europe with further

European Summit Conference, 1988, which included at the front, Jacques Delors (left), Margaret Thatcher (third from left), Helmut Kohl (West German Chancellor) and François Mitterand (French President).

progress in integration. He was supported by **Helmut Kohl**, Chancellor of Germany, who was anxious to allay any fears other countries had about German unification. In a common message, Helmut Kohl and François Mitterrand declared in 1990:

'We consider it necessary to speed up the political construction of the Europe of the Twelve. We think that this is the right moment to transform the whole of the relationships among the member States into a European Union and to endow it with the necessary means of action.'

TREATY OF EUROPEAN UNION – MAASTRICHT TREATY, 1992

After intense negotiations among the member states, the **Treaty of the European Union**, popularly known as the **Maastricht Treaty**, was signed in February 1992 but it did not come into operation until November 1993. This was largely because the Treaty went through a difficult process of **ratification** in some member states influenced:

- by poor economic circumstances;
- the failure of the European Community to achieve a ceasefire among the warring parties in Yugoslavia; and
- the fear of giving up more power to Brussels.

These factors undermined confidence in the European Community.

In **Denmark**, the Treaty was rejected in the first referendum (vote of the people). After renegotiation in relation to monetary and defence matters, it was accepted on the second referendum. The referendum in **France** had a slim majority (51·05%), while in **Britain** debates in the House of Commons dragged on until 1993 when it was passed by a very narrow margin. In **Germany** the Treaty was referred to the Constitutional Court before there was a ruling in favour.

Terms of the Maastricht Treaty

The Treaty of the European Union modified the previous treaties – Paris, Rome and the Single European Act:

- The EEC was renamed the **European Community (EC)** which is the core of the **European Union**.
- The Treaty affirmed: *'This Treaty marks a new stage in the process of creating an ever closer union among the peoples of Europe....'*
- It laid out the **timetable** for **Economic and Monetary Union**; it established the **European Central Bank (ECB)** and the conditions for the introduction of a **single** or **common currency**, later called the **euro**.

The Referendum on the Maastricht Treaty in 1992 led to widespread debate about the merits of European unity.

- It established a **citizenship** of the European Union.
- Many more decisions were based on **majority rule**.
- It increased the power of the **European Parliament** to influence European laws. This made the EC **more democratic**.
- The power of the **European Community** was **extended** in certain areas such as education, environment, health and consumer protection.
- It laid out guidelines for a **Common Foreign and Security Policy** (CFSP).
- There was to be increased co-operation in **Justice and Home Affairs**.

Conclusion

With the passing of the Maastricht Treaty, Western Europe had changed a great deal since 1945. The process of European unity had maintained peace in Western Europe for forty-five years. It had also created the largest single market in the world, as well as the largest trading power. The Maastricht Treaty laid the groundwork for further significant progress in European unity during the 1990s. It also set up structures for the expansion of the European Union with the advent of many Eastern European countries.

ORDINARY LEVEL AND HIGHER LEVEL HOMEWORK EXERCISES

ORDINARY LEVEL

1. Study the quotation from Churchill (p. 209) and answer the following questions:

(i) What is Churchill's wish or hope for Europe?

(ii) What does he mean when he says, 'We are with Europe, but not of it'?

(iii) What is he referring to when he says, 'We have our own dream and our own task'?

(iv) How does this quotation help to explain Britain's attitude in the 1950s to the movement toward European unity?

2. Study the quotations from Robert Schuman (p. 213) and answer the following questions:

(i) What industries did Schuman propose should come under a High Authority?

(ii) What would be achieved by this, according to Schuman?

(iii) How did he say **Europe** would be made? What does he mean by the word **Europe** here?

(iv) According to Schuman, what must happen to bring the nations of Europe together?

3. Study the cartoon on page 213 and answer the following questions:

(i) What does the steel bar (girder) represent?

(ii) What do 'mistrust' and 'suspicion' refer to?

(iii) Is the cartoon biased? Explain your answer.

(iv) Does the cartoonist favour Britain joining the European Coal and Steel Community (ECSC)?

4. Study the following document carefully and answer the questions below:

'The first reason for joining the Common Market (EEC) is peace and security. Another important reason is to provide a world role for Britain. As a nation of 55 million people Britain has some voice but not enough. Traditionally, Britain has always been part of a larger grouping, the Commonwealth. Most of the Commonwealth countries have become independent. The [European] Community opens windows on the whole world for Britain, which since the war have been closing.'

From a speech by Margaret Thatcher, Conservative government minister, in the House of Commons, April 1973

(i) Why was the EEC also called the Common Market?

(ii) What does Margaret Thatcher mean when she says *'a world role for Britain'*?

(iii) What has been happening to Britain *'since the war'*, according to Thatcher? What war is she referring to?

(iv) List the reasons Margaret Thatcher gives for Britain joining the EEC in 1973. Do you think she favoured Britain joining the EEC?

5. Write **paragraph answers** on each of the following questions:

(i) The political and economic factors that favoured European unity after the Second World War.

(ii) The Schuman Plan and the European Coal and Steel Community (ECSC).

(iii) Military alliances: NATO and the European Defence Community.

(iv) The Treaty of Rome 1957, and the setting up of the EEC.

(v) Margaret Thatcher and the development of European unity.

(vi) De Gaulle and the development of European unity.

(vii) The Maastricht Treaty – background and terms.

6. Write **long answers** on each of the following questions:

(i) The origins of European unity.

(ii) What steps were taken in the progress of European unity between the end of the Second World War (1945) and the setting up of the ECSC in 1951?

(iii) What role did Jean Monnet play in the development of European unity?

(iv) Britain and European unity, 1945–73.

(v) Britain and European unity, 1973–89.

(vi) What was the contribution of Jacques Delors to the development of European unity?

HIGHER LEVEL

1. How did the movement toward European unity develop between 1945 and 1957? (Department of Education, Sample Paper)

2. How did the movement toward European unity develop between the beginning of the EEC in 1958 and its first enlargement in 1973?

3. Account for the moves made toward European unity between 1945 and 1957 OR between 1957 and 1992.

4. Discuss the origins and development of the European Economic Community between 1945 and the Empty Chair Crisis of 1965.

5. Discuss the problems facing the European Economic Community from its first enlargement in 1973 to the Treaty of Maastricht in 1992.

6. To what extent has Britain been an **awkward partner** in the process of European unity?

7. Assess the contribution of Jacques Delors to the development of European unity.

TEST YOURSELF AT
my-etest.com

11. THE WESTERN ECONOMIES, 1945-90

The Era of Economic Growth

THE ECONOMIC EFFECTS OF THE SECOND WORLD WAR

One of the most serious effects of the Second World War was the huge **loss of life** – in all about forty million people died. However, the Western economies suffered much less than Eastern Europe and Russia. Indeed Britain, France and Italy lost only about one per cent of their pre-war population compared to nine per cent of Germans (six million) killed. Another serious effect of the war on the Western economies was the **physical destruction**. Roads, railways, factories, housing and merchant shipping were devastated. In all these cases, Germany was the worst hit. Not surprisingly, the **economic performance** of all countries was affected by the war. In 1945 some countries such as France, Italy and Holland were well below their pre-war levels. The only exception was Britain, but it suffered after war production ended in 1945. By this time international **trade** was disrupted and most economies had built up huge **debts**.

The European economies were disrupted by the Second World War. Millions of people were displaced. These refugees trudged from Poland to Berlin but Berlin was also in ruins. They faced a very harsh winter during 1945–6 in a war-torn continent.

RECONSTRUCTION

The Western powers, therefore, faced huge challenges in rebuilding their economies. In the immediate post-war period, America and Britain organised **relief efforts** to overcome the food shortages and the problem of refugees. Food rationing continued but food could also be obtained on the black market. Most of the relief was provided through the **United Nations Relief and Rehabilitation Administration** (UNRRA) which financed imports of food and raw materials. UNRRA also resettled thousands of displaced persons.

At the same time Western governments tried to restore the **normal working of the economy**. They encouraged farming production, tried to control inflation (rising prices) and encouraged the construction of new apartments and houses on the outskirts of war-bombed cities.

Some relief was provided by the United Nations Relief and Rehabilitation Administration (UNRRA). Here Argentine workers load grain for shipment to Italy as part of the supply donated by the Argentine government to UNRRA (1946).

Industrial production recovered surprisingly quickly. In most countries it had reached pre-war levels by 1947 with the exception of Germany, Italy and Holland. But European governments resisted any moves to co-ordinate their recovery efforts and trade continued well below pre-war levels. Western European economies looked to the US for supplies of machine tools and raw materials. But this highlighted a further problem – the **shortage of dollars** (dollar gap) needed to buy the imports.

The Marshall Plan

In these circumstances there was a danger that the recovery and reconstruction of the Western European economies would be stalled. To overcome the problems, the US Secretary of State, **General Marshall**, announced a programme of aid – the **European Recovery Programme (ERP)** or **Marshall Plan** – in July 1947. He said that the American government would provide aid if requested to do so by European governments. He wanted to integrate Western Europe into a single economic area, based on **free trade**. (See Chapters 9 and 10.)

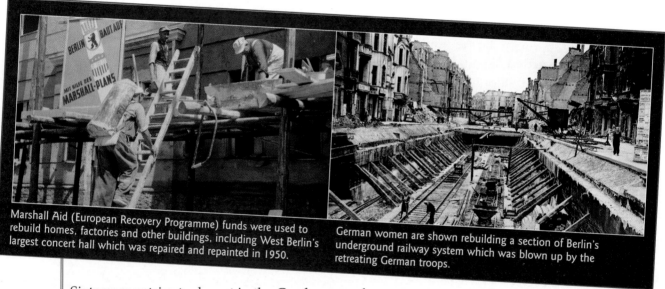

Marshall Aid (European Recovery Programme) funds were used to rebuild homes, factories and other buildings, including West Berlin's largest concert hall which was repaired and repainted in 1950.

German women are shown rebuilding a section of Berlin's underground railway system which was blown up by the retreating German troops.

Sixteen countries took part in the **Conference of European Economic Co-operation** (CEEC) in Paris and agreed to take part in a joint recovery programme. In setting up the European Recovery Programme, the American government under **President Truman** scaled down the amount of aid to ensure its passage through Congress. The **Organisation for European Economic Co-operation** (OEEC) was set up by the sixteen Western European countries to administer the money coming from America. It also reviewed the national plans and adjusted them to take into account their impact on other economies.

The Use of Marshall Aid

In total, the US spent **$13·7 billion** under ERP. Nine-tenths was in the form of **grants**, the rest in **loans**. The aid varied considerably from country to country. Britain received the largest amount followed by France, West Germany and Italy. ERP funds were used to import American food, raw materials and machinery. The governments sold the imported American goods onto firms. They were able to use the money which they received – called **counterpart funds** – to invest in **infrastructure** which benefited long-term economic development. In West Germany, for example, counterpart funds were used to build electricity stations; in France they were used to modernise the steel industry.

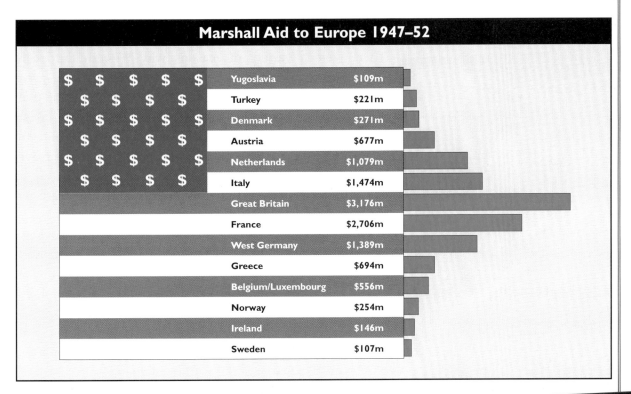

Marshall Aid to Europe 1947–52

Yugoslavia	$109m
Turkey	$221m
Denmark	$271m
Austria	$677m
Netherlands	$1,079m
Italy	$1,474m
Great Britain	$3,176m
France	$2,706m
West Germany	$1,389m
Greece	$694m
Belgium/Luxembourg	$556m
Norway	$254m
Ireland	$146m
Sweden	$107m

Marshall aid allowed the Western European countries continue their **recovery**. There were significant **increases** in industrial and agricultural production. It is likely that this recovery would have happened anyway but at a slower pace. However, one of the largest boosts was for **intra-European** trade. The OEEC countries agreed to cut quotas on trade between their countries. They also set up a system of payments to facilitate trade. Within six years, intra-European trade had more than doubled. This expansion of trade helped boost economic growth and further integrated their economies.

THE BOOM YEARS, 1950–73

The Western European economies prospered in the two decades of the 1950s and the 1960s. The economies grew rapidly, there was low unemployment and low inflation. Both workers and employers shared in the benefits. It was called the time of the **Great Boom** or the **Golden Age**.

Rising from the ruins: a decade after the war, Berlin was still rebuilding after the effects of Allied bombings. The tallest of the new buildings under construction was this 19-storey office block.

However, growth was not the same everywhere. The most significant growth was experienced in West Germany, while Britain suffered from the **British disease**. In Western European countries **unemployment** averaged about two per cent during these years, with West Germany on the lower side and Britain slightly higher than average. The pattern in **inflation** was much the same. All countries experienced growth in productivity, but once again West Germany was higher than most. There was also a strong growth of exports and investment.

WHY DID WESTERN EUROPEAN ECONOMIES PROSPER?

Italian migrant workers (called 'guest workers') came to West Germany to fill the labour shortage caused by the growing economy. Some found work in the Volkswagen factory in Wolfsburg because of the increased demand for cars in Western Europe.

There were a **variety of reasons** why Western European economies prospered in the 1950s and 1960s:

* The destruction of the Second World War meant that European countries could rebuild with the **latest technology**. This resulted in the transfer of American technology to Western Europe which made Europe more productive.
* Europe benefited from **low energy and raw material prices**.
* The **policies** adopted by Western European governments helped, in particular, the freeing of trade and economic integration through the establishment of the EEC and EFTA. This facilitated the transfer of **technology** and encouraged **large-scale production**.
* There were agreements between trade unions and employers which resulted in **wage moderation**, supported by the expansion of the **welfare state**.
* Competition from cheaper Asian economies did not begin to grow until the middle of the 1960s.

Moves Toward Free Trade

One of the factors which helped Western European economies to grow was the movement towards **free trade**. The Benelux countries began this in 1947, but the freeing of trade became more widespread after that under the influence of the **Marshall Plan**. With the advent of the **EEC** in 1958, free trade was extended through the further reduction in tariff barriers. In the case of **EFTA**, it applied to industrial goods. These changes were linked to the worldwide reduction in tariffs through the **General Agreement on Trade and Tariffs** (GATT). As a result of the EEC, trade within Western Europe grew faster than trade between Europe and the rest of the world.

IMMIGRATION

From the end of the Second World War in 1945 onwards, large numbers of immigrants entered Western European countries. In 1950 foreigners numbered about 5 million, but this rose to 15 million in 1982 and 18 million in 1992. The proportion of foreigners in the population grew from just over 1% in 1950 to 5% by the early 1990s. More than half the foreign-born population of Western Europe was concentrated in two countries. West Germany had the largest immigrant population of about 8%, along with **ethnic Germans** who had come from other European countries, while France had about 6%.

Immigration in the early years after the war was mainly **refugees**. It is estimated that some 25 million people were displaced persons, mostly ethnic Germans. Between 1945 and 1955, 8 million ethnic Germans moved to West Germany, followed by another 4 million before the Berlin Wall was built in 1961. They moved for political as well as economic reasons.

The Era of Economic Growth

But in the 1950s and 1960s **economic reasons** were more important as the Western European economies expanded and labour shortages were filled by migrants. Immigrants tended to do the jobs which local people did not want. In this way immigration became essential to keep the economic progress going. One-third of the workers in the Ford factory in Cologne in 1973 were Turkish.

Who Were the Immigrants?

The migrants came mainly from the **Mediterranean countries** and **North Africa** – the largest numbers coming from Turkey and southern Italy. The immigrants tended to **cluster** in

Italian migrant workers go on a shopping spree in Wolfsburg, West Germany.

groups in certain countries – three-quarters of the Turks, for example, lived in Germany in 1990; while most Algerians and Moroccans lived in France. The latter were mainly for historical reasons – they were former French colonies. This was also the case in Britain where immigrants from **ex-colonies** spoke the **mother tongue** and this made migration easier. Some of the migration came through **agreements** between the German and French governments and the emigrant countries.

Changes in Immigration

Many of the early immigrants – up to the 1970s – were **temporary**; they returned home once they had made money. Because of the First Oil Crisis in 1973, countries did not need labour and began to consider restrictions on immigration, but this did not stop immigration. Instead it changed from being **temporary to permanent**. Migrants now brought their families. With continuing unemployment in the 1980s, immigration restrictions were further tightened so that immigration fell. But it was at this time also, when jobs were scarcer, that attacks occurred on immigrants.

Immigration changed in another way in the late 1980s. The collapse of Communism in Eastern Europe in 1989 added **asylum seekers** to the immigrant trail. In contrast, migration within the EC declined as income levels in the **poorer** countries rose to the EC average. Now these countries such as Italy began to have their own immigrants – very often illegal – from North Africa.

Economic Effects

Immigration had a number of important **economic effects**:
- Immigration helped the economies of the receiving countries to overcome **labour shortages**.
- Immigrants sent back large amounts of money to their home countries.
- In spite of the fact that many of the immigrants were younger adults, they had **little effect** on the birth rate and consequently on changing the **ageing** population structure of the countries of Western Europe.
- Immigration created a **multiracial, multicultural society** in these countries.

The Welfare State

After the Second World War, Western European countries expanded their **welfare services**. Social expenditure doubled in the fifty years after 1945. This varied across countries with Denmark and Holland showing greater increases than Britain, France, West Germany and Italy. But overall there were similar **expansions** throughout Western Europe.

The welfare services which expanded include education, healthcare, social welfare benefits and pensions. They have also included many **more groups** in society so that the phrase *'from the cradle to the grave'* often applies to the new welfare states. Governments therefore had a large say in the living conditions of their people. The **role of the state** (governments) widened from providing security and protection to its people to that of caring for the economic and social condition of the people.

The Welfare State grew in many European countries after the Second World War. Education, health and social welfare benefits expanded. Here Guy's Hospital in London catered for forty dental patients at once.

> **KEY CONCEPT: WELFARE STATE.** This is a state in which the government plays a key role in promoting the health and general welfare of all its people. It is based on the idea of government responsibility for those who are unable to avail or provide for themselves the basic necessities for a good life. It involves state aid for people in all stages of their lives – *'from the cradle to the grave'*. It usually covers free education and insurance against unemployment, sickness and old age.

REASONS AND STRUCTURES

Many **reasons** contributed to the growth of the welfare state since 1945. A general feeling developed during the war that conditions should and would improve after the war. People wanted a **better and fairer society**. Political parties responded to this by forming **policies** to achieve this after the war. The **great boom** helped the expansion in welfare. As countries became more affluent, they spent more on social welfare. But they were also faced with ageing populations so more was spent on health and pensions.

The **structures** of the welfare states varied from country to country. The EC noted in 1995; *'Each nation has followed a distinct path in the development of its social policy which has greatly influenced the characteristics of the present system.'* West Germany developed a **fragmented** system which was built up piecemeal from the late nineteenth century. Other Western European countries followed much the same pattern. Britain was a definite exception. The pre-war system was radically changed between 1945 and 1948 under the influence of the **Beveridge Report**. After that time most parts of the British system were administered by **central government**.

EFFECTS OF THE WELFARE STATE

Economists disagree on the effect the welfare state had on economic development in Western Europe. Some economists saw the welfare state as **beneficial** in that it created a bond between the state and the individuals. Others have argued that the welfare state has created **economic inefficiency** by undermining the incentive to work through increased unemployment benefit. The welfare state also had a bearing on the amount of poverty in each country and the inequality of wealth. In overall terms, the Benelux and West Germany had lower levels of inequality, southern European higher, with France and Britain in between. Lower levels of income inequality were associated with higher levels of social spending.

The four major causes of poverty in post-war Europe were old age, unemployment, sickness and family breakdown. Since 1960 the incidence of three of these has risen a great deal – old age, unemployment and family breakdown – but poverty levels have risen by only **one-fifth** since the mid-1970s. This shows that the European welfare state continues to counter the consequences of economic and social change.

The Western Economies, 1973-90

BEFORE THE OIL CRISIS

Even before the Oil Crisis of 1973, the Western European economies were showing signs of problems. European inflation began to rise in the late 1960s caused by rising inflation in the US due to the Vietnam War. It was also caused by large wage increases in France in 1968 which spread to other countries. However, these problems seemed small compared to later difficulties.

THE SECOND OIL CRISIS 1979–80

No sooner had Western Europe begun to overcome the effects of the first Oil Crisis than it was hit by a second crisis (OPEC 2). A revolution in Iran in 1979 reduced the supply of oil and oil prices rose by over 100% during that year. The Western European countries faced the same problems as in the first Oil Crisis, but this time beginning with higher unemployment and inflation.

RECESSION AND THE RISE OF UNEMPLOYMENT

Inflation rose in Western European countries to an average of twelve per cent. But it declined soon after and remained fairly low for the remainder of the 1980s and early 1990s. However, **unemployment** hit much harder and remained high for most of the 1980s. Europe also experienced fluctuations in **exchange rates** (value of currencies) and this hurt international trade. This resulted in the establishment of the **European Monetary System** (EMS) which aimed at controlling inflation. Governments had more interest in controlling inflation than unemployment. **Britain** and **West Germany** led the way in controlling the money supply by reducing budget deficits. In **France**, on the other hand, President Mitterrand used expansionary (spending) policies to boost the economy but this led to further inflation. Thereafter, France changed its policy to be more in line with the other Western European countries.

OTHER ECONOMIC PROBLEMS

Western European countries faced **other economic problems** in the 1980s. There was competition from low-wage Asian countries, the stock market crash in the US in October 1987, living standards were low, and growth rates were even lower than the 1970s. Some economists said the **low growth** was due to the failure of business and workers to change their ways. This influenced governments who introduced policies which tried to open up markets.

One initiative was the full development of the **common** or **single market** in the EEC in 1992 to increase competition and provide larger markets. It was said that lower costs and prices would result, which would boost employment. **Other policies** included measures to increase banking competition, reduce taxes, privatise state industry (denationalisation), job training schemes and trade union reform. It would take some time before the impact of these policies would be felt.

SOLVING UNEMPLOYMENT – TWO APPROACHES

The recessions Western Europe experienced since the 1970s, along with an increase in the long-term unemployed, led to two approaches to solving unemployment. Economists said that wages should be more flexible, workers needed to be more mobile by moving to where the jobs were to be found and government policies should be able to help them. **Britain** followed one type of policy in the 1980s under **Margaret Thatcher**. There were changes to unemployment benefit, interviews with long-term unemployed and abolition of minimum wages. But **other EEC countries** were less inclined to follow these lines. They said that these policies might create more jobs but these jobs would often be lowly paid and unskilled. They believed that **the European approach** was better; strong trade unions, welfare support, and links between workers, employers and government to gain **consensus** and **agreement**. They said this approach was a more humane way of getting wage moderation and a flexible wage market. Only the 1990s and beyond would tell which of these two approaches was the right one.

ORDINARY LEVEL AND HIGHER LEVEL HOMEWORK EXERCISES

ORDINARY LEVEL

1. Study the graph on Marshall Aid (p. 229) and answer the following questions:

(i) Why did it get the name Marshall Aid or Plan?

(ii) Which country received the most aid under the Marshall Plan?

(iii) Why do you think that country would receive the most aid?

(iv) What was the purpose of Marshall Aid?

(v) What did Marshall Aid contribute to the Western European economies?

2. Study the graph on World Energy Use and World Population (Source 14) (p.241) and answer the following questions:

(i) When did energy use overtake world population?

(ii) What change took place in world energy use around 1960?

(iii) Write a brief explanation for the changes in world energy use after 1940. Would your explanation also be true for (a) Western Europe, and (b) Eastern Europe (Chapter 12)?

(iv) How useful are graphs for historians?

3. Study the following figures on the output of steel and answer the questions below:

Output of Steel (in millions of metric tons)

	1950	1960	1975
Britain	16·6	24·7	20·2
France	8·7	17·3	27·0
West Germany	12·1	30·1	40·4
Belgium	3·8	7·1	11·6
Italy	2·4	8·2	21·8

Figures quoted in T Morris and D Murphy, *Europe 1870–1991*

(i) Which countries had (a) the fastest growth, and (b) the slowest growth in steel production between 1950 and 1975?

(ii) What developments in European unity affected the output of steel in four of these countries? Which country is the exception? Explain your answers.

(iii) What other factors affected the output of steel between 1950 and 1975?

(iv) How useful are these figures in assessing the economic performance of these countries?

4. Study the following document carefully and answer the questions below:

'The causes of unemployment [in the 1970s and 1980s] are not easy to identify ... During the 1970s the main reason for the rising tide of British unemployment was thought to be a lack of demand for labour at a time when the working population was growing rapidly. Between 1971 and 1979, the total working population rose by 1·25 million but the only growth in jobs occurred in the part-time sector.... Deindustrialisation is another cause of unemployment. During the 1970s, one million jobs were lost in manufacturing industries in general, the hardest hit being construction, distribution, textiles and heavy engineering. Sometimes, when industry becomes more efficient, fewer people are required to manufacture goods ... Free competition between countries has also contributed to unemployment in Britain. Since Britain joined the EEC in 1973 ... this has made it easier for European nations to compete with British industry at home.... More worrying is the trade situation with Japan ... Poor industrial relations have also played a part in increasing unemployment.... Britain's industrial relations record has discouraged much needed investment and harmed productivity.'

M Gibson, *Let's Discuss Unemployment*

(i) When did Britain suffer high unemployment?

(ii) What reason was given for high unemployment in the 1970s?

(iii) What is 'deindustrialisation'?

(iv) What industries declined in the 1970s?

(v) What is another term for 'free competition'?

(vi) What competition did British industry lose out to, according to the author?

(vii) How did poor industrial relations play a part in increasing unemployment?

(viii) What major economic event in the 1970s is not mentioned here as a cause of British unemployment?

5. Study the following document carefully and answer the questions below:

'With the election of a Conservative government in 1979, the number of people out of work grew rapidly and by 1985 the figure had passed three million. Margaret Thatcher, the Conservative Prime Minister, has consistently replied to criticism of her government's employment record by saying governments cannot create "real jobs" and that employment is totally dependent on market forces.... Critics, however, maintain that there are many areas of British industry, such as construction, road-building and general manufacturing, in which there is room for a great number of new jobs, if only the government would either invest public funds or do more to encourage private investment.'

M Gibson, *Let's Discuss Unemployment*

(i) When did Britain's unemployment reach three million?

(ii) What was Margaret Thatcher's attitude to government job creation?

(iii) Explain the terms *'real jobs'* and *'market forces'*.

(iv) What did Thatcher's critics say the government should do?

6. Write **paragraph answers** on each of the following questions:

(i) The economic effects of the Second World War and Reconstruction.

(ii) The Marshall Plan and the economies of Western Europe.

(iii) Immigration in Western Europe in the post-war decades.

(iv) The growth of the Welfare State in Western Europe.

(v) Economic problems facing Western Europe after the second Oil Crisis, 1979.

(vi) The growth of free trade in Western Europe. (See also Chapter 10, European Unity.)

7. Write **long answers** on each of the following questions:

(i) Why did the Western European economies prosper in the 1950s and 1960s?

(ii) How and why did the Welfare State develop in Western Europe after the Second World War?

(iii) What were the immediate and long-term effects of the 1973 Oil Crisis on the European economy? (Department of Education, Sample Paper)

HIGHER LEVEL

1. How successful was Europe (Western and/or Eastern (Chapter 12)) in coping with the economic effects of the Second World War?

2. Why did Western Europe experience an economic boom in the 1950s and 1960s?

3. Discuss the role of governments (the state) in Western Europe in caring for the social condition of the people from the Second World War to 1990.

4. To what extent did free trade develop in Western European economies from the end of the Second World War to about 1990? (See also Chapter 10, European Unity.)

5. What economic problems did Western European countries face after the Oil Crises of the 1970s and how did they deal with them?

CASE STUDY: The Oil Crisis, 1973

INTRODUCTION

In October 1973, Egypt and Syria attacked Israel in the **Yom Kippur War**. America supported Israel with over $2 billion of military equipment and this helped Israel to defeat both countries.

In retaliation for the American help to Israel, on 17 October, the Organisation of Petroleum Exporting Countries (OPEC) introduced an **oil embargo** followed by a series of **prices rises**. In a period of about six months, oil prices rose by **400%**. Europe's high dependency on oil – about 80% came from Arab countries – along with the price rises, caused serious problems for the Western European economies.

Members of the Organisation of Petroleum Exporting Countries (OPEC) met to discuss increases in petrol prices. OPEC was founded in 1960 with five members – Iran, Iraq, Kuwait, Saudi Arabia and Venezuela. By 1973 it had seven more members. How useful are photos as evidence for historians discussing the Oil Crisis of 1973?

OPEC

The Organisation of Petroleum Exporting Countries (OPEC) was founded in 1960 with five members – Iran, Iraq, Kuwait, Saudi Arabia and Venezuela. By 1973 it had seven more members.

SOURCE 1 – OPEC and control of oil

'... It was in the 1970s that OPEC became a household name. The main oil-producing countries of the Middle East rebelled against control over their oil riches by the giant Western-owned oil companies, which made vast wealth for their owners by buying Arab oil cheap and selling dear. The OPEC members decided not only to take more control of their own oil, but also to use it as a political weapon. The resulting developments saw a quadrupling of the price of crude oil. It also saw the Arab states place an embargo on supplies to those countries which supported the expansionist policy of Israel....'

Oil, a Powerful and Profitable Business, The Spark, 20 September 2000, *home.clear.net.nz*

SOURCE 2 – OPEC oil embargo leaves world economy threatened

'If OPEC are trying to make America, and the West in general, sit up and take notice, they have succeeded. And spectacularly so. Another *DailyPast.com* correspondent, Nasser Aziz of our Middle East office, commented on the motives behind yesterday's OPEC move.

"OPEC has been gaining in strength and in confidence over the last five or so years. In doing what they have done, they are using just about the only weapon they have in the Middle East conflict which has become one of the Arab world against Israel and America. By cutting the oil to the US, they are saying 'you must listen to us'.... It seems unrealistic to assume the White House will now turn around and abandon their allies in Israel. OPEC, on the other hand, have declared the restrictions will stay in place 'until Israeli forces have left the occupied lands and restored the rights of Palestinians.' It is difficult to know who will blink first," Nasser Aziz says.

In the meantime, people in the West can expect some sort of fuel rationing and perhaps long lines to fill up their cars.'

Bringing the Past to Life, 21 October 1973, *www.dailypast.com*

THE IMPACT OF THE FIRST OIL CRISIS, 1973

The immediate impact was severe **oil shortage**. This resulted in petrol queues, rationing and the banning of Sunday driving in some European countries. Average **inflation** almost doubled by the mid-1970s. It declined later but was still as high as 10% in 1979, and in some countries such as Britain and Italy it remained as high as 16%. Increased inflation encouraged workers to demand **higher wages** to stop the decline in living standards. This led to widespread **strikes**.

SOURCE 3 – Cheap energy

'The great post-war boom had been propelled by cheap energy.... This fall in [the] price [of oil] was made possible by the rapid increase of exports of cheap Middle East oil. It is significant that the three leading sectors in the Western economic boom, motors, chemicals and electricity were all energy-intensive, indeed oil-intensive. By assuming energy would remain cheap, all the industrial nations were short-sighted...'

P Johnson, *Modern Times*

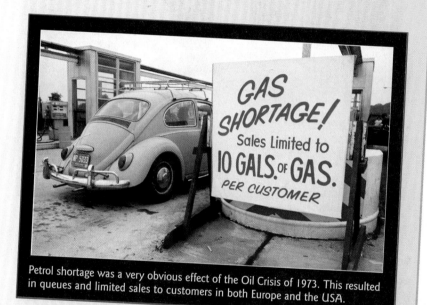

Petrol shortage was a very obvious effect of the Oil Crisis of 1973. This resulted in queues and limited sales to customers in both Europe and the USA.

SOURCE 4 – Voluntary petrol cuts fail to stop pumps running dry

'Petrol-hunting motorists created their own fuel-consuming traffic jams yesterday. When garages reopened after the weekend, forecourt rationing was almost universal. Some irate drivers rang the motoring organisations to report prices of up to 50p a gallon.

The AA estimated that a quarter of Britain's petrol stations remained closed yesterday. The extreme shortage was partially caused by motorists stocking up more than usual on Friday and Saturday, and many garages ran dry over the weekend.

The situation will only improve with fresh deliveries, and it becomes increasingly obvious that the Government's appeals for motorists to drive at 50 mph and stay off the roads on Sunday are inadequate.

When Mr Walker, Secretary for Trade and Industry, announced the issuing of petrol ration books he said a Sunday ban had been rejected by Britain as it had been by the majority of car-driving countries. That majority is now somewhat smaller. Switzerland, Holland, Germany, Belgium, Italy and Denmark have either introduced Sunday bans or are about to. And the threat of rationing becomes increasingly hard to ignore.'

Charles Cook,
Motoring Correspondent,
The Guardian, 4 December 1973

SOURCE 5 – British budget

'Anthony Barber, the Chancellor of the Exchequer, ... unveiled his pre-Christmas crisis budget.... It cut a massive £1,200 million from public spending, including axing one in five of the schools and colleges due to be built in 1974–5.... The mini-budget was more immediately concerned with the effects of OPEC's massive oil price increase, shown in November's £270 million trade gap.... The chancellor's priority has been to cut the nation's demand for non-oil imports in order to cope with the higher OPEC prices....'

Longman Chronicle of the 20th Century

UNEMPLOYMENT

It also resulted in higher **unemployment** as companies cut back production. This was made worse by the immediate response of governments to cut back spending. The combination of unemployment and inflation became known as **stagflation**. Some recovery began in 1975 but unemployment remained high during the 1970s.

Governments were faced with **high spending** on unemployment and **lower income** from taxes. This led to increased **borrowing** by countries. Governments made efforts to control wages with incomes policies. They also tried to introduce **employment schemes** and **industrial subsidies.**

EFFECTS ON COUNTRIES

However, some countries fared worse than others. The best performers were Austria and West Germany while Britain and Italy were among the worst.

In **West Germany**, the government was helped by the stronger economy before the crisis began. By the end of the 1960s West Germany was the strongest economy in Europe. During the crisis, it decided on a policy of controlling inflation. It reduced the money supply, employers negotiated good wage deals and inflation remained lower than other countries – about half the level. But unemployment rose to one million in the 1970s and doubled that in the 1980s after the second oil crisis.

Britain had economic problems even before the Oil Crisis in 1973. Bad management, powerful trade unions and strikes contributed to the economic problems. In 1972 striking British coal miners gathered outside the Tower of London after failing in their attempt to force their way into the House of Commons.

Britain suffered worst of all. It became 'the sick man of Europe' in the 1970s. Its economy was already weaker than others in the 1960s – bad management, powerful trade unions resisting change, a high level of strikes and poor productivity all contributed to slower growth in Britain in the 1960s. This situation was made worse by the oil crisis and membership of the EEC (1973). Its inflation rose to 25% in 1975. Unemployment rose to over one million in the 1970s and to four million in the 1980s; the latter partly due to the government's policy of controlling inflation.

The **Soviet Union** had a different experience. Its economy was already declining. But it was a major exporter of oil and gas so it benefited greatly from the increased prices. Indeed the revenue (money) the Soviet government got from the exports to the West covered up the weaknesses in the Soviet economy. These were eventually exposed in the later 1970s and 1980s and led to the downfall of Communism. The **satellite states** in Eastern Europe also benefited during the Oil Crisis because they still received Soviet oil and gas at a reduced rate.

SOURCE 6 – Changes in industry

'By 1972, the British Steel Corporation (BSC) was one of the world's biggest producers, but it struggled to stay competitive. The oil crisis of 1973 compounded its problems. The rise in energy prices meant customers wanted materials that were cheaper and used less energy, such as plastic. Steel consumption fell, and the recession of 1979 dealt the sector another blow. Within a year, BSC had brought in huge cuts.... In Wales alone, 25,000 steelmakers lost their jobs, a pattern that was repeated across the United Kingdom. But the strategy paid off. BSC, which had been losing up to £4 million a day, was making profits of £100 million a year by 1986. The industry was privatised.'

BBC News Online Business, 6 December 1999

FURTHER REACTIONS

In the medium term, governments in the West tried to **reduce dependence** on Arab oil and on oil in general. This included higher taxes on oil, encouraging greater insulation in buildings, promoting alternative sources of energy and exploring for European sources of gas and oil.

The economic crisis also created **political problems**. In many countries there were **changes of government** when they tried to bring in policies which were unpopular. This happened in Britain, for example, in 1974 when a Conservative government was replaced by a Labour government. There was also **disagreement** between Western Europe and America on the Arab-Israeli question because of Europe's dependence on Arab oil and America's commitment to Israel.

Gas heating became an attractive alternative to reduce dependence on oil. But governments also encouraged better insulation in buildings and the use of other power sources such as wind and coal.

SOURCE 7 – Europe in a dilemma

'The Arab decision [to stop supplying oil to the US] creates a cruel dilemma for America's allies in Europe, including Britain. There is an acute shortage of refining capacity in America, and another million barrels a day of refined products are shipped there. The European governments, if they continue these shipments of what was originally Arab crude oil to America, run the risk of having their own supplies affected in retaliation.'

Peter Hillmore,
The Guardian, 23 October 1973

SOURCE 8 – Europe and America

'The war in the Middle East has led to a crisis within NATO as its European members, under pressure from an oil embargo, split from the US in their policy towards the Arab-Israeli conflict. When the Americans organised a huge airlift of arms for Israel, four European members of NATO refused to let the US use bases on their territory or fly through their airspace.... All were anxious to avoid the oil embargo against the US widening to cover them, as it did in Holland, when the Dutch government came out in support of Israel....'

Longman Chronicle of the 20th Century

SOURCE 9

A Dutch cartoon from the 1970s commenting on the Oil Crisis showing four Western leaders – Brandt (West Germany), Pompidou (France), Nixon (USA) and Heath (Britain).

SOURCE 10 – Wind power

'It took the Middle East oil crisis of the 1970s to show that wind turbines had a potential far beyond self-sufficiency. Rising prices and uncertain supplies exposed the vulnerability of fossil fuels. At the same time, even before Chernobyl, the great white hope of nuclear energy was beginning to show its cracks.

Wind power offered an alternative which would never run out, was available locally and didn't produce the pollution which inevitably flowed from existing sources – everything from poisoned forests to tar-wrecked coastlines to the hazards of radioactive waste.'

Denmark – Birthplace of Modern Wind Power,
archive.greenpeace.org

SOURCE 11 – Too much oil

'The situation in the world oil market changed completely after the two oil crises in 1973 and 1979.... Energy savings became the priority, to the detriment of growth, and naturally the demand for oil fell. The net result was overcapacity. The oil crisis also led to a serious miscalculation. After the 1973 price explosion, it was generally assumed that prices for crude oil and refined products would remain high or go even higher. The opposite happened. As a result of energy savings and overcapacity, prices began to drop.'

Esso History,
www.essobenelux.com

SOURCE 12 – The Arab embargo – from oil crisis to OPEC crisis

'A quarter of a century after the Arab oil embargo, the West's lingering nightmare that the petrol pumps might again run dry has scarcely felt so remote. Awash with oil, the once-mighty OPEC cartel now suffers the lowest real crude prices since it tipped the world's leading industrial powers into crisis in 1973....

Twenty-five years later, in the worst oil glut for a decade, it is OPEC that is feeling the backlash of the first oil shock. This year's severe glut is only the latest in a series caused by persistent oil market overcapacity, partly a consequence of the 1973 embargo.... Vowing not to be caught out again, the West invested in its own oil. The major companies, sent packing by the nationalisations which swept OPEC producers, invested heavily in regions like the North Sea. New technologies were invented to slash the cost of finding crude. Power generators in nations without oil turned nuclear and then increasingly to cleaner fuels like natural gas. Consumers also became more efficient. High taxes in most parts of the industrialised world, with the exception of the US, have replaced high prices as the incentive for efficiency gains. In Europe, tax now counts for more than eighty per cent of the price of gasoline.... Oil demand growth this decade has been quelled to little more than two per cent a year, from seven per cent annually in the 20 years before the 1973 embargo.'

Richard Mably, London,
The Middle East Times, 1998

SOURCE 13 – Effects of crisis

'The worst hit were the poorest countries... The number of Africans and Asians who died in consequence of Arab oil policy in the decade after 1973 must be calculated in tens of millions.... It acted as a fierce brake on the energy-intensive leading sectors responsible for the prolonged expansion in the American, West European and Japanese economies, producing an abrupt decline in output and unemployment...'

P Johnson, *Modern Times*

Source 14 – World Energy Use and Population Growth

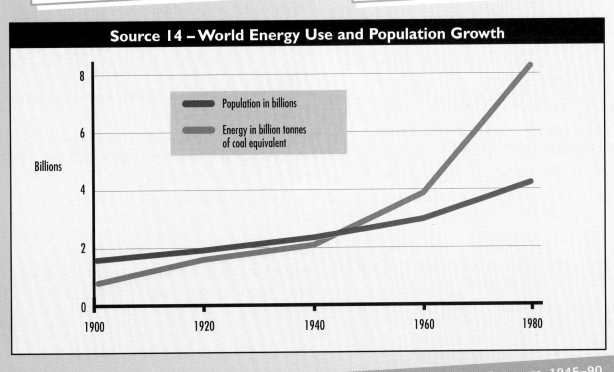

Population in billions

Energy in billion tonnes of coal equivalent

CASE STUDY QUESTIONS

COMPREHENSION

1. In Source 1, how did Western-owned oil companies make vast wealth?

2. What did OPEC decide to do in the 1970s?

3. In Source 2, why did OPEC do 'what they had to do'?

4. According to Source 3, what caused the post-war boom?

5. Why did Paul Johnson say 'all the industrial nations were short-sighted'?

6. In Source 4, why did a quarter of Britain's petrol stations remain closed?

7. What did the British government appeal to people to do?

8. What countries had introduced, or proposed to introduce, a ban on Sunday driving?

9. Explain one way in which the Chancellor proposed to save £1,200 million.

10. What was the Chancellor's main priority (aim) in the budget?

11. According to Source 6, how did the oil crisis affect the demand for steel?

12. How did the British Steel Corporation respond to the effects of the two recessions?

13. In Source 7, why were America's allies in Europe in a dilemma?

14. In Source 8, why did NATO split?

15. What NATO country had an oil embargo imposed on it like the US? Why?

16. What is the message of the cartoon in Source 9?

17. According to Source 10, what are the disadvantages of fossil fuels?

18. What are the advantages of wind power?

19. In Source 11, what did everybody assume would happen after the 1973 oil crisis?

20. In Source 12, who vowed not to be caught again? Why?

21. What action was taken so as not to be caught out again?

22. Who does Source 13 say were the worst hit by the oil crisis?

COMPARISON

1. Do Source 1 and Source 2 agree on the reasons for OPEC's actions?

2. Do Sources 1 and 2 lay heavier blame on OPEC for the oil crisis than Source 3?

3. Would you agree that the actions of the British government in Sources 4 and 5 were harsh?

4. In what way was the action of the British government in Source 5, and the British Steel Corporation in Source 6, similar?

5. According to Sources 7 and 8, how did the oil crisis affect relations between Europe and America?

6. How does Source 8 help you understand the cartoon in Source 9?

7. How did wind power in Source 10 lead to over-capacity in Source 11?

8. In Source 12, what actions increased oil supply and what actions led to energy savings?

9. How do the actions in Source 12 explain why 'prices began to drop' (Source 11)?

10. What 'energy-intensive leading sectors' (Source 13) are mentioned in Source 3?

11. How were they 'responsible for the prolonged expansion of the American, Western European and Japanese economies'?

12. Does Source 3 help explain Source 14?

CRITICISM

1. Source 1 and Source 2 are taken from websites. How would you judge their reliability as sources?

2. Source 4 is an English newspaper report of the time. What examples can you use from the report to show the advantages of newspapers as sources for history?

3. Source 6 is from the BBC News website. Does the extract seem favourable to the actions of the British Steel Corporation? Comment on the sentence, 'But the strategy paid off.' Is there any other viewpoint that could have been expressed?

4. Which side does the cartoon (Source 9) take on the Oil Crisis? Since it is a Dutch cartoon, does this account for the viewpoint of the cartoon? How helpful are political cartoons as historical sources? Does this cartoon help explain the origins of the Oil Crisis? Does it agree with the views in Source 1?

5. What evidence is there in Source 10 to show that the writer is biased?

6. Source 11 is taken from an oil company website – the Exxon Mobil website. Is there evidence of bias in the report?

7. In Source 12, what is the author's attitude to OPEC? Is he objective in his attitude? How well does his report help you to understand the issues of Source 11 – overcapacity and falling prices?

8. Source 3 and Source 13 are by the same author. Do you think he agreed with the Arab oil embargo?

9. Sources 1, 4, 7 and 12 are written by journalists, and Sources 3 and 13 by a historian. Which would you consider more reliable – journalists or historians? Can you provide evidence from the sources in support of your answer? What advantages do journalists and historians have over each other in writing about events?

10. What use are graphs in helping historians understand events such as the Oil Crisis of 1973?

11. Make your own notes on the usefulness (advantages and disadvantages) of the various types of sources used here.

CONTEXTUALISATION

1. How successful were the Western European economies in the decade before the Oil Crisis in 1973?

2. Using the sources above, write a short account of the immediate impact of the Oil Crisis on Europe.

3. How did the Oil Crisis affect the Western European economies?

4. How did Western Europe try to cope with the impact of the Oil Crisis?

5. Using the sources above and the account, write a report on the Oil Crisis, 1973 – origins, progress and results.

Post-war Economies

Eastern Europe and the Soviet Union **suffered** more in the Second World War than Western Europe. In Russia, after the war, there were 25 million killed and 25 million homeless. The country had experienced its own **scorched earth** policy as well as the **scorched earth** policy of the retreating Germans. There was enormous destruction of buildings, transport, industry and agricultural land – 1,700 towns and 70,000 villages were destroyed.

The Eastern European countries also experienced the sweep of two armies; and some countries, for example, Poland suffered even more than the Soviet Union. After the war, the Russians imposed Communism on these countries, and created the so-called **People's Democracies**.

Post-war Reconstruction in the Soviet Union

Before the Second World War, **Stalin** used Five Year Plans to **industrialise** and **collectivise** the Soviet economy. After the war, he approached the reconstruction of the country in the same way as he organised the earlier Five Year Plans. The aim of the fourth Five Year Plan (1946–50) was to restore the Soviet economy to pre-war levels. Gosplan (the State Planning Commission) set targets for both industry and agriculture.

Agriculture, however, failed to reach its targets. There were **shortages** of meat, milk and butter; there was even a famine in parts of the Ukraine in 1946. The number of collectives was reduced – from 250,000 in 1947 to almost 100,000 in 1952. But there was a **shortage of men** (because of the war) and of **tractors** (because of the failure to invest in agriculture). Stalin also imposed **higher taxes** on the peasants (farmers).

Instead, **heavy industry** was promoted, huge power stations were built and new towns were created. Industry surpassed its targets; industrial production in 1950 was **seventy per cent greater** than in 1940. Public amenities were also provided, such as libraries, parks

Male and female workers involved in the construction of a giant tractor plant in the Soviet Union in 1947 as part of Stalin's new Five Year Plan.

and theatres, and the Soviet Union was the **second largest** industrial power in the world. Industry was **more successful** for a variety of reasons:

- There were no restrictions on the use of **child labour**.
- Up to ten million workers – German prisoners of war, returning Russian soldiers and others – were used as **forced labour**.
- **Reparations**, such as coal, oil and industrial equipment – in some cases whole factories, were taken from Eastern Europe.
- Overall, Stalin imposed **hard work** on the Russian people.

Hydroelectric power stations played an important part in Soviet industrialisation. The Saratov hydroelectric plant was built in the mid-1950s in western Russia.

'*[Stalin] had to mobilise them again and extract from them every ounce of energy so that they should rehabilitate the wrecked and overworked industries and rebuild the scores of cities and towns reduced to ruins. He met the people's utter weariness with his unwearying ruthlessness.*' (Isaac Deutscher)

FURTHER PROBLEMS

However, while targets were often reached, industry still suffered from a number of other **problems**. One was a problem of **quality**. This could be seen in the case of housing. Many people were rehoused by 1950 but the housing was of a low standard. A second problem was the **waste** of money on projects built to glorify Stalin. An example was the Volga-Don Canal which had very little traffic but many statues of Stalin along its banks. A third problem was the huge spending on the **Soviet Army** which took money from other parts of the economy.

Magnitogorsk was one of the new towns created by Stalin's Five Year Plans in the 1930s. It continued its growth during the Second World War and after the war. These apartment blocks were constructed to house the steelworkers.

The People's Democracies in Eastern Europe

Immediately after the Second World War, the Communist parties shared power with other political parties in Eastern Europe. These governments controlled **mixed economies** with both public (government) and private ownership of industry. The most urgent problem they faced was **land reform.** They rejected collectivisation and instead divided landed estates among poorer peasants. Some of the land was also organised as state farms. However, once the Communist Parties had established complete control, they brought in a **Soviet-style economy** with **central planning**. *'There is only one road to socialism, the Soviet road.'* This meant government-control of industry and collectivisation of agriculture.

Agriculture: In **agriculture**, the process of collectivisation was accomplished in stages between 1948 and 1960 in most countries. It was justified on the basis that *'small-scale farming ... made the use of modern machinery and agricultural techniques impossible.'* There was much less resistance to collectivisation than had been the case in Russia itself thirty years before, except in Poland and Yugoslavia. By 1966, 90% of farming land was collectivised, except in Poland where only about 15% was collectivised. However, apart from collectivisation, there was **little investment** in agriculture and this often resulted in **food shortages**.

Industry: Instead, most investment occurred in **industry**. First, the government **nationalised** (took under government ownership) existing industry. This was accompanied by a policy of **rapid industrialisation**, with an emphasis on **heavy industry** – steel and machinery – as in Russia, and less emphasis on consumer industries. In following this pattern they were copying the Soviet example, but they were also strongly encouraged by Stalin who needed these supplies during the Korean War (1950–53).

The Eastern European economies grew rapidly, especially in the 1950s. The Communist revolution changed the countries from **agrarian** to **industrial** societies. This was accompanied by rapid **urbanisation** – by 1960 most Eastern European countries had a higher proportion of their people living in cities than in the countryside. Due to the rapid urbanisation, there was overcrowding and bad living conditions. Very often these economic changes were enforced by **political coercion**.

Post-war propaganda for the Five Year Plans (1946). A Soviet worker holds the Five Year Plan: 'With honour, we will fulfil and fulfil again Stalin's Five Year Plan'. How useful are propaganda posters as sources for historians?

Trade with the Soviet Union: The Soviet Union tried to control the economies of Eastern Europe by setting up **Comecon** (Council of Mutual Economic Assistance) in 1949, to regulate trade between the Communist countries and to co-ordinate national economic plans. Through Comecon, Stalin treated the countries largely as colonies of the

Soviet Union. The Soviet Union supplied much of the raw materials and the Eastern European countries manufactured the goods for the Soviet Union.

The People's Democracies after Stalin

Comecon took on new life after Stalin's death in 1953. There was **greater freedom** for each country to concentrate on what it was best able to do. By the middle of 1960s most of the countries believed in their right to reach Communism in their own way, some even trading with the West. However, all this was still within the **framework** of a Soviet-style economy with central planning, and heavy dependence on the Soviet Union. In spite of difficulties, this system provided strong economic growth in the 1950s and 1960s. The growth continued into the 1970s when they benefited from **cheaper Soviet oil** while the Oil Crisis hit the West.

Yugoslavia, also, experienced strong growth but the structure of its economy differed from the other Eastern European countries. After the government's attempt to enforce rapid industrialisation and collectivisation failed in the late 1940s, a different approach was taken in Yugoslavia. There was still government ownership of industry but the factories were **managed** differently. There was a shift from centralised planning to **worker management** with elected **workers' councils** and **management boards.** In agriculture, **private ownership** accounted for most of the farming land. The rest were state co-operatives. In this case the government-owned farms were more productive but agricultural productivity was still too low. With its own form of Communism, Yugoslavia also experienced rapid economic growth which was helped by an expanding **tourist industry** and **emigrants' remittances** from Yugoslavs who worked in the EEC.

The Soviet Economy after Stalin

After the death of Stalin in 1953, the Soviet economy continued to follow the pattern established by him – the economy was centrally planned and targets were set for all sectors of agriculture and industry. Successive leaders made some changes but these did not alter the basic structure of the economy.

The Soviet Economy under Khrushchev

One of those changes occurred under Khrushchev. He brought in **decentralisation** of planning. One hundred and five **regional councils** were set up to organise their own areas, with Gosplan responsible for overall planning. But there was **little co-ordination** between the councils so targets were often missed either through over- or under-production of different goods.

Khrushchev also changed the emphasis to more **modern industry** such as plastics and fertilisers. But his slogan of *'Catch up and overtake the US in per capita output by 1970'* was too ambitious. Even though the Soviet economy expanded considerably, heavy spending on **armaments** and the **space programme** held up economic progress.

Industry: In **industry**, the Soviet Union still emphasised **heavy industrial goods**, but now more **consumer goods** were produced – radios, cars and clothes. As Khrushchev said, *'You cannot put theory into your soup or Marxism into your clothes. If, after forty years of Communism, a person cannot have a glass of milk or a pair of shoes, he will not believe that Communism is a good thing, no matter what you tell him.'*

As a result, the **standard of living** improved – wages rose faster than prices, there was a shorter working week and free medical care. There were more houses and flats for the workers but these were often of poor quality.

Soviet space technology overtook the West when the Soviet Union sent the first satellite into space. It also sent the first man, Yuri Gagarin, into space.

Soviet technology: In a number of areas, however, the Soviet Union **equalled** or **surpassed** Western technology. The Soviet **space programme** surprised the West. The Soviets sent the first satellite and the first man into space. Soviet **military equipment** also matched that of the West. Furthermore, they developed a strong **nuclear industry** and their national airline, **Aeroflot**, expanded rapidly. Some of this technological progress was due to the expansion of **education**. There was free second- and third-level education and illiteracy disappeared. Contrary to Communist ideals, there were also specialist schools for talented people.

Agriculture: Khrushchev took a particular interest in **agriculture** with the aim of increasing agricultural production. He took the unusual step of touring the country, talking to officials and peasants, and encouraging production.

He began the **Virgin Lands project** which brought 75 million acres of new land into use, mainly in Siberia. About 300,000 people migrated there to farm the lands. After initial success in growing more maize, the project ran into difficulties due to overcultivation, lack of fertiliser and soil erosion.

He also gave **increased prices** to the collectives, and reduced their number; by 1967 there were less than 40,000 collectives, while the number of state farms was increased. But Russian agriculture still failed to produce enough food, especially in the early 1960s. Bread rationing was introduced and 12 million tons of grain was imported from Canada and Australia (1963) due to bad harvests.

Khrushchev could not overcome the **main problems** in agriculture. Agriculture had been neglected for too long. Overall it suffered from a **shortage of investment** – more fertiliser was needed, more irrigation and more agricultural machinery. Even where there were increases in tractor production, very often maintenance was so poor that tractor life was short.

The Soviet Economy under Brezhnev

Since Khrushchev's policies failed, agriculture still posed a problem into the late 1960s and the 1970s – indeed, it was the weakest link in the Soviet economy. The new leadership under **Brezhnev** amalgamated farms and gave huge financial support to agriculture. **Higher prices** were promised for the collectives and state farms, they paid **less tax**, there was **more investment** in machinery, trucks and fertiliser and there was **cheaper electricity**. There was also more encouragement for **private plots**.

However, poor harvests alternated with good harvests though there was an overall improvement in the late 1960s. This progress continued into the 1970s with a better standard of living for the peasants. By 1981, agricultural output was **twenty per cent higher** than 10 years earlier. The main reason for the increased production in the 1970s was greater use of fertiliser.

Soviet agriculture was inefficient in spite of huge amounts of money put into collectivisation. Sometimes Soviet soldiers had to be brought out to assist with the potato harvest as here on a collective farm near Moscow.

Problems with Agriculture

However, there were still **significant problems** with agriculture:

- Agriculture used a huge proportion of the Soviet Union's resources – much more than in the West. In 1981, this amounted to an investment of $33 billion dollars.
- A **quarter** of the Soviet workforce still worked on the land, which again was much higher than in the West. Yet, the country had to **mobilise** millions of townspeople and soldiers to harvest the crops in the mid-1980s.
- In spite of this, the country was still **importing food** from the West, and paying for this with oil exports. Twenty-three million tons were imported in 1973 as overall grain production fell despite the huge investment.

A giant metalworking plant in the Soviet Union. While Soviet technology matched western technology in iron and steel production, it fell behind in more modern industries such as computers, chemicals and consumer goods.

- **Machines** were often of poor quality and with poor maintenance they wore out quickly. The private plots showed up the problems of the collectives and the state farms. They produced 30% of total farm produce with only 4% of the farmland.
- Indeed, Brezhnev was throwing good money after bad. He was **failing** to solve the real problems of agriculture – shortage of skilled labour, a bad rural road system, compulsory quotas given to the state, poor technology, and lack of storage and refrigeration.

But whether these could be solved without abolishing the system of collectives and state farms was a question nobody dared discuss. If **decollectivisation** was necessary it could not be done because Communist ideas and the political power of the Communist Party were against reform.

Problems with Industry

In **industry** there were also problems. The Soviet Union was a match for the West in space, in military technology, and in iron and steel. But it lagged behind in more modern sectors – computers, chemicals, industrial research and in consumer goods. In the 1970s for the first time the Soviet Union planned a faster growth in consumer goods compared to industrial goods. Russians could buy more furniture, radios, refrigerators, TVs and watches. There was also a new housing programme which, as before, concentrated on apartments.

But during the 1970s there was a **slowdown** in economic growth which fell from 12% a year in the 1950s to 4% in the 1970s. This was well below planned targets. Falling growth rates led to Russians discussing how to improve the Soviet economic system. Was the slowdown in the economy **temporary** or due to **fundamental flaws** in the system?

Central Planning

Various changes were made to improve economic performance. Reforms in the mid-1960s abolished Khrushchev's decentralisation. Instead there was a return to the older system of **ministerial control** of each sector of the economy. Central planning was still in the hands of **Gosplan** (State Planning Commission). But there were many problems with central planning:

- Gosplan was **out of touch** with what was happening at the grassroots level and interfered in too much detail. Gosplan was still concentrating on **older products** while the economy was becoming more complicated so that it was impossible to plan in the old way for each factory.

Production of consumer goods was neglected in the Soviet Union under Communism. There were bread queues and shortages of bread and other products.

Some Soviet shops were small and old-fashioned as here – this man pays for his groceries through a hatch in the shop window.

Consumer goods such as cars, like this Lada, were based on out-of-date western technology. The Lada was based on an older Fiat car.

- Soviet economists suggested relaxing targets and emphasising **profits** rather than production. But managers were still under the control of state bureaucracy. At factory level, they were interested only in production, not sales – in spite of the fact that the wrong products were often produced with nobody to buy them.
- New designs or new methods were avoided because any temporary hold-up in production would affect targets.
- There was also a **lack of co-ordination** between the different ministries.

Communist Party officials preferred centralisation because it gave them more power. Maybe it was the Communist Party itself which was the problem.

Apart from central planning, two other problems were high-lighted. For one thing, **more research and technology** were needed. To solve this problem efforts were made to buy in **Western technology** from the 1960s onwards in the extraction of oil and gas, the manufacture of cars and trucks, and even Pepsi-Cola and jeans.

Others blamed the **workers**. There was a campaign against the **work-shy** in the 1980s. Workers were guaranteed jobs but that meant some took this for granted and had no incentive to work harder. As well as this, workers were kept on in factories and offices even when automation took over. This resulted in surplus workers in some factories but shortages in other areas.

But the problems of the Soviet economy were hidden for a while by the **Oil Crisis** in 1973. This benefited the Soviet Union because of its huge reserves of oil and gas. Oil and gas exported to the Western economies gained from the high prices. They were exported to pay for Western technology and grain. But even in these key industries targets were not met, and by the 1980s world prices of oil and gas were falling.

After the collapse of Communism in 1991, western consumer goods became widely available in the former Soviet Union as this billboard advertisement for Pepsi in Moscow shows.

Economic Reform and the Collapse of the Communist Economies

By the 1980s, the **Years of Stagnation**, it was clear the Soviet Union was badly in need of reform. Centralised planning was a failure. Economic performance was well behind the West. Agriculture was inefficient and there were substantial food imports. The country was heavily dependent on money earned from oil and gas exports. Shortages gave rise to corruption, bribery and hoarding. Investment in the military was too high. Some of the younger leaders, such as **Gorbachev**, knew this but older leaders were reluctant to change.

Gorbachev wanted to reform Communism so that it could compete with capitalism. He brought in his policies of **glasnost** (openness) and **perestroika** (reconstruction). He gave greater freedom to factories to decide what to produce and what prices to set. He allowed some **private ownership** of services and small-scale manufacturing.

But in changing from Communist central planning to a mixed economy, some of his policies made the economy worse rather than better. They led to increased wages, inflation (higher prices) and foreign debt. Neither did consumers benefit from the changes. Instead there were further **shortages** of meat, milk, tea and coffee, longer **food queues** and **rationing**. By 1990, the process of political and economic reform which Gorbachev began led to the **downfall of Communism** in the people's democracies in 1989, and in the Soviet Union in 1991. Communism had been unable to reform itself to provide the standard of living which the people demanded.

ORDINARY LEVEL AND HIGHER LEVEL HOMEWORK EXERCISES

ORDINARY LEVEL

1. Study the following document carefully and answer the questions below:

   'How well have the Communist economies grown? When Sputnik was launched [in 1957], Khrushchev promised that the Russian economy would overtake the American economy by 1970. It is hard to compare official statistics from Communist countries with Western ones. They ignore the very poor quality of consumer goods in the Eastern bloc and the shortage of certain services. Life is harsher with fewer luxuries than in the West. Communist economies are run from central planning offices. Officials have to decide how much each factory will produce, what prices they will charge and what wages they will pay. Trying to coordinate all this is too big and complex a task and grave mistakes are made which lead to shortages or to waste.'

   B Rigby, *The Western Alliance*

   (i) Who was Khrushchev? What was his promise?

   (ii) What are *'official statistics'*?

   (iii) Why is it *'hard to compare official statistics from Communist countries with Western ones'*?

   (iv) Give one example of differences in the economies between East and West.

   (v) How are Communist economies run *'from central planning offices'*?

(vi) What criticisms does the author make about the Communist system of economic planning?

(vii) Mention one other weakness in (a) Soviet industry, and (b) Soviet agriculture.

2. Write **paragraph answers** on each of the following questions:

(i) Post-war reconstruction in the Soviet Union.

(ii) Economic development in the People's Democracies after the Second World War from 1945 to 1953.

(iii) Khrushchev and the Soviet economy.

(iv) Problems in Soviet agriculture in the 1950s and 1960s.

(v) Problems in Soviet industry in the 1950s and 1960s.

(vi) Gorbachev's economic reforms.

3. Write **long answers** on each of the following questions:

(i) How did the Communist economies in Eastern Europe, including the Soviet Union, develop after the Second World War while Stalin was in power?

(ii) How did various Soviet governments attempt to solve the economic problems of the Soviet Union after the death of Stalin?

(iii) How did Gorbachev's reforms in the Soviet Union contribute to the downfall of Communism? (Department of Education, Sample Paper) (See also Chapter 9, The Cold War in Europe.)

HIGHER LEVEL

1. How did the Soviet government under Stalin cope with post-war reconstruction?

2. How successful was the development of Communist economies in the People's Democracies of Eastern Europe after the Second World War?

3. How did Khrushchev and Brezhnev respond to the economic problems facing the Soviet Union in the 1950s and 1960s and how successful were they?

OR

'After 1953, the Soviet economy faced fundamental problems in both agriculture and industry which the Soviet government failed to solve.' Discuss.

4. Discuss the view that the downfall of Communism under Gorbachev was largely due to the failure of the Soviet government to solve the economic problems of the country. (See also Chapter 9, The Cold War in Europe.)

TEST YOURSELF AT
my-etest.com

Marriage and the Family

In post-war Europe the family, based on marriage, remained the **basic unit of society**. In the immediate post-war years, the family was based on the breadwinner husband and the housekeeper wife. It was still assumed that the breadwinner had the last word in deciding how money was spent and on disciplining children.

The family fulfilled certain **functions** in society – reproductive, caring, social and cultural. Already some of these functions had begun to change in the previous century. But the pace of change speeded up considerably over the next forty years as **modern industrial society** spread. In the middle of the century, families in Europe were still characterised by low age of marriage, a high marriage rate and women working at home. But this had changed by 1990. Family life was then characterised by high age of marriage, low marriage rate, less women working at home and a high divorce rate.

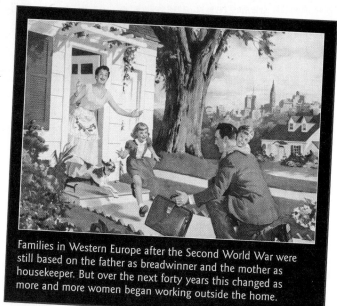

Families in Western Europe after the Second World War were still based on the father as breadwinner and the mother as housekeeper. But over the next forty years this changed as more and more women began working outside the home.

THE STRUCTURE OF THE FAMILY

The **legal position** of the father as head of the family and decider of things was abolished. The structure of the family changed from being **hierarchical** (based on authority) to being more **democratic**, somewhat like developments in society generally. This coincided with changes in the role of women, as more women continued in education and at work. The family was founded less on the **division of labour** between the breadwinner husband and the housekeeper wife than before. As the 1960s and 1970s progressed, marriage was seen more as a **partnership** in line with prevailing views on the equality of sexes. Increased leisure times allowed men to share in some of the household tasks.

YOU AND HIGH SPEED GAS!

Two out of three housewives (and the Sunday help) use High Speed Gas for cooking. The third would, as well, if she knew how much easier life was for the other two!

Advertising reflected the changes in family life as men took a greater part in household work from the 1960s onwards. What are the strengths and weaknesses of advertisements as sources for the historian?

THE ROLE OF THE FAMILY

The role of the family in society also changed. Families shed many of the functions they had in previous generations:

- The **reproductive** function of the family lessened with falling birth rates and the birth of children outside marriage. In the immediate post-war years, however, there was a **baby boom**. But soon more women worked outside the home and education prolonged the dependency of children on their parents into the teens or longer. Contraception and abortion made the limitation of families easier and so families had fewer children. The birth rate declined in both Western and Eastern Europe. In **Britain** it fell from 18 per 1,000 in the early 1960s to 13 per 1,000 in 1974. The birth rate in **Soviet Russia** declined from 25 per 1,000 in 1959 to 17 per 1,000 in the early 1970s.

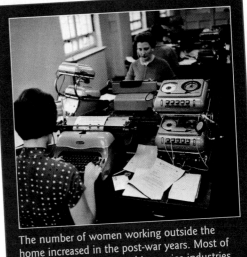

The number of women working outside the home increased in the post-war years. Most of the new jobs were created in service industries such as this typing pool in an office (1960).

- By the 1970s, more of those children were born **outside marriage**. In Sweden, almost forty per cent of children were born out of wedlock in 1979 and rates in other Western and Eastern countries began to increase in the late 1970s as well, as marriage became less fashionable. In 1990 about one-fifth of all births in Western Europe were illegitimate.
- The function of the family in **caring** for children and for older people was lessened by the spread of the **welfare state**.
- The **cultural** function of the family in passing on information and defining the roles of males and females was lessened by **outside forces** such as the media, education and peer groups.
- The function of the family in the **socialisation** of children declined as child care centres, nursery schools and **education** took over some of the responsibilities from parents.
- **Education** was expanded to meet the needs of modern industrial society for a better-trained workforce since families could not fulfil that function. **Primary education** became **compulsory** and illiteracy disappeared. Numbers staying to **secondary education** increased dramatically – in some countries such as Belgium they increased 4 times. University education also expanded rapidly – multiplying 5 or 6 times, admittedly from low numbers. This led to an increase in the number of universities and institutes of technology – in Britain there were 28 new universities, 5 in Portugal and 11 in Spain.

DIVORCE

These and other changes increased **pressures on families** and on relationships between husbands and wives. **Easier divorce** made it easier to end marriages. Divorce laws in the earlier part of the twentieth century worked largely on the principle of fault or guilt. In the early post-war years there was a rise in divorce and separation due largely to the disruption of war, movements of population, separation of families and easier divorce laws.

A women's liberation demonstration with conflicting messages. Divorce rates increased in the 1960s and 1970s as families experienced greater social pressures.

In the 1950s the levels of divorce fell, only to rise again in the 1960s and early 1970s. By the late 1960s substantial further changes were made to **divorce laws** which made divorce easier to obtain. Britain, the Netherlands, Belgium, France and even Italy (in opposition to the Catholic Church) passed liberal divorce laws. In Eastern Europe and the Soviet Union divorce was also easier to obtain. This led to an increase in divorces – in the West one-third to one-half of marriages ended in divorce in the 1970s. It was higher in most Eastern European counties than the West and higher also in Scandinavian countries.

Variations in the rate of divorce across Europe depended on the proportion of people living in cities, the influence of religion and public attitudes towards divorce. Countries such as Greece, Italy and Portugal, where more people lived in the countryside and where religion was strong, had lower divorce rates.

As families broke up through more divorces, the decreasing influence of religion and greater sexual freedom led to an increase in the numbers of **couples living together** (cohabitation). This began in Denmark and Sweden but by the late 1980s it had become the normal pre-marriage stage in France and Britain. It was much less so in Italy and Spain. However, in spite of the increase in couples living together, marriage still remained **fashionable** – very often those who divorced remarried and those who lived together did so prior to regular marriage.

The Role of Women

One of the most important changes in post-war society was the improving economic and political position of women. Simone de Beauvoir's *The Second Sex* highlighted the second-class role of women in the early post-war period. Forty years later, however, the role of women had changed greatly due to economic, social and technological factors.

> **KEY CONCEPT: FEMINISM** advocates equal political, economic and social rights for women. The Women's Movement was organised in the late 1960s to promote feminism.

SOCIAL AND TECHNOLOGICAL CHANGES

The **Great Boom** of the 1950s and 1960s created many more jobs for both men and women. Social and technological changes made it easier for women to fill these jobs. **Domestic appliances** – refrigerators, vacuum cleaners and washing machines – became more easily available from the mid-1950s onwards. As an indication of the changes, in France alone the amount of washing powder produced increased from 8,000 tons in 1952 to 164,000 tons in 1958 – an increase of more than 20 times. These changes allowed more married women to take up work outside the home in the late 1950s and 1960s.

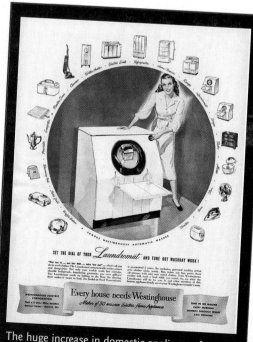

The huge increase in domestic appliances from washing machines to toasters helped with household work and made it easier for married women to work outside the home.

WOMEN AT WORK

As a result, the percentage of women in the **labour force** rose in most European countries from 1945 to the 1960s. It was highest in the Soviet Union, Austria and Sweden (50–60%), and lowest but increasing in Mediterranean countries (20–35%). In industrial **Britain** the main changes came from the end of the 1950s when the proportion of women in the workforce grew from 31% in 1951 to 36% in 1975. In more rural **Greece** the proportion grew from 18% in 1961 to 32% in 1971. In Eastern Europe, **Hungary** reflected the experience there when the proportion of women in the workforce grew from 29% in 1949 to 45% in 1980.

Not only were there more women in the workforce, the number of **married women** at work exceeded the number of single women. The increase in married women at work was due to increased marriage rates, smaller families, and the shorter time of childbearing reduced from an average of 15 years to 4 years. Many women returned to work after bringing up children. Modern appliances for housework helped this process.

THE WOMEN'S MOVEMENT

The growing number of women at work high-lighted some issues such as equal pay, crèches and schooling. But it wasn't until the late 1960s that a women's movement grew up to push the case of women. American in inspiration, the **Women's Movement** did not make an impact in Europe until after the student riots of 1968. **Feminism** gave encouragement to women to fulfil their potential in society. But it was more successful in northern Europe than in the south because a higher proportion of women had jobs and the Catholic Church had less influence.

The women's liberation movement became more widespread in the late 1960s and the early 1970s. It advocated equal political, economic and social rights for women. In this demonstration the message is clear.

Through protests and pamphlets, women campaigned for **legal changes** in their status. They showed that existing law discriminated against women and this led to changes to correct the legal system. In the countries of Western Europe **equal pay** for equal work was granted and **sexual discrimination** was outlawed. Sometimes change in the laws was slow – it took until 1977 before West Germany removed the condition that a wife had to get permission from her husband to work.

WOMEN IN SOCIETY

Feminists criticised the broader **portrayal of women** in society. They attacked children's books, comics, television, toys and schooling which they said reinforced the old fashioned division between boys and girls. They also criticised the portrayal of women in **advertising** and their use in beauty contests, which they said was exploitation for commercial profit.

There were significant increases in women in **professional** (doctors, solicitors) and **managerial** positions. This was helped by increasing numbers of women in higher education in both Eastern and Western Europe. Numbers at universities ranged from 26% (West Germany) to 41% (France). In Eastern Europe, the number of women students in university increased in Hungary from 14.5% in the 1930s to nearly 50% in the 1970s.

There were other areas where change was needed. In spite of significant progress, most women were **underpaid** and **underrepresented** in higher jobs. The average earnings of women were much lower than the average earnings of men – about half in Britain in 1975. **Politics** was one area where there was slow progress. Only a small proportion (about 4–5%) of members of parliament in Germany and Britain were women. Nevertheless, Britain had its **first** woman party leader and prime minister (1979) in Margaret Thatcher, while France had its first woman prime minister in 1994.

ORDINARY LEVEL AND HIGHER LEVEL HOMEWORK EXERCISES

ORDINARY LEVEL

1. Study the following document carefully and answer the questions below:

   'Women became more central to the economy, as both consumers and workers. Whereas it used to be that working-class women left the workforce after childbirth, taking only work they could do at home, women in post-war Europe remained in the workforce. This was due mainly to the fact that women were marrying and having all their children earlier than their mothers and grandmothers had. By the late 1960s the age at marriage for European women had dropped to 23. At the same time, women were having 80 percent of their children before they were 30. This helps to account for growing feminist dissatisfaction by the late 1960s and 1970s; women found that their traditional role as mother no longer absorbed the energy of a lifetime, yet new roles in the male-dominated world outside the family were slow to open. Nevertheless, even for middle-class wives, work outside the home became more common.'

   The Encyclopaedia of World History,
   www.bartleby.com

(i) What is a consumer?

(ii) Before the Second World War, when did working-class women leave the workforce?

(iii) What change occurred in the role of women in post-war Europe?

(iv) What caused the change, according to this account?

(v) Mention at least one other cause of this change which is not listed here.

(vi) Between what ages did many women have their children?

(vii) Explain the term 'feminist'.

(viii) Why were women dissatisfied by the late 1960s and 1970s?

2. Study the figures below and answer the questions that follow:

   Percentage of Parliamentary Seats
   Held by Women, 1990

Denmark	33·0
Norway	36·0
Austria	21·9
Belgium	9·0

France	5·0
Greece	5·3
Germany	20·5
Italy	12·7
Netherlands	27·3
Spain	13·4
Britain	6·8

P Snyder, *The European Women's Almanac*

(i) Which countries had (a) the highest and, (b) the lowest percentage of parliamentary seats occupied by women in 1990?

(ii) Based on the above figures, what assessment would you make of the following statements? (a) Catholic countries had a lower percentage of parliamentary seats occupied by women than Protestant countries? (b) Northern European countries had higher percentages of parliamentary seats occupied by women than southern European countries.

(iii) List some factors which you think would influence the percentage of parliamentary seats occupied by women.

(iv) What do you think these figures tell about the role of women in each of these countries?

3. Write **paragraph answers** on each of the following questions:

(i) The changing role of the family in post-war Europe.

(ii) The changing role of marriage in post-war Europe.

(iii) The changing role of women in relation to work and the family from the 1950s to the 1980s. (Department of Education, Sample Paper)

(iv) Divorce and the family in Europe from the 1950s to the 1980s.

4. Write **long answers** on each of the following questions:

(i) How, and why, did the structure and functions of the family change in Europe from the 1950s to the 1980s?

(ii) How, and why, did the role of women in the family and in society change in Europe from the 1950s to the 1980s?

HIGHER LEVEL

1. How were the structure and functions of the family in Europe from the 1950s to the 1980s influenced by economic and social factors?

OR

Account for the changing role of the family in Europe from the 1950s to the 1980s.

2. Discuss the view that feminism – the demand for equal political, economic and social rights for women – was largely successful in Europe from the 1950s to the 1980s because of economic and technological changes during that time.

3. To what extent do you agree that the role of women in Europe by the 1980s was very different from what it had been in the 1940s and 1950s?

TEST YOURSELF AT
my-etest.com

The Affluent Society

In 1957, Harold Macmillan told the English people they *'never had it so good'*. This could be applied even more to most of Western Europe. The majority of Western Europeans were better off than ever before. **Living standards** rose quickly after the Second World War. These were the years of the Great Boom, beginning in the early 1950s and lasting to the early 1970s. It was based on strong economic growth. In Britain, industrial production grew by 80% between 1950 and 1970. But the West German economy grew faster than all others. Workers became more productive because of greater use of technology. **Wages** rose faster than prices so everybody was better off. During the years from 1953 to 1965, real wages rose by between 36% (Britain) and 100% (Germany). As a result, people had greater amounts of money to spend (disposable income). This was the **Affluent Society**.

The increased standard of living in Western Europe in the 1950s and 1960s resulted in families buying greater quantities of food and other goods. Shopping became a family occasion.

The improved **standard of living** spread to all levels of society – middle class and working class. But it wasn't just urban dwellers who were better off. Peasants (farmers) were also better off even though there were still areas of poverty, such as the south of Italy. The increased standard of living could be seen in the provision of better quality housing with indoor toilets and bathrooms. By 1971 in Britain, 88% of all houses had a bathroom or a shower compared to 62% in 1951; 96% had their own toilet compared to 80% in 1951. There was more food and a greater variety of it, with less bread and more vegetables, meat, cheese and eggs. There was better clothing with more style, as people became more fashion conscious.

The Consumer Society

The Consumer Society grew out of the increased **affluence**. But it also grew out of improvements in **technology** which provided the basis for the new consumer lifestyles. New production techniques brought down the price of consumer goods while making it possible to pay higher wages. Food had been the largest single item in the family budget, but now the proportion of income spent on consumer goods grew. Spending on consumer goods in France grew five times between 1950 and 1974, for example.

The Consumer Society

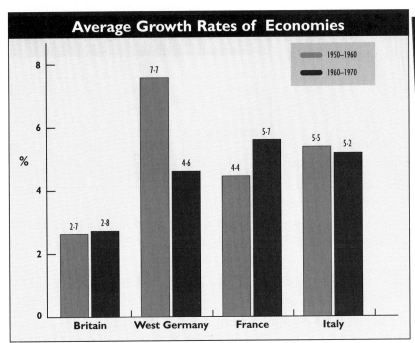

Average Growth Rates of Economies

Legend:
- 1950–1960
- 1960–1970

	Britain	West Germany	France	Italy
1950–1960	2·7	7·7	4·4	5·5
1960–1970	2·8	4·6	5·7	5·2

The motor car was the symbol of the consumer society. More and more families had cars so the number of cars in Western Europe increased rapidly from 1950 to 1990.

Growth of Cars in Britain	
1945	1·5 m
1955	3·5 m
1970	11·5 m

One of the largest increases was on **household appliances**. By 1975, 90% of homes in Britain had a vacuum cleaner, over 66% had a washing machine and 75% had a refrigerator. The increase in **automation** in the home helped increase the number of women going out to work. The standard of living was often measured by the number of appliances people had.

The **motor car** was the symbol of the consumer society. It affected all areas of life – work, leisure and family. As a means of transport, it provided greater **mobility** and changed the shape of cities. It also conferred **prestige** and **status**. In West Germany, 43% of households had a car in 1968; this increased to 80% by 1978. Overall in Western Europe, the number of cars grew from 6 million in 1950 to over 120 million in 1990.

Eastern Europe

Eastern Europe also grew more prosperous during the 1950s and 1960s. Production increased, wages rose and workers were often better off. But Eastern Europe was still **poor** compared to the West. As well as that, the deliberate policy of Eastern European Communist governments was to develop heavy industry (iron, steel and electricity) and not consumer goods. This was particularly the case up to the mid-1950s. There was some expansion of consumer goods after that. But Eastern Europe could not be considered a consumer society like the West.

Leisure

Leisure time was once confined to the rich, but during the 1950s and 1960s it became part of the **way of life** of everybody. Wages rose because of higher productivity and the average **working**

week was shortened. It was about 48 hours a week in most European countries before the Second World War. By the 1950s it had fallen to between 42 and 44 hours a week.

Average hours worked each year per person 1950-1986		
	1950	1986
Belgium	2,283	1,411
France	1,926	1,533
West Germany	2,316	1,630
Italy	1,997	1,515
Britain	1,958	1,511

TOURISM

The greatest development was in **mass leisure** activities. One of those areas was **tourism**. The shortening of the working week coincided with the spread of **paid holidays**. First introduced in France in the 1930s, paid holidays became common in other Western European countries after the Second World War. In 1955 Sweden had 29 days paid holidays, with West Germany and Italy having 28 each. This increased to between 32 and 35 days in the 1960s in all Western European countries.

In the early 1950s holidays were mainly confined to **day trips** or **weekend breaks**. Thereafter, home holidays continued to be an important feature of tourism. But foreign holidays developed very quickly in the 1950s. In 1950, the first **package tour** which included flight and accommodation was put together in Britain. The same year in France, **Club Mediterranean** was set up with its emphasis on holiday villages. By the middle of the 1950s, 30 million tourists crossed European borders each year. This grew to 100 million by 1966. **Cars** and **trains** provided the means of transport, and **planes** were used for long distances or **ferries** in the case of Britain.

The tourist industry grew in the 1950s and 1960s as the working week shortened, pay increased and paid holidays became common. Blackpool in England became increasingly popular. The Blackpool Tower – which was modelled on the Eiffel Tower – dates back to the 1890s.

Each country illustrated different **aspects of tourism.** In **France**, the urban working class, middle class and the rich each had separate holiday areas. Camping was popular with the lower middle class and the working class while young office workers and shop assistants preferred holiday villages. The **Italians** preferred hotels and guest houses to camping but some returned to the countryside to holiday with relations. In **Britain** those who did not go abroad – and four times more people went abroad in 1970 compared to 1951 – flocked to the **seaside resorts** such as Blackpool. The **Belgians** too had their holiday resorts by the sea. The **West Germans** tended to stay at home initially but by the later 1950s they could afford to go away. Most areas of Europe were accessible to the humble Beetle, or the lordly Mercedes, but Germans tended to head south to the Mediterranean and the hotter weather.

Package holidays were first organised in the 1950s. In France, Club Mediterranean built holiday villages to provide all the facilities on one site. What is the message of this advertisement? Are advertisements propaganda?

Earnings from tourism became an important contributor to the Italian and Spanish economies, the two most popular tourist countries. On the other hand, the Germans, French and British spent most abroad. Even though tourism suffered like everything else during the slower economic growth of the 1970s and 1980s, there was still a strong demand for home holidays as well as camping, sun holidays, and winter ski holidays abroad.

CINEMA AND THEATRE

Cinema was a very popular leisure activity in the 1930s and after the war. But all over Western Europe cinema **declined** in the late 1950s and early 1960s due to competition from television. In **West Germany**, for example, audiences declined from a peak of over 800 million in 1956 to 144 million in 1980. In **Britain** between 1957 and 1963, one-third of all cinemas closed and were converted to other uses. In the 1980s, cinema made a broad revival supported mainly by **younger audiences** in multiple cinemas built in the suburbs.

Cinema declined in popularity in the late 1950s due to competition from television. But there were still many stars such as James Dean and Elizabeth Taylor, here featured in *Giant* (1955).

Most audiences depended on **Hollywood films** portraying adventure and romance, except in France where the cinema industry was the largest in Europe. In some cases European films had limited appeal and were treated as **art-house movies** which failed to tell a story but appeared to delve deeply into the human mind. Not surprisingly they could not compete with Hollywood which went for more popular themes with the backing of much bigger budgets.

Theatre did not reach the same mass audience. It was based more in capital cities because it needed a large population to maintain it. **France** was Europe's most important country for theatre. Paris alone had over forty theatres after the Second World War. Theatre festivals spread theatre to the provincial towns and cities. In Britain, touring companies took the most popular London productions to the provinces. But theatre was largely a middle- or upper-class activity.

TELEVISION AND RADIO

Television was the most popular leisure activity. It drew audiences far larger than the other **mass media** and therefore had a greater impact on society. Most countries followed the British pattern of television ownership. In 1951 only 1 in 15 houses had a TV in Britain, by 1960 this had increased to 2 out of 3, and by 1975 9 out of 10 houses had a TV. By the mid-1990s almost all homes in Western Europe had a TV. **Average viewing time** in different countries was between 2 and 4 hours a day. Not surprisingly, in 1969 a quarter of all spare time was spent watching television.

Television was the most popular leisure activity. By the 1970s nine out of ten households had a television. Black and white sets were upgraded to colour when this became available.

Serious television programmes declined and sport and entertainment became more popular. By the 1980s **cable** and **satellite television** began to spread to satisfy the market – carrying more than 80 programmes in Europe by 1990. Broadcasts of the European Cup which began in 1955 and the Eurovision song contest brought one of the few European-wide dimensions to television which was hindered by language differences.

Radio developed earlier than television so most houses had radios by the 1960s. Most radio stations were licensed and owned by the government, the BBC in Britain, RAI in Italy and RTF in France. In reaction to government control and to satisfy the growing youth market, pirate stations flourished. These broadcasts were aimed at **younger audiences**. In **Britain** the pirate stations were replaced by local radio stations whereas in other Western European countries they were legalised as independent stations. In Belgium alone there were 650 independent stations.

Soccer was the most popular sport in Western Europe. The development of European competitions such as the European Cup gave it greater publicity. Here Brian Kidd of Manchester United heads goalwards against Real Madrid in the Bernabeu Stadium in the semi-final of the European Cup in 1968.

SPORT

Sport developed rapidly as a leisure activity. **Soccer** was the best example of the development of mass leisure time. In Britain in 1947–8, 11 million attended soccer matches. Soccer had working-class origins and during the 1950s in Britain it was mainly a working-class sport. This development came later in other Western European countries but with just the same impact. Huge stadia in Spain and Italy catered for the mass audiences of teams like **Real Madrid** and **AC Milan**. In Italy it had a huge following among the youth of the northern cities and it was partly based on inter-city rivalry. No other sport had such huge attendances who followed it with great intensity and regularity. However, even soccer experienced falling attendances in the late 1950s, partly due to the influence of television.

OTHER LEISURE PURSUITS

The increased leisure time was used in a **variety** of other ways. It led to the development of **hobbies** from stamp collecting to wine making. **Local societies** were developed to cater for anything from choirs or flower clubs. **Adult education** became more popular, both as a pastime to develop the person or to advance careers. In spite of all the new types of leisure, sometimes the **older habits** also stayed on. In Britain in 1974, **going out for a drink** was highly rated after television, along with reading books, house repairs or do-it-yourself for men, gardening for both men and women, as well as walking and climbing. There were also indoor pastimes with board games like Scrabble, chess in Spain or bridge in middle-class France.

Leisure

ORDINARY LEVEL

1. Study Source A and Source B carefully and answer the questions below:

Source A

'Ten years ago [in 1950], at Turin, the worker Giovanni B arrived at the factory on a bicycle. He was dressed in a leather jacket, a pair of ancient gloves, and had a beret pulled down over his eyes. In recent months, by contrast, from the moment he leaves the house to go to work he is dressed like some office worker in a public concern or some city enterprise. He wears a fine wool suit and a tie and drives a small car which he parks in a covered car park of recent construction. Previously there were two covered parking places at the factory, one for bicycles and the second for motorbikes, but the third one, for cars, will have to be enlarged still further.

'In the last few years the car has become the most obvious sign of the economic situation of the middle Italian. In the piazzas [squares], in front of offices, at the cinema, at the theatre, hundreds, no, thousands of cars are lined up ... the car, which was considered a luxury good, unnecessary, and which seemed destined only for the favourite children of respectable families, for popular singers, for owners of clinics, for big wholesalers, for stockbrokers, has sunk to the role of a pure and simple means of transport. Surveyors have them, skilled workers, clerks, teachers.'

From *Epoca*, an Italian magazine (1960) quoted in A Marwick, *The Sixties*

Source B
Ownership of Consumer Goods in Italy

	% of families in 1965	% of families in 1975
Owning TV sets	49	92
Owning refrigerators	55	94
Owning washing machines	23	76

A Marwick, *The Sixties*

(i) In 1950, how did Giovanni B get to work?

(ii) How was he dressed?

(iii) How was his life different by 1960?

(iv) Do you think Giovanni B was a real person?

(v) What does the term *'middle Italian'* mean?

(vi) How did the role of the car change?

(vii) Which people had cars for the first time in 1960?

(viii) What are consumer goods?

(ix) Use evidence from Sources A and B to show that Italy was becoming a consumer society.

(x) Were the changes in Italy similar to changes elsewhere in Europe?

(xi) Write a brief account to explain the changes here.

2. Study the following documents carefully and answer the questions below:

'Sports were also of great importance in eastern Europe. In 1952, East Germany set up the German College for Body Culture, and a 100,000-seat stadium was erected in Leipzig ... The Soviet Union had always encouraged physical fitness and also in 1952 participated in the Olympics for the first time.... If private enterprise supported sport in the west, in the east it was the state, who granted huge subsidies to gymnasia and training camps and made athletic victors the sort of heroes that they also became in the west.'

An Economic and Social History of Europe

'In 1948 the Soviet Communist Party called on the sporting institutions "to spread physical culture and sport to every corner of the land, and to raise the level of skill, so that Soviet sportsmen might win world supremacy in the major sports in the immediate future." Sport "provided the irrefutable proof of the superiority of the socialist culture over the decaying culture of the capitalist states."' (See p. 273)

(i) What did the East German government do to promote sport?

(ii) What did the Soviet government do to promote sport?

(iii) Why was the Soviet government interested in promoting sport?

(iv) How were athletic victors treated in both the West and the East?

3. Write **paragraph** answers on each of the following questions:

(i) The Consumer Society. (Department of Education, Sample Paper)

(ii) Tourism in Europe.

(iii) The role of the mass media in leisure.

(iv) Sport and leisure pursuits in post-war Europe.

4. Write **long answers** on each of the following questions:

(i) How did leisure patterns in Western Europe change from the 1950s to the 1980s?

(ii) How, and why, did a consumer society develop in Western Europe after the Second World War?

HIGHER LEVEL

1. How did Europe's affluent society after the Second World War influence the lifestyle of its people?

OR

Discuss the view that the growth of the economies of Western Europe after the Second World War gave rise to an affluent society dominated by consumerism.

2. To what extent did a consumer society develop in Western Europe after the Second World War?

3. 'In the post-war decades in Western Europe, the increase in leisure activities was just one aspect of the growing consumer society.' Discuss.

TEST YOURSELF AT
my-etest.com

15. Youth and Popular Culture (including Sport) and the Mass Media

Youth and Youth Culture

YOUTH

Youth is the stage between **childhood** and **adulthood** when experience and training fits young people for their role in society and culture. In older societies the **function** of youth was to continue the traditional way of life. But in modern industrial society youth is expected to question, experiment and criticise. In the 1950s there was a decided break between generations – **the generation gap** – which became more marked. The change in youth reflected various **causes** such as the earlier maturity of teenagers, their increased purchasing power and greater mobility. **Youth culture** was generally characterised by lack of interest in politics, lack of respect for authority, desire for greater freedom and individuality and a rejection of conformity.

Affluent Youth

> **KEY CONCEPT: TEENAGER.** Boys and girls who are in their teens, between the ages of 13 and 19.

The **full employment** of the **Great Boom** provided more jobs for young people and boosted their wages. Working-class youth took advantage of the better job and pay prospects while middle-class youth was still in full-time education dependent on his/her parents and part-time jobs. The affluent youth became the target for **manufacturers** who produced goods geared for the youth market – clothing, soft drinks and entertainment relied heavily on the spending power of youth.

Many followed American trends, particularly in Britain. Rock 'n' roll spread rapidly, helped by modern technology. The transistor radio, long playing and 45 rpm records popularised rock 'n' roll as well as its stars, such as **Elvis Presley** and **Buddy Holly**. The initial stars were American but soon Britain produced its own crop led by

> **KEY CONCEPT: POP STAR.** A musician or singer who has great appeal to, or is popular with, young people.

the **Beatles** in the early 1960s. Their long hair set a trend in fashion as it symbolised the **rejection** of adult or existing values. Their lyrics also reflected different values from the older generation.

First there were jeans. Now there are Falmers.

If you look good in jeans, you'll look great in Falmers.

Jeans became one of the symbols of the new youth culture.

Elvis Presley was the most popular rock 'n' roll star. His popularity spread from America to Europe. His clothes and hairstyle were imitated. He represented rebellious youth.

Key Personality: John Lennon

John Lennon was born in Liverpool in 1940. In secondary school, his **rebellious nature** came to the fore. It was at this stage that he began to develop his interest in music and art. His ambition was to become a famous musician. He led a band, the **Quarrymen**, with **Paul McCartney**. He played guitar and sang lead with McCartney, with whom he also **co-wrote** their songs. They changed their name to the **Beatles** and eventually had national success in 1962 with their record, *Love Me Do*. Very soon after their first Number One, *Please Please Me*, **Beatlemania** swept Britain and later the continent. Lennon's dream had come true.

Over the next few years a succession of Number One hits and albums increased their popularity, leading also to a breakthrough into the US market. At this time Lennon wrote **two books**, *In His Own Write* and *A Spaniard in the Works*, which combined his own poems and drawings. He also played in the **Beatles' films**, *A Hard Day's Night* and *Help*. But he was not always happy with the public side of Beatlemania. He had problems accepting the MBE from the Queen in 1963. His **interview** where he said the Beatles were now more popular than Jesus caused conflict with Christian groups, especially in America where he had to publicly apologise for his remarks. Lennon was a **restless** person, always moving on. He experimented with **LSD** in the psychedelic phase and **meditation** with the Indian master, Maharishi Mahesh Yogi. At this time, he forced the Beatles to give up touring. Afterwards they became solely recording artists.

Lennon's **marriage** to Cynthia, whom he knew since art college days in Liverpool, broke up and he married **Yoko Ono**, a Japanese artist. He became actively involved in **peace politics**. John and Yoko staged a **bed-in** honeymoon as a peace protest in a hotel bedroom in Amsterdam. In furtherance of his anti-war campaign, he released a song, *Give Peace a Chance*. He left Britain for good in 1971 and went to live in the US. His later songs, especially *Imagine*, reflected his concern for world peace. After a break from music to concentrate on family life, he was about to relaunch his music career when he was shot by a **psychopath** at the entrance to his apartment building – the Dakota Building – in New York in 1980. A 10-minute silence was observed worldwide in his memory.

Imagine

by John Lennon

Imagine there's no heaven
It's easy if you try
No hell below us
Above us only sky
Imagine all the people
Living for today...

Imagine there's no countries
It isn't hard to do
Nothing to kill or die for
And no religion too
Imagine all the people
Living life in peace...

Imagine no possessions
I wonder if you can
No need for greed or hunger
In a brotherhood of man
Imagine all the people
Sharing all the world...

You may say I'm a dreamer
But I'm not the only one
I hope some day you'll join us
And the world will be one.

The Beatles in London for their *Our World* TV Show in 1967.

YOUTH CULTURE

Youth culture reflected differences with adult or established culture. But some aspects of it showed greater rejection than others. The **teddy boys** were the original protesters. They began in south London among children of working-class parents. Their alienation from society was reflected in their clothes – the narrow drainpipe trousers, the long jackets and combed-back hair. Theirs was a world of jukeboxes and snack bars.

The **teddy boys** gave way to the **mods** and **rockers** of the 1960s. The **hippy** culture which spread from California rejected society entirely and sought an alternative lifestyle – flower power, pacifism and drugs. Amsterdam was the centre of their influence. Other groups such as **Hell's Angels**, the **skinheads** and the **punks**, who were often aggressive dropouts from society, reflected a stronger rejection of established values.

The 'teddy boys' developed amongst working-class youth in south London. Their clothes – narrow trousers and long jackets – and their hairstyle became popular. One of their heroes was Elvis Presley. They frightened the older generation, particularly because of their involvement in fights. They faded by the early 1960s.

The mods and rockers also grew out of working-class culture. The mods liked to imitate the middle classes. Their clothes were 'elegant'; some wore suits with narrow trousers and pointed toes. They sometimes wore Parka jackets, and armed themselves with flick knives. They rode Italian scooters, decked out with mirrors and headlights. Their music was ska, West Indian music, popularised by The Who and the Small Faces. They took 'speed' to suit their lifestyle.

The rockers were the opposite to the mods. They wore leather jackets with studs and rode motorbikes. They 'hung out' in cafés. They were the 'wild ones' who openly displayed an anti-authority attitude. The mods and rockers were sometimes involved in clashes such as the seaside riots in Brighton in 1964.
The skinheads followed later in the mid-1970s. They wore large boots, with jeans rolled up high to display them. Their hair was cut to the skin and they behaved violently. They followed football and took their violence onto the terraces. They also attacked hippies and other minorities. They supported conservative working-class values of hard work and patriotism.

The hippie culture spread from America. Hippies rejected middle-class society. They wore colourful clothes, preached peace and used drugs. Here a couple of hippies listen to one playing as others walk by at a fair.

The **French** developed a version of the teddy boys, the **blouson noirs**, with black leather jackets and bush moustaches. France also produced its own stars of American pop but soon the Beatles dominated popular (**pop**) music both there and in other Western European countries. **German** youth culture also developed with American and British influences because of their ability to speak English. But **Italy** did not develop a full youth culture because of strong family ties and a large rural population, particularly in the south. In **Eastern Europe**, the Cold War stopped the spread of this so-called American culture but illegal recordings and listenings still occurred.

Middle Class Dissent

Some – mostly middle-class youth – expressed **political dissent**. More of them were finishing second-level education and going onto university. Their numbers expanded rapidly in the 1960s. In **Britain** alone there were five times more students at university in 1971 than in 1950. They became more involved in politics, usually of a **radical** or **revolutionary** nature. This involved them in protests to reform the university system which had not kept pace with changes in society, particularly in France. But they also protested about wider issues such as the **Cold War**, **nuclear arms** and the **Vietnam War** in the 1970s.

The punks became a feature of the mid-1970s. They set out to shock, especially the middle classes. They wore outrageous clothes; their hairstyle was partly skinhead with a spikey middle. This was often dyed bright colours for effect. They had their own music style, punk rock, characterised by loud and abrasive music and extreme language. The Sex Pistols were an example of this. Their first single was called 'Anarchy in the UK', and the cover of their single 'God Save the Queen' showed the Queen with a safety pin through her lip. In the photograph, these young punks are attending a Campaign for Nuclear Disarmament (CND) rally in London.

Barricades made of overturned cars block a street in Paris in 1968 after rioting and demonstrations by students demanding major reforms at the Sorbonne University. This was part of a wider dissent by middle-class youth across Europe in the late 1960s when they protested against the Cold War, nuclear weapons and the Vietnam War.

Their influence was often very strong. In **Eastern Europe**, students were involved in protests in Poland and in the Hungarian Uprising in 1956 to reform the Communist system. In the **West**, they led the major protests against **President de Gaulle** in France in 1968 which indirectly led to his resignation. The level of student protest of the 1960s died down as universities were reformed, as governments learned to discuss matters with student leaders and because of the economic downturn after the Oil Crisis in 1973.

Other Aspects of Youth Culture

There were other aspects to youth culture. **Magazines** were published for the young audience which highlighted clothes, fashion, make-up and boy-girl relationships. **Fashion** also reflected this youth culture. Mary Quant designed **miniskirts** in London which shocked the older generation. Even though young men's fashions still retained the same basic structure of trousers and shirt, their clothes became more casual and colourful. **Sexual activity** was also a reflection of the rejection of older values. The **condom** and the **contraceptive pill** changed sexual habits. In Western Europe in 1968, a quarter of all men and a fifth of all women had **premaritial sex** before the age of twenty-one.

Miniskirts became a symbol of the freedom of youth in the 1960s. They shocked the older generation.

More Violence

By the 1980s youth culture had developed some unwelcome characteristics. **Drink** and **drugs** added to a violent image. In 1981, young people were responsible for over half of all violent crimes in Western European countries. The **hooligan** element, partly developed from the skinheads, became prominent in the 1970s, particularly at soccer matches. This violence led to the **Heysel disaster** in Belgium where Liverpool soccer fans attacked Italian fans causing the deaths of dozens of people. But the violence could also be seen in **holiday resorts** in Spain where money and drink combined for a **good time**.

Violence and crime were also part of youth culture. Some of this was displayed at soccer matches where rival fans clashed. In the Heysel Stadium, Brussels, in the 1985 European Cup Final, Liverpool fans attacked and killed dozens of Italian fans, who are seen here responding to some of the attacks.

Popular Culture

Youth culture was one aspect of the wider **popular culture** of the second half of the twentieth century. The mass culture was presented through the electronic media of **radio** and **television**. News, sport, music and general entertainment were available through radio to most people by the

1960s and through television a decade or so later. Europe had greater information about itself and the wider world than ever before. The jazz of the 1930s was replaced by the **rock 'n' roll** of the late 1950s and the 1960s – this in its turn shaped the folk music and reggae of later years.

Cinema was an influential part of popular culture. European films tried to compete with American films. But American stars, such as Faye Dunaway and Steve McQueen in *The Thomas Crown Affair* (1968), were very popular.

Fashion illustrated the popular culture of the time. The liberation of women was reflected in the dress of post-war Europe. The **knee-length dresses** of the post-war era suited the woman at work as well as the woman at home. The **miniskirt** of the 1960s was the younger woman's expression of independence, as was the **topless bathing** of the Mediterranean. The growing informality was represented by the popularity of the **blue jeans** of the young, male and female. These changes also covered over social or class differences.

Cinema was also a very popular medium, available to all classes. **Italian films** liked to portray the lives of ordinary people; the **French** on the other hand took a more intellectual look at society. They competed with the out-and-out entertainment of the American cinema which brought American culture to Europe.

Cinema and music were not just popular in their own right, they were built around the popularity of their **stars**. This helped to pack cinemas and sell millions of records. They created the popular entertainment industry helped by advances in technology such as the transistor radio, colour cinema, tapes, stereo equipment and, in the late twentieth century, videos, CDs and DVDs.

Sex became a trademark of popular culture. It was used to sell goods, it featured on magazine covers, it became a serious topic for discussion and analysis. Many people said the 1960s experienced a **sexual revolution** and it was condemned as **the permissive society.** In the 1970s, the sex industry came more into the open and was generally tolerated. *Emmanuelle* was the first successful semi-pornographic film seen in major cinemas. It was a huge success in the mid-1970s. It led the way for other such films, often shown on late night television or commercial video. **Prostitutes** and **pornographic books** were openly and legally available in some cities such as Amsterdam. The **sex shops** became big business. The easy availability of contraceptives changed sexual habits. More open attitudes to sex influenced the passing of laws on divorce and abortion which became more easily available.

SPORT

Sport played a crucial role in popular culture. It provided a focal point for discussion as well as a sense of comradeship and community as people followed particular teams or sportspeople. This was very important in **urban society** to give people a feeling of belonging.

Sport provided great **financial rewards** for a small section of sportspeople in the last quarter of the twentieth century. This was not so in the 1940s and 1950s, when **amateurs** were prized. As sport became more professional, it provided **new heroes** for society. The deliberate marketing of stars to sell their sport raised their profile and increased the money they earned. Golfers, tennis players, soccer players, boxers and jockeys were among some of the **highest earners** in Western Europe. **Television** was central to the development of professional sport. It provided the **mass audience** and the **market** for commercial sponsorship.

This was not the case in **Eastern Europe** before the fall of Communism in 1989–91. While sportspeople in Communist countries had special privileges, only those who could go abroad to live in the West such as the tennis player, **Martina Navratilova**, could benefit financially.

Sport and Society

Sport mirrored changes in society. As the **role of women** in society generally changed, so their participation in sport also changed. This change occurred at first with individual competitors, such as in tennis, golf, swimming and athletics. Then it spread to **team sports**, such as soccer.

Another way in which sport mirrored society was in greater use of drugs. Just as **drugs** became more widespread in society, sportspeople used them to gain a competitive edge. The growing **violence** in society was reflected in crowd violence, particularly at soccer matches. Sport also reflected divisions between **rich and poor**, particularly in the 1950s and 1960s. Soccer was the working-class sport while the rich followed the more expensive sports of polo, horseracing and yachting.

Sport also became involved in **politics** through the Cold War conflict between the US and USSR. In 1948, the Soviet Communist Party called on the sporting institutions *'to spread physical culture and sport to every corner of the land, and to raise the level of skill, so that Soviet sportsmen might win world supremacy in the major sports in the immediate future.'* Sport *'provided the irrefutable proof of the superiority of the socialist culture over the decaying culture of the capitalist states.'* The Olympics became the scene where much of this rivalry was played out, whether between Hungarians and Soviets in 1956, Czechs and Soviets in 1968 or between Americans and Soviets in the 1970s and 1980s.

Sport became more professional and tennis stars like Martina Navratilova were well paid. Navratilova, seen here lifting the Wimbledon Trophy in 1987, was from Communist Czechoslovakia, and she had to move to the West to benefit from professional sport.

As sport became more competitive, sports people used drugs to gain an advantage. The Canadian Ben Johnson won the 1988 Olympic 100 metres in Seoul. But he was later stripped of his medal when he tested positive for using steroids.

Mass Media

The mass media has developed since the late nineteenth century. Newspapers and magazines were joined by radio and cinema in the 1920s and 1930s. Television became widespread in the late 1950s and 1960s. However, language barriers meant that Western Europe did not develop a common media structure.

> **KEY CONCEPTS: MASS MEDIA.** This is the means of communication such as newspapers, radio, television and cinema which set out to reach large numbers of people.

Rupert Murdoch displays sample newspapers and magazines which he owned. He also owned Sky TV. Developments in newspaper and television ownership raised questions over the influence of the media on people and politics.

Newspaper sales rose steadily after the Second World War before stabilising in the 1960s. In **Britain**, two working-class daily newspapers had circulations over 4 million. This was far higher than equivalent newspapers in other Western European countries in that decade. In **Germany** the highest circulation was over 2 million in a much larger population. But newspapers also closed as press barons began to dominate the industry. **Rupert Murdoch** launched *The Sun* aimed at working-class readers. There were also links between **newspapers** and **television**. Murdoch launched Sky TV and in Italy **Silvio Berlusconi** owned both TV stations and newspapers. These developments raised concerns about the influence of the media and the dangers of its abuse.

Part of the reason for the success of British dailies was their huge coverage of **sport** which appealed to all classes but particularly working-class readers. This also meant that no specific **sporting newspaper** was successful there. In contrast, France, Italy, Spain and Greece had very successful sporting newspapers; in Italy the sporting dailies had a total daily circulation of over one million while *L'Equipe* in France sold 300,000 copies.

Even though newspapers faced competition from radio and television, they survived strongly and won a significant share of **advertising revenue**. The more serious dailies which relied on **politics** and **business** depended on a middle-class market, but the high circulation *The Sun* and the German *Bild* depended on **sensational stories** of sex and violence to succeed. This was obviously a successful formula for selling newspapers because *The Sun* sold 4 million copies daily and *Bild* over 5 million.

RADIO AND TELEVISION

Radio and television reached **greater audiences**. By the 1960s most homes had radios and by the 1990s most homes had televisions. Television had advantages over radio in that pictures told their own story. It had advantages over newspapers in its coverage of spectacular events, and its coverage of social conditions and documentaries. But it could not give coverage in depth. It had its greatest success in **light entertainment** where it drew in mass audiences and made household names of its presenters such as David Frost in Britain.

Initially, television was **state owned**, such as the BBC in Britain. This was joined in the mid-1950s by ITV, but the development of independent television came much later in other Western European countries. European-wide broadcasting was difficult because of different **languages**. This particularly hit news and documentaries, comedy shows and chat shows. But sport and musical entertainment were able to cross barriers. **Eurovision** was begun in 1954 as an association of national television stations.

This allowed broadcasting of European soccer matches, especially the **European Cup**, and also the **Eurovision Song Contest** where commentaries could be in the native language. Cable and satellite television spread in the 1980s and this brought more European-wide stations such as the American MTV Channel, the English Sky TV, and Eurosport.

Eurovision was begun in 1954 as an association of national television stations. It broadcast European soccer matches and the Eurovision Song Contest. In 1968 Cliff Richard, representing Britain, was second with the song 'Congratulations'.

The mass media played a very important role in **spreading popular culture**. Television, even more than radio and the newspapers, popularised different aspects of culture. Music and sport – two of the central features of popular culture – were ideally suited to television broadcasting.

ORDINARY LEVEL

1. Study the following document carefully and answer the questions below:

> 'One of the characteristics that sets pop music apart from the forms of entertainment that preceded it is its general emphasis upon rebellion. Obviously not all pop music bears this emphasis, but the vast majority of it carries the assumption that it is youth music and that it is therefore to some degree hostile to the interests of adults and the establishment. Elvis Presley and Chuck Berry, to name but two, offended the US and European establishments in the 1950s with what was considered their immoral emphasis on sexuality.... The importance of the link between youth and music is shown by figures relating to record-buying patterns in Britain [in 1987]. Although people between the ages of 15 and 19 make up only 8 per cent of the population over the age of 8, they purchase 36 per cent of all the singles sold in Britain. They also account for 21 per cent of all LPs [long-playing records] sold in Britain.'
>
> A Brown, *Let's Discuss Pop Music*

(i) How is pop music different from previous forms of entertainment, according to the author?

(ii) With what group in society is pop music associated?

(iii) To what is pop music hostile?

(iv) What is meant by *'US and European establishments'*?

(v) How did Elvis Presley and Chuck Berry offend the European establishment?

(vi) What evidence shows the importance of the link between youth and music?

2. Study the following document carefully and answer the questions below:

> 'Like so many other aspects of youth culture, the association between music and fashion began to develop in the 1950s. Teddy boys of the era adapted a style of dress based on a stylised version of the Edwardian suit. This outraged contemporary taste and immediately established a visual identity for all would-be teddy boys to adopt and imitate. In the late 1950s and early 1960s the popularity of rock 'n' roll was to a large extent responsible for a growing demand for denim jeans. Performers such as Elvis Presley wore jeans, which were at the time working-class clothes, in films which were seen right across North America and Europe. Denim suddenly became fashionable.'
>
> A Brown, *Let's Discuss Pop Music*

(i) When did the association between music and fashion begin, according to the author?

(ii) Who did the teddy boys imitate? How does this explain how they got their name?

(iii) What is a *'visual identity'*? Why would teddy boys want to establish a visual identity?

(iv) What led to the popularity of denim jeans?

(v) Using this source and the previous source, show how America influenced youth culture in Europe.

3. Study the following document carefully and answer the questions below:

> 'Twisting the night away and a-jiving – the music of John Lennon's youth was the jukebox tunes of the fifties and early sixties. John based his image on the slick Elvis Presley, whose *Heartbreak Hotel* inspired him to be a rock star, and on James Dean, who gave him the model for that anti-everything mood.... The early image that John had in mind for the [Beatles] was a rock 'n' roll, rebellious one ... [Manager] Brian Epstein believed that the Beatles would have the greatest chance of success if they smartened up their image. It was at his insistence that they wore jackets with rounded necks which became known as

"Beatles' suits". However, John could not stand them and would stamp his own personality on whatever he wore.... [The] smart respectable image was one he knew would get the Beatles success, but it wasn't what he wanted for the group. He felt the Beatles had "sold out" and lost their roots.'

M White, *John Lennon*

(i) What was *'twisting'* and *'a-jiving'*?

(ii) What was jukebox?

(iii) What influences had (a) Elvis Presley, and (b) James Dean, on John Lennon?

(iv) What image did John Lennon want the Beatles to have?

(v) What changes did the manager make to their image?

(vi) What was Lennon's attitude to the changes the manager insisted on?

(vii) What do we learn about John Lennon's character from this extract?

(viii) What do we learn about youth culture in Europe from this extract?

4. Write **paragraph answers** on each of the following questions:

(i) Youth culture in the 1950s and 1960s.

(ii) Sport in popular culture.

(iii) The role of the mass media in popular culture.

(iv) John Lennon.

5. Write **long answers** on each of the following questions:

(i) To what extent did youth culture in Europe reflect differences with adult or established culture?

(ii) To what extent did John Lennon represent the youth culture of his time? (Department of Education, Sample Paper)

(iii) What part did sport play in popular culture in Europe from the 1950s to the 1980s?

(iv) What part did the mass media play in popular culture in Europe from the 1950s to the 1980s?

HIGHER LEVEL

1. What were the influences on the development of youth and popular culture in Western Europe from the 1950s to the 1980s?

2. Discuss changes in popular culture in Western Europe in the post-war decades.

3. Discuss the role of sport both as a leisure activity and part of popular culture in Europe from the 1950s to the 1980s. (See also Chapter 14, Affluence, Leisure Time and the Consumer Society.)

4. Discuss the role of the mass media in leisure and in spreading popular culture in Europe from the 1950s to the 1980s. (See also Chapter 14, Affluence, Leisure Time and the Consumer Society.)

TEST YOURSELF AT
my-etest.com

Introduction

Religion, especially **Christianity**, has been an important part of the European heritage. After the **Reformation** in the sixteenth century, Europe was broadly divided into a Catholic South (Spain, Portugal, Italy and France but also including Belgium and Ireland); and a Protestant North (Scandinavia and Britain), a mixed group in the middle (Holland and Germany) and Eastern Europe which was mainly Catholic but with locally strong Protestant groups. Russia and Greece had Orthodox Churches, which pre-dated the Reformation. The pattern of religious adherence or belonging to church, established by the Reformation, remained largely the same by the middle of the twentieth century. Even by 1960, it was only in Holland, France and Britain that there was a sizeable number of people declaring that they had no religion.

Decline

By the middle of the twentieth century the **importance of religion** had declined. However, it still had considerable influence through popular ceremonies, politics and support for certain social values. Religious observance was also relatively high, though more so in Catholic countries than Protestant countries. Christians still regularly attended church and participated in other aspects of their religion.

Religious observance declined in Europe from the 1950s onwards. The decline was greatest in Britain and France.

In the case of **baptism**, over 90% of Belgian children and over 80% of French children were being baptised. At this time also **religious weddings** as a proportion of all weddings was still very high. In many countries they were still over 70% (Austria and France) or 80% (Belgium). The southern European countries of Italy (98%) and Greece (100%) had even greater numbers of church or religious weddings. Figures for **church attendance** were not as strong in some countries but they were still sizeable. In Holland over 80% attended weekly and in Britain over 65%, but France had a low of 20%.

Over the next 40 years, **religious adherence** (membership of religions) declined everywhere – in some countries by as much as 20% (France) or 30% (Belgium) – and the proportion with no religion had gone up from between 5% to 16% (Holland). Not surprisingly, figures for **church attendance** showed a rapidly declining proportion of practicing Christians. By 1990, a higher proportion of Europeans (40%) never attended church, compared with those who attended once a week (29%) or once a month (10%).

For many, attendance was limited to baptism, marriages, funerals, Christmas and Easter. **Baptism** was still significant for a majority of children, except in Britain. Around 1966, 55% of children were baptised in the Church of England but by 1985 that had fallen to 40%. But in Italy and Portugal there were high numbers of children being baptised. **Religious weddings** were also in the majority except in Holland. In Greece they were over 80%; while Portugal, Italy and Spain had over 50%. By the late 1980s therefore, while religious observance had shown significant decline, in some aspects numbers participating in religious ceremonies were still strong.

Catholic and Protestant Observance

However, while the decline was everywhere, it was not all at the same rate. One difference was between the **more religious Catholic** countries and the **less religious Protestant** countries. Overall, religious observance was much higher in Italy, Spain and Belgium than in Britain and the Scandinavian countries. Even within countries attendance was stronger in Catholic areas. In Germany, for example, attendance was lower in the more Protestant north and east compared to the Catholic south.

Frequency of church attendance in Western Europe 1990 (%)			
	Once a week	Once a month	Never
European average	29	10	40
Italy	40	13	19
Portugal	33	8	47
Spain	33	10	38
Belgium	23	8	52
Holland	21	10	56
West Germany	19	15	41
Britain	13	10	56
France	10	7	59
Denmark	-	11	
Norway	-	10	
Sweden	-	10	

The key exception to this was **France** which had the lowest proportion of weekly attenders at church, and in this regard was closer to Britain. Indeed it can be said that while France was culturally part of Catholic Europe, it was much more like Protestant Europe in religious practice. This was partly due to the historical legacy of conflict between church and state, and the revolutionary, republican tradition of French history.

Socio-economic factors

There were other patterns to be observed. There was a strong link between religious observance and socio-economic factors such as **occupation, gender and age**. There was greater attendance among women and rural dwellers. In **Greece** where the rural population was large, attendance at Orthodox churches was high. In **Portugal** there was a bigger attendance in the more rural north compared to the more urban and industrialised south. Italy and Spain also had smaller numbers attending church in **industrialised** areas. There was also much lower religious observance among **younger age groups**. This would indicate that religious observance will continue to decline.

Immigration

Immigration affected religious observance, as shown by the growth of Islam. The largest mosque in Europe was inaugurated in London in 2003.

Immigration also affected patterns of observance. Former colonial connections accounted for much of the growth of **non-Christian** religions in Europe. There has been a considerable growth of **Islam** and it has overtaken the other main non-Christian religion – **Judaism**. By the early 1990s, Islam was the largest non-Christian religion in Europe, making up about 3% of the population in Western European countries. Religious observance was high in these small communities.

However, in spite of the decline of religious observance there was still a strong sense of **religious belief**. Seventy per cent of Europeans still believed in God and there was also a strong commitment to other individual aspects of religious belief, such as heaven.

Eastern Europe

In the Soviet Union, **Khrushchev** conducted a major assault on Christian and non-Christian religions in the 1950s and 1960s. Christian and non-Christian churches were destroyed and only some were allowed to stand. The **Russian Orthodox Church** became an instrument of the Soviet state. A survey in 1970 in the Moscow district found that only 16% of men and 45% of women believed in God. As in Western Europe, younger people, richer people and city people believed less in God than older, poorer and more rural people.

While these actions, and continuous Communist propaganda, undermined religion, in some parts of the Soviet Union the harsh policies of the government strengthened the churches. In Poland, Latvia and Lithuania the Catholic Church remained strong, and Baptists grew in numbers in Russia.

What Caused the Decline in Religious Observance?

There are many explanations for these trends. Some are general and are connected to economic and social developments. But others are specific to individual countries. They largely account for the declining role of **organised religion**. As religion declined in importance and influence so the necessity for religious observance became less:

- In the first place the overall **political and social standing** of the churches declined. In many countries in the **West**, church and state were separated; while in the **East** the Communist governments were actively hostile to the churches. Even in Italy the power of the Vatican could not stop laws favouring contraception, abortion and divorce. **Poland** was an exception to this because the church was a rallying point for those opposed to the Communist state.

- The role of the church as the **provider of education and charity** was largely taken over by the state. Public schools grew substantially in Western Europe as education expanded to meet the needs of a changing society in the 1950s and 1960s. This resulted in reducing or excluding religious education from the school programmes. In the case of charity, the development of the Welfare State in particular since the Second World War enlarged the role of the state in providing care for its people.

- This was accompanied by a **spreading of individualism** and a rejection of traditional authority, whether it be political, social or religious. This applied to younger people rather than older people.

- The growth of **city life** and **migration** from the countryside along with alternative cultural outlets including cinema, television and radio reduced the role of the church in passing on values. Even once Christian festivals, such as Christmas, were **commercialised** by businessmen and advertisers, the growth of **prosperity** became much more the focus of people's lives.

- The explanation which religion provided for life and the purpose of life was replaced by **scientific explanations** which often did not agree with the religious explanation. The fear of life after death did not provide a bond with religion especially among young people.

- Religion suffered from its **own divisions** and identification with social divisions. Some of the divisions were sectarian as in Scotland and Northern Ireland and these reflected badly on religion generally.

CHRISTIAN RESPONSE

Christianity responded in many ways to the rise of the **secular worldly, lay society**. This was particularly true of the call of **Pope John XXIII** at the **Second Vatican Council** for updating the Catholic Church to meet the challenges of the modern world. Over three years from 1962 to 1965, the Catholic Church (through Vatican II) made huge changes to cope with the challenge of the decline in religion and to try to get the Christian message across. These changes included alterations to the ceremonies and constitution of the church to give a greater role to laity and to encourage commitment to the church and to religion. (See Case Study: The Second Vatican Council, p. 286)

The other major change has been the spread of the **ecumenical movement** to try to bring different branches of the Christian religion together. It arose from the sense of weakness among Christian churches and their failure to influence modern life. Its purpose was to lead to a strengthening of the role of Christianity in modern life.

The spread of the ecumenical movement resulted in a number of meetings between Pope Paul VI and the Greek Orthodox Patriarch Athenagoras. The two leaders were trying to end the division between the Eastern and Western churches which began 900 years before.

In 1948, the **World Council of Churches** was founded by Protestant churches, but by the early 1960s the Council included Orthodox churches from Eastern Europe. The ecumenical movement in the 1960s owed much to the work of Vatican II, even though the Catholic Church refused to join the World Council. Pope John invited observers from other churches to the Council. He supported the movement towards closer co-operation among Christians. This led to contacts at national and local level between the different churches. It also led to meetings between church leaders such as Pope Paul VI and Patriarch Athonagras of the Greek Orthodox Church and with Archbishop Fisher of the Church of England.

The **worker priests**, particularly in France, took an entirely different approach. They went to work in factories and elsewhere to spread the Christian religion. However, their impact was small.

Overall Effect on Religious Observance

In spite of the efforts of the Christian churches to modernise and to use the new means of communication to get their message across, the overall impact on religious observance was slight. By the 1990s some historians were calling Britain, France and other European countries **post-Christian societies**,

Crowds of young people welcome Pope John Paul II to Wales, which is one of over 110 countries he has visited.

where even social values were not being derived from religion. In the case of the Catholic Church, some of the good work of Vatican II was undone by **Pope Paul VI's** encyclical, *Humanae Vitae*, in which he outlawed artificial contraceptive methods for Catholics. This was widely ignored by Catholics and it undermined the authority of the Pope among Catholics and respect among non-Catholics. The **conservative trend** was carried on by **Pope John Paul II**. This slowed up the process of ecumenism (the coming together of the Christian churches). But he also expanded on the example set by Paul VI by **travelling widely** in Europe and the world in an effort to take the Christian message to the people.

> **KEY CONCEPTS: ECUMENICAL MOVEMENT.** This was the movement towards religious co-operation and unity among Christians. At a local level it involved contacts between parish churches and joint religious ceremonies, while at church level it involved discussion on beliefs and practices.

KEY PERSONALITY: POPE JOHN PAUL II

Pope John Paul II was born in **Poland** in 1920. He was ordained a priest in 1946, appointed a Professor of Theology in 1954 and made a bishop four years later. He attended the **Second Vatican Council** (1962–5) and became a cardinal two years after it ended. It was often said that to understand him, you had to go back to his Polish roots. Here he experienced life under the Nazis during the Second World War and under the Communists after the war.

In 1978, he was a surprise choice when he was selected the **first Polish Pope** ever and the **first non-Italian Pope** for over 450 years. He was a very active Pope, leading the Catholic Church in a changed world. He took his mission **out of the Vatican** and around Europe and the world. He became the most travelled Pope in history. During the 1980s, he made many **visits abroad** to countries including Poland, Ireland, Mexico, the US, France and Brazil. He continued this pattern in the 1990s, visiting over 110 countries. He also made many visits **inside Italy** as well as to the parishes of his diocese.

Pope John Paul continued the pattern of meeting people through his weekly **general audiences** in St Peter's in Rome. As he was going to a general audience in 1981 he was **shot** as he entered St Peter's Square. He survived the attack and two years later he visited his would-be assassin in jail. He took particular interest in the **youth** as the future of the Catholic Church. In 1985 he held the first World Youth Day. Since then he has continued to encourage young people to live their gospel message.

He has always used the **media** to reach as many people as possible. His ability to speak eight languages was very important in communicating his message. In his **message**, he promoted human rights, condemned the decline in values and the rise of materialism. He was very conservative in issues of sexual morality, opposing pre-marital and extra-marital sex, abortion and the use of artificial contraception. He worked to bring down **Communism** in his own country and in Eastern Europe. He worked constantly to improve relations with **Jews** and to open discussions with other religions. But his conservative Catholic message and issues over the role of women in the church have not helped relations with Protestant churches.

Pope John Paul **consulted** widely by holding many meetings with bishops and cardinals. He also created many **new cardinals**, particularly in Africa and Asia. But, he was also very traditional in **beatifying** (made them blessed) many holy people, and **canonising** many saints.

ORDINARY LEVEL AND HIGHER LEVEL HOMEWORK EXERCISES

ORDINARY LEVEL

1. Examine the table Frequency of Church Attendance in Western Europe (p. 279) and answer the following questions:

(i) Which countries had the highest percentage attendance (a) Once a week, and (b) Once a month?

(ii) Which country has the lowest percentage attendance (a) Once a week, and (b) Once a month?

(iii) How many countries are above and below the European average?

(iv) Which countries had (a) the highest, and (b) the lowest percentage of non-attendance?

(v) To what extent do these figures support the view that 'religious observance was higher in Catholic countries compared to Protestant countries'?

2. Examine the figures (%) below for **Baptisms and Religious Marriages** and answer the questions that follow:

Baptisms

	1960		1990		
	RC	A	RC	A	
Belgium	94		82		-12
France	82		64		-18
UK		50		33	-17

Religious Marriages

	1960		1990			
	RC	A	RC	A	RC	A
Belgium	86		57		-29	
France	78		50		-28	
UK	12	47	8	45	-4	-2

A = Anglican   RC = Roman Catholic

(i) Which country had the largest percentage decline in baptisms?

(ii) Which country had the largest percentage decline in religious marriages?

(iii) Which country had the smallest percentage of baptisms in (a) 1960, and (b) 1990?

(iv) Which country had the smallest percentage of religious weddings in (a) 1960, and (b) 1990?

(v) What do these figures tell us about religious observance in these countries?

(vi) State two reasons to explain the trends in religious observance in these countries.

3. Study the following documents carefully and answer the questions below:

Source A

'There are few more godless countries in Europe than this one [Britain], measured by belief and church-attendance. According to a survey conducted by Opinion Research Business and just published in the Catholic weekly, *The Tablet*, less than half the population (45%) now believes Jesus was the son of God: in 1957, the figure was 71%. Only a minority (48%) claimed to belong to any particular religion: it was 58% as recently as 1990.'

Hugo Young, *The Guardian*, 1 January 2000

Source B

'A recent survey showed that two-thirds of the British public still profess to believe in God, although the church's own statistics indicate that rather fewer than one in 10 of us actually make it there on a Sunday.'

Stephen Bates, *The Guardian*, 24 June 2000

(i) Explain the term **godless countries**.

(ii) How does the author measure **godless**?

(iii) What percentage of people in Britain believed that Jesus was the son of God in (a) 1957, and (b) 2000?

(iv) What percentage of people claimed to belong to a religion in (a) 1990, and (b) 2000?

(v) Do the figures in Source B confirm the trends in Source A?

(vi) Do the figures in Sources A and B continue the trends in baptisms and religious marriages in Question 2 above?

(vii) What do the figures in Sources A and B say about religious observance in Britain?

(viii) How useful and reliable are opinion polls (surveys) for historians?

4. Study the following document carefully and answer the questions below:

> 'I became a Catholic partly because of Pope John XXIII's Second Vatican Council, and because of Pope John himself. I saw, in that gathering of bishops in Rome, a spiritual inspiration at work, which had the force of a mushroom coming up through a paving stone. 'It was so powerful because it sprang from a sense of tradition stretching back to the Apostles in the upper room in Jerusalem, when fire came down on them from heaven at Pentecost. And in that pope anyone could see the successor of St Peter, the fisherman, casting out his nets.
>
> 'Pope John Paul II is a different sort of pope. This is Peter as the rock. Where John XXIII was a historian, seeing the tradition of the church in context, able to be pragmatic [practical], John Paul II is a philosopher, hewing [conforming, adhering] to the "inflexibility [rigid, unbending] principle", as he once called it in a sermon, having little time for casuistry [quibbling, argument]. He governs imperially from the centre, a super-bishop and a super-pope.'
>
> John Wilkins, *The Guardian*, 26 May 2001

(i) Why did John Wilkins become a Catholic?

(ii) What was *'that gathering of bishops in Rome'*?

(iii) What was the author's view of *'that gathering'*?

(iv) What was his view of *'that pope'*?

(v) What does the author mean when he says of Pope John Paul II, *'This is Peter as the rock'*?

(vi) Explain the term *'imperially'*.

(vii) What is the author's view of Pope John Paul II? Do you think he admires Pope John Paul II?

5. Write **paragraph answers** on each of the following questions:

(i) Describe the decline in religious observance in post-war Europe.

(ii) What were the factors which influenced the pattern of religious observance in Europe in the post-war years?

(iii) The patterns in religious observance in Catholic and Protestant countries in Europe.

(iv) The ecumenical movement.

(v) The role of Pope John Paul II in maintaining religious observance in Europe.

6. Write **long answers** on each of the following questions:

(i) How, and why, did religious observance decline in Europe in the post-war years?

(ii) How, and with what success, did the Christian churches respond to the decline in religious observance in post-war Europe?

(iii) What changes did the Second Vatican Council make to the Catholic Church in order to respond to the decline in religious observance in Europe?

HIGHER LEVEL

1. How successful was the Second Vatican Council in responding to the changing patterns of religious observance in Europe? (Department of Education, Sample Paper)

2. To what extent were the changing patterns in religious observance in Europe between 1945 and 1992 due to political, economic and social conditions outside the control of the churches?

TEST YOURSELF AT
my-etest.com

INTRODUCTION

By the end of the 1950s, the Catholic Church had become very **authoritarian**, with power centred on the Pope and the **Roman Curia** (the papal civil service). The Catholic Church spent much of its time attacking Communism and pointing out the errors of others. Shortly after he was elected Pope, **John XXIII** made the announcement in January 1959 of an Ecumenical Council of the Catholic Church. It was a call that surprised and angered the conservative bishops who had control over the Roman Curia. They did not see the need for change.

But Pope John issued a call for **aggiornamento** – the updating of the teachings and discipline of the Catholic Church – because he wanted to bring about a **spiritual renewal** of the church. He also wanted to join with other Christians in a search for **re-union**. The Council became known as the Second Vatican Council or Vatican II. It was the twenty-first general or ecumenical council of the Catholic Church. It was also the first to be held since Vatican I in 1870.

Pope John XXIII greeting crowds from the train on his way to inaugurate the 21st Ecumenical Council of the Catholic Church.

SOURCE 1 – Pope John's background

'A man of humble origin, he had known poverty in his childhood; during his diplomatic missions in the Balkans, and as Papal Nuncio in France he had become far more aware than most of his conservative colleagues in the Italian Curia that the Church needed to adapt itself to modern social and political developments.'

W Laqueur, *Europe Since Hitler*

SOURCE 2 – Pope John accepts the world as it is

'His experience of life among his own folk at Sotto il Monte, or later among the peasants of Bulgaria, or the Catholic poor of Istanbul, or again, in secularist and sophisticated France, had led him to accept the world as it is...'

P Hughes and E Hales, *A Short History of the Catholic Church*

SOURCE 3 – Open the windows of the Church

'While in many messages over the next three years he expressed his intentions in formal detail, one of the best known images is of Pope John, when asked why the Council was needed, opened a window and reportedly said, "I want to throw open the windows of the Church so that we can see out and the people can see in." '

Wikipedia, *The Free Encyclopedia at www.wikipedia.com*

SOURCE 4 – Aim of the Council

'...The Council ... will aim at re-invigorating [energising] the Church to meet the twentieth century challenge of atheism, materialism and apathy... Among the many topics likely to come up are the greater use of the modern languages instead of Latin; reform of the dress of priests and members of religious orders; more independence for bishops; less "Italianisation" in the Church machinery and better distribution of clergy throughout the world....'

The Irish Times, 11 December 1962

PREPARATORY WORK

Pope John set up **Commissions** based on the Roman Curia to draw up an agenda and to prepare documents for the Council. These were worked on for three years, reducing over 9,000 proposals to seven documents which were sent to the bishops of the world before the council opened.

The Council was held over **four separate sessions,** all in St Peter's Basilica in Rome. They were held each autumn from 1962–5. The discussions of the council were conducted in Latin, though the smaller working meetings were conducted in different languages.

THE FIRST SESSION

Pope John opened the first session of the council in October 1962. This was easily the **largest** church council in history. Present at the first session were over 2,500 cardinals, bishops and leaders of religious orders. Also present were **invited representatives** of the Protestant churches and, at later sessions, the Russian Orthodox Church. These observers did not have a right to take part or have a vote.

In his opening address, Pope John called on Catholic Church leaders to try to meet the **needs of the people** at this time. He said the aim of the council was to promote unity among Christians and all humankind, and not to repeat traditional teachings (doctrines) or to condemn errors. He said that the Church must show herself as *'the loving mother of all ... full of mercy and goodness toward the brethren who are separated from her.'*

SOURCE 5

A meeting of bishops and cardinals at the Ecumenical Council of the Catholic Church – Vatican II – in St Peter's Basilica in Rome in 1962.

SOURCE 6 – Pope and people rejoice together

'Church desires to show herself loving mother

...In his 35-minute sermon, Pope John severely criticised those to whom he had to listen to, much to his regret, who saw nothing in the present time except prevarication and ruin. He clearly had in mind those of the Hierarchy who see no point in holding the Council now. Divine Providence, the Pope said, was leading us to a new order of human relations and everything, even human differences, led to the greater good of the Church....'

Report from Rome by M Wall, The *Irish Times*, 12 October 1962

CONSERVATIVES AND PROGRESSIVES

From the beginning of the Council, there were conflicts between the **conservatives** (traditionalists) and the **progressives** (reformers). Some believed there was no need for change; others wanted to update ceremonies, teachings and the role of the church in the modern world.

Once the Vatican Council got underway, the Commissions were broadened to include Catholic leaders all over the world. The work of the Commissions and the discussions of the Council resulted in 16 documents being voted on by the Council. None were voted on in the first session, 2 in the second, 3 in the third and 11 in the fourth and final session.

NEW POPE

Pope John died in June 1963 but the work of the Council continued under his successor Pope Paul VI. The new Pope was also Italian and spent most of his priestly life in the Roman Curia (1924 to 1954). After this he spent eight years as Archbishop of Milan where he got his first experience of diocesan work.

SECOND SESSION

The second session was opened by **Pope Paul**. He said the **aims** of the Council were: to define more clearly what the Church meant, to renew the Church, to restore the unity of all Christians and to improve relations between the Church and the wider world. In the second session the Council endorsed the principle of **collegiality**, that the bishops share with the Pope in the government of the Church. It was also agreed to use the **vernacular** (native language) in the sacraments and in the Mass. This was the first decision of the Council which had a direct effect on ordinary people.

Pope Paul VI succeeded Pope John XXIII in 1963. It was his responsibility to reconvene the Vatican Council and to ensure that it concluded its business. The Council concluded in December 1965.

SOURCE 9 – Change in balance of power

'A few days later, Cardinal Ottaviani, prefect of the Holy Office (Curia), complained about revolutionary tendencies in the Council and charged that these would cause scandal among the faithful. When he went over his time, he refused to stop. When his microphone was turned off, the assembly applauded; another indication of a major change in the balance of power.'

The HarperCollins Encyclopedia of Catholicism

SOURCE 10 – Council rejected drafts

'Commissions directed by the Roman Curia, the Pope's administrative arm, prepared draft documents on a variety of subjects for Council consideration. However, many bishops in the Council found the drafts ... too conservative in tone. The council rejected these drafts and began, with the support of the Pope, to chart its own course, which led to many progressive and reforming actions.'

World Book Encyclopedia

SOURCE 11 – Membership of Commissions

'It was in the first session that the real revolution took place, when the Fathers (bishops) refused to accept the list of nominees, for its various Commissions, which had been prepared by the cardinals of the Curia who were to act as chairmen of these Commissions ...'

P Hughes and E Hales,
A Short History of the Catholic Church

SOURCE 12 – Progressives and conservatives

'During the first session of Vatican II ... the progressives with their strongholds in Western Europe and America realised, somewhat to their surprise, that they constituted a majority. During the interval between the sessions, the Roman Curia with its conservative supporters in Spain and some other countries, staged a counter-offensive ... the conservatives under Cardinal Ottaviani succeeded in slowing down the movement for reform; the declarations on religious liberty and the Jews (absolving them of deicide – killing of God) were watered down. But at the same time the powers of the Supreme Congregation of the Holy Office (the Curia) were limited.'

W Laqueur, *Europe Since Hitler*

In between the second and third sessions, Pope Paul went on a pilgrimage to Jerusalem. He was the first Pope to leave Italy since the fifteenth century and he was the first to visit the Holy Land. There he met the leader of the Greek Orthodox Church, **Patriarch Athenagoras**. The Catholic Church and the Greek Orthodox Church were in disagreement since the eleventh century.

SOURCE 14 – Pope Paul's trips abroad

'Pope Paul is given to a sign language that often speaks more eloquently than his prose. For example, his trips to three non-Christian countries, India, Jordan and Israel – all of which took place during the Council – dramatised the wider ecumenical spirit that distinguished this Council from any previous one. His cordial meeting with Patriarch Athenagoras established the mood of reconciliation that reached a high point yesterday when he and the Patriarch abolished from the "church's memory" a 911-year-old act of recrimination (accusation) for which both parties agreed, their predecessors shared blame.'

Report from Rome by J Cogley,
The *Irish Times*, 10 December 1965

SOURCE 13 – Vernacular languages

'Liturgically, it [the Council] took one very visible step towards discarding tradition where it no longer seemed helpful as a guide, by authorising the use of local, vernacular languages in the Mass ... only nineteen of those prelates attending the Council voted against the measure, while 2,158 voted for it.'

J H Roberts, *Twentieth Century*

THIRD SESSION

At the third session in the autumn of 1964, a statement on **ecumenism** was agreed. This opened the way to discussions between Catholics and other Christians. The Constitution of the Church was also agreed where the principle of collegiality was accepted. But also the doctrine of papal infallibility was agreed. However, this document indicated a shift in the balance of power between the Pope and the bishops. It led to the setting up of national councils of bishops and later to the announcement by Pope Paul of a Synod of Bishops to advise him on policy. The document also recognised the People of God and expanded the role and functions of the laity.

However, the Council failed to agree on a document on the **Church in the Modern World** and on **religious liberty**. These had to wait until the fourth session. But, the failure to agree on the document on religious liberty led to a rebellion by American bishops who organised a protest petition with 800 signatures.

FOURTH SESSION

In the fourth and final session, the Council proclaimed two more documents on Divine Revelation and the relationship of the Catholic Church with the modern world. There were also declarations on the relationship between the Catholic Church and non-Christian religions, on Christian education and religious liberty and a declaration removing the responsibility from the Jews for the death of Christ. At this session the Pope also announced his intention to establish a **Synod of Bishops** for **consultation and collaboration** with him in governing the church. The Pope proclaimed 1966 as Jubilee Year with the aim of ensuring the people would be familiarised with the Council's work and that they would put the intentions of the Council into practice. He also set up further Commissions to carry out the wishes of the Council.

CONCLUSION

- The work of the council had a huge **influence** on all aspects of church life and on the religious practice of Catholics. (See Summary of Changes following this section.)
- The Council opened up **divisions** between conservatives (traditionalists) and progressives (reformers). Some of the conservatives formed their own **Tridentine Church** which used Latin in its sacraments.
- It brought greater **lay participation** in Church activities. It reduced the authoritarian (strict) nature of the Church.
- It **improved relations** between the Catholic Church and other Christian and non-Christian religions.
- It is difficult to assess the impact of the Council on **religious observance** in Europe. It did not stop the decline but it may have slowed it down at the time, particularly among younger people. However, it strengthened the Catholic Church in Africa and South America.

SUMMARY OF CHANGES

• The Mass would be celebrated in the vernacular (the language of the country). Lay participation in the Mass would be increased, including involvement in readings and in distributing communion.

• There would be greater emphasis on ecumenism (the coming together of the churches) with both the Protestant churches and the Orthodox churches of Eastern Europe.

• The bishops were given greater authority in their own dioceses and when they met at national conferences. They would also meet in a synod with the Pope.

• The Church would become more involved in issues concerning justice and peace.

SOURCE 15 – Most important accomplishment of the Council

'In November 1996, I asked [Franz Cardinal Konig] what he considered the most important accomplishment of Vatican II. He immediately responded, "The empowerment [greater influence] of the laity and the corresponding reduction in the relative power of the clergy and the magisterium." '

I Shafer, *www.Vatican2.org*

SOURCE 16 – The People of God

'This constitution's favourite image of the church was that of the "people of God." ... The focus of the church as the whole people of God enabled the council to break with the one-sided emphasis of preceding centuries on the power of the clergy.'

World Book Encyclopedia

SOURCE 17 – Pope announces reform of the Holy Office

'Pope Paul, noting that the government of the Vatican must be adapted to "the necessities of the times", announced yesterday a series of reforms of the important Holy Office. The changes in the body, which deals with crucial matters of faith and morals, is the opening round of the Pontiff's [Pope's] planned reform of the entire Roman Curia. The Pope's action brings the biggest changes to the Holy Office since it emerged out of the Inquisition [Church court] of 1542.'

The *Irish Times*, 7 December 1965

SOURCE 18 – Council's work begins now

'After 168 frequently argumentative meetings, the Ecumenical Council was brought yesterday to a peaceful conclusion. The real work of the Council, however, is about to begin. It is claimed by Church historians that it took 30 years to implement the decrees of the sixteenth-century Council of Trent in the dioceses and parishes of the Church. This time, with communications speeded up, the spirit and reform of the Vatican Council can be communicated even to the far reaches of Catholicism much more rapidly.... The Church in the view of the vast majority is healthier today than it was when the Council ... began. The forces of reform and renewal are markedly stronger and the powers opposing the updating Pope John envisioned are notably weaker.'

Report from Rome by J Cogley, The *Irish Times*, 10 December 1965

SOURCE 19 – Changes to the Church

'Vatican Council II started the most far-reaching reforms within the Catholic Church in 1,000 years. Probably few participants in the council fully realised the magnitude of the changes they had put in motion. The Council helped transform the church from a European-centred institution toward a more genuinely world church, with most of its followers living in Third World countries outside Europe and North America.'

World Book Encyclopedia

SOURCE 20 – Effect of Vatican II

'The Pope in an interview after the end of the Council added: "... will everything go back to what it was before? Appearances and customs say Yes, but the spirit of the Council says No." '

W Laqueur, *Europe Since Hitler*

COMPREHENSION

1. According to Sources 1 and 2, where did Pope John XXIII work outside Italy? What influence did that work have on him?

2. In Source 3, why did Pope John say the Council was needed?

3. What, according to the *Irish Times* in Source 4, would be considered at the Council? What do you think the term Italianisation means?

4. In Source 6, how long was Pope John's opening sermon? Whom did he criticise? Who did not want to hold the Council?

5. Study Source 7. Which part of the world provided the largest number of bishops?

6. What modern means of communication had the Council available to it according to Source 8? How did the media get the news of the Council?

7. In Source 9, what did Cardinal Ottaviani complain about? What happened when he refused to stop speaking?

8. What was the reaction of many of the bishops to the draft documents produced by the Commissions, according to Source 10?

9. What did the Fathers (bishops) refuse to accept in Source 11?

10. In Source 12, what does progressives mean? Where was the stronghold of the progressives? Who were the supporters of the Curia?

11. In Source 13, what did the Council authorise? Comment on the majority in favour.

12. What trips abroad did Pope Paul take, according to Source 14?

13. According to Cardinal Konig in Source 15, what was the most important accomplishment of Vatican II?

14. In Source 16, what was the favoured image of the constitution?

15. What was reformed in Source 17? Why was it reformed? What else did the Pope plan to reform?

16. In Source 18, how many meetings were held during the Vatican Council? How long did it take to implement the changes of the sixteenth-century Council of Trent? Why would changes after Vatican II be quicker? What was markedly stronger in 1965 than in 1962 when the Council began?

17. According to Source 19, how did the Council transform the Catholic Church?

18. Study Source 20. Did the Pope believe that everything would go back to what it was before?

COMPARISON

1. According to Source 1, Pope John was aware that 'the Church needed to adapt itself to modern social and political developments.' Do Sources 2, 3 and 4 come to the same conclusion? Explain your answer.

2. What do Sources 5 and 7 tell you about the organisation of the Vatican Council?

3. In comparing Sources 7 and 8, why do you think the media came from all over the world? How reliable would their reports of the Council be?

4. Study Sources 9 to 12. List three points of information which showed there was a change in the balance of power in the Council. What change had occurred in the balance of power?

5. In Sources 13 and 14, what changes occurred? Did those changes support the conclusions of Sources 9 to 12?

6. Examine Sources 15 and 18. Do you think Cardinal Konig and John Cogley are optimistic about the changes in the Catholic Church?

7. According to Source 19, the Council transformed the Church 'from a European-centred institution toward a more genuinely world church.' What changes would have to be made

to the list of bishops in Source 7, if that was to happen?

8. How did the changes in Source 17 support the views of Source 12 that the 'progressives ... constituted a majority'?

CRITICISM

1. Classify Sources 1 to 4 as primary or secondary. What are the advantages (strengths) and disadvantages (weaknesses) of both types of sources for the study of history?

2. Source 3 is an extract from an internet site. What are the problems for historians of using internet sources as evidence? What are the Internet's advantages (strengths) for historical research?

3. What types of Sources are Sources 5, 6 and 7? What are the advantages (strengths) and disadvantages (weaknesses) of each of these in providing information on the opening of Vatican II?

4. In your opinion, which of the Sources 9 to 12 best explains the conflict between conservatives and progressives? What are the limitations (disadvantages) of relying on one of those sources for your information?

5. Are Sources 14 and 18 primary or secondary sources? How useful and reliable are they in providing information on the Vatican Council? Use information in and about the Sources to support your answer.

6. Are Sources 13, 19 and 20 primary or secondary sources? How useful and reliable are they in providing information on the Vatican Council? Use information in and about the Sources to support your answer.

7. Make your own notes on the usefulness (advantages/strengths and disadvantages/weaknesses) of the various types of sources used here.

CONTEXTUALISATION

1. Give a brief explanatory account of the trends in religious observance among Catholics and other Christian religions in Europe from the end of the Second World War to the 1960s.

2. Using the Sources and the account of the Second Vatican Council, write on the roles played by Pope John XXIII and Pope Paul VI in the Vatican Council.

3. What actions did the Second Vatican Council take to modernise the Catholic Church? How successful was the Council in achieving **aggiornamento** – the updating of the teachings and discipline of the Catholic Church?

4. Using the Sources above and the account, write a report on the Second Vatican Council – origins, progress and results.

The Impact of Advances in the Biological Sciences in Europe, 1945-92

The discoverers of the structure of DNA, James Watson and Francis Crick, with their model of part of a DNA molecule in 1953. Their discovery, made at Cambridge University, England, meant that the genes of some organisms could be changed.

THE BIOLOGICAL SCIENCES

'It is no exaggeration,' a group of British experts said in 1968, *'to suggest that biology today is in a phase as dynamic and productive as was physics during the first 25 years of the century.'* They attributed biology's success to advances in **molecular biology** – the study of the structure and function of the large organic molecules associated with living organisms, especially the nucleic acids (DNA and RNA) and proteins. However, while the most revolutionary advances were made in molecular biology, the overall impact of the biological sciences depended as much on the *'accumulated knowledge of previous decades'*. This was combined with work in the other sciences of chemistry and physics and aided by new advances in computers. The impact of advances in the biological sciences was felt most immediately in medicine, agriculture and industry.

DNA

Watson and Crick in Cambridge made the greatest advances in molecular biology through the discovery of the structure of DNA in 1953. This carried the genetic information which determined the pattern of life. Now the genes of some organisms could be changed to give them new characteristics. **Genetics** – the study of heredity – had already made its impact on European society before the Second World War. But it fell into disrepute during the war because of Nazi efforts to use it for **racial and political** purposes. After the war, public interest in genetics grew again as the biological scientists understood more and more about the workings of genes.

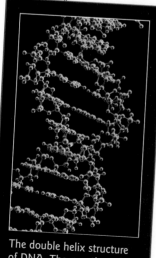

The double helix structure of DNA. The genetic code of the DNA controls the functioning and growth of every living organism.

MEDICINE

Medical advances occurred on all fronts, whether through the use of **penicillin** after the Second World War to kill bacteria or the production of **insulin** for diabetes in the late 1970s. There were three general areas where significant advances were made.

Surgery: In surgery much progress was made in **transplants** of kidneys, lungs and hearts. In the case of kidneys, the first workable kidney dialysis machines were made in Holland in the 1940s. The first transplants were also kidney transplants – the first successful one being made in Boston in 1954. Once kidney transplants were a success, then other transplants followed, including lung and later heart transplants. In the latter case most progress was achieved outside Europe but very soon heart transplants were taking place there too. Full success in all these transplants had to wait for the development of better drugs to help the body cope with the new organs.

Long before heart transplants were a success many thousands of people were helped by **heart pacemakers** which were developed in Sweden in 1959. Almost as widespread were **hip replacements** which were developed in the 1960s in Manchester Royal Infirmary. The first successful tests were conducted in 1972 and within four years over 9,000 people had benefited from successful hip operations. These advances in surgery both extended the lives of many people as well as making life more comfortable and less painful.

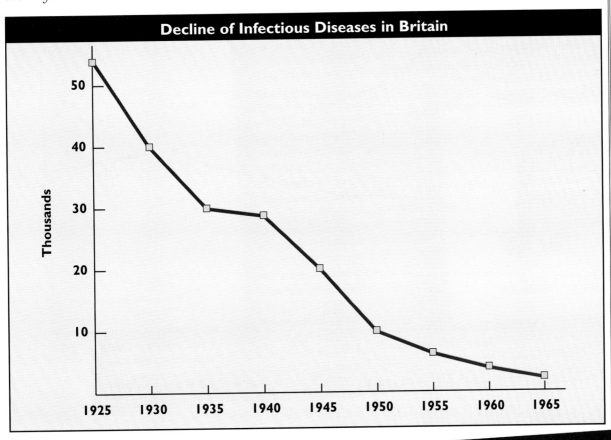

In 1968, Christiaan Barnard undertook the first heart transplant on dentist Philip Blaiberg (right) in Cape Town, South Africa. Later, European doctors undertook the same operations.

Infectious diseases: Campaigns against infectious diseases combined the results of biological research with public health issues. Research into the structure of viruses led to the development of vaccinations which helped eliminate some viral diseases such as **polio** which struck in regular epidemics. The campaign against **tuberculosis** appeared to be equally successful in the 1960s but in later decades it posed a threat in some European cities. Another infectious disease, **typhus**, was controlled by the use of **DDT**, first used on a large scale in a typhus epidemic in Naples at the end of the Second World War. DDT was also successful against **malaria** which was still prevalent in some parts of Europe in the 1940s. By the 1960s, a doctor who began practicing in the 1930s could say: *'the major threats to human life were tuberculosis, tetanus, syphilis, rheumatic fever, pneumonia, meningitis, polio and septicaemia of all sorts.... The problems of the 1930s and 1940s have literally vanished.'*

Decline of Infectious Diseases in Britain

Thousands

50 — 40 — 30 — 20 — 10 —

1925 1930 1935 1940 1945 1950 1955 1960 1965

Infertility: Many thousands of couples could not have children because of the problem of male and female infertility. **Genetic techniques** were particularly important in providing a solution for some of the problems relating to infertility. In Britain during the 1960s a gynaecologist, Patrick Steptoe, achieved fertilisation of human eggs outside the body. He used this technique – **in vitro fertilisation** – to produce the first **test-tube baby**, Louise Brown, in 1978. The initial success rate was about 10% but over the years further improvements in the process led to a 75% success rate.

One-year-old baby Louise Brown from England appearing on television in America. Louise was born in 1978 as the world's first 'test-tube' baby.

In vitro fertilisation and artificial insemination allowed many hundreds of thousands of couples in Europe and worldwide to have children – without this technique these couples could not have had children.

The overall impact of these advances was to reduce deaths and to lengthen life. These gave rise to **population pressures** – perhaps more serious in other parts of the world such as Africa and Asia than in Europe. However, even in Europe changing lifestyles influenced couples who sought to limit the **size of their families**. While some parents wanted more children, others used **birth control**. The slow down in population growth in Europe led to an **ageing population** which had social and economic effects.

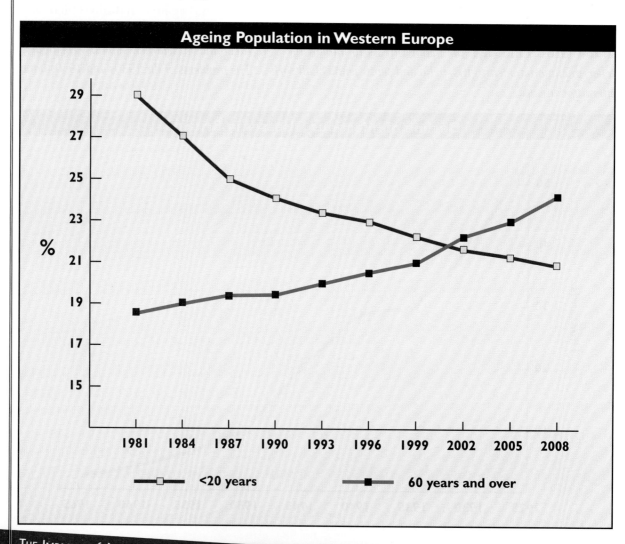

The Impact of (a) Advances in Biological Sciences, (b) Nuclear Power, and (c) the Computer

Moral Problems

The advances in the biological sciences posed ethical or moral problems for scientists. They now had to consider the social consequences of their work, particularly the possible **abuses** or **misuses** of their findings. This was especially true of genetic engineering because of the possibility that human traits or characteristics could be made to order. But who would decide which traits were desirable and which were not?

Transplants raised issues about the **sale of organs** and their trade particularly from the Third World. Some argued that the body could be disposed of like any other property. They proposed that people be paid in advance to donate their organs after death.

Another area which raised crucial ethical or moral questions and caused considerable controversy was **human reproduction**. The use of artificial methods of birth control, especially the Pill, led to their condemnation by the Catholic Church through Pope Paul VI's encyclical, *Humanae Vitae*. IVF, or test-tube fertilisation, caused further controversy. Critics condemned the use of fertilisation outside the womb. It also raised the issue of **surrogate mothers** (who received eggs and sperm from couples who could not have their own children). Governments were forced to put conditions on the use of IVF and payments to surrogate mothers were banned in some countries.

Growth of Health Industry

The huge advances in medical science led to a vast expansion of the **medical industry**, aided by the development of the **welfare state**. This brought the benefits of the latest medical research to ordinary people. It now seemed as if the political wish to care for everybody from the cradle to the grave could be accomplished by medicine.

The pharmaceutical industry grew rapidly after the Second World War, fuelled by the huge increase in spending on medicine by European governments. Here, quality control workers in an Italian pharmaceutical factory examine drug containers.

There was a huge increase in **spending** on medicine as state-supported medical schemes became widespread. In Britain about 90% of spending on health came from the government, while it was only 10% less in France and Germany. Between 1970 and 1992, spending on health as a proportion of Gross Domestic Product (GDP) doubled in many countries in Western Europe. The increased spending was partly caused by **more expensive medicines** as the health industry supported the pharmaceutical industry and the manufacture of sophisticated equipment. It was also partly caused by increasing **specialisation** and specialists usually earned more money than general practitioners.

Criticism of the Health System

The huge increase in the health industry led to increasing **criticism of the system**. Some believed that medicine was not being driven by care for patients but by professional ambition and company profits. Medicine was not fulfilling the huge expectations it had created.

Some investigations showed that new illnesses were brought on by the drugs and procedures used to treat the original condition of patients. As well as this, in spite of an elaborate medical system, the rich continued to live longer and to have healthier lives than the poor.

The high costs of modern medicine and dissatisfaction with its failure to deal with some medical problems led to a huge uptake of **alternative medicine** from about 1970 onwards. In Britain it was estimated that about 13 million visits were made to alternative medical practitioners in 1981. The range of alternative medicines also grew so that by the 1980s there were more people practicing alternative medicine than there were GPs. This trend seemed to suggest that many people were losing their faith in the ability of traditional medicine to provide all the cures.

Medicine became a **serious political issue** during the 1980s as governments in Europe tried to control the huge costs. Indeed medical improvements had created an ageing population which was being supported by a declining group of wage earners. In Britain, the Thatcher government introduced the market mechanism to cut costs so that hospitals were encouraged to compete with each other for patients. In France, the government cut costs by controlling medical expenses.

The Future of Medicine

However, as the 1980s came to a close, further advances in the biological sciences seemed to open the way to preventing and curing many major diseases. A huge project – **the Human Genome Project** – began to map the human genetic structure so as to identify the structure and function of every human gene. The leading laboratories were in **Britain** (in Cambridge and Oxford) and in the **US**. The success of this project will make it possible to identify defects underlying inherited diseases and to provide cures.

AGRICULTURE AND INDUSTRY

The work of the biological sciences also impacted on agriculture and industry:

* In agriculture, **genetic techniques** were used to improve plants and animals. This led to new species of plants more resistant to attack by insects. Animal breeders used **artificial insemination** to improve the quality of their animals. The genetic techniques also opened up the whole issue of genetically modified food. Once again the role of the biologist in society was examined. Would the benefits of genetically modified food outweigh its dangers? These were issues which only the future could resolve.

* In industry, **geneticists** were employed in the brewing industry to produce strains of wheat which yielded higher quantities of alcohol. In the pharmaceutical industry, geneticists were able to develop strains of bacteria with high yields of antibodies.

Undoubtedly, the overall impact of advances in the biological sciences was the improvement in the quality of everyday life.

Genetic engineering became a very controversial topic in the 1980s. Genetic techniques were used to produce genetically modified foods which some argued were dangerous. This scientist displays genetically modified food in jars and dishes.

The Impact of Nuclear Power in Europe, 1945-92

NUCLEAR POWER

During the Second World War, the US organised the **Manhattan Project** which developed the first atomic bombs. After the war, the Atomic Energy Act (1946) was passed by the US Congress which prevented classified atomic information from being passed to other countries. Countries in Europe therefore had to develop their own nuclear technology. In **Britain**, the Atomic Energy Authority and in **France** the Atomic Energy Commission worked independently on atomic weapons and nuclear energy. The **USSR** was also working independently and in 1949 exploded its first nuclear bomb.

Atomic and hydrogen bombs were tested in islands in the Pacific Ocean in the 1950s. The development of these bombs increased people's fear during the Cold War.

NUCLEAR WEAPONS

The development of the atomic bomb was one of the causes of the Cold War. (See The Cold War in Europe, Chapter 9.) The competition between the US and the USSR led to an **arms race** which included further development of nuclear weapons. By 1951 the US had developed the much more powerful **hydrogen bomb** to be followed two years later by the USSR. Britain also developed its own nuclear capacity with its first A-bomb test in 1952 and the H-bomb in 1957. France took until 1960 before it also became a nuclear power.

> **KEY CONCEPT: COLD WAR.** This was a time of hostility, tension and propaganda rivalry between the USSR (Soviet Union) and the countries of Western Europe and the US. It developed after the Second World War (1945) and lasted until the collapse of Communism in the Soviet Union in 1991. It resulted in a series of crises which brought the world to the brink of nuclear war.

The awesome power of these bombs added to the **fear** of both sides in the Cold War. It also led to developments in technology for delivering the bombs. Initially, **converted aeroplanes** were used to carry the bombs. The US and the USSR competed during the 1950s to build larger and more powerful planes to carry these bombs. In the meantime, American planes were based in Britain from the summer of 1949, and also in Morocco and Italy, to get within range of the USSR.

Nuclear Missiles

During the 1950s the power of the bombs increased and their size decreased. It then became possible to use **guided missiles** to deliver the bombs. Some of these missiles were air-launched from large planes, others were fired from submarines such as the American **Polaris**. These missiles were generally short-range so some were based on planes in Europe. By the late 1950s the US and the USSR invested considerable money in developing **ICBMs** (Intercontinental Ballistic Missiles). US intermediate missiles were based in Britain, Turkey and Italy. The USSR based **SS-20 missiles** in Eastern Europe and the Americans replied by basing the similar **Pershing** in Western Europe. When the USSR tried to install missiles in **Cuba** in 1962, this led to a crisis with America which almost resulted in a world war.

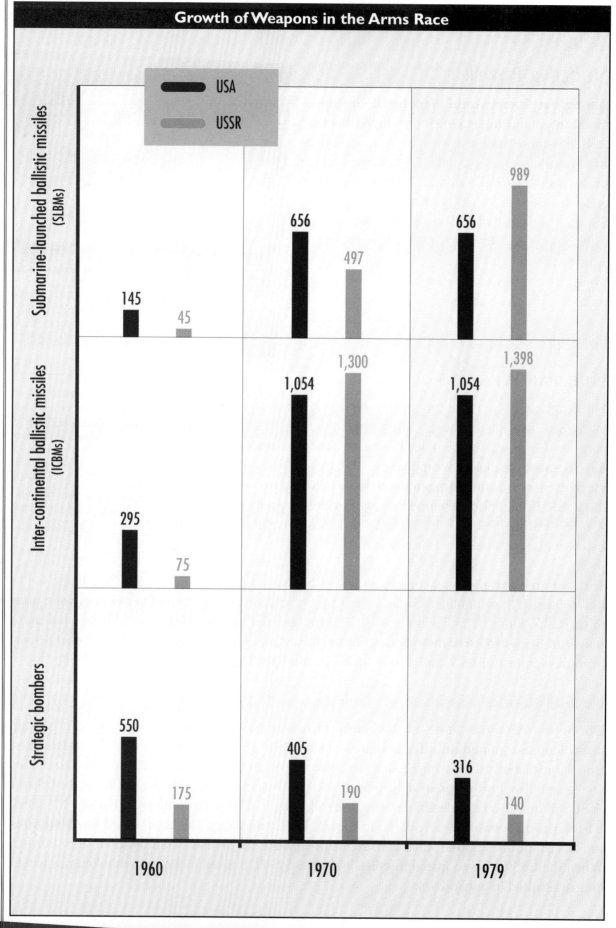

Growth of Weapons in the Arms Race

USA
USSR

Submarine-launched ballistic missiles (SLBMs)

145 · 45 · 656 · 497 · 656 · 989

Inter-continental ballistic missiles (ICBMs)

295 · 75 · 1,054 · 1,300 · 1,054 · 1,398

Strategic bombers

550 · 175 · 405 · 190 · 316 · 140

1960 · 1970 · 1979

The Impact of (a) Advances in Biological Sciences, (b) Nuclear Power, and (c) the Computer

By the early 1960s, the development of **long-range missiles** meant that each country could attack the other from their home bases. These increased the **tension and fear** of the Cold War. **Europe** was caught in the middle. The growth of nuclear power was spurred on by the belief in **nuclear deterrence**. Both sides believed that the only way to stop the other from attacking was to have the capacity for **huge retaliation**. A balance of terror developed, supported by a huge arms industry and the military, particularly in Britain, France and the USSR.

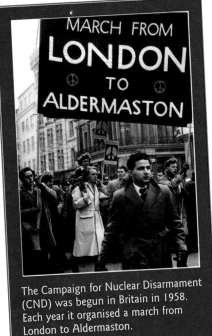

An imaginative drawing of a missile-launching submarine in the 1950s. The US developed the Polaris missile to be launched from submarines. Some countries, such as Britain, bought these missiles from the US.

While the USSR felt it was defending itself, Britain and France developed nuclear weapons to maintain their **status** as great powers. One way in which nuclear weapons were limited was through a series of treaties – **test ban treaties** – which controlled their testing. However, the huge cost of producing nuclear weapons (and maintaining a large army) contributed to the failure of the Soviet economy, to Gorbachev's reform movement in the Soviet Union and ultimately to the downfall of the Soviet Union.

Campaign for Nuclear Disarmament

The increasing danger of a nuclear war led to the development of an anti-war movement. The **Campaign for Nuclear Disarmament** (CND) was set up in Britain in 1958 to combat the use of nuclear weapons. It organised an annual march from **London** to **Aldermaston**, the centre of Britain's nuclear research, to **Ban the Bomb**. The Ban the Bomb movement spread to other Western European countries, such as Holland, West Germany and Sweden. As one of its founders said, *'To spread ruin, misery and death throughout one's own country as well as the enemy is the act of mad-men.... The question every human being must ask is "Can man survive?" '* Soon more active CND supporters organised **sit-down protests** which led to clashes with the police. The arrests which followed highlighted the issues for even more people.

The Campaign for Nuclear Disarmament (CND) was begun in Britain in 1958. Each year it organised a march from London to Aldermaston.

ELECTRICITY FROM NUCLEAR POWER

But nuclear power was not confined to military uses. The rapid expansion of the Western European economies, the reconstruction of the Soviet Union and the industrialisation of Eastern Europe after the war led to an increase in the demand for **electricity**. This was initially satisfied by electricity production based on water, coal, oil and gas. But in 1956 Britain built the world's **first nuclear power station** in Calder Hall. Other European countries soon followed:

- Nuclear energy was seen as an **alternative** for some countries who wanted to reduce their reliance on non-renewable fossil fuels such as coal and oil.

An aerial view of Calder Hall in Cumbria, England, the world's first nuclear power station, which opened in 1956.

- Some claimed that electricity produced by nuclear power plants was **cheaper** than that produced by coal-powered plants, even though the nuclear power plant was more expensive to build.

- Some countries such as Italy lacked their own energy sources.

Expansion of Nuclear Power

By 1973, Britain had 14 nuclear power stations. This increased to 33 by 1979. By the mid-1980s, 15 countries in both Eastern and Western Europe were using nuclear power stations. Nuclear power increased its **share** of electricity production from 4% in 1971 to 10% by 1978. Its rapid rise in the 1970s was due to the **cost** and **scarcity** of fossil fuels, particularly because of the **Oil Crisis** of 1973. Some countries depended on nuclear power far more than this, particularly **France** and **Belgium**. Both of these countries produced a higher proportion of electricity from nuclear power than any other countries in Europe. But **West Germany** also developed an ambitious nuclear power programme and by 1978 had become the largest single producer of nuclear power in Western Europe. In the **Soviet Union** very little electricity was generated by nuclear power in 1970. But rapid expansion occurred so that 10% was produced by 1986.

The attraction of nuclear power led to the formation of **Euratom** (European Atomic Energy Community) in 1957 at the same time as the EEC. However, alternative energy sources, such as

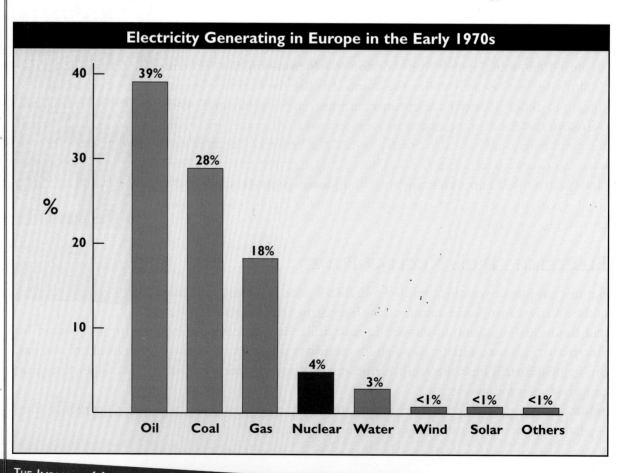

Electricity Generating in Europe in the Early 1970s

	%
Oil	39%
Coal	28%
Gas	18%
Nuclear	4%
Water	3%
Wind	<1%
Solar	<1%
Others	<1%

THE IMPACT OF (A) ADVANCES IN BIOLOGICAL SCIENCES, (B) NUCLEAR POWER, AND (C) THE COMPUTER

coal and oil, were more attractive during the 1960s. It took until the 1980s before a common policy on energy was developed at EU level because of differing national interests. It was the policy of the EU to encourage the development of nuclear power.

Dangers of Nuclear Power

However, the dangers of nuclear power soon slowed its development. A growing **anti-nuclear movement** was concerned about the long-term health effects, including cancer and birth defects; the problems of disposing of nuclear waste; the growing costs of building nuclear power plants; and the greater likelihood of explosions if the number of plants continued to increase.

In 1957, at **Windscale** (now called Sellafield) in England fire destroyed the core of one reactor leading to the escape of radioactive fumes into the air. More serious incidents occurred in the US at Three Mile Island before the **Chernobyl** disaster in the Soviet Union in 1986. Other serious explosions had occurred in the Soviet Union before this but these had all been covered up. However, it was not possible to cover up the Chernobyl accident and the Soviet leader, **Gorbachev**, had no desire to do so. An explosive leak caused the deaths of 31 people, more than 200 were seriously injured, many more died over the next number of years, thousands of square miles of local land was **contaminated** and clouds of radioactive material spread as far as Sweden.

The decontamination of the Chernobyl Power Station after the explosion in 1986. This was one of the serious incidents relating to nuclear power which led to some countries cutting back on their plans to expand nuclear power.

Serious issues also arose about the **disposal of nuclear waste** which stays active for several thousand years. Some waste was disposed at **sea** over 300 miles/450 kilometres off Land's End, England. Other waste material was disposed of in **disused salt mines** in West Germany. But these disposals only increased concern about the safety of the waste and its transportation.

Slow Down

Due to all these factors and growing public concern, there was a slow down in the development of nuclear power: in 1989, **Britain** decided to **postpone** the construction of new nuclear power stations; **Sweden** committed itself to decommissioning its reactors by 2010. In **Austria** a nuclear power plant was closed due to a referendum (vote of the people). But some countries such as **France** and the **USSR** went ahead with their nuclear programmes.

Greenpeace protesters wearing death masks lying on the road in London in opposition to the Thorpe nuclear reprocessing plant.

By the 1990s, the **controversy** over nuclear power continued. Some saw it as a **dangerous technology** which threatened the health and the future of people; others saw it as the **main replacement** when oil, gas and coal ran out. The lack of alternatives encouraged research into the development of other forms of energy, such as wind and water power. But only the future would tell what role they would play.

NUCLEAR REACTORS IN EUROPE IN THE EARLY 1980s			
COUNTRY	NO. OF REACTORS IN OPERATION	COUNTRY	NO. OF REACTORS IN OPERATION
Belgium	8	Italy	3
Bitain	38	Netherlands	2
Bulgaria	3	Spain	8
Czechoslovakia	2	Sweden	12
Finland	3	Switzerland	5
France	44	USSR	31
East Germany	5	Yugoslavia	1
West Germany	20		

PERCENTAGE OF ELECTRICITY GENERATED FROM NUCLEAR POWER	
France	70
Belgium	65
Hungary	50
Sweden	46
Spain	35
Finland	35
West Germany	33
Britain	18

WIDER NUCLEAR USE

Nuclear reactors also produced **radioactive isotopes** which were used in medicine and industry:
- In **medicine**, some were used for diagnosis such as testing for brain tumours; others were used for treating cancer by killing off cancerous cells.
- They were also used in **manufacturing industry**. In steel mills they were used to measure the thickness of steel sheets; or the thickness of tin plate for cans; they were also used in the filling of detergent packets, testing synthetic fibres and measuring the thickness of sheet glass.
- Isotope **batteries** were also used because of their long life in navigation lights, sonar beacons and weather stations.

The Impact of the Computer in Europe, 1945-92

COMPUTERS

The computer was developed rapidly in Britain, Germany and the US during and after the Second World War. But by the 1950s American technology overtook European technology and most significant later developments such as integrated circuits, microchips and computer languages were American in origin.

Limited Use

In the 1950s the use of computers was mainly confined to military, scientific and government use due to their size and expense. Their influence on business and industry was still limited. The LEO computer was produced in England in 1954 but it was only able to do routine office work. At about the same time in Germany, computers began to be used for the design of optical equipment. By 1961 there were only about 4,000 computers worldwide, and about a quarter of those were in Europe. Their impact on European society in general was therefore limited.

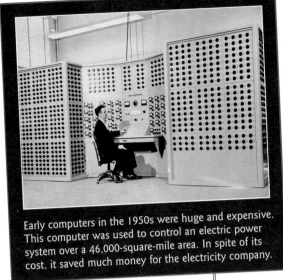

Early computers in the 1950s were huge and expensive. This computer was used to control an electric power system over a 46,000-square-mile area. In spite of its cost, it saved much money for the electricity company.

Rapid Growth

Government sponsorship in the 1940s and early 1950s was most important for the development of computers. But from the 1960s business and commerce spurred on the changes. Businesses had to set up separate **computer centres** with specialised staff. These cost so much that only businesses with large amounts of data such as banks and insurance companies could afford them and benefit from them. By the 1970s small and medium-sized companies took advantage of smaller, cheaper computers which did not need separate computer centres with all their extra costs. The 1970s and 1980s brought **computers for everybody** with the production of personal computers.

In the 1970s, Apple produced a personal computer which people could afford. Other companies such as IBM in America and Olivetti, Siemens and ICL in Europe soon followed. This was the beginning of a huge increase in the ownership and use of computers in the home.

By 1971 the number of computers had increased 10 times; twenty years later, in the early 1990s, this had increased to over 100 million machines. Half of these were in the US, about a quarter in Western Europe and only one per cent in the USSR. **Eastern Europe** lagged very far behind Western Europe. In Communist society information was considered **politically dangerous** so, apart from scientific and military research, governments tried to limit the use of computers to banks and state businesses.

All Areas of Life

The main impact of the computer on Europe was largely from the 1970s onwards. But its impact was widespread because it affected **all areas of life** – government, business, industry, transport, travel, education, medicine and the home. By the early 1990s much of the **daily life** which people took for granted would have been impossible without computers. They provided the means to organise a **more complicated world** and they promoted more rapid social change.

A New Industry: The development of the computer led to a new industry, beginning slowly in the 1950s and expanding rapidly in the 1980s, which provided employment in manufacturing, sales and servicing. But the European computer industry was on a smaller scale than the American and Japanese industries. **Olivetti** in Italy, **ICL** in Britain and **Siemens** were not able to compete with **IBM** in America. In the 1960s, IBM invested over ten times more in research and development than the largest European company, ICL. Not surprisingly, in 1966, IBM controlled three-quarters of the computer market in France, Germany and Italy; and half the British market. European companies were hindered by **smaller markets** and by **language barriers**.

From the 1970s the growth of the computer industry in Europe was dependent on American companies basing manufacturing facilities in Europe to service the growing European market. By the 1990s the European computer industry was still weak in both **hardware** and **software** products, its investment in research and development (R&D) was lower than that in the US and Japan and so was its labour productivity. After the merger of **Siemens** and **Nixdorf** in 1990, there was only one major European computer manufacturer.

Scientific Research: The great advantage of computers was their ability to handle vast quantities of information rapidly. In the 1950s they were used in scientific and engineering projects where calculations and information gathering would involve highly trained personnel over long periods of time. The computer's ability to update, revise and correct huge quantities of data rapidly overcame a limitation of the **printed media** on which Europe (and the world) had depended since the fifteenth century.

Government: As users of huge amounts of information, governments had an obvious need for computers. They were initially used in Britain to develop and control military equipment. But soon computers were used for all aspects of government work, from budgets to weather forecasting, from tax collecting to census gathering and counting.

The use of computers had a huge impact on car production. Assembly-line work was carried out by robots which increased efficiency and cut costs but also cut employment.

Industry: Industry too was influenced. Some feared rising unemployment because they believed that computers would make many people redundant. While this was true in certain areas, computers also led to the development of other industries and jobs.

Computers had a key role to play in providing greater accuracy in manufacture, controlling manufacturing processes by automation and even in organising the payroll. The increase in computer-controlled manufacturing was motivated by the necessity to cut costs and to ensure more efficient and cheaper production. The car industry was one of the first manufacturing industries to adopt computers on a wide scale. Computer-controlled robots became widespread in car manufacturing in the early 1980s – e.g. Fiat in Italy and Ford in Britain. They replaced about a quarter of the workforce. **Computer-aided design** (CAD) was used to design products large and small – from aeroplanes to bridges, buildings to cars. Computer technology also improved access to markets and contributed to movements in the EU towards a **single market**. But computers helped industry indirectly too as power, water and gas supplies were controlled by computer.

Business: Economics and finance were early users of computer power. **Economic research** made use of economic equations to predict business and economic growth. **Companies** worked out taxes, created company budgets and controlled investments. **Stock markets** in London, Paris and elsewhere in Europe needed reliable and fast information on the movement of stocks and shares, government bonds and currency movements. **ATM** (automatic teller machines) machines allowed customers to access information on accounts as well as withdraw cash. In France, the **Minitel** network reached 30 million private and business subscribers through 6 million small terminals which provided access to information on thousands of different services.

Transport: Transport systems were improved by the use of the computer. Traffic lights, trains and aircraft were controlled by computers in a central location. In the case of airlines, seat reservations were booked through travel agencies using a central reservation system.

Communications: The publishing of books and newspapers was revolutionised. Newspapers were able to adapt to meet the challenge of television. They increased in size and provided **special supplements** to cater for a variety of tastes. Newspapers were produced faster due to easier linking between journalists and the newsrooms, as well as new printing technology which was computer-driven. Just as national newspapers expanded, **desktop publishing** allowed local newspapers to be produced to satisfy a local market.

The first automated currency-dispensing machine was invented in Chicago in the early 1950s. Much later this led to the development of automatic teller machines (ATMs) which were linked by computer to each person's account.

But computers also helped newspapers' greatest competitor – **television**, particularly the development of satellite systems with set-top boxes. Undoubtedly computers and information technology widened the **sources of information** in Western democracies and in the dictatorships of Eastern Europe. They may have helped speed up the **downfall of Eastern regimes** because Western television stations were accessible through satellite transmissions which could not be blocked as easily as earlier radio signals.

Medicine: Computers were used in medical research to handle huge volumes of data. **Genetic research** in the 1950s and 1960s benefited from early computers while the Human Genome Project could not have been completed without the use of computers. Computers were also developed to control **medical equipment**. They were used, for example, with X-ray data in CAT scans of the head, heart or abdomen to help diagnose and treat diseases.

Cultural Diversity and Cultural Imperialism: Discussion of the impact of computers on culture led to two conflicting views:

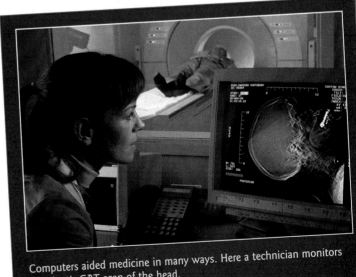

Computers aided medicine in many ways. Here a technician monitors a patient's CAT scan of the head.

- Some believed that computers would encourage **cultural decentralisation** or **diversity**, whereby people would identify more strongly with their local culture and regions and less with the nation-state. But the time span from the 1970s to the 1990s was too short to measure trends in this.

- Easier to observe was a trend towards **cultural imperialism** where some feared the domination of American culture or the **Americanisation** of European society. Some saw information technology contributing to **US cultural dominance** by facilitating the spread of all things American. They felt that this would make Europe more like America – e.g. more tolerant of differences in income and wealth and readier to accept that all countries would not achieve the same rates of economic development.

Population Movements: Some predicted that technology would stop or slow the growth of large European cities. This was based on the belief that computers and information technology would encourage people to move to the countryside and work from there through computer links. But the growth of cities in Europe had not stopped by the 1990s.

Computers had a very important role to play in controlling the large flows of money and currency changes in international money exchanges.

Data Security: Many people feared that computers would invade their **privacy** when personal data or information – medical, banking or tax records – stored about them would be misused. **Companies** also feared that business plans or information would become easily available to competitors. As far as **governments** were concerned, they wanted to ensure the secrecy of economic or military information. These concerns led to individual European countries passing their own laws to protect personal and company data. The EU tried to ensure that the national laws were harmonised.

The issue of data protection was part of a wider debate about the impact of computers and information technology on **democracy**. Some argued that computers would give governments **greater control over people**; others argued that they would give **greater power to people** by making it more difficult for governments to control access to information.

The Role of the EU: The slower production and adaptation of IT in Europe compared to the US and Japan concerned the European Union. There was a fear that if Europe did not play a fuller role in the IT revolution it would **fall behind** in the global economy. The European Commission was fully aware of the importance of the **information society** for future economic growth, competitiveness and improvement to the quality of life. In the 1990s, the report on **'Europe and the Global Information Society'** led to the first EU Information Society Action Plan which provided guidelines for the further development of the information society into the twenty-first century.

ORDINARY LEVEL

1. Study the graphs on the Decline of Infectious Diseases in Britain (p. 295) and Ageing Population in Western Europe (p. 296) and answer the following questions:

(i) What years after 1945 had the most rapid decline in infectious diseases?

(ii) What caused the decline in infectious diseases?

(iii) In 1981, what was the approximate percentage difference between the under-20s and the over-60s?

(iv) When did the percentage of over-60s pass out the percentage of under-20s?

(v) What advances in the biological sciences (a) decreased the percentage of people under 20, and (b) increased the percentage of people over 60 in Western Europe?

2. Study the graphs on the Growth of Weapons in the Arms Race (p. 300) and answer the following questions:

(i) How did the number of US weapons in each category compare with the USSR in 1960?

(ii) Refer to developments in the Cold War to explain why the number of weapons grew in the 1960s.

(iii) Can you suggest an explanation as to why the number of strategic bombers declined compared to the other two categories?

(iv) Can you suggest reasons why the growth of weapons slowed down or stopped in the 1970s?

(v) What was the impact of the growth of these weapons on Europe?

3. Study the following document carefully and answer the questions below:

'In 1970 [in the Soviet Union] the role of nuclear electricity was quite insignificant. It accounted for 0·5 per cent of all electricity generated in the Soviet Union. Thereafter, the rate of expansion of nuclear power generating facilities outstripped that of conventional fossil fuel thermal stations and all hydroelectric plants. By 1986, 10·1 per cent of all electricity generated came from nuclear stations.

Energy in the Soviet and Post-Soviet Eras

(i) Why do you think the Soviet Union had such a small percentage of its electricity generated by nuclear power in 1970?

(ii) Why did the rate of expansion of nuclear generating stations outstrip other types of electricity generating stations after this?

(iii) How does the Soviet percentage of electricity generated from nuclear stations in 1986 compare with (a) France, (b) Hungary, and (c) Britain? (See graphs on p. 304.)

4. Write **paragraph answers** on each of the following questions:

(i) The impact of medical advances in Europe.

(ii) The growth of the health industry and welfare state in Europe.

(iii) The development of nuclear weapons in Europe.

(iv) The use of nuclear power in generating electricity in Europe.

(v) Opposition to nuclear power in Europe.

(vi) The use of the computer in European business and industry.

(vii) How the use of computers improved life in Europe from the 1950s to the 1990s.

(viii) The growth of computers and their impact on information technology in Europe from the 1950s to the 1990s.

5. Write **long answers** on each of the following questions:

(i) The impact of the biological sciences in Europe, 1945–92.

OR

What impact had developments in the biological sciences on Europe between the 1940s and the 1990s?

OR

How did advances in the biological sciences improve the quality of life in Europe between the 1940s and the 1990s?

(ii) The impact of nuclear power in Europe, 1945–92.

OR

How, and why, did the use of nuclear power increase in Europe from the 1940s to the 1990s?

(iii) The impact of the computer in Europe, 1945–92.

OR

How did computers affect everyday life in Europe from the 1950s to the 1990s?

(iv) Write on the positive and negative impacts of advances in (a) the biological sciences, OR (b) nuclear power, OR (c) computers, on Europe from the 1940s to the 1990s.

HIGHER LEVEL

1. Discuss the view that *'the overall impact of advances in the biological sciences was the improvement in the quality of everyday life'*.

2. *'The development of nuclear power in Europe caused considerable controversy.'* Discuss.

3. How, and why, did the use of nuclear power in generating electricity increase in post-war Europe?

4. How did the use of computers change European society between the 1950s and the early 1990s?

OR

To what extent is it true to say that computers affected *'all areas of life'* in Europe by the early 1990s?

TEST YOURSELF AT
my-etest.com

The East: the Soviet Union

Stalin continued as dictator of the Soviet Union after the Second World War until his death in 1953. Not only was there strict censorship, there was also great fear. Writers dared not criticise the Stalinist regime. Instead they were expected to follow the path of **socialist realism**. This policy had been laid down by the Soviet Congress in the 1930s and continued until the 1980s. This meant that all novels, plays and poems had to serve the Communist revolution by glorifying socialism and its master, Stalin. In this way literature became a form of **state propaganda** and criticism of Communist society resulted in punishment.

THE THAW

The death of Stalin resulted in a gradual **thaw** under Khrushchev, particularly after he denounced Stalin at the twentieth Party Congress in 1956. This was illustrated by the book *The Thaw* by Ilya Ehrenburg which criticised Stalin's rule. It was also demonstrated by Dudintsev's *Not by Bread Alone* which described the struggle of the scientist-inventor against the party bureaucrat who tried to stifle new ideas. Dudintsev was criticised for blaspheming the Communist Party, but he was not arrested.

These new freedoms were illustrated by the poetry of **Yevgeny Yevtushenko** and others, who emphasised the importance of the individual. Even though their criticism of Communist society was mild to western eyes, in Soviet terms it was revolutionary. Yevtushenko's poem *Bari Yar* (1961) dealt with the massacre of Jews near Kiev in 1941. In the poem, Yevtushenko criticised not only Nazi, but also Soviet, anti-semitism. In another of his poems, *The Heirs of Stalin* (1961), he appealed to the Soviet government:

> KEY CONCEPT: **COMMUNISM** was based on the writings of Karl Marx, a German writer of the nineteenth century. He outlined his ideas in *The Communist Manifesto* and *Das Kapital*. Communists believed that the working class would revolt against the middle class who controlled industry. This would result in a Communist society where private property was abolished, the government would run the land and the factories for the benefit of the people and everybody would be equal.

'*to double*
and treble, the guard at the slab,
so that Stalin will not rise again,
and with Stalin – the past.'

These poets also organised public readings of their poetry and they had considerable popularity among young people.

Limits to the Thaw

However, there were limits to the thaw. While Khrushchev was prepared to allow criticism of the Stalinist system, he was not prepared to allow criticism of Communism in general. In 1957, he said writers should follow the party line. This was followed by an attack on '*rubbish*' – literature which was harmful to Communist thinking.

The limits allowed to writers in the Soviet Union are best illustrated by the lives of **Boris**

Pasternak and **Alexander Solzhenitsyn**. Pasternak's *Dr Zhivago* told the romantic story of a young doctor whose search for love took place during the Communist revolution in 1917 and the Russian Civil War. But these events were merely in the background. *Dr Zhivago* was refused publication in the Soviet Union but it was published in Italy in 1957 and in other countries after that. As a result, Pasternak was awarded the Nobel Prize for Literature in 1958. But Khrushchev refused to give him permission to travel to accept the award, and Pasternak was criticised in the Soviet press as a traitor. Pasternak was forced to reject the prize.

On the other hand, Solzhenitysn's *One Day in the Life of Ivan Denisovich* was written about his own experiences of Stalin's labour camps (or gulags). Its publication was backed by Khrushchev because of its criticism of Stalin's legacy. But it was also heavily criticised by Stalin's supporters. The book caused a sensation in the Soviet Union where the camps were never publicly referred to.

Boris Pasternak's novel *Dr. Zhivago* was first published in the West. It earned him the Nobel Prize for Literature but he was pressurised to refuse it by the Soviet government. The very successful film version was released in 1965.

Solzhenitsyn's novel *One Day in the Life of Ivan Denisovich* was based on his own experience in a labour camp, such as the one shown here in 1945.

Solzhenitsyn decided to publish

'During all the years until 1961, not only was I convinced that I should never see a single line of mine in print in my lifetime, but, also, I scarcely dared allow any of my close acquaintances [friends] to read anything I had written because I feared that this would become known. Finally, at the age of 42, this secret authorship began to wear me down. The most difficult thing of all to bear was that I could not get my works judged by people with literary training. In 1961, after the 22nd Congress of the U.S.S.R. Communist Party and Tvardovsky's* speech at this, I decided to emerge and to offer One Day in the Life of Ivan Denisovich. 'Such an emergence seemed, then, to me, and not without reason, to be very risky because it might lead to the loss of my manuscripts, and to my own destruction. But, on that occasion, things turned out successfully, and after protracted efforts, A.T. Tvardovsky was able to print my novel one year later. The printing of my work was, however, stopped almost immediately and the authorities stopped both my plays and (in 1964) the novel, The First Circle, which, in 1965, was seized together with my papers from the past years.'
*Alexander Tvardovsky – poet and editor of Novy Mir, a literary magazine.
From Alexander Solzhenitsyn, Autobiography, at *www.nobel.se/literature/laureates*

FROM THAW TO FREEZE

The thaw became a **freeze** when Khrushchev was ousted as leader and succeeded by **Brezhnev** in 1964. Solzhenitsyn's later novels such as *The First Circle* and *Cancer Ward* were published abroad. Their publication, and Solzhenitsyn's demand for greater artistic freedom, resulted in his expulsion from the Union of Soviet Writers. His next book, *The Gulag Archipelago*, which was a history of the Soviet labour camps from the 1920s onwards, was also published abroad. It resulted in his expulsion from the Soviet Union in 1974.

KEY PERSONALITY: ALEXANDER SOLZHENITSYN

Alexander Solzhenitsyn graduated in mathematics from university at the beginning of the **Second World War**. He fought in the war achieving the rank of captain of artillery. In 1945, however, a letter to friend in which he criticised Stalin was opened by the **censors**. *'I was arrested on the grounds of what the censorship had found during the years 1944–5 in my correspondence with a school friend, mainly because of certain disrespectful remarks about Stalin, although we referred to him in disguised terms.'* This resulted in him being sentenced without trial to eight years in **prison and labour camps** (gulags).

In 1952, he was diagnosed with **cancer** which was treated and cured. After finishing his sentence, he was forced to stay in exile in Siberia where he taught mathematics. During the process of **deStalinisation** begun by Khrushchev in the mid-1950s, Solzhenitsyn was allowed return to European Russia and he settled near Moscow.

During this time he also **wrote**. His novel, *One Day in the Life of Ivan Denisovich* (1962), told the story of his experiences in the labour camps. It was first published in *Novy Mir* – a literary magazine – and it became an immediate success. It described the typical day in the life of a prisoner of Stalin's labour camps. Solzhenitsyn's book encouraged others to write their accounts on their experiences in similar camps.

But with the downfall of Khrushchev, Solzhenitsyn lost favour and further novels were refused publication. Solzhenitsyn became openly critical of the growing **state censorship**. In 1967, he wrote to the **Union of Soviet Writers** demanding the abolition of censorship, the recognition of writers killed in earlier purges and the return of his personal papers, taken by the **KBG** (secret police).

Because of these difficulties, Solzhenitsyn's new novels were circulated as **samizdat** (self-published) literature – typed and secretly passed around. Some were also published abroad. These included *The First Circle* (1968) which was based on his time as a mathematician in a prison research institute. It showed the difficulties faced by researchers and scientists working for the secret police – they had little choice but to co-operate. If they refused, they were sent back to the harsh conditions of the labour camps. His next work, *Cancer Ward* (1968–9), was based on his experiences in hospital for cancer treatment.

Solzhenitsyn won the **Nobel Prize for Literature** in 1970 but he could not go to accept it because he feared he would not be allowed return to the Soviet Union. This award was soon followed by the publication of *August 1914* about Russian defeats in the First World War, and *The Gulag Archipelago* (1973–8). The *Gulag* recorded the history of the labour camps under communism. He was criticised fiercely in the Soviet press and was sent into **exile** in 1974.

He lived for a while in Switzerland before settling in the **US**. Here he published two more books – *The Oak and the Calf*, an account of his last ten years in the Soviet Union, and *The Mortal Danger* in which he warned about US misunderstandings concerning Russia.

While Solzhenitsyn was critical of Soviet Communism, he was also **critical of Western democracy** and individual freedom. He favoured a benevolent **authoritarian** (strict, controlling) **regime** based on traditional Christian values. He returned to Russia three years after the collapse of Communism in 1991.

Under Brezhnev and later Soviet leaders it became more difficult to publish. **Socialist realism** was still the official party policy on literature. The Communist leaders believed the trouble in Poland and the uprising in Hungary in 1956, and later in Czechoslovakia in 1968, were partly caused by **intellectuals** who had to be kept under control.

DISSIDENT WRITERS

Because of official censorship, writers used **samizdat** (self-publishing). They secretly circulated typed copies of their poems, novels and plays. At the same time laws became tougher and writers were branded as **criminals** and **traitors**, and some were treated as **psychiatric patients**. These were the **dissident writers** who wrote about and criticised the Communist system. They were part of a wider dissident movement but their writings were circulated within a small group.

Soviet dissident writers Yuli Daniel (left) and Andrei Sinyavsky on trial. They were sent to labour camps.

In some cases their protests resulted in arrest and trial. Such was the case of **Andrei Sinyavsky** and **Yuli Daniel** who had written novels which were published in the West. They were charged with spreading **anti-Soviet propaganda**. They were found guilty in 1966 and sent to labour camps.

This was followed by the trial of **Ginsburg** and others in 1968 for distributing leaflets. Some now began to fear that the full weight of the old Stalinist oppression was returning under Brezhnev. One of these, **Pavel Litvinov**, a grandson of one of Stalin's Foreign Ministers, compiled a report on the trial, together with protest letters from different parts of the Soviet Union. This was distributed in samizdat and later published in the United States as *The Trial of the Four*.

Others launched a journal – *Chronicle of Current Events* – which monitored all human rights abuses, especially the right to free speech. The work of publication had to be carried out in great secrecy because of the danger of the KGB. When many of those involved were arrested in 1971, publication stopped for about eighteen months. However, the *Chronicle* published reports on such varied topics as conditions inside prisons, mental hospitals, and the harsh treatment of ethnic and religious groups. It also published articles by **Solzhenitsyn** and by the dissident physicist Andrei **Sakharov**. Many of these were later translated and published in the West.

THE INFLUENCE OF GLASNOST

A change came with the arrival of Gorbachev to power in the 1980s. His policy of **glasnost** or openness led to a relaxation of the censorship rules. Journals (or magazines) such as *Novy Mir* and *Ogonyok* published previously banned writings and the KGB opened its files on writers. Yevtushenko's poem, *The Heirs of Stalin*, which had not been published again after its first publication in 1961, was republished in 1987. A further example of the new openness was *Dr Zhivago* which was published openly for the first time in the Soviet Union.

With the downfall of the Soviet Union in December 1991, all the Communist censorship structures such as the Union of Soviet Writers, the state publishing houses, the Ministry of Culture, and the censorship body, **Glavlit**, were reformed or dismantled. Independent publishers were allowed to operate and the social problems of the former Communist society, as well as contemporary problems, were widely discussed and written about.

The West

In the West, writers enjoyed greater freedom of expression. Their writings reflected a wide spread of interests and changes in society. They discussed many of the issues affecting western society – freedom, equality, feminism, the welfare state, the role of government and the growth of Europe.

FRANCE

Post-war French literature was heavily influenced by **existentialism**. This philosophy emphasised the **freedom** and importance of individual people. Each person was **responsible** for their own actions in a hostile world. *'In a godless universe, life has no meaning or purpose beyond the goals each man sets for himself.'*
This belief was mostly associated with **Jean-Paul Sartre** whose earlier books *Nausea* (1938) and *Being and Nothingness* (1943) defended freedom and individuality. In *Existentialism and Humanism* (1946) he said that freedom also had **social responsibility**. He expressed this message in his plays, such as *The Flies* (1943) and *Dirty Hands* (1948), and his novels, such as *The Age of Reason* (1945) and *The Reprieve* (1945). In these he dealt with the problems of freedom, responsibility and political commitment.

De Beauvoir

Other important writers were influenced by these ideas. One was Sartre's lifelong companion, **Simone de Beauvoir**. She used her philosophy, existentialism, to **criticise** aspects of society. This was clear in both her novels and works of non-fiction. In *The Blood of Others* (1944) she explored the choices facing a French Resistance leader during the Second World War.
In the late 1940s, de Beauvoir visited the **United States**. She wrote *America Day by Day* (1948) about her experiences there. She was highly critical of many of the social problems of the country. Later in *The Mandarins* (1954) she wrote about left-wing intellectuals whom she said should become more involved in political action, as she did herself in the 1950s and 1960s. In the 1950s, she took a more active involvement in politics, moving to the **left**. She defended the Soviet Union and

Communist China, and criticised capitalism. She also opposed France's role in Algeria.

Her most famous book was *The Second Sex* (1949). In this she explored the history of **women's oppression**, *'the slavery of half of humanity'*. *'Woman has always been, if not the slave of man, at least his vassal [servant].'* She outlined her views on the reasons for women's oppression and how they could be freed. She said woman was *'the Other'*; *'one is not born a woman, one becomes one.'* She argued **against marriage and motherhood** which she said was subjugation to male domination. To achieve freedom, women needed financial independence and *'the emancipation from the slavery of reproduction'*.

> **KEY CONCEPT: FEMINISM** advocates equal political, economic and social rights for women. The Women's Movement was organised in the late 1960s to promote feminism.

A Hostile World

The playwrights, **Eugene Ionesco** and **Samuel Beckett**, were also influenced by existentialism. Beckett, an Irish-born writer living in France and writing in French, was very pessimistic about human nature. This was made clear in his most famous play, *Waiting for Godot* (1952). Ionesco's plays also depicted people trying to survive in a hostile world. He was a supporter of human rights and he described his most famous play, *Rhinoceros* (1959), as *'an anti-Nazi play'*. When *Rhinoceros* was produced in Germany, he said, *'the papers wrote, "Ionesco shows us how we became Nazis". But in Moscow, they wanted me to rewrite it and make sure that it dealt with Nazism and not with their kind of totalitarianism.'*

KEY PERSONALITY: SIMONE DE BEAUVOIR

Simone de Beauvoir was born in Paris into a middle-class family. She graduated from the Sorbonne (Paris) and taught in secondary schools while still developing her **philosophy**. While in the Sorbonne, she met **Jean-Paul Sartre** and developed a lifelong relationship with him. Both became advocates of existentialism which stated that humans were free people with choice. In de Beauvoir's view, good acts increased freedom, bad acts limited freedom. She outlined those views in *The Ethics of Ambiguity* (1947) and co-founded and edited the journal (magazine), *Les Tempes Modernes*, with Sartre.

She used her philosophy, existentialism, to **criticise** aspects of society. This was clear in both her novels and works of non-fiction. These included *The Blood of Others* (1945), *America Day by Day* (1948) and *The Mandarins* (1954) In the 1950s, she took a more active involvement in politics, moving to the **left**. She defended the Soviet Union and Communist China, and criticised capitalism. She also opposed France's role in Algeria.

Her most famous book was *The Second Sex* (1949). In this she explored the history of **women's oppression**, *'the slavery of half of humanity'*. To achieve freedom, women needed financial independence and *'the emancipation from the slavery of reproduction'*.

Her ideas were ahead of her own times but they later became the **inspiration** for some of the leaders of the **women's liberation movement** in the late 1960s. Her book became one of the inspirations for Betty Friedan's *The Feminine Mystique* which had an important influence in beginning the women's movement in the US. It also encouraged modern **feminism** and gender studies. De Beauvoir herself became actively involved in **women's issues** in the 1960s, such as the social status of women, unmarried mothers, abortion rights and sexual violence.

In the 1970s, de Beauvoir explored the problem of ageing in *The Coming of Age*. She continued this theme in the last volume of her autobiography, *A Very Easy Death*, when she wrote about the death of her mother from cancer. She also wrote about Sartre's death in 1980 in *Adieux: Farewell to Sartre*.

De Beauvoir died in 1986 having lived her own philosophy; *'Each one of us is responsible for everything and to every human being.'* She was buried in the same grave as Sartre in Paris. Earlier in *Adieux*, she wrote, *'My death will not bring us together again. This is how things are. It is itself splendid that we were able to live our lives in harmony for so long.'*

West Germany

West German writers were critical of their past. At the end of the 1940s, a number of them came together in **Gruppe 47** to discuss German society critically. One of those was **Heinrich Boll** whose short stories and novels criticised the futility of war, attacked the materialism of his country and the viciousness of the popular press. Another member of Gruppe 47 was **Günter Grass**. He wrote *The Tin Drum* (1959) which satirised twentieth-century German society. In the 1960s he became active in politics, and his novels and plays advocated a Germany free from totalitarianism. He was also committed to the peace movement *(The Flounder)* and the environment *(The Rat)*.

Gunter Grass was a leading West German writer. His novels, such as *The Tin Drum*, were critical of German society.

Britain

In the immediate post-war years in Britain, writers were divided on the lessons and influences of the Second World War. For some, totalitarianism remained the great danger for Britain, others saw the spread of equality during the war which they did not like.

Fear of Totalitarianism

The dangers of the totalitarian state are dealt with by **George Orwell** in *Animal Farm* (1945). *Animal Farm* told the story of the rebellion of farm animals against their cruel owner. But the pigs then established control over their fellow animals even more ruthlessly than the farmer. Orwell feared that the **English Russophile intelligentsia** would set up a totalitarian, bureaucratic state. He wanted socialism with more feeling and humanity.

> **Key Concept: Welfare State.**
> This is a state in which the government plays a key role in promoting the health and general welfare of all its people. It is based on the idea of government responsibility for those who are unable to avail or provide for themselves the basic necessities for a good life. It involves state aid for people in all stages of their lives – 'from the cradle to the grave'. It usually covers free education and insurance against unemployment, sickness and old age.

Orwell also favoured a **socialist United States of Europe**. In his novel *1984* (1949) he portrayed a **socialist** Britain as a police state which supported Oceania (America) in its struggle against Eurasia (Soviet Eastern Europe) and Eastasia (China). Britain, Orwell argued, was subordinate to the US and neglected Europe.

Opposition to Equality

Other writers, such as **T S Eliot**, **Cyril Connolly** and **Evelyn Waugh**, were more concerned about the spreading **equality** which they saw happening during the war. Waugh in *Brideshead Revisited* (1945) regretted the decline of aristocratic life and complained about the mediocrity which he felt had spread in Britain during the war. These writers felt this tendency was being continued by the **welfare state**.

They also regretted the **social changes** which Britain experienced in the late 1940s and 1950s; the development of suburban houses, the consumer society, the lack of community, the high-rise flats, and West Indian and Asian immigration. Waugh and Wyndham Lewis regretted the spread of **godless**

Kingsley Amis criticised the educational system of the welfare state in Britain in *Lucky Jim*. He favoured a special relationship with the US.

materialism. Waugh's trilogy, *Sword of Honour*, said old-fashioned values of service and loyalty were replaced by grasping power. Wyndham Lewis in *Monstre Gai* (1955) and *Malign Fiesta* (1955) wrote about London falling to evil Communism and the effects of the welfare state. **Anthony Powell's** twelve volume *A Dance to the Music of Time* which he began in 1951 and concluded in 1975 also dealt with the decline of the English upper class.

Other writers were also critical of the **welfare state** for a different reason – its **bureaucracy**. **John Wain** in *Hurry on Down* (1953) and **Kingsley Amis** in *Lucky Jim* (1954) were critical of the institutions of the welfare state, in particular the hospitals and the education system. Amis's hero, Jim Dixon, was a working-class student who went to university. But it was a university still under middle-class domination in which he saw the snobbery and opposition to social change.

Alienation

Other writers were concerned by the **alienation** (hostility, isolation) caused by the social changes of the 1950s. The most prominent of these was **Alan Sillitoe** in *Saturday Night and Sunday Morning* (1958). He wrote about the young males whose lives revolved around the pay packet, the pub and sex without responsibility. In *The Loneliness of the Long Distance Runner* (1959), Sillitoe praised the hero who resisted authority.

Playwright John Osbourne criticised British middle-class society in the 1950s. His play *Look Back in Anger* portrayed a rebellious young man.

Angry Young Men

Some of these made up the so-called **Angry Young Men** or the **young angries**. They were discontented with middle-class society and its values. This was the case with **John Osborne** whose play, *Look Back in Anger* (1956), made an instant impact. The main character, Jimmy Porter, reflected the rebellious nature of youth and disliked the bureaucracy of the welfare state. Osborne, and others such as Arnold Wesker (in *The Wesker Trilogy*), highlighted what they saw as the dull and tedious lives of the working classes.

Decline of Britain

The Angry Young Men were made angrier by the **Suez Crisis** when Britain and France invaded Egypt because the Egyptian government nationalised the Suez Canal (1956). According to their view, the invasion displayed the arrogance of the English ruling class. But they also saw the powerlessness of a Britain which could do nothing to help the **Hungarian Uprising** against the Soviet Union at the same time. They began to favour the **special relationship** with America and attacked the anti-Americanism of the **pinkish intelligentsia**, as Amis did in *One Fat Englishman* (1963). Osborne's *The Entertainer* (1957) also portrayed the decline of Britain since the Second World War through the story of one family.

Other writers saw some hope for Britain. **C P Snow** in *Strangers and Brothers* (1940–70) or **Doris Lessing** in *Children of Violence* (1952–69) gave an account of the political, social and moral changes in Britain. They still saw the salvation of Britain in the abandonment of atomic power and the use of its resources to help solve world poverty.

William Golding challenged the idea that in some way the British were different or special. In *Lord of the Flies* (1954) he told the story of the English schoolboys who were stranded on a tropical island after a plane crash. Very soon the boys turned on each other and became killers. To Golding, this represented the **violent behaviour** of British society. '*And in the middle of them, with filthy body, matted hair, and unwiped nose, Ralph wept for the end of innocence, the darkness of man's heart....*'

Britain and Europe

The issue of **Britain's role in Europe** divided the writers in the 1960s. Those who opposed British entry into the EEC such as Kingsley Amis and Angus Wilson did so for different reasons. Some disliked Europe with '*its graying businessmen and technocrats*'; others feared the **uni-Europe** movement as Angus Wilson wrote in *The Old Men at the Zoo* (1961). Prominent among those who favoured entry was **Anthony Burgess**. In *A Clockwork Orange* (1962), he portrayed an Americanised Britain where moral feelings were wiped out. To stop this from happening, Burgess believed Britain needed '*European resources*'.

Social Problems

By the middle of the 1960s, English writers became aware of the social problems which the welfare state had failed to solve – housing, poverty, inequality and education. This was clearly seen in **drama**, both on stage and in the growing medium of television, where social and political issues were aired. **Jeremy Sandford's** *Cathy Come Home* highlighted the issue of **homelessness**. David Mercer's plays, such as his *Generations* trilogy (1961–3) which included *The Birth of Private Man* (1963), explored the conflict between people who wanted free expression and society which wanted conformity. *The Birth of a Private Man* takes a critical look at the Labour governments in Britain and Stalin's rule in Eastern Europe. The main character is killed at the Berlin

Saturday night drinking for men in a working-class British pub in the late 1940s. Sillitoe's *Saturday Night and Sunday Morning* portrayed the life of young working-class males.

Wall by gunfire from both sides. The role of women was also written about. **Margaret Drabble** in *The Millstone* (1965) dealt with the choices offered to women by the new freedom in the 1960s.

Conclusion

The post-war writers in Western Europe reflected the thoughts and feelings of different groups in society. In some ways they helped shape those thoughts, but very often they were just putting into literary form what many other people were thinking. In the Soviet Union, however, those who criticised society were small in number. During Stalin's rule they were not allowed to publish at all. But even under Khrushchev their publications were controlled to serve his political aims. Publications in samizdat were limited but nevertheless they kept alive a democratic tradition and opposition to the Communist system.

ORDINARY LEVEL

1. Study the following document carefully and answer the questions below:

> 'One of the first writers to dispense with Stalinist literary conventions [rules, practice] and thereby create a best-seller was Dudintsev, whose *Not By Bread Alone* [1956] showed how a talented, honest and potentially valuable individual was held back by a well-established group of bureaucrats [officials, administrators] who opposed innovations [improvements] as a threat to their vested interests. They even managed to get the hero sentenced to prison camp. Solzhenitsyn's *One Day in the Life of Ivan Denisovich* [1962], apparently published on Khrushchev's instructions after the censors had rejected it, was a short novel bringing home the miseries of daily life in a labour camp. A best-seller, it helped Khrushchev's campaign against the spirit of Stalinism.'
>
> Adapted from J N Westwood, *Endurance and Endeavour, Russian History, 1812–1971*

(i) How was Dudintsev's novel, *Not By Bread Alone*, different?

(ii) What, or who, held back the hero of the novel?

(iii) Why did they do so?

(iv) Who may have given instructions to allow the publication of Solzhenitsyn's novel?

(v) Why do you think he would favour the publication of the novel?

2. Study the following document carefully and answer the questions below:

> 'The seventies witnessed the growth of dissidence [protest] in the USSR. Alexander Solzhenitsyn, the famous novelist, took the lead in criticising the regime and set up the Russian Social Fund to help those charged with "anti-Soviet activities". When he left the USSR, his place was taken by Professor Yuri Orlov and Alexander Ginsburg, who was arrested on charges of "anti-Soviet agitation and propaganda". In May 1978, Orlov was found guilty and sentenced to seven years in a labour camp. A third leader, Anatoly Shcharansky, was also accused of working for the Central Intelligence Agency [CIA] although President Carter of the US indignantly denied it.'
>
> M Gibson, *The Communist Bloc*

(i) What decade witnessed the growth of dissidence in the Soviet Union?

(ii) Name two of the dissidents (protestors).

(iii) Why did Solzhenitsyn leave the Soviet Union?

(iv) What happened to those who took his place?

3. Study the extract, Solzhenitsyn decided to publish, on p. 312, and answer the following questions:

(i) Up to 1961, what did Solzhenitsyn think would happen to his writings?

(ii) Why did he not allow his friends see his writings?

(iii) What did he find was the most difficult thing to bear?

(iv) What happened in 1961 that changed everything?

(v) What was he afraid would happen when he **emerged** with his novel *One Day in the Life of Ivan Denisovich*?

(vi) What happened soon after this novel was published?

(vii) What happened in the Soviet Union which explains these changes?

4. Study the following document carefully and answer the questions below:

> 'The break came with the advent of a new generation, the angry young men ... Kingsley Amis's *Lucky Jim* was published in 1954, *Look Back in Anger* opened in 1956. These were followed within a very short time by several novels and films ... in a broadly similar vein. They constituted a clear break with tradition;

the children of the welfare state were not merely revolting against upper-class arrogance ... [and] against the hypocrisy of a genteel middle-class way of life; they were equally unhappy about the new, brave Socialist Britain, bored above all by the tedium of the welfare state. Rootless and classless men, they had been educated, as one critic said, to discontent and they were cheerfully biting the hand that was feeding them.... The common features of the Angry Young Men of the fifties were their youth and vitality, their delight in breaking certain taboos, the freshness of their approach and the originality of their topics.'

W Lacquer, *Europe Since Hitler*

(i) What books or plays does the author give as examples of the work of the angry young men?

(ii) What is meant by the phrase *'the children of the welfare state'*?

(iii) What were they revolting against?

(iv) What were they unhappy about?

(v) Explain the terms *'rootless and classless'* and *'educated to discontent'*.

(vi) What was the hand that was feeding them?

5. Write **paragraph answers** on each of the following questions:

(i) Literature and social criticism in the Soviet Union after the downfall of Stalin.

OR

The **Thaw** in literature under Khrushchev.

(ii) Dissident writers in the Soviet Union under Khrushchev.

(iii) Simone de Beauvoir and social criticism.

(iv) Literature and social criticism in Western Europe from the 1950s to the 1980s.

6. Write **long answers** on each of the following questions:

(i) How did the Communist system in the Soviet Union treat writers from 1945 onwards?

(ii) Outline the experiences of Alexander Solzhenitsyn and his writings under Soviet Communism.

(iii) What were Simone de Beauvoir's criticisms of Western society?

(iv) Assess the contribution of (a) Alexander Solzhenitsyn, OR (b) Simone de Beauvoir to social criticism in their countries.

(v) With reference to at least one Western European country, outline the main criticisms of society made by writers from the end of the Second World War onwards.

HIGHER LEVEL

1. To what extent did Soviet writers after the Second World War *'keep alive a democratic tradition and opposition to the Communist system'*?

2. What were the views of Soviet writers on Soviet society after the Second World War and to what extent were they allowed express those views?

3. To what extent did literature in Western Europe after the Second World War reflect *'a wide spread of interests and changes in society'*?

4. Discuss the main criticisms of Western society made by writers after the Second World War.

5. With reference to one country in Eastern Europe and one country in Western Europe, discuss the contribution of writers to social criticism in those countries.

TEST YOURSELF AT
my-etest.com

PART 3:
THE UNITED STATES AND THE WORLD, 1945-89

Overview

The United States of America ended the Second World War as the **most powerful country** in the world. It had a population of 140 million in 48 states (Hawaii and Alaska were added in 1959). Its power depended on the strength of its industry, agriculture, military and atomic might. Mainland America escaped direct destruction during the war, unlike its allies and enemies.

First grade pupils in 1948 reciting the pledge of allegiance before the US flag.

ECONOMY

Over the next forty-five years the US continued to grow. Its economy remained the most powerful in the world, and it was the leader in the development of new **high technology** industries, such as computers and electronics. Many of its industries developed into **multinational corporations** which invested in the other continents. It was not until the late 1960s that US economic growth slowed down and the US feared **competition** from other economies, particularly Japan and Germany.

SOCIAL CHANGE

During the post-war era the US also underwent rapid **social change**. This was fuelled by the **affluent (wealthy) society** which had developed. America developed a **consumer** society where houses, cars, televisions and household appliances became symbols of that society. For many it seemed the **American Dream** was coming true. It was a society whose culture was dominated by white middle-class values, characterised by the spreading suburbs of its cities.

But the US also faced many **social problems**. The most serious of these were racial segregation, urban poverty and rising crime. There was also a youth culture which began to reject the culture of the adult world. These came fully to the surface in the 1960s to make this a turbulent and exciting decade.

FOREIGN POLICY

During this time, US foreign policy was dominated by **Cold War rivalry** with the Soviet Union and, to a lesser extent, China. The US developed a **policy of containment**, resisting the spread of Communism, which shaped its response to all international incidents between the end of the Second World War and the downfall of Communism in Russia in 1991. It also led to the **arms race** which sometimes brought the world to the brink of a third world war.

Fear of Communism drove US foreign policy but it also led to the **Red Scare** in the US itself, and the growth of **McCarthyism**. The policy of containment dragged the US into the two major wars it fought in this period – **the Korean War** and the **Vietnam War**. US involvement in the Vietnam War coincided with the rising social problems of the 1960s. By the 1970s the US defeat in the Vietnam War, a worsening economy, and the problems of race, poverty and crime created a country which was very different from the booming 1950s.

19. US Politics

Structures and Tensions

The United States of America won its independence from Britain in the late eighteenth century. The leaders of the new America drew up a constitution which laid out the basic laws of the country. The new government was:

- A **representative democracy** – the people elected leaders who acted on their behalf.
- A **republic** which had a President, rather than a King, at its head.
- A **federal system** or structure with a central (or national) government in the capital, Washington, sharing power with state governments.

US States and Natural Resources

Federal and State Powers

The Constitution gave some powers to the **federal** (or central) government and some to the **states**. In general, the **federal government** controls war and peace, taxation, interstate and foreign trade, and foreign relations. The **states**, on the other hand, provide education, regulate trade within the state, maintain the police and levy local taxes. This **separation of power** between the federal and state governments creates **tension** between the two, but it was one way to avoid an abuse of power. The second way was to separate the powers within the federal government.

SEPARATION OF POWERS

The eighteenth-century leaders did not want any branch of government to have too much power so they devised a **separation of powers** between three separate branches – the **legislative** (which passed laws), the **executive** (which carried out the laws) and the **judicial** (which examined the laws). The separation of powers created a system of **checks and balances** which allowed each branch to have some control over the other two branches. This prevented any one branch becoming too powerful.

The Legislative Branch

Congress is the **legislative** or **lawmaking** branch of government. The power of passing laws is shared by the two houses of Congress – the House of Representatives and the Senate – based on Capitol Hill in Washington. The two Houses give a system of checks and balances – each house must co-operate and compromise with the other to get laws passed.

Congress has many important powers – to declare war, raise taxes and pay for the armed forces, establish federal courts of law, regulate trade with other countries and it can **impeach** (bring charges against) any member of the executive branch who may have committed a crime.

Political Parties

There are two main political parties in the US – the **Democratic Party** and the **Republican Party**. They are organised at national and local level, where they are run by county and state committees. Every four years the parties hold national conventions to choose Presidential and Vice-Presidential candidates and to decide a **platform**. This is a statement of the policies of the party which will guide elected representatives.

In general, the **Democrats** favoured federal government intervention in economic and social affairs. On the other hand, the **Republicans** were opposed to government intervention and preferred to give more power to the individual states.

Third parties have developed in the US but they have never lasted very long. After the Second World War, the Southern Democrats formed the **States' Rights** or **Dixiecrat Party** to protest at giving **civil rights** to black Americans. At a later stage, in the late 1960s, the American **Independence Party**, led by George Wallace, opposed **racial integration** (the coming together of the races). Very often those parties drew attention to important social and political issues.

The Republican Elephant, symbol of the Republican Party.

The Democratic Donkey, symbol of the Democratic Party.

The **House of Representatives** has 435 members who serve for two years. They represent the people of a congressional district. The House of Representatives chooses its own leader who belongs to the majority party in the House. The House of Representatives has a special role in taxation – all bills (proposed laws) for raising revenue (money) must begin in the House.

The Houses of Congress on Capitol Hill, Washington showing the US Senate (left) and the House of Representatives (right).

The **Senate** is much smaller with 100 members – two from each state, regardless of the population size. Each senator is elected for a six-year term, with elections being held for one-third of the senators every two years. The Senate has special responsibility for approving treaties with foreign countries; it is more influential than the House of Representatives in foreign affairs.

The Judicial Branch

The highest court in the US is the **Supreme Court**. Its principal function is to review laws passed by Congress or the state governments. It has the power to declare laws **unconstitutional** (or invalid). Judges are appointed by the President, and Presidents can therefore influence the general direction of the judgments of the Supreme Court.

The Executive Branch

The President of the US is elected every four years on the first Tuesday after the first Monday of November. Presidents can only serve for two terms. The successful candidate takes office after **inauguration** (the ceremony for swearing in the President) on 20 January of the following year. On that day the incoming President takes an oath of office: *'I do solemnly swear that I will faithfully execute the office of President of the United States, and will to the best of my ability, preserve, protect, and defend the Constitution of the United States.'*

Members of the US Supreme Court in 1993.

The White House

The White House in Washington, DC is the official residence of the President of the US. It also contains the offices in which the President and his staff conduct the business of the US government. The original building was begun in 1792, designed by Irish-born architect, **James Hoban**. He based his design on Leinster House, Dublin where the Dáil and Seanad meet now. The White House has been extended and redecorated many times since it was originally built.

The White House, home of the US President in Washington, District of Columbia.

The Executive Branch

The **executive branch** of the US government consists of the Executive Office of the President, executive departments and independent agencies. The executive departments run the federal government. Originally there were only 4 departments, these were expanded to 8 by 1945, and to 14 by the 1980s.

Original Four
Secretary of State
Secretary of War

Secretary of the Treasury

Attorney General (Justice)

Additional Departments
Secretary of the Interior
Secretary of Agriculture

Secretary of Commerce

Secretary of Labour

Added Since 1945
Secretary of Defence
Secretary of Health,
Education and Welfare
Secretary of Housing
and Urban Development
Secretary of Energy
Secretary of Transportation

The independent agencies have also grown in number. They administer federal programmes such as space, banking, communications, labour law and others.

The **federal bureaucracy** has grown since the 1930s as the federal government has become more involved in all phases of social and economic activity.

Number of federal employees (millions)

1930	0·6
1940	1·0
1950	1·9
1960	2·3
1970	2·7

Within the federal bureaucracy, there is also the **White House staff** who serve the President directly. By 1963 – President Kennedy's last year – 1,664 worked there. This jumped to 5,395 by 1971 when President Nixon was in power. The cost also jumped from $31 million to $71 million.

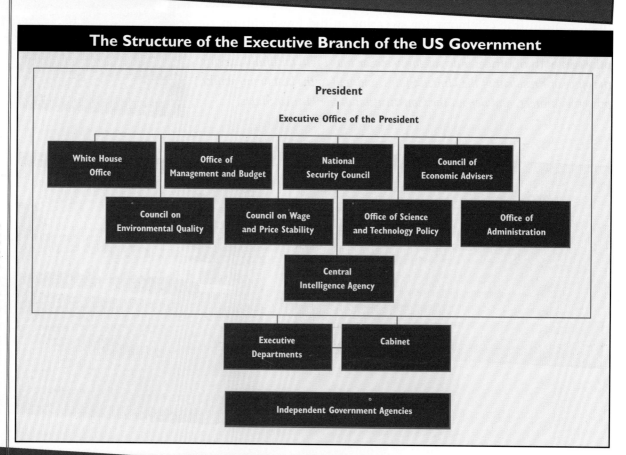

The Structure of the Executive Branch of the US Government

President
|
Executive Office of the President

- White House Office
- Office of Management and Budget
- National Security Council
- Council of Economic Advisers
- Council on Environmental Quality
- Council on Wage and Price Stability
- Office of Science and Technology Policy
- Office of Administration
- Central Intelligence Agency

Executive Departments — Cabinet

Independent Government Agencies

Roles of the President

Foreign → affairs
Domestic
imperial presidency

The President has **six main functions** or roles:

- Chief executive,
- Commander-in-chief,
- Foreign policy director,
- Legislative leader,
- Party leader,
- Head of state.

Chief Executive

As chief executive or chief administrator of the country, he has to enforce the laws of the country and to prepare a national budget. The President is assisted by his **Cabinet**. These are the heads of the government departments who are appointed by the President with the approval of Congress. As the power of the President grew, more departments were formed to run the country. Since 1945, six new departments were added, including Defence, Education and Transportation.

Commander-in-Chief

The President is commander-in-chief of the US Army, Navy and Air Force. In this way, he is responsible for the **defence of the country**. He appoints the top military officers with the approval of Congress. Only he can decide the use of nuclear weapons. He can also call up armed forces to put down disturbances in America itself.

Foreign Policy Director

The President can make treaties, appoint ambassadors and meet foreign diplomats. The **Secretary of State** is usually responsible for foreign policy but some Presidents have been more active than others in this area. As American power has grown, so has the power of the US President at home and abroad.

Legislative Leader

The President can propose laws for Congress in his **State of the Union** address, given to the Houses of Congress in January each year. He has a large influence on laws passing through Congress. He has to work to ensure the support of Congress for his proposals. He can veto a Bill passed by Congress. But if Congress passes it again with a two-thirds majority it becomes law. The President can also issue **Executive Orders** which do not need Congressional approval.

Party Leader

The President is **leader** of his Party. He works to form the Party's policies on all major issues. The President is in a strong position if his Party is in control (is in the majority) in the House of Representatives and in the Senate. But he still has to use his influence to win over support.

Head of State

This is mostly a ceremonial role where the President attends functions and meets the representatives of foreign countries.

The Presidency from Roosevelt to Reagan

INTRODUCTION

The power of US presidents has grown from being largely honorary at the end of the eighteenth century to being the most powerful person in the US (and the world) in the second half of the twentieth century:

Presidential Salary	
Date	**Salary ($)**
1789	25,000
1873	50,000
1909	75,000
1949	100,000
1969	200,000
2001	400,000

- The rise of the power of US Presidents has depended very much on **individual** Presidents. Some have been stronger leaders than others.
- It also depended on the circumstances of the time. Very often in times of **crisis** such as the American Civil War, the First and Second World Wars, the Great Depression and the Cold War, the power of the President has been expanded to lead the country.
- Presidential power has also grown because **American society** has become more complicated, with greater problems. Presidents have been given more powers to solve these problems. Sometimes this has happened because Congress failed to take action itself.
- It also depended on **political beliefs**. Some Presidents believed in active government, others believed in less active government, very often giving power back to the individual states.
- The President is listened to because of his position, so his policies are more likely to be acted upon. As one President called it, this was the *'bully pulpit'*. When a President raises issues, it will be more likely to become part of national debate.
- Some historians have argued that the power of the President is the *'power to persuade'*. In other words, the power of the President rests on bargaining and persuading Congress (House of Representatives and the Senate) to carry out presidential policies. Because of the separation of powers the President has to negotiate and bargain with other groups.
- The President is the only **unifying force** in a political system where power is so scattered. He speaks for the US, more than any of the other branches of government.

Some historians have called this the growth of the **imperial presidency** whereby more and more power was **centralised** in the hands of the President.

THE ROOSEVELT PRESIDENCY

By the time President Roosevelt (FDR) died in April 1945, he had expanded the power of the presidency considerably. He was the longest serving President and he was faced with two major crises – the Great Depression and the Second World War.

Recent Presidents of the US		
Franklin Delano Roosevelt	1933–45	Democrat
Harry S Truman	1945–53	Democrat
Dwight Eisenhower	1953–61	Republican
John F Kennedy	1961–3	Democrat
Lyndon Johnson	1963–9	Democrat
Richard Nixon	1969–74	Republican
Gerald Ford	1974–7	Republican
Jimmy Carter	1977–81	Democrat
Ronald Reagan	1981–9	Republican
George Bush Snr	1989–93	Republican
Bill Clinton	1993-2001	Democrat
George Bush Jnr	2001–	Republican

[handwritten margin note: Cold war: "Not a war of bombs or bullets, but of words and warnings"]

In trying to solve these problems, he was able to extend presidential power. It was Roosevelt's view that, *'The presidency is pre-eminently a place of moral leadership.'* This was the rise of the **imperial presidency** when more power was **centralised** in the hands of the President.

During the Great Depression, as part of Roosevelt's **New Deal** policies, the government took a more active interest in the economy. Roosevelt set up many emergency agencies *'to promote the general welfare'* (US Constitution). This was the beginning of the American **welfare state**. Even though the Supreme Court limited the spread of the New Deal policies by declaring some of them unconstitutional, others expanded the power of the federal government.

In 1939, Roosevelt created the **Executive Office** to control the work of the many agencies that operated directly for the White House.

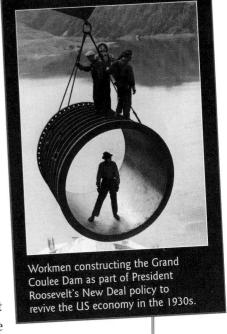

Workmen constructing the Grand Coulee Dam as part of President Roosevelt's New Deal policy to revive the US economy in the 1930s.

During the Second World War, Roosevelt extended federal government control over manufacturing. In foreign policy, he took part in the wartime conferences with Churchill (Britain) and Stalin (Soviet Union). He gave general direction to US foreign policy.

Roosevelt provided a direct link with the public (people) by speaking over the radio in his *'fireside chats'*. He was also the first President to speak on television. This increased his **popularity**.

KEY PERSONALITY: HARRY S TRUMAN

Harry Truman, a Democrat, was the thirty-third President of the United States of America (1945–53). He was elected a Senator in 1934 and again in 1940. He became Vice-President to President Roosevelt in 1944. When Roosevelt died in April 1945, Truman became President while the Second World War was still in progress. He told reporters he thought, *'the moon, the stars and all the planets had fallen on me.'*

However, he was inspired by the history and biographies which he had read. He believed in the role of **strong and honourable leadership**. On his desk he had a sign, *'The buck stops here'*, which reflected his view of his responsibility as President. Truman was also a straightforward person who liked simple food and pleasures.

Truman was faced with two immediate problems when he became President – one was relations with Stalin and the Soviet Union and the second was how to defeat Japan. After Germany was defeated, he met Stalin at **Potsdam** (July 1945) along with the British Prime Ministers, Churchill and Attlee (who replaced Churchill). At Potsdam, Truman demanded unconditional surrender from the Japanese. When they refused to surrender, he gave the go-ahead to drop atomic bombs on **Hiroshima** and **Nagasaki**. He believed this was necessary to prevent the invasion of Japan and reduce the loss of American and Japanese lives.

Very soon, relations with the Soviet Union deteriorated. Truman believed in a **policy of containment** – keeping Communism from expanding further. This remained US foreign policy for the remainder of the Cold War. He announced the **Truman Doctrine** to provide help to Greece and Turkey in fighting the spread of Communism. He also supported the **Marshall Plan** for European economic recovery. Named after George Marshall, Secretary of State, the Plan was one of the **most successful** US foreign policies.

In 1948-9, Truman was faced with the **Berlin Crisis** and Airlift and he achieved victory when Stalin lifted the Berlin blockade after nine months. Shortly after he formed the **North Atlantic Treaty Organisation** (NATO) with European countries for their defence.

In domestic policy, Truman wanted to add to the New Deal of Roosevelt but Congress (House of Representatives and Senate) blocked many of his ideas. However, he got re-elected in 1948 in a very close contest with Thomas Dewey, a Republican. He had more success in his second term and implemented parts of what he called his 'Fair Deal'. He also contributed to progress in civil rights by desegregating the armed forces and ending racial discrimination in the federal government.

In 1950, he sent US troops to support **South Korea** after it was invaded by North Korea. The war was still on and deadlocked when Truman's term of office was up in early 1953. During the last few years, he also experienced the growth of **McCarthyism** – anti-Communist hysteria – which he disliked.

THE TRUMAN PRESIDENCY

Truman was **Vice-President** so he became President when Roosevelt died in office (April 1945). He was soon faced with the biggest and most important decision he ever had to make – that was to drop **atomic bombs** on Hiroshima and Nagasaki to end the war against Japan.

Truman was prepared to take decisive action when it was necessary. '*The buck stops here'* was a sign he displayed on his desk to show how he viewed his responsibility as a President.

Truman maintained an **active foreign policy** providing presidential leadership. He won general approval for his foreign aid plans because of the advent of the Cold War. As Stalin imposed Communist satellite states on Eastern Europe, fear of Communism grew.

Truman got support for what became known as the **Truman Doctrine**, '*I believe that it must be the policy of the Unites States to support free people who are resisting attempted subjugation by armed minorities or by outside pressures.*' In this way Congress passed economic aid for Greece and Turkey after Britain could not continue to support those countries. Truman also received support for the **Marshall Plan** for the economic recovery of Europe after the Second World War.

A 1947 illustration showing American support for Turkey in response to the threat from Communist Russia.

Policy of Containment

By these two actions **Truman defined and shaped US foreign policy** for the next forty years as a **policy of containment** of Communism, i.e. not allowing Communism to expand beyond its current limits. In line with this, he also got Western European support for forming **NATO** (North Atlantic Treaty Organisation) in 1949 to build up forces to deter attack from the Soviet Union in Western Europe.

Even though according to the US Constitution only Congress can declare war, Truman ordered US troops to fight in the **Korean War** in defence of South Korea. He was able to do this because officially the Korean War was declared a *'police action'* under the United Nations – it was equal to war though none was declared.

Truman and Congress

However, Truman had far greater difficulties with **domestic** (internal) policies where Congress turned down many of his proposals. Here he was opposed by **Republicans** and **Southern Democrats**, especially after Republicans gained control of both houses of Congress in the 1946 Congressional elections. They formed a **conservative block** which did not want to see federal government influence expanded. But Truman was able to issue some **Executive Orders** which ended racial discrimination in federal employment, and he desegregated the US armed forces. Southern

Based on early election results in the 1948 Presidential election, the *Chicago Daily Tribune* ran a headline 'Dewey defeats Truman'. Here Truman laughs at the mistaken headline.

Democrates (Dixicret parties).

Truman and the People Protested against

Truman also carried on Roosevelt's style of relating directly to the American people. Instead of the radio, giving rights to black Americans.

Truman preferred to **meet people face to face**. In the 1948 presidential election he was faced with a Republican candidate, Thomas Dewey; Strom Trummond as a States' Rights (**Dixiecrat**) candidate; and Huey Wallace as a Progressive candidate. He criss-crossed the country by train – **whistle-stopping** – making speeches and meeting people. He was given very little chance of winning the election but his style pleased ordinary people: *'Give 'em Hell, Harry,'* they said. Not only did he win but he ensured the Democrats got back a majority in Congress.

After that he proposed a **Fair Deal** programme, some of which got through Congress. But Congress also passed the **Twenty-second Amendment** to the Constitution limiting the President to two terms in office. This was more a backlash against Roosevelt's four terms rather than against Truman.

THE EISENHOWER PRESIDENCY

Eisenhower became President in 1953. He had been a very successful Supreme Allied Commander in Europe during the Second World War; in particular he was in overall charge of the D-Day landings in 1944. He was now leader of the Republican Party which favoured cutting back taxes and cutting back **big government**.

Ike, as he was known, had a **limited view** of the presidency. He believed that the functions of the President were very different from those of the legislature and that Roosevelt and Truman had taken over some of the powers of Congress. But he still opposed efforts to pass a constitutional amendment which would reduce the power of the presidency to negotiate agreements and treaties with foreign powers.

Dwight Eisenhower acknowledges his nomination as the Republican candidate in the 1952 Presidential election. Eisenhower won the election and served two terms as President until 1961.

Business Dominated Cabinet

In domestic affairs, Ike believed in what he called **dynamic conservatism** – less government intervention in the economy along with continued federal support for individual welfare. He appointed a very business-dominated cabinet – *'eight millionaires and a plumber [a union leader]'*, it was said. He encouraged business by granting tax reductions. He also transferred the control of offshore oil deposits to the states, which opened the way to private development.

Ike and Congress

However, he did not attempt to repeal the social welfare laws implemented by Roosevelt and Truman; instead he extended social security and unemployment benefits, and raised the minimum wage. Ike worked equally well with **Republicans** and **Democrats** in Congress. He got much of his legislation through Congress. They were largely uncontroversial so he got 73 out of 83 Bills passed.

Domino Theory

Eisenhower maintained **the presidential role** in foreign policy. He followed **Truman's policy of containment**. He believed in the **Domino Theory** – that the fall of one country to Communism would lead to the fall of others. But he reduced the size of the US army. Instead he increased the size of the nuclear arsenal. He tried **peaceful co-existence** with the Soviets, which resulted in **summit meetings** with **Khrushchev** (the Soviet leader) in Geneva and Paris. He also set up **NASA** (National Aeronautics and Space Administration) in 1958 in response to the Soviets launching the Sputnik rocket.

But Eisenhower's **prestige declined** in his second term from 1956–60 due to a number of factors:
- There was a short economic recession.
- The rise of the civil rights agitation.
- The success of the Sputnik.
- Corruption among some officials.
- The shooting down of the **U2 spy plane** by the Soviets and the resulting collapse of the Paris Summit.

By 1960 some accused Eisenhower of not making full use of presidential power.

THE KENNEDY PRESIDENCY

John F Kennedy was elected America's youngest President after a hard-fought campaign against Richard Nixon. He appointed Lyndon Johnson as his Vice-President. He tried to imitate the New Deal by talking about a **New Frontier** which would *'get America moving again'*. He wanted to take a strong stand against the Soviet Union, and at home tackle poverty, civil rights, health and education.

President → Imperial → economic relationship with congress

The Presidency from Roosevelt to Reagan

Seen as Dynamite leader

But Kennedy faced problems with the **conservative coalition** in Congress between Republicans and Southern Democrats. He was able to increase spending on defence and space because of competition with Soviet successes. By doubling NASA's budget, he laid the foundation for the space project which eventually fulfilled his promise to have a man on the moon by the end of the 1960s. He had little difficulty getting these passed because much of the spending benefited the southern states.

Kennedy and Congress

However, he postponed a cut in taxes which was eventually brought in by his successor, Lyndon Johnson, because he feared failure in Congress. Kennedy did not want to send proposals to Congress which he thought would not pass. This would make him look weak and ineffective, and it would damage his chances of re-election. But he was partly to blame himself because he did not work very hard at improving relations with Congress.

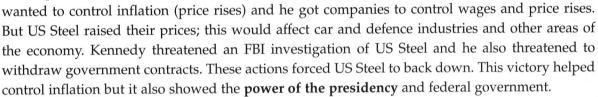

President J F Kennedy and his wife Jackie were pleased by the public support as they attended the premiere of the stage musical *Mr. President* in September 1962.

Kennedy was able to use the power of the presidency to win a battle against one of America's largest corporations, **US Steel**. He wanted to control inflation (price rises) and he got companies to control wages and price rises. But US Steel raised their prices; this would affect car and defence industries and other areas of the economy. Kennedy threatened an FBI investigation of US Steel and he also threatened to withdraw government contracts. These actions forced US Steel to back down. This victory helped control inflation but it also showed the **power of the presidency** and federal government.

Congress Blocked Policies

Poverty was a serious problem in the US by the early 1960s and Kennedy wanted to tackle the problem. He got agreement with Congress for a school- and job-based training programme. But he failed to get Congress's support for a huge public works programme. He also failed to get a healthcare programme passed, as well as a proposal to set up a Department of Urban Affairs to tackle the problems of the cities. The conservative coalition did not like federal interference in certain areas.

Kennedy was slow to act on **civil rights** partly because of the conservative coalition in Congress. Instead Kennedy was forced to act mainly through his brother Robert, as Attorney-General, to support desegregation. He introduced a **Civil Rights Bill** in 1963 but knew it would be difficult to get it passed. He was assassinated before it came to a vote in Congress.

Control of Foreign Policy

Under Kennedy, **foreign policy** was very much controlled by the White House. Indeed, he was more interested in foreign policy than in domestic policies. But he depended very much on his advisers. He increased involvement in **Vietnam** and took an aggressive stance against Khrushchev in the **Cuban Missile Crisis**. He also visited **Berlin** to inspect the Berlin Wall and show his support for Berliners. *'Ich bin ein Berliner! [I am a Berliner!]'*, he said in a speech there. But his time in government was short and historians still debate what might have happened if he had been re-elected in 1964.

The Johnson Treatment; President Johnson leans over a political colleague as he makes his point. He usually got his way.

> 'He'd come on just like a tidal wave sweeping all over the place. He went through walls. He'd come through the door, and he'd take the whole room over. Just like that. Everything.'

THE JOHNSON PRESIDENCY

When President Kennedy was assassinated in November 1963, his Vice-President, Lyndon Johnson, succeeded him. Johnson was able to use the shock of the assassination to continue the work of JFK. He supported the ideas of the **New Frontier** in trying to tackle poverty, healthcare and civil rights.

KEY CONCEPT: LIBERALISM was the political belief that was concerned with personal freedom and social progress. Liberals favoured gradual reform of political and economic matters. US liberals favoured government intervention in the economy.

FDR was Johnson's hero. Johnson believed that the **power of the federal government** should be used to improve the lives of the people. He wanted to create a **Great Society**. He believed that economic progress gave government the means to improve the lot of its people. He was helped by a huge Presidential victory in 1964 and by Democratic control of Congress. The 1964 Congressional elections weakened the conservative coalition which had dominated since the 1930s.

Johnson and Congress

Johnson **centralised control** in the White House. He showed his gifts as a negotiator in his dealings with **Congress**. In 1965, Congress felt it was the *'Three B Congress'* – bullied, badgered and brainwashed. He got **sixty bills** passed before and after his re-election.

Johnson got Kennedy's proposed tax cuts through Congress to encourage economic growth. He ensured the passage of two major laws which ended the legal basis for discrimination, and increased the powers of the President and the executive:

- **Civil Rights Act, 1964** which banned discrimination on grounds of race, religion, sex or national origin. It gave powers to the federal government to investigate cases.
- **Voting Rights Act, 1965** gave powers to the federal government to supervise state elections, mainly in the southern states because of their history of discriminating against blacks.
- He used **affirmative action** to ensure that the companies working on federal contracts reserved a certain quota of jobs for minority groups.

Johnson was a dealmaker who could get Congress to play almost any tune he wanted.

He used presidential power to begin a **war on poverty**:

- He set up schemes:
  - to improve employment prospects,
  - to give money to provide cheap housing and rent aid,
  - to provide grants for slum clearance,
  - to educate poor students in public schools.
- **Healthcare** – he set up the first federally funded healthcare system – **Medicare** and **Medicaid** – a proposal which previous Presidents had failed to get passed.

Johnson showed the federal government could tackle poverty. He also involved the **federal government** in creating national parks and many other conservation measures, limiting car pollution and supporting arts and culture.

In a period of eighteen months, as a *New York Times'* columnist wrote, Johnson had passed more reform legislation (laws) than most Presidents had put through in two full terms of office. In doing so he **extended the power** of the presidency.

Foreign Policy

As the situation in Vietnam escalated (worsened), Johnson got **increased powers** from Congress in the **Tonkin Resolution** to deal with them – *'all necessary steps including the use of military force'* to protect US interests. This created much greater US involvement in Vietnam until the US took over most of the fighting there at great cost to itself. But his actions here – and those of his successor, President Nixon – eventually led Congress to limit executive (presidential) authority. Congress felt that the Presidents had abused their power. (See Case Study: Lyndon Johnson and Vietnam, 1963–8.)

THE NIXON PRESIDENCY

Richard Nixon became President in 1969 after he defeated his main opponent, the Democratic candidate, Hubert Humphrey (as well as George Wallace of the American Independent Party) in November 1968.

Nixon and Congress

But the **Democrats** still dominated Congress. So Nixon's plans to follow a conservative domestic policy were not always successful:

- In spite of Nixon's opposition, in 1970 **Congress** lowered the voting age from twenty-one to eighteen.
- Congress also passed many environmental laws to control pollution from industry, power companies and from cars.
- Nixon's plan to end direct payments to the poor was rejected by Congress.
- Congress also increased social security benefits.

Nixon and the Supreme Court

Nixon also had difficulty with the **Supreme Court**. He wanted to prevent further desegregation in schools in Mississippi. But the Supreme Court demanded more school integration and supported bussing of children between black and white areas. However, Nixon was eventually able to appoint **more conservative judges** to the Court. He was also successful with his revenue-sharing plan to hand back power to the states for more control over the finances of social welfare matters.

Detente

President Nixon shaking hands with supporters in Ohio in 1972.

Nixon, Foreign Policy and the Imperial Presidency

Nixon still controlled and directed **foreign policy**. He showed this when he visited China and began negotiations to withdraw from Vietnam, eventually agreeing to the Paris Peace Agreement in 1973. He and his adviser, **Henry Kissinger**, used secret channels to organise the visit to China. He even bypassed the State Department which was mainly involved in foreign policy.

But the **Pentagon Papers** were leaked to the Press. They showed that the American government had lied about its involvement in the war. Nixon wanted to ensure there were **no further leaks** so he used his power over the intelligence agencies (the FBI and CIA) to spy on others. He also used private groups to gather information on political opponents. This led to the **Watergate break-in** at the Democratic National Headquarters in the Watergate building in Washington. When this was discovered and its roots traced back to Nixon aides in the White House, Nixon attempted a **cover-up**.

But by the early 1970s, Congress was concerned at the growth in the power of the presidency. In spite of his difficulties with Congress and the Supreme Court, Nixon's term in office was the high point of the **imperial presidency** (centralising government powers). More than any other President, Nixon concentrated powers in the presidency:

- He refused to spend money that Congress had allocated for health and the environment.

- He increased US involvement in Cambodia and Laos without approval from Congress.
- Congress began proceedings to impeach Nixon. He refused to co-operate, claiming **executive privilege**.
- He also claimed **executive powers** when he refused to hand over tapes of White House conversations on the Watergate affair.

However, the **Supreme Court** ruled against him and he had to hand over the tapes. Nixon then resigned rather than be impeached.

LIMITING THE POWERS OF THE PRESIDENT

Because of events in the Vietnam War and the Watergate Scandal, Congress began to limit the power of the President. Congress passed a series of laws to control presidential powers and to make the federal government more accountable:
- They set limits to political contributions for elections.
- They gave power to individuals to see government files on themselves.
- They passed the **Ethics in Government Act** to require senior government officials to declare their wealth.
- They made the CIA report to Congress.

The **War Powers Act, 1973** and the **Budget Reform Act, 1974** restored the powers of Congress in declaring war and in budgeting.

THE FORD PRESIDENCY

Nixon was succeeded by his Vice-President, Gerald Ford. He found himself in conflict with Congress. He wanted to increase military and space spending and reduce spending on social welfare programmes. He vetoed 18 Bills coming from Congress. Congress tried to overrule his veto on 9 occasions but only succeeded in having the necessary two-thirds majority on 3 occasions.

THE CARTER PRESIDENCY

Jimmy Carter defeated Ford in the 1976 presidential election. He was a former Governor of Georgia and an outsider to Washington politics. He promised a **new style** of presidency but, as an outsider, he failed to persuade Congress. He came across as being arrogant. However, he did have **some success** – he raised the minimum wage and provided money to clean up toxic waste sites. But he was not a decisive leader and his foreign policy was a failure. He cancelled the SALT II agreement after the Soviet Union invaded Afghanistan and he failed to rescue American hostages in Iran.

THE REAGAN PRESIDENCY

Ronald Reagan defeated Carter in the 1980 presidential election. This election also gave control of the Senate to the Republicans. Reagan became a two-term President when he won re-election in 1984.

Reagan's term in office is sometimes called the **Reagan Revolution**. He wanted to restore the **prestige** of the presidency. Reagan was helped by being a good communicator, and especially good at using **television**.

Reduce 'Big Government'

Reagan wanted to reduce the role of **big government**. He believed that *'Government is not the solution to our problem. Government is the problem.'* He wanted to dismantle the welfare state which had existed since Roosevelt's New Deal in the 1930s.

His economics policies were called **Reaganomics** – a promise to cut spending, reduce government regulation (control) of industry and lower taxes. In the economy he did this with major tax cuts and reducing federal spending on 300 programmes. He persuaded the Democrat-controlled House of Representatives to pass these. However, Reagan also began a massive build-up of US armed forces and this only increased government spending.

President Reagan and his wife, Nancy, waving and clapping hands in victory at Reagan's first inauguration as President in January 1981.

In **social policy**, Reagan wanted to give the **states** more responsibility for welfare. He also wanted to reduce the federal government by giving money to the states to use as they saw fit. But Congress refused to pass these plans.

Reagan increased defence spending and cut taxes for businesses and people on high incomes. He cut federal (government) spending on welfare programmes and aid to big cities which hit the poor.

Reagan mainly targeted the **health programme** – Medicare and Medicaid – with cutbacks. Reagan also believed that people did not need federal government intervention in their lives and he put this into practice when getting the private sector to do some of the job training. He gave less money to libraries, public radio, museums, national parks and education.

Iran-Contra Affair

In foreign policy, Reagan used the powers of the presidency to negotiate agreements with a new Russian leader, **Mikhail Gorbachev**. But he also used presidential power to sanction an invasion by US troops of the small West Indian island of Grenada without Congress's approval.

But Reagan's efforts to increase the prestige of the presidency took a more severe blow when details of the **Iran-Contra Affair** (1986–7) were revealed. It showed the government had given arms for the release of American hostages in the Lebanon. The money received for the arms sales was used to help Contra rebels fight the left-wing government of Nicaragua. This was specifically banned by Congress. Reagan was lucky to escape impeachment because the investigations into the affair could not show that he knew about the deal.

ORDINARY LEVEL AND HIGHER LEVEL HOMEWORK EXERCISES

ORDINARY LEVEL

1. Study the information on the Executive Branch of the US government in p. 328 and answer the following questions:

(i) What is the Executive Branch of the US government?

(ii) How many departments were there in the Executive Branch in 1945 and 1980?

(iii) What do the independent agencies do?

(iv) How many people were employed in the federal bureaucracy in 1970?

(v) What is the job of the White House staff?

2. Study the extract below and answer the following questions:

'The immediate crisis of the mid-1970s arose from the swollen powers of the presidency ... Richard Nixon believed that the presidency was an office almost kingly in its occupant's authority to act on his own. In the making of war, he claimed for himself unlimited powers over which Congress had no control. In domestic affairs he suddenly expanded a little-used and doubtful presidential tactic – the seizing of funds voted by Congress – into a major instrument of national government. Nixon believed he had the power to pick and choose which laws enacted by Congress he could carry out. By 1973 he had seized fifteen billion dollars and thereby eliminated a hundred federal programmes concerning health, housing, urban needs and environmental protection. Also he used executive privilege to stop Congress from getting any information on the actions of the various branches of government.'

Adapted from R Kelley, *The Shaping of the American Past*

(i) Why did the powers of the President of the US grow?

(ii) Nixon believed that the presidency was *'almost kingly'*. What does that mean?

(iii) Give three examples to show how Nixon used the power of the President.

(iv) To what extent did Nixon abuse the powers of the President?

(v) Do you think the writer agrees that Nixon abused the power of the President?

(vi) What crisis led to Nixon's downfall?

3. Study the cartoon, *The Voter*, on p. 341 and answer the following questions:

(i) Why did The Voter vote for Johnson? Was he happy with his vote?

(ii) Why did The Voter vote for Nixon? Was he happy with his vote?

(iii) Why did The Voter vote for Carter? Was he happy with his vote?

(iv) After these votes, what did The Voter conclude?

(v) Is The Voter happy with his vote for Reagan?

(vi) What is the overall message of the cartoon?

4. Write **paragraph answers** on each of the following questions:

(i) The separation of powers in the US Constitution.

(ii) The role of the US President.

(iii) Harry Truman as President.

(iv) Dwight Eisenhower as President.

(v) John F Kennedy as President.

(vi) Lyndon Johnson as President.

(vii) Richard Nixon as President.

(viii) Ronald Reagan as President.

5. Write **long answers** on each of the following:

(i) How effective were each of the following Presidents in using presidential power in their dealings with Congress and in foreign policy? (a) Truman, (b) Eisenhower, (c) Kennedy, (d) Johnson, (e) Nixon, and (f) Reagan.

(ii) Show how the power of the President (the imperial presidency) was increased from Roosevelt to Nixon.

Higher Level

1. To what extent did the power and role of the President increase between 1945 and 1973?

OR

How did the power of the President change between 1945 and 1973?

2. Assess the impact of the Vietnam War on the United States presidency under Lyndon Johnson and Richard Nixon. (Department of Education, Sample Paper)

3. How did the policies pursued by various Presidents from Roosevelt onwards increase the power and size of the US government?

TEST YOURSELF AT
my-etest.com

US Foreign Policy and the Cold War

TRUMAN TAKES OVER – USING THE ATOMIC BOMB

When Truman took over as President after the death of Roosevelt in April 1945, the Second World War was still in progress. One month later, war concluded in **Europe** (May 1945) but the war against **Japan** continued until August 1945.

In July 1945, Truman met **Stalin** face-to-face for the first and only time. This was at **Potsdam** in Germany where little was agreed. Truman could not afford to be seen to be weak when dealing with Stalin, particularly as some thought too much had been given away by **Roosevelt** at the **Yalta Conference** (February 1945). At Potsdam, Truman issued a warning to Japan to surrender uncondi-tionally or face *'prompt and utter destruction'*.

When Japan refused to surrender, Truman decided to bomb **Hiroshima** on 6 August, followed three days later by the bombing of **Nagasaki**. About 130,000 people were killed, mostly civilians; and as many again died over the next five years from the effects of radiation.

President Truman (right) and the Russian leader, Joseph Stalin, enjoy an amusing incident in between sessions of the Big Three meetings in Potsdam, near Berlin, in 1945.

Reasons for Truman's Decision

There were many **reasons** for Truman's decision to drop the atomic bomb. As commander-in-chief of the armed forces, he felt it was his duty to put an **end to the fighting**. He believed that this was the only way to stop the fighting as soon as possible. Otherwise it would involve a **land invasion** of Japan which would result in hundreds of thousands or even millions of American and Japanese lives. Truman saw how the Japanese had fiercely defended the Pacific islands; they also used **kamikaze pilots** and some regarded them as *'savages, ruthless, merciless and fanatic'*.

Truman's decision to use the atomic bomb had huge effects on US foreign policy. Now nuclear weapons could wipe out all people, especially after the USSR developed its own bomb in 1949. The US-USSR competition in the Cold War led to an **arms race** with wide political and economic effects. This was supported by a **policy of deterrence** – to maintain a strong nuclear force so that the Soviet Union would be deterred from attacking the US.

US Foreign Policy and the Soviet Union: Truman Doctrine and Marshall Plan

DEVELOPING US FOREIGN POLICY

When Truman took office, he had very little knowledge and experience of foreign affairs. However, he had **definite views** – he disliked dictatorships and countries which behaved aggressively toward other countries. These views led to his mistrust of the Soviet political system.

Because of his inexperience, Truman relied on his **senior officials** for advice:
- By 1946 they believed that the Soviet Union could **not be trusted**.
- Instead of acting defensively, the Soviet Union was acting **aggressively**.
- The Soviet Union should be faced with **firmness** so that war would not break out again.
- The US had the economic, political and military capacity to influence the behaviour of other countries.
- The US should **not appease** Russia like Hitler had been appeased before the Second World War. In Truman's view, *'Unless Russia is faced with an iron fist and strong language another war is in the making ... I'm tired of babying the Soviets.'*

Events in Europe and Asia seemed to confirm these conclusions. Stalin imposed a Soviet-controlled puppet government in Poland, as well as controlling Bulgaria and Romania; he made North Korea a satellite state, and he put pressure on Turkey and Iran. In a major speech **Stalin** said that, *'monopoly capitalism caused the Second World War'* and that it should be replaced by Communism to avoid future wars. Soon afterwards, **spies** were arrested in Canada for trying to steal atomic secrets for the Soviet Union. These events confirmed to Washington officials that, *'The ultimate aim of the Soviet foreign policy is Russian domination of a Communist world.'*

President Truman and Winston Churchill salute the crowds in Fulton, Missouri before Churchill's 'Iron Curtain' speech.

Keenan's Long Telegram

Crucial to the development of US foreign policy at this time was **George Keenan's Long Telegram**. Keenan was based in the US embassy in Moscow and was one of the few well-trained experts in Russian history and language. In Keenan's view, the Russians were using Communism as a cover for military growth, oppression at home and expansion abroad. He said the Soviets believed that there would be no agreement with the US, and they thought *'that it is desirable and necessary that the internal harmony of our society be destroyed, the international authority of our state broken.'* He concluded that the only way to deal with Soviet Communism was to contain it – *'firm, vigilant containment'*.

This secret memo was reinforced a few weeks later by **Winston Churchill's** speech in Missouri where he referred to the **iron curtain** descending across the continent of Europe and called for firmness against the Soviet Union. *'From what I have seen of our Russian friends and allies during the war, I am convinced that there is nothing they admire so much as strength, and there is nothing for which they have less respect than weakness, especially military weakness.'*

TRUMAN DOCTRINE AND MARSHALL PLAN

Truman was influenced by these arguments. Over the next year he took a progressively firmer stand against the Soviet Union. However, it was Britain's failure to continue helping Greece and Turkey which led to the full development of US foreign policy. America believed that the downfall of **Greece** and **Turkey** would lead to the **spread of Communism** all along the Mediterranean and into Iran, which provided much of Western oil. Truman played up the Communist threat to ensure congressional support for $400 million of military aid to Greece and Turkey. In his speech to Congress, he said, *'I believe that it must be the policy of the Unites States to support free people who are resisting attempted subjugation by armed minorities or by outside pressures.'* This became known as the **Truman Doctrine**.

A ceremony welcoming delivery of new freight wagons for West Germany, bought from Czechoslovakia with European Recovery Programme (Marshall Aid) money. The sign reads 'America helps rebuild Europe'.

The Truman Doctrine was complemented by the **Marshall Plan** (European Recovery Programme) to give economic aid to Western Europe. Truman said they were *'two halves of the same walnut.'* Marshall, the Secretary of State, said in his speech at Harvard University announcing the Plan, *'Our policy is directed not against any country or doctrine, but against hunger, poverty, desperation, and chaos.'* Truman and Marshall hoped that Marshall Aid would rebuild the European economy and strengthen Western Europe to stand up to Communism. It would also help Europe to import American goods.

Its passage through Congress was eased by **Stalin** establishing a pro-Soviet government in Hungary and supporting a Communist coup in Czechoslovakia. It was also eased when Stalin refused to accept any economic aid for Russia and when he forced Eastern European countries to refuse it also. Stalin felt the Plan was part of a US plot to encircle the USSR and undermine Communism.

Effects of Truman Doctrine and Marshall Plan

The effect of the Plan was to speed up the economic recovery of Europe after the war. It showed that the US was not going back to **isolationism** as it did after the First World War. Instead it was still committed to Europe. **Internationalism** – the belief that America should become involved in treaties and commitments with other countries – was now stronger in the country. The success of the Marshall Plan encouraged the US government to believe that they could undertake further schemes thinking that American strength would carry them through.

The **Second World War** had changed American foreign policy for the future. After the war, the US favoured intervention:

- As one political leader said, *'Pearl Harbour drove us to the conclusion that peace was indivisible.'*
- America also felt that **appeasement** before the Second World War had been a disastrous failure. The lesson to be drawn from the struggle against Hitler and Fascism was that there were some leaders who could only be held back by force.
- The US now had certain **responsibilities** in the world to protect **good** from **evil**. These lessons were applied to resistance to Communism.

This is why many people supported **internationalism** after the war. Now people wanted the US to lead the democratic and capitalist world.

Both the Truman Doctrine and the Marshall Plan highlighted **tension** between the US and the USSR. By 1948, the Cold War was fully established. For the next forty years all US policies revolved around the enmity between the US and the USSR. This influenced the arms race, patrolling by US fleets, round-the-clock flights by Strategic Air Command, the growth of the military in US life and the build up of the defence industry.

US FOREIGN POLICY AND BERLIN

Very soon Truman was faced with a new challenge. In June 1948, Stalin began the **blockade** of West Berlin. He responded to American policy in Germany. The wartime allies had agreed to divide Germany into **four zones** and Russia was allowed take **reparations** from the country. But soon the US gave Marshall Aid to rebuild their zone. The US and its allies, especially Britain, now believed that the economic recovery of Germany was necessary for the economic recovery of Europe. It was also necessary to build up Germany as a barrier to the expansion of Communism. On the other hand, Stalin feared that a prosperous West Germany would undermine Communism in Eastern Germany.

Extracts from Truman's speech to Congress announcing the Truman Doctrine

'... The foreign policy and the national security of this country are involved. The United States has received from the Greek Government an urgent appeal for financial and economic assistance. The very existence of the Greek state is today threatened by the terrorist activities of several thousand armed men, led by Communists, who defy the government's authority at a number of points....

The United States must supply that assistance.

The peoples of a number of countries of the world have recently had totalitarian regimes forced upon them against their will.

At the present moment in world history nearly every nation must choose between alternative ways of life. The choice too often is not a free one.

One way of life is based upon the will of the majority, and is distinguished by free institutions, representative government, free elections, guarantees of individual liberty, freedom of speech and religion, and freedom from political oppression.

The second way of life is based upon the will of a minority forcibly imposed upon the majority. It relies upon terror and oppression, a controlled press and radio, fixed elections, and the suppression of personal freedoms.

I believe that it must be the policy of the Unites States to support free people who are resisting attempted subjugation by armed minorities or by outside pressures.

I believe that we must assist free peoples to work out their own destinies in their own way.

I believe that our help should be primarily through economic and financial aid, which is essential to economic stability and orderly political processes....

If Greece should fall under the control of an armed minority... confusion and disorder might well spread throughout the entire Middle East....

The free peoples of the world look to us for support in maintaining their freedoms. If we falter in our leadership, we may endanger the peace of the world – and we shall surely endanger the welfare of our own nation.'

'We Are Going to Stay, Period'

Stalin was hoping to force the US out of West Berlin. But Truman did not want to abandon Berlin. It would mean a huge victory for Communism. It would also undermine the policy of containment. He was encouraged by his advisers to hold firm. The American commander in Berlin wrote, *'When Berlin falls, Western Germany will be next. If we mean to hold Europe against Communism, we must not budge.'* Truman agreed. He said, *'We are going to stay, period.'*

This resulted in a **huge airlift** by the US and British air forces which kept West Berlin going until Stalin lifted the blockade in May 1949. The Americans had won and containment had worked. The blockade also resulted in the establishment of **NATO** (North Atlantic Treaty Organisation) in 1949. The US and Canada joined with ten Western European countries. The US believed it needed to strengthen Europe militarily against the Soviet Union. This was the **first** time the US formed a **peacetime military alliance**. Under the terms of NATO, an attack on one was an attack on all. It resulted in the deployment of US troops to bases in Western Europe. (For US and Berlin; see also Part 2, Chapter 9, The Cold War in Europe; Berlin – Centre of Conflict, Building the Berlin Wall.)

US Foreign Policy and Korea

In 1949, China became Communist after a long civil war. This encouraged America to fear the further spread of Communism in Asia. It also led Republicans at home to accuse Truman of *'losing China'* by weak policies. American opinion was fully convinced of the danger of Communism, spurred on by **Senator Joe McCarthy**, and events in Europe and around the world. Therefore, it was not surprising that the US viewed the invasion by North Korea of South Korea in the same way. This was seen as **another test** of the policy of containment.

NORTH ATTACKED THE SOUTH

After the Second World War, Korea was divided along the **thirty-eighth parallel** between a Soviet-backed North and a US-supported South. This was meant to be a temporary arrangement until elections were held. The US went ahead with its elections in the South but the Soviet Union did not go ahead with elections in the North. Shortly after (in 1950), North Korea attacked and drove the South Koreans into one corner of the country.

US Marines halted on an icy trail in subzero temperatures in North Korea by Red Chinese soldiers after they crossed the Yalu River from China.

Truman had no choice but to intervene. Firstly, South Korea had suffered an unprovoked attack. Also, he believed that the Soviet Union was behind the attack – if he did not stop them they would *'swallow up one piece of Asia after another'*. *'I had to act as commander-in-chief and I did,'* he said. In this way **Truman bypassed Congress.** This was an increase in presidential power which was later used by Kennedy, Johnson and Nixon in Vietnam.

Truman immediately responded to the invasion by committing the US in the name of the **United Nations** (UN), to come to the rescue of South Korea. Truman got UN backing through a UN Security Council vote, when the Soviet Union was temporarily absent due to a dispute over recognition of Communist China.

US Success and Defeat

The US forces, led by **General McArthur** and aided by troops from twelve other countries, were very successful. McArthur invaded at **Inchon** behind North Korean lines and the North Korean invasion collapsed. By October, the North Koreans were pushed back behind the thirty-eighth parallel. America had been successful; this was another victory for the policy of containment.

But the US overreacted and invaded the North, easily taking it over in spite of Chinese warnings. This resulted in a Chinese invasion with 250,000 soldiers. They drove the Americans and their allies back and recaptured **Seoul**, the capital of South Korea. But in bitter and slow fighting the US eventually pushed them back to the thirty-eighth parallel again.

McArthur pressed for an attack on China and even the use of the **atomic bomb**. Truman had to dismiss him, but fighting dragged on for two more years. By 1953, the leadership of the USSR and the US had changed – Stalin died in Russia and Eisenhower was elected President of America. Eventually **peace** was agreed and the border was fixed on the thirty-eighth parallel. America lost over 50,000 soldiers and the war cost $20 billion.

Effects of the Korean War on US Foreign Policy

The war affected US foreign policy. Truman saw the need for strengthening the US military position in South-East Asia. He began by signing treaties with **Japan** and the **Philippines** (1951). He also formed a defence pact with **Australia and New Zealand** (ANZAC Pact). These were extended by Eisenhower who formed the **South-East Asia Treaty Organisation** (SEATO). This meant increased involvement of the US in Asian affairs. It also meant an **expansion of containment** which led to increased military spending. The war also worsened relations with **China** for two decades. The US was now more closely tied to hateful regimes in Taiwan and South Korea.

The war also affected **US policy in Europe**. The US felt that the defence of Western Europe needed to be strengthened. This led to US demands that West Germany should be allowed to rearm, and that the country should become a member of NATO. This eventually happened when West Germany became a member in 1955.

Gary Powers on trial in Moscow for spying after his U2 spy plane was shot down over the USSR.

US Foreign Policy under Eisenhower

Eisenhower maintained the general **policy of containment** laid out by his predecessor, Truman. He believed in the **Domino Theory** – that if any country fell to Communism, other countries nearby would do so also. He relied more on nuclear weapons rather than conventional weapons to back up his case. He thought a **policy of deterrence** would work against the Soviet Union. If he maintained a powerful nuclear arsenal then this would deter the Russians from attacking. But he also followed a **policy of peaceful co-existence** with the Russians and their new leader, **Khrushchev**. He hoped that both sides could get along peacefully with each other. But his policy here was upset when a U2 spyplane was shot down over Russia.

US Foreign Policy under Kennedy

THE CUBAN MISSILE CRISIS

Background

A number of factors heightened Cold War tension in the early 1960s and contributed to the Cuban Missile Crisis in 1962. First there was talk about a **missile gap**. The Military-Industrial complex, who hoped for greater defence spending, encouraged this. There was also increased anti-Communism caused by **Castro's Communist takeover** of Cuba. Many newspapers and magazines, such as *Time* and *Newsweek*, contributed to this. So also did the new President, John F Kennedy.

At his **inauguration speech**, President Kennedy said, *'We shall pay any price, bear any burden, meet any hardship, support any friend, oppose any foe to assure the survival and success of liberty.'* He followed this with a number of anti-Communist speeches. *'The enemy is the Communist system itself ... increasing in its drive for world domination.'* He too supported the view that there was a missile gap – that the USSR had overtaken the US in missile production.

Flexible Response

Kennedy took an active interest in foreign policy, even more so than domestic policy. He had his own ideas about that policy. He thought the US was over-reliant on nuclear weapons. Instead he wanted a policy of **flexible response** in order to be able to respond quickly to regional conflicts. He also supported the development of **counter-insurgency forces** (counter-terrorism) such as the Green Berets. These policies led to increased defence spending.

Kennedy also believed in firm and decisive action; he believed this displayed a certain **toughness**. This contributed to Kennedy's support for an attempt to overthrow Castro through an invasion in the **Bay of Pigs** in April 1960. This was a disastrous failure which was a huge embarrassment for the Kennedy government.

Soviet Views

Another factor in the development of the Cuban Missile Crisis was the attitude of **Khrushchev**, the Soviet leader. He pledged USSR aid to *'wars of national liberation'*. He was aggressive toward Kennedy when they met in **Vienna** in June 1960, and they failed to agree over East Germany. Khrushchev thought he was dealing with a weak and indecisive leader. Thereafter both increased military spending at home. It led to the building of the **Berlin Wall** to stop the flow of refugees from East Berlin to the West. This led to a further heightening of tension between the two sides.

The Soviet Union gave increased support to Cuba including the building of **missile bases** in the summer of 1962. Their range of over 1,000 miles meant that they could hit the major US cities. **U2** flights revealed that the missile sites were nearly ready.

American Reaction

Kennedy set up an **Executive Committee** (ExComm) to deal with the missile crisis. Over a period of thirteen days the world was on the brink of a third world war. There were various opinions in ExComm on what the US policy should be. Some advised an **invasion** of Cuba, others advised **air**

strikes on the missile bases. The more moderate members said that the US should agree to **demilitarise** Cuba, including withdrawing US forces from their naval bases in **Guantanamo**, and also remove their missiles from Turkey.

Kennedy believed he could not appear to be weak so he did not agree with the ideas of the moderates. He also rejected air strikes because they would not succeed in knocking out all the sites. Instead he decided on a **blockade** of Cuba to stop any further Soviet equipment reaching the island. He informed Khrushchev and later the public on television. The naval blockade demonstrated US will to resist Soviet pressure but it also gave Khrushchev a way out. There was huge **tension** in the US and worldwide. Some Soviet ships turned around, others with-

KASIMOV WITH IL-28 FUSELAGE CRATES ENROUTE TO CUBA
28 SEPTEMBER 1962

A Russian cargo ship carrying missiles to Cuba during the Cuban Missile Crisis, September 1962.

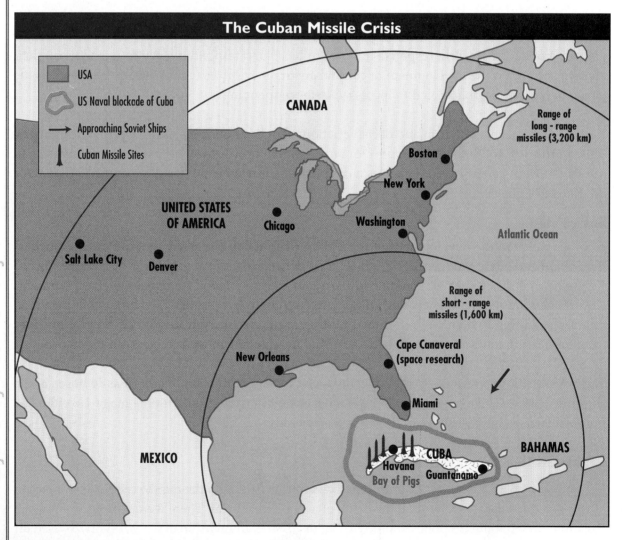

The Cuban Missile Crisis

USA

US Naval blockade of Cuba

Approaching Soviet Ships

Cuban Missile Sites

CANADA

Range of long - range missiles (3,200 km)

Boston

New York

UNITED STATES OF AMERICA

Chicago

Washington

Atlantic Ocean

Salt Lake City

Denver

Range of short - range missiles (1,600 km)

New Orleans

Cape Canaveral (space research)

Miami

MEXICO

CUBA

BAHAMAS

Havana

Guantanamo

Bay of Pigs

out weapons agreed to be searched. Kennedy demanded the dismantling of the missile bases. On the other hand, Khrushchev wanted the US to end the blockade and agree not to invade Cuba. He also wanted the US to dismantle their sites in Turkey.

Kennedy publicly agreed to lifting the blockade and to call off any invasion. But privately he assured the Soviets of the future dismantling of the Turkish sites. In return Khrushchev agreed to dismantle the Soviet missile bases.

Diplomatic Victory

While some US military leaders were angry that America did not strike, Kennedy's steady handling of the crisis earned him praise. One journalist said it was *'perhaps the greatest personal diplomatic victory of any US President in our history.'* It led to the establishment of a **hotline** between Moscow and Washington to improve future communications between the leaders and to lessen the dangers of nuclear war. It also led to a **Test Ban Treaty** which banned nuclear testing in the air, in space or underwater.

US Foreign Policy and the War in Vietnam

GRADUAL US INVOLVEMENT

The US became gradually involved in Vietnam. After the Second World War, **Truman** supported the French empire in Indo-China (Vietnam, Cambodia and Laos) in its battle against **Ho Chi Minh** and the Vietminh. He believed the Vietminh were backed by Stalin and the USSR and he looked on his support for the French in Cold War terms. By backing the French he believed he was containing Communism and following the Truman Doctrine.

President **Eisenhower** increased US involvement because he believed in the **Domino Theory** – that if Indo-China fell to Communism so would all the other countries around it. He sent in the first military advisers. After the French defeat, there was a peace agreement in Geneva which set up four countries – Laos, Cambodia, North Vietnam and South Vietnam. The US, however, refused to hold elections in the South because they feared a victory for the Communists. Instead they backed **Ngo Dinh Diem** in South Vietnam, sent in aid and increased the number of military advisers to 1,500 by 1960.

But Diem was an unpopular leader. He was accused of corruption and torture and he failed to win over the peasants (farmers). Instead popular support went to the South Vietnamese Communists called the **Vietcong**. These were supported by Ho Chi Minh, who was backed by the Soviet Union and China.

The Americans continued to believe in Vietnam as a **Cold War conflict**. They failed to see it as a **nationalist uprising** seeking independence. Their failure to do this led them to become more and more involved in Vietnam.

KENNEDY INCREASES US INVOLVEMENT

Kennedy believed he had to take a strong stand in South-East Asia since he had already accused the previous Eisenhower government (administration) of being soft. He believed in the **Domino Theory** too and was a strong supporter of the **policy of containment**. His advisers were equally strong in standing up to Communism in South-East Asia. However, Kennedy did not want to get the US militarily involved so he refused to send troops to Vietnam. But financial aid increased and there was a large increase in US advisers to 23,000 by 1963. It seemed inevitable that they would get involved in the fighting. Indeed, some of the so-called advisers were soon involved.

Kennedy believed in developing a **flexible response** to combat Communist expansion. This involved the US sending in Special Forces to train the South Vietnamese army in **counter-insurgency (counter-terrorism)** methods. But very often their tactics resulted in losing rather than winning the support of the people. Diem was assassinated in an internal plot in 1963. Even though the US knew about the plot they did not attempt to stop it. A few weeks later Kennedy himself was assassinated in Dallas.

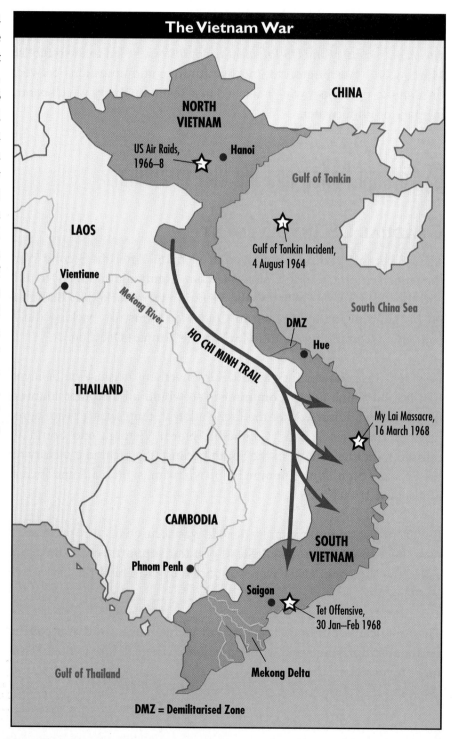

The Vietnam War

CHINA

NORTH VIETNAM

US Air Raids, 1966–8

Hanoi

Gulf of Tonkin

LAOS

Gulf of Tonkin Incident, 4 August 1964

Vientiane

Mekong River

South China Sea

DMZ

Hue

HO CHI MINH TRAIL

THAILAND

My Lai Massacre, 16 March 1968

CAMBODIA

SOUTH VIETNAM

Phnom Penh

Saigon

Tet Offensive, 30 Jan–Feb 1968

Gulf of Thailand

Mekong Delta

DMZ = Demilitarised Zone

Ordinary Level and Higher Level Homework Exercises

ORDINARY LEVEL

1. Study the extract from Truman's speech to Congress announcing the Truman Doctrine (p. 346) and answer the following questions:

(i) What appeal did the Greek Government make and why did they make the appeal?

(ii) What is Truman referring to when he says, *'The peoples of a number of countries of the world have recently had totalitarian regimes forced upon them against their will.'*?

(iii) What are the *'alternative ways of life'* between which every nation must choose?

(iv) What should be the policy of the US, according to Truman?

(v) What help will Truman provide?

(vi) Why will he help Greece?

2. Study the map on the Cuban Missile Crisis (p. 350) and answer the following questions:

(i) In each case, name two cities that would be hit by (a) Soviet short-range missiles, and (b) Soviet long-range missiles.

(ii) What other important US facilities were in danger from Soviet missiles?

(iii) What other countries besides the US were threatened by the Soviet missiles?

(iv) What was the importance of Guantanamo? What happened at the Bay of Pigs?

(v) In what ways does the map help you to understand the serious nature of the conflict over Cuba?

3. Write **paragraph answers** on each of the following questions:

(i) Truman and the development of US foreign policy toward the Soviet Union.

(ii) The role of US foreign policy in (a) the Berlin Crisis, 1948, (b) the Korean War, 1950–53, and (c) the Cuban Missile Crisis, 1962.

(iii) The Cuban Missile Crisis, 1962. (Department of Education, Sample Paper)

(iv) US foreign policy and the beginning of US involvement in the conflict in Vietnam under Truman, Eisenhower and Kennedy.

(v) US foreign policy and withdrawal from Vietnam. (See Chapter 22, Decline of Cold War Certainties, 1972–89.)

4. Write **long answers** on each of the following:

(i) What was US policy toward Berlin from the end of the Second World War to the early 1960s?

(ii) How effective was the US policy of containment in Korea?

(iii) How successful was President Truman's foreign policy in confronting Communism?

(iv) How did President Kennedy deal with the Cuban Missile Crisis?

(v) How did the United States become so heavily involved in Vietnam in the 1960s? (Department of Education, Sample Paper)

HIGHER LEVEL

1. What role did President Truman play in developing US policy toward the Soviet Union?

OR

How was US foreign policy developed under President Truman?

2. How effective was the US policy of containment in relation to at least two major crises of the Cold War?

3. Assess the impact of the Vietnam War on the United States presidency under Lyndon Johnson and Richard Nixon. (Department of Education, Sample Paper)

TEST YOURSELF AT
my-etest.com

JOHNSON AND VIETNAM

Instead of withdrawing from Vietnam, the new President, Lyndon Johnson, increased the number of US advisers by thirty per cent. Not only did Johnson support the **Domino Theory**, he believed that **US credibility** was at stake. He thought that if the US did not stand up for their ally – South Vietnam – nobody would trust them in future. Johnson's advisers, who also advised Kennedy, believed in a **military solution** to the problem. Even when doubts crept in a few years later about US policy, Johnson's **domineering personality** discouraged them from giving an alternative view. Johnson did not want to be 'the first President to lose a war.'

SOURCE 2 – Johnson's speach

'Most of the nations of Asia cannot by themselves and alone resist the growing might and grasping ambition of Asian Communism. Our power, therefore, is a vital shield. And an Asia so threatened by Communist domination would imperil the security of the US itself. Moreover, we are in Vietnam to fulfil one of the most solemn pledges of the American nation. Three Presidents over eleven years have promised to help defend this small and valiant nation. We cannot now dishonour our word.'

Speech by President Johnson in 1965

SOURCE 1 – The blind leading the blind

Four Presidents entangled in Vietnam.

SOURCE 3 – Phone call

'I don't think it's worth fighting for and I don't think we can get out. I don't see that we can ever hope to get out of there once we are committed. It's just the biggest damn mess.'

President Johnson in a private phone conversation in 1964

SOURCE 4 – Lessons from Munich

'We learned from Hitler at Munich that success only feeds the appetite of aggression.'

President Johnson

SOURCE 5 – The Movie JFK

'In the movie JFK ... director Oliver Stone makes much of an LBJ remark to a group of service chiefs at a White House reception on Christmas Eve 1963: "Just let me get elected, and then you can have your war." '

Quoted in H Evans, *The American Century: People Power and Politics*

THE 1964 PRESIDENTIAL ELECTION

In the 1964 Presidential election, Johnson was faced by **Barry Goldwater**, a Republican candidate. Goldwater wanted a 'total victory' in the war against world Communism. In relation to Vietnam, he suggested that atomic weapons should be used to 'defoliate' North Vietnam. Johnson, on the other hand, campaigned as a **candidate of peace**. However, Johnson soon began to realise:

• that limited American aid was not working,

• that the Vietcong were extending their hold on the country, and

• that the South Vietnamese government was not strong enough to stop them.

Johnson was faced with **two alternatives**: either withdrawing the US from Vietnam or else committing huge numbers of US troops to the country.

THE GULF OF TONKIN AND CHANGE IN US POLICY

During the election campaign in 1964, a dramatic change occurred in US policy. In August 1964, North Vietnamese boats fired on the **USS *Maddox*** while it was patrolling in the **Gulf of Tonkin** but they were easily driven off (see map). A couple of days later, the **Maddox** and the **C Turner Joy** were patrolling in the Gulf when they reported being fired on again. They returned fire but later investigators cast doubts on their account of what happened. Some historians suggest that the US patrols were deliberately set up to provoke a North Vietnamese response. At any rate, the incident was used by President Johnson to escalate US involvement in the war.

SOURCE 7 – Johnson's version of Tonkin

'The initial attack on the destroyer Maddox, on August 2, was repeated today by a number of hostile vessels attacking two US destroyers with torpedoes. The destroyers and supporting aircraft acted at once on the orders I gave after the initial act of aggression. We believe at least two of the attacking vessels were sunk. There were no US losses.'

President Johnson's television address, 4 August 1964

SOURCE 8 – Tonkin Gulf Resolution

'... Whereas naval units of the Communist regime in Vietnam, in violation of the principles of the charter of the United Nations and of international law, have deliberately and repeatedly attacked United States naval vessels lawfully present in international water, and have thereby created a serious threat to international peace; and ....'

Extract from 'The Tonkin Gulf Resolution', 7 August 1964, in the Pentagon Papers

SOURCE 6 – 'There is a Tonkin Gulf!'

"Only Thing We're Sure Of—There Is a Tonkin Gulf!"

Disagreement at the Senate Foreign Relations Committee hearings on the Tonkin Gulf incident.

Congress passed the **Tonkin Resolution** after Johnson gave a deliberately misleading account of the incident. This resolution gave Johnson almost unlimited power to wage war. This allowed the President to take 'all necessary measures, including the use of military force' to protect US interests in South-East Asia. It also allowed the US to attack North Vietnam, because Johnson claimed North Vietnam was supplying the Vietcong in South Vietnam.

THE ESCALATION OF THE WAR 1965–8

But Johnson waited until after his re-election before he took action. In response to an enemy raid on an American air base in South Vietnam early in 1965, he gave the go-ahead for **Operation Rolling Thunder**. This operation launched massive air assaults on North Vietnam to stop them helping the Vietcong. He also announced a $1 billion aid programme for the South.

Then he began a huge **build-up** of ground forces. In March 1965, the first US Marines landed in **Da Nang**. By the end of the year the US had over 180,000 soldiers in Vietnam. A year later this had increased to over 350,000 and it was a half a million by the end of 1967. By the end of 1968 the war was costing $30 billion a year.

In the meantime, Johnson rejected offers by the North Vietnamese government to negotiate on the basis of their **Four Points**. In turn, the US announced its **Fourteen Points** in January 1966 to form the basis of negotiations. But these were rejected by North Vietnam.

SOURCE 9 – Johnson's view

'We have kept our guns over the mantle and our shells in the cupboard for a long time now. I can't ask our American soldiers out there to continue to fight with one hand tied behind their backs.'

President Johnson at a meeting with his top advisers, February 1965, after the attack on a US air force base in which eight soldiers were killed.

THE FIGHTING

The US army used a variety of tactics to fight against the Vietcong and the North Vietnamese, including:

- **Search-and-destroy missions** in which villages suspected of helping the guerrillas were destroyed; it was one of these missions which caused the **My Lai massacre** in 1968, though news of it did not become public until after Johnson left office.
- Success in search-and-destroy missions was based on **body counts** or **kill ratios**.
- The US Air Force dropped **napalm** (jellied explosives) and **chemicals** (defoliants) on the forests of South Vietnam.

SOURCE 10 – Johnson and advisers

President Johnson meets with advisers in the Cabinet Room of the White House (May 1967).

- The US Air Force dropped a greater **tonnage of bombs** over North and South Vietnam between July 1965 and December 1968 than the Allies did in Europe in the Second World War.
- **Free fire zones** were laid out between the villages in which anybody there was regarded as a target.
- The US attempted to create a better South Vietnamese army but this failed.

Johnson took a close interest in the progress of the war. On Tuesdays, he met with his advisers and they decided the military targets for the bombers. Each morning the first information he looked for was the number of US personnel killed the previous day.

SOURCE 11 – Summary of North Vietnamese Four Points, for ending the war, 1965

1. Withdrawal of the US military from South Vietnam.

2. Neutrality of North and South Vietnam pending their re-unification.

3. The organisation of South Vietnam based on the programme of the Vietcong.

4. The peaceful re-unification of Vietnam without foreign intervention.

SOURCE 12 – Memo from Secretary of Defence McNamara

'With the situation continuing to deteriorate (in 1965), McNamara wrote a decisive memo in late July. It laid out three options: "cut our losses and withdraw," "continue at about the same level," or "expand promptly and substantially the U.S. pressure." ... He recommended the third. It would lead to "considerable cost in casualties and material" but would "offer a good chance of producing a favourable settlement in the longer run."'

Quoted in J Patterson, *Grand Expectations: The United States 1945–74*

SOURCE 13 – Statistics on the Vietnam War

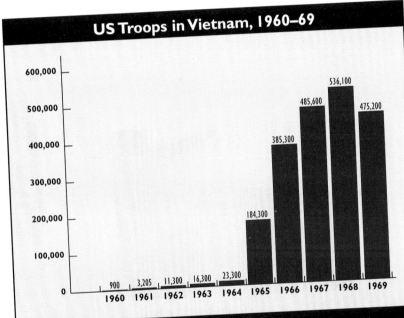

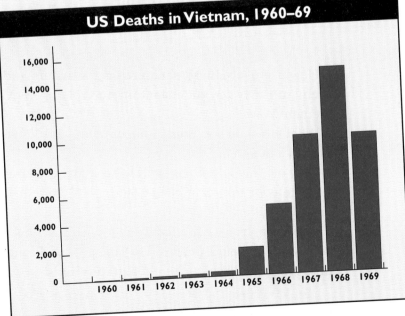

A US marine guards Vietnamese villagers who were rounded up after the troops discovered that most of the village's men had fled the area (1965).

SOURCE 15

The South Vietnamese Police Chief executes a Vietcong officer in Saigon, 1 February 1968.

SOURCE 16

A US soldier hurries away after setting fire to a house in South Vietnam during the Vietnam War (no date).

SOURCE 17

Bodies lie along the road after the US attack on the village of My Lai, South Vietnam (1968).

1. How useful are these photographs for understanding the US role in the Vietnam War? How useful are they for understanding the role of the Vietcong and the North Vietnamese in the Vietnam War?

2. What effect do you think Sources 15, 16 and 17 would have on US public opinion in relation to the Vietnam War?

3. How do photos compare with eyewitness accounts as historical sources?

4. Write your own captions to Sources 15, 16 and 17 to show how photographs can be interpreted in different ways.

5. 'Photographs have limited value to historians because they only show a moment in time, not what went on before or after.' Do you agree or disagree with this statement? To what extent does this statement apply to the photographs here?

PROGRESS OF THE WAR

Johnson claimed that the bombing was aimed at military targets but films showed otherwise. Johnson also claimed that the US was winning the war and that it would be over soon. His commander in Vietnam, **General Westmoreland**, always believed that if only he got more soldiers, he would win the war. But the use of **strategic bombing** failed to cripple a predominantly agricultural country, and the use of **artillery** and search-and-destroy missions failed in a **guerrilla** war.

US helicopters land under heavy sniper fire in South Vietnam during another military operation (1966).

SOURCE 18 – Johnson and the public

'However, Johnson was now so apprehensive about facing hostile audiences during domestic appearances that he asked the FBI to "send an advance man along with Secret Service to survey the situation" in Des Moines, Iowa, and Omaha, Nebraska. He "wanted the FBI's opinion as to whether or not it would be safe for him to go." ... [When he went there.] Aside from picketing by a few dozen anti-Vietnam demonstrators, the crowds were friendly and enthusiastic, and "there were no security problems of any sort."'

R Dallek, *Flawed Giant: Lyndon Johnson and his Times, 1961–1973*

A US B52 Stratofortress drops a load of 750-pound bombs over a coastal area in Vietnam in 1965. (Official US Air Force photo).

SOURCE 19

But Americans still largely supported the **President's handling** of the war. In 1964, eighty-five per cent of Americans supported the country's policy in Vietnam. But this began to decline as America became more involved in the war, and an **anti-war movement** began in 1965. Johnson himself was affected by the protests. The war soon became a media war as thousands of reporters and photographers from press, radio and television descended on Vietnam.

SOURCE 20 – Student slogan against the Vietnam War

Hey! Hey! LBJ! How many kids did you kill today?

THE TET OFFENSIVE, 1968

In the New Year of 1968, the Vietcong and North Vietnamese launched a large surprise attack on all the major cities of South Vietnam. They scored many significant victories, including an assault on the American embassy in **Saigon**, the capital. The offensive was only defeated after savage fighting. Almost 60,000 Communists were killed; 4,000 US troops; 2,000 South Vietnamese army (ARVN) and about 15,000 civilians:

- Even though the Tet Offensive was a military failure for the North Vietnamese, it **undermined Johnson's claim** that the US was winning the war in Vietnam. It seemed to show up his war policy as a failure.

- The US army commanders looked for **another 200,000 soldiers**. The only way the US could defeat the Vietcong, they said, was to use its full resources – a kind of total war.

- But Johnson did not want to do that since the war was already taking away resources from his **Great Society** programme. In March 1968 there was a **financial crisis** when speculators bought gold and sold dollars.

SOURCE 21 – Johnson listens

Sitting alone in the Cabinet Room, President Johnson listens to a tape-recorded message about the fighting in Vietnam from his son-in-law, Marine Captain Charles Robb (July 1968).

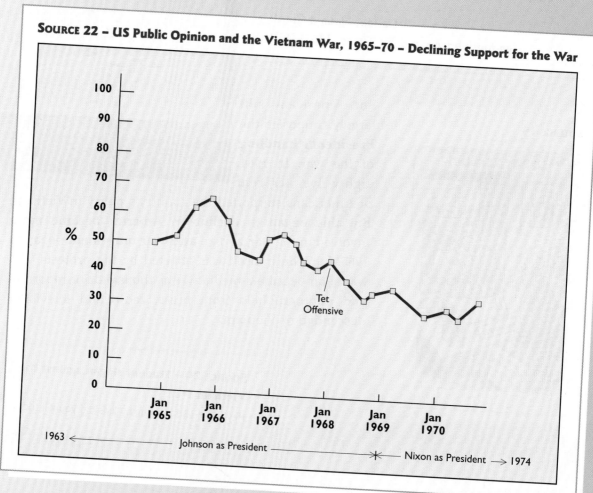

SOURCE 22 – US Public Opinion and the Vietnam War, 1965–70 – Declining Support for the War

- Johnson also knew that the American people would not let him expand the war. The Tet Offensive increased **US opposition** to the war. This was shown by the huge vote **Eugene McCarthy** got when he almost defeated Johnson in the New Hampshire Democratic primary election in 1968. A **credibility gap** was opening up because the people began to doubt what the government was telling them. The **anti-war movement** which began with university students spread to the wider public. This became more intense as the war progressed and culminated in the Chicago riots outside the Democratic Convention to select a presidential candidate in 1968 (see Chapter 27, Troubled Affluence).

A student anti-war rally in Iowa organised by the Students for a Democratic Society (SDS) in 1968.

JOHNSON CHANGES POLICY

Some of Johnson's advisers, including **Secretary of Defence McNamara**, had gone to other jobs. Others began to change their mind – they doubted the view of the military that they were winning the war. Johnson had to **change his policy**. He called a partial halt to the air bombing of North Vietnam. He also withdrew from the presidential election race. He made a proposal for peace talks which was accepted by the North Vietnamese. In May 1968, preliminary talks began in Paris, but the two sides were soon deadlocked. Later in 1968, just prior to the presidential election, Johnson announced the complete halt of the US bombing of North Vietnam. However, no agreement had been reached between the US and North Vietnam before Johnson left office in January 1969.

CONCLUSION – JOHNSON AND THE VIETNAM WAR

Johnson's involvement in the War in Vietnam:
- illustrated the **role** of the US President in shaping US foreign policy;
- highlighted the **growing power** of the US President and eventually led to a conflict between the White House and Congress during Nixon's Presidency;
- showed how foreign policy **distracted** from domestic policy and Johnson's efforts to create a Great Society;
- caused him to **withdraw** from the presidential election in 1968;
- caused **budgetary deficits** and **inflation** (rising prices) in the US;
- **expanded the war** from a small-scale local conflict to a full-scale war. By the end of Johnson's Presidency, the US suffered 200,000 casualties, including 30,000 dead.
- created **great divisions** in US society between the anti-war movement and Americans who felt they had to defend their country;
- demonstrated the **limits** of American military technology when faced with a well-supported guerrilla campaign;
- **distracted** the US and Johnson from foreign problems elsewhere.

SOURCE 23 – Great society

'This confused war has played havoc with our domestic destiny.... The promises of the Great Society have been shot down on the battlefields of Vietnam.'

Martin Luther King, 1967

SOURCE 24 – Stalemate

'It seems now more certain than ever that the bloody experience of Vietnam is to end in stalemate....'

Walter Cronkite, CBS News, 27 February 1968

SOURCE 25 – Effect on Johnson

'For Lyndon Johnson, the Vietnam War represented a personal as well as a national tragedy. Johnson had not created the commitment in Vietnam, and he would have preferred to shun what he once called "that bitch of a war" and concentrate on "the woman I really loved", his cherished Great Society. But the war he took on so reluctantly and struggled unsuccessfully to conclude eventually destroyed the Great Society, tore the nation apart, and inflicted great pain on Johnson himself.'

G Herring, *The War in Vietnam in the Johnson Years*, Vol. 1, ed. R Divine

CASE STUDY QUESTIONS

COMPREHENSION

1. Who are the Presidents featured in the cartoon in Source 1? What is the message of the cartoon?
2. What reason does President Johnson give in Source 2 for the US involvement in Vietnam?
3. What is 'the biggest damn mess', according to President Johnson in Source 3.
4. What happened with Hitler in Munich (Source 4)? (See Part 1, Chapter 6.)
5. What does President Johnson mean when he says in Source 5, 'Just let me get elected, and then you can have your war.'?
6. What is the message of the cartoon in Source 6?
7. What happened in the Tonkin Gulf, according to President Johnson in Source 7?
8. In Source 8, who are the neighbours of North Vietnam? Who are the nations joined with them?
9. What does President Johnson mean by saying in Source 9, 'We have kept our guns over the mantle and our shells in the cupboard for a long time now'?
10. Which of the North Vietnamese Four Points (Source 11) is, in your opinion, most important to them?
11. In Source 12, what were Robert McNamara's three options for US policy in South Vietnam? Which did he favour?
12. In the graph of US Troops in Vietnam, 1960–69 (Source 13), which two years had the biggest build-up of troops?
13. In the graph of US Deaths in Vietnam, 1960–69 (Source 13), which year had the highest number of deaths?
14. In Source 18, why did President Johnson send the FBI to survey Des Moines and Omaha? What happened when President Johnson spoke there?
15. Who does the Johnson administration fear in the cartoon in Source 19?
16. What is the message of the students' slogan in Source 20?
17. What is President Johnson doing in Source 21?

18. In Source 22, US public opinion and the Vietnam War, 1965–70, when was support for US involvement in Vietnam at its, (i) highest, and (ii) lowest, during President Johnson's term in office? What is the overall trend of the graph during the Johnson presidency?
19. What does Martin Luther King blame on the Vietnam War in Source 23?
20. What is Walter Cronkite's view of the war in Source 24?

COMPARISON

1. Study Sources 1 and 2. What information in Source 2 is linked to the cartoon in Source 1? How do the two sources differ in their attitudes to the same information?
2. How does President Johnson's attitude in Source 3 compare with his views in Sources 2 and 4? Can you explain the differences?
3. What evidence is there from Sources 1–5 to show that President Johnson was conscious of the influence and importance of History? Explain how History influenced him?
4. How does President Johnson's remark in Source 5 compare with his views in Source 3? Do his comments in Source 3 support the remark in Source 5?
5. Are both cartoons in Sources 1 and 6 favourable or unfavourable toward US policy in Vietnam? Explain your answer.
6. Are Sources 7 and 8 in agreement on what happened in the Tonkin Gulf? Explain your answer.
7. What do Sources 9 and 10 tell us about the role of President Johnson in forming US foreign policy during his administration?
8. The historian James Patterson calls Robert McNamara's memo of July 1965 'a decisive memo' (Source 12). What do you think he meant by that? Compare the memo with the graph of US Troops in Source 13. Does the graph show that

the memo was 'decisive'? How does the memo influence your view of the role of President Johnson in forming US foreign policy on Vietnam (Question 7)?

9. Examine Sources 18, 19, 20 and 22. What do they tell us about Johnson's fear of 'facing hostile audiences'? Was his fear justified? Do you think his fear was well known to the public?

10. What impression does the photo in Source 21 give you of Johnson's attitude to the war? Is it supported by Source 25?

11. Do the views of Sources 23, 24 and 25 explain the trend of the opinion polls in Source 22?

12. Do the views of Sources 23 and 24 support the conclusions of Source 25?

CRITICISM

1. Examine the political cartoons in Sources 1, 6 and 19. How useful are political cartoons as sources for historians?

2. How does the attitude of Source 1 compare with President Johnson's views in Source 2? Are Sources 1 and 2 biased? To what extent do you think Sources 1 and 2 are propaganda?

3. Source 2 is a transcript of a public speech made by President Johnson. How useful are such speeches as sources for historians? How reliable are public speeches?

4. How reliable are movies as sources for historians? How useful are movies for understanding History? Do you think the author Harold Evans agrees with the use made of the LBJ remark by the director, Oliver Stone?

5. In assessing President Johnson's attitude to the Vietnam War which of the Sources 2, 3, 4 and 5 would you rely on most? Explain your answer.

6. What is the difference in the style of language of Sources 7 and 8? Explain the difference.

7. President Johnson exaggerated/lied about the account of what happened in the Tonkin Gulf. Why do you think he did this? Do Sources 9, 10, 11 and 12 help us understand why he escalated the war in Vietnam? Explain your answer.

8. Examine Sources 9 and 12. How useful are records of government meetings and government memos as sources for historians? What are their advantages/strengths and disadvantages/limitations as sources compared to political speeches?

9. Examine Source 13. What are the strengths and weaknesses/limitations of graphs for presenting historical information?

10. How do the photos in Sources 10 and 21 help our understanding of the role of President Johnson in US involvement in the Vietnam War?

11. What is the role of slogans in politics? How would that affect their usefulness and reliability as sources in history? (Source 20)

12. List the Sources from 18–25 according to whether they are primary or secondary. Based on your listing, do the primary or the secondary sources provide a better understanding of Johnson's role in the Vietnam War? Support your answer by referring to information provided by the sources.

13. Which of the Sources 18–25 would be kept in (i) archives, (ii) libraries, and (iii) museums?

14. Walter Cronkite was a very influential and respected commentator for CBS News. He made his comment (Source 24) after the Tet Offensive. How influential would this be? How useful are written extracts of television commentaries as historical sources?

15. Outline one fact and one opinion from Source 25.

16. In view of the conclusions of Source 25, consider again the impact or influence of Source 20 on Johnson himself.

17. Source 25 is an historian's assessment of the influence of the Vietnam War on President Johnson. Do you think the historian is favourable or unfavourable toward Johnson?

18. What other types of sources, apart from those used in this Case Study, would you consider helpful for a better understanding of Lyndon Johnson and Vietnam, 1963–8? Explain your answer.

CONTEXTUALISATION

1. Outline the stages through which the US became more involved in the Vietnam War from 1960 onwards.

2. Using the sources and the account of the Vietnam War, explain how the US tried to impose a military solution on Vietnam.

3. Discuss the Gulf of Tonkin and the Tet Offensives as turning points in US involvement in the Vietnam War.

4. Using your knowledge of Johnson's aims and policies, do you think the Vietnam War was a 'personal tragedy' for Johnson (Source 25)? How was the Vietnam War a 'national tragedy'?

5. Using the account above and the sources, write a report on Lyndon Johnson and Vietnam 1963–8 under the headings – Johnson's attitude to US involvement, Johnson's escalation of the war, Johnson changes his policy, the impact of the Vietnam War on Johnson's presidency.

6. How did the US eventually withdraw from Vietnam? (See p. 373.)

US foreign policy was influenced by many domestic factors. Presidents were very conscious of public opinion, particularly in the run-up to congressional and presidential elections.

As well as this, various interest groups within the US tried to influence foreign policy from the Military-Industrial complex to the press.

From the 1940s to the 1980s three other factors had an important influence. These were:

- McCarthyism (and the Red Scare),
- the anti-war movement,
- race relations.

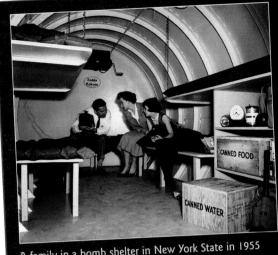

A family in a bomb shelter in New York State in 1955 ready for the possibility of a nuclear war.

> **Key Concept: PUBLIC OPINION.** The views and attitudes of the people. This is measured in elections or in between elections in opinion polls. In a democracy, political parties have to get elected so they have to pay attention to public opinion. They also try to influence and manipulate public opinion in their favour. This is often done through the media – press, radio and television.

> **Key Concept: MILITARY-INDUSTRIAL COMPLEX** was the combination of the armed forces, the politicians who supported them and the industries who supplied them. They had a strong influence on government decisions.

Key Personality: Senator Joe McCarthy – 'Tail Gunner Joe'

Joe McCarthy was born in Wisconsin in the American Mid–West. He served in the Second World War, mostly in a desk job. After the war, he was elected to the **US Senate** for Wisconsin in 1946. He had a **poor record** as a Senator – he liked playing poker and drinking – and he seemed likely to be defeated in the next congressional election. He needed an issue to fight the election and friends advised him to go after **subversives**. 'That's it,' he said, 'The government is full of Communists. We can hammer away at them.'

In February 1950, he claimed that the **State Department** had 200 employees who were Communists. This was the beginning of the accusations which brought him fame – he was on the cover of *Time* and *Newsweek* – and re-election. But it also intensified the growing anti-Communism (the **Red Scare**) which spread fear around the US for the next four years.

McCarthy was a **strong and dramatic speaker** who cleverly stoked up fears. He attacked individuals and groups with a wicked and nasty tongue. He said of a fellow Republican that he was 'a living miracle in that he is without question the only man who has lived so long with neither brains nor guts.' He attacked the Protestant clergy (he was a Catholic), the civil service, writers and scientists.

He detested what was called the **Eastern Establishment** – the well-educated, often wealthy, mainly Protestant young men who ran government and much of industry at the time. He linked **liberalism** and the **New Deal**, which he hated, with **socialism** and **Communism**.

He was supported by the **Republicans** who encouraged his attacks on Truman and the Democrats, accusing them of being **soft** on Communism. After President **Eisenhower** was elected McCarthy continued his attacks on Democrats. It even seemed Eisenhower was afraid of him because the President dropped a section of a speech defending George Marshall, a friend, when he was attacked by McCarthy.

McCarthy became chairman of the Senate Committee on subversion. His attacks on the US army, and the **Army-McCarthy** hearings which were televised, led to his downfall. His downfall came in 1954 and he died two years later of **liver disease** due to his drinking. But his influence continued long after. Many Americans now look back on McCarthyism as a disgraceful episode in their history.

1. McCarthyism (and the Red Scare)

McCarthyism was the most extreme form of **anti-Communist hysteria** which developed in the US after the Second World War. It was a **witch hunt** of federal and state government employees. It got its name from **Senator Joe McCarthy**. As part of the general **Red Scare** in the US, it influenced public and political opinion against the Soviet Union, and, in this way, it shaped US foreign policy.

THE BEGINNINGS OF MCCARTHYISM

A prime mover in spreading the Red Scare was **Senator Joe McCarthy**. In February 1950, McCarthy claimed to have a list of over 200 State Department employees who were Communists. He continued to repeat his allegations, varying the numbers though without any proof. He added to the anti-Communist hysteria as well as improving his political standing. He got a widespread following particularly in the Mid-West of America, among recent immigrants from Eastern Europe and among working-class Catholics.

His success in whipping up anti-Communist hysteria helped to get him **re-elected** to the Senate in 1952. But some of his critics failed to get re-elected in the same elections. This undermined the position of other critics who feared they would soon be called pro-Communist.

THE SPREAD OF MCCARTHYISM

McCarthy won support because his **message** was simple – America was in trouble in the Cold War because of traitors within the US government. *'The reason we find ourselves in a position of weakness is because ... of the traitorous actions of those who have been treated so well by this nation.'* He accused the **State Department** – *'the bright young things who were born with silver spoons in their mouths ... have been the worst'* – of being *'thoroughly infested with Communists.'* He believed the State Department was partly responsible for the **loss** of China to the Communists in the civil war in 1949.

Senator Joe McCarthy speaking about the Communist Party organisation in the US at the Army-McCarthy hearings in 1954.

His resentment against *'the bright young things'* was partly based on class, religion and regional divisions. He came from a small-town background, they were wealthy; he was Catholic, they were Protestant; he was from the Mid-West, they were from the East Coast.

Senior Republican leaders supported him. Republicans accused **Democrats** of associating with **socialists and Communists** through Roosevelt's New Deal. They accused them for being *'soft on Communism'*. In return, Democrats had to show how tough they were by denouncing it as strongly as possible. In this way both political parties encouraged the spread of McCarthyism.

THE DOWNFALL OF MCCARTHY

In 1952, he became chairman of the **Committee on Government Operations** and its **Subcommittee on Investigations**. He began hearings on Communist infiltration in the federal government but he did not uncover anything. His campaign led to the banning of over **400 writers** by the State Department. His downfall came when he accused the army of harbouring Communists. The **Army-McCarthy hearings** were televised from April to June 1954. These showed the public what a **bully** he was as he shouted at witnesses and interrupted them. Public opinion changed and his support dropped from 50% to 34%, with 45% disapproving of his actions. The Senate censored him in 1954 for bringing that body into disrepute.

THE INFLUENCE OF MCCARTHYISM ON US FOREIGN POLICY

The Red Scare and McCarthyism set the tone for American foreign policy in the late 1940s and for the next thirty years. By heightening fear of Communism McCarthyism clouded much of American thinking on foreign policy. It contributed to making the Cold War more extreme. It reinforced the view that all events everywhere should be viewed as part of a Communist conspiracy, led by the Soviet Union and Communist China. Both Democrats and Republicans agreed that anti-Communism should be the main aim of US foreign policy. It brought America into supporting corrupt governments once they appeared to be anti-Communist, particularly in Asia and South America. In Asia, for example, it led the US into supporting the corrupt and incompetent **Chiang Kai-shek** in Taiwan and also into refusing to recognise the Communist government in China.

The **State Department** lost many of its finest people. In particular, the Far East and Asia department lost many able people. Some historians link the **US failure in Vietnam** and their misreading of the situation to the lack of knowledge or information on the area. The US viewed Vietnam as a Cold War conflict when it was much more a **nationalist uprising** against the French colonial government.

McCarthy also undermined respect for American policy in **Europe**, particularly among the young who developed an anti-American view. They looked on his actions as being **undemocratic**. In this way McCarthyism damaged America's reputation abroad.

2. The Anti-war Movement

The majority of Americans supported government policy during the Vietnam War. But as the war progressed greater and greater numbers began to criticise American actions in the war.

The anti-war movement began among university students. The first **teach-in** was held in the University of Michigan in 1965.

As the number of university students grew in the 1960s, some of them were committed to improving society, as well as abolishing racism and poverty. These were members of the **New Left** who formed the **Students for a Democratic Society** (SDS).

REASONS FOR ANTI-WAR PROTEST

They protested about the war for a variety of **reasons**:
- They believed the war was taking away money from Johnson's Great Society Programme.
- They said the Vietnam War was really a civil war in which the US should not intervene.
- They said the US had no interest in South-East Asia.
- They regarded the war as morally wrong.
- Television brought pictures of the war into US homes – this was the first *'living room war'*.
- Many criticised the way the US was fighting the war – saturation bombing, the use of napalm, and the deaths of civilians. The cruelties and savagery of the Vietcong were not televised and did not have the same impact.
- Some feared they would be called up in the draft to fight.

However, they did not want to see the US defeated and instead hoped for a divided Vietnam with two governments.

STUDENT PROTEST

The students organised **demonstrations** and **protest marches**. Their placards read 'STOP THE KILLING: WAR ON POVERTY, NOT ON PEOPLE'. Some songs such as *Eve of Destruction* expressed their bitterness:

The Eastern world, it is explodin'
Violence flarin', bullets loadin'
You're old enough to kill, but not for votin'
You don't believe in war, but what's that gun you're totin'
And even the Jordan River has bodies floatin'

In 1969, 300,000 anti-war protesters marched past the White House in silent protest. Each carried the name of a dead soldier or a destroyed Vietnamese village.

However, until the late 1960s their protests were confined to a few universities. It was not only the majority of students who were supporters of the war, so also were labour unions, churches, Congress and the media. Anti-war demonstrators angered some Americans who did not like the protestors' criticisms of American institutions and they did not like people avoiding the draft (military service). *'Here were those kids, rich kids who could go to college, didn't have to fight. They were telling you your son died in vain.'* Instead they believed what their leaders told them. But soon the huge cost of the war, the greater numbers of soldiers fighting and the increasing casualties, made people question what was happening.

TET OFFENSIVE AND THE ANTI-WAR MOVEMENT

A crucial turning point was the **Tet Offensive** in New Year of 1968. The success of the Offensive in threatening most South Vietnamese cities undermined the view of the American government that they were winning the war.

Public approval of Johnson's handling of the war fell to twenty-six per cent. The anti-war protests became more violent. The police were called **pigs**, students burnt draft cards, protestors surrounded the Pentagon, and some left the country to avoid the draft.

CREDIBILITY GAP

By now the anti-war movement **spread** well beyond the students. The **credibility gap** arose as people did not believe what the government was saying about the war. Senior politicians began to go against the war. These included **Eugene McCarthy** who almost defeated Johnson in a Democratic Presidential primary election and **Robert Kennedy** who began campaigning for the presidency. The **media** – press, radio and television – were also angry because they had broadcast the government reports about winning the war. One of the country's most respected newsmen, **Walter Cronkite** of CBS News, publicly questioned US participation in the war.

The anti-war movement forced Johnson to **withdraw** from the presidential election campaign. It also forced him to change his policies on Vietnam and led to him calling a partial halt to the bombing of North Vietnam and beginning talks with the North Vietnamese.

KENT STATE

When Nixon came to power in 1969, he had to continue the process of disengaging from Vietnam – he continued the talks, he began a policy of **Vietnamisation** (getting the South Vietnamese army, the ARVN, to take more responsibility for the war) – which satisfied most people. However, when US troops invaded Cambodia in 1970, this led to the most serious incident in the **anti-war campaign.** Four students were shot dead protesting in **Kent State University** by Ohio National Guardsmen. This caused a national outcry and 500 universities were closed temporarily due to protests.

One of four students lies dead after being shot by National Guardsmen at Kent State University, Ohio during an anti-war protest (May 1970).

Soon afterwards the student anti-war protest lost impetus when the various groups, especially the **SDS**, split over other issues. But by now the momentum toward peace had been established. Americans were now thoroughly opposed to the war as incidents such as the **My Lai massacre** became public in 1969. Then the **Pentagon Papers** were leaked to the *New*

York Times and the *Washington Post* in 1971. These showed how the federal government became more involved in Vietnam and that it had **deceived** the public in the process. The anti-war movement had now become a widespread public feeling. However, it took two more years of talks and bombings before the war eventually ended in 1973.

Undoubtedly the anti-war movement undermined American will to keep on fighting. But it was only **one factor** among many which shaped US foreign policy in relation to Vietnam and South-East Asia.

3. Race Relations

US IMAGE ABROAD

US Presidents were concerned about the image that bad race relations gave the US abroad. This was one of the factors which led to **Truman** and **Eisenhower** desegregating the armed forces.

Kennedy also was worried that racial unrest in the US would damage the national image abroad and sabotage foreign policy goals. In 1960, as he prepared to meet the Soviet leader Khrushchev in Vienna, Kennedy was looking for national unity prior to the summit.

In a clash in Birmingham, Alabama police treated black protesters brutally. Kennedy was concerned about the bad publicity as television showed pictures around the world. This undermined US claims to lead the Free World because they were shown to be trampling on the rights of their own people.

BLACKS AND VIETNAM WAR

As the American commitment to **Vietnam** expanded from 1961 onwards, American black men were just as committed as anybody else to the war. Between 1961 and 1965 the percentage of American soldiers who were **black** was in line with the proportion of the available draft age population. In fact, by 1966 they were three times as likely as whites to re-enlist when their tour of duty was over.

A young soldier is carried piggy-back style after being rescued in South Vietnam (1967).

In spite of advances in civil rights in the 1960s, **race relations worsened** by the end of the decade. This was partly because rising expectations among blacks were not fulfilled. The bitter race relations affected black attitudes to all issues including foreign policy and the Vietnam War.

By 1965, a higher percentage of blacks were being killed in the war. This was largely because fewer blacks (compared to whites) could avoid the draft in order to finish college. Black political leaders were also turning against the war. **Martin Luther King** spoke against expanding the war in 1965. He wanted money for social and economic improvements. In a speech in 1967, he feared that 'the Great Society has been shot down in the battlefields of Vietnam.' Two important black civil rights organisations openly opposed the war in 1966.

By the early 1970s, opinion polls showed that a greater proportion of blacks (83%) than whites (67%) thought that the US had made a mistake sending troops to Vietnam in the first place. Not surprisingly, blacks were less willing to serve than before. Also, they would not put up with **racial discrimination** at the front. As a result, American army leaders made changes which resulted in a reduction in the proportion of black deaths.

ORDINARY LEVEL AND HIGHER LEVEL HOMEWORK EXERCISES

ORDINARY LEVEL

1. **Study this extract from Senator Joe McCarthy and answer the following questions:**

   'This is the time of the 'cold war'. This is the time when all the world is split into two vast, increasingly hostile camps.... The reason why we find ourselves in a position of weakness is not because our only potential enemy has sent men to invade our shores, but rather because of the traitorous actions of those who have been treated so well by the nation. It has not been the less fortunate or members of minority groups who have been selling this nation out, but rather those who have had all the benefits that the wealthiest nation on the earth has to offer – the finest homes, the finest college education, and the finest jobs in government we can give.
   This is glaringly true in the State Department. There the bright young things who were born with silver spoons in their mouths are the ones who have been the worst ... In my opinion, the State Department ... is thoroughly infested with Communists.'

   (i) According to Senator Joe McCarthy, why was America in a weak position in the Cold War?

   (ii) Who is the 'potential enemy'?

   (iii) Who does he blame for 'selling out the nation'?

   (iv) What is his attitude to those who work in the State Department?

   (v) What role has the State Department in the US government?

   (vi) Show how McCarthy uses a variety of words to turn his listeners against the people he dislikes.

2. **Study the verse of the song, Eve of Destruction (p. 368), and answer the following questions:**

   (i) What does 'The Eastern world, it is explodin' ' refer to?

   (ii) What is meant by 'You're old enough to kill, but not for votin' '?

   (iii) Explain 'You don't believe in war, but what's that gun you're totin''.

   (iv) What does the reference to the Jordan River mean?

   (v) Why would this song be considered anti-war?

3. Write **paragraph answers** on each of the following questions:

   (i) McCarthyism.

   (ii) Student protests against the Vietnam War.

   (iii) The attitude of Black Americans to the Vietnam War.

4. Write **long answers** on each of the following:

(i) How did Senator Joe McCarthy and McCarthyism influence US foreign policy?

(ii) How and why did an anti-war movement develop in the US in the 1960s and 1970s?

(iii) How did the anti-war movement influence US policy toward Vietnam?

(iv) How did race relations influence US foreign policy?

HIGHER LEVEL

1. Assess the importance of two of the following in influencing US foreign policy between 1945 and 1972 (a) McCarthyism, (b) the Anti-war Movement, and (c) Race Relations.

OR

To what extent was US foreign policy between 1945 and 1972 influenced by (a) McCarthyism, (b) the Anti-war Movement, and (c) Race Relations?

Withdrawal from Vietnam

When Richard Nixon became President in 1969, he wanted to end US involvement in Vietnam. He wanted this because:

- Opposition at home was growing.
- The costs of the war were increasing.
- Huge numbers of American soldiers were killed.
- The US did not seem to be able to win the war.
- But Nixon also had other foreign policy aims. He wanted to improve relations with Communist China and to do this he needed peace in Vietnam.

But Nixon knew he could not pull out of Vietnam because this would look like a defeat for America. He hoped for **peace with honour** which would mean separate governments for South and North Vietnam. He began a policy of **Vietnamisation** – the gradual withdrawal of US troops and the strengthening of the South Vietnamese army (ARVN) to take a greater part in the war. By 1971, Nixon had withdrawn almost half of the 550,000 US soldiers based in Vietnam. By September 1972, only 40,000 were left. He also announced the **Nixon Doctrine** – the US would give help to countries fighting internal attack but he would not send in US troops.

Since the talks in Paris were dragging on, Nixon also increased **aerial bombing**, particularly of North Vietnam and the Ho Chi Minh trail. This was part of his **mad man** strategy where he wanted to give the impression that he was prepared to even use atomic bombs to end the war.

INVASION OF CAMBODIA

He also secretly ordered the **invasion of Cambodia** to destroy Vietcong dumps and to destroy their supply lines along the Ho Chi Minh trail. The invasion of Cambodia had serious consequences for Nixon when it was made public:

- It increased **anti-war demonstrations** at home, and led to the deaths of four students at Kent State University in Ohio.
- It widened the **credibility gap** as more people doubted what the government was telling them.
- It led to a **rebellion in Congress** where it was felt that Nixon was overstepping his power. Congress repealed the Tonkin Resolution and cut off all military aid from Cambodia. It also passed the **War Powers Act, 1973** which controlled the President's use of troops.

PEACE TREATY

Negotiations were still going slowly in Paris, but eventually a combination of heavy bombing, pressure from China and the Soviet Union and the continued fighting brought peace. The US and North Vietnam signed a **peace treaty** in Paris in January 1973. They agreed:

- The US would withdraw from South Vietnam.

A North Vietnamese tank leads North Vietnamese troops in the fall of Saigon in 1975.

- All prisoners-of-war would be released.
- There would be further negotiations to decide the future of North and South Vietnam.

VIETNAM BECAME COMMUNIST

The US continued to give aid to South Vietnam after it withdrew in 1973. They hoped to maintain a non-Communist government in South Vietnam. But the North Vietnamese launched an attack in 1975 which led to the capture of **Saigon**, the capital. North and South Vietnam were united under a Communist leadership. In explaining the Vietnamese victory, Nixon's National Security Adviser, **Henry Kissinger**, later said, *'Because there were always more Vietnamese prepared to die for their country than foreigners, their nationalism became the scourge of invaders and neighbours alike.'*

THE EFFECTS OF THE VIETNAM WAR ON THE US

1. The US lost 58,000 soldiers **killed** and 150,000 **wounded**.
2. The war cost the US $150 billion – it contributed to weakening the **US economy** and rising inflation. It also took money away from Johnson's Great Society programme.
3. The US **policy of containment** in the Cold War had **failed**. Not only had the US been defeated in South Vietnam but Laos and Cambodia were also weakened. They soon had Communist governments.
4. American **propaganda** in the Cold War had painted themselves as the good guys against the cruel Communists. But American conduct of the war (e.g. My Lai, the use of chemical weapons and napalm) undermined America's image at home and abroad.
5. **Respect** for the US government system and politicians was **undermined** as they were shown to have lied about US involvement and about the progress of the war.
6. The Vietnam War contributed to the **great divisions** in American society which caused so much violence and conflict at the end of the 1960s.
7. Congress reduced the **power of the President** whom they felt had increased commitments to Vietnam without Congress's permission.
8. The US government used the **CIA** to break many laws during the conflict; the CIA was forbidden by law to conduct secret operations inside the US. But in Operation Chaos, it kept files on thousands of Americans, infiltrated college groups and opened private letters.

Nixon and Détente

Nixon's other main foreign policy concern was Cold War relations with the Soviet Union and China. He developed his foreign policy with **Henry Kissinger**, his National Security Adviser and later his Secretary of State. They believed that the US must look after its own interests. They were both **suspicious people** so they often negotiated in **secrecy** and set up secret channels of communication which bypassed the State Department (which was also responsible for foreign policy) and

Congress. This was called **shuttle diplomacy**. This was another aspect of the **imperial presidency** which reached its peak during Nixon's term of office.

Nixon still believed in the **policy of containment** but he approached it in a different way. He developed a policy of **détente** – that is trying to improve relations with the Soviet Union and China. This was linked to the **Nixon Doctrine** (getting countries which faced internal Communist aggression to take on more responsibility of fighting for themselves). He was hoping that détente would ease tensions so that he could cut military spending.

VISITS TO CHINA AND RUSSIA

Nixon and Kissinger used **back channels** to organise Nixon's visit to China in 1972. His visit caught many people in the US and outside by surprise because Nixon had a reputation as a **Cold War warrior** and the US had tried to **isolate Communist China** since 1949.

However, Nixon hoped to improve relations with China, increase US-China trade, put pressure on North Vietnam in the peace negotiations, and to play off China and the USSR against each other. It also helped Nixon in the presidential election year of 1972 because television pictures of his visit to the **Great Wall** of China were beamed back to the US. In spite of Nixon's claim that *'This was the week that changed the world'*, his visit was mainly symbolic.

President Nixon holds his chopsticks ready as Chinese Prime Minister, Chou En-lai (left) reaches in front of him at a farewell banquet in Shanghai (February 1972).

However, Nixon did successfully play off China and the USSR. The Soviets feared that they would be isolated. So two months after his visit, Nixon had a summit meeting in **Moscow** with **Brezhnev**, the Soviet leader. This was the first visit by a serving American President to the Kremlin. The leaders agreed on the **Strategic Arms Limitation Treaty** (SALT I). This Treaty put a limit to the number of ICBMs (intercontinental ballistic missiles) and submarine-based missiles for five years. Even though there was still much scope for developing other types of nuclear weapons, **SALT I** showed that both sides realised the dangers of the arms race. The two countries signed a further agreement to work together for **peaceful co-existence**, *'to do their utmost to avoid military confrontation and to prevent the outbreak of nuclear war.'* This was a significant victory for the policy of détente, which was strengthened by **Brezhnev's visit** to the US in 1973.

ARAB-ISRAELI WAR, 1973

However, détente was put to a **severe test** when Egypt and Syria attacked Israel in October 1973 (in the Arab-Israeli – Yom Kippur – War). The USSR had supported Egypt and Syria before the war and the US supported Israel. There was a danger that détente would be destroyed. **Kissinger** was sent to Moscow to work out a truce. The Israelis refused to agree and the Soviets said it should be enforced by the two superpowers. Nixon disagreed and put the US on **nuclear alert**. One year after SALT I, détente seemed to be collapsing. But both sides backed down and a truce was agreed.

CHILE AND THE CIA

In spite of Nixon's visits to China and Russia, it was clear that Cold War tensions were still strong. Some accused Nixon of mainly undertaking his visits for **election purposes** in the election year of 1972. Indeed, Nixon's treatment of **Chile** showed he was still the Cold War warrior. He tried to prevent the election of the socialist **Salvador Allende** as President of Chile. When that failed, he used the CIA to undermine Allende's rule and this led to Allende's overthrow and assassination in 1973. In this way, Nixon was following the traditional **policy of containment**.

Ford and Détente

President Ford, who succeeded Nixon after he resigned over the Watergate Scandal, continued the policy of **détente**. He relied on Henry Kissinger as his Secretary of State and this provided continuity of policy. Ford met **Brezhnev** in Vladivostok in 1974 and agreed on a second round of SALT talks.

President Ford (right) and the Soviet leader, Leonid Brezhnev, share a toast at their final dinner in Vladivostok after the Strategic Arms Limitation Treaty (SALT) talks in 1974.

Détente took another major step when Ford and Brezhnev, along with thirty-three other government leaders, signed the **Helsinki Agreement** in 1975. They agreed to:
• respect each others borders, which applied particularly to Europe;
• allow freedom of travel, and encourage trade and cultural links;
• respect human rights.

But Congress was opposed to other aspects of Ford's policies. It refused to send military aid to the collapsing **South Vietnamese government** which was attacked by North Vietnam in 1975. It also rejected his proposals to send arms and equipment to anti-Communist forces in **Angola**. Congress feared that the US would be dragged into another foreign war.

Carter's Foreign Policy and SALT II

Carter's foreign policy differed from that of Nixon and Ford. He wanted a foreign policy based on **moral principles** – based on honour and right. But Carter was very **inexperienced** in foreign policy. Because he relied for advice on two different points of view – that of his Secretary of State, **Cyrus Vance**, as well as his Secretary of Defence, **Zbigniew Brzezinski** – his policy was often inconsistent.

He wanted to reduce arms but he was also critical of the Soviet Union for its treatment of **dissidents** (political protestors) in Czechoslovakia and the Soviet Union itself. This criticism upset the Russians and this put détente under pressure. Further difficulties were caused between the two superpowers when Carter arranged a peace agreement between **Egypt and Israel** in 1978, without involving the Soviet Union (the Camp David Agreement).

SALT II

The SALT talks continued slowly and once again the US played the **China card** when the Chinese leader, **Deng Xiaoping**, visited the US. The Soviet Union feared isolation again and soon agreement on arms limitation – **SALT II** – was reached with the US in 1979. This put a limit (on missiles and bombers) of 2,400 per country. But this did not stop the USSR installing SS-20 missiles in Eastern Europe and the US countering with Pershing missiles. SALT II was also criticised in the US where the liberals said it did not go far enough and the conservative right wing said it went too far.

Soviet leader, Brezhnev, holds a signed copy of the SALT II Treaty as he kisses President Carter of the US in June 1979 in Vienna.

However, even the limited agreement was halted when the USSR invaded **Afghanistan** in December 1979 and Congress **refused to ratify** the Treaty. In his State of the Union speech, Carter said the Soviet invasion was *'the most serious threat to peace since the Second World War.'* He caused relations with the Soviet Union to deteriorate by suspending grain sales to that country and by boycotting the **Olympic Games** in Moscow in 1980. This was the end of détente.

Reagan and Star Wars

By the late 1970s and the early 1980s Cold War tensions between the US and USSR increased:
- The **Soviet invasion** of Afghanistan confirmed to the US that the Soviet Union had not changed since 1945 – it was still aggressive and expansionist.
- Reagan introduced an **aggressive tone** to his foreign policy – he wanted military superiority over the Soviet Union which he said was **the evil empire** aiming for world domination.

Reagan began a huge **arms build-up**. Over $550 billion a year was spent on conventional and nuclear weapons. New weapons such as the **stealth bomber** were developed. At the same time, however, Reagan was prepared to discuss **arms reduction**. But, because of mistrust between the two sides, the **Strategic Arms Reduction Talks** (START) which began in 1982, failed.

In 1982, Reagan wrote a **private letter** which explained his approach to the Soviet Union.

> *'I don't underestimate the imperialist ambitions of the Soviet Union.... I want more than anything to bring them into realistic arms-reduction talks. To do this they must be convinced that the alternative is a build-up militarily by us. They have stretched their economy to the limit to maintain their programme. They know they cannot match us in an arms race if we are determined to catch up. Our true ultimate purpose is arms reduction.'*

To achieve this he was prepared to tolerate huge **budget deficits**.

The following year Reagan announced that the US was developing the **Strategic Defence Initiative** (SDI), popularly called **Star Wars**. This was a plan to develop a **defence shield** in space which would destroy any missiles fired at the US. Some scientists doubted if the US could develop such as shield. Others said they could and that it would make all Soviet missiles obsolete.

STAR WARS AND RELATIONS WITH THE SOVIET UNION

SDI was a barrier to US-Soviet agreement when **Reagan and Gorbachev**, the new Soviet leader, met in **Geneva** and **Reykjavik**. Gorbachev objected to extending the arms race into space, while Reagan said the US would share the Star Wars technology. But Gorbachev did not believe him. However, agreement was eventually reached in 1987 when they signed the **Intermediate-range Nuclear Forces Treaty** (INF) in Washington. This led to the dismantling of the Soviet SS-20 missiles and the US Pershing missiles in Europe. But Reagan still refused to abandon the Star Wars project.

US President Ronald Reagan shakes the hand of a baby held by Soviet leader Mikhail Gorbachev, during a tour of Moscow's Red Square in 1988. The Kremlin and Lenin's tomb are in the background on the left.

Some historians believe that **Reagan's tough policy** and his increase in armaments forced the Soviet Union to see that it could not compete. Others think that the **growing understanding** between Reagan and Gorbachev was more important. At any rate, it was clear that Gorbachev wanted to reform the Soviet Union and reduce arms, and Reagan was prepared to negotiate. A further improvement in relations occurred between the two states when Reagan visited **Moscow** in 1988.

The Policy of Containment – a Successful Policy?

Shortly after, however, **Gorbachev's reform** movement led to a process which caused the collapse of the Soviet empire in Eastern Europe (1989) and finally the **downfall of Communism** in Russia (1991). The US policy of containment **contributed** to this downfall. It forced the Soviet Union to maintain huge spending on armaments which would have been better used in improving the economy and social conditions in the USSR. Ultimately the USSR could not compete with the spending of the stronger US economy. But reforms to reduce military spending in the USSR undermined Communism and led to its collapse and the end of the Cold War. The US became the world's most dominant power.

One of the authors of the policy of containment in the 1940s assessed the **cost of the victory** of that policy:

'We paid with forty years of enormous and unnecessary military expenditures [spending]. We paid through the cultivation of nuclear weaponry to the point where the vast and useless nuclear arsenals had become a danger to the very environment of the planet…. We paid all this because we were too timid to negotiate.'

But those who supported the policy of containment also argued that it avoided war with the Soviet Union, and discouraged or prevented a Soviet invasion of Western Europe.

ORDINARY LEVEL

1. Study the extract from President Reagan's letter on p. 377 and answer the following questions:

(i) What is meant by *'the imperialist ambitions of the Soviet Union'*?

(ii) What does Reagan want the Soviets to do?

(iii) How does he intend to make them do what he wants?

(iv) What is the purpose of an arms race as far as he is concerned?

(v) How successful was his policy?

2. Study the extract from one of the authors (George Keenan) of the policy of containment on p. 378 and answer the following questions:

(i) What does he say is the cost of the Cold War?

(ii) What is the result of the *'cultivation of nuclear weaponry'*?

(iii) This was written when the Cold War came to an end. Does the author now agree with his views in the 1940s? Explain your answer fully.

3. Write **paragraph answers** on each of the following questions:

(i) The effects of the Vietnam War on the US.

(ii) Nixon and Détente.

(iii) Carter and SALT II.

(iv) President Reagan's relations with the Soviet Union.

4. Write **long answers** on each of the following:

(i) How and why did the US withdraw from Vietnam?

(ii) How successful was the policy of détente from Nixon to Carter?

(iii) What was the role of US foreign policy in ending the Cold War?

HIGHER LEVEL

1. How successful was President Nixon's foreign policy?

OR

What impact did the Nixon presidency have on US policy toward Vietnam and China?

2. Assess the progress of the policy of détente from Nixon to Carter.

3. How did US foreign policy help bring about the end of the Cold War?

4. How successful was the US in trying to contain the spread of Communism, both internally and externally? (See also Chapter 20, US Foreign Policy, 1945–72 and Chapter 21, Domestic Factors in US Foreign Policy, 1945–72.)

TEST YOURSELF AT
my-etest.com

The Boom

During the Second World War the US economy entered a boom period which lasted until the end of the 1960s. After the war was over some Americans feared the return of the Great Depression but this did not happen.

Instead the US economy **grew rapidly** in the late 1940s and through the 1950s and 1960s. Indeed the economy more than doubled in size between 1945 and 1960. Throughout this time unemployment remained low, and inflation averaged

Huge spaghetti junctions and large highways (motorways), as shown here in California, were symbols of the economic boom in the US in the post-war years.

only 2·5% a year from 1951–70 as the US enjoyed *'the greatest prosperity the world has ever known.'* In the process, the US became the **world's dominant economic power**. The US population in the late 1940s was only 7% of the population of the whole world; yet the country produced half the world's manufacturing output and it possessed over 40% of the world's income.

By the end of the 1960s many Americans had become home owners, high consumers and were well educated. Generally Americans were much better off. By 1960, for example, families could buy about thirty per cent more than they could in 1950.

US PRODUCTION AS % OF THE WORLD'S PRODUCTION (LATE 1940s)	
Steel	57
Electricity	43
Oil	62
Cars	80

THE INFLUENCE OF THE SECOND WORLD WAR ON THE US ECONOMY

The huge expansion in **war industries** eliminated the high unemployment of the Great Depression of the 1930s. It also brought millions of **women** into the workforce. Family earnings increased during the war and so did **savings** because there was nowhere to spend the money. By 1945, there was $140 billion in private savings. These savings were used after the war to boost **consumer spending**.

The war also increased **government revenue** as more people were brought into the tax net. In 1940, the government collected $7 billion in tax. This rose to $51 billion by 1945. This paid for war expenses, along with borrowing. The economy grew enormously because of the extra spending. The US economy almost **doubled** during the war, even allowing for inflation.

Companies also gained out of the war as their profits increased, especially those on government contracts. Many companies grew much bigger because of **mergers** (joining of companies). By the end of the war three-quarters of manufacturing industry was controlled by 100 companies (or corporations). These companies had the resources to develop **new technology** which kept American companies ahead of their competitors.

> **KEY CONCEPT: TECHNOLOGICAL DEVELOPMENT** is the application or use of scientific discoveries in industry.

America also benefited from the war in another way. The US mainland was **undamaged** during the war so the country did not have to spend money on reconstruction like European and Asian countries. The US also benefited by **exports** to these areas. In the case of countries in Western Europe, for instance, Marshall Aid funds were used by those countries to buy in American goods.

PUBLIC INVESTMENT

US government spending (or public investment) increased dramatically from $10 billion in 1940 to $580 billion in 1980. Much of government spending went on the huge military budget; from 1945–70, sixty per cent of all federal spending went on **defence**. But there was also increased spending on **highways** (roads), **education** and **welfare**. This gave a huge boost to the economy. Its importance can be seen in the mild recessions of 1953–4 and 1957–8 which were mainly due to cutbacks in government spending.

Four guided surface-to-air missiles point skywards. The US government invested heavily in weapons research and development.

The **defence spending** was due to Cold War rivalries. A conscript army was maintained, some of it abroad in Western Europe and Asia. The US was directly involved in **two major wars** – the Korean War and the Vietnam War, as well as a number of smaller conflicts. There was also huge spending on **weapons research and development** – military aircraft, missiles, ships and submarines. The US also benefited from sales of its weapons to other countries. This led to the growth of many **corporations** and involved many thousands of workers. States in the South and South-West from Florida to California – known as the **Sun Belt** – flourished. The latter benefited most from the new high-tech and defence industries.

Government was also involved in other areas of the economy. The **Employment Act** stated that the federal government should try to achieve maximum employment, production and purchasing power. Many government economists followed **Keynesian economic ideas** which stated that government spending had a large influence on economic growth and employment.

In 1944, the government passed the **GI Bill of Rights**. This gave aid to veterans to buy houses, start businesses and educate themselves. By 1956, about eight million veterans benefited from further education. This helped the economy grow through the provision of increased **skills** and a boost to the **construction industry** (more schools and colleges).

Government investment in the **Highways Act, 1956** had an important influence on economic growth. Over fifteen years the government invested $43 billion in major roads crossing the continent. This gave an immediate boost to construction and employment in the various states involved. But it also gave an indirect boost to the car industry and to interstate trade and commerce.

The government spent a great deal on the **social welfare programme** put in place by the New Deal in the 1930s. This was added to during the 1950s and especially during President Johnson's **Great Society** programme in the 1960s. By the end of the 1960s this had the effect of reducing the amount of poverty in the country.

OTHER FACTORS

The American economy also benefited from **cheap energy** (oil) and **technological advances**. There were significant advances in research and development – these increased **productivity** (output per worker) and **real per capita income**. Output per worker rose by about thirty-five per cent in each decade.

The rapid technological expansion occurred in electronic and electrical companies, tobacco, soft drinks, chemicals, plastics and pharmaceutical industries. The number of scientists and engineers involved in industrial research grew six times between 1945 and 1961. Some inventions were more influential than others. In particular, **transistors**, which were invented at the end of the 1940s, were used in machines from computers to hearing aids. In another example, **medicine**, it was estimated that eighty per cent of drugs prescribed in 1956 had been developed in the previous fifteen years.

The Development of the US Industrial Structure

> **KEY CONCEPT: CORPORATE CAPITALISM** was part of the economic, political and social system based on private property, business and industry. The large companies or corporations which controlled the system wanted to make increased profits.

THE MULTINATIONAL CORPORATION, 1945–68

After the Second World War one of the features of the changing American economy was the **concentration of economic power** in business and industry. In 1945, there were over 300 recorded mergers in manufacturing and mining; this had increased to over 2,000 in 1969. These mergers created very large companies or corporations. In 1955, 30% of manufacturing sales was controlled by just 50 of over 300,000 manufacturing companies.

Some of these companies became **multinational corporations** – that is, they built and operated factories or plants outside the US. Some of the largest were Exxon, Standard Oil, Ford and General Motors. They

The McDonald's Museum in Des Plaines, Illinois. This replica of the first corporate McDonald's opened in 1955. The McDonald's Corporation became a large multinational business with franchised outlets all over the world.

operated on a worldwide scale because they bought raw materials from a variety of countries and sold their products in these and other countries. In the process the US became the **world's largest overseas investor**. In 1950, foreign investment amounted to $19 billion but this increased to over $160 billion by 1973. It was estimated that by the end of the 1960s over 1,200 US companies had manufacturing or marketing subsidiaries abroad. They became a form of **economic imperialism**.

[handwritten margin note: not just economically, but military investment]

However, US **foreign investment declined** in the late 1970s and into the 1980s as the US economy itself was in trouble. Between 1945 and the 1960s, the US accounted for most of the world's foreign investment. But by 1980 this had declined to less than half. But the type of investment also changed. By the 1980s most US multinationals were investing in service industries – banking, fast food, hotels and financial services – as US home industry changed to more service-orientated industries.

Causes of Multinational Expansion

The expansion of the US multinational corporation was due to a number of factors:

- Many businesses became **successful** in the home market in the US and these businesses tended to invest abroad.
- US multinationals had **advantages** of greater technology, higher productivity and better management skills compared to European or Asian competitors.
- The multinational corporations developed partly in response to the **growth of world markets** – it became easier to control widespread operations by improvements in communications and transportation.
- Another factor in the rise of the American multinational was the **huge investment in research and development** which paid off with many new products. However, the costs of exporting these were high so it was easier to build a factory in or near the foreign market to cater for that market.
- Federal **tax laws** encouraged firms to invest abroad. US firms were liable for tax in the host country, but not in the US unless their earnings were brought back to the US. But the attraction of host countries was **lower corporation tax** than the US.
- The federal government also helped by **insuring companies** against losses in politically unstable countries, particularly in South America.
- The **US dollar** became the world's main currency.
- The growth of the **European economy** in the 1950s and 1960s, especially the development of the European Economic Community (EEC), provided another prosperous market.

A number of factors influenced the **pattern** of US foreign investment. Most of the foreign investment was in Western Europe and Canada. In Western Europe most of the investment was in **manufacturing** but in some of the less developed countries there was investment in producing raw materials. This concentration of investment in a couple of areas was caused by a number of factors:

- The spread of Communism in Eastern Europe and Russia excluded these areas.
- The growing **independence movements** (or decolonisation) in Africa and Asia created unstable political conditions which put off investors. This was sometimes followed by the **nationalisation** (government ownership) of industry and raw materials.
- **Japan** deliberately kept out foreign investment.

Concerns about Multinationals

But the growth of the multinational corporation caused **concern** over the ability of the US government and foreign governments to control their operations. These corporations were able to take advantage of host country economic policies designed to build-up their own economies. Some were involved in **transfer pricing** where they were able to avoid making profits in high-tax countries. The US government, **supported** by Congress, was also concerned about the growth of the huge corporations because they wanted to maintain **competition**. They feared that a smaller number of companies would control the prices of products to increase their profits.

Foreign investment became increasingly important to corporations and this can be seen in the use of **bribes to politicians**. These were illegal payments to political campaign (election) funds, and also to federal government officials. By 1976, 150 corporations admitted to involvement in these activities. Exxon, Lockheed Aircraft and Gulf Oil Corporation were some of the major corporations involved.

THE GROWTH OF US FOREIGN INVESTMENT ($ BILLIONS)	
1950	11·8
1951	13·0
1952	14.7
1953	16.3
1954	17.6
1955	19.4
1956	22.5
1957	25.4
1958	27.4
1959	29.8
1960	31.8
1961	34.7
1962	37.3
1963	40.7
1964	44.5
1965	49.5
1966	54.8
1967	59·5
1968	64·8

Levi's

The growing popularity of Levi's worldwide was one example of the Americanisation of the world. Levi's and other products were part of the globalisation process.

GLOBALISATION

The growth of US multinational corporations was one part of the **globalisation** process – the closer **integration** of the world's economies and growing **interdependence** between different places. Through this growing integration, the fortunes of the US economy affected other parts of the world. US multinational corporations were part of the growing **internationalisation** in both trade and politics. They spread new ideas, especially cultural values, to other countries. Indeed their success depended on a world based on **consumer** goods, particularly American goods, such as **Coca-Cola, IBM** and **Levi jeans**. They were part of the **Americanisation** of the world with similar pop music – jazz and rock 'n' roll – and films. Critics accused them of spreading American culture and undermining local cultures. In spite of the increasing popularity and acceptance of American products in Europe, Americanisation also gave rise to **anti-American feelings** in some countries.

> **KEY CONCEPT: GLOBALISATION** is the spread of institutions, organisations and culture on a worldwide or global scale. It is usually associated with the spread of trade and industry by large companies or corporations to many different countries. Goods, services and culture gradually become the same in all parts of the world.

Global Trade System

The growth of the multinational corporations was eased by the development of a number of international agreements and organisations which created conditions for free trade. Some historians suggest that the US set up a trade system that suited their interests:

- The **International Monetary Fund** was established in 1946 to promote international co-operation in finance and to encourage stability in exchange rates. The US dollar became the cornerstone of the currency market.
- The **World Bank** provided loans for development programmes.
- At the same time the **General Agreement of Tariffs and Trade** (GATT) was signed in 1947. This began a process of reducing tariffs on goods which was continued with further agreements, or **rounds** in later years, such as the Kennedy Round in the 1960s.

This structure made greater trade and globalisation possible.

Supporters and Critics of Globalisation

The intense conflict between those who favoured globalisation and those who opposed it did not come until the 1990s. However, the arguments of the debate were outlined long before in the 1970s and 1980s.

Supporters: Those who favoured globalisation argued that increased world trade reduced worldwide poverty. By boosting economic growth, they said it helped poorer countries catch up with richer countries.

They also pointed out that less developed countries increased their share of world trade.

Supporters also said that when industry was set up in foreign countries, it improved the skills of the local workforce.

Critics: Critics of globalisation argued against that. They said larger US corporations invested in poorer countries only because they made greater profits from lower wages. Freer trade they said only opened markets for the benefit of multinational corporations. They also argued against the spread of American culture.

This globalisation increased the wealth of the better-off states (initially the US and later Western Europe and Japan) at the expense of the less developed world – adding to the growing rift between the **richer** and **poorer** countries. Some regarded globalisation as a form of **imperialism**.

THE MILITARY-INDUSTRIAL COMPLEX

Another aspect of the US industrial structure which developed in the 1950s and 1960s was the **Military-Industrial complex**. In 1961, President Eisenhower in his farewell speech to the American people, warned about the dangers of the **complex** whose influence was felt in *'every city, every State house, every office of Federal Government'*. This was the **link** (or connection) between the Department of Defence and the major corporations which provided military equipment. He was concerned that the political leadership might not be able to control this powerful and growing combination.

> **KEY CONCEPT: IMPERIALISM** occurs when one country has a great deal of power or influence over others, especially in political and economic affairs. Sometimes the imperial power may actually take over the weaker countries.

Eisenhower was concerned that its influence would undermine the values of the **republic** and the **democratic process**. He feared its influence would dominate domestic and foreign policy, heightening tensions with the Soviet Union. He was afraid that it would favour an **aggressive anti-Communist policy** and not favour peaceful co-existence. The Cold War threatened to make the military too powerful in American life, and that was a potential threat to freedom of education and scientific research. He urged Americans to guard against its increased power.

The **corporations** involved in the Military-Industrial complex included McDonnell Douglas, Lockheed and Boeing. The generals and admirals benefited from increased money for the armed forces. The complex also included the **politicians** whose states or cities benefited from armaments contracts and the growth of the armaments industry. This involved the space programme by the end of the 1950s. In the early 1960s, 22 of the 50 states of the US had a great dependency on military spending. However, it was not only selfish gain which motivated politicians and army commanders. They firmly believed in keeping the US strong in its struggle against Communism.

The Missile Gap

The relationship between lobbyists (for the arms industry), politicians and arms contractors became known as the **Iron Triangle** and its influence posed problems for political leaders. In the Presidential election of 1960, John F Kennedy campaigned on the issue of the **missile gap** between the USSR and the US. This suited arms contractors and army leaders who encouraged talk of a missile gap, even though there was none, in the hope of increased military spending. They used their influence with members of Congress. This was one of the factors – along with heightened Cold War tensions – which encouraged Kennedy to increase defence spending by over ten per cent for each year from 1961–3 when he became President.

Demographic Growth: Population Increase and Movement

One of the most significant aspects of post-war American history was the rapid growth in population and its geographic distribution. The US population increased from 131 million in 1940 to 226 million in 1980 – an increase of 95 million (or almost 75%). Each decade from 1940–80 saw large percentage increases in population – the largest occurring during the 1950s when the population grew by almost 20%.

GROWTH OF US POPULATION (MILLIONS)			
	Population (millions)	% Urban	% Rural
1940	131·7	56·5	43·5
1950	150·7	64·0	36·0
1960	179·3	69·0	31·0
1970	203·2	73·5	26·5
1980	226·5	73·7	26·3
1990	250·0	-	-

CAUSES

Birth and Death Rates

The most important cause of the rising population was the increased **birth rate**. The birth rate increased after the Second World War with the return of twelve million servicemen and the improving economy. This caused the post-war **baby boom** which lasted into the 1960s. There were 3·5 million births in 1947, and 4·3 million births in 1960.

Along with the increased birth rate, there was a decline in the **death rate** due to **better food** and improvements in **medicine**. New drugs such as **penicillin** controlled sickness and disease. The new polio vaccine eliminated polio, and tuberculosis, which was once a serious killer, was controlled by new medicines and improved living standards. Even when the birth rate declined in the 1970s and 1980s, there was still a further decline in the death rate so that the population continued to rise.

BIRTH AND DEATH RATES (PER THOUSAND OF POPULATION)		
	Birth Rate	Death Rate
1940	19·4	10·8
1950	24·1	9·6
1960	23·7	9·5
1970	18·4	9·5
1980	15·9	8·9
1990	16·7	8·6

Immigration

Immigration contributed also to population growth, though to a much lesser extent. In all about eleven million immigrants came to the US between 1940 and 1980. Some were refugees from mainly Eastern and Central Europe after the Second World War. Others came in after the Hungarian Rising in 1956 and after Castro took over Cuba in 1959. In total, refugees amounted to about twenty per cent of all immigration.

Mexican wetbacks (illegal immigrants) who were caught in a freight train in Los Angeles in 1953.

Greater numbers of immigrants came from **Canada** and **Mexico**. In the latter case, this was because of a shortage of **farm labour** in the South-West states. Legal Mexican immigrants were far outnumbered by **wetbacks** – those who swam across the Rio Grande to get to the US. By the 1970s America was experiencing large **Asian immigration** but this was controlled by new immigration laws (1965) which allowed in people with special skills or qualifications. However, the overall impact of immigration was small between 1945 and 1980 so that the proportion of foreign-born people living in the US declined to five per cent in 1970. But the new immigration of the 1970s and 1980s pushed that proportion up again by 1990.

% OF US POPULATION FOREIGN-BORN	
1940	8·8
1970	4·8
1990	7·9

Population Structure and Mobility

The increase in the birth rate and the decline in the death rate changed the **age structure** of the population. There were now **more younger people** and **more older people**. The younger people became the **teen market** – the so-called Pepsi Generation – for clothes, music, cars and increased college places. This contributed to the **general consumer boom** of the 1950s and 1960s which itself was caused by a growing, wealthier population. In the case of the increased numbers of older people, there was greater federal spending on health and welfare to cater for their needs.

The rapidly growing economy created **greater mobility** in the population. There was movement from cities to the suburbs, and from the countryside to the cities, within states and between states. By 1960 over 60% of the population lived in cities of half a million or more; this increased to over 75% by 1980. The spread of these cities, particularly from Washington through New York to Boston created the idea of a **conurbation** or **megalopolis** – a vast sprawling built-up area. At the same time the farm population declined rapidly in the US. Increased farm mechanisation and farm size resulted in the farm population dropping from seven million in 1935 to less than two million by 1980.

Growth of Suburbs

Within the cities there was huge move from the inner or central city to the **suburbs** helped by new roads, the widespread use of cars and cheaper houses. It was here that the vast new housing estates and new towns, such as Levittown in Long Island, were created. Between 1950 and 1970, American cities lost population to their suburbs ranging from 10% in New York to 35% in Detroit, and the overall population of the suburban areas grew by 35 million.

The growth of the suburbs had a number of **social consequences**:

- The people of the suburbs were **white and middle class**. This left the centre of the city to the poor and the wealthy.

- It also **divided the races** as blacks migrating from the South largely took over the central city areas. No blacks were allowed to buy houses in Levittown.

Levittown, New York, which sprang up from potato farmland in Long Island in the late 1940s. The builders, Levitt and Sons, used mass production methods to keep down costs. The suburbs of US cities expanded rapidly in the post-war decades.

- The suburbs were mainly for living in so that huge **traffic jams** were caused by husbands commuting to work. It wasn't until the 1970s that significant numbers of people both lived and worked in their communities as schools, churches, shops, businesses and industries developed.

- **Businesses declined** in the city centre – some newspapers, cinemas, hotels and shops closed and buildings decayed. The decay was contributed to by the failure of urban renewal projects and housing projects.

- Some criticised the sameness or **conformity** of the suburbs – Mam, Dad, two kids and the dog.

'Suburbs are small, controlled communities where for the most part everyone has the same living standards, the same weeds, the same number of garbage cans, the same house plans, and the same level in the septic tank.' They saw it as a **threat to individualism**. Some criticised them as places where everyone *'buys the right car, keeps his lawn like his neighbours, eats crunchy breakfast cereal and votes Republican.'* William Whyte in *The Organization Man* said that white suburbs had some good points. But he also said that they were similar to a large corporation which threatened to squash the individual drive or spirit that made America great.

- But later observers noted that the suburbs **provided houses** when there was a shortage. They also noted that **individualism** did break out so that with additions and changes no two houses looked the same.

A suburban home in the mid-1950s, the desire of many middle-class Americans.

Interstate Mobility

There was also mobility from **state to state**. By 1960, one-quarter of Americans were living in a different state to the one they were born in. The greatest beneficiaries of the movement were the states of the **Sun Belt** in the South and South-West, from California on the west coast to Florida on the east coast. The new people were largely following the spread of the new high-tech industries, though the elderly who moved to Florida and Arizona followed the sun. As a result of this movement, California became the most populous state in the US.

There was also the opposite movement from the southern states with the large migration of **blacks** to the North and North-West. Between 1940 and 1970, 4·5 million blacks left the South for the North. This migration changed the population structure in the cities. In 1950, there was no city in the US with a majority black population. By 1970 there were four, and a number of others had significant black populations. **Washington DC**, which was three-quarters white in 1940, became three-quarters black by 1970. This movement of blacks to the cities coincided with the movement of whites to the suburbs. It highlighted the **racial differences** between the central cities and the suburbs.

ORDINARY LEVEL

1. Study the figures on the Growth of US Population (p. 386) and answer the following questions:

(i) Which decade had (a) the largest population increase, and (b) the largest percentage increase?

(ii) Which decade had the lowest percentage population increase?

(iii) What conclusions can you draw from your answers to (i) and (ii)?

(iv) Describe the change in the balance between urban and rural populations?

(v) How do the figures for Birth and Death Rates (p. 387) help explain the growth of the US population?

2. Write **paragraph answers** on each of the following questions:

(i) Government investment in the US economy.

(ii) The multinational corporation.

(iii) US industry and globalisation.

(iv) The military-industrial complex.

(v) Changes in the US population.

(vi) US immigration.

(vii) The growth of the suburbs in US cities in the post-war decades.

3. Write **long answers** on each of the following:

(i) What caused the US economic boom after the Second World War?

(ii) How, and why, did the US population change between the end of the Second World War and the 1980s?

(iii) The role of US public investment in the economic boom of the 1950s and 1960s.

(iv) How, and why, did US corporations develop into multinational corporations?

(v) Outline criticisms of the US multinational corporation and globalisation.

(vi) What was the impact of US population change on society and the economy?

HIGHER LEVEL

1. Why did the US experience an economic boom in the 1950s and 1960s?

   OR

   What were the causes and consequences (results) of the US economic boom in the 1950s and 1960s?

2. How did US public investment contribute to the economic boom of the 1950s and 1960s?

3. Assess the development of US multinational corporations in the post-war decades.

4. Outline the changes in the population of the US after 1945 and assess the impact of those changes on US society and economy.

TEST YOURSELF AT
my-etest.com

"69

The booming American economy of the 1950s and the 1960s began to show signs of decline by the late 1960s.

During the twenty years prior to 1965, the US experienced economic stability and increasing output and employment. Minor recessions were corrected by government policy. Many came to believe that this would continue.

However, in 1965 these conditions began to change. The cost of the Vietnam War led to inflation (price rises). This was worsened by the Oil Crisis in 1973 which quadrupled the price of oil. The Iranian Revolution of 1979 further increased the cost of oil. Between 1981 and 1983, the US experienced its worst economic recession since the Great Depression of the 1930s.

The Economic Consequences of the Vietnam War

In 1966, President Johnson said to Congress, *'I believe that we can continue the Great Society while we fight in Vietnam.'* Like most Americans at the time, Johnson believed that the American economy was powerful enough to pay for both. In the late 1960s, President Johnson increased spending on the Great Society programme and on the Vietnam War.

Budget Deficit

Balancing the federal budget was the normal target of US governments in the 1950s. Deficit budgeting began under President Kennedy – but it was on a small scale.

Part of the prosperity of the 1960s was due to increased government spending. But this increased spending was not matched by increased taxes. Indeed, in 1964 the Johnson government brought in tax cuts. So government revenue (taxes) did not equal spending. This caused a **budget deficit**.

There was a federal deficit in previous years. But throughout the 1960s under the influence of Keynesian economics, the budget was in deficit every year from 1961–8. However, these deficits were small compared to the 1970s and 1980s. The average deficit in the 1960s (1% of GDP) doubled in the 1970s and doubled again in the 1980s. Since the government did not increase taxes to pay for the deficit, it **borrowed**. This put more money into the economy which caused **inflation** (price rises).

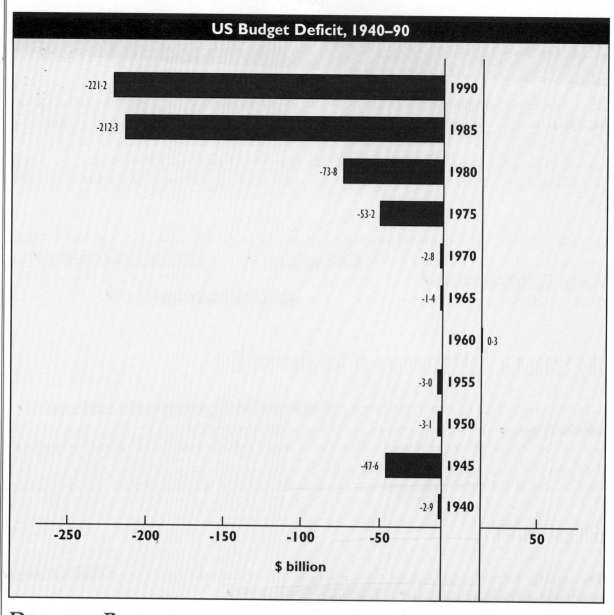

US Budget Deficit, 1940–90

	$ billion
1990	-221·2
1985	-212·3
1980	-73·8
1975	-53·2
1970	-2·8
1965	-1·4
1960	0·3
1955	-3·0
1950	-3·1
1945	-47·6
1940	-2·9

DOMESTIC RECESSION

From 1965 prices rose. They had risen only 2% in each of the years 1963–5. But they increased to 3% in 1966 and reached over 6% by the early 1970s.

Labour costs also rose. This was partly due to wage rises but it was also due to the fall in productivity (output per worker).

The US also faced increased **unemployment** – this began about 1969. In 1971, there were 7 million unemployed and the average duration of joblessness rose from 9 weeks to 12 weeks. By 1975–6, after the

In spite of US prosperity, there were also scenes of squalor like this one, typical of Washington slums, with the Capitol Building dome in the background.

impact of the Oil Crisis of 1973, unemployment rose to 8·5%. Unemployment hit teenagers, women, blacks and other minority groups hardest. During the 1970s the US was hit by both unemployment and inflation troubles. Unemployment averaged over 6% compared to 4% during the 1960s. Inflation went from over 2% to 13%. The combination of unemployment and inflation became known as **stagflation**.

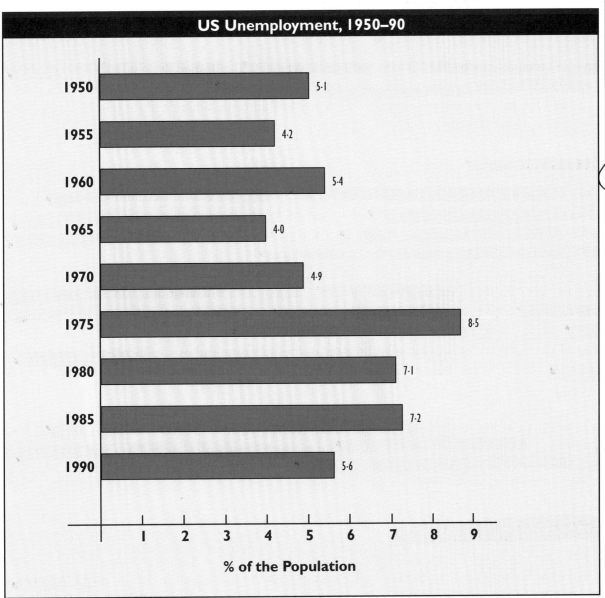

The US **balance of payments** (the balance of imports and exports) also worsened. At the end of the 1940s, the US held large gold reserves. But during the 1950s and early 1960s the US gave over $140 billion in economic and military aid abroad. This was mostly balanced by US exports but gradually the US gold reserves fell to one-third of what they had been. By the end of the 1960s, US imports were greater than exports so the US had a huge deficit (shortage).

GOVERNMENT REACTION

Nixon took measures to improve the economy in the early 1970s. In 1971, he put a **freeze** on wages and prices for three months, later making them voluntary. He also abandoned the **fixed exchange**

rate system set up after the Second World War. The US dollar was the backbone of the system. The US dollar was **devalued**, which made exports cheaper and imports dearer. Nixon also placed a **tariff** (taxes) on imported Japanese cars. But these actions only led to temporary improvements.

The economic policies followed by **Ford** and **Carter** did not help the economy either. Ford cut government spending, while Carter tried the opposite. When Carter increased government spending, this only added to inflation, as well as increasing imports, including foreign cars.

By 1980, inflation reached 13% and interest rates were 20%. The Iranian Revolution led to a doubling of the price of oil and Carter was given powers to ration petrol. At the same time, the states reacted against **big-spending governments**. This began in California where a state referendum passed Proposition 13 which cut state taxes.

REAGANOMICS

When Ronald Reagan became President in 1980, he rejected Carter's economic policies. In his **Programme for Economic Recovery**, he wanted to create employment and growth through improvements in productivity and output. He intended to do this with major **tax cuts** to encourage people to work, and to reduce government spending.

At the same time as cutting taxes by 25%, Reagan also cut spending on 300 government programmes. This action helped economic recovery. The economy grew by 10% by the end of 1984, unemployment fell to 7% and inflation dropped to 4%.
But while Reagan cut federal spending on domestic programmes, he increased spending on defence. This was the biggest peacetime build-up of US armed forces. This created a huge **federal deficit**.

In 1985, Congress passed the **Gramm-Rudman Act** to reduce the federal deficit gradually. It was planned to disappear by the 1991 Budget. But the next President, George Bush Snr, continued to face these problems when he took office in 1989.

International Competition

One of the factors which worsened the US economy in the 1970s and the 1980s was **international competition** from Western Europe and Japan. While the US remained the largest economy, other economies were catching up. Between 1966 and 1987, other economies grew faster than the US (3·3%), e.g. the Japanese (6·5%) and the West German (13%). These countries also invested more of their income in business.

The increased international competition led to more imports coming into the US, the decline of some manufacturing industry, rising unemployment and a worsening balance of payments.

GROWTH OF JAPAN AND WEST GERMANY

One of the competing economies was the **Japanese** which grew faster than the US economy in the 1970s. Japanese productivity also grew faster than the US. In manufacturing the average output per worker grew at three times the US average between 1960 and 1973. Some believed that Japanese success was due to their management style.

Another country was **West Germany** which led the Western European challenge to the US. West Germany recovered rapidly in the 1950s, aided by the Marshall Plan and its own economic policies of free trade, government support for industries, large firms and cartels, the banking sector and skilled workers. Between 1965 and 1979, German productivity grew faster than the US. The West German economy depended more on exports (30% of manufacturing output) compared to the US (7%) and Japanese (11%). West Germany was the world's leading exporting country because it spent less on consumer goods and paid its employees less than the US.

Even though the US economy was still much larger then the Japanese or West German, these countries had improved their position. In particular, they closed the gap in chemicals, machinery, communications equipment, cars and trucks. They competed against the US in a global market and in the US domestic market.

The US share of **world trade** also declined from 25% in 1948, to 15% in 1964, and 10% by 1970. The US was no longer the largest trading block – the EEC was. The US was no longer the fastest growing economy – Japan was. US imports amounted to 6% in the early 1960s; by 1970 this had risen to 16%.

Some claimed that the US was going through a process of **deindustrialisation** – as shown by the decline of such basic industries such as steel, and the shift out of manufacturing to the service industry, the transfer of manufacturing facilities abroad, the loss of some foreign markets and the increased share of the domestic market taken by foreign goods.

However, the decline was only relative; the US economy continued to be far larger than the others.

ORDINARY LEVEL

1. Study the graphs on the Budget Deficit 1940–90 (p. 392) and US Unemployment 1950–90 (p. 393) and answer the following questions:

(i) What is a budget deficit?

(ii) Why was there a budget deficit in the years 1941–6?

(iii) When was the Korean War fought? Can you connect the budget deficit to the war? Explain your answer.

(iv) What year had the most serious deficit in the 1960s?

(v) How many years between 1970 and 1991 was the budget in surplus?

(vi) What caused the deficits in the years 1970–91?

(vii) What was the highest unemployment figure in the 1950s?

(viii) Describe the trend in unemployment in the 1960s.

(ix) How did unemployment in the 1960s compare with unemployment in the (a) 1970s, and (b) 1980s?

2. Study the cartoon below (which dates from 1989) and answer the following questions:

(i) What is the newspaper headline on the left referring to?

(ii) What is the newspaper headline on the right referring to?

(iii) What is the message of the cartoonist?

(iv) What techniques is the cartoonist using to get his message across? How effective is he in getting his message across?

(v) Is this propaganda? Explain your answer. How useful and reliable is this cartoon as a source for historians?

3. Write **paragraph answers** on each of the following questions:

(i) The economic consequences of the Vietnam War.

(ii) US government economic policy in the 1970s and 1980s.

OR

Reaganomics.

(iii) International competition in the US economy.

(iv) The US budget deficit.

4. Write **long answers** on each of the following:

(i) How and why did the US economy decline in the 1970s and 1980s?

(ii) How did US governments cope with the decline in the economy in the 1970s and 1980s?

(iii) What effect had international competition on the US economy?

HIGHER LEVEL

1. Why did the US economy decline from the mid-1960s and how successful were government policies in trying to solve the economic problems?

OR

What were the causes and consequences (results) of the US economic decline from the mid-1960s to the 1980s?

25. The Affluent Society

Affluence and Consumerism

Post-war US culture was characterised by a desire (demand) for **consumer goods**. This was based on the **affluence** (wealth) and **productivity** of the country. In the 1950s, US Gross National Product (GNP) grew from $318 billion in 1950 to $488 billion in 1966. Average household incomes were twice that of the 1920s, and a whole new middle class was created amounting to 60% of American families. In the 1940s and 1950s the average working week was reduced by 10% while real wages rose. This increased wealth led to the growth of a **mass consumer culture**. But there were other factors involved as well.

A sign of affluence: the growth of consumerism – a middle-class American family with food for a year.

The growth of **consumerism** was partly fuelled by the rapidly **rising population**. Between 1950 and 1960 the population grew by 29 million, boosted by the post-war **baby boom** which lasted into the 1960s. This increased demand for houses, schools, household appliances, cars and so on.

> **KEY CONCEPT: CONSUMERISM**
> is the stage in industrial society when a great deal of goods are bought and sold. It is also called the consumer society.

The increased spending was financed by **wartime savings**. But consumers were also encouraged to spend with **low interest loans** or **instalment payments**; *'Buy Now, Pay Later'* was the slogan. **Credit cards**, first introduced in 1950, also made money more easily available. Not surprisingly, private debt more than doubled in the 1950s.

Advertising persuaded people that they needed all these products for the **Good Life**. The people were presented with a whole range of new goods – electric clothes dryers, Polaroid cameras, vacuum cleaners and refrigerators.

CARS, FAST FOOD AND HOUSES

There was a huge expansion in **car sales** because a car represented status and freedom, as well as being necessary for work and shopping. There were 2·1 million new car sales in 1946 but this increased to 8 million by 1956. By 1960, there were over 70 million cars registered in the US. By 1974, this increased to over 130 million. Only a small proportion were imported cars. The growth of the car industry led to the expansion of gas (petrol) stations,

A car showroom in the 1960s. Admiring looks at a new model car, part of the huge expansion in car sales in the US.

roadside motels and restaurants. It also contributed to expanding the suburbs and suburban shopping centres. The latter increased from 8 in 1946 to over 4,000 by the end of the 1950s.

The growth of **fast-food outlets** also reflected the new consumer society. **McDonald's** created a food production line to increase efficiency and reduce costs. Their successful operation, begun in San Bernardino, California in 1955, was later franchised throughout the US. They were generally based in the new suburbs and along the new highways. They influenced the change in eating habits of Americans who, before this, rarely ate out because of the expense.

There was a also a huge expansion in **house construction**, partly to compensate for the lack of it during the war. The **GI Bill of Rights** guaranteed mortgages for veterans, and the **Housing Act, 1949** committed the federal government to building subsidised housing for poorer families. Fifteen million houses were built in the US between 1945 and 1955 and many of these were in suburbs. By 1960, sixty per cent of Americans owned their own homes. They were aided by mass production techniques in housing which created vast new towns but also reduced the cost of housing. The new houses had to be fitted out with **household goods**, increasing the demand for washing machines, dishwashers and furnishings, as people's lives became more comfortable.

CARS AND HOUSEHOLD APPLIANCES (% OWNERSHIP IN POPULATION)					
	Cars	Radios	Televisions	Fridges	Washing Machines
1940	58	81	-	71	-
1946	-	88	0·002	-	-
1950	-	95	9	91	73
1960	75	95	87	90	70
1970	79	99	98	100	73
1980	86	99	98	100	75
1990	84	99	98	100	75

TELEVISION

Television was part of the consumer demand but it also caused it. By 1948, few Americans had seen television as only 172,000 families had a set. But then a huge boom in television sales began. By 1952, there were over 15 million television sets and by 1960 over 90% of houses owned at least one set. This expansion continued as colour replaced black and white, so that by 1970 almost 40% of houses had colour sets.

Increased sales of televisions were part of the growing consumer demand but it also caused it by advertising other products of the consumer society.

Television dominated **home life**. Household activities stopped as families tuned into their favourite programmes. Forty-four million people saw an episode of *I Love Lucy*, a weekly comedy show in 1953. By 1960, 50% of Americans listed television as their favourite leisure activity. It also contributed to the spread of the **consumer culture** or **consumerism** by advertising and standardising tastes. It helped create the **mass market** and thus reinforced the rising consumerism of the 1950s and 1960s. **Advertisers** saw the potential of television. They geared their ads in the 1950s to young, middle-class families. *'We are after a specific audience, the young housewife ... with two to four kids who has to buy clothing, the food, the soaps and the home remedies.'*

There was also a new **teenage market** for records, record players, juke-boxes and clothes. Teenagers earned money working part-time in shops or fast-food outlets or got increased allowances from their more prosperous parents. Sales of records of the new rock 'n' roll jumped three times in six years between 1954 and 1960. But teenagers also wanted **cars**. By 1958, 6 million teenagers had licences to drive, and about 1·5 million of them owned cars.

This big General Electric Spacemaker gives you almost twice as much room inside...

GENERAL ⊛ ELECTRIC

The new kitchen with the large fridge and freezer well stocked with food.

CRITICS OF THE CONSUMER SOCIETY

Critics of the new mass consumer culture said it was **tacky** and **showy**. They disliked the ugly roadside hoardings, criticised the mass entertainment of the movies and Disneyland, and laughed at the huge **gas-guzzling** cars with their flashy designs – *'like jukeboxes on wheels'*, they said. In his book, *The Affluent Society*, J K Galbraith said Americans were too concerned with materialism. He said more money should be spent on improving the quality of life.

A more effective critic of **consumerism** and the **corporate capitalism** which gained from it was **Ralph Nader**. He was a graduate of Harvard Law School who began a one-man campaign against the giants of American business and industry. His book, *Unsafe at Any Speed*, highlighted defects in a General Motors' car and led to improvements in motor safety. But this one-man operator was soon joined by his **Nader's Raiders** – young lawyers and researchers – as they investigated the food industry, federal commissions, pollution and much more. Their campaigns led to many laws to protect the consumer.

The consumer advocate, Ralph Nader, with a young girl demonstrating the automobile airbag in 1977. Nader's Raiders led many campaigns to improve laws to protect the consumer.

Equally strong criticism came from Michael Harrington's book *Other America* where he highlighted the **poverty** in the midst of affluence. Whatever the spending of the middle classes, he pointed out that more than twenty per cent of the US population lived below the **poverty line** – the amount of money needed to maintain a family at a minimum standard of living.

The consumer culture was rejected by the **Beat generation** of the 1950s and the **counter-culture** of the 1960s. The **beats** (or beatniks) rejected middle-class consumerism and followed a **bohemian** way of life. They were generally in their 30s and 40s but their numbers were small – no more than a thousand or so – and their movement didn't last long. But their message was spread wider through witty poems, books and songs. In the 1960s, the **Hippies** rejected consumer culture by wearing army surplus gear and second-hand clothing.

Yuppies of the 1980s

The consumer culture took a downturn as the American economy worsened in the late 1960s and 1970s. However, consumerism and the consumer culture were by then established trademarks of the American economy and an integral part of economic progress. Consumer spending revived again in the **1980s** when new wealth was created out of stock market speculation. More than 100,000 millionaires were created each year and this fuelled a new surge in consumer spending. The **yuppies** (young upwardly mobile professionals) of the 1980s spent their money on luxury goods such as imported quality cars, designer clothes, expensive hi-fi equipment or they fitted out a home gym. Their attitude was expressed in 1987 by Gordon Gekko in the film *Wall Street*, when he said, *'greed is good'*.

In spite of its critics, the consumer culture provided people with a more comfortable life, especially better food and housing than had existed before. It also increased employment to provide those products. All this encouraged even greater expectations that other aspects of the American way of life could be improved.

Leisure

In the 1950s, *Business Week* magazine said, *'Never have so many people had so much time on their hands – with pay.'* This was the key to the huge expansion of the leisure industry, which had begun in the early twentieth century but expanded enormously after the Second World War.

Sport

Sport benefited enormously from the greater demand for leisure time activities. Increased wealth, the greater amount of leisure time, the use of the car and the television increased the popularity of sport. It was estimated that 35 million attended football matches, including college football, in 1953; this was followed by 15 million at major league baseball matches and over 2 million at professional basketball matches. But television also popularised sport, as radio had done so in the 1920s and 1930s. Fifty million watched the football playoff in 1958 and the success of this, and later playoffs, gave rise to the launch of the **Super Bowl** in 1966 as a marketing device to heighten interest in football. By now, of course, many sportsmen were professionals, ensuring a good living from their chosen sport.

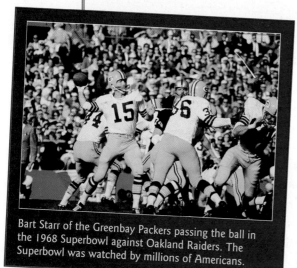

Bart Starr of the Greenbay Packers passing the ball in the 1968 Superbowl against Oakland Raiders. The Superbowl was watched by millions of Americans.

The changing pattern of **golf** playing illustrated how sport responded to the greater demand. Before the Second World War, golf was played by the **privileged few** in private clubs. But in the 1950s, spurred on by television and the example of President Eisenhower who loved to play golf, the sport was taken over by the **middle classes**. From the late 1950s to the 1970s there was a huge **construction boom** in golf courses. Six thousand golf courses were built in those years to cater for the new participants. In the process, too, golf had to gradually open its doors to **blacks**. However, the building of new golf courses slowed down due to increased construction and land costs. But in 1988 – the centenary year of golf in America – 20 million people played over 400 million rounds of golf on over 12,000 courses.

Changing work practices influenced the forms of leisure people enjoyed. Before the Second World War, workers experienced hard labour with longer working hours. Leisure time was relaxing, watching a game or listening to radio. After the war, **mechanisation** made tasks easier and more routine; these did not offer enough stimulation for workers; *'I felt so stifled, my brain wasn't needed anymore,'* said one. This led to greater participation in sports. In addition to just watching the popular sports, there was also increased **participation** in more extreme sports such as skiing, skydiving, mountain biking, surfing as well as mountain and rock climbing. The new work practices also led to the growth of fitness clubs and the sale of sports equipment.

WEEKLY HOURS OF RECREATION AND WORK, 1975	Men (Hours)	Women (Hours)
Working on the job	33·1	16·9
Working in the house and shopping	13·5	30·1
Total Recreation	33·3	31·9
Television	14·8	14·0
Sports, entertainment, travel, hobbies	14·0	13·9
Meals out, gardening, movies, bars	4·5	4·0

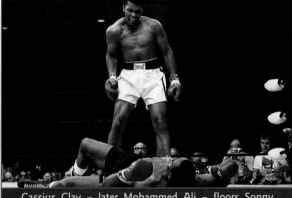
Cassius Clay – later Mohammed Ali – floors Sonny Liston in 1965 to win the World Heavyweight title.

KEY PERSONALITY: MUHAMMAD ALI

Muhammad Ali was born **Cassius Clay** in Louisville, Kentucky in 1942. He took up **boxing** at 12, and over the next 6 years fought 108 fights as an amateur. In 1960, at the age of 18, he won an **Olympic Gold medal** in Rome. He returned to a victory parade in Louisville.

However, Louisville was then part of the **segregated South** and so even though he was an Olympic champion, Clay was refused service at a local restaurant. Clay was openly critical of the treatment of his fellow blacks or African-Americans – some time later he threw his Olympic medal in the river as a protest.

Soon after his Olympic victory, Clay became a **professional heavyweight boxer**. His success depended on dedicated training, his **dancing** style of boxing and his constant talk. He used his speed and mobility to dance his way to victory – it was said that *'he floated like a butterfly and stung like a bee'*. He invented what was later called the **Ali Shuffle**, a rapid foot movement which confused his opponents. His constant talking both inside and outside the ring was also part of his style – he even predicted the rounds in which he would defeat opponents; *'To prove I'm great he will fall in eight.'* He became known as the **Louisville Lip** which got him great publicity, but it also turned some people against him.

In 1964, Clay defeated **Sonny Liston** to become Heavyweight Champion of the World for the first time. Also, at this time he came under the influence of **Malcolm X**, the Black Muslim leader. After the Liston fight, Clay announced he was converting to the Muslim religion and becoming a member of the **Nation of Islam**. He changed his name to Cassius X, to signify the former slave status of blacks, and later to **Muhammad Ali**. When Malcolm X left the Nation of Islam, or Black Muslims as they were also called, Ali did not follow him.

Ali continued his successful career as heavyweight champion by defending his title against all-comers. In 1967, however, his career changed dramatically when he was called up for the **draft** (military service) in **Vietnam**. He refused to go on religious grounds, as a practising Muslim minister. *'I ain't got no quarrel with the Vietcong,'* he said. Ali's refusal to join the army caused huge controversy. His boxing licenses were revoked, he was stripped of his title and his passport was taken up. He was jailed, but let out on bail while he appealed against his conviction through to the Supreme Court.

Public opinion began changing against the war, and Ali made his comeback after two and a half years. In 1970, he defeated Jerry **Quarry**, the Great White Hope. However, he lost to the champion, Joe **Frazier** as a result of his long layoff. But, soon after, the **Supreme Court** reversed his conviction and upheld his position as a conscientious objector.

Ali continued to fight – his most famous victories were the **Rumble in the Jungle** against George **Foreman**, who had beaten Frazier; this was followed by his great fight – the **Thrilla in Manila** – against Frazier. Ali then lost his title to Leon **Spinks** before winning it back a third time. He retired at 38 in 1979, probably the greatest heavyweight boxer of all time.

Ali was also involved in **politics** – he supported Jimmy Carter's Presidential campaign in 1980 and worked for the release of four US hostages captured in Lebanon. Ali was diagnosed with **Parkinson's Disease** in 1982.

Television as Leisure

But in spite of the growth of sports and other leisure activities, **television was the main source of leisure** – *'the piece of furniture that stares back at you,'* said comedian Bob Hope. Record audiences watched *I Love Lucy* and 65 million people watched *Peter Pan* in 1955. Successful radio programmes moved over to television such as the *$64,000 Question* (a quiz show) and *Gunsmoke* (a Western series). The first **soap operas** appeared in 1956 and they were targeted at women. Many shows portrayed middle-class families in suburban homes. To ease the burden on the working mother, inside or outside the home, companies produced **TV dinners** and 25 million were sold in 1955.

But not everybody was happy with these developments. Critics said television was *'chewing gum for the mind'*. Some blamed increased violence and changing behaviour patterns on television.

Movies, Books and Musicals

Movies went into decline in the 1950s and 1960s. The weekly audience was down to 36 million from a high of 86 million in 1946. The rise of television – entertainment at home – and the movement of people from the city centres where the cinemas were located contributed to the decline. Movies fought back with new **technological advances** – widescreen format, improved colour, the drive-in cinema and **epics** such as *Ben Hur* and *The Ten Commandments*. But they failed to stop the decline. Movies had to wait until the 1970s before they experienced rising numbers again as teenagers and those in their twenties increased its popularity.

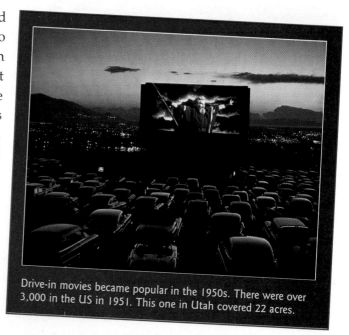

Drive-in movies became popular in the 1950s. There were over 3,000 in the US in 1951. This one in Utah covered 22 acres.

Book publishing boomed, helped by the **paperback revolution**. Americans bought fifty per cent more books in the 1950s compared to the previous decade. Publishers put their success down to television. They said Americans stayed at home to watch their favourite programmes and when the show was over, it was *'too late to go out and too early to go to bed'*. So they read books ranging from *Peyton Place* (a mixture of adultery, drunkenness, greed and murder) to self-help guides such as *The Power of Positive Thinking*.

Musicals were also popular in the 1950s. They packed theatres to see *Guys 'n' Dolls*, *The King and I*, *West Side Story* and the most successful of all, *My Fair Lady*. All these became successful films in later decades. But the costs of production, the movement of the middle classes from the city centres and the attraction of other forms of entertainment contributed to the **decline of theatre and musicals** in the 1960s and 1970s.

The leisure industry also catered for **younger people**. The television stations had children's shows in the mornings. The Disney company used television to promote its first **Disneyland®** built in California in 1955. It created Fantasyland, Frontierland and Main Street USA, as well as attracting four million visitors in its first seven weeks. Later **Walt Disney World®** was built in Florida on the same successful pattern. There were also new fads or gimmicks aimed at the youth market and some of these such as Frisbees and hula-hoops were very successful. By the late 1970s and the 1980s **computer games** became a huge attraction which fuelled a new industry.

The Role of Work

Work was highly valued in American society in the 1950s and 1960s. Some said America's success was based on the **work ethic** – a code of behaviour which valued thrift, discipline, hard work and individualism. Work was important for a good life. *'Work made men useful.'*

The work ethic was part of the **American dream** – work provided the means of improving a person's life. Americans believed that individuals were rewarded for their work according to their merits and not according to their birth, family ties or length of service.

UNEMPLOYMENT

For twenty years up to the end of the 1960s there was plenty work for everybody. Unemployment remained low, and there was much part-time work available for students.
It was not until the 1970s that unemployment became a serious issue in America. As the economy declined due to the impact of the Vietnam War, and the two oil crises of the 1970s, US unemployment grew to ten per cent.

Unemployment in the US was higher among women than men, higher among blacks than whites, higher among young than adults and higher among less educated and skilled compared to more educated and higher skilled.

Decline of Manufacturing Work

But the **nature of the work** also changed. In the 1950s, manufacturing industry (blue-collar work) was an important part of US employment – in steel mills, factories and engineering works. But this began to change as service industry (white-collar work) became more important. By the 1960s and 1970s, the service industry occupied three-quarters of the labour force. This change in the type of work opened up opportunities for women in the workforce – their numbers increased.

New York commuters pack this station in the city as they head out to the suburbs after work. Many of them were employed in the growing service industries.

The **structure** of the workforce also changed:

- By 1947, 28% of the US labour force was **female**. This expanded in the 1950s and 1960s until it reached over 40% by 1977. They were mainly older women returning to the workforce after their children reached school age.
- Workers became **younger** with a growing population. The under-35 age group grew from 37% of the workforce in 1960 to 50% by 1977.
- The workforce was also better **educated**. Between 1958 and 1977 the percentage of college graduates in the workforce more than doubled. But black male participation in the workforce fell – from 85% in 1954 to 71% in 1977.

THE ASSEMBLY LINE

Work in American manufacturing industry followed the **assembly line system** devised in the early twentieth century by Henry Ford to produce his Model T cars. This involved the production of many identical parts and their assembly into finished products. His system cut the time involved in manufacturing goods and their cost. This increased worker **productivity** (output per worker).

It also meant the replacement of skilled workers by cheaper unskilled labour. The production was dictated by the speed of the assembly line which caused conflict between workers and management. It also created dull, repetitive work on the assembly line, and this bored the workers. Managers reported **absenteeism** and **poor workmanship** on the assembly line.

By the 1950s manufacturing industry was divided into unskilled workers, a large body of supervisors and production managers, and an office management staff of accountants, engineers, chemists, as well as distribution and sales staff.

THE ORGANISATION OF WORK

A **scientific approach** to the organisation of this work developed. It was based on the ideas of Frederick **Taylor**, an American mechanical engineer. He emphasised the job of **management**.

His view was that the job of management was to decide the best way for the worker to do the job and to provide incentives for good work. Out of his ideas, **time and motion studies** developed.

These ideas led to the development of **industrial psychology**. This said that the attitudes of workers to their jobs and toward the company was just as important as the assembly line. The managers should try to improve motivation by rotating jobs, and making them more challenging. This led to the new study of industrial relations to ensure that management and workers sorted out their problems.

> **KEY CONCEPT: TECHNOLOGICAL DEVELOPMENT** is the application or use of scientific discoveries in industry.

AUTOMATION

Throughout the post-war period there was increased **mechanisation** and **automation**. Some argued that the introduction of automatic machinery would cause mass unemployment. But the alarm and panic caused by these predictions was eased as time went by and other industries grew to provide employment for displaced workers.

Automation increased efficiency and quality control; it provided the basis for higher wages and more leisure time. The increased production changed worker-employer pay negotiations as productivity was now included to the advantage of the worker.

The role of the **manager** also changed. Originally managers were often recruited from the factory floor or supervisory staff, but now more and more managers were recruited from university graduates. This frequently involved further on-the-job training. Management promotion often meant moving to another city in the US.

Blue-collar workers often changed employees and jobs. On average over a 25-year period of working, they changed to very different jobs five times. The most skilled and the least skilled workers were the most mobile – the skilled because they could avail of higher pay elsewhere, the least skilled because they did not have any particular attachment to their work.

Migrant work also played its part, though at a declining rate. About 600,000 were involved annually in the 1950s; this declined to about 400,000 in the 1960s. This was largely because of improvements in the economy and the demand for permanent labour. Migrant workers were mainly young, male and often from the southern states of the US. They were usually employed in agricultural work and followed the ripening of the crops from citrus fruits in Florida to vegetables further north. Their work was casual, hard and badly paid.

CRITICISMS OF WORK

In the 1950s, there were criticisms of the changing nature of work. In *The Organization Man*, William Whyte said that corporations were forcing **middle managers** to conform to the values of the company. He said that this was getting rid of individuality and experimentation. Instead, loyalty and obedience to the corporation had become more important.

KEY PERSONALITY: THE ORGANISATION MAN

In 1956, **William H Whyte** wrote *The Organization Man*. Whyte was a journalist with *Fortune* magazine and he was critical of many developments in US society.

Whyte was an admirer of the spirit and freedom of the **individual**. The (Protestant) work ethic valued hard work, thrift and a competitive struggle. He was concerned that it was being crushed by organisations.

Whyte was concerned about the impact of the organisation on the individual. His views highlighted the role of **corporate culture** (the values, ideas and ways of doing things) in the operation of companies and other organisations. The corporate culture brought pressures on the managers to conform for the good of the company.

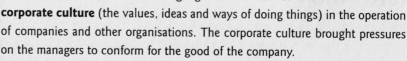

Whyte's typical organisation men were **middle managers** in large organisations (especially companies). The **organisation man** did not only **work** for the organisation, he also **belonged** to them. The organisation man conformed to the **culture** of the company, mainly to get **promoted** in his career.

The organisation man believed that his own well-being was linked to the well-being of the company. Many assumed that they would work for the company all their lives. **Loyalty, reliability and obedience** were important characteristics of the organisation man. These guaranteed job security and long-term careers.

Top managers worked very long hours – 50 to 60 hours a week – and more in work-related entertaining and reading. They looked on this as part of the job and promoted those who thought like themselves.

'We have, in sum, a man who is so completely involved in his work that he cannot distinguish between work and the rest of his life – and is happy that he cannot.'

The organisation had layers of **bureaucracy**. Each layer had certain power and the organisation man knew his place in this set-up. He knew he had to **conform**. He could not show creativity, experimentation, enterprise or independence.

In the world of organisation man, he was the breadwinner and his wife kept house. He lived in the suburbs and took the train to work each day. *'This is the new suburbia, the packaged villages that have become the dormitory of the new generation of organisation men.'* He wore a suit to work – he was also *The Man in the Grey Flannel Suit*. His wife availed of new **household appliances** which speeded up housework. This gave time for coffee mornings with friends – the so-called *Kaffeeklatsch*.

TRADE UNIONS

Union members grew in the US during the Second World War. The workers were organised by the **American Federation of Labour** (AFL) and by the **Congress of Industrial Organisations** (CIO), who merged in 1955. But unions faced difficulties after the war. The **Taft-Hartley Act, 1947** gave greater government control of unions:

• Closed shop agreements in which employers only hired union labour were outlawed.

• Workers' right not to join a union was protected.

While the numbers joining unions increased up to the early 1960s, the percentage of workers who belonged to unions declined throughout the post-war years. Thirty-five per cent of workers were unionised in 1954, but this started to decline, reaching 27% by 1970. There was a more rapid decline in the 1980s during the economic recession. By the early 1990s only 15% of workers were in unions.

The overall decline in union membership was due to:

- a shift from blue-collar to white-collar work;
- anti-union laws in the states;
- union corruption in the late 1950s;
- regulations on picketing tightened;
- inter-union squabbles;
- growth in part-time work.

The Changing Role of Women and the Family

THE ROLE OF WOMEN

In the 1940s and 1950s the **traditional role** of women was still popular. This was the role of woman as wife and mother. This view was reinforced by television programmes and films. However, at the same time **economic and social influences** were at work which eventually changed the traditional role.

Women at Work

In 1940, only 25% of women over 14 were at work – this was the same as in 1910. They were mostly young, unmarried and poor. Many were blacks or foreign-born whites. The Second World War and the post-war era changed all that. By 1970, there were over 31 million women at work, 43% of the workforce. Married women

More women went out to work. Many worked in the new service industries but some worked in factories such as the women seen here supervising the spinning machines at this nylon factory in South Carolina.

now outnumbered single women, and a large proportion were over thirty-five. The greatest growth was among well-educated, middle-class wives.

These changes were partly **caused** by the growth of the tertiary (or service) industry, labour-saving devices in the home, and cultural change (**the feminist movement**).

WEEKLY HOURS OF HOUSEWORK			
	Meals and Washing-up	**Laundry**	**Cleaning**
1925–7	24	6	9
1965	15	n/a	n/a
1975	10	1	7

But women were still a **depressed class** as they continued to experience **prejudice**. There was still the view that 'For the sake of every member of the family, the family needs a head. This means Father, not Mother.' The Atlantic Monthly expressed the view that 'What modern woman has to recapture is the wisdom that being just a woman is her central task and greatest honour.' They were still discriminated against in employment and wages. Relatively few were in skilled crafts or the professions. In 1973, 34% had clerical jobs and 22% were in service occupations. These were generally low-paid and low-prestige jobs. They were also paid much less than men doing the same job.

The Women's Movement

The Civil Rights movement provided the spur to the **women's movement**. In 1963, **Betty Friedan** published *The Feminine Mystique*. This attacked the idea that women could only get satisfaction and fulfilment when rearing children and minding the house. Her views sparked off a national debate.

Friedan took a further step when she founded the **National Organisation for Women (NOW)** in 1966 *'to take action to bring American women into full participation in American society.'* Its main aim was to end sexual discrimination in employment. It later developed other issues such as child care centres, legal abortion and paid maternity leave. It sponsored the **Equal Rights Amendment (ERA)** which guaranteed sexual equality. NOW depended on legislation and the law to improve the position of women. It publicised its message with demonstrations and protests. In 1977, thousands of women took part in a 2,610 mile marathon walk from New York to Houston, Texas to publicise the first National Women's Conference.

> **KEY CONCEPT: FEMINISM** was the belief that women should be treated equally as men with the same rights and opportunities.

Radical feminists were more aggressive than Friedan. They wanted to overthrow society which they saw as male-dominated. They burned bras, attacked advertising that *'demeaned women'* and insisted that men help with housework. They invaded men's bars and restaurants or picketed the Miss America Pageant. They developed feminist publishing houses, health organisations and child care centres. These were women-run organisations. Some hated all men. They expressed this in bumper stickers – *'Don't Cook Dinner Tonight, Starve a Rat Today'*. They were a small number but they got a great deal of publicity.

KEY PERSONALITY: BETTY FRIEDAN

Betty Friedan was born in 1921 and graduated from Smith College, Massachusetts in 1942 with a degree in **psychology**. It was at Smith that she developed a questioning of authority and a belief in social change. In 1949, she married Carl Friedan – becoming a housewife, mother of three children and an occasional freelance writer. In 1963, Friedan published ***The Feminine Mystique*** which sold three million copies in a year. She based her ideas on a questionnaire which she issued in 1957 to fellow graduates of Smith College at a 15-year reunion. She discovered that they were as unhappy with their lives as she was with her own. This led her to a series of studies resulting in *The Feminine Mystique*. This book inspired the women's movement.

The 1950s was the period of growing **suburbanisation** and the **baby boom**. *The Feminine Mystique* concentrated on the white **middle-class wife** who lived in the suburbs. The main idea of the book was that women were victims of a set of values and culture (the feminine mystique) which said they would find their fulfilment through their husbands and children. Friedan said women were in a trap and to escape they must finally exercise *'their human freedom and recapture their sense of self.'*

Friedan said women were not being given a chance to develop their talents. Women were expected to stay in the kitchen and nursery, get involved in voluntary community work, look pretty and get frustrated. She called it **The Problem That Has No Name** *'which is simply the fact that American women are kept from growing to their full human capacities.'* Friedan said that the media (press, TV, radio and cinema) manipulated women in order to keep them at home to sell them their vacuum cleaners and dishwashers.

'The feminine mystique has succeeded in burying millions of American women alive.' She felt women were not complete in themselves. *'The problem lay buried, unspoken, for many years in the minds of American women.... Each*

suburban wife struggled with it alone. As she made her beds, shopped for groceries, matched slipcover material, ate peanut butter sandwiches with her children, chauffeured Cub Scouts and Brownies, lay beside her husband at night – she was afraid to ask even of herself the silent – "Is this all?" '

She claimed that suburban women were **frustrated and unhappy**, comparing them to the prisoners of a Nazi concentration camp – they had become *'Dependent, passive and childlike.'* She criticised the second-class status of women. She emphasised that women could find happiness in careers outside the family.

More recent **critics** have questioned her account of her own life in *The Feminine Mystique*. They said her own account was unreliable and misleading. Some claimed she was bad-tempered, selfish and arrogant. Her 21-year marriage was troublesome; *'Although her marriage was violent, ... she and Carl were a match; she egged him on, and she gave as good as she got....'* Their marriage ended in divorce in 1969.

Some have also raised doubts about her **sources** and the questionable research methods of the sources she used. They said the experts she quoted were unreliable. However, Friedan and her book helped to change not only the thinking but also the lives of many American women. Her book coincided with other developments which were making women reconsider their role in society.

In 1966, Friedan co-founded the **National Organisation of Women** (NOW) which campaigned to achieve equality of opportunity for women. She was also a founding member of the **National Women's Political Caucus** in 1971 which fought to ratify the **Equal Rights Amendment**, but lost. Ten years later, she wrote *The Second Stage* which assessed the current state of the women's movement. She said that feminists must reclaim the family and deal with child care, maternity leave and flexible work arrangements. She disagreed with the extreme feminists – *'the disrupters of the women's movement',* she called them – who were advocating *'lesbianism and the hatred of men'.*

Success

The women's movement had considerable **success**. The Civil Rights Act, 1964 outlawed discrimination on the basis of sex. The federal and state governments passed equal opportunities laws, and presidential executive orders did away with the legal basis for discrimination. President Johnson signed an executive order requiring employers on federal contracts to take **affirmative action** to ensure more women and underprivileged minorities were hired. Skilled trades, such as carpenters and electricians, as well as professions were opened up to women; the numbers of women accountants grew more rapidly than men.

Greater participation in education was the key to success. **Yale and Princeton**, two of America's most prestigious universities, opened their doors to women. In 1950, from 5% to 8% of students in medical, law and business schools, were women – by the mid-1980s this had grown to 40%.

Legalised **abortion** was a very controversial issue. Seventeen states made abortion easier. As a result, in 1970 there were 200,000 legal abortions, which was ten times greater than 1968. In 1973, the Supreme Court, in the Roe v. Wade decision, upheld a woman's right to abortion in the early stages of pregnancy.

Women also became more successful in **politics**. There were women mayors elected in Chicago, San Francisco and San Jose (California). The first woman governor was elected in Connecticut.

The Limits of Success

But women still held few of the **top jobs**. In 1970, only five per cent of the country's three million managers and executives were women. The **ERA** passed Congress but there was stiff opposition in the states and it failed to get ratified before its deadline.

Poorer Women

The benefits of the women's movement were confined mainly to middle- and upper-class women. Hardly any of the benefits trickled down to poorer women. **Race**, **class** and **gender** operated against them. Poor, black or Hispanic women still suffered. A third of black families were headed by women who apart from being husbandless were also jobless. Women without skills or training were usually stuck in dead-end, low-paying jobs; but so were men in a similar situation. Between 1955 and 1981, women's earnings fell from 64% to 59% of men's; and even by the late 1980s only climbed back to 62%. Eighty per cent of all women workers were employed in the lowest-paying jobs and women comprised 70% of the adult poor.

Traditionalists

Some women were still **traditionalists**. They believed that women's place was in the home as wife and mother. They attacked the women's liberation movement. They were part of the rising new political force in the 1970s and 1980s – the conservative New Right which developed in response to the social problems of the time. **Phyllis Schlafly** headed this movement whose main aim was to '*Stop the ERA*' – and this they did.

THE FAMILY

Marriage rates grew and remained high after the war. Many married young in the 1950s – the average age for men was 22 and 20 for women. Public opinion polls showed that young people expected to marry and raise children. Divorce rates dropped sharply after 1947. Despite more liberal divorce laws in the 1950s, the divorce rates remained lower in the 1950s and early 1960s than since 1942. Illegitimacy rates also remained stable.

The **change in family life** came in the 1960s. Family life changed as the role of mother and father changed. With more women at work outside the home, fathers had to take a greater share of family and housekeeping duties. Increased social pressures led to the break-up of families. Families also became more isolated due to **mobility** – from city centre to suburbs, or from state to state. Connections to the extended family of grandparents and uncles and aunts were weakened or broken.

Divorce and Illegitimacy

In these circumstances, **divorce** and **illegitimacy rates** rose sharply. The divorce rate rose from 9·2 per 1,000 married couples in 1960 to 11·2 per 1,000 married couples in 1968. This was partly caused by more women at work who now had the resources to break away from unhappy marriages. The instability of marriage and the sexual revolution contributed to the rise of **trial** marriages or partnerships.

The illegitimacy rates also rose quickly after 1963. In 1963, 23% of births among blacks were illegitimate and 2% among whites. This rose to 30% among blacks and 3% among whites by 1970. By 1990, almost 30% of all births were illegitimate. The sexual liberation of the 1960s and the increased use of drugs and alcohol were blamed for the change.

By the 1970s and 1980s there were concerns that the break-up of family life would cause **further social problems** in the years ahead. In 1965, the **Moynihan Report** argued that the biggest single cause of poverty in the US was the instability of black marriages, as black husbands abandoned their families. He argued that government policy should help to establish a *'stable family structure'*.

RISE OF ILLEGITIMATE BIRTHS		
	Totals	% of All Births
1940	89,500	3·5
1950	141,600	3·9
1960	224,300	5·3
1970	398,700	10·7
1980	665,800	18·4
1990	1,165,400	28·0

ORDINARY LEVEL AND HIGHER LEVEL HOMEWORK EXERCISES

ORDINARY LEVEL

1. Study this extract on Ralph Nader and answer the following questions:

'Ralph Nader became America's best-known and influential critic of corporate practices through the direct assistance of America's largest corporation, General Motors.... In 1966, at a Senate hearing on auto safety, General Motors admitted that its response to Nader's charges [in his book, *Unsafe at Any Speed*, that one of its cars was faulty] had been to send out private detectives to find some 'dirt' on Nader.... All leads' checked out negative. Nader got wind of the snooping and filed a $26 million lawsuit. GM's president tried to get off with a private apology to Nader. Four years later, Nader settled out of court for $425,000 ... But, by then, Nader had already become a virtual legend. GM's action had made him famous and focused attention on his investigations.... Young lawyers and researchers flocked to work for his Center for the Study of Responsive Law and later his Corporate Accountability Research Group – groups known more popularly as 'Nader's Raiders'. ... [Their reports] have helped pass laws in several areas [motor vehicle safety, meat inspection, and safety in mining, for example].'

Adapted from A Weinstein, R Jackson Wilson, *Freedom and Crisis, An American History.*

(i) What are *'corporate practices'*?

(ii) Why did Nader criticise General Motors in his book, *Unsafe at Any Speed*?

(iii) How did General Motors respond?

(iv) What were the effects of their response?

(v) What have Nader's Raiders achieved?

2. Write **paragraph answers** on each of the following questions:

(i) The origins of the consumer society in the US.

(ii) The consumer society.

(iii) Critics of the consumer society.

(iv) The development of leisure in US society after the Second World War.

(v) The role of television in leisure.

(vi) Muhammad Ali.

(vii) Changes in US work in the post-war decades.

(viii) Automation and its effects.

(ix) The Organisation Man.

(x) The changing role of women at work.

(xi) The women's movement.

(xii) Betty Friedan and the women's movement.

(xiii) The changing role of the US family.

3. Write **long answers** on each of the following:

(i) How did the consumer society develop in the US from the late 1940s onwards?

(ii) What were the effects of the growth of the consumer society on the US?

(iii) How, and why, was there a huge expansion of leisure in the US after the Second World War?

(iv) Describe the changing images of women in America between the 1950s and the 1980s, making reference to Marilyn Monroe and Betty Friedan. (Department of Education, Sample Paper) (See also Chapter 26, Consensus? 1945–68.)

HIGHER LEVEL

1. Assess the growth of the consumer society, or consumerism, in the US from 1945 to the 1980s.

2. How and why was there a huge expansion of leisure in the US after the Second World War?

3. To what extent is it true to say that Americans *'worked hard and played hard'* from the 1940s to the 1980s?

4. What were US attitudes to work and changes in the role of work in the post-war decades?

5. To what extent was there a change in women's role in US society and in the US economy between the 1940s and the 1980s?

   OR

   How, and why, did the role of women change in the US from the 1940s to the 1980s?

6. What were Betty Friedan's criticisms of women's role in the US and what were the effects of those criticisms?

7. Assess the successes and failures of the Women's Rights Movement in America between the 1950s and 1980s? (Department of Education, Sample Paper)

TEST YOURSELF AT
my-etest.com

The Age of Consensus

The period from the early 1950s to the mid-1960s is often regarded as an **age of consensus** in American history. The majority of Americans seemed to agree on many of the same things.

The affluence of the 1950s created a growing **optimism** in America about the ending of class, religion and racial divisions. Some talked about a **post-industrial society** which provided a consensus about American society and how it would develop:

- There was a feeling that ethnic divisions were declining – the **melting pot** was working and people were becoming part of the American Way of Life.
- There was a rise of **patriotism** in the prevailing Cold War conditions.
- Organised **religion** grew stronger.
- There was agreement to **oppose Communism**.
- Many believed there were opportunities to be had for everybody. This was the **American dream** that hard work was the key to success; that people could improve in society and their children would do better than themselves. America was the land of opportunity. It rested on the idea that Americans could move up in society.

Overall, Americans were **confident** of their place in the world. This confidence was based on American prosperity – the affluent society. The people generally had very little fear or concern for the future – only their health and the danger of war and the Soviet threat. Americans were **optimistic** – their athletes expected victory; their economists expected economic growth; doctors expected to cure diseases and social problems too could be solved. They expected to be the best in the world.

ECONOMIC SYSTEM

The new economic prosperity was supported by the **New Economics**. *'American capitalism works, and in the years since the Second World War, quite brilliantly'*, said the respected economist John Kenneth Galbraith. Based on the ideas of the English economist, **J M Keynes**, it was felt that **US governments** could manage the economy and end economic depressions. They would keep down unemployment and inflation, and create economic growth and prosperity.

The American **free enterprise** (capitalist) system created **abundance** which would lessen social injustice. They believed the economy would continue to grow and this would satisfy people's needs. They believed it was creating greater equality in society; indeed everybody was getting better off. The prosperity of the 1950s was so widespread that some claimed that everybody was now middle class.

No Left Wing

There was **no left-wing** (socialism) in politics. No party wanted great social and economic change and supported the interests of the disadvantaged (the poor) against the rich or more powerful groups in society.

There was also consensus in **foreign policy**. Americans believed that foreign affairs were more important than domestic matters. They also believed that the **policy of containment** should be followed everywhere – not only in Europe but also in South-East Asia. This meant America should intervene wherever necessary to defend the **Free World** against the spread of Communism. Americans now supported **internationalism** over isolationism.

Looking Back

Looking back from the 1960s, people remembered the calmness of the 1950s. In fact it took the 1960s to show that much of the calmness of class, race and religion of America of the 1950s was **superficial**. The cracks began to appear openly in the troubled 1960s. Apart from that, not everybody in the 1950s shared the view of harmony and consensus. They pointed to problems with suburban growth and the consumer society. They also pointed to the unspoken poverty. But for most people all this was covered over.

The Red Scare

There was a steady build-up of **anti-Communism** in the US after the Second World War. It traced its origins to the **Communist Revolution** in Russia in 1917. The victory of the Communists there created a fear in the West and in the US that Communists would take over property and establish a **totalitarian system** of government. Some called it the **Red Menace**.

A member of the House Un-American Activities Committee (HUAC) reading a newspaper in 1953 which claimed that the actress, Lucille Ball, was registered as a Communist in the 1930s.

Even though the US and the Soviet Union worked together during the Second World War, the alliances created to fight Hitler and Japan quickly broke down as the Cold War spread. A series of incidents and events in the late 1940s and early 1950s increased anti-Communist feeling in the US. These gave rise to the belief that the US was **infiltrated** by Communist sympathisers and spies:

- Six hundred **US government documents** were found in a raid on the office of a Communist magazine in America.
- Canada announced it had caught a **network of spies** working for the Soviet Union.
- Truman played up the **fear of Communism** to get congressional support for the Truman Doctrine, the Marshall Plan and to set up the National Security Council to advise on security matters. By exaggerating the Communist threat abroad, Truman heightened fears about Communists in America.

- Truman also passed **Executive Order (EO) 9853** to get federal Loyalty Boards to remove employees if *'reasonable grounds existed for the belief that the person involved is disloyal to the government of the US.'* States passed their own anti-Communist laws and employees had to take loyalty oaths or lose their jobs.
- The development of the **first Soviet atomic bomb** in 1949, the takeover of **China** by Communists and the beginning of the **Korean War** in 1950 all heightened tension in relation to Communism.
- The main **newspapers** – the *New York Times* and the *Washington Post* – and **magazines** – *Time* and *Newsweek* – were strongly anti-Communist. Their message was that America was losing the Cold War.
- The **Catholic Church** in America was strongly anti-Communist. So also were the **Protestant Evangelical preachers** such as **Billy Graham**. He preached that, *'The world is divided into two camps! On the one side we see Communism has declared war against God, against Christ, against the Bible, and against all religion....'*
- The **Internal Security (McCarron) Act, 1950** was passed – all Communist organisations had to register and no Communist could be employed in defence projects.

> **KEY CONCEPT: PUBLIC OPINION.** The views and attitudes of the people. This is measured in elections or in between elections in opinion polls. In a democracy, political parties have to get elected so they have to pay attention to public opinion. They also try to influence and manipulate public opinion in their favour. This is often done through the media – press, radio and television.

HUAC (HOUSE UN-AMERICAN ACTIVITIES COMMITTEE)

As part of the growing fear of Communism, the HUAC began hearings in 1947 to investigate subversive activities in the US. Witnesses were asked, *'Are you now or have you ever been a member of the Communist Party?'* Witnesses were also expected to *'name names'*, that is give names of other alleged Communists. Witnesses could not plead the **Fifth Amendment** which says nobody has to implicate (connect) himself or herself to a crime. The Committee took the view that this was an admission of guilt. Gradually the constitutional rights of Americans were being whittled away.

The House Un-American Activities Committee in action in Washington investigating Communist activities in the film (movie) industry.

HUAC and Hollywood

In 1947, and again from 1951–4, HUAC concentrated on **Hollywood**. HUAC claimed Hollywood was infiltrated by Communists. They disliked the influence movies had over **public opinion**. Actors and actresses who failed to co-operate were blacklisted and some were jailed.

In 1947, the **Hollywood Ten** refused to discuss their political views with HUAC. They were jailed for terms of four to ten months for contempt of Congress. They were supported by prominent Hollywood actors and actresses who formed the **Committee for the First Amendment** (which guaranteed free speech in the US Constitution). But very soon a public backlash saw support for the Ten disappearing. Some towns boycotted films in which supporters of the Ten appeared. On one occasion, stones were thrown at the screen when Katherine Hepburn, one of the Committee for the First Amendment, appeared. Under this pressure,

Hollywood producers and directors withdrew support from the Ten, who were often blacklisted during the 1950s.

Between 1951 and 1954, 90 actors, actresses, producers and directors were questioned by HUAC. The Committee cited over 300 people in Hollywood as Communists, and these were blacklisted by the studios. They looked with suspicion on anybody with **liberal views**.

Even the actors' union, the **Screen Actors' Guild**, headed by **Ronald Reagan**, later US President, co-operated in *'naming names'* and blacklisting alleged Communists.

Prominent film stars, Lauren Bacall and Humphrey Bogart, head for the Capitol Building in Washington to protest at the hearings by HUAC into the film industry.

Alger Hiss, accused of Communist spying, takes an oath during hearings of the House Un-American Activities Committee (HUAC) in Washington in 1948.

The Hiss Case

One of the HUAC members was **Richard Nixon**, later President of the US. Nixon rose to fame over the **Alger Hiss** case. Hiss was a graduate of two of America's most famous universities and he served in the State Department where he had been one of President Roosevelt's closest advisers. He was brought before HUAC in 1948 where he denied he had been a Communist. But constant cross-questioning by Nixon, who was supplied with information by the FBI, broke Hiss down. Hiss was later charged with perjury and found guilty, and Nixon became a national hero.

The Hiss case encouraged people to believe that Communists could be found in high places. This was reinforced when **Julius and Ethel Rosenberg** were arrested for spying. They were part of a spy ring which passed **atomic secrets** to the Soviet Union. The Rosenbergs were tried, found guilty and executed by electric chair in 1953.

EFFECTS OF THE RED SCARE

Education too was affected by the Red Scare. Some feared that schools and universities would be used for Communist propaganda. They warned about the *'little Red schoolhouse'* and wrote articles saying that *'Your Child is Their Target'*. In high schools, **600 teachers** lost their jobs because they were accused of being Communists; blacklists ensured they did not get jobs elsewhere. HUAC demanded reading lists from universities and colleges, and some university lecturers who were alleged to be Communists were fired.

The Red Scare affected **other aspects** of American life in the 1950s and 1960s. **Movies** and **books** reflected the main thinking. Some wartime films had praised Soviet resistance to the German invaders. Now in the Cold War, Hollywood wanted to confirm its loyalty. Communists were portrayed in fifty films and many documentaries as traitors and spies. *The Iron Curtain*, *I Was a Communist for the FBI* and *My Son John* were examples of films where the Communists or **Reds** were uncovered and defeated. Books reinforced this thinking.

Civil liberties suffered, particularly **free speech**. Federal workers faced severe loyalty tests. They could be brought before Boards to answer for their views, and dismissed if *'reasonable doubt'* existed about their suitability. The **FBI**, headed by **J Edgar Hoover**, was virulently anti-Communist. The organisation kept records on suspected Communists, used surveillance and tapped phones. They leaked information about the activities of *'subversives'* to the press, which heightened tensions.

The Rosenbergs, Ethel and Julius, separated by a wire screen as they are transported to prison after their conviction for spying in 1953. They were later executed.

These demonstrators made clear their views during the trial of the Rosenbergs.

KEY CONCEPT: LIBERALISM was the political belief that was concerned with personal freedom and social progress. Liberals favoured gradual reform of political and economic matters. US liberals favoured government intervention in the economy.

All these actions generated an **atmosphere of fear**. Librarians took books off their shelves in case they would come under suspicion themselves. People were afraid that innocent comments would be reported to the FBI. **McCarthyism** was the high point of the Red Scare. The overall feeling of fear helped McCarthy to maintain his position for so long and, in the end, he was largely responsible for his own downfall. (See '1. McCarthyism (and the Red Scare)' in Chapter 21.)

Hollywood – the American Dream

The American film industry was dominated by Hollywood. The studio system which grew up in the 1920s and 1930s controlled both the production (making) and the distribution (showing) of films. Movies enjoyed huge audiences up to and including the Second World War.

However, after the war, the studios declined. But Hollywood still held its attractions. For many there was still the desire to go to Hollywood to become a **star**. For most people it was an illusion because very few reached stardom. However, Hollywood continued to have great appeal, and stories of actors and actresses, such as **Marilyn Monroe**, who made it to the top, inspired others.

The **success story** was also the theme of many Hollywood films, which needed a **good ending** to satisfy popular taste. Hollywood made everybody's dream come true – some called it the dream factory.

DECLINE AND CHANGE

But Hollywood went through huge changes in the 1950s and 1960s. This was brought on by:

- declining ticket sales due to television;
- government anti-trust laws;
- suburban living and new forms of leisure.

Declining sales led to a cutback in production: box office receipts declined from over $1·6 billion in 1946 to $1·3 billion in 1956 – a drop of nearly 20%. The revenue (income) of the ten leading companies fell by a quarter, while profits fell by three-quarters.

The number of people employed in Hollywood – the majority were craftsmen – fell from over 22,000 in 1946 to 13,000 in 1956. Actors, writers, directors and producers were taken off long-term contracts.

Hollywood was also affected by the **anti-trust lawsuit** against the studios by the US government. In 1948, the **Supreme Court** ruled that the studios could not control both production and distribution. This forced the studios to sell off their cinemas and to stop the practice of block booking and price fixing. This created a boom in **independent productions**. The major studios provided the money and studio space for independent directors and handled their films afterwards.

ATTACK ON HOLLYWOOD

The **HUAC** (House Un-American Activities Committee) hearings also affected Hollywood. The hearings which were hunting for Communists in Hollywood led to blacklisting of actors, actresses and others. The HUAC hearings, along with McCarthyism and the general Red Scare, eliminated **liberalism** in Hollywood. They also affected the **content** of movies. Prior to this, some films showed an interest in social problems, and some of them were box-office successes. But after the hearings, film producers were rarely involved in social comment. Instead, Hollywood emphasised **pure entertainment**. They also produced some anti-Communist films – about fifty were made in the late 1940s and early 1950s – but they were not successful. (See Chapter 29, The Mass Media in Modern American Culture, p. 457.)

THE STAR SYSTEM AND NEW TECHNOLOGY

While there were **fewer movies** in the 1950s, the quality was still maintained. *From Hell to Eternity, On the Waterfront, Bridge over the River Kwai* and *A Streetcar named Desire* all became classics. There were also some outstanding westerns such as *High Noon, The Searchers* and *Shane*.

Hollywood developed the **star system** in the 1920s and 1930s to sell their movies. The lives and actions of movie stars were given great publicity. In the 1950s, male stars such as Cary Grant, Robert Mitchum, James Stewart, Gary Cooper and Marlon Brando were matched by the female stars such as Marilyn Monroe, Grace Kelly, Debbie Reynolds, Lana Turner and Doris Day.

Marlon Brando, one of the stars of the 1950s, in *A Streetcar Named Desire*.

Hollywood also tried to innovate. They tried to give the audiences *'something television can't'*. The first of these was improved **colour** (colour was already used in the 1930s) – next came **Cinerama** and **3-D**. But these had short-term success, and could not compare with the success of **cinemascope**. The huge costs of production and the new technology which could not be afforded by smaller companies ensured that Hollywood was still dominated by **about ten major companies**.

KEY PERSONALITY: MARILYN MONROE

Marilyn Monroe, Hollywood sex symbol of the 1950s, was born **Norma Jean Mortenson** in 1926 to a single mother. Her mother's single status and mental illness meant that Marilyn spent many of her early years in **orphanages and foster homes**. *'The whole world around me at the time was kind of grim. I had to learn to pretend in order to ... block the grimness,'* she said. One of her foster parents encouraged her, *'Don't worry Norma Jean. You're going to be a beautiful girl when you grow big ... an important woman, a movie star.'* Monroe herself said Jean Harlow, star of the 1920s, was her idol.

Monroe experienced a **failed teenage marriage**. But she was spotted by a photographer while working in a factory during the Second World War. He advised her to join a **modelling** agency. By 1947, she appeared on the cover of thirty-three national magazines. She was spotted by Twentieth Century Fox, one of the big studios, and **changed her name** to Marilyn Monroe. However, for the next few years she only got **small parts** in movies. It was at this time that she also posed nude for a calendar.

Gradually, however, her career took off in the early 1950s. She starred in a series of hits such as *Niagara*, *The Seven Year Itch*, *Gentlemen Prefer Blondes*, *Bus Stop*, and *Some Like It Hot*. *The Seven Year Itch* had the famous skirt-blowing scene. She was partly helped by the controversy surrounding her earlier appearance nude in a calendar. Hollywood exploited this to achieve **sex-symbol** status for her.

Monroe, however, had an **unhappy life**. Her second marriage to **Joe DiMaggio**, a former baseball star, was a failure which only lasted a year. *'I didn't want to give up my career, and that's what Joe wanted me to do most of all.'* A third marriage to playwright, **Arthur Miller**, was also a failure which ended in divorce. She also had affairs with other movies stars, such as **Robert Mitchum** and **Frank Sinatra**. There were also reports of affairs with **President John F Kennedy** and his brother, **Robert**.

Marilyn Monroe suffered two miscarriages while married to Miller. She was also taking **tranquilisers**. She was sometimes difficult to work with and had a record of being late for work.

On 4 August 1962, she died from an **overdose** of sleeping pills. Controversy still surrounds her death. Even without any evidence, many believe that the US government was involved to cover up affairs with Robert and JFK. Her fame continued long after her death. Indeed, her death contributed to that fame. In 1999, she was named the Number One Sex Star of the Twentieth Century. Elton John composed *Candle in the Wind* as a tribute to her.

She once said, *'I knew I belonged to the public and to the world, not because I was talented or even beautiful, but because I had never belonged to anything or anyone else.'*

FOREIGN MARKETS

But Hollywood also looked for other markets. It increased its sales **abroad**, particularly as most of the European film industry had collapsed during the Second World War. Hollywood was encouraged by the US government who saw American films as important **propaganda** weapons during the Cold War – *'ambassadors of goodwill'*, in Truman's words.

Very soon the major companies began to **invest abroad** in genuine locations and to take advantage of lower labour costs and tax benefits. In 1949, Hollywood made 19 films abroad; in 1969 it made 183. Not surprisingly, Hollywood films dominated much of the Western European market. By the 1960s, half of Hollywood's revenue came from abroad. This compensated for declining revenues at home.

SOME BENEFITS FROM TELEVISION

Even though Hollywood suffered from declining audiences due to television, television provided **benefits** in other ways. Small independent production companies made low-budget films for television, usually a half an hour in length. The series *I Love Lucy* was the most successful example of this.

Hollywood soon realised it had to **co-operate** with the new medium, television. The major companies began to show regular filmed programmes. By the end of the 1950s most of the prime-time shows came from Hollywood. This replaced live broadcasting on TV.

Hollywood also supplied old **feature films** and **shorts** for television. Older films became features of **movie nights** on the main television channels. Very soon networks competed with each other for film rights. In 1966, ABC paid $2 million for *Bridge on the River Kwai*. When it was shown on ABC, in September 1966, it created history by having an audience of sixty million.

By the 1960s, television had become an important **market** for movies. Indeed film projects were now assessed partly on their potential for television. Television distribution usually took place about eighteen months after films were shown in the cinemas.

There was also the **made-for-television movie** which relied on low-budget production costs. In this way advertising covered the costs of production. By the late 1960s, there was a glut of films being shown on television so that film companies and television networks suffered losses. This resulted in companies cutting back operations. Ten years later Hollywood was making half the number of films it made in the 1960s.

By the 1970s and 1980s, huge prices were being paid by the networks for the television rights to show films such as *Aliens* ($15 million). By the end of the 1970s, pay TV, cable, satellite and video provided outlets for Hollywood productions. As well as this, new **marketing techniques** tried to exploit other areas of leisure. Books and soundtracks as well as the merchandising of toys, games and clothing all created new income for Hollywood.

ORDINARY LEVEL

1. Study carefully this advertising poster for the Hollywood film, *Runaway Daughter* (1953) and answer the questions that follow:

(i) What was **the Red Menace** referred to in the poster?

(ii) Why does the film claim to be timely in 1953?

(iii) What attitudes toward young people does the poster reveal?

(iv) What attitudes toward education in America does the poster reveal? (Department of Education, Sample Paper)

2. Write **paragraph answers** on each of the following questions:

(i) The Age of Consensus.

(ii) The origins of the Red Scare.

(iii) The House Un-American Activities Committee and the Red Scare.

(iv) The Effects of the Red Scare.

(v) How Hollywood coped with the challenge of television.

(vi) Marilyn Monroe and the Hollywood Star system.

3. Write **long answers** on each of the following:

(i) How did the Red Scare affect the US in the 1940s and 1950s?

(ii) Marilyn Monroe and the Hollywood film industry.

(iii) Hollywood – the American Dream? The film industry from the 1950s to the 1980s.

(iv) Describe the changing images of women in America between the 1950s and the 1980s, making reference to Marilyn Monroe and Betty Friedan. (Department of Education, Sample Paper) (See also Chapter 25, The Affluent Society.)

HIGHER LEVEL

1. How, and why, did the Red Scare develop in the US in the late 1940s and the 1950s?

2. To what extent was the period from the early 1950s to the mid-1960s an age of consensus in American history?

3. To what extent did the Hollywood movie business reflect changing cultural attitudes in the United States between the 1950s and 1980s? (See also Chapter 29, Religion, the Mass Media and Higher Education.)

4. How successful was the Hollywood film industry in adapting to changing circumstances from the 1940s to the 1980s?

TEST YOURSELF AT
my-etest.com

27. TROUBLED AFFLUENCE

Racial Conflict

BACKGROUND

The **American Constitution** (1791) said that *'all Men were created equal, that they are endowed by their Creator with inalienable rights.'* But the Constitution allowed **slavery** which was not abolished until the American Civil War in the 1860s. Even after the abolition of slavery, black America did not have civil, political and social equality. An important episode in American history is the struggle of Black Americans to achieve these rights.

A segregated drinking fountain in use in the American South.

Once the Civil War was over, whites in the **southern states** used their power to make the blacks second-class citizens. They did this by passing **Jim Crow** laws which introduced the **segregation** of blacks and whites. The laws stated that blacks and whites had to use **separate** public facilities such as toilets, benches and schools. They were supported by a Supreme Court ruling in the 1890s which upheld separate but equal treatment.

Blacks were also banned from voting. In addition, they suffered from violence and intimidation, particularly by the **Ku Klux Klan**, a **white supremacist** group, and some were even **lynched**.

> **KEY CONCEPT: DISCRIMINATION** was to treat a group of people differently because of their colour, religion, sex, age etc.

White tenants trying to prevent black Americans from moving into a government housing project in Detroit.

The Second World War was a **major turning point** for blacks. Thousands of blacks served in the armed forces and worked in the war industries in defence of democracy and freedom. But after the war they were still second-class citizens in their own country. However, **conditions had now changed** and over the next forty years black Americans (and other ethnic minorities) gradually, and often painfully, won civil and political equality.

THE CONDITIONS OF CHANGE

- By 1945, many black Americans had **migrated** from the South (where they worked on subsistence farming) to northern cities. This continued into the 1950s and 1960s, so many benefited from the greater prosperity (affluence) of the times. Others migrated to southern cities. Because blacks were **concentrated in cities**, they were easier to organise.

- Black **education** had expanded in the North and South with more schools, colleges and universities. This progress continued over the next forty years. A new, **educated black leadership** emerged.

- Blacks also depended a great deal on their **Christian churches** and on **Christian leadership**. Some of their most important leaders were clergymen and these gave them unity and a belief to carry on.

- When black Americans returned from the **Second World War**, they had **higher expectations** for greater civil and political rights and they were not prepared to accept less.

- There was a decline in colour prejudice as **whites** believed less and less that blacks should be denied equal opportunity simply because they were black. This was part of **liberalism** or liberal ideas. This was helped by leaders such as President Roosevelt and his wife, Eleanor, during the war.

- The development of the **Cold War** from the late 1940s onwards had a significant influence on the progress of black rights. The US portrayed itself as the leader of the **Free World** against evil Communism. This position was difficult to maintain when the **Old South** continued segregation and legal discrimination against blacks. If the US wanted to maintain respect in Europe and the new countries of Africa and Asia it would have to reform itself.

- The influence of the **mass media**, especially television which became widespread in the 1950s, was very important. All Americans became aware of the issues affecting black Americans. Very often television highlighted the brutal and oppressive treatment of blacks in various incidents in the South.

- Blacks themselves were **better organised**. The **NAACP** (National Association for the Advancement of Coloured People) founded in 1909, fought a series of successful Supreme Court challenges to laws in the South. The NAACP were later joined by other organisations such as **CORE** (Congress of Racial Equality) who worked in different ways for racial desegregation.

> **KEY CONCEPT: MASS MEDIA** was a medium of communication (newspapers, magazines, radio and television) which reached a large audience or the mass of the people.

THE PROCESS OF DESEGREGATION

The Army: One of the first areas to be desegregated was the **armed forces** – army, navy and air force. President Truman issued an **Executive Order** in 1948 ending segregation in the armed forces. This process was speeded up by the **Korean War** when it was easier to organise mixed units of blacks and whites. By 1954, the armed forces were desegregated, though the officer class was largely white.

> **KEY CONCEPT: LIBERALISM** was the political belief that was concerned with personal freedom and social progress. Liberals favoured gradual reform of political and economic matters. US liberals favoured government intervention in the economy.

Education: A much more difficult and controversial area was education. The battle here was carried on by the NAACP who took test cases all the way to the **Supreme Court.** In 1953 a new Chief Justice, **Earl Warren**, was appointed by President Eisenhower. Over the next sixteen years his Court provided a succession of judgments which opened up not only education, but many other areas of life.

One of the most important decisions was **Brown v. The Board of Education, Topeka, Kansas** in 1954. Here the Court said, *'We conclude that in the field of public education the doctrine of separate but equal has no place. Separate education facilities are inherently unequal.'* It declared state laws which required public school segregation **unconstitutional**. In a follow-up judgment, it said that public schools should be integrated *'with all deliberate speed.'*

In spite of the Supreme Court ruling, there was huge **resistance** to **integration** (mixing people of different colours) in the South where **seventeen states** had segregated education. White **Citizens Councils** and **Governors** all over the South resisted and they were sometimes backed up by a revived **Ku Klux Klan**. This resistance led to conflict as in **Little Rock, Arkansas** in 1957 where angry whites tried to prevent desegregation.

In Arkansas the state's school Board of Education planned a process of desegregation for September, 1957. But when **nine black students** attempted to enter the **Central High School** in Little Rock, national guardsmen stopped them. But, the Governor was forced to withdraw the National Guards and the students entered the school under police protection. Very soon an angry mob attacked the school. Newspaper coverage highlighted the incidents and forced **President Eisenhower** to send 1,000 federal troops. These had to stay on guard for a few months until tempers cooled.

Bussing: Although legal segregation in the South was ended by the Brown case, **segregated housing** in other parts of America resulted in separate black and white schools. Supreme Court decisions supported the bussing of black and white students across cities to achieve a **racial balance** in public schools. In the North, this resulted in widespread resistance – even rioting in Boston and Detroit – because black students were moved from inner-city ghettoes to suburban schools and vice versa. Eventually the Supreme Court softened compulsory bussing.

Federal troops stand guard outside Central High School in Little Rock, Arkansas, in 1957 after Federal courts ordered the desegregation of the schools there.

However, while these and other legal battles were won, by 1964 only 2% of blacks attended multiracial schools in 11 southern states. Even in the North, by the late 1980s two-thirds of black children attended public schools where they formed over 50% of the students. This indicated that in spite of Supreme Court judgments there were other social and political conditions which hindered desegregation. In part this was caused by **white middle-class families** sending their children to private schools, and leaving the public schools to black students.

University of Mississippi: In 1962, **James Meredith**, a 29-year-old air force veteran, attempted to attend the all-white University of Mississippi. He was opposed by the Governor who believed in state power over federal power; *'We must either submit to the awful dictate of the federal government or stand up like men and tell them.'* Meredith was only admitted when President Kennedy sent federal marshals to protect him. However, a few days later, a white mob attacked the university and two onlookers were killed. Regular army troops had to be sent in to control the situation.

Racial Conflict

Transport: Transport was also segregated in some parts of the South. Blacks had to sit at the back of buses and whites at the front. The battle to desegregate transportation was highlighted by the Montgomery Bus Boycott, 1955–6. (See Case Study: The Montgomery Bus Boycott, 1955–6; p. 436.)

KEY PERSONALITY: MARTIN LUTHER KING

Martin Luther King was born in Atlanta, Georgia, the son of a **Baptist** minister. He was encouraged by his father to enter the Baptist ministry instead of law or medicine which was his preference. He studied for the ministry and completed his education at Boston University where he was a awarded a PhD in 1955.

At the same time, he was appointed pastor of a Baptist church in **Montgomery**, Alabama. It was here that he came to national prominence as leader of the **Montgomery Bus Boycott**, 1955–6. He was inspired by the teachings of Mahatma Gandhi on the use of **non-violent protest**, which he put into practice in Montgomery. The Bus Boycott was eventually successful when the Supreme Court ruled that buses should not be segregated.

Soon after, King founded the **Southern Christian Leadership Conference**. He made good use of his gifts as a powerful and moving speaker to publicise the problems of blacks. In the early 1960s, he was involved in many **non-violent demonstrations** against segregation and he was arrested several times. He was involved in leading demonstrations in **Birmingham**, Alabama, over segregated hotels and restaurants. He deliberately provoked the Birmingham police to use savage methods which were publicised by press, radio and TV. Late in 1963, he led 200,000 people in a civil rights march in Washington. It was here he made his *'I have a dream'* speech.

'I have a dream that one day this nation will rise up and live out the true meaning of its creed: We hold these truths to be self-evident, that all men are created equal ....'

In 1964, he was awarded the **Nobel Peace Prize** and he also saw the passing of the **Civil Rights Act, 1964**. He was involved also in the **Selma to Birmingham** march to highlight voting discrimination against blacks. This led to the passage of the **Voting Rights Act, 1965** which gave power to the federal government over voter registration.

However, by now King's leadership was being challenged by younger, **more radical** (extreme) black leaders, such as **Malcolm X**. King himself became more critical of other **social and economic problems** faced by blacks. He was also investigated by the **FBI** who were trying to uncover any **dirt** to undermine his campaign. He became very critical of the **Vietnam War** which he believed was taking away money from the reform programmes to help the poor. He was planning a **Poor People's March** on Washington when he was assassinated in Memphis, Tennessee in 1968 on the balcony of a motel by a hired assassin, **James Earl Ray**. His death gave rise to widespread riots in the black areas of many American cities.

THE CIVIL RIGHTS PROTEST CONTINUED

Lunch Counter Protests: Non-violent protest became an important part of the methods used to change segregation. It was used in 1960 in the lunch counter protests. A group of black students sat at a **Whites Only** lunch counter. Their action set off a widespread lunch counter protest in fifty-four cities in the Old South These protests were highlighted in the press and on television. Their success in **desegregating lunch counters** led to greater student involvement.

The Freedom Riders: In 1961, black and white college students took **interstate buses** to test that the law against segregating interstate buses was being applied. One bus was firebombed and other Freedom Riders were attacked by crowds. Once again the **media** highlighted the issues and forced the federal government to enforce desegregation on interstate buses.

Birmingham, Alabama: In each of these cases the protestors encouraged a **white backlash** against their actions to get national and world media coverage. This was also the case in Birmingham, Alabama in 1963 when Martin Luther King used school children as demonstrators. The overreaction of the police chief, **Eugene 'Bull' Connor**, and his men when they used **dogs and water cannon** was featured on television.

Martin Luther King acknowledges the crowds at the Lincoln Memorial during the March in Washington in August 1963 when he made his 'I Have a Dream' speech.

Washington: Soon after, in August 1963, a huge peaceful rally of 250,000 civil rights protestors marched in Washington to advance their cause. It was here that Martin Luther King made his famous **'I have a dream'** speech.

Selma to Birmingham March: In 1965, half of the population of Selma county, Alabama were black, but only one per cent of blacks were registered to vote. Efforts by black leaders to register black voters were stopped by police and state troopers in **Selma**. When they attempted to march from Selma to Montgomery, the state capital, to protest, they were attacked by state troopers. But this shocking violence was covered by national **television**. President Johnson sent national guardsmen to Selma to protect the marchers who were now joined by **Martin Luther King** and other black leaders. Three thousand began the march in Selma and this had increased to 25,000 by the time the march reached Montgomery. This march won support for the **Voting Rights Act** which became law in August 1965.

Extracts from Martin Luther King's Speech in Washington, August 1963

'...I say to you today, my friends, that in spite of the difficulties and frustrations of the moment, I still have a dream. It is a dream deeply rooted in the American dream.

I have a dream that one day this nation will rise up and live out the true meaning of its creed: "We hold these truths to be self-evident: that all men are created equal." I have a dream that one day on the red hills of Georgia the sons of former slaves and the sons of former slave owners will be able to sit down together at a table of brotherhood. I have a dream that one day even the state of Mississippi, a desert state, sweltering with the heat of injustice and oppression, will be transformed into an oasis of freedom and justice. I have a dream that my four children will one day live in a nation where they will not be judged by the colour of their skin but by the content of their character. I have a dream today....

With this faith we will be able to transform the jangling discords of our nation into a beautiful symphony of brotherhood. With this faith we will be able to work together, to pray together, to struggle together, to go to jail together, to stand up for freedom together, knowing that we will be free one day.'

Division in the Civil Rights movement – conflict among blacks

But by now the civil rights movement was dividing. Martin Luther King's influence began to decline. He criticised American involvement in the **Vietnam War** and he also looked for **social equality** between blacks and whites. In March 1968, he was shot by a **white assassin in Memphis**. His assassination sparked off huge **rioting** and **looting** in 130 cities across the US. Sixty-five thousand troops were called out to quell the riots, in which 35 people were killed.

But blacks were also demanding more than civil rights. *'What use is a mouthful of civil rights and a empty stomach?'* said an unemployed black youth. Large proportions of the unemployed were black. They were **frustrated** by the slow progress of racial integration, the poverty of the **black ghettoes** and by white violence against civil rights marchers.

Out of this grew a more **radical** (extreme) black voice. Led by **Malcolm X**, the radical black movement advocated violence, and supported **black nationalism**. They advocated **Black Power** which expressed a growing pride in being **African-American**. They sought the development of a separate black identity. The black power slogan was adopted by many different groups. The most extreme of these were the **Black Panthers**, who wanted to gain black power *'through the barrel of a gun'*.

Bad social and economic conditions in inner-city ghettoes, combined with a growing violence, led to **race riots** in a number of cities, ranging from **Harlem** in New York to **Watts** in Los Angeles to Chicago between 1965 and 1968. (See Chapter 27, Urban Poverty.)

The Government and Civil Rights

The federal government was concerned about racial conflict and about the image which US racial segregation gave to the world. In opposition to southern state governments, the federal government played a vital role in getting civil rights for blacks and other minority groups:
- Both Truman and Eisenhower ended segregation in the armed forces.
- In the **Civil Rights Act, 1957** Eisenhower set up a Civil Rights Commission to investigate places where blacks were denied the vote.
- Kennedy brought in the **Civil Rights Bill** but it was not until Johnson became President that it was passed. The **Civil Rights Act, 1964** outlawed discrimination in public places including restaurants, theatres, sport stadiums and cinemas. It also set up the **Employment Opportunities Commission** to outlaw job discrimination.
- The **Voting Rights Act, 1965** organised **voters' registration** and banned literacy tests for voter registration. In 1968, discrimination in housing was ended.
- The government extended **affirmative action** by ensuring that companies on federal contracts had to provide jobs for minorities.

Reagan, however, tried to withdraw federal support for the civil rights programme. He also appointed more **conservative judges** to the Supreme Court. He also dismantled some of the welfare programmes set up under the **New Deal** and the **Great Society**, and these had mostly benefited blacks.

BLACK SUCCESS

Many African-Americans benefited from the civil rights struggle as a new economic and social black leadership was created – in sports, films, politics, and music. More blacks were registered to vote, and more were elected to state and federal Houses of Congress. This was accompanied by a much greater white acceptance of blacks. Opinion polls showed clear majorities of whites in support of desegregation.

However, this still left a large number of blacks in **poverty**. Black society itself became divided. Around 40% of black society achieved a **middle-class lifestyle** during the 1970s, but about 30% were still below the poverty line. The condition of these blacks was a class issue as much as it was a race issue.

CHICANOS AND NATIVE AMERICANS

Chicanos (Mexican-Americans) and Native Americans (American Indians) were encouraged by the civil rights movement to fight for their rights. Chicanos were used legally and illegally as farm labourers in the US. They suffered general white hostility, particularly in California and Florida. In the early 1960s, **Cesar Chavez** used non-violent methods of **boycotting** to gain improved working and living conditions for agricultural labourers.

Native Americans were even worse off. They suffered from over 100 years of discrimination and repression. By the end of the 1960s, their one million members suffered the worst education and housing, and the highest disease and death rates among any ethnic group in the US. Some founded the **American Indian Movement** (AIM) and took over Alcatraz Island and government buildings to highlight their conditions. This worked. The **Indian Self-Determination Act, 1975** was passed which gave Indians control of their reservations. Other laws gave Indians **religious freedom** and **educational support**. Tribes also won legal battles to get the return of lands taken from them in the past by the federal government.

Urban Poverty

BACKGROUND

In the 1950s and early 1960s, most Americans were happy with their way of life. The affluence (wealth) of the country led people to believe that if poverty existed it was only in **small pockets**. Then in 1962, Michael Harrington wrote *The Other America* which revealed the poverty behind the affluence – forty million Americans were living in poverty. This was about twenty-five per cent of the population.

A street scene in East Harlem, New York.

Traditionally poverty in America was associated with rural poor blacks in the South. But since the Second World War a number of changes had occurred which created the problem of **urban poverty**.

CAUSES – BLACK GHETTOES

During the 1940s and 1950s, there was **huge movement of black Americans** from the South to the northern cities. They fled poverty, racial discrimination, white violence and lynching to find a better life in the urban North. They sought jobs in the booming manufacturing industries. They concentrated in the inner areas or the centre of cities.

At the same time, there was **movement of whites** from the cities to the suburbs. This was often accompanied by a movement of industry to the suburbs. This left many decayed and abandoned buildings and factories in the centre. This was also a time of change in industry, as **manufacturing declined** in the 1950s and 1960s so also did the need for unskilled – mostly black – labour.

Instead of the better life for many migrant black families, the inner cities became places with high concentrations of unemployment, poverty, low educational levels and poor housing. They became **black ghettoes**.

TAXES AND HOUSING

The movement of the whites to the suburbs had another result; it deprived cities of **tax revenue** which could be used to maintain streets, schools, and public areas. In spite of federal funding, many cities were in **financial trouble**. In 1975, New York City was almost bankrupt and was only saved by huge federal funding.

The cities were made worse by government **housing policies**. The cities built over two million new houses by the early 1970s but this was not enough to house people. These public housing projects were often a cause of further problems because the high rise apartments only included the **very poorest people** and those with **serious social problems**. The government also provided billions of dollars from the 1940s for slum clearance or **urban renewal**, as it was called. This often meant replacing the old tenements with office blocks and luxury apartments, which increased the number of homeless.

WAR ON POVERTY

In the 1940s and 1950s Presidents Truman and Eisenhower had increased **social security payments** and established a **minimum wage**. President Kennedy continued on the same path but he also provided federal money for **school and job-based training**.

The federal government established a **poverty line** in 1964 – this was an income level below which people were regarded as poor. This included more than half the black population, almost a half of female-headed families, and a third of elderly people.

President Johnson wanted to use government resources to improve the condition of poor people as part of his **Great Society** programme. He believed that a **war on poverty** would give people a chance to help themselves. He set up the **Office of Economic Opportunity**. This organised:
• **Head Start** – where children went to pre-school classes.
• **Job Corps** – to provide skills for inner-city youth.
• **Community Action Programmes** which set up clinics and law centres.
He also provided $1 billion to help poor students in **public schools** but this was often spent by school boards on middle-class children instead. He also gave $3 billion to fund low- and middle-income **housing** as well as rent aid. He set up **Medicare** for the elderly and **Medicaid** for the poorer welfare recipients.

Johnson's war on poverty had some success. The number of people below the poverty line dropped from 40 million in 1959, to 28 million in 1968, and 25 million in 1970. This was also helped by the growth in the economy in the 1960s. When the economy took a downturn in the 1970s and 1980s, government spending was cut back and this, along with rising unemployment, made urban poverty worse.

URBAN RIOTS

However, before Johnson's policy could have any effect, riots broke out in 1965 in **Watts, Los Angeles**. These were sparked off by an incident between a young black driver who was drunk and a white policeman. The rioters looted and burned shops and businesses and threw bottles and stones at police. Thirty-four people were killed, almost all black, and over 900 were injured and 4,000 arrested.

Watts was the beginning of a series of urban riots which lasted from 1965–8, and affected many US cities – Chicago, Cleveland, San Francisco, Newark (New Jersey) and Detroit. There were 38 riots in 1966, in which 7 people were killed, 400 injured and 3,000 arrested. In 1967, the worst year, there were 164 riots. The 2 most serious riots – in Newark (New Jersey) and Detroit – resulted in 23 and 34 dead respectively and thousands of buildings looted and burned.

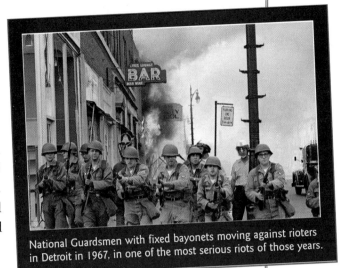

National Guardsmen with fixed bayonets moving against rioters in Detroit in 1967, in one of the most serious riots of those years.

Causes

Many **causes** were given to explain these riots:

- There was a **concentration of poverty and unemployment** in these areas, and most of the rioters were poor or working class. They were class riots every bit as much as they were racial riots.
- But for others there were **Rising Expectations** – much of the legal discrimination against blacks had been overcome, the civil rights movement give hope of a better life to blacks. But now there were other social and economic **barriers to improvement**. Indeed, blacks were better off on average than the 1950s when there was no violence. The black ghettoes in Detroit and Watts were better off than those in other cities.

> 'You go into a local store in Watts. Besides the rats and the roaches, the food was rotten. There would be some Jewish guy or white guy standing there saying, "The Hell with you, you're going to have to buy this anyway." Those were the first places people went, to burn down the store. What we didn't have in Watts wasn't civil rights. It was jobs, housing and education. It was a positive image of ourselves. We didn't know what they were complaining about in the South.'
>
> **A Watts rioter**

- There was also a concentration of **young people**, especially young men – the group most likely to be involved in violence.
- **Malcolm X** – Martin Luther King was not the hero of the young rioters. Instead of the message of non-violence they preferred the message of Malcolm X. He wanted blacks to be black, he preached black nationalism and spoke about inequality. *'I'm not going to sit at your table and watch you eat,'* he said, *'with nothing on my plate and call myself a diner.'* Some preached a message of black power with violence.
- There was growing tension between the **police and black youths**. Most of the riots were sparked off by incidents between white police and black residents.

Malcolm X, speaking at a Black Muslim rally in 1961, preached a message of Black Nationalism.

- The influence of **television** which made people aware what was happening elsewhere and spread a general discontent.
- There were also growing levels of **violence in society** generally and guns were easy to get.

Drugs and Crime

Poverty, unemployment and slum conditions were major causes of crime in the US. But they were not the only causes. There was also:
- The widespread availability of guns – almost one gun per person in a population of 250 million.
- Drug addiction and the cost of drugs.
- Inadequate number of police.

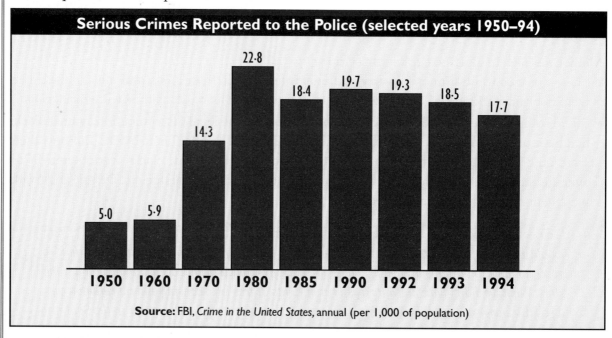

Serious Crimes Reported to the Police (selected years 1950–94)

1950	1960	1970	1980	1985	1990	1992	1993	1994
5.0	5.9	14.3	22.8	18.4	19.7	19.3	18.5	17.7

Source: FBI, *Crime in the United States*, annual (per 1,000 of population)

Crime levels began to rise after the Second World War. However, they jumped rapidly from the early 1960s onwards. Violent crime, for example, trebled between 1960 and 1977. The problem was more serious in the US than elsewhere. Compared with other industrialised countries, the US had the highest rate of reported murders, rapes and robberies.

Rising crime was largely an **urban** phenomenon. In the 1970s, 30% of all reported crimes in America took place in the **six largest cities**. But these cities only contained 12% of the country's population. New York, a city with a population roughly equal to Sweden's, had 20 times more murders.

Criminals tended to be **young, male, poor and black**. In 1975, three-quarters of all people arrested for violent crime were males under twenty-five. But the average age of criminals dropped in the 1980s. Crime was largely confined to a small proportion of society. US criminologists estimated that two-thirds of all violent crimes were committed by seven per cent of the people. These people were habitual offenders with a number of arrests. Crime also paid, particularly in relation to burglaries where arrest and conviction rates were very low.

DRUGS

By the 1970s, much crime was **drug-related** as the US became the largest **consumer** of illegal drugs. This pattern began in the late 1950s and grew more rapidly in the 1960s, partly encouraged by being fashionable among pop and film stars. By 1990, 6% of all Americans were drug addicts, but many more had experienced drugs. Surveys showed that 44% of high school students had taken drugs at least once, and about 12% were frequent users.

A warning sign to drug dealers, users and gang members, posted in a New York street around 1970.

By the 1980s, drug trafficking became a huge **multinational business** operated by **organised crime**. There were Columbian cartels linked with the Mafia and Jamaican, Puerto Rican, black or Mexican gangs in various cities across the US. Most of the drugs originated in poorer countries such as Columbia, Peru, Turkey and Afghanistan. Poorer peasants were dependant on the cash they got for their crops. In some places, guerrilla groups depended on the money from drug sales to fund their war against a local government.

Drugs were linked to **other crimes** and **problems**:
- Many drug addicts began to steal to feed their habit until they were stealing up to ninety per cent of what they spent on drugs.
- About half the US murders were drug-related. These were often caused by gang wars between drug dealers competing for territory.
- The spread of AIDS was partly caused by dirty needles being shared among drug addicts.

CONCERNS ABOUT CRIME

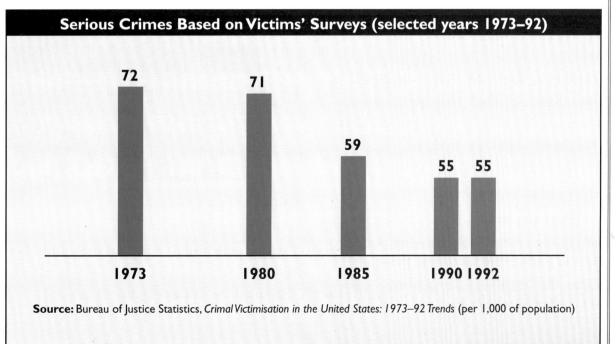

Serious Crimes Based on Victims' Surveys (selected years 1973–92)

1973	1980	1985	1990	1992
72	71	59	55	55

Source: Bureau of Justice Statistics, *Crimal Victimisation in the United States: 1973–92 Trends* (per 1,000 of population)

Drugs and Crime

In the US, many **feared** the spread of crime. By the late 1960s, **crime in the streets** was the country's main problem according to opinion polls. Blacks as well as whites worried about the growth of crime because blacks were often the targets of crime from fellow blacks. Working-class whites were angry about crime – it led to increased racial tension. A white resident of Brooklyn, New York said, *'You can't walk anywhere. It's because these people don't know how to live. They steal. They got no values. They say it's history. It's not history, it's the way they live. They live like animals.'*

The **US government** reacted to the people's concerns. Crime became an issue in presidential and congressional elections. Government policies tried to tackle the causes of crime by investing in job-training schemes and improving education and housing. They also tried to **crack down** on crime by increasing penalties, building more prisons and putting more police on the street.

Similar approaches were tried in the case of **drug trafficking**. In 1986, President Reagan increased funding for police and increased penalties for drug traffickers. He also proposed **economic sanctions** against drug-producing countries to force them to deal with the problem there.

ORDINARY LEVEL AND HIGHER LEVEL HOMEWORK EXERCISES

ORDINARY LEVEL

1. Study the extract from Martin Luther King's speech, *'I have a dream'*, on p. 427 and answer the following questions:

(i) When and where did Martin Luther King make this speech?

(ii) What according to King is the American creed?

(iii) Why do you think he calls Mississippi a *'desert state'*?

(iv) What is his dream about his children?

(v) What does he hope *'this faith'* will do?

(vi) What is the purpose of this speech?

(vii) Is this speech propaganda?

2. Study the graphs on Serious Crime on p. 432 and p. 433 and answer the following questions:

(i) According to the FBI figures, which year was the worst year for serious crime?

(ii) According to the Bureau of Justice Statistics, which year was the worst year for serious crime?

(iii) Briefly describe and explain the trends in the graphs.

(iv) Can you suggest explanations for the differences in the figures for 1980, 1985, 1990 and 1992?

(v) How do these graphs help you understand the problems of using statistics as sources in history?

3. Study the photograph of the sign on p. 433 and answer the following questions:

(i) Who put up this sign?

(ii) Who is being warned?

(iii) What are they told to do?

(iv) What is said about dope addicts and dope gangsters?

(v) What must law enforcement officers do?

(vi) What, do you think, is the purpose of erecting a sign like this?

(vii) How effective would a sign like this be?

4. Write **paragraph answers** on each of the following questions:

(i) Desegregation in education in the US.

(ii) Chicano and Native Americans.

(iii) Urban poverty in the US from the 1950s to the 1980s.

(iv) Urban riots in the US in the 1960s.

(v) Johnson's war on poverty.

(vi) The rise of crime.

5. Write **long answers** on each of the following:

(i) What role did Martin Luther King play in the movement for civil rights for black Americans?

(ii) What was the role of the US federal government in achieving civil rights for black Americans?

(iii) What were the causes of urban poverty?

(iv) What was the role of the US federal government in combating urban poverty?

(v) How badly affected were US cities in the 1970s and 1980s by rising crime and the rise in the use of drugs?

HIGHER LEVEL

1. How successful were black Americans in their attempts to achieve civil and political rights from 1945 to the 1980s?

   OR

   Assess the successes and the failures of the Civil Rights Movement in America between the 1950s and the 1980s. (Department of Education, Sample Paper)

2. What role did Martin Luther King play in the civil rights movement?

3. How important was the role of the US federal government in the achievement of civil and political rights for black Americans?

4. To what extent did black Americans have to rely on their own organisation to achieve civil and political rights?

5. What caused urban poverty in the US and what were its effects?

TEST YOURSELF AT
my-etest.com

INTRODUCTION

Montgomery was the capital of the state of Alabama in the Deep South. It was a city of 70,000 whites and 50,000 blacks. It enforced **Jim Crow** by having segregated schools and other public facilities. Most blacks were employed in **low-paid unskilled jobs**; 60% of black women worked as domestics, and 50% of black men worked as domestics or labourers. The **average income** of blacks was half that of whites.

The **bus company** followed the pattern of the rest of the city. It employed no blacks as drivers. It also segregated buses with blacks sitting at the back and whites at the front. Black passengers often complained about verbal abuse from the white bus drivers.

SOURCE 1 – Negroes' most urgent needs

FOLLOWING ARE A FEW OF THE MOST URGENT NEEDS OF OUR PEOPLE. IMMEDIATE ATTENTION SHOULD BE GIVEN EACH OF THESE. WHAT IS YOUR STAND TOWARD THEM?

1. The present bus situation [in relation to segregated seating] ....
2. Negro representation on the Parks and Recreation Board ....
3. Sub-division for housing [of Negroes stopped] ....
4. Jobs for qualified Negroes [not open to them] ....
5. Negro representation on all boards affecting Negroes ....
6. Congested areas, with inadequate or no fireplugs. Fire hazards are inviting.
7. Lack of sewage disposals make it necessary to resort to outdoor privies [toilets], which is a health hazard.
8. Narrow streets, lack of curbing, unpaved streets in some sections ...

Gentlemen, what is your stand on these issues? What will you do to improve these undemocratic practices? Your stand on these issues will enable us to better decide on whom we shall cast our ballot in the March election.

Very truly yours,

Montgomery Negroes

Inez Jessie Baskin Papers, in Alabama Department of Archives and History, Montgomery

---

SOURCE 2 – Code of the city of Montgomery

Section 10. Separation of races – Required.

Every person operating a bus line in the city shall provide equal but separate accommodation for white people and negroes on his buses, by requiring the employees in charge thereof to assign passengers seats on the vehicles under their charge in such manner as to separate the white people from the negroes, where there are both white and negroes in the same car ....

Section 11. Some powers of persons in charge of vehicle; passengers to obey directions.

Any employee in charge of a bus operated in the city shall have the powers of a police officer while in actual control of any bus, for the purpose of carrying out the provisions of the preceding section, and it shall be unlawful for any passenger to refuse or fail to take a seat among those assigned to the race in which he belongs, at the request of any such employee in charge, if there is such a seat vacant.

Alabama Department of Archives and History, Montgomery

ROSA PARKS

One of those who used the buses regularly was **Rosa Parks**, a 42-year-old black woman. She worked as a **seamstress** in a downtown department store. She was also a member of the local **NAACP** (National Association for the Advancement of Coloured People). She had been put off a bus in the mid-1940s for refusing to do as she was told. She had recently completed a workshop on race relations.

On 1 December 1955, she boarded a bus after a day's work and some shopping. She took a seat in the black section at the rear. When all the seats filled up, she was told by the driver to get up and give her seat to a white man – but she refused. The driver called the police and Rosa Parks was booked for breaking city laws. She had to appear in court four days later.

SOURCE 3

Rosa Parks being fingerprinted in Montgomery after being charged with violating segregation laws.

SOURCE 4

A painted wood sculpture of the arrest of Rosa Parks.

SOURCE 5 – Rosa Parks

'I had first met Rosa Parks during the time that I was a member of the NAACP. She had always impressed me. She was just an angel walking. When things happened that would upset most people, she would just give you this angelic smile, and that was the end of that.'

Inez Jessie Baskin, quoted in P Jennings and T Brewster, *The Century*

SOURCE 6 – Why Mrs Parks was chosen

'Mrs Parks was a married woman. She was morally clean, and she had a fairly good academic training ... If there was ever a person we would've been able to [use to] break the situation that existed in the Montgomery city line, Rosa L Parks was the woman to use ... I probably would've examined a dozen before I got there if Rosa Parks hadn't come along before I found the right one.'

E D Nixon, quoted by Gary Younge in *The Guardian*, 16 December 2000

SOURCE 7 – Not yield one inch

'The City Commission, and we know our people are with us in this determination, will not yield one inch but will do all in its power to oppose the integration of the Negro race with the white race in Montgomery, and will forever stand like a rock against social equality, intermarriage and mixing of the races under God's creation and plan.'

Statement from the Montgomery City Commission at the start of the boycott quoted in M Walker, *Makers of the American Century*

Organising the Boycott

Local black leaders decided to take action. **E D Nixon** was leader of the Montgomery NAACP and **Jo Ann Robinson** was leader of the Women's Political Council of Montgomery.

Nixon asked Parks if the NAACP could use her case to fight for desegregation, even though it might put her life in danger. She discussed it with her husband and mother and decided to let the NAACP go ahead with a lawsuit to contest the constitutionality of the segregation law.

Robinson along with the Women's Political Council decided to ask blacks to **boycott** the buses on the following Monday, the day of Parks's trial. They issued 35,000 leaflets to spread the word. The boycott decision was supported by **black ministers** in their church sermons on Sunday.

The organisers looked around for a **leader**. They found one in **Martin Luther King**, a 26-year-old clergymen who had come to Montgomery just a year before. King was an inspirational leader and an outstanding speaker. As one historian wrote, 'As King spoke in a singsong cadence [tone, lilt], his followers would cry and clap and sway, carried away by the magic of his oratory.' He became President of the **Montgomery Improvement Association** (MIA) which was set up to lead the boycott.

King was inspired by the teachings of the leader of Indian independence, **Mahatma Ghandi**, and **Reinhold Niebuhr**, a theologian. From these people he adopted the method of **non-violent protest**. This belief spread to others and it gave his followers a strong feeling of unity and determination.

In court on Monday 5 December, Parks was convicted and was fined $10. Her lawyer appealed against the conviction. But the bus boycott that day was successful. Most blacks supported it in spite of great inconvenience.

SOURCE 8 – The weapon of protest

'Since it had to happen, I'm happy it happened to a person like Mrs Parks, for ... nobody can doubt the height of her character. Nobody can doubt the depth of her Christian commitment.... And you know my friends, there comes a time when people get tired of being trampled on by the iron feet of oppression. The only weapon that we have in our hands this evening is the weapon of protest. If we were incarcerated behind the iron curtains of a Communistic nation, we couldn't do this.... But the great glory of American democracy is the right to protest for right ... We are not wrong in what we are doing. If we are wrong, the Supreme Court of this nation is wrong. If we are wrong, God almighty is wrong.'

Martin Luther King, speaking at a public meeting at the beginning of the boycott

---

SOURCE 9 – Martin Luther King speaking

'Martin Luther King spoke in a very soft, rich voice, and as he was going along, you'd get the feeling ... that here was a person who really cared.... He was able to make all of us – the washerwoman, the domestic, the teenager – feel like he was talking directly to each of us.'

Inez Jessie Baskin, quoted in P Jennings and T Brewster, *The Century*

SOURCE 10 – This is not a war

'There are those who would try to make this a hate campaign. This is not a war between the white and the Negro but a conflict between justice and injustice ... We must use the weapon of love.'

Speech by Martin Luther King

SOURCE 11 – Communist view

'No day passed but the Italian Communists pointed to events in our South to prove that American democracy was a "capitalist myth" ... No man has ever waged the battle for equality under our law in a more lawful and Christian way than you have.'

Clare Booth Luce, American Ambassador to Italy, wife of the founder of *Time* magazine. January 1957 in a private letter to Martin Luther King quoted in M Walker, *Makers of the American Century*

CONTINUED BOYCOTTING

After the success of the **Monday boycott**, the Montgomery Improvement Association decided to continue with the boycott until the bus company gave in to its demands:

- that black drivers be employed on the buses;
- that drivers should be courteous to passengers;
- that seats should be filled on a first come, first served basis.

The policy of boycotting was **risky** because it needed widespread support. Blacks would have to walk to work or co-operate with sharing cars. But boycotting also had **advantages**:

- It allowed people take action without violence.
- It could create a sense of solidarity.
- It would hit the bus company because it would lose money.

In organising the boycott, black leaders collected money to buy station wagons for a private **taxi service**. Some of the money came from local black workers (who donated twenty per cent of their wages), the NAACP, the United Auto Workers Union, sympathetic whites and the Montgomery Jewish community. The leaders set up a **Transportation Committee** to form **car pools**, while some black workers took bicycles or walked to work. When local insurance agents tried to cancel **insurance** for the car pool, the boycotters insured with Lloyds of London.

The **black churches** played a vital role in organising the boycott. The churches raised $30,000 for the car pool, and the churches became the despatch centres where people gathered to wait for rides. During the year, twenty-four ministers were arrested for helping the boycott.

Blacks walking to work during the Montgomery Bus Boycott.

The empty interior of a Montgomery Transit bus during the boycott.

SOURCE 14 – A protest of the people

'The amazing thing about our movement is that it is a protest of the people. It is not a one-man show. It is not the preachers' show. The masses of this town, who are tired of being trampled on, are responsible.'

Jo Ann Robinson, 1955

SOURCE 15 – Came together

'I had been living in Montgomery most of my life, and up until then, you couldn't even get three people to stay together for two hours. And here we had all come together as one for 381 days.'

Inez Jessie Baskin, quoted in P Jennings and T Brewster, *The Century*

WHITE OPPOSITION

City authorities tried to undermine the protest. When black-owned taxis (cabs) took customers for 10 cents a trip – the same as a bus fare – the city authorities threatened to shut them down. At the same time, the **Ku Klux Klan** became active. They marched in the streets and poured acid on cars involved in the car pooling. The homes of King and other leaders were bombed.

The **police** also interfered. Those involved in car pools were stopped regularly by police trying to find any excuse to disrupt the boycott. **King** was arrested for doing 30 miles an hour in a 25 miles an hour zone. In February 1956, 89 blacks, including King, were arrested under an old law banning boycotting. Black **churches** were bombed.

But the boycott held out during 1956 in spite of great pressure. This was partly helped by the increasing outside interest, both in America and abroad. Television and newspapers publicised the boycott and the local white reaction to it.

SUPREME COURT JUDGMENT

At the same time, the lawsuit by the NAACP was proceeding through the law courts. It eventually reached the **Supreme Court** in Washington. The Court ruled on 13 November 1956 that the city laws relating to buses violated (broke) the Constitution. It said that the seating arrangements must stop on 20 December.

When the city officials gave in, King and his Montgomery Improvement Association called off the boycott. On 21 December 1956, 381 days after it began, King and other civil rights leaders took seats at the front of the bus. But this led to a new round of violence when snipers shot at buses, and churches and houses were bombed. However, this white backlash soon quietened down.

After it was over, King got on the front cover of *Time* magazine which regarded him as the **American Ghandi**. He was also invited to the independence ceremony for the African country of Ghana.

SOURCE 18

The arrest of Martin Luther King in Montgomery

SOURCE 19

Martin Luther King is welcomed by his wife, Coretta, after leaving court in Montgomery, March 1956. He was found guilty of conspiracy to boycott city buses in a campaign to desegregate the bus system. The judge suspended the $500 fine pending an appeal.

> **SOURCE 16 – Listen, nigger**
>
> 'Listen, nigger. We've taken all we want from you. Before next week, you'll be sorry you ever came to Montgomery.'
>
> **Late night phone caller speaking to Martin Luther King, quoted in P Jennings and T Brewster, *The Century***

> **SOURCE 17 – We want to love our enemies**
>
> 'We believe in law and order. Don't get panicky. Don't do anything at all. Don't get your weapons. He who lives by the sword will perish by the sword. Remember, that is what God said. We are not advocating violence. We want to love our enemies. We must love our white brothers no matter what they do to us.'
>
> **Martin Luther King, after his house was bombed**

CONCLUSION

The **significance** of the Montgomery Bus Boycott:

- The success of a **well-organised and peaceful resistance** set an example for further action against segregation. Many historians regard it as the beginning of the modern civil rights movement.
- This was a **new method** that blacks could use to promote civil rights, and not just the NAACP (National Association for the Advancement of Coloured People) way of testing the laws.
- The boycott involved **local black leaders** and **followers** who had to face violence and pressure. The organisation and commitment involved was a source of great pride to black people all over America.
- It saw the rise to prominence of **Martin Luther King**. Following on from this, he founded the **Southern Christian Leadership Conference** in 1957 which became prominent in fighting for civil rights for blacks.
- The boycott got support from the **press and television**, especially outside the South, and highlighted the issues for northern whites.
- It highlighted the role of the **black churches and religious leaders** in the fight for civil rights.
- But the Boycott was eventually ended by a **Supreme Court decision**; on its own it might have failed to force the Montgomery city officials to change.
- But it also **failed to end Jim Crow** in other areas of Montgomery life; schools, hotels and theatres were still segregated and bus drivers were still white.
- **Rosa Parks** lost her job and had her life threatened several times. She and her husband left Montgomery in 1957 and settled in Detroit where she worked as an administrative assistant in a politician's office. In 1994, she was **attacked** and beaten by a young black man who wanted money. Two years later she was awarded the **Presidential Medal of Freedom**.

SOURCE 20 – There lived a great people

'If you will protest courageously and yet with dignity and Christian love, when the history books are written in future generations the historians will pause and say, "There lived a great people – a black people – who injected new meaning and dignity into the veins of civilisation." '

Martin Luther King, 1956, quoted in P Jennings and T Brewster, *The Century*

SOURCE 21 – We won't bow down again

'We got our heads up now, and we won't ever bow down again – no sir – except before God.'

A black janitor in Montgomery, quoted in J Patterson, *Grand Expectations*

SOURCE 22

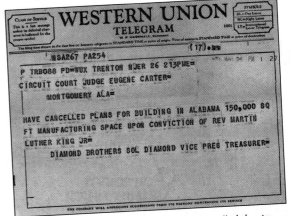

Telegram showing business investment cancelled due to Martin Luther King's conviction.

Case Study Questions

Comprehension

1. In Source 1, who are 'our people'? List three of the 'most urgent needs of our people'. How many of the most urgent needs are (i) political, (ii) social, and (iii) economic? Why do the 'Montgomery Negroes' want to know 'What is your stand on these issues?'

2. What was outlawed according to Section 10 of the Montgomery City Code (Source 2)? What power was given to bus employees by Section 11? What was it unlawful for passengers to do?

3. What does Inez Jessie Baskin say about Rosa Parks in Source 5?

4. What did E D Nixon mean when he said '[to] break the situation that existed on the Montgomery city line'? Why did he select Rosa Parks '[to] break the situation'? (Source 6)

5. What was the Montgomery City Commission opposed to according to Source 7? Who supported them, according to the Source?

6. According to Martin Luther King (Source 8), what is the 'great glory of American democracy'? Where does he say people can't protest?

7. What impressed Inez Jessie Baskin about Martin Luther King when he spoke?

8. What is Martin Luther King's message in Source 10?

9. According to Source 11, what did Italian Communists use the example of the South to prove? Who is the 'man' the writer is referring to?

10. In Source 12, why are people walking?

11. What impression is given by this photo in Source 13?

12. What is 'the amazing thing about our movement', according to Jo Ann Robinson in Source 14? Who are the preachers?

13. In Source 15, what do you think the figure '381 days' refers to?

14. What is the message of the phone caller to Martin Luther King (Source 16)?

15. What is Martin Luther King's message in Source 17?

16. How is Martin Luther King being treated in this photo (Source 18)?

17. Why are people happy in this photo (Source 19)?

18. According to Source 20, why will historians 'pause and say, "There lived a great people – a black people" '?

19. What does the janitor in Source 21 mean when he says 'we won't ever bow down again'?

Comparison

1. Which of the issues listed in Source 1 is referred to in Source 2?

2. What evidence is there to suggest that Source 1 was written before the Montgomery Bus Boycott?

3. Examine Sources 3 and 4. Are the same impressions given by the photo (Source 3) and the wood sculpture (Source 4)?

4. Is E D Nixon's view of Rosa Parks (Source 6) supported by Source 5? How do the views of Rosa Parks in these two statements compare with Martin Luther King's statement in Source 8? Why did E D Nixon intend go to so much trouble to find 'the right one'?

5. How do the views expressed in Source 7 conflict with the 'most urgent needs' of Source 1?

6. Source 7 refers to 'God's creation and plan'. How does this differ from the views expressed by Martin Luther King in Source 8 when he says, 'If we are wrong, God almighty is wrong'?

7. What do these and other sources tell us about the role of religion in the Montgomery Bus Boycott?

8. Do you think Clare Booth Luce (Source 11) would support the Montgomery City Commission (Source 7)? Explain your answer.

9. Read Source 8 carefully. Is there evidence in this extract from Martin Luther King's speech to support the views expressed in Source 9?

10. Read Sources 8, 10 and 17. What are the main points of Martin Luther King's message? Is the message the same in each extract?

11. What aspects of Source 8 support the views of Source 11?

12. What evidence do the photos in Sources 12 and 13 provide to support the view that the Bus Boycott is effective? Do they support Source 14 and Source 15?

13. What is the main difference between the views of Source 16 and 17?

14. Is there evidence in Sources 12, 14 and 21 to support the conclusions of Martin Luther King in Source 20?

CRITICISM

1. Sources 1 and 2 are held in the Alabama Department of Archives and History. What are archives? Why is it necessary to have archives? How does an archive differ from a museum?

2. Which of the Sources 1–7 are primary and which are secondary?

3. In general, what are the advantages/strengths and disadvantages/limitations of primary compared to secondary sources?

4. How do documentary sources (Sources 1 and 2) compare with the wood sculpture (Source 4) as historical sources for studying the Montgomery Bus Boycott? How would you compare the wood sculpture to a political cartoon as a source?

5. Source 6 is taken from a newspaper report. How useful and reliable are newspapers as sources? How do they compare as sources with official documents (public records) such as the Code of the City of Montgomery (Source 7)?

6. Source 8 is an edited extract from a speech by Martin Luther King. What do you think was the purpose of the speech? How useful is it as a source? How reliable is it? Outline one of its main disadvantages.

7. Source 11 is a private letter. How useful and reliable are private letters as sources? Using the information in the letter, give an example of fact and opinion.

8. How reliable an opinion is that of Jo Ann Robinson in Source 14?

9. Source 15 is a later memory (recollection). What problems are presented by evidence based on memory? Do you think that is the case with Source 15?

10. How reliable is Source 16? What use is the Source?

11. Which of the following sources – Sources 1, 4, 7, 8, 11, 20 – are biased? Which are propaganda? Justify your answer.

12. Examine the photos (Sources 3, 12, 13, 18, 19). What use are they as evidence for the Montgomery Bus Boycott? Is there bias or propaganda in them? If that is the case, does that make them less reliable and useful?

13. Which of the Sources 16–21 would be kept in (i) archives, (ii) libraries, and (iii) museums?

14. What other types of sources, apart from those used in this Case Study, would you consider helpful for a better understanding of the Montgomery Bus Boycott? Explain your answer.

CONTEXTUALISATION

1. Outline the process of desegregation in post-war US.

2. Write about the role of Martin Luther King in the Civil Rights Movement.

3. What were the origins of the Civil Rights Movement and how successful was it?

4. Using the sources and the account above, write a report on the Montgomery Bus Boycott using the following three headings – cause/origins, progress and results.

Introduction

Historians look on the 1950s and early 1960s as a time of **consensus** in US history. By the middle of the 1960s, however, the US experienced a series of shocks which undermined that consensus. There was the assassination of President Kennedy in Dallas in 1963, differences in the civil rights movement, and the escalation of the war in Vietnam – all these undermined US confidence in its ability to change the world and to improve its own country. By the late 1960s, American society was **polarised** – divided between different groups and viewpoints. Three aspects of those divisions were:

• Youth culture;

• Counter-culture; and

• Multiculturalism.

Youth Culture

America had a **large, youth population** in the 1950s and 1960s due to the post-war **baby boom**. In contrast to the early decades of the century when most children were at work by fifteen, a higher proportion of the post-war children stayed on in high schools (secondary schools), in colleges and universities – this extended the youthful years. In addition, at this time, the young population shared the benefits of the **affluent society** – some through parental support, others through the rise of part-time jobs. This better-off and more numerous young population developed their own culture.

The front cover of *Seventeen*, a magazine aimed at the growing teenage market in post-war US.

The word **teenager** began to be used to describe this youthful time in life between childhood and adult years. Teenagers became a target for **business** who saw a new market. They became the focus of **advertising campaigns**, largely using the new medium of **television**. By the end of the 1950s, American teenagers were spending more on themselves than the national income of some smaller European countries.

The **youth culture** which developed in the 1950s and 1960s highlighted the differences with the adult lifestyle; this became the **generation gap**. Youth wanted to express its independence and freedom: doing things its own way. J D Salinger's **The Catcher in the Rye**, published in 1951, told the story of the restless life of a teenager, Holden Caulfield, who rejected the phoniness of adult life. *'If you want to know the truth, they're all a bunch of phonies,'* he said. It was banned in high schools in fifteen states but it became a must read for many teenagers.

ROCK 'N' ROLL

Rock 'n' Roll and **dance** was one way of expressing the generation gap. Parents called rock 'n' roll the devil's music. Radio helped to spread its popularity with disc jockeys and the Top Twenty, along with cheap 45 rpm singles, the invention of the LP (in 1948) and jukeboxes. Record sales soared to over $500 million in 1960.

The stars of the new music were **Chuck Berry** and **Elvis Presley**. Presley, above all, shocked the older generation with his stage performances – his slicked-back hair, his gyrating hips and his moody look. He became **Elvis the Pelvis** and his audiences screeched excitedly. Adult critics said his performances were *'not only suggestive but downright obscene.'*

Elvis Presley, the king of rock 'n' roll, singing to adoring fans who reach out to touch him.

The **car** also became a symbol of **restless youth**. Six million teenagers had driving licences by the end of the 1950s, and 1·5 million of these owned their own cars. Cruisin' around on a Saturday night became a popular pastime. New drive-in diners with carhops and drive-in movie theatres were developed for the mobile teenage and youth market.

DELINQUENTS

Adults became alarmed at the **rise of delinquents** – young people who ran into trouble with the law. There seemed to be an increasing number of fights and teenage drinking parties. Even the US Senate investigated the delinquent problem. Some blamed the publication of a huge number of **comics** with their recipe of violence and action. Many states passed regulations to control their publication and distribution.

Others worried about the influence of **movies**, such as *Rebel Without a Cause* which featured James Dean as a rebellious teenager, and *The Blackboard Jungle* which featured rebellious students. Some blamed rock 'n' roll music. They feared an **open revolt against society**. *'The gangster of tomorrow is the Elvis Presley of today.'*

THE SIXTIES

In the 1960s, the **twist** and the **Beatles** were the highlights of the music scene. When the twist became popular after 1961, adults objected to the movements and exhibitionism. They condemned it as lustful. This coincided

Twistin' the night away: the Twist, a teenage dance which became popular with college students and young clubbers in the late 1950s and 1960s.

with the advent of *Beatlemania* from 1964 onwards. The Beatles influenced not only the music but also the fashion of the time as they changed from their **mod** style to the long-haired, colourful costumes of the late 1960s. **Drugs** became more freely available. Middle-class youth, in particular, liked to experience or experiment.

SEXUAL REVOLUTION

The 1960s also experienced a **sexual revolution**. This was part of a feeling of greater freedom for young people. It also arose from the greater freedom from pregnancy due to the invention of the Pill in 1961. The women's movement also encouraged women to seek greater freedom and fulfilment whether sexual or otherwise. The sexual freedom was also encouraged by Supreme Court decisions which made sexually explicit books and magazines more easily available, even if still illegal for teenagers. Movies also became more sexually explicit and encouraged the view of a right to sexual pleasure.

However, by the late 1970s, the spread of **venereal diseases** and the deadly **AIDS** caused many young people to avoid casual sexual relations. For some the ideas of celibacy and virginity became more common by the late 1980s. Nevertheless, the dominant trends in youth culture remained – independence, freedom, the consumer market and wealth. Pop music, fashion, smoking and drugs continued to be the most obvious expressions of the youth culture.

KEY PERSONALITY: NORMAN MAILER

Norman Mailer was brought up in Brooklyn, New York. He is one of America's best-known writers of the twentieth century. He wrote widely on history, psychology, politics and current affairs.

Mailer was educated at **Harvard University** and graduated in **aeronautical engineering**. He was drafted into the **US army** during the Second World War and spent two years in the Pacific and South-East Asia. His acclaimed novel, *The Naked and the Dead* (1948), is based on his personal experiences of the war. One review of the book said, *'Most people who reach three times twenty-six [his age] never tumble to a fraction of what Mr. Mailer has already found out about the psychology of the men who want power.'*

Mailer was a **prolific** writer. He published thirty-nine books (including eleven novels), plays, screenplays, poems and many articles in newspapers and magazines. Mailer co-founded the *Village Voice* (one of the earliest underground papers) in 1955, and he edited *Dissent* for about 10 years. He also wrote essays and short stories. In some of his books, he used the techniques of a journalist to write about real events and people. This was sometimes called the **New Journalism**.

Some called Mailer the prophet of **machismo** – the macho man; *'macho means taking the dares that come your way,'* he said. He had a reputation for aggression, fist fights, head-butting and drunken brawls. He was critical of both the US and the Soviet Union which he saw as **totalitarian societies**. In the case of America, he felt the country's power structure destroyed individualism. Totalitarianism, he said, is a force that *'beheads individuality, variety, dissent ... it blinds vision, deadens instinct.'* He supported **resistance to conformity**.

Mailer's writings are a commentary on American society:
- In *The White Negro* (1959) he wrote about the **hipster** who rebelled against cultural conformity; *'Hip is the sophistication of the wise primitive man in a giant jungle.'*
- *An American Dream* (1965), in which a man murders his wife, concerned the sacrifice of personal integrity (honesty) in the pursuit of material success.
- He also wrote *Why Are We in Vietnam?* (1967) about the role of violence in the Vietnam years.
- In *Armies of the Night* (1968) he wrote about the **anti-Vietnam march** on the Pentagon in which he took part and was arrested.
- His *Of a Fire on the Moon* (1970) was an account of the **Apollo 11** moon landing.

- In *Miami and the Siege of Chicago* (1968), he wrote about the Republican and Democratic Conventions of 1968. In this book and in *Armies of the Night* he was also concerned with the difficulties of trying to give an accurate account of a mass event.
- In *The Prisoner of Sex* (1971) he was **critical** of the feminist or women's liberation movement. He proposed that gender (male/female) could influence the way a person sees events and happenings. He was attacked as a *'male chauvinist pig'* by feminists. He angered them with his public statement, *'All women should be locked in cages.'* *'This notion of the women's movement that women are good and men are evil is about as useful as Hitlerism or Communism or Political Correctness or any kind of ideology that is limiting or constricting.'*
- He wrote a biography of **Marilyn Monroe** (1973) in which he said that the right wing (conservatives) murdered the sex goddess to frame the Attorney General, Robert Kennedy. He claimed later that this *'was not good journalism.'*
- His book *The Fight* (1975) was an account of the legendary **Rumble in the Jungle** between Muhammad Ali and George Foreman.
- He wrote *The Executioner's Song* (1979) about the life and death of a convicted killer Gary Gilmore.

He won two **Pulitzer Prizes** for his books. He also wrote, produced and directed several films. Apart from anti-war action, he also sought the Democratic nomination for Mayor of New York, but failed to get it.
Mailer was married six times and had nine children.

Counter-culture

Other influences in the 1960s developed a **counter-culture** which rejected the prevailing culture of the decade:
- The influence of the civil rights movement.
- The growing anti-war movement.
- The feeling that everybody had rights.
- The huge expansion of the university population from 16 million in 1960 to 25 million in 1970.
- The rise of drugs.

All these contributed to the development of the counter-culture, which looked for an alternative to the prevailing culture.

HIPPIES

Those who favoured the counter-culture followed a **hippie** lifestyle. They were mainly middle class and white who **dropped out** of college or university. They rejected material wealth and the consumer society. They also rejected the defects of the established culture – war, poverty and injustice. They promoted freedom of expression and a questioning of authority.

They expressed this rejection in a number of ways. They sought freedom from authority. They wore colourful clothes with beads, and they grew their hair long. The

A hippie family with their psychedelic bus in a commune in New York State.

men often added beards. They lived together in **communes**, or in **tribes** or **families**, practicing free love. They burned incense, took drugs, particularly marijuana and LSD and listened to **acid rock**. Some experimented with different religions, particularly Asian.

Their numbers were small, living in two main areas in the **Haight-Ashbury** district of **San Francisco** and the **East Village of New York City**. They spoke of peace, love and beauty. They were the **flower people**.

ROCK FESTIVALS

The music of **peace and love** of groups like the Grateful Dead and Jefferson Airplane was an important part of the counter-culture. A number of **rock festivals** gave expression to this. In 1967, Crosby, Stills and Nash and others performed at the San Francisco Bay Area **Human Be-In** or **A Gathering of the Tribes**. But the most famous was at **Woodstock**, New York in 1969 when between 300,000 and 400,000 people turned up for a weekend of rock, drugs and sex. In spite of the unexpectedly large crowd on a rainy and muddy three days, there was no disturbance.

This was in contrast to the **Rolling Stones'** Altamont festival later in 1969. Here, hired Hell's Angels acted as security guards and treated the audience brutally, resulting in some deaths. The **Manson family** showed another aspect of the counter-culture. Led by Charles Manson, the **family** ritually murdered a young actress, Sharon Tate, and four friends in 1969.

The widespread publicity the hippies received also created a **strong antagonism** among working-class youth, workers generally and much of middle-class America which increased social or class tensions. Ronald Reagan, as Governor of California, expressed that antagonism when he defined a hippie as a person who *'dresses like Tarzan, has hair like Jane, and smells like Cheetah.'*

END OF THE COUNTER-CULTURE

The counter-culture did not last long, from about 1966 to 1970. Some claimed the publicity they got destroyed them. It attracted drug pushers, criminals and mentally disturbed people to their areas. Violence increased as hippies became easy targets of rapes, assaults and murders. But their influence lasted longer than this as some of their ideas, music and fashions were commercialised in the 1980s and 1990s.

> ### Haight-Ashbury in the Counter-culture
>
> *'The counter-culture was beginning to blossom in the neighbourhood [Haight-Ashbury].... (The area) was soon lined with alternative shops, coffee shops, and book-stores that sold psychedelic gear, posters, drug paraphernalia, hip clothes and books with information about transcendentalism, LSD and mushrooms ... You would get up every morning and you had no idea what the day would bring. You didn't need money; you could get food without it. You could crash at anybody's house. You didn't need to look good or wear your hair in a certain way. It didn't matter if you didn't look like Tab Hunter or Debbie Reynolds [film stars]. There was a sense of adventure...'*
>
> Quoted in P Jennings and T Brewster,
> *The Century*

Woodstock Festival, New York, in 1969 where between 300,000 and 400,000 people turned up for a weekend of rock, drugs and sex.

Counter-culture

Multiculturalism

Throughout the nineteenth century and the early twentieth century, America became the **melting pot** with the arrival of immigrants from many different European countries and from Asia. While people from different countries lived in separate neighbourhoods, they were expected to follow the American Way of Life. The dominant view was that social unity was needed to develop a strong national state. Gradually many people became **Americanised** through schools, the spread of popular culture and growing prosperity.

ETHNIC PRIDE

However, in the 1960s there was a growth of **ethnic pride**, as well as the beginning of the women's movement. These challenged the existing American culture. A number of factors were responsible for the growth of ethnic pride:

- The growth of the **civil rights movement** made people aware of their cultural identity. The growth of rights consciousness in the 1960s led to demands to respect the many different cultures of the US.
- Many people wanted to establish a distinct cultural identity to counteract the spread of the consumer culture of the 1950s and 1960s.
- **US immigration laws** were changed in 1965. They eliminated the **national origins** quota which had previously favoured European immigration. Now more could come from Asia, Latin America and the Caribbean. From 1965 to the 1990s, over eighty per cent of all new immigration was non-European.

As a result of the growth of ethnic pride, racial and dialect jokes were frowned on. Descendants of European emigrants discovered their roots. Some of this was encouraged by the home country who saw a market for tourism and a source of influence in America. In other cases, the **white ethnic** movement, as it was called, did not last long.

BLACK, CHICANO AND NATIVE AMERICAN

During the 1960s, **black leaders** encouraged black pride in themselves and their history. They wanted to trace their heritage and roots to Africa. They demanded the establishment of black studies courses in schools and colleges. Some wanted to be called **African-American** to highlight their origins.

In the late 1960s, **Mexican-Americans** inspired by earlier battles for improved economic conditions, demanded to be called **Chicanos**. They formed groups in the south-western states where many lived – New Mexico, Colorado, California and Texas. They rejected the main American values. They also wanted education in **Spanish** and the teaching of **Chicano culture** in public schools and universities. Some used the slogan **Brown Power** to express control of their own community.

A Chicano (Mexican-American) protesting at an anti-discrimination rally in California.

Mexican-Americans were part of the wider **Hispanic** community – people from Latin America and the Caribbean. By the 1990s, they had surpassed blacks as the largest minority group. They sometimes adopted **Latino** as an alternative to Hispanic. Latino music and dancing gained popularity, and some of their food – tacos, fajitas and salsa – entered the main US diet.

Native Americans (Indians) saw their culture largely wiped out in the nineteenth century. But in the 1960s American Indians, numbering about one million, recalled their origins and culture. They shared in the general feeling of **cultural revival**. They asserted their rich heritage and forced the white government to help their economic and social conditions.

CULTURAL DIVERSITY

The growth of ethnic pride emphasised the **cultural diversity** of America. Many believed that **multiculturalism** should be encouraged. They saw multiculturalism as the study of the social, cultural and historical influences that shaped the development of America's different peoples.

In that way, multiculturalism influenced many aspects of **education** from elementary school to university. In particular, **US history and literature curricula** changed to include the experiences and writings of Americans of different backgrounds. They included new courses on black studies and women's studies. Multiculturalists believed that this provided **greater tolerance and inclusiveness** in society.

OPPOSITION TO MULTICULTURALISM

Those who opposed multiculturalism argued that previous migrants were integrated into American society to create a **united country**. By stressing multiculturalism they said that this created divisions between Americans and undermined the beliefs that held the country together. Those against multiculturalism were part of the **New Right** under President Reagan.

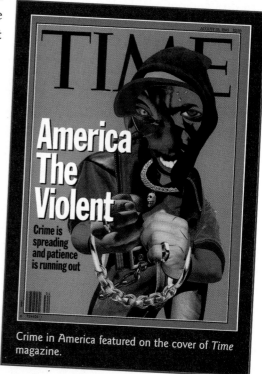

Some have argued that multiculturalism has led to a **dumbing down** (reducing to a lower level of understanding) of education. They said that reading levels had declined in elementary schools by trying to accommodate the various cultures. Higher education also became a battleground between multiculturalists and those opposed to them. The largely white, male-dominated system had to change to allow for other cultures and viewpoints.

The **problem for America**, as one historian argued, was how to cherish different cultures and traditions without breaking the common political institutions, language, culture and ideals *'that holds the country together.'*

Crime in America featured on the cover of *Time* magazine.

The difficulty faced by the country was that often the different ethnic groups while living together, **operated separately**. In the past, for example, the blending of races through marriage was rare. Interracial marriage increased a little from the 1960s. But all the different racial groups from European Americans to African, Asian and Latino Americans have almost entirely chosen their husbands and wives (or partners) from within their own ethnic group.

In the circumstances, those opposed to multiculturalism argued that increasing cultural divergence and rivalry could cause **serious social problems** and conflicts if developments continued. They argued that in cities there was a likelihood of fragmented and separate communities which could cause **racial and class conflict** in the future. In response, those who favour a multicultural society said that neglecting the various cultures is more likely to cause this conflict.

ORDINARY LEVEL AND HIGHER LEVEL HOMEWORK EXERCISES

ORDINARY LEVEL

1. Study this extract on the counter-culture and answer the following questions:

   'In the '60s, a group of young people – mostly college age and middle class – started living differently from most Americans. They wore different clothes; they marched; they demanded power in their schools and colleges; sometimes they went off to live in their own little communities, called 'communes'; some refused to serve in the army because they didn't believe in fighting. They thought the Vietnam War was wrong and immoral. They were part of something that was called the counterculture.... Some people called them 'hippies'; some people called them strange.... Many wore their hair long and their clothes loose and colourful. Many lived in California. They questioned everything, refused to conform, and made their favourite music – rock music – a national passion.'

   Adapted from J Hakim,
   All the People, 1945–2001

(i) When did the counter-culture begin?

(ii) How were the young people of the counter-culture different?

(iii) What were their little communities called?

(iv) Why would some people call them strange? Who would those people be?

(v) Why did the hippies wear their hair long and their clothes loose?

(vi) Is this a primary or secondary source?

(vii) What is the author's attitude toward the hippies and the counter-culture?

2. Write **paragraph answers** on each of the following questions:

(i) The development of youth culture in the US in the 1950s and 1960s.

(ii) Norman Mailer – critic of US society.

(iii) The counter-culture in the US.

OR

The Hippies in the US in the 1960s and 1970s.

(iv) The growth of ethnic pride among Black, Chicano and Native Americans from the 1950s to the 1980s.

3. Write **long answers** on each of the following:

(i) How did the development of a youth culture lead to a collapse of consensus in the US in the 1960s and 1970s?

(ii) How did the development of a counter-culture lead to a collapse of consensus in the US in the 1960s and 1970s?

(iii) How did the development of multiculturalism lead to a collapse of consensus in the US in the 1960s and 1970s?

HIGHER LEVEL

1. *'By the late 1960s, American society was polarised – divided between different groups and viewpoints.'* Explain how, and why, this developed with reference to the youth culture, counter-culture and multiculturalism.

2. How, and why, did a youth culture develop in the US from the 1950s onwards?

3. How, and why, did a counter-culture develop in the US from the 1950s onwards?

4. Assess the impact of the development of multiculturalism on American history from the 1960s onwards.

29. Religion, the Mass Media and Higher Education

Religion in Modern American Culture

POST-WAR REVIVAL

In the US, the drift away from **organised religion** in pre-war days was reversed after the Second World War. Church membership soared in the 1950s, there was increased money spent on church buildings and religious leaders grew in respect.

CHURCH MEMBERSHIP IN US (AS % OF POPULATION)	
1940	49
1950	55
1960	69
1970	63

SPENDING ON CHURCH RECONSTRUCTION ($ MILLION)	
1945	26
1950	409
1960	1,016

The influence of religion could be seen at all levels in US life. In the **movies**, for example, *The Ten Commandments* broke box-office records. Semi-religious **songs** became hits. The **pledge of allegiance** recited every day by children in school included the words *'under God'*. In the 1950s, the words, *'In God We Trust'*, were added to the currency. In 1954, *Time* magazine said that the Christian faith was *'back at the centre of things.'*

Causes of Revival

Cold War tensions helped the rise in religious feelings. Religious leaders said that Communism was a *'great sinister anti-Christian movement'*. Some Americans viewed their foreign policy in **moralistic** terms (right versus wrong). They believed in the rightness of their cause and the evil of Communism which they saw as godless. They believed it was the god-given duty of Americans to spread the blessings of democracy. More cynical observers said, however, that in the era of McCarthyism and the Red Scare, being an active church member was a good way to avoid being branded a subversive.

But there were **other reasons** for the growth in church membership. It was partly due to the need for Americans to **belong** in such a rapidly changing society as the 1950s and 1960s, and the churches provided **stability**. To help them get their message across, the churches made use of modern technology – especially radio and television.

Evangelical Preachers

One factor which appealed to many in the 1950s was the simplified gospel message of **evangelical preachers**. One of the most influential was **Billy Graham**, a North Carolina Baptist whose **crusades** attracted large audiences. Billy Graham began in a one-room office with a secretary in 1950. By 1958, he had 200 working out of a four-storey office building. He also had a weekly television show and Presidents liked to meet and be photographed with him. Another evangelist, **Oral Roberts**, owned a large ranch, a private plane, a TV and radio show, a university called in his name and he collected $50 million a year.

Billy Graham, one of the most popular of the evangelical preachers, shaking hands with admirers.

The preachers used **radio and television** (there were 1,200 religious radio stations and 36 religious television stations), **mass mailings** and **advertising language and methods** to preach against the materialism of American life. In this way their appeal was particularly widespread among **poorer Americans** who did not share the affluence of the middle class.

Billy Graham meeting President Kennedy in the White House in 1961.

KEY PERSONALITY: BILLY GRAHAM

Billy Graham was born in North Carolina and educated at Bob Jones University, the Florida Bible Institute and Wheaton College. He was ordained as a Baptist minister in 1939.

After a very successful mission in Los Angeles in 1949, he set up the **Billy Graham Evangelistic Association** in 1950. He was a powerful and dynamic preacher supported by an efficient organisation. He used advertising and publicity campaigns and a staff of specialists (including prayer leaders, singers and counsellors). He developed religion as a form of mass popular entertainment.

He preached to over 200 million people in 185 countries. In New York in 1957, his 16-week crusade (or mission) was attended by 2 million people. *Time* magazine called him the **Pope of Protestant America**.

Graham preached an **Evangelical Protestantism** which emphasised personal commitment to Christ, the authority of the Bible, and the literal truth of the Bible. He differed from more conservative **Fundamentalists** of the Christian Right. He said, *'I don't think Jesus or the Apostles took sides in the political arenas of their day.'*

Graham depended not only on large public meetings or crusades. He also used the **mass media** to get across his message:

- The *Hour of Decision*, a radio programme, was broadcast weekly.
- Television crusades began in 1957.
- A newspaper column was published by papers across America.

Graham also wrote twenty-five books, including *Peace with God, The Jesus Generation* and *How to be Born Again*. Graham's influence and reputation were so strong that many **Presidents** consulted him, from Eisenhower and Kennedy to Johnson, Nixon and Ford. He began in the 1950s as a strong **anti-Communist** and an admirer of

Senator Joe McCarthy. *'I thank God for men who ... go loyally on in their work of exposing the pinks, the lavenders and the reds [Communists].'* But by the 1980s he had moved with the times and instead he now advocated **world peace** and **reconciliation** (understanding) with Soviet Russia and Communist China.

Graham received many honours, including the **Congressional Gold Medal** (1996), which was also presented to his wife, Ruth, for *'outstanding and lasting contributions to morality, racial equality, family, philanthropy [charity] and religion.'* Unlike some other preachers, no financial or sex scandals were associated with Graham. Instead he represented the **strong religious tradition** of the US.

CHANGES

After 1960, there was a **change** in the balance of religious membership. Protestant membership rose from 52 million in 1950 to 68 million in 1980, but membership changed between the different Protestant religions. In numbers, Methodists were overtaken by Baptists, while the Lutherans overtook Presbyterians. Catholic membership grew faster from 29 million to 50 million, partly helped by the increase in **immigration** from Latin America.

There were other changes. In the 1960s, **churchgoing fell** from its peak but it was still high. In 1970, over 60% of Americans were still active church members. This compared to 10–15% in England and France.

CATHOLIC CHURCH

The US had the **largest national grouping of Catholics**. In response to this, the number of **US cardinals** grew from 4 in 1946 to 11 in 1980. There was also the growth of Catholic education and cultural institutions. But the Catholic Church faced difficulties in the 1960s. There was a general acceptance of the changes proposed by **Vatican II**. But there was **resistance** among US Catholics to Pope Paul VI's encyclical, *Humanae Vitae*, banning artificial methods of birth control. Partly as a result of that, between 1966 and 1969, the Catholic Church lost 14,000 nuns and there was a thirty per cent reduction in those studying for the priesthood. However, the Catholic Church had its own revival movement with the growth of the Catholic **Pentecostals** and the youthful **Jesus Movement**.

RELATIONS BETWEEN RELIGIONS

But relations between the religions were not good; anti-Catholic feeling was still strong in the 1940s and the Jews also felt resentment against themselves. There was **little religious intermarriage**. Between 80% and 90% of Protestants married Protestants, similarly for Catholics and Jews. The differences continued between religions in the 1960s. Even though the religious distinction

> **KEY CONCEPT: FUNDAMENTALISM** was a conservative religious movement among Protestants in the US which emphasised the strict truth of the Bible, the virgin birth, the death and resurrection of Jesus Christ and the Second Coming of Christ. Fundamentalism was particularly influential in the southern states of the US. They became actively involved in politics.

in marriage began to break down, there was no spirit of ecumenism. Catholics maintained their beliefs and anti-Catholic feeling was still present – a former President of Harvard University, one of America's most prestigious universities, called Catholics undemocratic.

FUNDAMENTALISTS

The tradition of the evangelical preachers was continued in later decades by the fundamentalists of the 1970s and 1980s. They believed in a **strict reading** of the Bible. They were super-patriotic and reactionary (very conservative) in politics. Their leaders were white, upper and middle class while many of their followers were poor working class who wanted clear and simple answers.

Christian fundamentalists were the **backbone** of the conservative movement in the US – the **religious Right** – in the late 1970s and the 1980s. They were a sizeable group in society – in 1977, 70 million Americans described themselves as *'born-again Christians'*. One of the best-selling books of the 1970s was Hal Lindsay's, *The Late Great Planet Earth*, which described the return of Jesus to earth to save mankind.

Christian fundamentalists were angered by **Supreme Court** rulings in favour of abortion, and also by the teaching of evolution and influences against prayer in public schools. They felt they had to become more **active in politics** to protect their religion and shape society according to their religious views. They brought a religious tone and influence to politics.

> **KEY CONCEPT: THE MORAL MAJORITY** were those people who supported the application of strict or severe Christian standards of behaviour to society.

The Moral Majority

Jerry Falwell, an evangelical minister, organised the **Moral Majority** in 1979 *'to bring about a conservative revolution.'* The Moral Majority was particularly influential among southern Baptists. At a time when overall church membership was declining, the number of southern Baptists increased by thirty per cent. They used television to get their message across. In 1978, 25 channels broadcast religion on television. By 1989, this had increased to over 300.

The Moral Majority campaigned against abortion, divorce, homosexuality, federal involvement in education, and the ERA (Equal Rights Amendment). This movement and the **Christian Coalition** (led by Pat Robertson) were especially influential in the **Republican Party** where they worked to change it into a party of *'traditional family values'*. They were particularly influential during the Republican Presidency of **Ronald Reagan**. In 1988, Pat Robertson became the first major religious leader in US history to campaign for a party presidential nomination, even though he failed to get it.

Rev. Jerry Falwell, who organised the Moral Majority, giving an anti-abortion speech in 1981.

However, the Christian fundamentalists showed signs of **bigotry**, particularly anti-semitism. *'With all due respect to these dear people, God does not hear the prayer of a Jew,'* said one leader. Some blamed all America's troubles on a Jewish conspiracy. This anti-semitism, along with financial and sex scandals, undermined some of the fundamentalist leadership by the early 1990s.

BLACK COMMUNITIES

Religion played an important part in the life of black communities. **Baptism** and **Methodism** were especially influential in the rural South. Religious leaders and church buildings were important in the **social life** of the community. The Civil Rights movement was spearheaded by religious leaders such as **Martin Luther King** and **Ralph Abernathy**. When many blacks **migrated** to northern and southern cities so also did their churches. In the huge change in social life from rural to urban, from agriculture to industry, religion provided a constant source of **stability**, in church buildings which were often small and intimate.

The **Islamic tradition** also developed among the black community in northern cities. The **Black Muslims** (Nation of Islam) grew from about 1,000 members in 1946 to about 100,000 members in 1960. They rejected the term **Negro** (they said it was a slave term) for black. They enforced strict rules of behaviour and called for separate black development. Their most outstanding spokesman in the 1960s was **Malcolm X**. But they attracted high-profile members such as **Muhammed Ali**, the world heavyweight boxing champion, and their message spread well beyond their own members. When Malcolm X split with the leadership of the Black Muslims in 1965, he was assassinated. In spite of this crisis, Black Muslims still appealed to sizeable numbers of blacks.

Elijah Muhammad, leader of the Black Muslims, addressing their National Meeting in 1966 with Muhammed Ali beside him.

The Mass Media in Modern American Culture

The spread of many aspects of modern American culture was dependent on the mass media which itself was an integral part of that culture. **Newspapers** and **movies** continued as important elements of the mass media but the new medium, **television**, became the dominant aspect of the mass media.

NEWSPAPERS

> KEY CONCEPT: MASS MEDIA was a medium of communication (newspapers, magazines, radio and television) which reached a large audience or the mass of the people.

Newspaper circulation expanded rapidly in the decades before the Second World War. But in the second half of the twentieth century the coming of television influenced both their **content** and **circulation**. Americans turned more to television for their daily news, so newspapers had to change. There was a greater concentration of ownership as some newspapers were bought out. The number of US cities with more than one daily newspaper dropped. By 1960, over eighty per cent of cities had only one daily newspaper. As a result, the number of newspapers in the country also dropped to about 1,500. While the daily circulation of newspapers remained steady, the population rose by ninety per cent so that a smaller proportion of people bought newspapers.

NEWSPAPER CIRCULATION (MILLIONS)	
1949	53
1965	59
1995	57

Newspaper Influence

Nevertheless, the influence of newspapers remained strong. Newspaper **investigations** played an important role in monitoring government policy. The *New York Times* broke the story of the Pentagon Papers which revealed the deceit of American foreign policy in relation to Vietnam. Some years later Woodward and Bernstein, two journalists working for the *Washington Post*, revealed the corruption at the centre of the Nixon Administration and the conspiracy over the Watergate Affair. The impact of these revelations was to roll back the powers which **presidents** (the imperial presidency) had accumulated over the previous forty years.

There was no **national daily newspaper** in the US until the 1980s due to the vast size of the country and the different time zones. But early in the decade, *USA Today*, the first daily national newspaper was published. Its style of short articles and colour made it a success. It was soon followed by the *Wall Street Journal* and the *New York Times* with national editions of their own newspapers using satellite transmission and regional printing.

MOVIES

Movies too declined in post-war America. This was partly caused by the **movement of population** from the centre cities (where cinemas were located) to the suburbs. But it was also caused by the rise of **television**.

The film industry, largely based in Hollywood (Los Angeles) responded by building drive-ins, using wide screens, 3-D and stereo sound. The film industry also responded to changes in popular culture. As a commercial operation, it needed to satisfy the mass market. Therefore, new productions were aimed at the popular taste.

Westerns were popular, as were **Cold War** stories. So also were spectacular shows such as *The Ten Commandments* and *Ben Hur*. These reinforced popular images of brave men, gentle women and the evils of Communism. However, some films broke with general consensus, such as the anti-war movie, *Paths of Glory*, or *Rebel Without a Cause* which highlighted rebellious youth.

But these failed to reverse the decline. However, these figures underestimate the influence and role of movies in modern American culture. From the 1950s, many movies (films) were rerun on television and some were made for television only. By the 1970s and 1980s, videos and pay TV channels such as **Home Box Office** (HBO) widened the audience and the influence of films.

Throughout all this time Hollywood maintained a **code of conduct** in relation to portraying sex or violence on screens. This was not relaxed or eased until 1966, after which films became more obscene, violent and sexual to reflect the more turbulent 60s. *Bonnie and Clyde*, which featured a couple of young robbers on the run from the law, and *The Wild Bunch* were early examples which reflected the changes.

The 1970s saw the appearance of many young directors such as **Francis Ford Coppola** whose *The Godfather* series told the story of a Mafia family. These directors followed the pattern of **realistic portrayals** of life. But there were also **action movies**, such as *Star Wars* and *Raiders of the Lost Ark*, which harped back to the earlier decades of the cinema. Very often some of the best movies were directed by **independent directors** outside the Hollywood studio system which controlled the film industry. This, along with new suburban cineplexes (multiple-cinema complexes), helped to attract a growing younger audience back to the cinema.

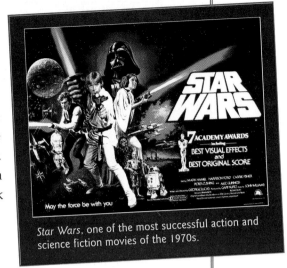

Star Wars, one of the most successful action and science fiction movies of the 1970s.

TELEVISION

Television grew **rapidly**. In 1948, less than 200,000 families had televisions. But this boomed in the next few years to 15 million by 1952, and 35 million in 75% of homes by 1955. By 1960, 90% of homes had televisions. Colour took over in the 1960s. It was not until the late 1970s that **cable** began to spread – only 12% of homes had cable in 1974; but by 1990 about 70% had cable television.

The use of **satellite transmissions**, beginning with Telstar and Early Bird in the 1960s, made national live broadcasts possible. Their link up with cable TV gave rise to new channels geared to specific **mass audiences** such as **MTV** (Music Television) and **CNN** (Cable News Network) which both began in 1981. But some feared that the effect of the wider range of channels specialising in religion, sport and business, might lead to a **splintering of society** and reduce the overall national feeling of identity. However, as others pointed out, there was also the likelihood of **oversaturation**. As pop star, Bruce Springsteen sang:

'I can see by your eyes friend you're just about gone
Fifty-seven channels and nothin' on...'

Television and Family Life

Television became the centre of the **family life** influencing the time of meals, sometimes even what was eaten in the shape of TV dinners. Television provided many hours of **leisure**, some said too much because it produced a **lazy lifestyle**. To cater for **mass audiences** television went for general interest programmes, variety entertainment, quiz shows, sitcoms, and talk shows. Some criticised the **mindlessness** of these programmes. Even before television became very popular, the President of Boston University said in 1950, *'If the television rage continues ... we are destined to have a nation of morons.'*

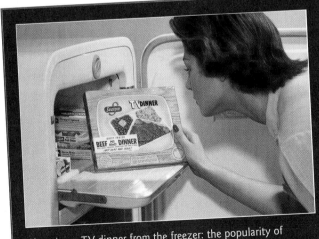

Choosing a TV dinner from the freezer: the popularity of television influenced the time of meals.

Television affected other aspects of **American life**. Along with movies it reinforced the **image** of the white, suburban, middle-class family. In this way it also reflected the woman's role as a house-wife. *'A career is just fine,'* said Debbie Reynolds in *The Tender Trap*, *'but it is no substitute for marriage.'* Television also increased the value and attractiveness of **advertising** and in this way contributed to the growing consumer society. The advertisers *'had a more potent force available for selling purposes. Radio was abandoned like the bones at a barbecue.'*

Television raised the profile of sports stars, including Michael Jordan, one of the all-time great basketball players.

Since television depended largely on **sponsorship**, the advertisers had a huge influence on what was shown on television. One of the most influential and provocative current affairs programmes of the early 1950s was changed to an occasional documentary before it was dropped when the sponsoring company withdrew its support.

Televised **sport** was ideal for the mass audiences. Television money paid for more **professionalism** in sport, especially by the 1970s and 1980s when multi-million dollar contracts became normal. But it also dictated breaks in sport to cater for advertising. It also raised the profile of black and Hispanic sports stars, such as **Michael Jordan** in basketball and **Muhammed Ali** in boxing. In its entertainment programmes, it had to change gradually to reflect **the racial mix of society** by moving from blacks as servants and slaves to portraying them with a fuller role in society.

Television and Politics

Television also influenced **politics** by shaping **public opinion**. It contributed to the downfall of **Senator Joe McCarthy** when his bullying style was shown up badly by live television broadcasts at the Army-McCarthy hearings in 1954. Television also influenced the outcome of **presidential elections**, particularly the very close 1960 race between John F Kennedy and Richard Nixon. Kennedy's performance on the first live television presidential debates and his youthful image helped to give him a narrow victory.

It influenced politics in another way. By increasing the **costs of campaigning**, it opened politicians to charges of influence when they got money from businesses to cover their costs. Television could not deal with more complicated problems so it tended to **simplify issues**. In this way advertisers and polit-ical consultants emphasised the importance of **sound bites** – short, snappy comments which caught attention – rather than serious discussion.

> **KEY CONCEPT: PUBLIC OPINION.**
> The views and attitudes of the people. This is measured in elections or in between elections in opinion polls. In a democracy, political parties have to get elected so they have to pay attention to public opinion. They also try to influence and manipulate public opinion in their favour. This is often done through the media – press, radio and television.

Television had a large influence on the progress of the **civil rights movement**. It exposed to national and international audiences police efforts to prevent school desegregation in Little Rock, Arkansas in 1957, **Bull Connor** and his police force's brutal treatment of black protestors in Birmingham, Alabama and the police violence against the Selma-Montgomery marchers. It brought **Martin Luther King** to national prominence as a black spokesman. In this way television encouraged northern liberal white support for civil rights and it provoked government action.

In the 1960s and 1970s, Americans watched the first **living room war** as they saw action from Vietnam. But producers of NBC, ABC and CBS cut out **bloody incidents** from evening news broadcasts. This helped shield the public from the horrors of war. For the most part television gave the **government's version** of the war – that America was winning – until the Tet Offensive in early 1968. After this, television played an important role in the growth of anti-war opinion. Just like the newspapers, television felt betrayed by government misinformation.

Mass Higher Education

EXPANSION OF HIGHER EDUCATION

There was a **huge interest** in education in post-war America. Dozens of books on education and educational articles were published. This reflected parents higher aspirations for their children. A more complex and technical world also demanded higher levels of education. The booming economy of the 1950s created a strong demand for college educated students by corporations providing large salaries.

Colleges and universities faced problems of coping with the increased demand for places. Enrolment grew because of veterans attending under the **GI Bill of Rights**, it fell off slightly during the Korean War, but grew rapidly again afterwards when the post-war **baby boomers** reached college age. By the time the GI Bill was wound up in 1956, eight million had benefited. University enrolment also grew because of the **greater prosperity** – college fees grew slower than family incomes. As well as this, full employment made part-time jobs more easily available for students who needed to fund some of their education.

Enrolment went from 1·5 million (16% of the 18–21 age group) in 1945 to 7·9 million (over 40%) in 1970. Of those in college in 1970, 60% of whites and 75% of blacks came from families with no previous experience of higher level education. In 1970, 26% of workers were college educated, this increased to 46% by 1989. To cope with this increase, the **number** of colleges and universities grew – from 1,500 in 1940 to over 2,000 in 1960, and over 3,000 in 1975.

COLLEGE AND UNIVERSITY NUMBERS (MILLIONS)	
1945	1·5
1950	2·3
1960	3·6
1970	7·9
1975	9·7

PROBLEMS

Because of the rapid increase, the **quality** of the universities and colleges varied from the high-flying ones such as **Yale** and **Harvard** to colleges which offered courses in anything. Some even accused these colleges of **dumbing down** education.

Universities also grew in **size** – 39 had over 20,000 students each in 1969. This made them more **bureaucratic** and **impersonal**. This led to conflict between the strict campus regulations about lifestyle and behaviour inherited from olden days and the youth of the 1960s, some influenced by a culture of long hair, untidy clothes, rock music, drugs and the sexual revolution.

This contributed to **mass campus uprisings** in the mid-1960s, partly spurred on by opposition to the Vietnam War and to the **draft**. The first protest – the **Free Speech Movement** at the University of California at Berkley in 1964 – was due to college attempts to restrict political activity on campus. In 1965, 25,000 students marched through Washington to protest against the Vietnam War. The **campus riots** spread over the next few years, with over 200 major university demonstrations in 1968. The climax of the demonstrations was a pitched battle between students and the Chicago police and national guards outside the Democratic Convention being held in Chicago in late 1968.

There was also more widespread **criticism of American society**, in particular the economic system and the role of the universities as part of it. The **New Left**, in particular **Students for a Democratic Society** (SDS), argued that acceptance of large **research grants** from government and corporate industry posed a threat to independent scholarship. The **Massachusetts Institute of Technology** (MIT), for example, was part of the Military-Industrial complex. Even *Time* magazine worried about the development. *'Is the military about to take over US science lock, stock and barrel?'*

The universities responded to these criticisms by relaxing entry requirements and changing courses to reflect changes in society such as introducing Black Studies and Women's Studies, as well as abolishing officer training courses. (See also Chapter 21, Domestic Factors in US Foreign Policy, 1945–72; The Anti-war Movement, p. 368.)

RACIAL CONFLICT

Universities also became the scene of **racial conflict**. In southern universities, blacks, like James Meredith at the University of Mississippi, had to battle to gain entry to all-white universities. In other places, some colleges and universities had **special admission policies** for blacks and other minority groups in the 1960s. This was part of the government's **affirmative action** programme which increased black enrolment. However, it also caused a white complaint of **reverse discrimination** that they were failing to gain admission to university because of special schemes for blacks, and not on the basis of merit or ability. In 1978, a white Californian student challenged his failure to get into medical school because of the admissions policy. The Supreme Court ruled in his favour, and declared that **other factors** along with ethnic and racial background had to be considered in admissions policies.

There was a **decline** in student political activity after 1973. This was due to the ending of the Vietnam War and the Draft and also to worsening economic conditions which concentrated minds on jobs. The reduction in federal support, higher costs of courses and the fact that a degree did not guarantee a good job, reduced enrolments. As a result of cutbacks in colleges, some even closed.

ORDINARY LEVEL

1. Study the figures on Church Membership and Spending on Church Reconstruction on p. 453 and answer the following questions:

(i) Which decade had the largest percentage increase?

(ii) In which decade did a decline occur?

(iii) Suggest one reason for this decline.

(iv) Compare these figures with the US population figures on p. 386. What conclusions can you draw about the religious revival?

(v) Suggest two reasons for the huge increase in spending on church reconstruction.

2. Write **paragraph answers** on each of the following questions:

(i) The causes of the religious revival in the US from the 1940s onwards.

(ii) Christian Fundamentalism and the Moral Majority.

(iii) The role of religion in the Black communities.

(iv) The role of (a) newspapers, (b) movies, and (c) television, in the US mass media during the post-war decades.

(v) The expansion of higher education in the US after the Second World War.

3. Write **long answers** on each of the following:

(i) Billy Graham and the religious revival in the US.

(ii) Why was the evangelist Billy Graham so influential in American life in the second half of the twentieth century? (Department of Education, Sample Paper)

(iii) What influence had television on modern American culture from the 1940s onwards?

(iv) Why did higher education expand so rapidly in post-war America and what problems were associated with that expansion?

HIGHER LEVEL

1. Assess the impact of the post-war religious revival on modern American society.

2. Assess the impact of the mass media on modern American society.

3. Assess the impact of the expansion of higher education on modern American society.

TEST YOURSELF AT
my-etest.com

Advances in Military Technology

In the second half of the twentieth century, America led most advances in military technology. Its involvement in a series of wars – hot and cold, its powerful economy, advanced research and technology, its superpower status and public opinion have all contributed to continuous advances in military technology:

- The **wars** provided the reason for developing weapons and the final testing of them.
- The **economy** provided the resources to fund the development of military technology.
- **Research and development** came up with new ideas and built them.
- **Superpower status** needed to be maintained.
- American **public opinion** supported the strengthening of the military.

NUCLEAR WEAPONS

The most spectacular and dangerous advances in military technology occurred in **nuclear weaponry**. Already during the Second World War, the US had developed the atomic bomb in the **Manhattan Project**. When they dropped the bombs on Hiroshima and Nagasaki in August 1945, the atomic age truly began.

> KEY CONCEPT: **TECHNOLOGICAL DEVELOPMENT** is the application or use of scientific discoveries in industry.

These bombs were delivered on board **B-29 bombers**. In the post-war era, the US began to develop more powerful planes, particularly after the USSR exploded its own atomic bomb in 1949. Now the US needed a plane that could attack the USSR directly. This became the **B-52 Stratofortress** which entered service in 1955. The B-52 was the backbone of Strategic Air Command for the next thirty-five years, with 650 in operation at its peak in 1963. It had a dual role both in delivering atomic bombs and in conventional bombing, as in Vietnam.

At the same time, President Truman gave the go-ahead for a crash programme to develop the **Hydrogen bomb** (H-bomb), largely in response to the USSR's A-bomb and to counteract the possibility that the USSR would develop a Hydrogen bomb itself. **Computer technology** played a key role in the development of nuclear bombs. The US tested its first H-bomb in the Pacific Ocean in 1952. The explosion sent a radioactive cloud twenty-five miles into the sky and developed a crater one mile wide.

ROCKETS

The development of **rockets** gave much greater precision to nuclear warfare. They were also much more difficult for the enemy forces to shoot them down. US rocket development was boosted enormously when the best German staff working on rockets of the Second World War, and headed by **Werner von Braun**, surrendered to US troops. The US also captured some of the rockets (the V2s) which they tested in America between 1945 and 1951.

The US used their experience of these rockets to develop short- and medium-range missiles such as the **Snark** and **Corporal**. These were developed to supplement the long-range bomber, not replace it. By the 1960s, the US had replaced earlier rockets with the **Pershing** which had a range of 400 miles (640 kilometres) and was based in Europe. They could all carry either nuclear or conventional warheads.

A Polaris missile being tested off the coast of Florida in 1963.

ICBM

The development of **inter-continental ballistic missiles** (ICBMs) began in the mid-1950s. President Eisenhower speeded up the arms race with his preference for nuclear missiles over conventional ones. He said nuclear weapons gave *'more bang for the buck'*. The development of the H-bomb, the improved rocket guidance systems and new rocket fuels made the building of the ICBMs possible. The launching of the **Russian Sputnik** into space made it necessary. Now Americans feared the Russians would attack from space.

The first ICBM rocket was the **Atlas**, launched in 1958, followed by **Titan** and later by the **Minuteman** which could be fired from an **underground silo**. Further development of the Minuteman gave it a longer range (7,000 miles) and **multiple warheads** (MIRV).

At the same time the Navy developed the **Polaris missile** which could be fired from nuclear powered submarines. By the 1970s, these were being replaced by the **Poseidon**, with a longer range and carrying MIRV warheads.

WARNING SYSTEMS

The similar development of Soviet planes and missiles made it necessary for the US to develop an **early warning system** to detect an attack and to initiate counter-attacks. The US worked with Canada to develop the **DEW** (Distant Early Warning) system – a series of radar stations stretched across Northern Canada and Alaska. The US also developed **airborne search radars** such as AWACS (Airborne Warning And Control System) which are constantly in the air. In 1960, they launched the first **reconnaissance satellite**, SAMOS, which provided early warning.

In the 1980s, President Reagan announced his **Strategic Defence Initiative** (SDI) – popularly known as **Star Wars** – which would be able to defend US territory against Soviet attack by launching intercepting missiles from space. However, the huge costs involved in developing such a missile defence system ($1,000 billion) and the end of the Cold War meant that this was not developed by the end of the 1980s.

CONVENTIONAL TECHNOLOGY

In spite of President Eisenhower's wish in the 1950s to cut back on spending on conventional weapons, these were not neglected either. In fact, the awesome power of nuclear bombs made their use unlikely and the US was involved in a number of conventional wars – Korean War, 1950–53 and the Vietnam War in the 1960s, for example.

To cope with this kind of fighting, the US continued with the development of planes, a variety of missiles such as air-to-air or surface-to-air, tanks, reconnaissance aircraft, chemical and biological warfare, aircraft carriers and submarines. In spite of the huge advances in military technology, **tactics and strategy** remained much as they were, and these weapons were used in the same way as in the Second World War. As well as this, the Vietnam War showed that superior technology did not guarantee victory in fighting unconventional **guerrilla warfare**.

Air War

The development of the **jet engine** at the end of the Second World War increased the speed and range of aircraft. Fighter aircraft were equipped with missiles to attack enemy aircraft, but also other missiles to attack tanks, troops, fuel depots and airfields. By the late 1950s, supersonic air-to-air missiles such as the **Sidewinder**, **Phoenix** and **Falcon** were developed to cope with faster aircraft.

Bomber aircraft were also developed with greater range and accuracy. They were used in the **Korean War** and in **Vietnam**, where they **carpet-bombed** areas of the Vietnamese jungle. But they had to wait for the development of computer-controlled, radar-guided bombs in the 1990s to increase their accuracy and effectiveness.

Reconnaissance aircraft were also developed, especially the supersonic **U2** which was involved in spying over the USSR and also over Cuba before and during the Cuban Missile Crisis. In more recent decades **drones** or **pilotless aircraft** were developed for spying.

Helicopters

The helicopter was one of the most significant developments in military technology. After their use in the Second World War, helicopters came into their own in the Korean War. They were used for scouting and troop-carrying, as well as search and rescue. Their ability to evacuate casualties from particularly difficult countryside was given as a reason for the reduced death rate. In the Vietnam War, **helicopter gunships** became symbolic of the action there. They were fast, heavily armed and used in support of ground troops.

Aircraft carriers gave increased mobility to the US armed forces who could respond rapidly to small or large conflicts.

To combat the power and speed of enemy aircraft, **surface-to-air missiles** were developed to replace conventional artillery. The US Army and Navy developed separate types – the Army developed the **Hercules** which had a range up to eighty-five miles, while the Navy developed the **Terrier** and the **Sea Sparrow**. But as well as these the **Redeye**, a shoulder-mounted missile, was developed for ground troops. All these used various methods such as radar and heat seeking to guide their missile on to the target.

Aircraft Carriers

The growing significance of air war increased the importance of **aircraft carriers**. These gave mobility and rapid response to cater for small and larger scale wars. The advent of jet aeroplanes after the Second World War meant that aircraft carriers had to be larger and stronger. It also led to the development of the **catapult** (a British device) to cater for larger and faster planes.

The *Enterprise*, a nuclear-powered aircraft carrier, was the most powerful of the new carriers with great speed, manouverability and endurance. It was equipped with a wide range of military technology to meet the needs of modern warfare – radar, missile guidance, guided missiles, and sophisticated communications equipment.

Land War

Tank development proceeded similarly to the Second World War. The essential design of the tank remained the same but there were significant improvements in engines, suspension and firepower. By the 1960s and 1970s the **M60** and **MBT-70** tanks had gun launchers to fire missiles as well as conventional shells.

To cope with the vast range and power of the new weaponry developed against them, the **soldiers** also had improved military technology. Apart from the Redeye missile, they were equipped with heavy machine guns, anti-tank grenade launchers, recoilless rifles with armour piercing bullets and night-viewing glasses. Soldiers also had to be equipped to meet new threats from **chemical** and **biological** warfare.

PERMANENT WAR ECONOMY

close relationship between department of defence and the major companies and corporations.

The huge advances in US military technology from 1945 onwards cost a great deal of money. Indeed, so much money was spent on weapons and the military that some claimed America was a **permanent war economy**. On average, ten per cent of national income was spent each year on such technology.

Most of the money was spent on a small number of companies – General Dynamics, Lockheed, IBM, Boeing and a few others. Their manufacturing plants were located largely in the states of the **Sun Belt**, the South and South-West of the US from California to Florida.

This led to the development of what **President Eisenhower** called the **Military-Industrial complex** – the link between the Defence Department, industries, certain states and their political representatives. He warned about the danger of the Military-Industrial complex and its influence on government policy, in particular, its interest in pushing for an aggressive foreign policy. (See Chapter 20.)

Advances in Space Technology

> **KEY CONCEPT: MILITARY-INDUSTRIAL COMPLEX** was the combination of the armed forces, the politicians who supported them and the industries who supplied them. They had a strong influence on government decisions.

ROCKETS AND SOVIET COMPETITION

During the 1950s there were considerable developments in **rockets**. But these were mainly to power nuclear missiles. Then in 1957, the Russians sent a modified rocket into space called **Sputnik**. In contrast, the Americans first attempt to send a rocket into space – the Vanguard – was destroyed by an explosion on its launch pad a few months after the Sputnik's success. According to the press, it was a case of *'Flopnik'* and *'Kaputnik'*.

This – and later Russian **firsts** such as Yuri Gagarin becoming the first man in space – shocked the Americans. They had believed that American technology was superior to the Russians and the Russian successes were a severe blow to American **morale**. They also saw the Russian successes as a danger to national security, a very important consideration in the middle of the **Cold War**.

NASA (National Aeronautics and Space Administration) was set up in 1958 to catch up to, and beat, the Russian space technology. The Americans launched their first satellite, **Explorer I**, also in the same year. In 1961, President Kennedy, inspired by Cold War competition and Yuri Gagarin's success, promised that the Americans would have a man on the moon *'before the decade is out.'* During the 1960s the Americans spent $25 billion to achieve that aim.

A Russian postcard celebrates Yuri Gagarin's successful voyage as the first man in space.

MERCURY AND GEMINI PROJECTS

This was done in stages. First the **Mercury Project** sent Americans into space. The first was **Alan Shepard** in 1961, a month after Gagarin. This flight lasted fifteen minutes. Five more flights followed, including **Freedom Seven** in February 1962, in which **John Glenn** orbited the earth three times.

In the **Gemini Project**, two-man flights were organised to test **rendezvous** and **docking** techniques – this included space walks. The US also used the **Surveyor** space flights to test soft landings on the moon, as well as photographing and testing the surface. Then a series of **Lunar Orbiter** craft photographed possible landing sites for manned flights to the Moon. By now American technology had overtaken the Russian.

MAN ON THE MOON

The next stage was the development of a **three-man spacecraft**. This was the **Apollo Mission**. In 1968, Apollo 8 made a successful manned orbit of the moon sending back television pictures for millions of viewers at Christmas. Later missions tested the operation of the lunar module. In July 1969, Apollo 11 with **Neil Armstrong, 'Buzz' Aldrin** and **Michael Collins** on board, lifted off from Cape Kennedy, Florida for the moon. On 20 July 1969, Neil Armstrong stepped out of the lunar module, **Eagle**, to become the first man to set foot on the moon.

Later Apollo missions continued with further **landings** – in some of which the astronauts used a moon buggy to get around – and scientific investigations of the moon until 1972.
Apollo 12, later in 1969, collected soil samples from the Moon, took photographs and set up scientific experiments.
Apollo 13 took off in 1970 but ran into difficulties when an oxygen tank burst. The astronauts had to cancel their planned landing on the Moon. Instead they had to use the power of the Lunar Module to bring them back to Earth.

Apollo 14 (1971) carried out the mission intended for Apollo 13. They landed in a rugged part of the Moon and set up scientific experiments and collected rock samples.

The crew of **Apollo 15** (1971) spent almost three days on the Moon. They used a **moon buggy** to travel away from their spacecraft. They collected some of the oldest samples of Moon rock and set up further experiments. They also launched a **lunar mini-satellite** to send back data about the Moon's environment. This was the first crew which did not have to be quarantined.

Apollo 16 (1972) and **Apollo 17** (also 1972) followed the same pattern as previous Moon visits. Apollo 17 was the last of the Missions to the Moon.

SPACE STATIONS AND SPACE SHUTTLES

Much of the later advances of space technology were in **unmanned spacecraft**. This involved unmanned space flights to distant parts of the **solar system**, and also the development of **space stations** and the **space shuttle**.

A succession of space flights in the 1970s were sent to **Jupiter**, **Mars**, **Mercury** and **Venus** followed by flights to **Saturn** in the 1980s. These flights were mostly scientific investigations of the surface and atmosphere of these planets, with the main aim being to try and find signs of life.

The Skylab space station orbits the Earth during the Skylab 4 mission in 1973–4.

At the same time NASA was developing the **Skylab** programme to maintain a space station above the earth. Skylab was designed as a laboratory to carry out experiments in space, to test the effects of long periods of weightlessness on crew members, and to observe the Sun. Skylab was launched in 1973 and eventually crashed to Earth in western Australia in 1979.

At the same time the US developed the **space shuttle** – a reusable space vehicle which could cut the cost of space research and exploration, and reduce the amount of space litter. The first successful flight was made in 1981 by the space shuttle **Columbia** with a crew of seven. But the explosion of **Challenger** in January, 1986 and the deaths of its seven astronauts (including the first US civilian in space) raised doubts about the organisation of the space programme. A special commission on the disaster did not hold NASA responsible for design flaws in the shuttle, but it recommended that the agency be reorganised. By the end of the 1980s there was declining public interest and declining support from Congress for space flights. **Budget cutbacks** limited research and development. This led to fewer manned space flights.

OTHER SATELLITES

The advances in space technology led to other developments. In 1960, the US launched its first **weather satellite** which gave much greater understanding of global weather patterns. This was followed in the mid-1960s by commercial **communications satellites**, the first was called **Early Bird**. These provided a faster, worldwide system of communications by television, radio and phone.

In military and security, the US competed with the Russians by putting **spies in the sky**. These were satellites which used high definition cameras and infra-red technology to survey each other's country in great detail. But President Reagan's plan for the **Strategic Defence Initiative** (SDI), or Star Wars as it was called, was too ambitious for its time. This would have developed a space technology to intercept incoming Soviet or Russian missiles by exploding them before they reached America.

Advances in Information Technology

Information technology (IT) is the equipment and methods used to handle information. The information is collected, processed and stored. As the twentieth century progressed, more and more information needed to be handled to organise a more complex society. The development of the computer was central to the new information age and the development of modern information technology.

This was the ENIAC, the first general purpose computer, which was based at the US Proving Ground in Maryland. It weighed 30 tons and it was 8 feet high, 3 feet deep and 100 feet long.

The needs of the **American government** and **military** in the middle of the century were crucial to the development of the computer. Their need to handle vast amounts of data concerning atomic weapons gave a spurt to the development of the early computers. They linked with **business** (mostly IBM) and the **universities** to design and build the first US computers.

FIRST COMPUTERS

Computers developed rapidly during and after the Second World War. **Mark 1** was developed in 1943 through co-operation between Harvard University and IBM (International Business Machines). But this used **mechanical switches** to do its calculations. Much faster was **ENIAC**, which was the first **all-electronic computer**. It was developed for the army for calculations of thermonuclear fusion. Both machines were huge – ENIAC weighed 30 tons – and were very expensive. They needed a team of operators to work them.

One of those who contributed to the development of computers was **John von Neumann**, a Hungarian-born mathematician working in the US. He devised the logic which became the basis for the **mainframe computers**, particularly those built by IBM. His work led to the development of **EDVAC**, which influenced the building of IBM mainframe computers. They next developed **UNIVAC 1** which became the first commercially available computer. It was used to count the US Census in 1951 and the Presidential election results in 1952.

INVENTION OF THE TRANSISTOR

However, computers were still very large. This began to change after the invention of the **transistor** in 1947 by **William Shockley** at Bell Telephone Research Laboratories. It was mostly made of silicon and it replaced the electronic valves, produced no heat, eliminated miles of wiring, was very small and cheap to produce. In 1958, Seymour Cray designed the **first, fully-transistorised** computer. IBM produced its own version a year later.

The spread of this new form of information technology was gradual. Twenty computers were sold in 1954, this rose to 1,000 in 1957 and 2,000 in 1960.

Further advances in integrated circuits in the early 1960s led to the development of the **microchip**. Now the entire workings of the computer could be put on a few microchips. Smaller, personal computers became possible with the development of **Intel's microprocessor** in 1971.

PERSONAL COMPUTERS

The first **personal computer** (PC) was produced in 1975 but its use was mainly confined to electronic engineers. Two years later, however, **Steve Jobs** and **Steve Wozniak** introduced the **Apple II** which brought personal computers within the range of small business, families and schools. Shortly afterwards, **IBM** entered the personal computer market and the market expanded dramatically in the 1980s. The development of new operating systems, begun by Apple, and later spreading to others, in particular **Bill Gates** of **Microsoft**, made computers much more user-friendly. The number of computers rose quickly from less than 2 million to over 65 million in 1991.

COMPUTER INDUSTRY

By 1958, the US produced about $1 billion worth of computer equipment. Ten years later, this had grown to almost $5 billion, and to $17 billion by 1978. This was all part of the move away from heavy manufacturing to the **high technology industries** which also included genetic engineering, lasers and fibre optics. In 1952, 50% of workers were employed in manufacturing industry; by 1992 this had fallen to 20%.

By 1990, the US had the **largest computer industry** in the world, employing one million people with a revenue of $100 billion. Companies such as Dell, Compaq, Apple and Microsoft dominated hardware and software production. It also had the greatest number of computers – 50 million – half of the world's computers, compared to Japan with 11% and Europe with about 25%.

However, the industry split between the high-cost **research and development** side and the **production** side. Research and development was largely confined to **core areas** in the US – Silicon Valley in California, the Route 128 corridor around Boston, and the Research Triangle in North Carolina. On the other hand, much of the routine production and assembly functions were transferred to **peripheral locations**, particularly in Asia. This is how **multinationals** in information technology have developed. In this way, they have increased the gap between the **haves** and the **have-nots** on a worldwide scale.

THE INTERNET

In 1969, fear of a Cold War nuclear attack resulted in the beginning of the **internet**. This was the Defence Department's Advanced Research Project Agency (**ARPANET**) to allow military scientists to communicate over computers in the event of a nuclear explosion. It was expanded in 1986 to the National Science Foundation to include researchers at American universities. By the late 1980s, the **internet** as it had become known was widely used by businesses and individuals.

But the huge expansion of the internet, or the World Wide Web as part of it, did not come until the early 1990s.

IMPACT OF INFORMATION TECHNOLOGY

- By the late 1980s, computers had made a huge impact on **all aspects of American life**, from home to shopping and from work to entertainment.
- They caused a rapid **rise in productivity**. Indeed they caused a debate about the danger of **technological unemployment**.
  - ○ Some point to the fact that the Fortune 500 companies in the US shed over **four million jobs** in the 1980s. These used information technology to replace workers with machines. At the same time, these companies' sales and assets grew, and their **chief executives** increased their own income by six times. This increased the gap between the rich (haves) and poor (have-nots) within America during the 1980s.

  > **KEY CONCEPT: GLOBALISATION** is the spread of institutions, organisations and culture on a worldwide or global scale. It is usually associated with the spread of trade and industry by large companies or corporations to many different countries. Goods, services and culture gradually become the same in all parts of the world.

  - ○ Others argue that the fears that computer technology would replace people are exaggerated. They say that while some industries have declined, others have replaced them.
- An **example** of how the computer and information technology industries have made many people extremely **wealthy** is Bill Gates of Microsoft. Gates dropped out of college, founded Microsoft and produced the MS-DOS and Windows operating systems for IBM computers. By the age of 32 in 1987, he was worth $1 billion.
- Information technology had a major influence in the **globalisation** of industry, finance and culture. Computers speeded up communications and the transfer of money, and made it easier to transmit television channels worldwide.
- There was a **greater concentration of industry** because of the expense of the new technology which only the largest corporations could afford.
- Computer technology gave rise to a debate about the **invasion of privacy** and **dangers to democracy** of storing information on people. The US government passed a law to protect the privacy of individuals.

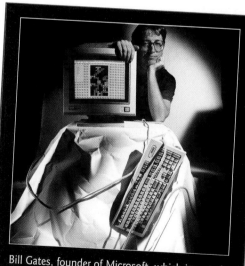

Bill Gates, founder of Microsoft, which invented the operating system running most personal computers.

ORDINARY LEVEL

1. Study the cartoon from *Punch* on p. 479 and answer the following questions:

(i) Who is represented in this cartoon?

(ii) What is the message of the cartoon?

(iii) Is the message happy or sad?

(iv) What techniques does the cartoonist use to get across his message?

(v) Is the cartoon biased? Explain your answer.

(vi) How useful and reliable are cartoons as sources for historians?

2. Write **paragraph answers** on each of the following questions:

(i) Advances in military technology.

(ii) Developments in nuclear weapons.

(iii) Developments in conventional weapons.

(iv) Advances in space technology. (Department of Education, Sample Paper)

(v) Advances in information technology.

3. Write **long answers** on each of the following:

(i) How did technology influence the development of nuclear warfare in the US from the 1940s to the 1980s?

(ii) How did technology influence the development of conventional weapons in the US from the 1940s to the 1980s?

(iii) How did technology influence the development of space exploration in the US from the 1940s to the 1980s?

(iv) How, and why, did computer technology develop in the US in the post-war decades?

HIGHER LEVEL

1. How, and why, was there a huge expansion in military technology in the US from 1945 to the 1980s?

2. What was the impact of advances in rockets in the US in the post-war decades?

3. Outline advances in information technology in the US in the post-war decades and assess the impact of that technology.

INTRODUCTION

The Russian space successes in the late 1950s and early 1960s surprised and shocked the US. The country was going through its greatest economic boom and its technology appeared to be well in advance of all other countries. Then the Russians proved otherwise.

To counter the Soviet success, the US set up **NASA** (National Aeronautics and Space Administration) in 1958 to take charge of US space exploration. Now the space race became fully part of Cold War rivalry. It forced **President Kennedy** to commit the US to landing a man on the moon before the end of the 1960s.

THE APOLLO PROGRAMME

The Apollo Programme was developed to land the first man on the moon. The first six Apollo missions were unmanned. They were used to test the giant **Saturn** rocket. But soon after, it hit disaster. In 1967, three astronauts in **Apollo 7** died when a fire broke out in the spacecraft on the launch pad. The next three missions successfully tested various aspects of the moon journey:

Apollo 8 undertook an important mission in December 1968 by orbiting around the moon and returning.

Apollo 9 practiced docking the command ship and the lunar module in earth orbit.

Apollo 10 went to the moon to test the lunar module further by flying to within 15 kilometres of the moon's surface before rejoining the command module.

APOLLO 11

Apollo 11 was destined to make the first moon landing. It was powered by the most powerful Saturn rocket yet, 111 metres tall. It had three **modules** (parts) to it:

• The **command module** (called Columbia) to carry the astronauts to the moon and back.

• The **service module** which held the rockets and fuel needed for the moon journey.

• The **lunar module** (Eagle) to land on the moon. It had four landing legs, each with a large footpad to prevent it from sinking into the lunar soil.

At the top was the **launch escape tower** to allow the astronauts to escape from the command module if there were problems on the launch pad.

THE ASTRONAUTS

The three astronauts were selected some years before:

• **Neil Armstrong**, the commander, was a pilot in the Korean War and later a test pilot. He flew in Gemini 8 in 1966.

• **Edwin 'Buzz' Aldrin** was also a pilot in Korea. He flew in Gemini 12 when he also walked in space. He was pilot of the lunar module.

• **Michael Collins**, also a pilot, flew in Gemini 10. He was the pilot of the command module.

The astronauts went through intensive training. They practiced in **simulators**, similar to the Apollo spacecraft. They also experienced **weightlessness** in underwater tanks and in special aeroplane flights.

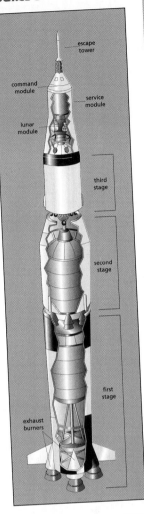

SOURCE 5

escape tower

command module

service module

lunar module

third stage

second stage

first stage

exhaust burners

SOURCE 6

The crew of Apollo 11 ready to go to the Moon; Neil Armstrong, Michael Collins and Edwin 'Buzz' Aldrin.

'**Neil Armstrong**: Devoted to duty, he has little time for anything but his job and sets himself apart from people except for his family and close friends. He has been described as a modern day soldier of fortune because he likes to be where the excitement is, whether as a test pilot of the X-15 rocket plane or flying 78 combat missions during the Korean War.

Edwin 'Buzz' Aldrin: The young man seemed to know everything in his chosen profession. West Point honours graduate, Distinguished Flying Cross with Oak Leaf cluster, 56 combat missions in Korea with two MiGs shot down and one damaged, but, at the age of 33, his blond hair already thinning, he was back in school ... Writing the dissertation (study, thesis) that won him a Doctor of Science degree in Astronautics, he dedicated it to "the men in the astronaut programme".

Michael Collins: How will he feel about acclaim after the flight? "I've really enjoyed the programme immensely. This job is the most fascinating in the world. On the other hand, I say in all candour [truth] that I appreciate remaining anonymous, and I'll do the best I can to keep that going. I like to live a normal private life." '

The *Irish Times*, 16 July 1969

THE LAUNCH

On 16 July 1969, the three astronauts ate a large breakfast of steak, eggs, toast and orange juice in the Kennedy Space Centre in Florida. They then dressed in bulky **spacesuits** and went aboard the command module, **Columbia**, two hours before take-off. Aldrin sat in the centre, with Armstrong on his left and Collins on his right. Thousands of spectators watched the launch some distance from Apollo, while millions more watched on television. The news of the launch was covered by 3,000 press, radio and television reporters.

SOURCE 7 – Largest turnout in history

'An estimated 750,000 to one million persons witnessed the launching (at Cape Kennedy) ... The turnout was the largest in history to witness a space launch ... Traffic was tied up even further with about 160 members of the Poor People's Campaign, with four mules, who marched about one mile along the highway to emphasise the plight of the nation's hungry.'

New York Times News Service, the *Irish Times*, 17 July 1969

SOURCE 9

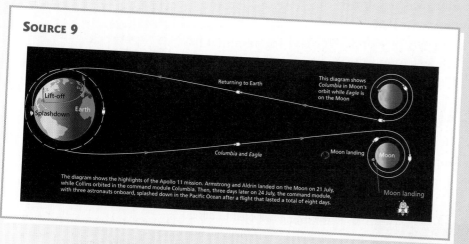

The diagram shows the highlights of the Apollo 11 mission. Armstrong and Aldrin landed on the Moon on 21 July, while Collins orbited in the command module Columbia. Then, three days later on 24 July, the command module, with three astronauts onboard, splashed down in the Pacific Ocean after a flight that lasted a total of eight days.

THE JOURNEY

At 9.32 a.m. Apollo was cleared for take-off. Saturn 5 had **three rocket stages** – each one was jettisoned (dropped off) when its fuel was used up. It was loaded with 2,000 tonnes of fuel which it burned at a rate of 15 tonnes a second:

- At 3 minutes, the **launch escape tower** was jettisoned; now the astronauts could see out from the command module.
- At 9 minutes the second-stage rocket was jettisoned.
- At 11 minutes Apollo and its three astronauts reached Earth orbit. It was ready for its journey to the moon.

At this point, **Collins** separated the command module from the third-stage rocket, then reconnected with the lunar module before heading for the moon. On the journey, the astronauts checked the lunar module, participated in live television broadcasts and rested in sleeping bags. They did not have to wear their spacesuits except at certain stages of the voyage, such as the launch and re-entry. Their food included bacon strips, peaches, chicken, salmon and beef stew and they had drinks of coffee and orange juice. The food was freeze-dried and sealed in small plastic bags and sometimes had to have water added. On 19 July, they reached the moon.

SOURCE 12

SOURCE 13

Buzz Aldrin takes his last step off the Eagle lunar module onto the surface of the Moon.

Buzz Aldrin prepares to deploy a scientific package to investigate the Moon.

SOURCE 14

SOURCE 15

Buzz Aldrin poses on the Moon beside the US flag.

The impression of an astronaut's shoe on the Moon's surface.

1. Describe the lunar landscape in Source 12.
2. What impression of the Moon landing does Source 13 give?
3. Why was the American flag erected?
4. What does the photograph of the footprint tell us about the Moon's surface?
5. How useful are these photographs in helping us to understand the First Moon landing?
6. Why were these photographs taken and why were they published? Is there evidence of bias or propaganda in the photographs? If that is the case, does that make them less reliable and useful?
7. 'Photographs have limited value to historians because they only show a moment in time, not what went on before or after.' Do you agree or disagree with this statement? To what extent does this statement apply to the photographs here?

MOON LANDING

The next day, 20 July, Armstrong and Aldrin went into the lunar module, **Eagle**. They separated from Collins in the command module and landed in the **Sea of Tranquility**. Armstrong had to manually guide Eagle to ensure a safe landing place. Then he reported back to Earth, 'Contact light on. Engine off. The Eagle has landed.' When Armstrong came out of the module and stepped on the moon, he said, 'That's one small step for man, one giant leap for mankind.' Aldrin followed later and they planted an **American flag**, stiffened with wire.

The **spacesuit** for walking on the moon was similar to the suit for the launch, except that it had an extra layer for added protection. They also had special underwear cooled by plastic tubing filled with water. Their backpack or **Portable Life Support System** (PLSS) supplied cooling water for the underwear and oxygen to breathe. Their helmets had a plastic shell, and two visors for added protection.

They spent 21·5 hours on the surface conducting **scientific experiments** and **collecting rock samples**. They were able to walk quite easily on the Moon without having to take the kangaroo-like steps they thought they would have to. They also placed a **metal plaque** on the moon, commemorating the landing; 'Here men from the planet Earth first set foot upon the Moon, July 1969 AD. We came in peace for all mankind.'

THE RETURN

When Eagle took off from the moon, the descent stage of the module was left behind. The lunar module then docked with Columbia. After Armstrong and Aldrin returned to the command module, Eagle was detached and left to float in Moon orbit.

The command module returned to Earth, protected by its **heat shield** as it came through the Earth's atmosphere. Parachutes then slowed down the entry speed. The command module splashed down in the **Pacific Ocean**, a thousand miles south-west of Hawaii, on 24 July, one mile from the target area. The capsule landed upside down in the sea, but it was soon righted. The astronauts were taken on board the **USS *Hornet*** and placed into quarantine for 21

days in case they brought back any dangerous germs. Their mission had lasted 8 days. The quarantine chamber was taken to Houston Space Centre, Texas.

SOURCE 19 – Lynch sends message

'We fervently hope that the sense of community which united the world-wide audience with the astronauts' families and the people of the United States in following the critical phases of the mission will lead mankind to the unity of minds and hearts which alone can bring peace in the world.'

Message from Taoiseach, Jack Lynch, to President Nixon after the return of the astronauts, the *Irish Times*, 25 July 1969

SOURCE 20 – By 1984

'Although Space Agency engineers have not yet put their computers to work ... It appears likely that by 1984 a round-trip economy-class rocket-plane flight to a comfortably appointed orbiting station can be brought down to a cost of several thousand dollars ... By 1984 there should be a permanent lunar orbiting space station passing over each point on the moon every 14 days and the establishment of an initial lunar surface base.'

Thomas O Paine, Administrator of the National Aeronautics and Space Administration, in 'Winning New Worlds for Our Descendants', the *Irish Times*, 18 July 1969

SOURCE 21 – Coming home

'What they have done is to push outward not only into space, but into untapped reserves of hope. A generation or so from now their contribution will move into a more settled perspective. By then, there may be interplanetary space stations and hotels on Mars. But the men on the Moon began it all.'

Editorial, the *Irish Times*, 22 July 1969

SOURCE 22 – Crossing national boundaries for magnificent achievement

'Apollo 11 will always be remembered as a magnificent achievement in the history of applied science and technology in the United States, and we Americans are justifiably proud of it. In reality, however, the team that brought Apollo 11 to fruition cuts across national boundaries. The mission itself had its beginning not on 16 July 1969, but several centuries ago. The sense of history involved in this realisation of man's ancient dream of voyaging to the Moon is easily overlooked and we tend to consider this feat as the product of twentieth-century science and technology ... [quoting Frank Borman, a previous astronaut] "Yet when we say this was an American achievement, we really have to go back to Newton and paraphrase him ... How can anyone think of [the Apollo mission] without thinking of Galileo or Copernicus or Kepler or Jules Verne or Oberth or Tsiolkovski or Goddard or Kennedy or Grissom or White or Chaffee or Komarov." We truly stood on the shoulders of giants.'

Dr Werner Von Braun, the *Irish Times*, 17 July 1969

SOURCE 23

A cartoon from *Punch*, an English magazine, in 1969.

CONCLUSION

The **significance** of the Moon landing, 1969:

- It fulfilled the **commitment** of the US, through its President, John F Kennedy, to land a man on the moon before the end of the 1960s.
- The Apollo mission was part of a **huge project** which involved over 400,000 people in assembly plants and control rooms.
- The US now led the **space race** against the Russians; it was portrayed as a victory for the democratic, capitalist system in the West.
- The Soviet Union launched an unmanned space-craft, Luna 15, shortly before the Apollo launch. It was aimed to reduce the publicity of Apollo 11, but it crash-landed on the moon. After this, the Soviet Union concentrated more on developing **space stations** where it had a clear lead over the US. However, these were not as spectacular as the first moon landing.
- **Budget cuts** in the 1970s meant that since 1972 no one has gone to the moon.

- The three astronauts were affected in different ways by the landing:
  o **Armstrong** was a quiet personality so he rarely talked publicly about the moon landing afterwards. He became a professor and chair-man of a computer company.
  o **Aldrin**, who had a brilliant mind, had a nervous breakdown and became an alcoholic. But he recovered and became a professor.
  o **Collins** published an account of the space voyage. He was a business executive.
- The cost of the space programme caused public debate. Some argued that the vast amount of money involved in putting the first men on the moon could have been spent on **America's social and economic problems** which were very evident in the 1960s.
- The **rocks** which they brought back, and others from later voyages, provided new information about the structure and formation of the moon.

SOURCE 24 – It's official: US did land on moon

'The US moon landings, as any good conspiracy theorist knows, were staged on a movie set by Americans eager to outstrip the Russians in the space race. You can tell because the flag they plant there ripples in a gust of wind, because the film-makers forgot to include stars in the night sky and because Neil Armstrong and 'Buzz' Aldrin have never spoken about their lunar adventures.

But in a move the doubters will surely dismiss as just another plank in the conspiracy, NASA has finally been goaded into responding. The space agency is to launch a publication setting out the evidence that the 1969 Apollo landing really did take place, NASA's former chief historian told *The Guardian* yesterday, in response to a flood of questions from school students and their teachers. "Hardcore conspiracy theorists," Roger Launius said, "are not the audience – nobody believes you can convince them of anything. But teachers are always saying they were asked in class and want to know how to respond."

The missing stars are easily dealt with: the photographs in question also show Earth, a huge patch of brightness hard to combine on the same exposure with dimmer flickering lights. Awkwardly for those who see evidence of deception, Armstrong and Aldrin have both spoken of the mission.

The rippling flag is explained as follows: the astronauts had to twist the flagpole to insert it into the moon's surface, and doing so caused it to ripple. In the absence of any atmosphere, the rippling continued long after they had moved away.'

Oliver Burkeman in New York,
The Guardian, 6 November 2002

COMPREHENSION

1. What was the battle between 'freedom and tyranny' which President Kennedy refers to in Source 1? What does he mean when he says 'men everywhere ... are attempting to make a determination of which road they should take'? What did Sputnik do in 1957?

2. According to Source 2, what effect did President Kennedy's commitment to put a man on the moon have?

3. What was Khrushchev's theme according to Source 3? What had 'a traumatic impact on the US'?

4. In Source 4, who designed the Saturn rockets? What two countries did he work for? What is 'man's greatest venture'?

5. List the different stages of the rocket and the most important parts of the spacecraft in Source 5.

6. Examine Source 6. What kind of person was Neil Armstrong? Why was he described as a 'soldier of fortune'? Is the young man who 'seemed to know everything' a good description of 'Buzz' Aldrin? What kind of person was Michael Collins?

7. Refer to the account, what achievements had the three astronauts in common?

8. In Source 7, how many people gathered in Cape Kennedy to watch the launch? Why was the Poor People's Campaign there?

9. In Source 10, what did Armstrong say he could not hear when he listened to the radio reception on Earth?

10. How many people were estimated to have watched the first steps on the Moon on television? What proportion of the world's population was that? How many countries saw the pictures?

11. In Source 16, who are the 'temporary inhabitants' of Tranquility Base? Why do you think it is called Tranquility Base? What two instruments were left on the Moon? How would they help scientists?

12. According to Source 17, why will the astronauts be quarantined? For how long?

13. In Source 18, why is President Nixon talking to the astronauts through a microphone? What has 'only been 8 days'? Why did President Nixon say it was 'the greatest week in the history of the world'?

14. What is the Taoiseach's hope in Source 19?

15. What does Thomas O Paine say will happen by 1984 (Source 20)? How many years later is that?

16. What does the *Irish Times* editorial (Source 21) say the astronauts have done apart from push outward into space? What may happen a 'generation or so from now'?

17. In Source 22, what are Americans justifiably proud of? How, according to Werner von Braun, did the mission have its beginning 'several centuries ago'? What is meant by the words, 'We truly stood on the shoulders of giants'?

18. What is the message of the cartoon in Source 23?

19. In Source 24, what do the conspiracy theorists say happened with US moon landings? What evidence do they produce to support this? What is NASA doing to counteract the conspiracy theory? How does NASA explain the **evidence**?

COMPARISON

1. Is the conclusion of Source 3 – 'a traumatic impact' – supported by Sources 1 and 2? Explain your answer.

2. How does the drawing in Source 5 help us understand the work of Werner von Braun (Source 4)?

3. Source 6 includes a photograph and a brief account of each astronaut. What information is provided in the accounts which is not provided in the photographs?

4. What information is provided in the drawing of the Moon voyage (Source 9) which helps understand the information in the drawing of the Apollo space craft (Source 5)?

5. Why would people in Source 7 be kept well back from the launch (Source 8)?

6. Refer to the photographs in Sources 12–15 and to other sources to explain why the largest crowd in history came to watch the launch (Source 7) and why 600 million watched television pictures from the Moon (Source 11).

7. Refer to Sources 13 and 14 to explain why there was little danger of the contamination feared in Source 17.

8. Why is President Nixon not able to talk to the astronauts directly (Source 18)?

9. What evidence is there in Sources 1–3 that the 'hope' of Jack Lynch in Source 18 may not be fulfilled?

10. What have Sources 20 and 21 in common about the future of space exploration?

CRITICISM

1. Which of the Sources 1–3 are primary and which are secondary?

2. What was the context/background of President Kennedy's Special Message to Congress in May 1961? How useful is a public speech like this in assessing America's reasons for landing a man on the Moon?

3. Sources 2 and 3 were written by commentators on current affairs (politics). Select one fact and one opinion in each source. Do the writers show bias? How useful and reliable are they as sources for historians?

4. Source 4 is taken from a newspaper summary of Werner von Braun's work. Is it favourable or unfavourable to him?

5. Sources 5 and 9 are artist's drawings of the Apollo rocket and the moon journey. What is the main purpose of drawing them? How useful are they as sources to historians?

6. Source 6 contains publicity photographs of the three astronauts. Why would these be published? What impression is being given of the astronauts?

7. Source 10 is oral history. How long after the event is the press conference? What are the advantages/strengths and disadvantages/limitations of oral history as a source for historians? Is there evidence in this extract to support strengths or limitations? From the extract, what advantages do modern people have over previous generations in trying to remember the past?

8. Some of the sources in this Case Study are taken from newspapers. In the case of the moon landing what difficulties did newspapers face in reporting what happened? How would this affect their usefulness and reliability?

9. In general, what are the advantages/strengths and disadvantages/limitations of newspapers as sources for historians? Explain your answer fully by referring to any sources in this Case Study.

10. Why, do you think, Jack Lynch sent this message to President Nixon (Source 19)?

11. Can you identify bias in Source 20? To what extent do you think that the author of the article, Thomas O Paine, is using propaganda? Explain your answer.

12. To what extent is the *Irish Times* in Source 21 influenced by propaganda?

13. Select one fact and one opinion in Source 22. Is there bias or propaganda in the article by Werner von Braun?

14. Is the cartoon in Source 23 propaganda? How useful and reliable are political cartoons as sources for historians studying the moon landing?

15. The conspiracy theory in Source 24 is called an urban legend. What are urban legends? Why do urban legends spread so easily? Why are they difficult to counteract? Do they have any effects on history sources and on history teaching?

16. How would each of the following types of sources contribute to our understanding of the First Moon Landing: (i) television broadcasts, (ii) radio broadcasts, (iii) documentaries, and (iv) rock samples?

CONTEXTUALISATION

1. Write about US advances in Space Exploration up to 1969.

2. Write about the Space Race and the Cold War.

3. How did Space Exploration develop after the First Moon Landing?

4. Using the account above and the sources, write a report on the First Moon Landing in 1969 under the following headings: Reasons; Preparations and launch; The journey to the moon; Moon landing; The return journey; and Results.

What is History?

The word **history** can have different meanings. It can refer to:
- The past itself.
- Surviving evidence of the past.

But the principle underlying the syllabus is that:
- **The study of history is the exploration of what historians believe happened, based on an enquiry into the available evidence.**

> EXPLORATION → ENQUIRY → EVIDENCE

History deals with the experience of human life in the past. The study of history involves an investigation of the surviving evidence relating to such experience.

Since **change** is an essential aspect of the human condition, it is a matter of fundamental concern to the student of history. Time and change, indeed, may be described as the essence (spirit, core) of history.

The study and writing of history changes over time. New evidence and new insights can lead to **revision** of the historical record and to a deepening of our **historical understanding**.

The Historian at Work – What is the Job of the Historian?

The job of the historian is to investigate what happened in the past based on the available evidence. He/she uses sources to find **evidence** of the past. The historian uses those sources to **reconstruct the past**.

Everything that survives from the past is a source – letters, newspapers, diaries, photographs, film, clothes, machines, government records and many other examples.

Primary source	**Secondary source**
A primary source is a source which comes from the time which is being studied.	A secondary source is a source which is based on other sources.

Sources are divided into **Primary** and **Secondary**.

How Do We Know Whether a Source is Primary or Secondary?

Whether a source is primary or secondary will depend on what the historian wants to use the source for, or what he/she is studying or researching. If the historian is studying Hitler's Germany or post-war America, then this textbook is a secondary source for those topics. But in future years, when historians are researching the Irish education system, this textbook will be a primary source for what history students learned.

THE HISTORIAN AT WORK

Questioning the Sources

Historians need to ask questions about their sources before they use them. They need to know if they are genuine or authentic. These questions can be summarised as When, Who, What and Why.

What aspect of history is to be investigated or researched?

EVIDENCE

Locate the sources – all history writing is based on sources.

Held in museums, archives, libraries and on the Internet.

RESEARCH

Use variety of primary and secondary sources – record information/data.

INTERPRETATION

Assess the evidence; making judgments, drawing conclusions from the evidence.

Communicate the information; write up the history.

Explain the process of continuity and change, cause and consequence.

Try to be fair-minded, balanced, objective.

Revise interpretations in the light of new evidence.

When?

When was it created or written? Was it at the time of the events it records, or later?

Who?

Who wrote or created the source? What do we know about the author or the organisation that produced it?

What?

What type of document is it? Is it an eyewitness account, a government report, a newspaper report, a letter, a photograph, a cartoon?

Why?

Why was the source produced or created? Was it done for a particular purpose?

How Useful is the Source?

Is it **relevant** to what is being researched or investigated?

This will be decided by what the historian wants to know. The source is useful if it can provide direct or indirect information on what is being researched or investigated.

How Reliable is the Source?

Is the information accurate? If it is a **document**, it will depend on **bias**, whether the person was

an **eyewitness** or not, and the **purpose** of creating the document. If it is a **book** on the topic, it will depend on whether the author read a wide range of sources, and whether they were used accurately. We can also assess the reliability of a source by checking it against other sources. This is **cross-referencing** or **corroborating**.

Is the Source Biased?

A source is biased if it is one-sided, when the writer deliberately selects information to strengthen his/her own case and undermine the other cases. Is the source **propaganda**? Is the source used to influence and control people's beliefs, ideas and attitudes?

What is the difference between **fact** and **opinion**? Historians have to sort out fact from opinion. A fact is something that actually happened. An opinion is a person's view of what happened. Opinions can be biased or can be used for propaganda.

How do we evaluate sources on the Internet?

The internet provides a vast amount of information. Many of the same criteria which are used to evaluate documents in archives or books must also be used for Internet sources.

The author:
Is the author named? What do we know about the author? Does he/she provide information on their education and background? What is the author's expertise or qualifications?
Does the author provide a contact address?
Is there evidence that the author is trying to be fair and objective? Balanced?
Does the author list sources?

The organisation and site:
Is the information from a well-known organisation? Does the organisation have a good reputation?
What is the purpose of the Internet site? Is it to provide information? Is it trying to persuade or propagandise?

The information:
Is the information accurate?
How comprehensive is the source? Does it deal with all aspects of the topic or only with some?
Can you get other sources to corroborate (support) this source?
Are there links to other sites?

Where are the sources stored?

Sources are stored in:

Archives
An archive is a place where **historical records** or **documents** are held and preserved.

Museums
A museum is a place where **historical and archaeological objects** are stored and preserved. **Artefacts** are objects made by people. They range from household appliances to space rockets, from weapons to CDs, from clothes to shoes.

Libraries
A library is a place where books, newspapers, videos, records, microfilms and films are kept for **reading and reference**.

Types of Sources

There are many different types of sources. Sources can be **written**, **visual** or **oral**. Each source must be judged in relation to the particular topic under investigation or research. But below is a general outline of the **strengths** and **weaknesses** (or limitations) of the more common sources used in modern history.

'Each type of source possesses certain strengths and weaknesses; considered together and compared one against the other, there is at least the chance that they will reveal the true facts – or something very close to them.'

J Tosh, *The Pursuit of History*

TYPE OF SOURCE	STRENGTHS	WEAKNESSES
Written		
Eyewitness Account	• Saw what happened. • Direct evidence of the events. • Better if written down soon after the event.	• Could be mistaken. • Eyewitness accounts can differ. • Could be biased.
Public Records Government Records	• Provide information on the workings of government. • Give information on a wide range of political, economic and social topics.	• Too much information to analyse. • May attempt to cover up information. • Politicians concerned with their place in history may write carefully.
Statistics including the Census	• Accurate. • Available for political, economic and social topics.	• Must be used in context. • Can be distorted; *'lies, damned lies and statistics'*.
Memoirs and Autobiographies	• Directly involved in the events. • First-hand account. • Explain motives or reasons. • Explain political relationships.	• Memory can be faulty. • Could be biased. • Only one person's view. • Can exaggerate own role in events. • Could be propaganda. • Could be written by researchers and so would not be true memoirs or autobiographies. • *'A form of oral history set down to mislead historians.'* A J P Taylor
Biography	• Often based on private papers of person. • Can provide new information.	• Could be biased. • Could favour and exaggerate the part of the person. • May be too dependent on private papers.

TYPE OF SOURCE	STRENGTHS	WEAKNESSES
Letters and Diaries	• Private views of writer. • Usually not intended to be published. • Explain motives or reasons. • Information on topics not found in other sources. • Can provide information on the lives of ordinary people.	• Could be biased. • Private letters of politicians often intended for publication. • Might only record what they want people to know.
Newspapers	• Daily or weekly record of events. • First-hand accounts; can include eye-witness accounts taken immediately after the events. • Include political, economic and social information. • Use of different newspapers to counteract bias.	• Can get facts wrong. • Could be biased. • Could be propaganda. • Could be dependent on leaked stories from government which might deliberately mislead.
History Books	• Place events in a wider context. • Wide range of facts and information available on which to make a judgment – use of primary and secondary sources. • Can judge the influence/impact of events. • Fair and balanced account. • Detailed and comprehensive account. • Reputable author. • Use of index and illustrations.	• Could be biased. • Might not use wide range of primary and secondary sources. • Might not provide any sources. • Could be used for propaganda in totalitarian states.
Internet	• Many primary sources, both written documents and visual sources. • Many secondary articles. • Many reputable sites – archives, universities, libraries. • Easily accessed. • Signed by author, notes cited.	• Can be biased. • Can be used for propaganda. • Information may not be reliably researched and checked. • Anyone can set up an internet site. • Author unknown or not identified.
Survey and Opinion Polls	• Show trends in public opinion.	• Show opinion at one point in time. • Based on sample which may not reflect the whole population. • Only show connections between different topics – not causes.

TYPE OF SOURCE	STRENGTHS	WEAKNESSES
Visual		
Photographs	• First-hand evidence. • Useful for political, economic and social history. • Can give information on topics other than the main topic of the photograph.	• Can be altered for propaganda purposes. • Captions can mislead. • Only record a moment in time.
Political Cartoons	• Show political and social attitudes of the time.	• Biased. • Propaganda. • Used to persuade people, to get across a point of view.
Maps	• Usually accurate. • Variety of information on political, economic and social matters. • Can show changes.	• Must be compared to the written record. • Official government maps will be more accurate than secondary maps which may have errors. • Some maps are only drawn for illustration purposes, not for accuracy.
Imaginative Painting or Drawing	• May be the only visual evidence available. • Useful for political, economic and social history. • Accuracy and usefulness depends on whether the artist was an eyewitness.	• Could be biased. • Could be propaganda. • Artist may not have witnessed the event or seen the person.
TV Documentaries	• Sound and action added to picture. • Better understanding of events than photograph.	• Director can be biased. • Documentaries can be used for propaganda.
Oral		
Interviews, Tape Recordings or Transcripts	• May be an eyewitness to events. • Can help fill gaps in documents, and provide additional information on relationships between people. • Useful sources for recent history before official papers are released.	• Reliance on memory which can be faulty. • Interviews usually done with leaders, not always with ordinary people. • Can falsify or mislead. • Can exaggerate own role in events. • Hindsight can distort the memory. • Interviewer may not ask the right questions.

Evaluating a Source

You are researching the topic **Britain at the Outbreak of the Second World War**. Examine the source right and apply the questions to evaluate the source.

If the topic of research was changed to **Germany at the Outbreak of the Second World War**, what would your answers be to the same questions?

CASE STUDIES

Each topic has three Case Studies. These are **document-based** studies.

By studying these, students should develop the ability to:

- Recognise **different types of sources**.
- **Extract information** from sources to answer historical questions.
- Evaluate the **usefulness** of sources and their **limitations**.
- Detect **bias**.
- Identify **propaganda**.

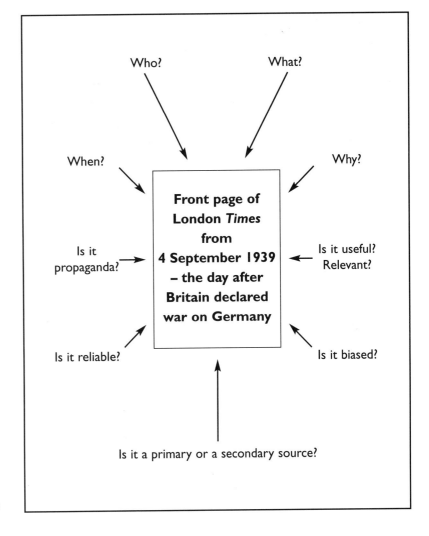

In the examination, the document-based questions will involve the use of **short**, **thematically linked extracts**. The format of the questions will be as follows:

- **Comprehension** – to **extract** relevant information from the document.
- **Comparison** – to **compare two or more sources or accounts** of the events in order to explain the **similarities** and **contrasts**.
- **Criticism** – to **assess the sources** for bias or propaganda, and to assess for usefulness and reliability.
- **Contextualisation** – to place the subject matter of the documents in a **historical context**; to show understanding of the wider issues connected with the Case Study.

In the examination, more marks will be given for **Comprehension** at **Ordinary Level** and for **Contextualisation** at **Higher Level**.

THE RESEARCH STUDY

The Research Study aims to develop a spirit of enquiry about the past and a range of skills that will help with the enquiry. It will involve the study of a subject of **historical significance** chosen by the student, under the direction of the teacher.

The Research Study will be **20% of the final exam**.

Guidelines for Choosing a Topic for Research

The topic of the study:
- Should be **clearly defined** with a narrow focus.
- Should deal with a **significant event or person**.
- Should reflect **your own interests**.
- Should be a **good story** with interesting detail.
- Should have **good sources**.

- Begin with a **shortlist of possible topics** (two or three) because good sources are not always available for topics; the sources will eventually decide which topic you will do.
- Use either **primary or specialist secondary sources**.
- Use a minimum of **two** sources at **Ordinary Level** and a minimum of **three** sources at **Higher Level**.
- The topic can be chosen from **any period or place in history**.
- If you choose a topic from **within the course**, this will help give **better understanding** of some aspect of your course.
- If you choose from **outside the course** (any event or person at any time), this will **widen your interest**.

The Format of the Study

The Research Study will form a report which will be divided into **three parts**:
- **The Outline Plan**: this will define and justify the proposed subject of study, identify the aims, the intended approach and the sources to be consulted (3% of the marks) – about one **A4 page** in length.
- **Evaluation of Sources**: this will examine the relevance of the sources to the topic chosen and comment on their strengths and weaknesses (5% of the marks) – about one **A4 page** in length.
- **Extended Essay**: this will set down the **main findings and conclusions** of the study. It should include a **review of the process** undertaken and how **useful** that process was in achieving the aims of the outline plan. The essay should have a clear introduction, paragraphs developing the main arguments of the essay and a conclusion (12% of the marks) – about **1,000 words** in length for **Ordinary Level**; about **2,000 words** in length for **Higher Level**.

The Report will be **pre-submitted**.

Sample Research Study for Higher Level

BLACK AMERICAN VOTING RIGHTS AND THE SELMA TO MONTGOMERY MARCH, 1965

Outline Plan

What is My Research Study?

I intend to research the question of black American voting rights and the Selma to Montgomery March in 1965. This march was organised by black American leaders to protest at laws in the state of Alabama, and elsewhere in the Southern States of the US, which deprived black Americans of the vote. The march led President Johnson to pass the Voting Rights Act 1965 to ensure federal control of voter registration in the Southern States. It was a major step on the road to political and civil rights for black Americans (and other minority groups).

Why I Chose This Topic

I chose this topic for research study because I am interested:

- in the progress of black Americans to political and civil rights in the US.
- in the use of non-violent protest and its influence.
- in the impact of television.
- in the role of Martin Luther King in the civil rights movement.

Aims of the Research Study

- To develop **research skills** which I can use in further research or work; to gain experience in the **work of the historian**.
- To develop the ability to **think independently**; to develop a spirit of inquiry and critical thinking.
- To gain experience in **self-directed learning** which will be of importance to me in my future career.

How I Will Research the Topic: the Intended Approach

I will consult sources in:

- my school library,
- the local county library branch,
- the reference section of the county library, and
- the Internet.

I will read **general accounts** of the civil rights movement in the US, such as my school textbook, *Modern Europe and the Wider World* by Dermot Lucey, to get understanding of the period. Then I will consult **more detailed** primary and secondary sources. In each case I will take notes. In the case of the Internet, I will print off various sources. I will evaluate all the sources and use them to write up my research study.

> **Referring to sources**
>
> In referring to **sources** you should include the following information:
> **Books and articles**: author(s), title (including title of the article and magazine) and publisher.
> **Internet sites**: the title page of the site, the full website address or URL, author (if available), the date information was written and updated on site (if available) and the date it was downloaded from the site.

The Sources I Will Consult

Books and Articles

Dermot Lucey, *Modern Europe and the Wider World*, Gill & Macmillan, for general background.
James T Patterson, *Grand Expectations, The United States, 1945–1974*, Oxford University Press.
David J Garrow, *Bearing the Cross: Martin Luther King and the Southern Christian Leadership Conference*, Vintage Books.
Taylor Branch, *Parting the Waters: Martin Luther King and the Civil Rights Movement, 1954–63*, Macmillan.
John Hope Franklin & Alfred A Moss, *From Freedom to Slavery, A History of African Americans*, Volume Two: 'From the Civil War to the Present', Seventh Edition, McGraw-Hill.

Internet Sources

The History Place, Great Speeches Collection. Lyndon Johnson's 'We Shall Overcome' at www.historyplace.com/speeches/johnson.htm
'Selma in Retrospect' at http://bob.swe.uni-linz.ac.at/EUU/Unifier200006/selma.html
'The Selma March' in the Civil Rights section of *Spartacus Educational* at www.spartacus.schoolnet.co.uk/USAselma.htm
Map of the Selma to Montgomery March at *America's Byways* at www.byways.org/browse/byways/2050/
The internet sources were downloaded between 10–15 December 2003.

Evaluation of the Sources

James T Patterson, *Grand Expectations, The United States, 1945–1974*, **Oxford University Press**

This is a **general history** of the US from 1945 to 1974. However, it provides a very good account of the Selma to Montgomery March and details of the Voting Rights Act 1965.

For evaluating sources, see Questioning the Sources (page 484), How Do We Evaluate Sources on the Internet? (page 485), Types of Sources (pages 486–8).

This is a **secondary source** for my research study. But Professor Patterson uses both **primary and secondary sources** for his account. Some of these he uses as **footnotes** in the pages; others are listed in a **bibliographical essay** at the end of the book. The book also has a detailed **index** and **photographs** of the main people involved in the March and the voting rights campaign.

Professor Patterson has a **good reputation** as a historian. He is Ford Professor of History at Brown University and he has also written other books and articles on US history. This book was awarded the 1997 Bancroft Prize.

The account in *Grand Expectations* is **detailed** and **comprehensive** because the author writes about the economic and social aspects of the topic as well as the political. He **explains** what happened as well as **describing** what happened. The author attempts to be **balanced** and **fair**. He also puts the March in its **historical context** – the progress of the civil rights movement and developments in Johnson's Great Society. He has a very nice **style of writing** which is easy to read and provides interesting details.

David J Garrow, *Bearing the Cross: Martin Luther King and the Southern Christian Leadership Conference*, **Vintage Books**

This is a detailed account of the role of Martin Luther King and the Southern Christian Leadership Conference in the civil rights campaign in the US. It has a very long account of the voting rights campaign and the Selma March.

Professor Garrow uses many **primary and secondary sources** for his account – the full list of his **bibliography** comes to almost 50 pages. He also provides **notes** to refer to specific sources. He was given access to Martin Luther King's personal papers and to FBI documents. He also **interviewed** many of the people who took part in these events. This book also has a detailed **index** but it has no photographs.

Professor Garrow has **written other books** which deal with Martin Luther King and with the Selma protest. He was also senior advisor to a major television documentary history of the American civil rights movement, *Eyes on the Prize*. He worked in the Institute for Advanced Study at Princeton and was also Professor of Political Science at the City College of New York. This book won the Pulitzer Prize.

Bearing the Cross is a very **comprehensive** account of the Selma campaign in 1965. It deals with the **origins** of the campaign and how local and national politics were linked together. It highlights the role of many individuals even though it concentrates more on the role of Martin Luther King. It gives a very good **narrative account** of what happened as well as **analysing** the **causes** and **consequences** of what happened. The account has many **direct quotations** from sources in support of its conclusions. The account attempts at all times to be **balanced** and **fair**. It also places the events in Selma and Montgomery in the **wider historical context** of the progress of the civil rights movement. It was well written and full of interesting detail.

Taylor Branch, *Parting the Waters: Martin Luther King and the Civil Rights Movement, 1954–63*, **Macmillan**

This is a **detailed account** of the civil rights movement. It was mainly useful in providing **background information** since its account stops in 1963. However, it provides some information on the voting rights issue in the Southern States of the US.

Taylor Branch was a journalist but he cites **notes** and he has a full list of Major Works cited in the notes at the end of the book. He also has a detailed **index** and **photographs** of the main people involved in the events of the books.

John Hope Franklin and Alfred A Moss, *From Freedom to Slavery, A History of African Americans*, Volume Two: 'From the Civil War to the Present', Seventh Edition, McGraw-Hill
This provides an overall account of the progress of the civil rights movement. It places the Selma to Montgomery March in its historical context. But it does not provide the detailed information which some of the other books provided.

Internet Sources

There were many internet sources for the Selma March. A search with Google provided over 140,000 sites but some of these were duplicated. Instead I concentrated on a small number.

***The History Place*, Great Speeches Collection. Lyndon Johnson's 'We Shall Overcome' at www.historyplace.com/speeches/johnson.htm**
'Selma in Retrospect' at http://bob.swe.uni-linz.ac.at/EUU/Unifier200006/selma.html
'The Selma March' in the Civil Rights section of *Spartacus Educational* at www.spartacus.schoolnet.co.uk/USAselma.htm
Map of the Selma to Montgomery March at *America's Byways* at www.byways.org/browse/byways/2050/

Overall, the internet sites were disappointing. Most of the sites had secondary information. However, *The History Place* provided President Johnson's full speech on 15 March when he spoke live on television before a joint meeting of the Houses of Congress. This is a reliable site, set up by a US graduate, with many awards and commendations for its content.

The *Spartacus Educational* site also provided a good deal of information on the overall civil rights movement. It had a briefer account of the Selma March, but it also included extracts from speeches around the time, including Martin Luther King's speech in Montgomery at the end of the March. The Spartacus site is very reliable.

'Selma in Retrospect' provided an account of a participant in the Selma March. He was also attacked along with James Reeb by white segregationists. His account provides first-hand information which other sites do not have. This site was set up by the Unitarian Church – the writer and James Reeb were both ministers of that church.

The *America's Byways* site provided the only map I could find of the route. It also included the camp sites. I think the information was accurate. I got other illustrations, mostly photographs, through 'Google-Images'.

The Extended Essay

A Review of the Research Process

> For the research process see The Historian at Work (pages 484–5).

- I first of all **read the sources**. I took **notes** from each source, after writing down the title, author and publisher or details of the internet source. I extracted the key information, identified **bias** and sorted out causes and effects. I had difficulty getting **primary sources**, except the extracts which were quoted in the secondary sources. Some of the main primary sources were photographs of the events. I **evaluated** the sources as I used them.
- My History teacher got permission from the Computer teacher to give the class access to the **Internet** for a couple of class periods. We were able to print off the main sources. I also visited the **libraries** and was able to borrow books. Since I had to return the books, I found it useful to **photocopy** the cover, the title page, contents list and (some of the) sources of each book in case I needed them for future reference.
- I **compared** the information in the sources to get my facts right and to understand clearly what happened. When this was done, I was able to **plan** the structure of my report, with an introduction, paragraphs and

a conclusion. I used **one main idea** for each paragraph and **sorted my notes** around each of those main points. I got information from each of the sources to support the main points of each paragraph. I then wrote a **draft** of each paragraph. I had difficulty **condensing** all the information into a short essay. I tried to be **fair** and **objective** in writing the report.

- Some of this work was done in **class**, under the supervision of the teacher. My History teacher assessed the paragraphs I wrote and made some recommendations which I followed. Some of my paragraphs were too long, with too much detail.

- I **re-drafted** the report, word processed it, did a spell-check and a word count. Once I was satisfied with my report, I also included some additional information in **text boxes** which provided background to some of the places, events, organisations and personalities involved. This included brief information on Selma and Montgomery in the 1960s, Martin Luther King's role in the wider civil rights campaign, Governor George Wallace, President Johnson's role in civil rights, the Student Non-violent Co-ordinating Committee (SNCC) and the Southern Christian Leadership Conference (SCLC).

- I used Microsoft **Publisher** to lay out the Research Study in a report format. I could also have used Microsoft Word, on which I typed my report, but the templates in Publisher made it easier to lay out the report. I combined text and illustrations which I got from **scanning** books or **downloading** from Google-Images – I also gave **references** in the report in the case of each illustration. Apart from photographs, I also included a **map** of the route from Selma to Montgomery.

- I printed off the full Research Study, including Outline Plan, Evaluation of the Sources and the Extended Essay, on an **inkjet printer** and bound it in a **folder**.

- The research I undertook helped to develop **my research skills**. I had never used the County Library before. Also, I had never used the Internet to research a topic in history. I had to undertake most of the work **on my own**. I had to **decide** between information in different sources. I learnt a great deal about **taking notes** and using the notes in **writing** the report. I had to learn about the **report structure** in providing an introduction, paragraphs and a conclusion. By the end of the Research Study, I had a much clearer idea about the **work of the historian** and the **process of historical research**.

The Report

Note: Ordinary Level students – The Research Study for Ordinary Level follows the same pattern as Higher Level except for a shorter extended essay and report (1,000 words).

BLACK AMERICAN VOTING RIGHTS AND THE SELMA TO MONTGOMERY MARCH, 1965

Introduction

Black Americans gained many civil and political rights between the end of the Second World War and the 1960s. The armed forces were desegregated and so also was education. In 1964, President Johnson passed the Civil Rights Act which outlawed discrimination and segregation against blacks in many areas of American life, including voting. But in many parts of the Deep South of the US, Jim Crow laws still prevented black Americans from registering for the vote. One of those places was Selma, Alabama. Here in a town of almost 30,000 people, including 15,000 blacks of voting age, only 151 of them were registered in 1961. The registration board only met twice a month and they used severe literacy tests to disqualify blacks from registering.

In late 1964, the Southern Christian Leadership Conference (SCLC) decided that black voter registration was going too slowly. They selected Selma for a huge campaign in voter registration in the belief that a white reaction would lead to violence, widespread television coverage and subsequent government action. In the previous year, another black civil rights organisation, the Student Non-violent Co-ordinating Committee (SNCC), was active in Selma. But in spite of hard work, it only increased the black vote to 355. By the end of 1964, the SNCC campaign was running out of steam. The SCLC sent workers to Selma to assess the possibility of a successful campaign there. They reported that the Sheriff, Jim Clark, was an active segregationist and was likely to overreact to black marchers and demonstrators. In these circumstances, local black community leaders invited Martin Luther King and the SCLC to Selma.

Dr King was the recognised leader of black Americans. His first major involvement in civil rights began with the Montgomery Bus Boycott in 1955–6. He believed strongly in non-violent protest and in late 1964 he was awarded the Nobel Peace Prize for his work. He was conscious of the need for a successful campaign in Selma to maintain the progress of non-violent action. But he was also under pressure from the FBI who had information on his sexual involvement with a number of women. His phone was tapped, his house and hotel bedrooms he used were bugged and he was under surveillance. Any leak of this information would have been disastrous for him, the Selma campaign and the civil rights movement.

In Selma, King encouraged blacks to register for voting. When groups marched to the courthouse they were held up by the Sheriff, Jim Clark. Over the space of a few months from January to March 1965, a series of incidents increased the pressure and led to police attacks on the marchers. Soon groups of workers who marched to the courthouse were arrested, in all over 3,000 were jailed for short periods. The SCLC decided that it was necessary for King to get himself arrested – which he did – to increase the pressure and the national media coverage. From jail, he advertised in the *New York Times* in the form of a letter; '...THIS IS SELMA, ALABAMA. THERE ARE MORE NEGROES IN JAIL WITH ME THAN THERE ARE ON THE VOTING ROLLS.'

On Sunday, 7 March, 600 people – mostly black – gathered at Brown Chapel in Selma to begin a walk to Montgomery, the state capital. They intended to demand protection for black voters from the Governor, George Wallace. On the Edward Pettus Bridge, on the outskirts of Selma, they were met by a force of state troopers and local police, armed with bullwhips, billy clubs and wearing gas masks. The troops and police advanced on foot and on horseback, firing tear gas and cutting a deep wedge into the marchers. Eyewitnesses reported:

'The first 10 or 20 Negroes were swept to the ground screaming, arms and legs flying, and packs and bags went skittering across the grass divider strip and on to the pavement on both sides. Those still on their feet retreated.... The mounted possemen [policemen] spurred their horses and rode at a run into the retreating mass. The Negroes cried out as they crowded together for protection, and the whites on the sidelines whooped and cheered.'
'Fifteen or twenty nightsticks could be seen through the gas, flailing at the heads of the marchers.'

The actions of Sheriff Clark and his men were shown that evening on television all over the US, and they were widely reported the next day in the newspapers. **Bloody Sunday**, as it became known, shocked white, middle-class opinion in the northern cities.

At this time King was in Atlanta, but when he heard reports of the events and saw them on television, he telegraphed other clergymen to join him for a ministers' march to Montgomery. King was joined by many high-profile figures and clergymen from different religions. One of those was James Reeb, a Unitarian minister from Boston. His tragic end illustrated the awful conditions of Selma. Along with some colleagues, he ate in a black café in Selma and he was fatally clubbed by white thugs when he left. His death had a large impact in the northern cities because he was both white and a minister.

On Tuesday, 9 March, a second march began from Selma, this time led by Martin Luther King. Once again this march was banned by Governor George Wallace, and King wanted to wait for the decision of a court hearing to avoid being in contempt of court. But militants pressed him to go ahead. King agreed with the police authorities that he would lead a march to the Pettus Bridge and then turn back to Selma. In this way he hoped to stay within the law but also save face. King's decision to turn round led to a split between the SCLC and the SNCC.

Two days later, a federal judge lifted Wallace's ban on the march from Selma to Montgomery. This infuriated Governor Wallace who said state and local police officials could not guarantee the safety of the marchers. President Johnson intervened and commissioned the state troopers as federal troops to protect the march. He spoke directly to Wallace in Washington. Their meeting was a bruising encounter of bad words and bad temper. Johnson's direct manner impressed and temporarily quietened Wallace.

The events of Selma had a major influence on President Johnson. Early in 1965, he told Martin Luther King that he could not introduce a voting rights bill to Congress that year because he had other proposals in his Great Society programme to implement. But in a televised address on 15 March before both Houses of Congress and watched by 70 million people, he said:

'I speak tonight for the destiny of man and the dignity of Democracy.... At times, history and fate meet at a single time and in a single place to shape a turning point in man's unending search for freedom.... So it was last week in Selma, Alabama. There, long-suffering men and women peacefully protested the denial of their rights as Americans. Many of them were brutally assaulted. One good man – a man of God – was killed.'

He announced that he was introducing a Voting Rights Bill to Congress 'designed to eliminate illegal barriers to the right to vote'. 'Their [American Negroes] cause,' he said, 'must be our cause too. Because it's not just Negroes, but really it's all of us, who must overcome the crippling legacy of bigotry and injustice. And we shall overcome.'

The march eventually set off on 21 March, led by King at the start and also at the end. Over 3,000 marchers set off from Selma on the 54-mile journey to Montgomery. However, only 300 were allowed march along the two-lane middle section of the route. Each night the marchers camped in fields. After four days marching and singing, they reached the outskirts of Montgomery where they were entertained that night by folksingers and comedians. The following day, King and other leaders led the marchers, now 25,000 strong, into Montgomery. Here they addressed the crowd in front of the capital buildings. King said during his speech, 'I know you are asking today, "How long will it take?" ... How long? Not long, because you still reap what you sow! ....' The crowd responded with We Shall Overcome, the anthem of the civil rights movement. That night, however, a Detroit housewife, Viola Gregg Liuzzo, who came to Selma to help the marchers was shot dead by Ku Klux Klan members as she drove back to Selma.

Conclusion

The events in Alabama inspired Johnson to work incessantly to get the passage of his Voting Rights Bill. The bill stated that the federal government could control federal, state and local elections – particularly banning literacy tests and other restrictions preventing black Americans from voting. It authorised federal officials to register minority voters. On 6 August 1965, President Johnson signed the bill into law before an audience of civil rights leaders, including King, and congressmen. 'The vote,' he said, 'is the most powerful instrument ever devised by man for breaking down injustice.'

This was true in part. Within two years, fifty per cent of black voters in the South were registered and black leaders were elected in state and local elections. Even white politicians, including Wallace, had to pay more attention to the black vote. But the vote was not everything, as Martin Luther King well knew. He had already begun to shift the focus of the SCLC and non-violent protest to the northern cities, where blacks still suffered from poor economic and social conditions. But, five days after President Johnson signed the Voting Rights Act, a major riot broke out in the Watts district of Los Angeles. It resulted in the deaths of 34 people and $40 million of damage. The road to equality had many more miles to go, and it was a much more difficult road.